FROMMER'S
EasyGuide

To
S0-AZM-152

SAN FRANCISCO

By
Erika Lenkert

Easy Guides are ✦ Quick To Read ✦ Light To Carry
✦ For Expert Advice ✦ In All Price Ranges

FrommerMedia LLC

FEB 2 2 2016

Published by
FROMMER MEDIA LLC

ISBN 978-1-62887-082-4 (paper), 978-1-62887-083-1 (e-book)

Editorial Director: Pauline Frommer
Editor: Lorraine Festa
Production Editor: Lindsay Conner
Cartographer: Liz Puhl
Cover Design: Howard Grossman
Front cover photo: San Francisco houses © Preve Beatrice
Back cover photo: Golden Gate Bridge © Preve Beatrice

For information on our other products or services, see www.frommers.com.

Frommer Media LLC also publishes its books in a variety of electronic formats. Some content that appears in print may not be available in electronic formats.

Manufactured in the United States of America

5 4 3 2 1

3 9082 12206 6361

CONTENTS

ABOUT THE AUTHOR

Native San Franciscan **Erika Lenkert** has been writing about food, wine, and travel for top lifestyle publications, such as "Food Network," "Travel & Leisure," "InStyle," "Food & Wine," "Los Angeles Magazine," "San Francisco Magazine," and Frommer's for the past 20 years. She is also the founder and Editor-in-Chief of "Gluten-Free Forever Magazine." Her propensity to bounce around the region, living in San Francisco, Napa, and Marin County in the past decade, has given her an insider and outsider's perspective of her hometown, while motherhood has afforded her yet another fresh vantage point on local travel. Throughout, a love for food, simple pleasures, luxury indulgences, kitsch, and local dives, has only heightened her appreciation for the glorious, idyllic region she calls home.

ABOUT THE FROMMER'S TRAVEL GUIDES

For most of the past 50 years, Frommer's has been the leading series of travel guides in North America, accounting for as many as 24% of all guidebooks sold. I think I know why.

Though we hope our books are entertaining, we nevertheless deal with travel in a serious fashion. Our guidebooks have never looked on such journeys as a mere recreation, but as a far more important human function, a time of learning and introspection, an essential part of a civilized life. We stress the culture, lifestyle, history and beliefs of the destinations we cover, and urge our readers to seek out people and new ideas as the chief rewards of travel.

We have never shied from controversy. We have, from the beginning, encouraged our authors to be intensely judgmental, critical—both pro and con—in their comments, and wholly independent. Our only clients are our readers, and we have triggered the ire of countless prominent sorts, from a tourist newspaper we called "practically worthless" (it unsuccessfully sued us) to the many rip-offs we've condemned.

And because we believe that travel should be available to everyone regardless of their incomes, we have always been cost-conscious at every level of expenditure. Though we have broadened our recommendations beyond the budget category, we insist that every lodging we include be sensibly priced. We use every form of media to assist our readers, and are particularly proud of our feisty daily website, the award-winning Frommers.com.

I have high hopes for the future of Frommer's. May these guidebooks, in all the years ahead, continue to reflect the joy of travel and the freedom that travel represents. May they always pursue a cost-conscious path, so that people of all incomes can enjoy the rewards of travel. And may they create, for both the traveler and the persons among whom we travel, a community of friends, where all human beings live in harmony and peace.

Arthur Frommer

THE BEST OF SAN FRANCISCO

San Francisco's reputation as a rollicking city where almost anything goes dates back to the boom-or-bust days of the California gold rush. It's always been this way: This city is so beautiful, so exciting and diverse, and so cosmopolitan that you can always find something new to see and do no matter if it's your 1st or 50th visit. Oh, and bring a warm jacket: Bob Hope once remarked that San Francisco is the city of four seasons—every day.

THE best ONLY-IN-SAN FRANCISCO EXPERIENCES

- **A Powell–Hyde Cable Car Ride:** Skip the less-scenic California line and take the Powell–Hyde cable car down to Fisherman's Wharf—the ride is worth the wait. When you reach the top of Nob Hill, grab the rail with one hand and hold your camera with the other, because you're about to see a view of the bay that could make you weep. See p. 98.

- **An Adventure at Alcatraz:** Even if you loathe tourist attractions, you'll dig Alcatraz. Just looking at the Rock from across the bay is enough to give you the heebie-jeebies—and the park rangers have put together an excellent audio tour with narration by former inmates and guards. Heck, even the boat ride across the bay is worth the price. See p. 102.

- **A Sourdough Bread Bowl Filled with Clam Chowder:** There is no better way to take the chill off a freezing July day in San Francisco than with a loaf of bread from Boudin Bakery, hollowed out to form a primitive chowder vessel, filled with hot steamy clam and potato soup. See p. 104.

- **A Walk Across the Golden Gate Bridge:** Don your windbreaker and walking shoes and prepare for a wind-blasted, exhilarating journey across San Francisco's most famous landmark. It's one of those things you have to do at least once in your life. See p. 127.

- **A Stroll Through Chinatown:** Chinatown is a trip—about as close to experiencing Asia as you can get without a passport. Skip the camera and luggage stores and head straight for the food markets, where a cornucopia of critters that you'll never see at the grocery store sit, slither, or hop around in boxes waiting for the wok. Better yet, take one of Shirley Fong-Torres's Wok Wiz tours of Chinatown. See p. 114.

- **Night of Comedy at Beach Blanket Babylon:** Giant hats, over-the-top costumes, and wicked humor are what it's all about at this North Beach classic, the longest running musical review in the country. See p. 178.

- **A Visit with the California Sea Lions:** These giant, blubbery beasts are probably the most famous residents of the City by the Bay. Though they left en masse for greener pastures—or bluer seas—back in 2009, they are now back in full force, barking, belching, and playing king of the mountain for space on the docks at Pier 39. See p. 107.

THE best HOTEL EXPERIENCES

- **Best Service:** The **Ritz-Carlton** is the sine qua non of luxury hotels, offering near-perfect service and every possible amenity. Even if you can't afford a room, come for the mind-blowing Sunday brunch—and get the royal treatment. See p. 57.
- **Best Beat Generation Hotel:** The **Hotel Bohème** is the perfect mixture of art, funky style, and location—just steps from the sidewalk cafes and shops of North Beach. If Jack Kerouac were alive today, this is where he'd stay—an easy stagger home from his favorite bar and bookstore. See p. 65.
- **Best Old Luxury:** Hands down, the **Palace Hotel.** Built in 1875, and quickly rebuilt after the 1906 earthquake, the regal lobby and stunning Garden Court atrium—complete with Italian marble columns, and elegant chandeliers—will take you back 100 years to far more simple times. See p. 61.
- **Best Hotel in the Woods:** Surrounded by trees in a national park just south of the Golden Gate Bridge, the **Inn at the Presidio** is the perfect place for nature lovers. With a golf course close by, hiking trails out the back door, and a fire pit on the back patio, you may never make it to Fisherman's Wharf. See p. 66.
- **Best for Families:** The **Argonaut Hotel** is set in the heart of Fisherman's Wharf, with sea lions, ice cream sundaes at Ghirardelli's, the beach at Aquatic Park, and the Musee Mechanique, all only a few minutes away. With its cool nautical theme throughout, and a toy-filled treasure box in the lobby that kids can dig into, you tikes may never want to leave. See p. 61.
- **Coolest Doormen:** Nothing can possibly compete with the **Sir Frances Drake Hotel** in this category. The jovial doormen greet guests wearing their signature red Beefeater costumes—complete with frilly white collar, top hat, and tights. The most famous doorman in the city, Tom Sweeney, has been blowing his whistle and handling bags at the Sir Francis Drake for over 35 years. Heavy bags are nothing for him; he used to play football with Joe Montana and Dwight Clark. See p. 51.

THE best DINING EXPERIENCES

- **The Best of the City's Fine Dining:** A sleeper restaurant if ever there was one, Italian **Acquerello** (p. 82) has been creating extremely special dining experiences for 25 years in its stunning, unlikely location. Expect perfectly prepared, gorgeous food with service to match *and* plenty of elbow room. For a French-influenced counterpart, **Restaurant Gary Danko** (p. 87) never disappoints with refined food, polished service, an amazing cheese cart, and flambéed finales.
- **Best Value:** For less than $6, you can buy a plate of handmade, succulent potstickers—each one the size of your fist; add a plate of noodles, and a couple of drinks, and you can feed two for less than $20. Believe it or not, it's also on Nob Hill, at **U-Lee Restaurant.** See p. 83.
- **Best Authentic San Francisco Dining Experience:** Even top local chefs can't get enough of **Swan Oyster Depot,** where patrons have been bellying up to the narrow

bar to indulge in fresh crab, shrimp, oysters, and clam chowder since 1912. See p. 83.

o **Best Dim Sum Feast:** At **Ton Kiang** (p. 97), you'll be wowed by the variety of dumplings and mysterious dishes.

o **Best-Kept Secret:** Far, far away from Fisherman's Wharf, hidden on a residential street a few blocks from the heart of the Castro, step through the heavy curtain at the front door and enter **L'Ardoise,** which has the look and feel of an old, romantic Paris bistro. See p. 95.

o **Best View:** Fog permitting, **The Cliff House** (p. 137) is where to take in the Pacific coastline. Perched high on a cliff above Ocean Beach, it offers an expansive scope of the crashing Pacific Ocean, sunsets, and sea lions out front on the rocks. At the other end of town, **Waterbar** (p. 80) has bayfront tables and an upstairs cocktail area with a patio looking directly onto the Bay Bridge and its twinkling lights.

o **Best Out-of-This-World Decor:** Chances are, no matter where you hail from, you have never seen a place like **Farallon,** with its giant hand-blown jellyfish lamps, glass clamshells, kelp columns, and a sea-life mosaic underfoot. You'll feel like you're on the bottom of a beautiful ocean floor while you munch on its inhabitants. See p. 79.

o **Best in the Country:** According to the recent James Beard foodie awards—and judging by the throngs waiting hours just to stand at the bar to eat, this one goes to **State Bird Provisions.** With its dim sum–style service—and no Chinese food in sight—this is the perfect place to try a few bites of all sorts of fab food. See p. 90.

THE best THINGS TO DO FOR FREE (OR ALMOST FREE)

o **Cross the Golden Gate Bridge:** See above.

o **Meander Along the Marina's Golden Gate Promenade and Crissy Field:** There's something about strolling the promenade that just feels right. The combination of beach, bay, boats, Golden Gate views, and clean, cool breezes is good for the soul. Don't miss snacks at the Warming Hut. See p. 129.

o **Take a Free Guided Walking Tour:** With over 90 tours to choose from—Murals and the Multi-Ethnic Mission, Castro: Tales of the Village, or Gold Rush City, to name a few—**San Francisco City Guides** is one of the best deals in town. See p. 133.

o **Pretend You're a Guest of the Palace or Fairmont Hotels:** You may not be staying the night, but you can certainly feel like a million bucks in the public spaces at the **Palace Hotel** (p. 61). The extravagant creation of banker "Bonanza King" Will Ralston in 1875, the Palace Hotel has one of the grandest rooms in the city: the **Garden Court,** where you can have high tea under a stained-glass dome (definitely not free). Running a close second is the magnificent lobby at Nob Hill's **Fairmont San Francisco** (p. 59).

o **Tour City Hall:** Come see where, in 2004, Mayor Gavin Newsom made his bold statement to the country about the future of same-sex marriage in this beautiful Beaux Arts building. Free tours are offered to the public. See p. 117.

o **Cocktail in the Clouds:** One of the greatest ways to view the city is from a top-floor lounge in hotels such as the **Sir Francis Drake** (p. 51), or the venerable **Inter-Continental Mark Hopkins** (p. 58). Drinks aren't cheap, but considering you're not paying for the view, it almost seems like a bargain.

○ **Browse the Ferry Building Farmers' Market:** Stroll booth to booth sampling organic food. Buy fresh produce alongside some of the big name chefs of the Bay Area. People watch. It is always a party and always free. Held rain or shine every Tuesday, Thursday, and Saturday, this is one of the most pleasurable ways to spend time the city. See p. 111.

○ **Visit the Wells Fargo Museum:** Have a look at pistols, mining equipment, an original Wells Fargo stagecoach, old photographs, other gold rush-era relics at the bank's original location. See p. 111.

○ **Hang Out in Golden Gate Park:** Stroll around Stow Lake, watch the disco roller skaters who dance around the area closed to traffic on Sundays, hang out in Shakespeare's Garden, or just find a sunny patch of grass to call your own. There's tons to do in the city's communal backyard that doesn't cost a cent. (See below for the stuff that'll cost you.)

○ **Take Advantage of Free Culture Days:** Most every museum in San Francisco opens its doors to the public for free on certain days of the week. See the complete list on p. 118.

THE best OUTDOOR ACTIVITIES

○ **A Day in Golden Gate Park:** Exploring Golden Gate Park is an essential part of the San Francisco experience. Its arboreal paths stretch from the Haight all the way to Ocean Beach, offering dozens of fun things to do along the way. Top sights are the **Conservatory of Flowers** (p. 123), the **Japanese Tea Garden** (p. 124), the fabulous **de Young Museum** (p. 123), and its eco-fabulous cross-concourse neighbor, the **California Academy of Sciences** (p. 123). The best time to go is Sunday, when main roads in the park are closed to traffic. Toward the end of the day, head west to the beach and watch the sunset. See p. 122.

○ **A Walk Along the Coastal Trail:** Stroll the forested **Coastal Trail** from Cliff House to the Golden Gate Bridge, and you'll see why San Franciscans put up with living on a fault line. Start at the parking lot just above Cliff House and head north. On a clear day, you'll have incredible views of the Marin Headlands, but even on foggy days, it's worth the trek to scamper over old bunkers and relish the cool, salty air. Dress warmly. See p. 129.

○ **A Wine Country Excursion:** It'll take you about an hour to get there, but once you arrive you'll want to hopscotch from one winery to the next, perhaps picnic in the vineyards. And consider this: When the city is fogged in and cold, especially in summer, Napa and Sonoma can be more than 50 degrees warmer. See chapter 11 and plan your tour.

○ **A Climb up or down the Filbert Street Steps:** San Francisco is a city of stairways, and the crème de la crème of scenic steps is Filbert Street between Sansome Street and the east side of Telegraph Hill, where steep Filbert Street becomes Filbert Steps, a 377-stair descent that wends its way through flower gardens and some of the city's oldest and most varied housing. It's a beautiful walk down from Coit Tower, and great exercise going up.

○ **Bike the Golden Gate Bridge:** Go see the friendly folks over at Blazing Saddles in Fisherman's Wharf and ask them to hook you up. Rent a bike and pedal over this San Francisco icon on your own. Take a guided tour over the bridge down into

Sausalito, and return to the city by ferry. Heck, they even rent electric bikes—now that is my kind of outdoor adventure. See p. 135.

THE best OFFBEAT TRAVEL EXPERIENCES

o **A Grumpy Old Man Passing out Cookies and Insults in Chinatown:** A San Francisco institution for years, no visit to Chinatown is complete without visiting **Uncle Gee** in front of his tea shop on Grant Street. He will give you a Chinese name, offer you some sound advice . . . and threaten to take you downstairs and beat you if you don't follow that advice. Yes, it sounds weird, but Uncle is hilarious; people line up for his abuse. See p. 144.

o **A Soul-Stirring Sunday Service at Glide Memorial Church:** Every city has churches, but only San Francisco has the Glide. An hour or so with Reverend Cecil Williams, or one of his alternates, and his exuberant gospel choir will surely shake your soul and let the glory out. No matter what your beliefs may be, everybody leaves this Tenderloin church spiritually uplifted and slightly misty-eyed. See p. 115.

o **A Cruise Through the Castro:** The most populated and festive street in the city is not just for gays and lesbians (though some of the best cruising in town *is* right here). This neighborhood shows there is truth in San Francisco's reputation as an open-minded, liberal city, where people are free to simply love whomever they want. If you have time, catch a flick and a live Wurlitzer organ performance at the beautiful 1930s Spanish colonial movie palace, the Castro Theatre. See "Neighborhoods in Brief," beginning on p. 22, for more info.

o **Catching Big Air in Your Car:** Relive "Bullitt" or "The Streets of San Francisco" as you careen down the center lane of Gough Street between Ellis and Eddy streets, screaming out "Wooooeee!" Feel the pull of gravity leave you momentarily, followed by the thump of the car suspension bottoming out. Wimpier folk can settle for driving down the steepest street in San Francisco: Filbert Street, between Leavenworth and Hyde streets.

o **AsiaSF:** The gender-bending waitresses—mostly Asian men dressed *very* convincingly as hot-to-trot women—will blow your mind with their performance of lip-synched show tunes, which takes place every night. Bring the parents—they'll love it. Believe it or not, even kids are welcome at some seatings. See p. 81.

o **Browse the Haight:** Though the power of the flower has wilted, the Haight is still, more or less, the Haight: a sort of resting home for aging hippies, ex-Deadheads, skate punks, and an eclectic assortment of young panhandlers. Think of it as a people zoo as you walk down the rows of used-clothing stores, hip boutiques, and leather shops. See p. 120.

o **The Sisters of Perpetual Indulgence:** A leading-edge "Order of queer nuns," these lovely "ladies" got their start in the Castro back in 1979 when a few men dressed in 14th century Belgian nun's habits "and a teensy bit of make-up so as not to be dowdy on a Friday night" to help chase away visiting church officials who regularly came to town preaching about the immorality of homosexuality. With their Adam's apples, and sometimes beards, these dames appear at most public events, and have devoted themselves to community outreach, ministry, and helping those on the fringes of society. Amen.

THE best ARCHITECTURE

- **The Transamerica Pyramid:** Without this tall, triangular spire gracing its presence, the skyline of San Francisco could be mistaken for almost any other American city. Though you can't take a tour to the top, on the Plaza Level—off Clay Street—there is a Visitor Center with videos and facts, a historical display, and a live feed from the "pyramid-cam" located on the top. Did you know this icon appears white because its façade is covered in crushed quartz? Located at 600 Montgomery St.

- **The Palace of Fine Arts:** This Bernard Maybeck–designed stunner of Greek columns and Roman ruins is one of the only structures remaining from the 1915 Panama-Pacific International Exhibition which was held, in part, to show that San Francisco had risen from the ashes of the 1906 earthquake destruction.

- **Mission Dolores:** Also known as Mission San Francisco de Asís, this was the sixth in a chain of missions ordered built by Father Junipero Serra. Built in 1776, it is the oldest surviving building in the city. See p. 116.

- **Sentinel Building/Columbus Tower:** Real estate is at such a premium in our city; every speck of land has to be used if at all possible. There is no better proof of this than Francis Ford Coppola's triangular-shaped flatiron building, located at the corner of Columbus and Kearny Streets. Under construction in 1906, it was one of the few structures in the city to survive the earthquake and ensuing fires. See p. 150.

- **Recycled Buildings:** Since San Francisco was the first city in North America to mandate recycling and composting; it only follows we would be good at recycling our old buildings as well. The **Asian Art Museum** (p. 117) was once the city library. The **Contemporary Jewish Museum** (p. 109) was created from an old power substation designed by Willis Polk. Built in 1874 to hold the "diggings" from the gold rush, the old US Mint (at 5th and Missions sts.) is currently being recycled and will eventually house the San Francisco Museum at the Mint. The **Ferry Building Marketplace** (p. 111) was—surprise—the old ferry building. Built between 1895 and 1903, 170 ferries were docked here daily.

- **The Painted Ladies of Alamo Square:** Also known as the Six Sisters, these famous Victorian homes on Steiner Street (p. 116) are among the most photographed sights in the city. The characters from the sitcom "Full House" lived here in TV land.

THE best MUSEUMS

- **Palace of the Legion of Honor:** Located in a memorial to soldiers lost in World War I, this fine arts museum features Renaissance and pre-Renaissance works—many from Europe—spanning a 4,000-year history. See p. 131.

- **de Young:** Appropriately housed in a new modern building in Golden Gate Park, the Legion of Honor's modern fine arts sister, the de Young, features works from more recent times. Both can be entered on the same day with one admission ticket. See p. 123.

- **California Historical Society:** Established in 1871, this little-known gem invites visitors to explore a rich collection of Californiana, including manuscripts, books and photographs pertaining to the Golden State's fascinating past. See p. 108.

- **Contemporary Jewish Museum:** Even if you have absolutely no interest in Jewish culture, history, art, or ideas, go to visit the old-meets-new building, created when New York architect, Daniel Libeskind, "dropped" shiny steel cubes onto the roof of the 1907 Willis Polk–designed Beaux Arts brick power substation. See p. 109.

o **Asian Art Museum:** Located in the big showy Civic Center space, across the way from City Hall, this is my favorite museum in the city. I never tire of looking at the variety of treasures from countries I had no idea were in fact a part of "Asia." See p. 117.

THE best THINGS TO DO WITH CHILDREN

o **The Exploratorium:** Imagine a hands-on science museum where kids can play for hours, doing cool things like using a microscope to search for miniscule sea creatures, and then watch them attack each other with teeny, tiny claws. Throw in a drinking fountain in a real toilet and you've got the sweetest science museum on the planet. See p. 111.

o **Pier 39 and the California Sea Lions:** Featuring ice cream and candy stores, bungee jumping, a puppet theater, and lots of cool shops, Pier 39 is every kids' dream come true. To top it all off, this pier is home to the famous barking sea lions. See p. 107.

o **Musee Mechanique:** Filled with old fashioned penny arcade games, kids love to pop in quarters and experience what their great, great grandparents did for fun 100+ years ago. See p. 105.

o **Aquarium of the Bay:** Stand on a conveyor belt. Move through a tube in an aquarium while all sorts to sea creatures swim over and around you. Repeat. What's not to love? See p. 104.

o **Cable Car Museum:** Kids love to learn what makes things work. They'll be fascinated when they enter this cool museum in action, especially if they've just hopped off a cable car. On the main level you can see giant wheels turning the very cables that pull the cars around the city. Below, you might catch a gripper actually grabbing a cable. See p. 113.

o **California Academy of Sciences:** At this 150-year-old institution located in the middle of Golden Gate Park, kids' favorite activities include watching Claude, the cool albino alligator, and learning about the planets while laying back in their chairs at the Morrison Planetarium. See p. 123.

SAN FRANCISCO SUGGESTED ITINERARIES

S an Francisco may be only 7 miles squared, but it's got enough dramatically diverse environments and attractions to make forging any "best of" itinerary challenging. Along with information about the city's vibrant neighborhoods—almost all of which are worthy of exploration—I've outlined a good deal of the classic must-sees below. But should you stray, you can rest assured that you're bound to have an experience that's uniquely San Francisco.

BEST OF SAN FRANCISCO IN 1 DAY

If you've got only 1 day to explore the city and haven't been here before, follow this whirlwind jaunt of the classic highlights. It starts with a scenic cable car ride, includes a tour of Alcatraz Island (Get tickets in advance—it regularly sells out!), and meanders through two of the city's most colorful neighborhoods—Chinatown and North Beach—for lunch, shopping, browsing, cocktails, dinner, cappuccino, and a show. Get an early start and wear comfy walking shoes because you're about to embark on a long, wonderful day in the City by the Bay. *Start: F-Line Streetcar to Union Square.*

1 Union Square

Named for a series of pro-union mass demonstrations staged here on the eve of the Civil War, Union Square is literally that—a square. The epicenter of the city's shopping district, the open space dotted with lingering tourists and pigeons is surrounded by Macy's, Saks, and Tiffany & Co. (and, at press time, a new Apple store was in the works) and blocks of other high-end boutiques. Major sales aside, there are few bargains or independent retailers to be found, but if shopping is your thing, you won't find more places to spend your money than this bustling area.

Just 3 blocks down, at Powell and Market streets, is the cable car turnaround where you'll embark on a ride on the nation's only moving National Historic Landmark. See p. 98.

2 Cable Cars & Lombard Street ★★★

Yes the line of people at the cable car turnaround at Market and Powell streets is long. But the ride is worth the wait. The $5 thrill starts with a steep climb up Nob Hill, and then passes through Chinatown and Russian Hill before clanging its way down Hyde Street to Fisherman's Wharf—all with a picturesque bay backdrop. (*Note:* If you want to check out the famous winding stretch of Lombard Street, hop off the cable car at the intersection of Hyde and Lombard streets and, when you've seen enough, either walk the rest of the way down to Fisherman's Wharf or take the next cable car that comes along.) For maximum thrill, stand on the running boards during the ride and hold on Doris Day–style. See p. 119.

3 Buena Vista Cafe ☕

After you've completed your first Powell–Hyde cable car ride, it's a San Francisco tradition to celebrate with an Irish coffee at the Buena Vista Cafe, located across from the cable car turnaround. It's crowded and touristy for sure, but it's a good time and you can tell your friends you threw one back in the bar that served the first Irish coffees in America in 1952. See p. 87.

To get to Fisherman's Wharf from here, cross the street and head toward the water for 1 block, to Jefferson Street. Take a right onto Jefferson and follow it to Pier 33 to catch the ferry to Alcatraz. (Be sure to buy tickets in advance!)

4 Alcatraz Tour ★★★

To tour "the Rock," the Bay Area's famous abandoned prison on its own island, you must first get there—and that's half the fun. The brief but beautiful ferry ride offers captivating views of the Golden Gate Bridge, the Marin Headlands, and the city. Once inside, an excellent audio tour guides you through cellblocks and offers a colorful look at the prison's historic past as well as its most infamous inmates. Book well in advance because these tours consistently sell out in the summer. Bring snacks and beverages for the ride (ferry's pickings are slim and expensive, and nothing is available on the island). See p. 102.

If you've got time, when you get off the ferry follow the sidewalk fronting the bay toward the Bay Bridge (the opposite direction from the Golden Gate Bridge) and take round-trip stroll on the Embarcadero toward the Bay Bridge. On a nice day, the views are breathtaking, and more and more attractions are popping up along the thoroughfare's piers, including the recently relocated Exploratorium (see p. 111). Then hop back on a cable car to Chinatown. There are two locations for cable cars near Fisherman's Wharf. The Powell–Hyde line (PH) and the Powell–Mason line (PM). The PH line is located at Beach and Hyde streets; the PM line is at Bay and Taylor streets. Both lines intersect each other. Best place to get off is Washington and Mason streets or Powell and California streets. Walk down a few blocks and you will be in:

5 Chinatown ★★

Despite the number of international visitors pounding this small neighborhood's pavement, Chinatown remains its own authentic world. San Francisco has one of the largest communities of Chinese people in the United States, and more than 80,000 of them are condensed into the blocks surrounding Grant Avenue and Stockton Street. Join the locals and peruse the vegetable and herb markets, restaurants, and shops and check out the markets along Stockton Street hawking live frogs, armadillos, turtles, and odd sea creatures—all destined for tonight's dinner table. *Tip:* The dozens of knickknack shops are a great source of cheap souvenirs. See p. 114.

6 Great Eastern Restaurant ☕
You can't visit Chinatown and not try food so terrific that President Obama himself popped in back in 2012. Walk to the Great Eastern Restaurant and order salt-and-pepper fresh crab and sizzling chicken in a clay pot. See p. 86.

7 North Beach
San Francisco's "Little Italy" celebrates cafe (and bar) culture like no other part of town. Here dozens of Italian restaurants and coffeehouses brim with activity in what is still the center of the city's Italian community. A stroll along Columbus Avenue will take you past the eclectic cafes, delis, bookstores, bakeries, and coffee shops that give North Beach its Italian-bohemian character. See p. 112.

8 Mario's Bohemian Cigar Store ☕
The menu's limited to coffee drinks and a few sandwiches (the meatball is our favorite), but the convivial atmosphere and large windows perfect for people-watching. It's at 566 Columbus Ave. (☏ 415/362-0536).

9 Dinner at Original Joe's ★
The best thing about North Beach is its concentration of old-school restaurants—many of them owned by the same family for generations. **Original Joe's** is a classic, where patrons sit in red leather booths and dine on Italian-American comfort food. See p. 84.

10 Caffè Greco ☕ ★
By now you should be stuffed and exhausted—which is the exact right time for a cappuccino at Caffè Greco (423 Columbus Ave.; ☏ 415/397-6261). Sit at one of the sidewalk tables and watch the area's colorful citizens come and go.

11 Beach Blanket Babylon at Club Fugazi ★★
This whimsical live show is so quintessentially San Francisco, there may be no better way to end the day. Buy tickets in advance and prepare for the outrageous costumes and giant hats of the longest-running musical revue in the country. See p. 178.

BEST OF SAN FRANCISCO IN 2 DAYS
If you follow the 1-day itinerary above and have a day to spare, use it to get familiar with other famous landmarks around the city. Start with breakfast, a science lesson, and a pleasant bayside stroll in the Marina District. Next, cross the famed Golden Gate Bridge on foot; then take a bus to Golden Gate Park. After exploring the city's beloved park, it's time for lunch and power shopping on Haight Street, followed by dinner and cocktails back in the Marina District. Smashing. *Start: Bus nos. 22, 28, 30, 30X, 43, or 76.*

1 Good Morning Marina District
The area that became famous for its scenes of destruction after the 1989 earthquake has long been one of the most picturesque and coveted patches of local real estate. Here, along the northern edge of the city, multimillion-dollar homes back up to the bayfront **Marina,** where flotillas of sailboats and the mighty Golden Gate Bridge make for a magnificent backdrop on a morning stroll.

Start the day with a good cup of coffee on Chestnut Street; then get some postcard perfect snapshots at the stunning **Palace of Fine Arts,** built for the Panama Pacific Exhibition of 1915, and then walk over to **Crissy Field** (p. 129), where restored wetlands and a beachfront path lead to historic **Fort Point** (p. 129) and to the southern underside end of the **Golden Gate Bridge.**

2 The Grove ▣

If you can't jump-start your brain properly without a good cup of coffee, then begin your day at The Grove (2250 Chestnut St.; ☏ 415/474-4843), located in the Marina District—it's as cozy as an old leather couch and has big, killer breakfasts, too.

3 The Golden Gate Bridge ★★★

It's one of those things you have to do at least once in your life—walk across the fabled Golden Gate Bridge, the most photographed man-made structure in the world (p. 127). As you would expect, the views along the span are spectacular and the wind a wee bit chilly, so bring a jacket. It takes at least an hour to walk northward to the vista point and back.

When you return to the southern end, board either Muni bus no. 28 or 29 (be sure to ask the driver if the bus is headed toward Golden Gate Park).

4 Golden Gate Park ★★★

Stretching from the middle of the city to the Pacific Ocean and comprising 1,017 acres, Golden Gate Park is one of the city's greatest attributes. Since its development in the late 1880s, it has provided San Franciscans with respite from urban life—offering dozens of well-tended gardens, museums, a buffalo paddock, a Victorian greenhouse, and great grassy expanses prime for picnicking, lounging, or tossing a Frisbee.

Have the bus driver drop you off near John F. Kennedy Drive. Walking eastward on JFK Drive, you'll pass five of the park's most popular attractions: Stow Lake (p. 125), the de Young Museum (p. 123), the Japanese Tea Garden (p. 124), the California Academy of Sciences (p. 123), and the Conservatory of Flowers (p. 123).

5 Cha Cha Cha ▣ ★★

By now you're probably starving, so walk out of the park, past the throngs of young squatters (don't worry—they tend to be harmless) and into the Haight to Cha Cha Cha (1801 Haight St.; ☏ 415/386-7670). Order plenty of dishes from the Caribbean tapas-style menu and dine family-style. Oh, and don't forget a pitcher of sangria—you've earned it.

6 Exploring the Haight-Ashbury District ★★★

Despite the overall gentrification of San Francisco, the birthplace of the Summer of Love and Flower Power remains gritty. The several blocks of Haight Street lined with inexpensive restaurants and shops are popular with young and old nonconformists, who congregate on the sidewalk over beers, bongos, and buds. Spend at least an hour strolling up Haight Street (p. 120), browsing the cornucopia of used-clothes stores, leather shops, head shops, and poster stores. There are some great bargains to be found here, especially for vintage clothing.

When you get to the intersection of Haight and Masonic streets, catch the Muni no. 43 bus heading north, which will take you through the Presidio and back to the Marina District.

The Best of San Francisco in 3 Days

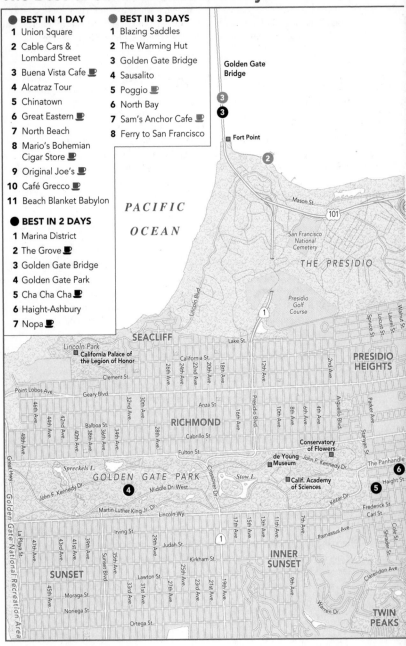

● BEST IN 1 DAY
1 Union Square
2 Cable Cars & Lombard Street
3 Buena Vista Cafe ☕
4 Alcatraz Tour
5 Chinatown
6 Great Eastern ☕
7 North Beach
8 Mario's Bohemian Cigar Store ☕
9 Original Joe's ☕
10 Café Grecco ☕
11 Beach Blanket Babylon

● BEST IN 2 DAYS
1 Marina District
2 The Grove ☕
3 Golden Gate Bridge
4 Golden Gate Park
5 Cha Cha Cha ☕
6 Haight-Ashbury
7 Nopa ☕

● BEST IN 3 DAYS
1 Blazing Saddles
2 The Warming Hut
3 Golden Gate Bridge
4 Sausalito
5 Poggio ☕
6 North Bay
7 Sam's Anchor Cafe ☕
8 Ferry to San Francisco

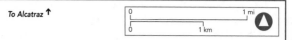

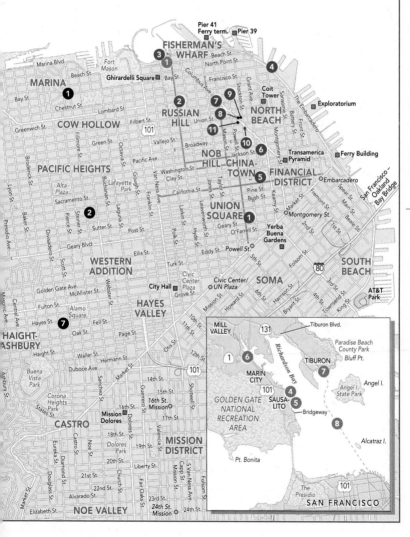

7 Dinner & Drinks

After such a full day on your feet, you deserve a memorable San Francisco dinner, and **Nopa** (p. 90) is a great place to get it. Located nearby but off the tourist path, it's got a vibrant bar scene, killer cocktails, and a fantastic menu offering "urban rustic" food—which translates to contemporary American cuisine with seasonal, farm-fresh influences.

BEST OF SAN FRANCISCO IN 3 DAYS

You've done lots of sightseeing, time for a change of pace. Today we're going to do one of our all-time favorite things to do on a day off—ride a bike from Fisherman's Wharf to Sam's Anchor Cafe in Tiburon (that small peninsula just north of Alcatraz Island). The beautiful and exhilarating ride takes you over the Golden Gate Bridge, through the heart of Sausalito, and along the scenic North Bay bike path, ending with a frosty beer and lunch at one of the most festive outdoor cafes in the Bay Area. And here's the best part: You don't have to bike back. After lunch, you can take the passenger ferry across the bay to Fisherman's Wharf—right to your starting point. Brilliant. ***Start:*** *Powell–Hyde cable car line. Bus nos. 19, 30, or 47.*

1 Rent a Bicycle

Walk, take a bus, or ride the Powell–Hyde cable car (which goes right by it) to one of the bike shops (p. 137) near Ghirardelli Square. Rent a single or tandem bike for a full day, and be sure to ask for: 1) a free map pointing out the route to Sam's in Tiburon, 2) ferry tickets, 3) a bicycle lock, and 4) a bottle of water. Bring your own sunscreen, a hat (for the deck at Sam's), and a light jacket—no matter how warm it is now, the weather can change in minutes. Each bike has a small pouch hooked to the handlebars where you can stuff your stuff.

Start pedaling along the map route to Golden Gate Bridge. You'll encounter one short, steep hill right from the start at Aquatic Park, but it's okay to walk your bike (hey, you haven't had your coffee fix yet). Keep riding westward through Fort Point and the Marina Green to Crissy Field.

2 The Warming Hut ☕

At the west end of Crissy Field, alongside the bike path, is the Warming Hut (p. 129), a barnlike building where you can fuel up with a light (organic, sustainable) snack and coffee drinks. Several picnic tables nearby offer beautiful views of the bay.

3 Biking the Golden Gate

After your break, there's one more steep hill up to the bridge. Follow the bike path to the west side of the bridge (pedestrians must stay on the east side), cross the bridge, and take the road to your left heading downhill and crossing underneath Hwy. 101. Coast all the way to Sausalito.

4 Exploring Sausalito

You'll love Sausalito (p. 199). Cruising down Bridgeway is like being transported to one of those seaside towns on the French Riviera. Lock the bikes and explore on foot for a while.

5 Poggio Trattoria 🍺
If it's sunny, ask for a table outside at Poggio Trattoria (777 Bridgeway; ☎ 415/332-7771; www.poggiotrattoria.com) and order a cocktail, but save your meal for later.

6 North Bay Tour

Back on the bike, head north again on the bike path as it winds along the bay. When you reach the Mill Valley Car Wash at the end of the bike path, turn right onto East Blithedale Avenue, which will cross Hwy. 101 and turn into Tiburon Boulevard. (This is the only rough part of the ride, where you'll encounter traffic.) About a mile past Hwy. 101, you'll enter a small park called Blackie's Pasture. (Look for the life-size bronze statue erected in 1995 to honor Tiburon's beloved "mascot," Blackie the horse.) Now it's an easy cruise on the bike path all the way to Sam's.

7 Sam's Anchor Café 🍺
Ride your bike all the way to the south end of Tiburon Boulevard and lock your bike at the bike rack near the ferry dock. Walk over to the ferry loading dock and check the ferry departure schedule for "Tiburon to Pier 39/Fisherman's Wharf." Then walk over to Sam's Anchor Café (27 Main St.; ☎ 415/435-4527; www.samscafe.com), request a table on the back patio overlooking the harbor. You may have to wait, but hang in there. Once you're relaxing with a burger, oysters, and cool drink, you'll see why this is a famous local trek.

8 Ferry Ride Back to San Francisco

When it's time to leave, board the ferry with your bike (bike riders board first, so don't stand in line) and enjoy the ride from Tiburon to San Francisco, with a short stop at Angel Island State Park. From Pier 39, it's a short ride back to the rental shop (the rental shops close around 7:30pm, but there's 24-hr. drop-off).

After all this adventuring, it's time to reenergize your body and soul with another Irish whiskey at the **Buena Vista Cafe** (p. 87), across from the cable car turnaround, a short walk from the bike rental shop. After libations, take the cable car back to your hotel for some rest and a shower; then spend the rest of the evening enjoying dinner.

SAN FRANCISCO FOR FAMILIES

Knowing kids have different interests than their folks, we've put together a couple of kid-friendly days to make sure you and your offspring cover some of the "musts" with a bit of time to hang and relax.

BEST OF SAN FRANCISCO WITH KIDS IN 1 DAY

If you've only 1 day to explore the city, the best place to spend it is around every kid's favorite—Fisherman's Wharf—and The Embarcadero. First stop of the day is a tour to Alcatraz, then a short walk to Pier 39, where you should see the sights, including the sea lions, grab some lunch, and then head to the aquarium. Next stop will be one of the greatest science museums in the world, and then a really cool underwater restaurant for dinner. Finish the night with a cable car ride. *Start: F-Line Streetcar to Pier 33.*

1 Alcatraz ★★★

The boat ride over is half the fun. Once onto the Rock, if you're lucky, one of the wardens, or even a former prisoner, might be there to greet your boat. Watch a quick movie about the place, and then get your audio tour. Step into a real cell and grab the bars for a photo op. Check out solitary confinement. Look at the dummy masks that three escapees left in their beds to fool the guards. When you feel like leaving, take the ferry back to Pier 33. See p. 102.

Walk a few minutes towards Golden Gate Bridge to Pier 39.

2 Pier 39 ★★

Yes, it's touristy and crowded. But with a carousel, nonstop puppet shows and magicians on the stage (behind the carousel), a store with barrel after barrel of candy, cool shops, and bungee jumping, it also happens to be a lot of fun. See p. 107.

3 Crepes for Lunch ☕

Why have a healthy lunch when you can have a crepe dripping with melty Nutella instead? OK, have a ham and cheese crepe for lunch, and save the Nutella crepe for dessert. The Crepe Café is located about halfway down Pier 39. See p. 87.

Now, sneak out the back door to:

4 The California Sea Lions ★★

Watch the sweet-faced swimmers bark, splash, sleep, and fight for space on the docks. If you're lucky, naturalists from the Aquarium of the Bay will be on hand to answer questions. See p. 107.

5 Aquarium of the Bay ★

We're not quite done with Pier 39. At yet another "kid favorite" place, you'll be able to see all sorts of sea critters in their near-to-natural habitat (we love the conveyor belt that slowly takes you through a tube under a giant tank filled with sharks and rays). There's an area where you can touch bats and starfish (which are deep enough to make you roll your sleeve up to your armpit) and a large otter habitat. Located streetside, where Pier 39 meets the Embarcadero. See p. 104.

Now, walk 15 minutes, or take that historic F-Line streetcar, from Pier 39 to Pier 15.

6 The Exploratorium ★★★

One of the best science museums in the world moved from its old Presidio location to new waterfront digs. It tends to be crowded as all get out and on busy days lines for food in the cafeteria can be long, but that's only because kids LOVE this multi-room, multimedia, hands-on experience, which could easily captivate for an entire day. Pier 15. See p. 111.

Right next door, walk to Pier 17.

7 Tcho Chocolate Factory ★

It's warehouse looks belie the quality of this local chocolatier. Take a tour if you have arranged it ahead of time. If not, no worries; stop in for a few samples, and buy a treat. Pier 15. See p. 169.

Walk 15 minutes, or hop back on the F-Line streetcar, back to Pier 39.

8 Dinner at The Ferry Building Marketplace ☕ ★★

You've had a long day exploring and it is time to take a break. Luckily, you're close to one of the top stops for delicious downtown eats. Inside the Ferry Building, you'll find gourmet burgers and shakes at Gott's Roadside, famous upscale Vietnamese at the Slanted Door, ridiculously good Japanese takeout at Delica (come early; they close most days by or before 6pm), and healthy Mexican enjoyed at crowded tables at Mijita, and more. See p. 111.

BEST OF SAN FRANCISCO WITH KIDS IN 2 DAYS

On Day 2, it's time to leave Fisherman's Wharf and get familiar with a couple of the other famous spots in the city. Start with a tour over that big orange bridge, lunch in Sausalito, and a ferry ride across the bay. Next, stop to play a few old-fashioned video games, and then it's off to a working museum. End your tour at the crowded, colorful world that is Chinatown. *Start: Historic F-Line streetcar to Fisherman's Wharf.*

1 Guided Golden Gate Bridge Bike Tour

The perfect way to start your day is a pedal across one of the most recognized landmarks in the world. Don't worry, you are not alone! You'll have a great guide from one of the Fisherman's Wharf area bike shops (p. 137) to show you the way.

Bring a jacket and meet a few minutes early for a safety briefing. Follow your guide up and over the bridge, then down into Sausalito.

2 Sausalito ★

Say goodbye to your guide and stop for lunch or refreshments anywhere along Bridgeway (the main drag through Sausalito). Two of my favorites are **Barrel House Tavern** (660 Bridgeway; ✆ 415/729-9593; www.barrelhousetavern.com), which has spectacular bay-front patio seating, and the beachside bocce ball and fire pits at **Bar Bocce** (1250 Bridgeway; ✆ 415/331-0555; www.barbocce.com). Explore the town, and then take the ferry from Sausalito back to the city. It is a quick ride back to ditch the bikes.

Walk 3 blocks to the corner of Taylor and the Embarcadero at Pier 45.

3 The Musee Mechanique ★★

Give the kids a roll of quarters and let them run free at this antique penny arcade where everything works. Capture the moment in black and white at the classic photo booth. Located at Pier 45. See p. 105.

Walk back towards the corner of Beach and Larkin sts.

4 Ghirardelli for Ice Cream ★

Aptly located in historic Ghirardelli Square, this ice cream parlor of the same name is pricy, but it's one of the best places to grab a sweet treat in the city. See p. 104.

Walk back to the corner of Jefferson and Hyde sts.

5 Powell–Hyde Cable Car to Nob Hill ★★★

Take a cling clang over the hills; kids of all ages really can't get enough of it. Stay on long enough and the spot they've been dying to sit or stand in is sure to open up. See p. 98.

Best of San Francisco with Kids

● **BEST IN 1 DAY**
1 Alcatraz
2 Pier 39
3 Crepe Cafe ☕
4 California Sea Lions
5 Aquarium of the Bay
6 Exploratorium
7 Tcho Chocolate
8 Ferry Building
  Marketplace ☕
9 Cable Cars

● **BEST IN 2 DAYS**
1 Golden Gate Bridge
  Bike Tour
2 Musee Mechanique
3 Ghirardelli ☕
4 Cable Car
5 Cable Car Museum
6 Chinatown

● **BEST IN 3 DAYS**
1 California Academy
  of Sciences
2 Stow Lake
3 Golden Gate Park
4 Cliff House
5 Japantown ☕

SAN FRANCISCO BAY

Golden Gate Bridge

Fort Point

PACIFIC OCEAN

Mason St.

101

San Francisco National Cemetery

THE PRESIDIO

Presidio Golf Course

Lincoln Blvd

SEACLIFF

Lincoln Park

California Palace of the Legion of Honor

Lake St.

California St.

26th Ave.
24th Ave.
22nd Ave.
20th Ave.
18th Ave.
12th Ave.
2nd Ave.

PRESIDIO HEIGHTS

Clement St.

Point Lobos Ave.

Geary Blvd.

46th Ave.
44th Ave.
42nd Ave.
40th Ave.
38th Ave.
36th Ave.
34th Ave.
32nd Ave.
30th Ave.

Balboa St.

Anza St.

16th Ave.

10th Ave.
8th Ave.
6th Ave.
4th Ave.

Presidio Blvd.

Arguello Blvd.
Parker Ave.
Spruce St.
Locust St.
Walnut St.

Stanyan St.

RICHMOND

Cabrillo St.

Fulton St.

48th Ave.

Spreckels L.

GOLDEN GATE PARK

Conservatory of Flowers

de Young Museum

John F. Kennedy Dr.

The Panhandle

Haight St.

John F. Kennedy Dr.

Middle Dr. West

Stow L.

Calif. Academy of Sciences

Kezar Dr.

Great Hwy

Martin Luther King Jr. Dr.

Lincoln Wy.

Crossover Dr.

17th Ave.
15th Ave.
13th Ave.
11th Ave.
9th Ave.
7th Ave.

Frederick St.
Carl St.
Cole St.
Shrader St.

Irving St.

Judah St.

29th Ave.

Parnassus Ave.

Golden Gate National Recreation Area

La Playa St.
47th Ave.
45th Ave.
43rd Ave.
41st Ave.
39th Ave.
35th Ave.
33rd Ave.
31st Ave.
27th Ave.
25th Ave.
23rd Ave.
21st Ave.
19th Ave.

Sunset Blvd.

Kirkham St.

Lawton St.

INNER SUNSET

Clarendon Ave.

SUNSET

Moraga St.

Noriega St.

Ortega St.

Warren Dr.

TWIN PEAKS

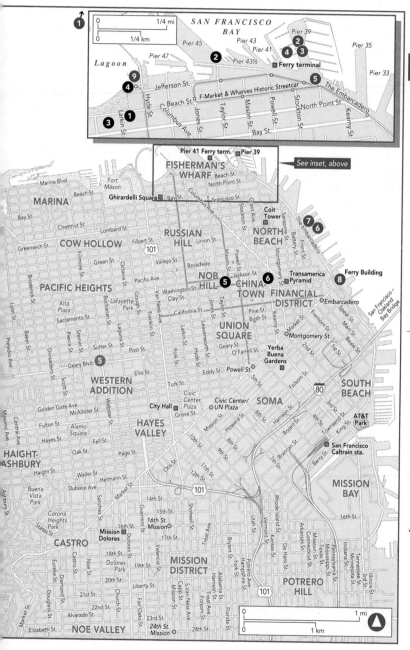

SAN FRANCISCO BAY

Pier 45
Pier 43
Pier 39
Pier 41
Pier 35
Pier 43½
Pier 33
Lagoon
Ferry terminal
Jefferson St.
F-Market & Wharves Historic Streetcar
The Embarcadero
Beach St.
North Point St.
Hyde St.
Columbus Ave.
Larkin St.
Jones St.
Taylor St.
Mason St.
Powell St.
Stockton St.
North Point St.
Kearny St.
Bay St.

0 ————— 1/4 mi
0 ————— 1/4 km

Pier 41 Ferry term. Pier 39

See inset, above

FISHERMAN'S WHARF

Beach St.
North Point St.

MARINA
Marina Blvd
Fort Mason
Beach St.
Ghirardelli Square
Bay St.
Francisco St.
Columbus Ave.
Bay St.
Chestnut St.
Greenwich St.
Lombard St.
Filbert St.
Union St.

COW HOLLOW
RUSSIAN HILL
101
Coit Tower
NORTH BEACH
Sansome St.
Battery St.
The Embarcadero

Green St.
Vallejo St.
Broadway
Pacific Ave.
PACIFIC HEIGHTS
Octavia St.
Buchanan St.
Laguna St.
Gough St.
Franklin St.
Van Ness Ave.
Polk St.
Larkin St.
Hyde St.
Leavenworth St.
Jones St.
Taylor St.
Mason St.
Powell St.
Stockton St.
Jackson St.
NOB HILL
Washington St.
Clay St.
CHINA TOWN
California St.
Pine St.
Bush St.
Transamerica Pyramid
FINANCIAL DISTRICT
Embarcadero
Ferry Building
San Francisco – Oakland Bay Bridge
Spear St.
Main St.
Beale St.
Fremont St.

Brederick St.
Lyon St.
Baker St.
Broderick St.
Filmore St.
Steiner St.
Pierce St.
Scott St.
Divisadero St.
Presidio Ave.
Masonic Ave.
Central Ave.
Alta Plaza
Lafayette Park
Sacramento St.
Sutter St.
Post St.
Geary Blvd.
UNION SQUARE
Geary St.
O'Farrell St.
Market St.
Montgomery St.
2nd St.
1st St.

WESTERN ADDITION
Ellis St.
Turk St.
Golden Gate Ave.
McAllister St.
Fulton St.
Alamo Square
Webster St.
Civic Center Plaza
City Hall
Civic Center/ UN Plaza
Grove St.
Eddy St.
Powell St.
5th St.
Yerba Buena Gardens
SOMA
Howard St.
Folsom St.
Bryant St.
Brannan St.
3rd St.
4th St.
Townsend St.
King St.
SOUTH BEACH
AT&T (Park)

HAIGHT- ASHBURY
Ashbury St.
Buena Vista Park
Corona Heights Park
States St.
HAYES VALLEY
Hayes St.
Oak St.
Page St.
Fell St.
Haight St.
Waller St.
Hermann St.
Duboce Ave.
101
Mission St.
10th St.
9th St.
8th St.
7th St.
11th St.
12th St.
Sanchez St.
Market St.
14th St.
15th St.
16th St. Mission
17th St.
San Francisco Caltrain sta.
Berry St.
MISSION BAY
16th St.
Rhode Island St.
Kansas St.
De Haro St.
Carolina St.
Wisconsin St.
Arkansas St.
Connecticut St.
Missouri St.
Texas St.
Mississippi St.
Pennsylvania Ave.
Minnesota St.
Indiana St.
3rd St.
Illinois St.
Tennessee St.

CASTRO
Castro St.
Noe St.
Eureka St.
Diamond St.
Douglass St.
21st St.
22nd St.
Church St.
Fair Oaks St.
Dolores St.
Guerrero St.
Valencia St.
Mission St.
S.Van Ness Ave.
Capp St.
Shotwell St.
Folsom St.
Harrison St.
Alabama St.
Treat Ave.
Bryant St.
York St.
Hampshire St.
Florida St.
Bryant St.
Potrero Ave.
Utah St.
Vermont St.
POTRERO HILL
Mission Dolores
Dolores Park
MISSION DISTRICT
18th St.
19th St.
20th St.
Liberty St.
Alvarado St.
23rd St.
24th St. Mission
24th St.
Elizabeth St.
NOE VALLEY
101

0 ————————— 1 mi
0 ————————— 1 km

Hop off at the corner of Washington and Mason sts. on Nob Hill for the:

6 Cable Car Museum ★★

After riding these moving landmarks, kids will love this quick museum that shows how the cable cars work. The actual cables that pull all the cars through the city are right here spinning on giant wheels. See p. 113.

Walk a few blocks down Washington St. to:

7 Chinatown ★★★

The perfect way to end the day is a stroll through this very colorful neighborhood. Kids will love the shops selling everything from air guns to kites to fireworks to live animals. For a detailed tour itinerary, see p. 140. When it's time for dinner, the possibilities are endless (see box on p. 86).

BEST OF SAN FRANCISCO WITH KIDS IN 3 DAYS

If you are lucky enough to have 3 full days in San Francisco with your kids, head to the other side of town on Day 3 and hit Golden Gate Park. There you'll visit a science museum, go for a boat ride, wander through the park some more, then go relax at the beach, and have yummy shabu shabu for dinner. *Start: Bus nos. 5, 28, or 44.*

1 California Academy of Sciences

Anchored in Golden Gate Park is this family favorite spot where you can visit a planetarium, find an albino alligator, climb through a tropical rainforest, learn about earthquakes, see penguins splash about, and check out jellyfish and other sea creatures. Grab a gourmet snack at the surprisingly good cafe if hunger hits. See p. 123.

Walk west for a few minutes until you reach Stow Lake.

2 Rent a Boat on Stow Lake

Frogs, ducks, seagulls, strolling residents, pretty much everyone loves this picturesque little lake with a walk-able center island called Strawberry Hill. Rent a pedal boat, a rowboat, or a low-speed electric boat at the Boathouse (p. 125) and take in a classic San Francisco experience.

Head over to Strawberry Hill in the middle of the lake.

3 More Golden Gate Park

By now the kids are probably tired of having an agenda—enjoy this beautiful park. Maybe the Japanese Tea Garden (p. 124)? Perhaps the Conservatory of Flowers (p. 123)? There's even a fantastic and elaborate Children's Playground complete with a carousel. For a list of things to do, see p. 122.

Either walk or hop on a bus and head to the beach. Use www.511.org to figure out which bus to take, depending on where you are in the park.

4 Cliff House

Stop in for a drink and a bathroom break. Look at the pictures all over the walls showing what it looked like in this area 100 years ago. Once refreshed, head outside and look for wildlife on Seal Rocks. Walk to the right and climb around the ruins of the Sutro Baths. Go relax on the beach and take a nap, or dig a hole. Do not go swimming here; the currents are dangerous. The **Cliff House,** see p. 137.

Take the bus no. 38 to the corner of Geary and Fillmore sts.

5 Japantown for Dinner ☕

Chinese last night—how about Japanese tonight? Fun options inside Japan Center include perennial kid favorite Benihana (1737 Post St., 🕐 415/563-4844; reserve in advance!) and Isobune Sushi (in Japan Center, 1737 Post St., 🕐 415/563-1030; drop-in OK), where you'll pluck plates of surprisingly affordable sushi off of little boats floating around a circular centerpiece stream. See p. 120.

CITY LAYOUT

San Francisco occupies the tip of a 32-mile peninsula between San Francisco Bay and the Pacific Ocean. Its land area measures about 46 square miles, although the city is often referred to as being 7 square miles. At more than 900 feet high, towering Twin Peaks (which are, in fact, two neighboring peaks), mark the geographic center of the city and make a great place to take in a vista of San Francisco.

With lots of one-way streets, San Francisco might seem confusing at first, but it will quickly become easy to navigate. The city's downtown streets are arranged in a simple grid pattern, with the exceptions of Market Street and Columbus Avenue, which cut

tips **FOR GETTING AROUND**

Here are a few strategies for making your way around the city:

1. San Francisco is really a small city. If you're in reasonably good shape, and you leave your stilettos at home, you can hoof it quite easily between many of the sights we suggest in this book, without stressing about taxis, buses, cable cars, and such.

2. If you only remember the "F-Line" historic streetcar, you will be able to get almost anywhere you want to go in the Eastern half of the city. The F-Line starts at the Castro, close to Mission Dolores in the Mission District, and runs northwest "up" Market Street to within a couple of blocks of City Hall, the Asian Arts Museum, and many of the performing arts venues in the Civic Center area. The route continues along Market Street to within a couple of

blocks of Union Square and the Yerba Buena District, through the Financial District, and on to the historic Ferry Building. Then the F-Line turns left, running along the Embarcadero passing right in front of the Exploratorium, past streets leading to Coit Tower in North Beach, and on to Pier 39 and the rest of Fisherman's Wharf, where the route ends. Add in the no. 5 Fulton bus, which runs east-west from downtown to the ocean, and you have most of the city covered with only two routes to remember.

3. If all else fails, use your smart phone to search www.511.org. You can input your current and desired addresses and this foolproof site will give you all your public transportation options and tell you when the next vehicle will be along to save you.

across the grid at right angles to each other. Hills appear to distort this pattern, however, and can disorient you. As you learn your way around, the hills will become your landmarks and reference points.

MAIN ARTERIES & STREETS **Market Street** is downtown San Francisco's main thoroughfare. Most of the city's buses travel this route on their way to the Financial District from the outer neighborhoods to the west and south. The tall office buildings clustered downtown are at the northeast end of Market; 1 block beyond lies the Embarcadero and the bay.

The **Embarcadero**—an excellent strolling, skating, and biking route—curves along San Francisco Bay from south of the Bay Bridge near the Giants' home at AT&T Park to the northeast perimeter of the city. It terminates at the famous tourist-oriented Fisherman's Wharf. Aquatic Park, Fort Mason, and Golden Gate National Recreation Area are on the northernmost point of the peninsula.

From the eastern perimeter of Fort Mason, **Van Ness Avenue** runs due south, back to Market Street. This area forms a rough triangle, with Market Street as its southeastern boundary, the waterfront as its northern boundary, and Van Ness Avenue as its western boundary. Within this triangle lies most of the city's main tourist sights.

Another main artery, which is less on the tourist track, is **Geary Boulevard**, which stretches from Union Square, through the bedroom-community Richmond District, and all the way out to Ocean Beach.

FINDING AN ADDRESS Because most of the city's streets are laid out in a grid pattern, finding an address is easy when you know the nearest cross street. Numbers start with 1 at the beginning of the street and proceed at the rate of 100 per block. When asking for directions, find out the nearest cross street and your destination's neighborhood, but be careful not to confuse numerical avenues with numerical streets. Numerical avenues (Third Ave. and so on) are in the Richmond and Sunset districts in the western part of the city. Numerical streets (Third St. and so on) are south of Market Street in the east and south parts of town.

Major Neighborhoods in Brief

See the "San Francisco Neighborhoods" map on p. 24.

UNION SQUARE Union Square is the commercial hub of San Francisco. Most major hotels and department stores are crammed into the area surrounding the actual square, which was named for a series of violent pro-union rallies staged here on the eve of the Civil War. A plethora of upscale boutiques, mediocre restaurants (soon to be improving), and galleries occupy the spaces tucked between the larger buildings. A few blocks west is the **Tenderloin** neighborhood, a patch of poverty and blight brimming with drug addicts and homeless people. While most keep to themselves, this is definitely a place to keep your wits about you. The **Theater District,** also populated by down-on-their-luck residents, is 3 blocks west of Union Square.

THE FINANCIAL DISTRICT East of Union Square, this area sometimes referred to as Fi-Di—bordered by the Embarcadero and by Market, Third, Kearny, and Washington streets—is the city's business district and home to many major corporations. The pointy Transamerica Pyramid at Montgomery and Clay streets is the district's most conspicuous architectural feature. To its east sprawls the Embarcadero Center, an 8½-acre complex housing offices, shops, and restaurants. Farther east still at the water's edge is the old Ferry Building, the city's pre-bridge transportation hub. Ferries to Sausalito and Larkspur still leave from this point. However a renovation in 2003 made the building an attraction all its own; today it's packed with outstanding restaurants and gourmet food—and wine-related shops, and surrounded by a farmers' market a few days a week that attracts residents and top chefs looking to fill their fridges.

NOB HILL & RUSSIAN HILL
Bounded by Bush, Larkin, Pacific, and Stockton streets, Nob Hill is a genteel, well-heeled district occupied by the city's power brokers and the neighborhood businesses they frequent. Russian Hill extends from Pacific to Bay streets and from Polk to Mason streets. It contains steep streets, lush gardens, and high-rises occupied by both the moneyed and the bohemian.

CHINATOWN
A large red-and-green gate on Grant Avenue at Bush Street marks the official entrance to Chinatown. Beyond lies a 24-block labyrinth, bordered by Broadway, Bush, Kearny, and Stockton streets, filled with restaurants, markets, temples, shops, apartment buildings, and a substantial percentage of San Francisco's Chinese residents. Chinatown is a great place for exploration all along Grant and Stockton streets, Portsmouth Square, and the alleys that lead off them, like Ross and Waverly. Chinatown's incessant traffic and precious few parking spots mean you shouldn't even consider driving around here.

NORTH BEACH
This Italian neighborhood, which stretches from Montgomery and Jackson streets to Bay Street, is one of the best places in the city to grab a coffee, pull up a cafe chair, and do some serious people-watching. At night, the restaurants, bars, and clubs along Columbus and Grant avenues attract folks from all over the Bay Area. Down Columbus Avenue toward the Financial District are the remains of the city's Beat Generation landmarks, including Ferlinghetti's City Lights Booksellers. Broadway Street—a short strip of sex joints—cuts through the heart of the district. **Telegraph Hill** looms over the east side of North Beach, topped by Coit Tower, one of San Francisco's best vantage points.

FISHERMAN'S WHARF
North Beach runs into Fisherman's Wharf, which was once the busy heart of the city's great harbor and waterfront industries. Today it's a popular tourist area with little, if any, authentic waterfront life, except for a small fleet of fishing boats and some noisy sea lions. What it does have going for it are activities for the whole family, with honky-tonk attractions and museums, restaurants, trinket shops, and beautiful views everywhere you look.

THE MARINA DISTRICT
Created on landfill—actually rubble from the 1906 earthquake—for the Panama Pacific Exposition of 1915, the Marina District boasts some of the best views of the Golden Gate, as well as plenty of grassy fields alongside San Francisco Bay. Elegant Mediterranean-style homes and apartments, inhabited by the city's well-to-do singles and wealthy families, line the streets. Here, too, are architectural wonder the Palace of Fine Arts, the artcentric warehouses of Fort Mason, and dog and jogger-lover's paradise, Crissy Field. The main street is Chestnut, between Franklin and Lyon streets, which abounds with shops, cafes, and boutiques. Because of its landfill foundation, the Marina was among the hardest-hit districts in the 1989 quake.

COW HOLLOW
Located west of Van Ness Avenue, between Russian Hill and the Presidio, this flat, graze-able area supported 30 dairy farms in 1861. Today, Cow Hollow is largely residential and largely post-colligate young professionals. Its two primary commercial thoroughfares are Lombard Street, known for its relatively cheap motels, and Union Street, an upscale shopping sector filled with restaurants, pubs, cafes, and boutiques.

PACIFIC HEIGHTS
The ultra-elite, such as the Gettys and Danielle Steel—and those lucky enough to buy before the real-estate boom—reside in the mansions and homes in this neighborhood. When the rich meander out of their fortresses, they wander down to the neighborhood's two posh shopping and dining streets—Fillmore or Union—and join the pretty people who frequent the chic boutiques and lively neighborhood restaurants, cafes, and bars.

JAPANTOWN
Bounded by Octavia, Fillmore, California, and Geary streets, Japantown shelters only a small percentage

San Francisco Neighborhoods

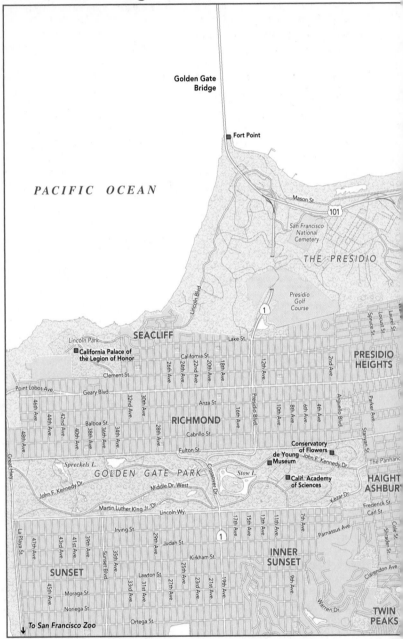

PACIFIC OCEAN

Golden Gate Bridge

Fort Point

Mason St.

101

San Francisco National Cemetery

THE PRESIDIO

Presidio Golf Course

1

Lincoln Park

SEACLIFF

Lake St.

California Palace of the Legion of Honor

California St.

PRESIDIO HEIGHTS

Clement St.

Point Lobos Ave.

Geary Blvd.

Anza St.

RICHMOND

Cabrillo St.

Balboa St.

Fulton St.

Conservatory of Flowers

de Young Museum

John F. Kennedy Dr.

The Panhand

Spreckels L.

GOLDEN GATE PARK

Stow L.

Calif. Academy of Sciences

HAIGHT ASHBUR'

John F. Kennedy Dr.

Middle Dr. West

Martin Luther King Jr. Dr.

Lincoln Wy.

Kezar Dr.

Frederick St.

Carl St.

Irving St.

Judah St.

Parnassus Ave.

Kirkham St.

INNER SUNSET

Lawton St.

SUNSET

Moraga St.

Clarendon Ave.

Noriega St.

Ortega St.

TWIN PEAKS

To San Francisco Zoo

Great Hwy.

46th Ave. 48th Ave. 44th Ave. 42nd Ave. 40th Ave. 38th Ave. 36th Ave. 34th Ave. 32nd Ave. 30th Ave. 28th Ave. 26th Ave. 24th Ave. 22nd Ave. 20th Ave. 18th Ave. 16th Ave. 12th Ave. 10th Ave. 8th Ave. 6th Ave. 4th Ave. 2nd Ave.

Lincoln Blvd.

Presidio Blvd.

Arguello Blvd.

Parker Ave. Stanyan St. Spruce St. Locust St. Laurel St.

La Playa St. 47th Ave. 45th Ave. 43rd Ave. 41st Ave. 39th Ave. 35th Ave. 33rd Ave. 31st Ave. 29th Ave. 27th Ave. 25th Ave. 23rd Ave. 21st Ave. 19th Ave. 17th Ave. 15th Ave. 13th Ave. 11th Ave. 9th Ave. 7th Ave.

Sunset Blvd. Crossover Dr. Cole St. Shrader St.

Warren Dr.

To Alcatraz ↑

0   1 mi
0   1 km

SAN

FRANCISCO

BAY

Pier 41
Ferry term. ■ Pier 39
FISHERMAN'S
WHARF

Beach St.   North Point St.
Fort
Mason   Beach St.
MARINA   Francisco St.   Coit   ■ Exploratorium
Ghirardelli Square ■ Bay St.   Tower
Bay St.   NORTH
Chestnut St.   BEACH
Greenwich St.   Lombard St.   Filbert St. RUSSIAN
COW HOLLOW   HILL   Union St.
Green St.   Ferry Building
Vallejo St.   Broadway
Pacific Ave.   NOB   Jackson St.   Transamerica
PACIFIC HEIGHTS   HILL CHINA-   Pyramid
Washington St.   TOWN FINANCIAL
Alta   Lafayette Clay St.   DISTRICT Embarcadero
Plaza   Park   California St.
Sacramento St.   Pine St.
Bush St.
Sutter St.   UNION   Montgomery St.
Post St.   SQUARE   Geary St.
Geary Blvd.   O'Farrell St. Yerba
Ellis St.   Powell St. Buena   SOUTH
WESTERN   Eddy St.   Gardens BEACH
ADDITION   Turk St.   Folsom St.
Golden Gate Ave.   Civic   80
McAllister St.   Center   Civic Center/ SOMA
City Hall ■ Plaza   UN Plaza   AT&T
Fulton St. Alamo   Grove St.   Park
Square HAYES   Mission St.   San Francisco
Hayes St.   VALLEY   Howard St.   Caltrain sta.
Fell St.   MISSION
Oak St.   Page St.   BAY
Haight St.
Waller St.   16th St.
Buena   Duboce Ave. Hermann St.
Vista   Market St.
Park   14th St.
Corona   15th St.
Heights   16th St.
Park   Mission
CASTRO   Mission Dolores ■ 17th St.
18th St.
Dolores MISSION   POTRERO
Park 19th St. DISTRICT   HILL
20th St.
21st St.
22nd St.
23rd St.
NOE VALLEY   24th St.   24th St.
Mission

SAN FRANCISCO - OAKLAND BAY BRIDGE

of the city's Japanese population. At its epicenter is Japan Center, a dated but fun 2-block indoor mall featuring Japanese knickknack shops, bookstores, noodle restaurants, and more. Duck inside one of the photo booths and take home a dozen Hello Kitty stickers as a souvenir.

CIVIC CENTER Although millions of dollars have gone toward brick sidewalks, ornate lampposts, and elaborate street plantings, the southwestern section of Market Street can still feel a little sketchy due to the large number of homeless people who wander the area. The Civic Center at the "bottom" of Market Street, however, is a stunning beacon of culture and refinement. This large complex of buildings includes the domed and dapper City Hall, the Opera House, Davies Symphony Hall, the new SFJAZZ building, and the Asian Art Museum. The landscaped plaza connecting the buildings is the staging area for San Francisco's frequent demonstrations for or against just about everything.

SOMA This expansive flatland area within the triangle of the Embarcadero, Hwy. 101, and Market Street is characterized by wide, busy streets and old warehouses and industrial spaces with a few scattered underground nightclubs, restaurants, and shoddy residential areas. But over the years the addition of the Museum of Modern Art, Yerba Buena Gardens, the Jewish and African Diaspora museums, Metreon, and AT&T Park, and later offices for major companies like Twitter have infused the gritty area with multimillion-dollar lofts, fancy high-rise residences, and a bevy of new businesses, hotels, restaurants, and nightclubs.

MISSION DISTRICT Mexican and Latin American populations made this area home, with their cuisine, traditions, and art creating a vibrant cultural area, but more recently, the Mission is home to San Francisco's hipsters and hippest restaurants. Some parts of the neighborhood are still poor and sprinkled with the homeless, gangs, and drug addicts, but young urbanites have declared the place their own, lured

by the endless oh-so-hot restaurants and bars that stretch from 16th and Valencia streets to 25th and Mission streets. Less adventurous tourists may just want to duck into Mission Dolores (San Francisco's oldest building), cruise past a few of the 200-plus amazing murals, and head back downtown. But anyone who's interested in hanging with the hipsters and experiencing the hottest restaurant and bar nightlife should definitely beeline it here.

THE CASTRO One of the liveliest districts in town, the Castro is practically synonymous with San Francisco's gay community, who moved here back in the 1970s, turning this once Irish working-class neighborhood into a bustling hotbed of shops, bars, and restaurants. Located at the top of Market Street, between 17th and 18th streets, the Castro offers a thoroughly entertaining dose of street theater, and while most businesses cater to the gay community, it's more than welcoming to open-minded straight people.

HAIGHT–ASHBURY Part trendy, part nostalgic, part funky, the Haight, as it's most commonly known, was the soul of the psychedelic free-loving 1960s and the center of the counterculture movement. Today, thanks to a never-ending real estate boom, the gritty neighborhood straddling upper Haight Street on the eastern border of Golden Gate Park is more gentrified, but the commercial area still harbors all walks of life. But you don't need to be groovy to enjoy the Haight—the ethnic food, trendy shops, and bars cover all tastes. From Haight Street, walk south on Cole Street for a more peaceful neighborhood experience.

RICHMOND & SUNSET DISTRICTS San Francisco's suburbs of sorts, these are the city's largest and most populous neighborhoods, consisting mainly of small homes, shops, cafes, and neighborhood restaurants. Although they border Golden Gate Park and Ocean Beach, few tourists venture into "the Avenues," as these areas are referred to locally, unless they're on their way to the Cliff House, zoo, beach, or Palace of the Legion of Honor Museum.

SAN FRANCISCO IN CONTEXT

Often referred to as America's most European city, regularly topping travel magazine favorite cities lists, and famed for its postcard-perfect vistas, San Francisco is indeed, as John Steinbeck described, "a golden handcuff with the key thrown away." But it's more than topography that makes the City by the Bay one of the top places for 16.5 million visitors to leave their hearts each year. The colorful Molded and refined politically, socially, and physically and refined by a variety of natural and manmade events outlined here, the city's character is like no other.

SAN FRANCISCO TODAY

While San Francisco's international character began to take shape during the 1849 Gold Rush (discussed below), over the past two decades, California's fourth largest and most densely populated city (second in the nation, behind New York, with 826,000 residents), has weathered the wild ride of two more boom-or-bust economies. The first, in the late 1990s, was the famed "Dot-com boom," which, when it went bust in the early 2000s, left the city's residents, businesses and real estate market reeling from economic whiplash. Today, it's on an upswing again. Only this time, there's no end in sight to the growth and influx of new wealth. With the Bay Area as the epicenter of the now-established Internet industry and San Francisco the most compelling crash pad for young entrepreneurs and tech workers (who have access to big luxurious private busses that shuttle them to Silicon Valley), the face of the city is changing at wireless Internet speed. Teardown homes in nice neighborhoods are selling for upward of $2 million. Room rentals in shared homes regularly go for more than $1,200. Once-desolate industrial areas are now being developed into multi-use communities teeming with glistening new luxury condos, chic restaurants and trendy businesses.

Not surprisingly, there's backlash. Reports show that middle-income residents are moving out at rates much faster than they are moving in. The Occupy SF movement, itself part of Occupy Wall Street, brought the city's economic struggles front and center in the fall of 2011, as hundreds camped out and protested in San Francisco, Oakland, and throughout the Bay Area. (A legitimate question heard from the encampment in Justin Herman Plaza: Why can't everyone who works in San Francisco afford housing in or near San Francisco?) And, of course, there are the typical big-city problems: Crime is up along with drug use, and despite efforts to curb the ubiquitous problem of homelessness and panhandling, it's still a thorny—and very visible—issue.

Still, the spirit of San Francisco is still alive and well. Its convention halls are fully booked and, the Giants and 49ers are riding high, and since the U.S. Supreme Court struck down "Prop 8" in June 2013, Governor Jerry Brown has instructed all county clerks to issue same-sex marriage licenses. San Franciscans are lining up for hot, new restaurants and nightspots, packing theaters and film festivals, and crowding into Apple Stores to get their hands on the latest iPhone. Though it may never relive its heady days as the king of the West Coast and it's hard to predict just how much the continued flood of privileged new residents will affect its tolerant, alternative soul, San Francisco continues to embrace diverse lifestyles and liberal thinking and will undoubtedly retain the title as everyone's favorite California city.

3 LOOKING BACK AT SAN FRANCISCO

In the Beginning

Born as an out-of-the-way backwater of colonial Spain and blessed with a harbor that would have been the envy of any of the great cities of Europe, San Francisco boasts a story that is as varied as the millions of people who have passed through its Golden Gate.

THE AGE OF DISCOVERY After the "discovery" of the New World by Columbus in 1492, legends of the fertile land of California were discussed in the universities and taverns of Europe, even though no one really understood where the mythical land was. (Some evidence of arrivals in California by Chinese merchants hundreds of years before Columbus's landing has been unearthed, although few scholars are willing to draw definite conclusions.) The first documented visit by a European to northern California, however, was by the Portuguese explorer João Cabrilho, who circumnavigated the southern tip of South America and traveled as far north as the Russian River in 1542. Nearly 40 years later, in 1579, Sir Francis Drake landed on the northern

DATELINE

1542 Juan Cabrillo sails up the California coast.

1579 Sir Francis Drake lands near San Francisco, missing the entrance to the bay.

1769 Members of the Spanish expedition led by Gaspar de Portolá become the first Europeans to see San Francisco Bay.

1775 The *San Carlos* is the first European ship to sail into San Francisco Bay.

1776 Captain Juan Bautista de Anza establishes a presidio (military fort); San Francisco de Asís Mission opens.

1821 Mexico wins independence from Spain and annexes California.

1835 The town of Yerba Buena develops around the port; the United States tries unsuccessfully to purchase San Francisco Bay from Mexico.

1846 Mexican-American War.

1847 Americans annex Yerba Buena and rename it San Francisco.

California coast, stopping for a time to repair his ships and to claim the territory for Queen Elizabeth I of England. He was followed several years later by another Portuguese, Sebastian Cermeño, "discoverer" of Punta de los Reyes (King's Point) in the mid-1590s. Ironically, all three adventurers completely missed the narrow entrance to San Francisco Bay, either because it was enshrouded in fog or, more likely, because they simply weren't looking for it. Believe it or not, the bay's entrance is nearly impossible to see from the open ocean. It would be another 2 centuries before a European actually saw the bay that would later extend Spain's influence over much of the American West. Gaspar de Portolá, a soldier sent from Spain to meddle in a rather ugly conflict between the Jesuits and the Franciscans, accidentally stumbled upon the bay in 1769, en route to somewhere else, but then stoically plodded on to his original destination, Monterey Bay, more than 100 miles to the south. Six years later, Juan Ayala, while on a mapping expedition for the Spanish, actually sailed into San Francisco Bay and immediately realized the enormous strategic importance of his find.

Colonization quickly followed. Juan Bautista de Anza and around 30 Spanish-speaking families marched through the deserts from Sonora, Mexico, arriving after many hardships at the northern tip of modern-day San Francisco in June 1776. They immediately claimed the peninsula for Spain. (Ironically, their claim of allegiance to Spain occurred only about a week before the 13 English-speaking colonies of North America's eastern seaboard, a continent away, declared their independence from Britain.) Their headquarters was an adobe fortress, the Presidio, built on the site of today's park with the same name. The settlers' church, built a mile to the south, was the first of five Spanish missions later developed around the edges of San Francisco Bay. Although the name of the church was officially Nuestra Señora de Dolores, it was dedicated to St. Francis of Assisi and nicknamed San Francisco by the Franciscan priests. Later, the name was applied to the entire bay.

In 1821, Mexico broke away from Spain, secularized the Spanish missions, and abandoned all interest in the Indian natives. Freed of Spanish restrictions, California's ports were suddenly opened to trade. The region around San Francisco Bay supplied large numbers of hides and tallow for transport around Cape Horn to the tanneries and

1848 Gold is discovered in Coloma, near Sacramento.

1849 In the year of the gold rush, San Francisco's population swells from about 800 to 25,000.

1851 Lawlessness becomes acute before attempts are made to curb it.

1869 The transcontinental railroad reaches San Francisco.

1873 Andrew S. Hallidie invents the cable car.

1906 The Great Earthquake strikes, and the resulting fire levels the city.

1915 The Panama Pacific International Exposition celebrates San Francisco's restoration and the completion of the Panama Canal.

1936 The Bay Bridge is built.

1937 The Golden Gate Bridge is completed.

1945 The United Nations Charter is drafted and adopted by the representatives of 50 countries meeting in San Francisco.

1950 The Beat Generation moves into the bars and cafes of North Beach.

continues

factories of New England and New York. The prospects for prosperity persuaded an English-born sailor, William Richardson, to jump ship in 1822 and settle on the site of what is now San Francisco. To impress the commandant of the Presidio, whose daughter he loved, Richardson converted to Catholicism and established the beginnings of what would soon became a thriving trading post and colony. Richardson named his trading post Yerba Buena (or "good herb"), because of a species of wild mint that grew there, near the site of today's Montgomery Street. (The city's original name was recalled with endless mirth 120 years later during San Francisco's hippie era.) He conducted a profitable hide-trading business and eventually became harbormaster and the city's first merchant prince. By 1839, the place was a veritable town, with a mostly English-speaking populace and a saloon of dubious virtue.

Throughout the 19th century, armed hostilities between English-speaking settlers from the eastern seaboard and the Spanish-speaking colonies of Spain and Mexico erupted in places as widely scattered as Texas, Puerto Rico, and along the frequently shifting U.S.–Mexico border. In 1846, a group of U.S. Marines from the warship *Portsmouth* seized the sleepy main plaza of Yerba Buena, ran the U.S. flag up a pole, and declared California an American territory. The Presidio (occupied by about a dozen unmotivated Mexican soldiers) surrendered without a fuss. The first move the new, mostly Yankee citizenry made was to officially adopt the name of the bay as the name of their town.

THE GOLD RUSH   The year 1848 was one of the most pivotal years in European history, with unrest sweeping through Europe and widespread disillusionment about the hopes for prosperity throughout the eastern coast of the United States. Stories about the golden port of San Francisco and the agrarian wealth of the American West filtered slowly east, attracting slow-moving groups of settlers. Ex-sailor Richard Henry Dana extolled the virtues of California in his best-selling novel *Two Years Before the Mast* and helped fire the public's imagination about the territory's bounty, particularly that of the Bay Area.

The first overland party crossed the Sierra and arrived in California in 1841. San Francisco grew steadily, reaching a population of approximately 900 by April 1848,

1967   A free concert in Golden Gate Park attracts 20,000 people, ushering in the Summer of Love and the hippie era.

1974   BART's high-speed transit system opens the tunnel linking San Francisco with the East Bay.

1978   Harvey Milk, a city supervisor and America's first openly gay politician, is assassinated, along with Mayor George Moscone, by political rival Dan White.

1989   An earthquake registering 7.1 on the Richter scale hits San Francisco during a World Series baseball game, as 100 million

watch on TV; the city quickly rebuilds.

1991   Fire rages through the Berkeley/ Oakland hills, destroying 2,800 homes.

1993   Yerba Buena Center for the Arts opens.

1995   New San Francisco Museum of Modern Art opens.

1996   Former Assembly Speaker Willie Brown elected mayor of San Francisco.

2000   Pacific Bell Park (now AT&T Park), the new home to the San Francisco Giants, opens.

but nothing hinted at the population explosion that was to follow. Historian Barry Parr has referred to the California gold rush as the most extraordinary event to ever befall an American city in peacetime. In time, San Francisco's winning combination of raw materials, healthful climate, and freedom would have attracted thousands of settlers even without the lure of gold. But the gleam of the soft metal is said to have compressed 50 years of normal growth into less than 6 months. In 1848, the year gold was first discovered, the population of San Francisco jumped from under 1,000 to 26,000 in less than 6 months. As many as 100,000 more passed through San Francisco in the space of less than a year on their way to the rocky hinterlands where the gold was rumored to be.

If not for the discovery of some small particles of gold at a sawmill that he owned, Swiss-born John Augustus Sutter's legacy would have been far less flamboyant. Despite Sutter's wish to keep the discovery quiet, his employee John Marshall leaked word of the discovery to friends. It eventually appeared in local papers, and smart investors on the East Coast took immediate heed. The rush did not start, however, until Sam Brannan, a Mormon preacher and famous charlatan, ran through the streets of San Francisco shouting, "Gold! Gold in the American River!" (Brannan, incidentally, bought up all the harborfront real estate he could get and cornered the market on shovels, pickaxes, and canned food, just before making the announcement that was heard around the world.)

A world on the brink of change responded almost frantically. The gold rush was on. Shop owners hung GONE TO THE DIGGINGS signs in their windows. Flotillas of ships set sail from ports throughout Europe, South America, Australia, and the East Coast, sometimes nearly sinking with the weight of mining equipment. Townspeople from the Midwest headed overland, and the social fabric of a nation was transformed almost overnight. Not since the Crusades of the Middle Ages had so many people been mobilized in so short a period of time. Daily business stopped; ships arrived in San Francisco and were almost immediately deserted by their crews. News of the gold strike spread like a plague through every discontented hamlet in the known world. Although other settlements were closer to the gold strike, San Francisco was the

2002 The San Francisco Giants make it to the World Series but lose to the Anaheim Angels in Game 7.

2004 Thirty-six-year-old supervisor Gavin Newsom becomes the city's 42nd mayor and quickly makes headlines by authorizing City Hall to issue marriage licenses to same-sex couples. Six months later, the state supreme court invalidates 3,955 gay marriages.

2005 The new, seismically correct $202-million de Young Museum opens in Golden Gate Park.

2006 The 100-year anniversary of the Great Earthquake and fire of

1906, the greatest disaster ever to befall an American metropolis, is commemorated.

2007 A tiger escapes from its pen at the San Francisco Zoo, killing one man and injuring two others before the police shoot and kill it.

2008 The California Supreme Court overturns the ban on same-sex marriage, touching off short-lived celebrations at San Francisco City Hall. The ban is reinstated in an election later that year, added to the ballot as "Proposition 8."

continues

famous name, and therefore, where the gold-diggers disembarked. Tent cities sprung up, demand for virtually everything skyrocketed, and although some miners actually found gold, smart merchants quickly discovered that more enduring hopes lay in servicing the needs of the thousands of miners who arrived ill-equipped and ignorant of the lay of the land. Prices soared. Miners, faced with staggeringly inflated prices for goods and services, barely scraped a profit after expenses. Most prospectors failed, many died of hardship, others committed suicide at the alarming rate of 1,000 a year. Yet despite the tragedies, graft, and vice associated with the gold rush, within mere months San Francisco was forever transformed from a tranquil Spanish settlement into a roaring, boisterous boomtown.

BOOMTOWN FEVER By 1855, most of California's surface gold had already been panned out, leaving only the richer but deeper veins of ore, which individual miners couldn't retrieve without massive capital investments. Despite that, San Francisco had evolved into a vast commercial magnet, sucking into its warehouses and banks the staggering riches that overworked newcomers had dragged, ripped, and distilled from the rocks, fields, and forests of western North America.

Investment funds were being lavished on more than mining, however. Speculation on the newly established San Francisco stock exchange could make or destroy an investor in a single day, and several noteworthy writers (including Mark Twain) were among the young men forever influenced by the boomtown spirit. The American Civil War left California firmly in the Union camp, ready, willing, and able to receive hordes of disillusioned soldiers fed up with the internecine war-mongering of the eastern seaboard. In 1869, the transcontinental railway linked the eastern and western seaboards of the United States, ensuring the fortunes of the barons who controlled it. The railways, however, also shifted economic power bases as cheap manufactured goods from the east undercut the high prices hitherto charged for goods that sailed or steamed their way around the tip of South America. Ownership of the newly formed Central Pacific and Southern Pacific railroads was almost completely controlled by the "Big Four," all iron-willed capitalists—Leland Stanford, Mark Hopkins, Collis P. Huntington, and Charles Crocker—whose ruthlessness was legendary. (Much of the

2009 The economic downturn has San Francisco in a financial tailspin, but amazingly, tourism dollars keep pouring in. After a dismal start, hotel occupancies resurge. Small businesses continue to struggle, however, battling high rents and a cash-strapped public.

2010 The San Francisco Giants baseball team wins the World Series against the Texas Rangers; thousands of fans fill Civic Center Plaza for the parade and celebration.

2011 Ed Lee is elected San Francisco's 43rd mayor.

2012 The San Francisco Giants beat the Detroit Tigers to win the World Series, again.

2013 California Governor, Jerry Brown, instructs county clerks to begin issuing same-sex marriage licenses after the U.S. Supreme Court strikes down "Prop 8."

bone-crushing labor for their railway was executed by low-paid Chinese newcomers, most of whom arrived in overcrowded ships at San Francisco ports.) As the 19th century came to a close, civil unrest became more frequent as the monopolistic grip of the railways and robber barons became more obvious. Adding to the discontent were the uncounted thousands of Chinese immigrants, who fled starvation and unrest in Asia at rates rivaling those of the Italians, Poles, Irish, and British.

During the 1870s, the flood of profits from the Comstock Lode in western Nevada diminished to a trickle, a cycle of droughts wiped out part of California's agricultural bounty, and local industry struggled to survive against the flood of manufactured goods imported via railway from the well-established factories of the East Coast and Midwest. Often, discontented workers blamed their woes on the now-unwanted hordes of Chinese workers, who by preference and for mutual protection had congregated into teeming all-Asian communities.

Despite these downward cycles, the city enjoyed other bouts of prosperity around the turn of the 20th century, thanks to the Klondike gold rush in Alaska and the Spanish-American War. Long accustomed to making a buck off gold fever, San Francisco managed to position itself as a point of embarkation for supplies bound for Alaska. Also during this time emerged the Bank of America, which eventually evolved into the largest bank in the world. Founded in North Beach in 1904, Bank of America was the brainchild of Italian-born A. P. Giannini, who later funded part of the construction for a bridge that many critics said was preposterous: the Golden Gate.

THE GREAT FIRE   On the morning of April 18, 1906, San Francisco changed for all time. The city has never experienced an earthquake as destructive as the one that hit at 5:13am. (Scientists estimate its strength at 8.1 on the Richter scale.) All but a handful of the city's 400,000 inhabitants lay fast asleep when the ground beneath the city went into a series of convulsions. As one eyewitness put it, "The earth was shaking . . . it was undulating, rolling like an ocean breaker." The quake ruptured every water main in the city, and simultaneously started a chain of fires that rapidly fused into one gigantic conflagration. The fire brigades were helpless, and for 3 days, San Francisco burned.

Militia troops finally stopped the flames from advancing by dynamiting entire city blocks, but not before more than 28,000 buildings lay in ruins. Minor tremors lasted another 3 days. The final damage stretched across a path of destruction 450 miles long and 50 miles wide. In all, 497 city blocks were razed, or about one-third of the city. As Jack London wrote in a heart-rending newspaper dispatch, "The city of San Francisco is no more." The earthquake and subsequent fire so decisively changed the city that post-1906 San Francisco bears little resemblance to the town before the quake. Out of the ashes rose a bigger, healthier, and more beautiful town, though latter-day urbanologists regret that the rebuilding that followed the San Francisco earthquake did not follow a more enlightened plan. So eager was the city to rebuild that the old, somewhat unimaginative gridiron plan was reinstated, despite the opportunities for more daring visions that the aftermath of the quake afforded.

In 1915, in celebration of the opening of the Panama Canal and to prove to the world that San Francisco was restored to its full glory, the city hosted the Panama Pacific International Exhibition, a world's fair that exposed hundreds of thousands of visitors to the city's unique charms. The general frenzy of civic boosterism, however, reached its peak during the years just before World War I, when investments and civic pride might have reached an all-time high. Despite Prohibition, speakeasies did a thriving business in and around the city, and building sprees were as high-blown and lavish as the profits on the San Francisco stock exchange.

WORLD WAR II   The Japanese attack on Pearl Harbor on December 7, 1941, mobilized the United States into a massive war machine, with many shipyards strategically positioned along the Pacific Coast, including San Francisco. Within less than a year, several shipyards were producing up to one new warship per day, employing hundreds of thousands of people working in 24-hour shifts. (The largest, Kaiser Shipyards in Richmond, employed more than 100,000 workers alone.) In search of work and the excitement of life away from their villages and cornfields, workers flooded into the city from virtually everywhere, forcing an enormous boom in housing. Hundreds found themselves separated from their small towns for the first time in their lives and reveled in their newfound freedom.

After the hostilities ended, many soldiers remembered San Francisco as the site of their finest hours and returned to live there permanently. The economic prosperity of the postwar years enabled massive enlargements of the city, including freeways, housing developments, a booming financial district, and pockets of counterculture enthusiasts such as the beatniks, gays, and hippies.

THE 1950s: THE BEATS   San Francisco's reputation as a rollicking place where anything goes dates from the Barbary Coast days when gang warfare, prostitution, gambling, and drinking were major city pursuits, and citizens took law and order into their own hands. Its more modern role as a catalyst for social change and the avant-garde began in the 1950s when a group of young writers, philosophers, and poets challenged the materialism and conformity of American society by embracing anarchy and Eastern philosophy, expressing their notions in poetry. They adopted a uniform of jeans, sweaters, sandals, and berets, called themselves Beats, and hung out in North Beach where rents were low and cheap wine was plentiful. "San Francisco Chronicle" columnist Herb Caen, to whom they were totally alien, dubbed them *beatniks* in his column.

Allen Ginsberg, Gregory Corso, and Jack Kerouac had begun writing at Columbia University in New York, but it wasn't until they came west and hooked up with Lawrence Ferlinghetti, Kenneth Rexroth, Gary Snyder, and others that the movement gained national attention. The bible of the Beats was Ginsberg's "Howl," which he first read at the Six Gallery on October 13, 1955. By the time he finished reading, Ginsberg was crying, the audience was chanting, and his fellow poets were announcing the arrival of an epic bard. Ferlinghetti published "Howl," which was deemed obscene, in 1956. A trial followed, but the court found that the book had redeeming social value, thereby reaffirming the right of free expression. The other major work, Jack Kerouac's "On the Road," was published in 1957, instantly becoming a bestseller. (He had written it as one long paragraph in 20 days in 1951.) The freedom and sense of possibility that this book conveyed became the bellwether for a generation.

While the Beats gave poetry readings and generated controversy, two clubs in North Beach were making waves, notably the hungry i and the Purple Onion, where everyone who was anyone or became anyone on the entertainment scene appeared—Mort Sahl, Dick Gregory, Lenny Bruce, Barbra Streisand, and Woody Allen all worked here. Maya Angelou appeared as a singer and dancer at the Purple Onion. The cafes of North Beach were the center of bohemian life in the '50s: the Black Cat, Vesuvio, Caffe Trieste and Tosca Cafe, and Enrico's Sidewalk Café. When the tour buses started rolling in, rents went up, and Broadway turned into strip club row in the early 1960s. Thus ended an era, and the Beats moved on. The alternative scene shifted to Berkeley and the Haight.

THE 1960s: THE HAIGHT The torch of freedom had been passed from the Beats and North Beach to Haight-Ashbury and the hippies, but it was a radically different torch. The hippies replaced the Beats' angst, anarchy, negativism, nihilism, alcohol, and poetry with love, communalism, openness, drugs, rock music, and a back-to-nature philosophy. Although the scent of marijuana wafted everywhere—on the streets, in the cafes, in Golden Gate Park—the real drugs of choice were LSD (a tab of good acid cost $5) and other hallucinogens. Timothy Leary experimented with its effects and exhorted youth to turn on, tune in, and drop out. Instead of hanging out in coffeehouses, the hippies went to concerts at the Fillmore or the Avalon Ballroom to dance. The first Family Dog Rock 'n' Roll Dance and Concert, "A Tribute to Dr. Strange," was given at the Longshoreman's Hall in fall 1965, featuring Jefferson Airplane, the Marbles, the Great Society, and the Charlatans. At this event, the first major happening of the 1960s, Ginsberg led a snake dance through the crowd. In January 1966, the 3-day Trips Festival, organized by rock promoter Bill Graham, was also held at the Longshoreman's Hall. The climax came with Ken Kesey and the Merry Pranksters Acid Test show, which used five movie screens, psychedelic visions, and the sounds of the Grateful Dead and Big Brother and the Holding Company. The "be-in" followed in the summer of 1966 at the polo grounds in Golden Gate Park, when an estimated 20,000 heard Jefferson Airplane perform and Ginsberg chant, while the Hell's Angels acted as unofficial police. It was followed by the Summer of Love in 1967 as thousands of young people streamed into the city in search of drugs and free love.

The '60s Haight scene was very different from the '50s Beat scene. The hippies were much younger than the Beats had been, constituting the first youth movement to take over the nation. Ironically, they also became the first generation of young, independent, and moneyed consumers to be courted by corporations. Ultimately, the Haight and the hippie movement deteriorated from love and flowers into drugs and crime, drawing a fringe of crazies like Charles Manson and leaving only a legacy of sex, drugs, violence, and consumerism. As early as October 1967, the "Diggers," who had opened a free shop and soup kitchen in the Haight, symbolically buried the dream in a clay casket in Buena Vista Park.

The end of the Vietnam War and the resignation of President Nixon took the edge off politics. The last fling of the mentality that had driven the 1960s occurred in 1974 when Patty Hearst was kidnapped from her Berkeley apartment by the Symbionese Liberation Army and participated in their bank-robbing spree before surrendering in San Francisco in 1975.

THE 1970s: GAY RIGHTS The homosexual community in San Francisco was essentially founded at the end of World War II, when thousands of military personnel were discharged back to the United States via San Francisco. A substantial number of those men were homosexual and decided to stay on in San Francisco. A gay community grew up along Polk Street between Sutter and California streets. Later, the larger community moved into the Castro, where it remains today.

The modern-day gay political movement is usually traced to the 1969 Stonewall raid and riots in Greenwich Village. Although the political movement started in New York, California had already given birth to two major organizations for gay rights: the Mattachine Society, founded in 1951 by Henry Hay in Los Angeles, and the Daughters of Bilitis, a lesbian organization founded in 1955 in San Francisco.

After Stonewall, the Committee for Homosexual Freedom was created in spring 1969 in San Francisco; a Gay Liberation Front chapter was organized at Berkeley. In fall 1969, Robert Patterson, a columnist for the "San Francisco Examiner," referred to homosexuals as "semi males, drag darlings," and "women who aren't exactly women." On October 31 at noon, a group began a peaceful picket of the "Examiner." Peace reigned until someone threw a bag of printer's ink from an "Examiner" window. Someone wrote "F--- the Examiner" on the wall, and the police moved in to clear the crowd, clubbing them as they went. The remaining pickets retreated to Glide Methodist Church and then marched on City Hall. Unfortunately, the mayor was away. Unable to air their grievances, they started a sit-in that lasted until 5pm, when they were ordered to leave. Most did, but three remained and were arrested.

Later that year, an anti-Thanksgiving rally was staged at which gays protested against several national and local businesses: Western and Delta airlines, the former for firing lesbian flight attendants, the latter for refusing to sell a ticket to a young man wearing a Gay Power button; KFOG, for its anti-homosexual broadcasting; and also some local gay bars for exploitation. On May 14, 1970, a group of gay and women's liberationists invaded the convention of the American Psychiatric Association in San Francisco to protest the reading of a paper on aversion therapy for homosexuals, forcing the meeting to adjourn.

The rage against intolerance was appearing on all fronts. At the National Gay Liberation conference held in August 1970 in the city, Charles Thorp, chairman of the San Francisco State Liberation Front, called for militancy and issued a challenge to come out with a rallying cry of "Blatant is beautiful." He also argued for the use of what he felt was the more positive, celebratory term *gay* instead of *homosexual,* and decried the fact that homosexuals were kept in their place at the three B's: the bars, the beaches, and the baths. As the movement grew in size and power, debates on strategy and tactics occurred, most dramatically between those who wanted to withdraw into separate ghettos and those who wanted to enter mainstream society. The most extreme proposal was made in California by Don Jackson, who proposed establishing a gay territory in California's Alpine County, about 10 miles south of Lake Tahoe. It would have had a totally gay administration, civil service, university, museum—everything. The residents of Alpine County were not pleased with the proposal. But before the situation turned really ugly, Jackson's idea was abandoned because of lack of support in the gay community. In the end, the movement would concentrate on integration and civil rights, not separatism. They would elect politicians who were sympathetic to their cause and celebrate their new identity by establishing National Gay Celebration Day and Gay Pride Week, the first of which was celebrated in June 1970 when 1,000 to 2,000 marched in New York, 1,000 in Los Angeles, and a few hundred in San Francisco.

By the mid-1970s, the gay community craved a more central role in San Francisco politics. Harvey Milk, owner of a camera store in the Castro, decided to run as an openly gay man for the board of supervisors. He won, becoming the first openly gay person to hold a major public office. He and liberal mayor George Moscone developed a gay rights agenda, but in 1978 both were killed by former supervisor Dan White, who shot them after Moscone refused White's request for reinstatement. White, a Catholic and former police officer, had consistently opposed Milk's and Moscone's more liberal policies. At his trial, White successfully pleaded temporary insanity caused by additives in his fast-food diet. The media dubbed it the "Twinkie defense," but it worked, and the murder charges against White were reduced to manslaughter. That day, angry and grieving, the gay community rioted, overturning and burning police cars in a night of rage. To this day, a candlelight memorial parade is held each year on the anniversary of Milk's death, and Milk's martyrdom remains both a political and a practical inspiration to gay candidates across the country.

The emphasis in the gay movement shifted abruptly in the 1980s when the AIDS epidemic struck the gay community. AIDS has had a dramatic impact on the Castro. While it's still a thriving and lively community, it's no longer the constant party that it once was. The hedonistic lifestyle that had played out in the discos, bars, baths, and streets changed as the seriousness of the epidemic sunk in and the number of deaths increased. Political efforts shifted away from enfranchisement and toward demanding money for social services. The gay community has developed its own organizations, such as Project Inform and Gay Men's Health Crisis, to publicize information about AIDS, treatments available, and safe sex. Though new cases of AIDS within the gay community are on the decline in San Francisco, it still remains a serious problem.

THE 1980s: THE BIG ONE, PART TWO The '80s may have arrived in San Francisco with a whimper (compared to previous generations), but they went out with quite a bang. At 5:04pm on Tuesday, October 17, 1989, as more than 62,000 fans filled Candlestick Park for the third game of the World Series—and the San Francisco Bay Area commute moved into its heaviest flow—an earthquake of magnitude 7.1 struck. Within the next 20 seconds, 63 lives would be lost, $10 billion in damage would occur, and the entire Bay Area community would be reminded of its humble insignificance. Centered about 60 miles south of San Francisco within the Forest of Nisene Marks, the deadly temblor was felt as far away as San Diego and Nevada.

Though scientists had predicted an earthquake would hit on this section of the San Andreas Fault, certain structures that were built to withstand such an earthquake failed miserably. The most catastrophic event was the collapse of the elevated Cypress Street section of I-880 in Oakland, where the upper level of the freeway literally pancaked the lower level, crushing everything. Other structures heavily damaged included the San Francisco–Oakland Bay Bridge, shut down for months when a section of the roadbed collapsed; San Francisco's Marina district, where several multimillion-dollar homes collapsed on their weak, shifting bases of landfill and sand; and the Pacific Garden Mall in Santa Cruz, which was completely devastated.

President George H. W. Bush declared a disaster area for the seven hardest-hit counties, where 63 people died, at least 3,700 people were reported injured, and more than 12,000 were displaced. More than 18,000 homes were damaged and 963 others destroyed. Although fire raged within the city and water supply systems were damaged, the major fires sparked within the Marina district were brought under control within 3 hours, due mostly to the heroic efforts of San Francisco's firefighters.

After the rubble had finally settled, it was unanimously agreed that San Francisco and the Bay Area had pulled through miraculously well—particularly when compared to the more recent earthquake in northeast Japan, which killed thousands. After the San Francisco quake, a feeling of esprit de corps swept the city as neighbors helped each other rebuild and donations poured in from all over the world. Though it's been over 2 decades since, the city is still feeling the effects of the quake. That another "big one" will strike is inevitable: It's the price you pay for living on a fault line. But if there is ever a city that is prepared for a major shakedown, it's San Francisco.

THE 1990s: THE DOT.COM BUBBLE During the 1990s, the nationwide recession influenced the beginning of the decade, while the quiet rumblings of the new frontier in Silicon Valley escaped much notice. By the middle of the decade, San

Francisco and the surrounding areas were the site of a new kind of gold rush—the birth of the Internet industry.

Not unlike the gold fever of the 1800s, people flocked to the western shores to strike it rich—and they did. In 1999, the local media reported that each day 64 Bay Area residents were gaining millionaire status. Long before the last year of the millennium, real estate prices went into the stratosphere, and the city's gentrification financially squeezed out many of those residents who didn't mean big business (read: alternative and artistic types, seniors, and minorities who made the city colorful). New businesses popped up everywhere—especially in SoMa, where start-up companies jammed warehouse spaces.

As the most popular post-education destination for MBAs and the leader in the media of the future, San Francisco no longer opened its Golden Gate to everyone looking for the legendary alternative lifestyle—unless he or she could afford a $1,000 studio apartment and $20-per-day fees to park the car.

The new millennium was christened with bubbly in hand, foie gras and caviar on the linen tablecloth, and seemingly everyone in the money. New restaurants charging $35 per entree were all the rage, hotels were renovated, the new bayfront ballpark was packed, and stock market tips were as plentiful as million-dollar SoMa condos and lofts. Though there were whispers of a stock market correction, and inklings that venture capital might dry up, San Franciscans were too busy raking in the dough to heed the writing on the wall.

THE MILLENNIUM When the city woke up from the dot.com party, San Franciscans found themselves suffering from a major new millennium hangover. In the early 2000s, dot.coms became "dot.bombs" faster than you could say "worthless stock options," with companies shuttering at a rate of several per day. The crash of the Internet economy brought with it a real estate exodus, and scads of empty live-work lofts sprouted up in SoMa. But from the ashes of the collapse grew the seeds of innovation, and by mid-decade, San Francisco was back on the cutting edge with a little search engine called Google. Wikipedia, YouTube, and new skyscrapers followed, holding steady even as Wall Street and big banks fell around their feet in 2008. It's an undeniable testament to the resilience and mettle of San Franciscans, who always seem to have an ace in the hole, even when things seem at their worst.

SAN FRANCISCO & THE ARTS

Getting acquainted with San Francisco through the work of authors and filmmakers will provide an extra dimension to your trip and perhaps some added excitement when you happen upon a location you recognize from a favorite cinematic moment or literary passage. San Francisco's own Chronicle Books publishes a great variety of material on the city, for children, cooks, art and architecture students, and readers of memoirs and fiction. One of Chronicle's best books to stimulate your interest and curiosity is "San Francisco Stories: Great Writers on the City," edited by John Miller. This collection of short pieces covers the personal and the political as recalled by acclaimed authors including Mark Twain, Jack Kerouac, Tom Wolfe, and Amy Tan. To find out about a smaller, more intimate city, check out "Good Life in Hard Times: San Francisco in the '20s and '30s," by former journalist and San Francisco native Jerry Flamm (published by Chronicle Books).

One of the more famous and beloved pieces of modern fiction based in San Francisco is Armistead Maupin's "Tales of the City" (published by Perennial). If you've seen the miniseries, and especially if you haven't, this is a must-read for a lei-surely afternoon—or bring it with you on the plane. Maupin's 1970s soap opera covers the residents of 28 Barbary Lane (Macondry Lane on Russian Hill was the inspiration), melding sex, drugs, and growing self-awareness with enormous warmth and humor.

A work of fiction featuring San Francisco during the gold rush is "Daughter of Fortune," by acclaimed novelist and Marin County resident Isabel Allende (published by HarperTorch). Allende's depiction of life in California during the mid–19th century is vividly described and is one of the novel's strengths.

As one of the loveliest spots on the planet, San Francisco has been a favorite of location scouts since the beginning of the film industry. Hundreds of movies and television shows have been shot or placed in San Francisco, making the hills and bridges among the most recognized of backgrounds. It may be difficult to locate at your local video store, but the 1936 Clark Gable/Jeanette MacDonald romance, "San Francisco," is lauded for its dramatic reenactment of the 1906 earthquake and for MacDonald's rendition of the song of the same name. "The Maltese Falcon" (1941), Dashiell Hammett's classic detective story, with Humphrey Bogart starring as Sam Spade, includes shots of the Bay Bridge, the Ferry Building, and Burritt Alley (above the Stockton Tunnel). John's Grill, mentioned in the novel, continues to flog its association with Hammett's hero from its location at 63 Ellis Street (btw. Stockton and Powell sts.).

Alfred Hitchcock's "Vertigo" (1958), starring James Stewart and Kim Novak, is admittedly an obvious choice on the list of great San Francisco films, but it's always worth viewing. Stewart plays a former detective hired to tail the wife of an old college friend, but the woman's identity is less than clear-cut. In the meantime, Stewart becomes obsessed with his prey as they make their way around the Palace of the Legion of Honor, Fort Point, Mission Dolores, and the detective's apartment at 900 Lombard Street. The city also fared well in the 1968 thriller "Bullitt," starring a young Steve McQueen. Along with the hair-raising car chase over many hills, you'll see the Bay Bridge from a recognizable point on the Embarcadero, Mason Street heading north next to the Fairmont Hotel, the front of the Mark Hopkins Hotel, Grace Cathedral, and the fairly unchanged Enrico's Sidewalk Café.

For a change of pace and no tragic law-enforcement characters, screen the romantic comedy "What's Up, Doc?" (1972) with Barbra Streisand and Ryan O'Neal. Along with being very funny, it's got one of cinema's all-time classic car chase scenes, with shots of Lombard Street, Chinatown, and Alta Plaza Park in Pacific Heights. If you have kids to rev up, the 1993 comedy "Mrs. Doubtfire," starring Sally Field and the city's favorite son, Robin Williams, shows San Francisco under blue skies and cable cars with plenty of room. The house where the character's estranged wife and chil-dren live is located in Pacific Heights at 2640 Steiner Street (at Broadway St.), in case you care to gawk.

Finally, "24 Hours on Craigslist" is a documentary that covers a day in the life of the Internet community bulletin-board phenom. The filmmaker posted an ad on Craigslist, followed up with a handful of volunteers—an Ethel Merman impersonator seeking a Led Zeppelin cover band; a couple looking for others to join a support group for diabetic cats; a single, older woman needing a sperm donor—and sent film crews to cover their stories. Unlike other films that show the physical splendors of San Francisco, "24 Hours on Craigslist" will give you a sense of the city's psyche, or at least offer an explanation of why non–San Franciscans think the place is populated with . . . um . . . unusual types.

Sounds of the '60s

During its heyday in the 1950s and 1960s, San Francisco was the place to be for anyone who eschewed the conventional American lifestyle. From moody beatniks to political firebrands, the city was a vortex for poets, writers, actors, and a bewildering assortment of free thinkers and activists. Drawn by the city's already liberal views on life, liberty, and the pursuit of happiness, thousands of the country's youth—including some of America's most talented musicians—headed west to join the party. What culminated in the 1960s was San Francisco's hat trick of rock legends: It was able to lay claim to three of the rock era's most influential bands—the Grateful Dead, Big Brother and the Holding Company and Janis Joplin, and Jefferson Airplane.

THE GRATEFUL DEAD　Easily the most influential band to be spawned from the psychedelic movement of the 1960s, the Grateful Dead was San Francisco's own music guru. Described as the "house band for the famous acid tests that transformed the City by the Bay into one endless freak-out," the Dead's music was played simultaneously on so many stereo systems (and at such high volumes) that the group almost seemed to have set the tone for one enormous, citywide jam session.

Though the group disbanded in 1995 after the death of its charismatic lead vocalist, Jerry Garcia, the group's devoted fans had already elevated the Grateful Dead to cult empire status. Tie-dyed "Deadheads" (many of whom followed the band on tour for decades) can still be found tripping within the Haight, reminiscing about the good old days when the group never traveled with a sound system weighing less than 23 tons. In fact, more than any other band produced during the 1960s, the Grateful Dead were best appreciated during live concerts, partly because of the love-in mood that frequently percolated through the acidic audiences. Many rock critics remember with nostalgia that the band's most cerebral and psychedelic music was produced in the 1960s in San Francisco, but in the 1980s and 1990s, permutations of their themes were marketed in repetitive, less threatening forms that delighted their aficionados and often baffled or bored virtually everyone else.

For better or for worse, the Grateful Dead was a musical benchmark, expressing in new ways the mood of San Francisco during one of its drug-infused and most creatively fertile periods. But the days of the Dancing Bear and peanut butter sandwiches will never be quite over: Working from a proven formula, thousands of bands around the world continue to propagate the Dead's rhythmical standards, and several of the band's original members still tour in various incarnations.

But reading about the Grateful Dead is like dancing to architecture: If you're looking for an album whose title best expresses the changing artistic premises of San Francisco and the ironies of the pop culture that developed here, look for its award-winning retrospective "What a Long Strange Trip It's Been" at any of the city's record stores.

BIG BROTHER & THE HOLDING COMPANY AND JANIS JOPLIN　The wide-open moral and musical landscape of San Francisco was almost unnervingly fertile during the 1960s. Despite competition from endless numbers of less talented singers, Texas-born Janis Joplin formulated much of her vocal technique before audiences in San Francisco. Her breakthrough style was first acknowledged at the Monterey Jazz Festival in 1967. Audiences reached out to embrace a singer whose rasping, gravely, shrieking voice expressed the generational angst of thousands of onlookers. "Billboard" magazine characterized her sound as composed of equal

San Francisco & the Arts

SAN FRANCISCO IN CONTEXT

portions of honey, Southern Comfort, and gall. She was backed up during her earliest years by Big Brother & the Holding Company, a group she eventually outgrew.

Warned by specialists that her vocal technique would ruin her larynx before she was 30, Janis wailed, gasped, growled, and staggered over a blues repertoire judged as the most raw and vivid ever performed. Promoters frantically struggled to market (and protect) Janis and her voice for future artistic endeavors but, alas, her talent was simply too huge for her to handle, the time and place too destructive for her raw-edged psyche. Her style is best described as "the desperate blues," partly because it never attained the emotional nonchalance of such other blues singers as Bessie Smith or Billie Holiday.

Parts of Janis's life were the subject of such lurid books as "Going Down with Janis," and stories of her substance abuse, sexual escapades, and general raunchiness litter the emotional landscape of modern-day San Francisco. The star died of a heroin overdose at the age of 27, a tragedy still mourned by her thousands of fans, who continue to refer to her by her nickname, "Pearl." Contemporary photographs taken shortly before her death show a ravaged body and a face partially concealed behind aviator's goggles, long hair, and a tough but brittle facade. Described as omnisexual—and completely comfortable with both male and female partners—she once (unexpectedly) announced to a group of nightclub guests her evaluation of the sexual performance of two of the era's most visible male icons: Joe Namath (not particularly memorable) and Dick Cavett (absolutely fantastic). The audience (like audiences in concert halls around California) drank in the anecdotes that followed as "Gospel According to Janis."

JEFFERSON AIRPLANE   In the San Francisco suburbs of the late 1960s, hundreds of suburban bands dreamed of attaining stardom. Of the few that succeeded, none expressed the love-in ethic of that time in San Francisco better than the soaring vocals and ferocious guitar-playing of Jefferson Airplane. Singers Grace Slick and Marty Balin—as well as bass guitar player Jack Casady—were considered at the top of their profession by their peers and highly melodic even by orchestral standards. Most importantly, all members of the band, especially Paul Kantner and Jorma Kaukonen, were songwriters. Their fertile mix of musical styles and creative energies led to songs that still reverberate in the minds of anyone who owned an AM radio during the late 1960s. The intense and lonely songs such as "Somebody to Love" and "White Rabbit" became the musical anthems of at least one summer, as American youth emerged into a highly psychedelic kind of consciousness within the creatively catalytic setting of San Francisco.

Although in 1989 the group reassembled its scattered members for a swan song as Jefferson Starship, the output was considered a banal repetition of earlier themes, and the energy of those long-faded summers of San Francisco in the late 1960s was never recovered. But despite its decline in its later years, Jefferson Airplane is still considered a band inextricably linked to the Bay Area's historic and epoch-changing Summer of Love.

WHEN TO GO

If you're dreaming of convertibles, Frisbee on the beach, and tank-topped evenings, change your reservations and head to Los Angeles. Contrary to California's sunshine-and-bikini image, San Francisco's weather is "mild" (to put it nicely) and can often be downright bone-chilling because of the wet, foggy air, and cool winds—it's really

Even if it's sunny out, don't forget to bring a jacket and dress in layers; the weather can change almost instantly from sunny and warm to windy and cold—especially as you move between microclimates. Also bring comfortable walking shoes or your feet will pay the price.

nothing like Southern California. **Summer,** the most popular time to visit, is often the coldest time of year, with damp, foggy days; cold, windy nights; and crowded tourist destinations. A good bet is to visit in spring or, better yet, autumn. Just about every **September,** right about the time San Franciscans mourn being cheated (or fogged) out of another summer, something wonderful happens: The thermometer rises, the skies clear, and the locals call in sick to work and head for the beach. It's what residents call "Indian summer." The city is also delightful during **winter,** when the opera and ballet seasons are in full swing; there are fewer tourists, many hotel prices are lower, and downtown bustles with holiday cheer.

San Francisco's temperate, marine climate usually means relatively mild weather year-round. In summer, chilling fog rolls in most mornings and evenings, and if temperatures top 70°F (21°C), the city is ready to throw a celebration. Even when autumn's heat occasionally stretches into the 80s (upper 20s Celsius) and 90s (lower 30s Celsius), you should still dress in layers, or by early evening you'll learn firsthand why sweatshirt sales are a great business at Fisherman's Wharf. In winter, the mercury seldom falls below freezing and snow is almost unheard of, but that doesn't mean you won't be whimpering if you forget your coat. Still, compared to most of the state's weather conditions, San Francisco's are consistently pleasant, and even if it's damp and chilly, head north, east, or south 15 minutes and you can usually find sun again.

The coastal fog is caused by a rare combination of water, wind, and topography. The fog lies off the coast, and rising air currents pull it in when the land heats up. Held back by coastal mountains along a 600-mile front, the low clouds seek out any passage they can find. The easiest access is the slot where the Pacific Ocean penetrates the continental wall—the Golden Gate.

San Francisco's Average Temperatures (°F/°C)

	JAN	FEB	MAR	APR	MAY	JUNE	JULY	AUG	SEPT	OCT	NOV	DEC
AVG. HIGH	56/13	59/15	61/16	64/18	67/19	70/21	71/22	72/22	73/23	70/21	62/17	56/13
AVG. LOW	43/6	46/8	47/8	48/9	51/11	53/12	55/13	56/13	55/13	52/11	48/9	43/6

Holidays

Banks, government offices, post offices, and many stores, restaurants, and museums are closed on the following legal national holidays: January 1 (New Year's Day), the third Monday in January (Martin Luther King, Jr., Day), the third Monday in February (Presidents' Day), the last Monday in May (Memorial Day), July 4 (Independence Day), the first Monday in September (Labor Day), the second Monday in October (Columbus Day), November 11 (Veterans Day/Armistice Day), the fourth Thursday in November (Thanksgiving Day), and December 25 (Christmas). The Tuesday after the first Monday in November is Election Day, a federal government holiday in presidential-election years (held every 4 years).

San Francisco–Area Calendar of Events

For more information on San Francisco events, visit **www.onlyinsanfrancisco.com** for an annual calendar of local events, as well as **http://events.frommers.com**, where you'll find a searchable, up-to-the-minute roster of what's happening in cities all over the world.

FEBRUARY

Chinese New Year, Chinatown. Public celebrations spill onto every street in Chinatown, beginning with the "Miss Chinatown USA" pageant parade, and climaxing a week later with a celebratory parade of marching bands, rolling floats, barrages of fireworks, and a block-long dragon writhing in and out of the crowds. The action starts at Market and Second streets and ends at Kearny Street. Arrive early for a good viewing spot on Kearny Street. You can purchase bleacher seats online starting in December. Make your hotel reservations early. For dates and information, call ✆ **415/680-6297** or visit www.chineseparade.com.

MARCH

St. Patrick's Day Parade, Union Square, and Civic Center. Everyone's an honorary Irish person at this festive affair, which starts at 11:30am at Market and Second streets and continues to City Hall. But the party doesn't stop there. Head down to the Civic Center for the post-party, or venture to the Embarcadero's Harrington's Bar & Grill (245 Front St.) and celebrate with hundreds of the Irish-for-a-day yuppies as they gallivant around the closed-off streets and numerous pubs. Sunday before March 17. For more information, visit **www.saint patricksdaysf.com**.

APRIL

Cherry Blossom Festival, Japantown. Meander through the arts-and-crafts and food booths lining the blocked-off streets around Japan Center and watch traditional drumming, flower arranging, origami making, and a parade celebrating the cherry blossoms and Japanese culture. Call ✆ **415/563-2313** or visit www.sfcherry blossom.org for information. Mid- to late April.

San Francisco International Film Festival, around San Francisco with screenings at the Sundance Kabuki Cinemas (Fillmore and Post sts.), and at many other locations. Begun in 1957, this is America's oldest film festival. It features close to 200 films and videos from more than 50 countries. Tickets are relatively inexpensive, and screenings are accessible to the public. Entries include new films by beginning and established directors, and star-studded tributes. For a schedule and to purchase tickets, visit **www.festivalsffs.org**. Mid-April to early May.

MAY

Cinco de Mayo Festival, Mission District. This is when the Latino community celebrates the victory of the Mexicans over the French at Puebla in 1862; mariachi bands, dancers, food, and revelers fill the streets of the Mission. The celebration is usually in Dolores Park (Dolores St. btw. 18th and 20th sts.). Contact the Mission Neighborhood Center for more information at ✆ **415/206-0577** or www.sfcincodemayo.com.

Bay to Breakers Foot Race, the Embarcadero through Golden Gate Park to Ocean Beach. Even if you don't participate, you can't avoid this giant, moving costume party (which celebrated its 100th year in 2011) that goes from downtown to Ocean Beach. More than 75,000 entrants gather—many dressed in wacky, innovative, and sometimes X-rated costumes—for the approximately 7½-mile run. If you don't want to run, join the throng of spectators who line the route. Sidewalk parties, bands, and cheerleaders of all ages provide a good dose of true San Francisco fun. For more information, call ✆ **415/231-3130,** or check their website, www.baytobreakers.com. Third Sunday of May.

Carnaval Festival, Harrison St. between 16th and 23rd Sts. The Mission District's largest annual event, held from 9:30am to 6pm, is a day of festivities that includes food, music, dance, arts and crafts, and a parade that's as sultry and energetic as the Latin American and Caribbean people behind it. For one of San Franciscans' favorite events, more than half a million spectators line the parade route, and samba musicians and dancers continue to entertain on 14th Street, near Harrison, at the end of the march, where you'll find food and craft booths, music, and more revelry. Call ⟨ 415/206-0577 for more information. Celebrations are held Saturday and Sunday of Memorial Day weekend, but the parade is on Sunday morning only. See www.carnavalsf.org for more information.

JUNE

Union Street Art Festival, Pacific Heights along Union Street from Steiner to Gough streets. This outdoor fair celebrates San Francisco with themes, gourmet food booths, music, entertainment, and a juried art show featuring works by more than 250 artists. It's a great time and a chance to see the city's young well-to-dos partying it up. Call the **Union Street Association** (⟨ **415/441-7055**) for more information or see www.unionstreetfestival.com. First weekend of June.

Haight-Ashbury Street Fair, Haight-Ashbury. A far cry from the froufrou Union Street Fair, this grittier fair features alternative crafts, ethnic foods, rock bands, and a healthy number of hippies and street kids whooping it up and slamming beers in front of the blaring rock-'n'-roll stage. The fair usually extends along Haight Street between Stanyan and Ashbury streets. For details, visit www.haightashburystreetfair.org. Second Sunday of June.

North Beach Festival, Grant Ave., North Beach. In 2009, this party celebrated its 55th anniversary; organizers claim it's the oldest urban street fair in the country. Close to 100,000 city folk meander along Grant Avenue, between Vallejo and Union streets, to eat, drink, and browse the arts-and-crafts booths, poetry readings, swing-dancing venue, and *arte di gesso* (sidewalk chalk art). But the most enjoyable parts of the event

are listening to music and people-watching. Visit **www.sresproductions.com/north_beach_festival.html**.

Stern Grove Music Festival, Sunset District. Pack a picnic and head out early to join the thousands who come here to lie in the grass and enjoy free world-class classical, jazz, and ethnic music and dance in the grove, at 19th Avenue and Sloat Boulevard. The free concerts take place every Sunday at 2pm between mid-June and August. Show up with a lawn chair or blanket. There are food booths if you forget snacks, but you'll be dying to leave if you don't bring warm clothes—the Sunset District can be one of the coldest parts of the city. Call ⟨ **415/252-6252** for listings or go to www.sterngrove.org. Sundays, mid-June through August.

San Francisco Lesbian, Gay, Bisexual, Transgender Pride Parade & Celebration, downtown's Market St. This prideful event draws up to one million participants who celebrate all of the above—and then some. The parade proceeds west on Market Street until it gets to the Civic Center, where hundreds of food, art, and information booths are set up around several soundstages. Call ⟨ **415/864-0831** or visit www.sfpride.org for information. Usually the third or last weekend of June.

JULY

Fillmore Jazz Festival, Pacific Heights. July starts with a bang, when the upscale portion of Fillmore closes to traffic and the blocks between Jackson and Eddy streets are filled with arts and crafts, gourmet food, and live jazz from 10am to 6pm. For more information visit **www.fillmorejazzfestival.com**. First weekend in July.

Fourth of July Celebration & Fireworks, Fisherman's Wharf. This event can be something of a joke—more often than not, fog comes into the city, like everyone else, to join in the festivities. Sometimes it's almost impossible to view the million-dollar pyrotechnics from Pier 39 on the northern waterfront. Still, it's a party, and if the skies are clear, it's a darn good show.

San Francisco Marathon, San Francisco and beyond. This is one of the largest marathons in the world. It starts and ends at the Ferry Building at the base of Market Street, winds 26-plus miles through virtually every neighborhood in the city, and crosses the Golden Gate Bridge. For entry information, visit **www.thesfmarathon.com**. Usually the last weekend in July.

SEPTEMBER

Sausalito Art Festival, Sausalito. A juried exhibit of more than 20,000 original works of art, this festival includes music—provided by jazz, rock, and blues performers from the Bay Area and beyond—and international cuisine, enhanced by wines from some 50 Napa and Sonoma producers. Parking is difficult; make it easier and take the ferry (www.blueandgoldfleet.com) from Pier 41 to the festival site. For more information, call © 415/332-3555 or log on to www.sausalitoartfestival.org. Labor Day weekend.

Opera in the Park. Usually in Sharon Meadow, Golden Gate Park. Each year, the San Francisco Opera launches its season with a free concert featuring a selection of arias. Call © **415/861-4008** or visit www.sfopera.com to confirm the location and date. Usually the Sunday after Labor Day.

Folsom Street Fair, along Folsom St. between 7th and 12th sts, the area south of Market Street (SoMa, From 11am to 6pm). This is a local favorite for its kinky, outrageous, leather-and-skin gay-centric blowout celebration. It's hardcore, so only open-minded and adventurous types need head into the leather-clad and partially dressed crowds. For info visit www.folsomstreetfair.org. Last Sunday of September.

OCTOBER

Hardly Strictly Bluegrass, in Golden Gate Park's Hellman Hollow (formerly Speedway Meadows), Lindley, and Marx meadows. This free annual music event lures thousands into Golden Gate Park for 3 days of awesome music, beer drinking, and pot smoking. It's about as groovy, happy-go-lucky San Francisco as it gets.

Fleet Week, Marina and Fisherman's Wharf. Residents gather along the Marina Green, the Embarcadero, Fisherman's Wharf, and other vantage points to watch incredible (and loud!) aerial performances by the Blue Angels and other daring stunt pilots, as well as the annual parade of ships. Call © 650/599-5057 or visit www.fleetweek.us for details and dates.

Artspan Open Studios, various San Francisco locations. Find an original piece of art to commemorate your trip, or just see what local artists are up to by grabbing a map to over 800 artists' studios that are open to the public during weekends in October and May. Visit www.artspan.org for more information.

Castro Street Fair, the Castro. Celebrate life in the city's most famous gay neighborhood. Call © **800/853-5950** or visit www.castrostreetfair.org for information. First Sunday in October, from 11am to 6pm.

Italian Heritage Parade, North Beach and Fisherman's Wharf. The city's Italian community leads the festivities around Fisherman's Wharf, celebrating Columbus's landing in America with a parade along Columbus Avenue. But for the most part, it's a great excuse to hang out in North Beach and people-watch. For more information, visit **www.sfcolumbusday.org**. Observed the Sunday before Columbus Day.

Halloween, the Castro. This once huge street party has been tamed down by city officials in recent years to curb violence and prevent the increasing influx of out-of-towners into the neighborhood. Castro denizens still whoop it up with music and drag costume contests, but if you go to gawk, you'll be disappointed. October 31.

Treasure Island Music Festival, Treasure Island. Bands and crowds take over this East Bay landfill island (and former U.S. Navy base) for the weekend. Free shuttle from AT&T Park. Visit **www.treasureisland festival.com**. Mid-October.

DECEMBER

The Nutcracker, War Memorial Opera House, Civic Center. The **San Francisco**

Ballet (© 415/865-2000) performs this Tchaikovsky classic annually. (It was actually the first ballet company in America to do so in 1944.) Order tickets to this holiday tradition well in advance. Visit www.sfballet.org for information.

SantaCon, various San Francisco locations. Get into the holiday spirit and join thousands as they booze their way across the city. Dress up as Santa, Mrs. Clause, an elf, or your own interpretation for a full day of drinking, singing, and being merry. This is an adults-only pub crawl that, true to San Francisco style, includes nudity. The time, date, and location change annually and the details are released only a few days before the event, so follow SantaCon on twitter or check out the website at **www.santacon.info/San_Francisco-CA**.

WHERE TO STAY

From luxury resorts to funky motor inns to charming B&Bs, San Francisco is more than accommodating to its 15.7 million annual guests. Most of the city's 200-plus hotels cluster near Union Square, but smaller, independent gems are scattered around town. Stay in the heart of the tourist action for easy access to shopping and museums or shack up in the city's quieter residential neighborhoods for a more authentic, local experience. Whatever you do, the city's small enough that you'll have easy access to everything you want to do and see.

PRACTICAL MATTERS: THE HOTEL SCENE

Getting the Best Deal

The listings in this chapter give you an idea of the kind of deals that may be available at particular hotels. All rates showcase the low and high end of each hotel's price structure. Since there is no way of knowing what the offers will be when you're booking, consider these general tips if you want to get the best prices:

Choose your season carefully. Room rates can vary dramatically—by hundreds of dollars in some cases—depending on what time of year you visit. Winter, from November through March, is best for bargains, excluding Thanksgiving, Christmas, and New Years, of course—though the days between Christmas and New Years can offer amazing deals, and these just happen to be some of the best shopping days all year in Union Square. Occupancy rates hover around 90 percent from June through October; rates adjust upwards accordingly. Bizarrely enough, when the city fills up, lesser quality hotels will often charge prices that are equal to or even higher than what the luxury hotels are asking. So it's important to *never* assess the quality of a hotel by the price it's asking. Instead, read the reviews carefully and compare the prices you're being quoted to make sure you're not getting taken.

Remember to factor in the extras. Most folks simply look at the price when booking a room, without considering the value of the extras thrown in with a slightly more expensive place. For example, the Hotel Drisco (see p. 66) is a lovely place in Pacific Heights. At $285 per night, many might not even consider booking a room here. But when you factor in free parking (about a $50 value if you have a car and parked downtown), free full breakfast (worth at least $40 per couple), evening cocktails and hot appetizers (easily another $20 per couple), and free Wi-Fi ($10), all of a sudden it's as if you're only paying $165 for the room itself. For one of the

The Price You'll Pay

With the average price for a double room topping $200 per night, occupancy rates as high as 90 percent in peak season, and $300 hotel rooms going for $75 through Priceline on an off night, getting a good deal on a bed in this city is a bit like playing roulette—you never know what number will come up. If you have your heart set on a particular neighborhood or hotel, by all means book it. But you're likely to save money if you shop around, check the discount hotel sites, and stay in neighborhoods less central than Union Square.

finest boutique hotels in the country, that's a darn good deal. Whenever possible, we've tried to focus on hotels that offer free breakfast, cocktails, nibbles, parking, and Wi-Fi—it adds up.

Stay in a hotel away from Fisherman's Wharf—or SoMa, Nob Hill, and Union Square for that matter. The advantages of staying in the popular tourist locations are overrated, particularly so when money is an issue. Muni buses and, especially, the historic F-Line streetcars, can take you to most tourist sites in minutes. Even if you stay as far away as The Castro, you can be at the ferry launch for Alcatraz in about half an hour; your daily ride up and down Market Street on these old beauties will likely be a lovely lasting memory of your visit. You'll not only get the best value for your money by staying outside the tourist areas, in the residential neighborhoods where real San Franciscans live, but you'll have a better overall experience: you won't constantly be fighting crowds, you'll have terrific restaurants nearby, and you'll see what life in the city is really like. Lodgings in The Castro, Haight-Ashbury, Civic Center, The Marina, and quiet Japantown offer particularly good savings.

Visit over a weekend. If your trip includes a weekend, you might be able to save big. Business hotels tend to empty out, and rooms that go for $300 or more Monday through Thursday can drop dramatically in cost, to as low as $150 or less, once the execs have headed home. These deals are especially prevalent in SoMa. Also, you'll find that Sunday nights are the least expensive, no matter the neighborhood. Check the hotel's website for weekend specials. Or just ask when you call. None of this applies in Fisherman's Wharf—it's always expensive there.

Do what they do in Europe and share a bathroom. What is the value of a private loo? In San Francisco, I'd say it's at least $100 per night. If the thought of "sharing" brings back dreaded memories of the high school locker room scene, don't worry; "sharing" usually means you can lock the door to the bathroom—as you would visiting a friends' house. The bathroom won't be in your room, it will be down the hall, and will be used by fellow guests.

Shop online. There are so many ways to save online and through apps, we've devoted an entire box to the topic. See p. 50.

Try the chains. Since you probably know what you will get with a Hyatt, Hilton, or Holiday Inn, we focused on smaller, unknown, independent properties with character—and a good local feel—in this chapter. That said, the big brand names are usually in good locations, and, depending on how booked they are, can offer great deals since they have loads of rooms to let. Most chain hotels let kids stay with parents for free using existing bedding and they accept loyalty points. Ask for every kind of discount; if you get an unhelpful reservation agent, call back, and try calling the local number.

Practical Matters: The Hotel Scene

WHERE TO STAY

For your convenience, we have listed all of the major chains—including neighborhood, website, address, and local phone number—on p. 54.

Avoid excess charges and hidden costs. Little things add up big in hotels. If you're cash-conscious (and who isn't?) consider

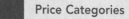

Price Categories

Expensive: $250 and up
Moderate: $150–$250
Inexpensive: Under $150

skipping the mini bar, use your cell phone or prepaid phone cards instead of pricy hotel phones, and look for hotels that offer free Wi-Fi. (For information about free Wi-Fi throughout the city, see p. 237.) Most important, if you've rented a car, check parking rates. Downtown rates are as high as $60 a day! Also, if a hotel insists upon tacking on an "energy surcharge" that wasn't mentioned at check-in, you can often make a case for getting it removed.

Buy a money-saving package deal. A travel package that combines your airfare and your hotel stay for one price may just be the best bargain of all. In some cases, you'll get airfare, accommodations, transportation to and from the airport, plus extras—maybe an afternoon sightseeing tour or restaurant and shopping discount coupons—for less than the hotel alone would have cost had you booked it yourself. Most airlines and many travel agents, as well as the usual booking websites (Priceline, Orbitz, Expedia) offer good packages to San Francisco.

Alternative Accommodations

Consider private B&B accommodations. You can easily rent a bed, a room, and sometimes a whole house or apartment, from a private owner. This type of accommodation is usually much cheaper than a hotel room, it allows you to meet a friendly local, and it places you in a residential neighborhood where you live like a local. One of the best companies to use for this type of booking is Airbnb.com, though many also turn to websites www.homeaway.com, www.flipkey.com, or www.bedandbreakfast. com. Be sure to get all details in writing and an exact price for the stay, including applicable taxes and fees, before booking.

Try a Home Exchange. There are three types of home exchanges: simultaneous (you stay in someone's house while they stay in yours), non-simultaneous (you stay at someone's home, no one stays in yours), and a hospitality exchange (you stay in someone's home while they are there). Sound like a weird, new trend? **Homelink** (www.homelink.org), one of the premier home-exchange companies, has been in business for over 60 years. You pay a small fee to join (though you can take a look for free), and then connect with homeowners around the world.

I have never done a home exchange, but friends have, and swear by it. They say that by the time the exchange happens, they have emailed and spoken on the phone with their exchange partners so often, they feel like old friends. Two more companies specializing in exchanges are **HomeExchange** (www.homeexchange.com), and **Intervac** (www.intervac.com). Most experts warn against using **Craigslist** for swaps, because it's had problems with scammers. Those clubs that charge a fee—and all those listed above do—are able to weed out the ne'er do wells.

UNION SQUARE

The streets surrounding Union Square's 1-block open-air spot are crammed with department stores, hotels, and tourists.

FINDING HOTEL DISCOUNTS online

Turn to the Internet to get deep discounts on hotels. There are four types of online reductions to look out for:

o **Extreme discounts on sites where you bid for lodgings without knowing which hotel you'll get.** You'll find these on such sites as Priceline.com and Hotwire.com, and they can be real money-savers, particularly if you're booking within a week of travel (that's when the hotels get nervous and resort to deep discounts to get beds filled). As these companies use only major chains, you can rest assured that you won't be put up in a dump. For more reassurance, visit the website www.BetterBidding.com. On it, actual travelers spill the beans about what they bid on Priceline.com and which hotels they got. I think you'll be pleasantly surprised by the quality of many of the hotels that are offering these "secret" discounts to the opaque bidding websites.

o **Discounts on the hotel's website itself.** Sometimes these can be great values, as they'll often include such nice perks as free breakfast or parking privileges. Before biting, though be sure to look at the discounter sites below.

o **Discounts on online travel agencies as Hotels.com, Venere.com, Quikbook.com, Expedia.com, and the like.** Some of these sites reserve rooms in bulk and at a discount, passing along the savings to their customers. But instead of going to them directly, I'd recommend looking at such dedicated travel search engines as **Hipmunk.com, HotelsCombined. com, Momondo.com** and my

favorite, **Trivago.com**. These sites list prices from all the discount sites as well as the hotels directly, meaning you have a better chance of finding a discount. *Note:* Sometimes the discounts these sites find require advance payment for a room (and draconian cancellation policies), so double check your travel dates before booking. Be careful when one of these sites says "just a few blocks from Union Square," as you could find yourself stepping over homeless people and around drug dealers and prostitutes in the Tenderloin—which is just a few blocks from Union Square. Always read the reviews! **Tingo.com**, a site founded by TripAdvisor, is another good source, especially for luxury hotels. Its model is a bit different than the others. Users make a pre-paid reservation through it, but if the price of the room drops between the time you make the booking and the date of arrival, the site refunds the difference in price.

o **Try the app HotelsTonight.com.** It only works for day of bookings, but—Wow!—does it get great prices for procrastinators and spontaneous people who decide to travel on a whim—up to 70 percent off in many cases. A possible strategy: make a reservation at a hotel, then, on the day you're arriving try your luck with HotelsTonight.com. Most hotels will allow you to cancel without penalty, even on the date of arrival.

Yes, it's a lot of surfing, but with the potential to save hundreds of dollars over a few days, it can certainly pay off.

Expensive

Hotel Triton ★★   This hotel has just as much funky character and personality as San Francisco itself. Wild colorful murals cover the lobby, employees wear their own clothes instead of uniforms, the bathrobes are zebra-printed, and the evening wine reception features poetry and tarot card readings. (Don't drink wine? Your freebies are the fresh baked cookies that are served every afternoon at 3pm.) Using bright colors and an eclectic collection of furniture, Kimpton does a good job making you forget that the rooms are a little small and the bathrooms are tiny. Entertainers such as Kathy Griffin and Jerry Garcia designed a few specialty rooms, complete with original water-colors painted by the late great Garcia. Another specialty room has a Häagen-Dazs ice cream theme, including a custom-designed ice cream cabinet filled with pints in an assortment of flavors. Dogs are not only welcomed, but greeted with a message board announcing their arrival, and offered spa treatments. The location, on the border of chic Union Square and historic Chinatown, is also a draw at this vibrant hotel. On one side you have the upscale luxury shops and trendy restaurants of the world famous Union Square neighborhood; on the other, you'll find old men mixing ancient recipes with Chinese herbs, simple noodle shops and tea stands through the gates and under the red lanterns of old Chinatown.

342 Grant Ave. (at Bush St.). ✆ **415/394-0500.** www.hoteltriton.com. 140 units. From $139–$459 double; $239–$559 suite. Parking $53. Cable car: Powell–Hyde or Powell–Mason line (2 blocks west). **Amenities:** Cafe; 24-hr fitness center; room service; concierge; raid the mini bar (up to $10); and free Wi-Fi for Kimpton InTouch members (no charge to join).

Sir Francis Drake ★★   The Sir Francis Drake isn't just a luxurious hotel, but a city landmark that's as much beloved by the locals for its sweeping views and swanky bars as it is by visitors for the royal treatment it offers. In operation since 1928, the Renaissance architecture, grand lobby, ornate chandeliers, swirling staircases and British pomp and circumstance seems to pre-date San Francisco. Upon arrival, the fully costumed Beefeater doormen will help you with your bags, setting the tone for the type of service you can expect at this regal hotel. As with most vintage hotels, the rooms are small and well loved. But they're also filled with rich wood furnishings and the striped wallpaper gives them a plush, old European feel. Ask for a higher floor for the best views and quieter rooms. Even if you don't stay here, the hotel is still worth a visit. Pop in for a drink and gorgeous city views from **The Starlight Room** on the 21st floor. At **Sunday's a Drag Brunch**, cross-dressers perform while you sip mimosas and gorge on omelets, is also a classic San Francisco experience worth looking into.

450 Powell St. (at Sutter St.). ✆ **415/392-7755.** www.sirfrancisdrake.com. 416 units. $150–$400 double. Valet parking $50. Cable car: Powell–Hyde or Powell–Mason line (direct stop). Pets welcome. **Amenities:** 2 restaurants; bar; concierge; exercise room; room service; raid the mini bar (up to $10) and free Wi-Fi for Kimpton InTouch members (no charge to join).

Westin St. Francis ★   If you're looking for a hotel exuding classic San Francisco elegance, the Westin St. Francis with its massive lobby, crown molding, marble columns, and iconic Grandfather Clock delivers. Built in 1904 by "Bonanza King" Charles Crocker and his wealthy friends, the St. Francis has hosted a who's who of world famous celebrities including Mother Teresa, Helen Keller, Charlie Chaplin, Douglas Fairbanks, Mary Pickford, Queen Elizabeth, as well as a number of U.S. presidents. The Westin comprises two buildings: The historic Landmark Building fronts the square (so it can be noisy), and rooms feature turn-of-the-century charm including high ceilings and ornate crystal chandeliers. The 32-story Tower Building was built in 1972 and features larger rooms and bathrooms with a sleeker aesthetic. The floor-to-ceiling windows offer majestic views of the city on higher floors. The St. Francis is especially lovely around the holidays when executive pastry chef Jean-Francois Houdre unveils an elaborate gingerbread mansion, sugar castle, or an entire village and Union Square's Christmas tree can be seen from most rooms. Chef Michael Mina's restaurant Bourbon Steak, as well as the swanky tourist-friendly Clock Bar, also draw visitors.

335 Powell St. (btw. Geary and Post sts.). © **415/397-7000.** www.westinstfrancis.com. 1,195 units. $199–$699 double; $299–$4,999 suite. Children stay free w/parents when using existing bedding. Valet parking $57 ($7 more for SUV/larger vehicles). Cable car: Powell–Hyde or Powell–Mason line (direct stop). Pets under 40lbs. accepted. **Amenities:** 2 restaurants; concierge; health club and spa; room service, Wi-Fi ($15 per day).

Moderate

Hotel Abri ★★   The building is more than 100 years old, but the interior is pure 21st century, making this boutique spot a desirable and stylish urban crash pad. Several iPads mount one wall, while architectural art and lounge music sets a trendy tone. A sitting area with high-backed, mid-century leather chairs and a fireplace adds a cozy vibe. Rooms are spacious by San Francisco standards, but vary a bit due to the building's history as an apartment building. The bathrooms have been recently updated so you'll enjoy tons of storage space and new bathtubs. Suites include a sitting area, with a pullout sofa bed, and a desk area. Alas, you won't find all the big-hotel amenities here, such as room service or a fitness center. Next door, a lively, family-friendly restaurant and bar **Puccini & Pinetti** serves Italian food (and a great happy hour deal from 3 to 6pm) in a spacious, comfortable setting. Like all hotels in this area, exercise caution at night, as the area can get a little dicey.

127 Ellis St. (btw. Cyril Magna and Powell sts.). © **415/392-8800.** www.hotelabrisf.com. 115 units. $169–$299 double; $299–$499 suite. Valet parking $40, oversized vehicles $50. Bus: 38, 27, 45. Cable car: Powell–Hyde and Powell–Mason lines. **Amenities**: Business center; restaurant; concierge; Wi-Fi (free).

Hotel Diva ★★   Instead of the typical mid-century modern decor, custom shades featuring burlesque images, and sleek, steel headboards set the hip and modern tone at this cute boutique hotel. Guests can enjoy a hosted sake happy hour every evening, a tea lounge on the 7th floor, and the 24/7 business and fitness center. Kids will go wild for the Little Divas Suite—a completely tricked out room featuring bunk beds, a computer, toys, games, a drawing table, Wii game, and a karaoke machine. Parents, stay in the adjoined room. Restaurants, galleries, and high-end stores are all close by, as are the cable cars and historic F-Line streetcars.

440 Geary St. (btw. Mason and Taylor sts.). © **415/885-0200.** www.hoteldiva.com. 116 units. $199–$470 double; $470–$700 suite. Dogs welcome for $25/per dog. Valet parking $40–$45. Bus: 38 or 38L. Cable car: Powell–Mason line. **Amenities:** Concierge; restaurant; 24-hr. exercise room; free Wi-Fi.

Hotel Vertigo ★   Hitchcock buffs might recognize this hotel from his movie "Vertigo." It was here that Kim Novak's character gazed out the bay window in her green dress. Today the hotel embraces its cinematic history. The renovated rooms and lobby feature mid-century furnishings, the signature tangerine and white colors from the movie's promotional materials, and wall art featuring the "Vertigo" spiral motif. The film plays constantly in the lobby where complimentary coffee and tea are offered each morning. If you're not into the ornate aesthetic of many Victorian hotels in the area, you'll appreciate Vertigo's bold simplicity. *Note*: The area can be a bit sketchy at

Union Square Hotels

Beresford Arms Hotel **23**
Beresford Hotel **19**
The Fairmont San Francisco **3**
The Golden Gate Hotel **18**
The Grant Hotel **17**
Hotel Abri **13**

Hotel Diva **20**
Hotel Palomar **10**
Hotel Triton **8**
Hotel Vertigo **24**
Hotel Zetta **12**
Inn at Union Square **15**
InterContinental Mark Hopkins **2**

The Mosser **11**
Omni San Francisco Hotel **7**
The Palace Hotel **9**
The Ritz-Carlton, San Francisco **6**
Scarlet Huntington Hotel **1**
Serrano Hotel **22**

Sir Francis Drake **16**
Stanford Court Hotel **4**
The University Club of San Francisco **5**
The Warwick **21**
Westin St. Francis **14**

NAME-BRAND hotels

Because this is a small pocket guidebook with limited space, we chose to write about independent hotels that offer uniquely San Francisco experiences (or really great deals). But we understand that many readers alleviate the cost of travel with free stays through hotel loyalty programs. So for those readers, we've compiled the following list of hotels, in all prices ranges, but not all areas (we only chose the ones we feel are well-located).

Hyatt (www.hyatt.com)

○ Hyatt Regency **FiDi** ($381), 5 Embarcadero Center, Ⓒ **415/788-1234**

○ **Fisherman's Wharf** ($299), 555 North Point St., Ⓒ **415/563-1234**

○ **Union Square** Grand Hyatt ($279), 345 Stockton St., Ⓒ **415/398-1234**

Marriott (www.marriott.com)

○ Courtyard **Downtown** ($169), 299 Second St., Ⓒ **415/947-0700**

○ **Fisherman's Wharf** ($279), 1250 Columbus Ave., Ⓒ **415/775-7555**

○ Courtyard **Fisherman's Wharf** ($299), 580 Beach St., Ⓒ **415/775-3800**

○ JW Marriott **Union Square** ($239), 500 Post St., Ⓒ **415/771-8600**

○ **Union Square** ($229), 480 Sutter St., Ⓒ **415/398-8900**

○ Marquis **SoMa** ($179), 780 Mission St., Ⓒ **415/896-1600**

Starwood (www.starwoodhotels.com)

○ Le Meridien **Embarcadero** ($469), 333 Battery St., Ⓒ **415/296-2900**

○ Sheraton **Fisherman's Wharf** ($299), 2500 Mason St., Ⓒ **415/362-5500**

○ St. Regis **SoMa** ($625), 125 Third St., Ⓒ **415/284-4000**

○ W San Francisco **SoMa** ($446), 181 Third St., Ⓒ **415/777-5300**

○ Westin Market St. **SoMa** ($436), 50 Third St., Ⓒ **415/974-6400**

night. Ask the concierge which way to walk when heading out sightseeing and use caution after dark.

940 Sutter St. (btw. Leavenworth and Hyde sts.). Ⓒ **415/885-6800.** www.hotelvertigosf.com. 102 units. $149–$499 double; $224–$650 suite. Rates include morning beverages in lobby, wine 5:30pm weekdays. Valet parking $35–$40. Bus: 2 or 3. **Amenities:** Concierge; exercise room.

Inn at Union Square ★★   For a boutique hotel right next to Union Square, you can't get much better than this little gem. It's narrow and quaint, reminiscent of many of the apartment buildings in the area, but well maintained enough to resist any drabness. Morton's Steak House, located next door, provides the room service to guests. A hearty continental breakfast and hosted evening wine hour are just two of the perks found here. But be warned: Rooms and bathrooms are small, though each has a built-in dresser and sufficient storage. The windows open (not always the case in city hotels), which adds to the hotel's light and airy feel.

440 Post St. (between Powell St. and Mason St.). Ⓒ **415/397-3510.** www.unionsquare.com. $209–$300 double; $289–$399 Jr. suite, $349–$600 suite. 30 units. **Amenities:** Concierge; continental breakfast, hosted wine happy hour; complimentary Peet's coffee and tea; room service from Morton's Steak House; access to Club One fitness center ($15/day).

- Westin St. Francis **Union Square** ($350), 335 Powell St., ℂ **415/397-7000**

Hilton (www.hilton.com)
- **FiDi** ($275), 750 Kearney St., ℂ **415/433-6600**
- **Union Square** ($249), 333 O'Farrell St., ℂ **415/771-1400**

Holiday Inn (www.holidayinn.com)
- **Civic Center** ($164), 50 Eighth St., ℂ **415/626-6103**
- Express **Fisherman's Wharf** ($265), 550 North Point St., ℂ **415/409-4600**
- **Fisherman's Wharf** ($247), 1300 Columbus Ave., ℂ **415/771-9000**
- **Nob Hill** ($197), 1500 Van Ness Ave., ℂ **415/441-4000**

Best Western (www.bestwestern.com)
- The Tuscan at Fisherman's Wharf ($263), 425 North Point St., ℂ 415/561-1100
- **SoMa** ($158), 121 Seventh St., ℂ **415/626-0200**

- **Union Square** ($235), 580 Geary St., ℂ **415/441-2700**

Travelodge (www.travelodge.com)
- **The Castro** ($158), 1707 Market St., ℂ **415/621-6775**
- **Fisherman's Wharf** ($179), 1450 Lombard St., ℂ **415/673-0691**
- **Marina** ($144), 2230 Lombard St., ℂ **415/922-3900**
- **Marina** ($175), 2755 Lombard St., ℂ **415/931-8581**
- **North Beach** ($127), 1201 Columbus Ave., ℂ **415/776-7070**

Days Inn (www.daysinn.com)
- **Civic Center** ($146), 465 Grove St., ℂ **415/864-4040**
- **Marina** ($99), 2322 Lombard St., ℂ **415/921-4980**
- **Marina** ($144), 2358 Lombard St., ℂ **415/922-2010**
- **SoMa** ($99), 10 Hallam St., ℂ **415/431-0541**
- **Sunset** ($126), 2600 Sloat Blvd., ℂ **415/665-9000**

Serrano Hotel ★★ Located at the intersection of tourist action and local hangouts, the beautifully appointed Serrano boasts amenities and luxury not usually available at a boutique urban hotel (as in, a 24-hour fitness center with dry sauna). A stunning lobby featuring intricately painted and carved ceilings, grand flower arrangements, and baroque furnishings give way to spacious, elegantly appointed rooms. Alas, the carpet and yellow wallpaper is a bit dated and, because the building is old, the rooms vary in shape and size and bathrooms are small. But most accommodations are large enough for a desk, and higher floors boast views from Union Square to Twin Peaks. The adjoined Jasper's Corner Tap provides room service and a complimentary continental breakfast for guests. It's also a fun place to grab a beer—they have 18 on tap—or dinner, where upscale bar bites and progressive American cuisine are served tapas-style. With extensive breakfast, brunch, lunch, pre-theater, dinner, and late-night menus, you surely won't go hungry.

405 Taylor St. (at O'Farrell St.). ℂ **415/885-2500.** www.serranohotel.com. 236 units. $159–$300 double; $169–$500 suite. Valet parking $52, oversized vehicles $69. Bus 38, 27, 3. **Amenities:** Restaurant; 24-hour business center and fitness center with dry sauna; room service; Wi-Fi ($20/night). Cable car: Powell–Hyde or Powell–Mason lines.

The Warwick ★   An ever-reliable choice in the theater district, this boutique hotel upped its understated-opulence game with a complete makeover, from its rooms to its restaurant. Streamlined and visually pleasing accommodations feature new everything, French doors, and large bathrooms with walk-in marble showers. Downstairs, the hotel's bar and lounge, is a great place to start your night with a craft cocktail in front of the fireplace and its restaurant, features inventive Californian cuisine and an open kitchen. *Tip:* Book directly with the hotel, instead of a third party, to get the best rates and free Wi-Fi.

490 Geary St. (btw. Mason and Taylor sts.). ℂ **415/928-7900.** www.warwicksf.com. 90 units. $199–$399 double; $249–$1,299 suite. Parking $42, oversized vehicles $59. Bus: 2, 3, 27, or 38. Cable car: Powell–Hyde or Powell–Mason line. **Amenities:** Restaurant; concierge; access to nearby health club ($15 per day); 24-hour room service; Wi-Fi ($10/day).

Inexpensive

Beresford Arms Hotel ★★★   As a low-cost hotel in the stylish Nob Hill neighborhood, the Beresford Arms is an especially good choice for large families or groups: A family of up to seven can stay in a two-bedroom suite with a full kitchen, including a complimentary continental breakfast, afternoon wine, cheese, and cookies, for around $210—a practically unheard-of deal. Listed on the National Register of Historic Places, the public areas have a '20s feel, complete with parlor furniture, white columns, elegant chandeliers, and a grandfather clock. The regular rooms are also large, and all suites—not just the two-bedrooms—have a kitchenette or wet bar. Want to bring Fido with you? No problem; pets are welcome. The downsides: It's a little dated, a little noisy, there's no AC (although, San Francisco almost never needs it) and the beds are not the most comfortable. The property's sister hotel, **Beresford Hotel ★**, at 635 Sutter St. (ℂ **415/673-9900;** www.beresford.com; $89–$165 double, extra person $15), is another budget option in an old Victorian serving free continental breakfast but the rooms are downright tiny and basic. Still, if you're just looking for a crash pad, the price is right.

701 Post St. (at Jones St.). ℂ**415/673-2600.** www.beresford.com. 95 units. $159–$209 double. Parlor Suite $210. Extra person $15. Children 12 and under stay free in parent's room. Rates include continental breakfast, afternoon wine and tea. Valet parking $27 per night; oversized vehicles $35. Bus: 2, 3, 27, or 38. Cable car: Powell–Hyde line. **Amenities:** Access to nearby health club ($10 per day).

The Golden Gate Hotel ★   Staying here is like visiting Grandma's house—quaint, friendly, and filled with antiques. There's even a ginger cat on staff that goes by the titles "Feline Overlord" and "Room Service Cuddle Provider." Rooms are tiny, decorated with floral curtains and wallpaper, but there's a European charm to this B&B. Coffee, tea, juice, and croissants are served in the parlor each morning and homemade cookies each afternoon. The family-run staff is helpful, and it's an easy walk to Union Square, Chinatown, and Nob Hill.

775 Bush St. (btw. Powell and Mason sts.). ℂ**415/392-3702.** www.goldengatehotel.com. 25 units. From $135 double (with shared bathroom); from $190 (with private bathroom). Rates include continental breakfast, afternoon tea and cookies. Parking $30. Cable car: Powell–Hyde or Powell–Mason line. BART: Powell and Market. **Amenities:** Concierge; free Wi-Fi.

NOB HILL

Nob Hill is where San Francisco's railroad and mining barons once lived and modern barons stay during their visits. A few very steep blocks away from Union Square, it's also where most of the city's finest hotels are perched.

Expensive

The Ritz-Carlton, San Francisco ★★★ Superior service, stately environs, an abundance of amenities, and the Ritz reputation make this luxury stalwart the premier choice for most dignitaries and celebrities since its 1991 opening. The entrance may be understated, but it leads to grand rooms, including one of the top spots to have tea in the city (a great way to visit if a stay isn't in your budget). Rooms are spacious and well appointed, although bathrooms in some of the smaller accommodations are surprisingly basic. Guest amenities include a fitness center, spa, and an indoor pool. Their flagship restaurant, once formal, has been overhauled to become **Parallel 37,** a relaxed, bistro-chic dining room presided over by well-known city chef Ron Siegel, who serves top-notch contemporary American cuisine. The **Lounge** is where you'll find that legendary afternoon tea. (If you're here for the holidays with a tot in tow and have money to burn, don't miss the teddy bear tea.)

600 Stockton St. (at California St.). ✆ **415/296-7465.** www.ritzcarlton.com. 336 units. From $335–$668 double; $359–$1,100 suite. Buffet breakfast $39. Pet friendly for dogs under 10lbs. Parking $65. Cable car: California St. line (direct stop). **Amenities:** 2 restaurants; 3 bars; concierge; outstanding fitness center; spa; Jacuzzi; indoor pool; room service, gift shop, Wi-Fi in room $15 per day (no charge in bar and lobby areas).

Moderate

The University Club of San Francisco ★★ By far the best value on Nob Hill, this elite, private social club offers the history and old-world charm of its neighboring luxury behemoths in a more intimate (and less expensive) setting. First and foremost, it's a social club catering to San Francisco's elite—think wood paneling, leather chairs, floor-to-ceiling bookshelves, and grand fireplaces—but the club opens its doors (and swanky restaurant, bar, and fitness center) to non-members. While by no means modern, rooms are elegantly appointed and homey. Suites have sitting areas large enough for a rollaway bed. The best part of this hotel, besides its stunning views from every window, is the convivial collegiate atmosphere in the Black Cat Bar, which hasn't changed in close to a century. Another great perk is use of one of the finest gym facilities in the city, complete with exercise room, squash courts, yoga studio (with scheduled classes), steam, and sauna. Continental breakfast is included.

800 Powell St. (at California St.). ✆ **415/781-0900.** www.univclub.com. 16 units. 5 are suites with a sitting room. $219 double; $219–$249 suite. Children are free using existing bedding. Rates include continental breakfast. Limited parking $35 per day. **Amenities:** Restaurant and bar Tues–Fri only; gym; sauna.

Omni San Francisco Hotel ★ Italian marble, crystal chandeliers, and rich wood paneling in the lobby set the elegant tone in this award-winning hotel that beckons the business traveler. Located at the base of Nob Hill at the entrance of the Financial District on iconic California Street where cable cars roll up the steep incline and flanked by city skyscrapers, the hotel boasts ballrooms, a health center, and a popular steakhouse. While it has all the trappings of a luxury Omni hotel—spacious rooms, sheets with a high thread count, all the expected amenities—its location gears it to the business trip than the family vacation or romantic getaway.

500 California St. (at Montgomery St.). ✆ **415/677-9494.** www.omnihotels.com/FindAHotel/san francisco.aspx. 362 units. $189–$799 double; $399–$1,500 suite. **Amenities**: 24-hour health club; restaurant, bar, 24-hour room service, business center, in-room fitness kits and treadmills in select rooms, free weekly guided walking tour (Sat), kid's program with free milk and cookies.

HOTELS WITH A past

We can thank early San Francisco businessmen (some would say swindlers and rapscallions) for some of the city's most luxurious and historic hotels. Founded on new-moneyed competition, The Big Four, also known as the Southern Pacific Railroad group Leland Stanford, Colis P. Huntington, and Charles Crocker, competed with each other to see who could build the largest, most lavish home on Nob Hill with their new found railroad wealth. Though their homes burned to the ground after the 1906 earthquake, their legacy lives on with hotels, a park, and a church built on the sites.

Leland Stanford was president of the group, loved the limelight, and served as governor of California and U.S. Senator. After his 15-year-old son passed away, Stanford converted his horse farm in Palo Alto into a university named for the boy, now a world-famous institution considered the Harvard of the West. He loved to spend money and was first of the group to build on Nob Hill. At one point, he could brag his mansion had the largest private dining room in the West. On the site you'll find the aptly named **Stanford Court Hotel** ★ (905 California St. at Powell St.; ℂ **415/989-3500;** www.stanfordcourt.com; 393 units; $180–$429.) Compared to its luxury-minded Nob Hill neighbors below, the Stanford Court strives for "modern classic" and caters more to the no-fuss business travelers who might appreciate the high-tech touches, such as the iPad minis set up in the lobby and complimentary Wi-Fi, as well as the 24-hour fitness center. The carpets are due for a replacement and there is no room service, but this option is comfortable with a great location.

Known for his ruthlessness, **Collis P. Huntington** was vice president of the Big Four. He spent time behind the scenes greasing palms and lobbying for favorable treatment of the group's interests with politicians. The site of his

mansion is now Huntington Park (at California and Taylor sts.). He has a Nob Hill hotel named in his honor: the **Scarlet Huntington Hotel** ★ (1075 California St. btw. Mason and Taylor sts.; ℂ **415/474-5400;** www.huntingtonhotel.com; 136 units; $329–$629), which completed a $15-million renovation in 2014—and added "Scarlet" to its name. The makeover lent a much-needed modernization to the guest rooms, complete with new bathrooms adorned with hand-carved vanities and marble showers, and made improvements to the public spaces with Asian-inspired touches and a new color scheme featuring rich jewel tones accented with gold. Rooms are large and tastefully decorated; the lobby is small and elegant. The hotel restaurant, suitably named **The Big Four** (ℂ **415/474-5400;** www.big4restaurant.com), has walls covered with photos and historical objects commemorating the group; it serves fine tycoon-fare such as truffled lobster mac and cheese and its breakfast goes for $18—a steal compared to the $49 it cost before the renovation.

Mark Hopkins was considered the most frugal, making his role as the group's treasurer fitting. Though he was happy living in small, rented quarters on Sutter Street, his social-climbing wife had other ideas. At a cost of $3 million, she commissioned the Gothic, wooden fairytale castle, complete with towers and spires. Hopkins died just before it was completed and his wife lived there only a few years before moving to the East Coast. On the castle's site, you can sleep at the **InterContinental Mark Hopkins** ★★ (1 Nob Hill at California and Mason sts.; ℂ **415/392-3434;** www.intercontinentalmarkhopkins.com; $199–$500; pets welcome). Hopkins' widow would approve of the hotel named after her husband. The lobby is part French chateau, part Italian renaissance with high ceilings, light-drenched sitting areas, and ornate chandeliers. The rooms and suites, all with city views, feature rich woods and fine fabrics, though they are on the smaller side thanks to the Victorian architecture style. While steeped in history, the hotel has added modern touches to its farm-to-table restaurant and lounge, Nob Hill Club, which is now equipped with a self-serve espresso bar that uses touchscreens to deliver the goods. It's all very Luxury 2.0, considering the classic furnishings and historic surroundings. Enjoy grab-and-go pastries from the bakery, or sit down to a daily breakfast buffet amid the aubergine-colored walls, high-backed chairs, and gold details. The chef from the Top of the Mark (upstairs) developed the seasonal menu, offering guests another option for modern Californian cuisine.

Charles Crocker was the group's construction supervisor—too bad he built his mansion out of wood. After the 1906 fire, the Crocker family donated the entire city block where their home had stood to the Episcopal church, which built the beautiful **Grace Cathedral** (see p. 113) on the site.

The Big Four's counterparts were known as the **Bonanza Kings,** four Irish buddies who made their fortune from a silver mine in Nevada. While their wealth far out-paced that of The Big Four, their names are less well known today. Members **John William Mackay** and **William S. O'Brien** left little mark on San Francisco, whereas the mansion of partner **James C. Flood** can still be seen today at 1000 California Street on top of Nob Hill as home to the private Pacific-Union Club. Because it was built using Connecticut sandstone, it was one of the few structures in the area to survive the 1906 earthquake fires. You can't go inside, but you can take an up-close look from the street and admire the original bronze fence, which still exists on three sides of the property.

The last Bonanza King partner, **James Fair,** died before he could build his mansion on Nob Hill. His daughters, Tessie and Virginia, built a hotel to honor their father, but, because they got in a little over their heads financially, had to sell it to the Law brothers. The property changed hands on April 6, 1906, less than 2 weeks before the great quake. The hotel burned, though some of the structure survived. It was completely rebuilt with the help of architect, Julia Morgan—of Hearst Castle fame—and reopened 1 year to the date of the quake in 1907 as **The Fairmont San Francisco ★★★** (950 Mason St. at California St.; ℂ **415/772-5000;** www.fairmont.com/sanfrancisco; 591 units; $399–$899). Perched high atop Nob Hill, the majestic Fairmont completed a $21-million refresh in 2014 to its 591 rooms bringing contemporary, custom-made furnishings, hand-blown glass lamps, and a "jewel box" theme featuring bright sapphire blues with accents of contemporary pewter and platinum. The large marble bathrooms and walk-in closets have remained constant. While the revamped guest rooms showcase the Fairmont's of-the-moment aesthetic and commitment to modern amenities, the opulent lobby, with its vaulted ceilings and Corinthian columns trimmed in gold is a nod to its timeless grandeur.

The Fairmont isn't all pomp and circumstance. For a fun dance floor and tropical drinks, head down to the basement (the site of the Fairmont's original pool) and visit the whimsical **Tonga Room and Hurricane Bar** (p. 183), where guests enjoy Asian fusion food and umbrella drinks while sitting in tiki huts. Every so often thunder rumbles and warm, tropical rain pours down into the center pool, where a live band plays on the little floating pontoon boat in the middle.

Inexpensive

The Grant Hotel ★ Choose this lower Nob Hill crash pad if all you care about is an awesome location and basic but clean accommodations. Minutes away from Union Square yet far from Tenderloin sketchiness, the Grant is a rare find. Its bedspreads are dated, the bathrooms are tiny, and there's no AC (though almost never an issue in this temperate town—but who cares? The price is right and you're here to enjoy the town, not the room. Complimentary continental breakfast is served in the lobby, where there is a spacious seating area and old piano. There's a 24-hour front desk person, but don't expect him to be your travel agent. This is bare bones at its best.

753 Bush St. (btw. Mason and Powell sts). ✆ **415/421-7540.** www.granthotel.net. 76 units. $100–$169 double. Rates include continental breakfast. Garage parking across the street $21 per night with unlimited ins and outs. Amenties: 24-hour front desk; Wi-Fi (free).

SoMa

SoMa, which starts only a few blocks away from Union Square and stretches for several long blocks toward the Mission District, offers an eclectic mix of lodgings, from some of the highest thread counts in the city to budget motels. Hotels are generally located near the Moscone convention center, the Museum of Modern Art, the Yerba Buena Center for the Arts, and AT&T Park.

Moderate

Hotel Palomar ★★ At a Kimpton hotel, like this one, you get a lot for your money in the way of service and personality. Plus you're in a great location, inches away from Union Square (though technically South of Market), convention centers, museums, and tons of shopping. The hotel itself was remodeled in 2014, which gave the lobby a facelift complete with an elegant chandelier, art deco touches, modern art, and a new home for the adorable, sleepy chocolate Labrador on staff. Rooms are on the large size for the area and bathrooms offer plenty of counter space. The biggest improvement is the rooftop addition of a restaurant, bar, and patio, which will surely draw locals and visitors alike since it's one of few rooftop spaces in the city. The previously unused middle courtyard has been transformed into an urban oasis, adorned with fountains and a fire pit. And just off the elevated patio is a whiskey bar. There's a fitness center on site, but if you can't stand treadmills, the resident wellness expert leads a run every morning at 7am. Exercise and guided sightseeing—what's not to love about that?

12 4th St. (at Market St.). ✆ **415/348-1111.** www.hotelpalomar-sf.com. $189–$500 double; $300–$1,200 suite. Pets stay free; Valet parking $48. **Amenities**: Hosted wine happy hour daily; morning coffee and tea, fitness center, business center; free Wi-Fi for Kimpton InTouch Members (free to join); in-room spa services (surcharge).

Hotel Zetta ★ Sleek, masculine, and trendy with an L.A. sensibility, this hotel embodies San Francisco's young professionals' "work hard, play hard" motto by providing a proverbial adult playground for the tech crowd. For starters, it has an interactive lobby complete with a Plinko Game and a playroom, featuring a pool table, shuffleboard, and video games. Guest rooms start at a spacious 250 square feet and feature large butcher-block desks, pillow-top mattresses, smart TVs, and illy espresso machines; the large bathrooms feature mosaic-tiled walk-in showers. The sexy lobby bar and comfy-cool Cavalier restaurant also lure.

55 5th St. (btw. Minna and Market sts). ✆ **415/543-8555.** www.viceroyhotelgroup.com/en/zetta. 116 units. $249–$399 double; $449–$699 suite. Valet parking: $50 per night. Pet friendly with a $75

cleaning fee. **Amenities**: Restaurant; bar; fitness center; game room; access to spa at Westfield Shopping Center; Wi-Fi (free in common areas, $15/per day in-room).

The Palace Hotel ★★★   Enter the Palace Hotel and its stunning Garden Court and you might think you've stepped into a Parisian castle. Marble columns, massive chandeliers, crowned by an atrium of over 80,000 panes of stained glass, will take your breath away. While completely rebuilt after the 1906 earthquake, its history dates back to 1875 when it was considered the largest, most expensive hotel in the world. For a historic hotel, the rooms are a good size (even the least expensive standard rooms have enough space for a comfy chair to relax in and a desk set). The surprisingly high ceilings help give the illusion that rooms are a little larger. A stately hotel of this magnitude wouldn't be complete without plenty of options to eat and imbibe, and the Palace delivers. Enjoy breakfast, lunch, afternoon tea, and Sunday brunch in the Garden Court, which doubles as the only indoor historic landmark in the city. Or cozy up to the swanky Pied Piper Bar, where you can sip an expertly crafted classic cocktail or dine on upscale American cuisine, while gazing upon the $3-million Pied Piper mural that hangs behind the bar.

2 New Montgomery St. (at Market St.). *©* **415/512-1111.** www.sfpalace.com. 553 units. $249–$799 double; $449–$5,000 suite. Extra person $40. Children 17 and under sharing existing bedding stay free in parent's room. Parking $59, oversized vehicles $64. Pets welcome (up to 80 lbs.) $100/stay. Bus: All Market St. buses. Streetcar: All Market St. streetcars. Bart: Market. **Amenities:** 2 restaurants; bar; room service; concierge; health club w/skylight-covered, heated lap pool; Jacuzzi; sauna; spa; Wi-Fi (free in lobby, $20/day in-room).

Inexpensive

The Mosser ★   Considering its location—nestled next to the Moscone Convention Center, Westfield Centre shopping mall, Union Square, and amid high-end hotels—this quaint hotel is a spectacular deal. You'll make some compromises for the price and location, however. The rooms are tiny and the en suite showers are about 3 square feet. Rates get lower if you opt to use a shared bathroom (if that doesn't appeal, be sure to double check what kind of room you're reserving when you book). Free Wi-Fi and continental breakfast add to the deal. Just don't expect luxury and you'll be happy here.

54 Fourth St. (at Market St.). *©* **415/986-4400.** www.themosser.com. 166 units, $110–$359 double with bathroom; $89–$144 double w/out bathroom. Rates include continental breakfast. Valet parking $39, $49 for oversize vehicles. Streetcar: F-Line, and all underground Muni. BART: All trains. **Amenities:** Restaurant; bar; concierge; access to Marriott fitness center and spa for $15 per day.

NORTH BEACH/FISHERMAN'S WHARF

North Beach is the birthplace of the Beat Generation, where Little Italy meets and mixes with neighboring Chinatown's Big China. It's home to a few boutique hotels, family-run restaurants, and a lively nightlife scene, including bustling bars, restaurants, cafes, and a half-block of topless clubs. Fisherman's Wharf is the heart of all the tourist action. You'll pay more to stay in this neighborhood, because it's where many visitors want to be.

Expensive

Argonaut Hotel ★★★   If you want to stay in a beautiful, historic building and walk right out your door into the heart Fisherman's Wharf action—and are willing to

San Francisco Hotels

0 ___ 1/2 mi
0 ___ 0.5 km

Marina Blvd.   Marina Green

MARINA

Mason St.

Cervantes Blvd.

North Point St.

Fort Mason

101

Lincoln Blvd.

Richardson Ave.

Divisadero St.

Pierce St.

Avila St.

Chestnut St.

Moscone Rec. Ctr.

Bay St.

Francisco St.

6 **7**

Octavia St.

Franklin St.

San Francisco National Cemetery

4 101

Lombard St.

5

THE PRESIDIO

Greenwich St.

Filbert St.

COW HOLLOW

Union St.

2

Green St.

Fillmore St.

Vallejo St.

Laguna St.

Gough St.

Lyon St.

Broderick St.

Broadway

Pacific Ave.

Jackson St.

Scott St.

Alta Plaza

PACIFIC HEIGHTS

Lafayette Park

Presidio Golf Course

3

Washington St.

Clay St.

Sacramento St.

Buchanan St.

Locust St.

Laurel St.

Walnut St.

California St.

Maple St.

PRESIDIO HEIGHTS

Baker St.

Pine St.

Bush St.

15

14

5th Ave.

Lake St.

Cherry St.

Commonwealth Ave.

Parker St.

Spruce St.

Presidio Ave.

Lyon St.

Sutter St.

Post St.

Japan Center

Cornwall St.

Euclid Ave.

Collins St.

Wood St.

Hamilton Sq.

Geary Blvd.

WESTERN ADDITION

Clement St.

Jordan Ave.

Palm Ave.

Anza St.

O'Farrell St.

Steiner St.

Eddy St.

Jefferson Square

←1

2nd Ave.

3rd Ave.

Arguello Blvd.

Ellis St.

Webster St.

6th Ave.

4th Ave.

UNIVERSITY OF SAN FRANCISCO

Turk Blvd.

RICHMOND

Masonic Ave.

Golden Gate Ave.

Balboa St.

U.S.F.

McAllister St.

Fulton St.

Cabrillo St.

Parker Ave.

Grove St.

Central Ave.

Hayes St.

Divisadero St.

Alamo Square

Fell St.

Fulton St.

Willard St.

Stanyan St.

Cole St.

Oak St.

Pierce St.

Fillmore St.

HAYES VALLEY

Laguna St.

Octavia St.

Conservatory of Flowers

Fell St.

Page St.

John F. Kennedy Dr.

The Panhandle

Clayton St.

Ashbury St.

Haight St.

Duboce Park

Waller St.

Duboce Ave.

Hermann St.

GOLDEN GATE PARK

Shrader St.

HAIGHT-ASHBURY

Buena Vista Park

Alpine Terr.

Sanchez St.

16

19

Buena Vista Ave.

14th St.

Castro St.

Noe St.

Kezar Dr.

20

Kezar Stadium

Frederick St.

Downey St.

15th St.

Guerrero St.

Dolores St.

Lincoln Wy.

Carl St.

Corona Heights Park

Hugo St.

Belvedere St.

States St.

16th St.

CASTRO

INNER SUNSET

Parnassus Ave.

Cole St.

18

Church St.

Mission Dolores

6th Ave.

5th Ave.

UNIVERSITY OF CALIFORNIA– SAN FRANCISCO

Carmel St.

17th St.

Market St.

Castro Theatre

17

18th St.

Dolores Park

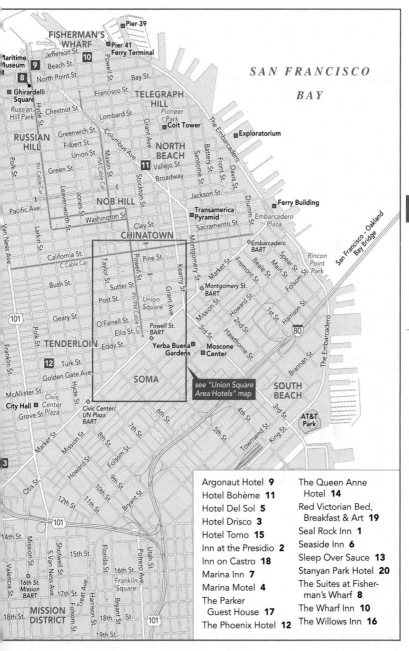

Argonaut Hotel **9**	The Queen Anne Hotel **14**
Hotel Bohème **11**	Red Victorian Bed, Breakfast & Art **19**
Hotel Del Sol **5**	Seal Rock Inn **1**
Hotel Drisco **3**	Seaside Inn **6**
Hotel Tomo **15**	Sleep Over Sauce **13**
Inn at the Presidio **2**	Stanyan Park Hotel **20**
Inn on Castro **18**	The Suites at Fisher-man's Wharf **8**
Marina Inn **7**	The Wharf Inn **10**
Marina Motel **4**	The Willows Inn **16**
The Parker Guest House **17**	
The Phoenix Hotel **12**	

THE most FAMILY-FRIENDLY HOTELS

Argonaut Hotel (p. 61)   Not only is it near all the funky kid fun of Fisherman's Wharf and the National Maritime Museum, but this bayside hotel also has kid-friendly perks like scavenger hunts, board games, kid-friendly movies, the chance for each child to grab a gift from the hotel's "treasure chest," and a Wii system in the lobby.

Beresford Arms Hotel (p. 56)   The Parlor Suite can sleep up to a family of seven and comes with a full kitchen and dining room—all for around $200. The Junior Suite sleeps six and costs only $159. Located a few blocks from Union Square, this Victorian charmer is perfect for families on a budget wanting a little extra space.

The Fairmont San Francisco (p. 59)   While the glamorous lobby and spectacular city views will please parents, kids will be thrilled by the hotel's **Tonga Room,** a fantastically kitsch Disneyland-like tropical bar and restaurant where "rain" falls every 30 minutes.

Hotel Del Sol (p. 67)   It's colorful enough to represent a Crayola selection, but tots are more likely to be impressed by the "Kids are VIPs" program that includes a lending library, toys and movies, evening cookies and milk, a heated pool, and a nearby park. Parents will be happy to find a two-bedroom family suite.

Hotel Diva (p. 52)   The sleek, mod Diva has all sorts of fun kid-friendly perks. Check out SF's version of the Walk of Fame right outside the door, and definitely ask about their two-room Little Divas Suite, with bunk beds, drawing tables, and a TV loaded with kids' movies.

Ritz-Carlton (p. 57)   The Ritz has a Very Important Kid program with a kid-sized in-room tent for your room, coloring books, and milk and cookies at turndown.

Seal Rock Inn (p. 67)   The Seal Rock's setting—surrounded by parks, across the street from the beach, and just a few minutes from the zoo—is a real draw as are the hotel's suites with kitchenettes.

Stanyan Park Hotel (p. 71)   Plenty of elbow room and a half-block walk to Golden Gate Park's Children's Playground make this a prime spot for crashing family-style. But the biggest bonuses are the suites, which come with one or two bedrooms, a full kitchen, and a dining area.

Westin St. Francis (p. 51)   A classic San Francisco hotel down to its hospitality, the Westin welcomes little ones with gifts and toys, including coloring books, crayons, and a rubber ducky. Kids love riding in the glass elevators.

pay for the privilege—this nautical-themed hotel is perfect for you. Owned by upscale Kimpton Hotels, the Argonaut is housed in the exposed red brick and wooden beams of the old 1908 cannery. Guest rooms are done up in navy and beige and decorated with tasteful nautical knickknacks (and feature free Starbucks coffee). Kids love the treasure chest at the front desk and the Wii system in the lobby, plus Ghirardelli ice cream is around the corner. Visiting dogs are equally pampered, with a dog bed, dog toys, and even doggie room service. Each afternoon at 5pm, the hotel's Master Sommelier hand selects a few vintages for guests to enjoy at a hosted wine reception in the Living Room, a comfortable lounge area with a fireplace, plush red chairs, and all sorts of nautical paraphernalia mounted on the walls, such as maps, compasses, and wooden steering wheels. The nautical theme carries over to the Blue Mermaid Chowder House & Bar, a sea-faring room of thick-hewn timber and braided ropes. You don't even need to leave the hotel to soak up San Francisco's maritime past—an interactive museum kids and adults will love is located off the lobby and has made this location a historical national landmark since the '70s.

495 Jefferson St. (at Hyde St.). © **415/563-0800.** www.argonauthotel.com. 252 units. $179–$379 double; $358–$649 suite. Rates include evening wine in the lobby. Pet friendly (no charge, no size limit). Parking $46, oversized vehicles $61. Bus: 30 or 47. Streetcar: F-Line. Cable car: Powell–Hyde line. **Amenities:** Restaurant; bar; concierge; in-room spa services; 24-hr fitness center, Wi-Fi free and "raid the mini bar" program for Kimpton InTouch members (no charge to join).

Moderate

The Hotel Bohème ★
What this historic boutique hotel located in the center of North Beach restaurant and cafe activity lacks in space, it makes up for in European charm. Harnessing the bohemian culture that dominated North Beach back when Beat Poet Allen Ginsberg hung his hat at this very hotel, this tiny hotel with rooms up a flight of stairs (no elevator) is painted in colorful '50s colors and adorned with black and white photographs of Beat Generation greats. Accommodations and bathrooms are tiny, and the smell of fresh cannoli wafting up from **Stella Pastry & Café** downstairs add to the cozy feel. Sit at the cabaret table in your shabby-chic room while you enjoy complimentary sherry (served in the lobby each evening) to experience the hotel as Ginsberg likely did, or meander next door in either direction for a taste of North Beach's cafe culture.

444 Columbus Ave. (btw. Vallejo and Green sts.). © **415/433-9111.** www.hotelboheme.com. 15 units. $174–$254 double. Rates include afternoon sherry. Parking at nearby public garages $30–$35. Bus: 12, 30, 41, or 45. Cable car: Powell–Mason line. **Amenities:** Concierge.

The Suites at Fisherman's Wharf ★★
Located right on the Hyde–Powell cable car line, a block away from Aquatic Park and the famous Buena Vista Restaurant, this hotel offers a home-away-from-home right in the middle of the tourist action. Choose between a one- or two-bedroom suite with an upscale apartment vibe and the amenities of a hotel to get perks like a pullout couch, two flatscreen TVs, and a kitchenette. Rooms facing Bay Street also have a balcony where you can watch the cable cars roll by and see the lights of the famous Ghirardelli Square sign. While the lobby and rooms are clean and tasteful, the thing you'll be writing home about is the roof deck, which offers views of both bridges, Alcatraz, and the neighboring Victorian houses (weather permitting). Do as San Franciscans do and bring a bottle of wine to the deck around sunset for your very own happy hour.

2655 Hyde St. (at North Point St.). © **415/771-0200.** www.shellvacationsclub.com/club/resorts/suites_fisherman/index.jsp. 24 units. $250–$399 double. **Amenities:** Limited on-site parking for $20 per day; coin-operated laundry; 24-hour front desk; Wi-Fi (free). Bus: 30. Cable car: Powell–Hyde line.

The Wharf Inn ★
Though this basic hotel is a little dated, the Wharf Inn is the rare example of a really good deal right in the heart of Fisherman's Wharf. Pier 39, the cable car turnaround, and Boudin Bakery are all just steps away. Guest rooms are clean, if frill-free. The helpful staff, free parking, and free coffee, tea, and hot chocolate all day in the lobby help most guests forgive the inn's lack of style.

2601 Mason St. (at Beach St.). © **415/673-7411.** www.wharfinn.com. 51 units. $127–$160 double. Free parking. Bus: 39 or 47. Streetcar: F-Line. Cable car: Powell–Mason or Powell–Hyde line.

THE MARINA/PACIFIC HEIGHTS/PRESIDIO

The Marina is a young, lively neighborhood full of 1950-and-later motor inns that have been updated for the modern traveler. Pacific Heights boasts old-moneyed mansions (Getty, Danielle Steel), quiet streets, and outrageous views. And for the nature-lover, the Presidio will make you forget that you're mere minutes from urban hustle.

Expensive

Hotel Drisco ★★★ If you're looking to pretend you're a real San Francisco resident—and a wealthy one at that—stay at this elegant yet understated hotel nestled among the multimillion dollar mansions of swanky Pacific Heights. What looks like an upscale apartment building from the outside is actually *the* place for guests seeking discreet, high-class service and amenities, without the showy feel of a big-city luxury property. Guests enjoy generous rooms, many with commanding views of the city. Complimentary continental breakfast includes such delicacies as currant scones with lemon curd and clotted cream, local organic sheep's milk yogurt, and a selection of meats and cheeses. The evening wine reception allows guest to socialize in the renovated parlor while noshing on cheese, charcuterie, and hot hors d'oeuvres. Boutique shopping and great restaurants (without the tourists) on Fillmore or Union Streets are short scenic walks away. The quiet location means only the soothing foghorn will haunt your dreams. Still, the sights, shopping, restaurants, and nightlife are all only a few minutes away. Hop on the 1 bus to be in the heart of Chinatown or Financial District in less than 30 minutes.

2901 Pacific Ave. (at Broderick St.). ☏ **415/346-2880.** www.hoteldrisco.com. 48 units. $285–$475 double. Rates include gourmet continental breakfast, afternoon tea and cookies, and evening wine, cheese, and hot hors d'oeuvre. Free street parking available. Bus: 3 or 24. **Amenities:** Concierge; exercise room and free pass to YMCA; room service; bikes to borrow.

Inn at the Presidio ★★ If you prefer nature to the traffic, crowds, and skyscrapers of a big city, this former officers' quarters, converted to an inn in 2011, was created just for you. Set on over 1,400 acres of coastal dunes, forests, and prairie grasslands, this stately red brick Georgian Revival–style building puts you in the middle of San Francisco's natural beauty—as well as a flashback to the U.S. Army days when the Presidio played an important role defending the new territories on the West coast. Though Pershing Hall, as the inn was formerly called, is on the National Register of Historic Places, it's anything but a musty old boys club. Rooms are modern and elegant, featuring high ceilings and original moldings; most are suites with fireplaces; many have views of the bay. At almost 300 square feet, even the basic queen rooms are large by San Francisco hotel standards. Public spaces are warm and inviting; guests enjoy complimentary continental breakfast and an evening wine and cheese reception. The inn has been such a success that in the summer of 2013, Funston House—a Victorian-style home that used to house officers and their families—opened as a four-bedroom cottage that can be rented in part or as a whole by groups or extended families for $220 to $1,000 per night. If you want to see the city sights, the PresidioGo shuttle offers rides downtown on weekdays; Muni buses serve the area daily. Though, with miles of hiking trails just outside the door, a fire pit out back, and rocking chairs on the fporch, you might not make it to Fisherman's Wharf.

Main Post, 42 Moraga Ave. (at Funston Ave.). ✆ **415/800-7356.** www.innatthepresidio.com. 26 units. $229–$385 double. $25 extra person charge; children under 16 stay free. Rates include continental buffet breakfast & evening wine and cheese reception. Pet friendly $40 fee. Self-parking $7. Bus: 28, 43, or PresidioGo shuttle bus.

Moderate

Hotel Del Sol ★★ Funky, colorful Hotel del Sol is strategically located in the family-friendly Marina District, just a couple of blocks from the bustling thoroughfare of Lombard Street. Children will be thrilled to know they are not far from the Disney Museum, and hiking trails of the Presidio, as well as the noise and excitement of Fisherman's Wharf. When little ones tire of touring, they can cool off in the hotel's sparkling outdoor heated pool. Two-bedroom family suites are available; make sure to ask about the "Kids-are-VIP's" program featuring books, toys, and movies. Rooms are light and airy, with colorful decor—think more 1970s funk than old world Victorian like most of the city. Though it's built in the style of a mid-century motor lodge, it has all the style and amenities of a boutique hotel.

3100 Webster St. (at Greenwich St.). ✆ **415/921-5520.** www.thehoteldelsol.com. 57 units. From $143–$224 double; $161–$296 suite. Rates include continental breakfast and free newspapers in the lobby. Free parking. Bus: 22, 28, 30, or 43. **Amenities:** Heated outdoor pool.

Seaside Inn ★ What this motor inn lacks in ambience, it makes up for in its friendly staff, walkability in a lively neighborhood, and free parking. Thought it's not much to look at from the outside, its proximity to the Golden Gate Bridge and great bars and eateries makes it a worthy contender for the budget traveler. Rooms and bathrooms are just a step above basic, but they were completely renovated in 2012 so they're sparklingly new with fresh bedding, desks, and entertainment units, sleek black and white furnishings, and perks like minifridges, microwaves, and coffeemakers. Free parking, Wi-Fi, and continental breakfast add to the very good deal.

1750 Lombard St. (btw. Laguna Buchanon sts.) ✆ **415/921-1842.** www.sfseasideinn.com. 19 units. $90–$179 double. Rates include continental breakfast. Free parking.

seaside **SLEEPS**

Established in 1959, the **Seal Rock Inn** ★★, 545 Point Lobos Ave. (at 48th Ave.) (✆ **415/752-8000;** www.sealrockinn.com), is San Francisco's only ocean-front motor inn. The perfect spot for a family stay, the inn is surrounded by parks and trails and sits across the street from the beach—great for relaxing, but don't swim here; there is a nasty current. The zoo and Golden Gate Park are just a few minutes away. The motel's restaurant is popular among locals and it serves a great brunch. Rooms are large, and some feature kitchenettes or fireplaces; all have fridges and free parking. As of March 2014, the pool was temporarily closed (call ahead if a pool is important). Doubles go for $110 to $167 per night, with a 2-night minimum on weekends and holiday; it's $10 per night for additional guests 16 and above, $5 for guests under 16.

ACCOMMODATIONS WITH free parking

With parking fees averaging $45 to $60 a night at most hotels, you might want to consider staying at one of these hotels that offers free parking:

- **Hotel Del Sol,** Marina District/ Cow Hollow (p. 67)
- **Hotel Drisco,** Pacific Heights (no garage, but lots of free street parking; p. 66)
- **Marina Motel,** Marina District/ Cow Hollow (see below)
- **Phoenix Hotel,** Civic Center (p. 69)
- **Seal Rock Inn,** Richmond District (p. 67)
- **The Wharf Inn,** North Beach/ Fisherman's Wharf (p. 65)
- **Seaside Inn**, Marina District (p. 67)

Inexpensive

Marina Inn ★ Here's a great option for the traveler on a budget who doesn't mind a busy street. Set in a 1920s Victorian building, the floral wallpaper and heavy pine furniture give the place a cozy, cottagelike feel. Rooms are quaint, though a little noisy if close to busy Lombard Street (ask for a room in the back). With prices as low as $69 for a double, it's hard to find a better deal in the city.

3110 Octavia St. (at Lombard St.). ℂ **415/928-1000.** www.marinainn.com. 40 units. $69–$205 double. Rates include continental breakfast. No parking. Bus: 28, 30, or 49. **Amenities:** Concierge; barber shop; nail salon.

Marina Motel ★ If you're looking for simple, convenient accommodations, the Marina Motel is one of your best bets. Guests enter the property on a cobblestone driveway, and pull their cars into a courtyard with cascading flowers, reminiscent of a European inn. They then park in their own private garage—unheard of at most San Francisco hotels, and, for that matter, most San Francisco houses too. Rooms are small and clean, though a little noisy if they front Lombard Street. (Ask for a room in the back if you're a light sleeper.) All rooms have fridges, and complimentary coffee, tea, and hot chocolate. About half of the units have fully equipped kitchens, making this a great choice for extended stays and families. This sweet and simple "auto courtyard" motel was built to celebrate the opening of the Golden Gate Bridge in 1939, and has been owned by the same Gold Rush–era pioneer family ever since. Trendy restaurants and shops on Chestnut and Union Streets are just a few blocks away.

2576 Lombard St. (btw. Divisadero and Broderick sts.). ℂ **415/921-9406.** www.marinamotel.com. 39 units. $109–$179 double; $119–$279 suite. Rates include discount coupons for nearby cafe. Pet friendly ($15 per night for the first pet and $10 for an additional). Free parking. Bus: 28, 30, 43, 45, or 70.

JAPANTOWN & ENVIRONS

If you're staying in or near Japantown, it might be because you found a lodging deal you couldn't pass up. Though a few miles from the typical tourist sights, this historic neighborhood is centrally located, providing a good launching pad to tourist destinations and lesser-known gems.

Moderate

Hotel Tomo ★★   Where else would you expect to find an anime-themed hotel but in the heart of Japantown? The rooms at this Joie de Vivre property are high design, each with its own colorful wall mural by Heisuke Kitazawa, comfy beds, and lots of light. Rooms are large by San Francisco standards, and offer guests a fridge and a Keurig coffeemaker. Decor is sleek and modern—no Victorian fussiness here! If you're not sure where to dine in Japantown, **Mums,** the hotel's onsite restaurant, serves all-you-can-eat shabu shabu with all-you-can-drink beer and sake.

1800 Sutter St. (at Buchanan St.). ✆ **415/921-4000.** www.hoteltomo.com. 125 units. $175–$335 double. Parking $29. Bus: 2 or 3. **Amenities:** Restaurant, fitness center, business center.

The Queen Anne Hotel ★   Visitors are certain this historic Victorian mansion is haunted by a Miss Mary Lake, the former headmistress of the school that occupied this building 100 years ago. Her office was in room 410, and experts swear there is paranormal activity in the area. But don't be scared away by the ghost rumors. This "haunted hotel" is one of the best values in the city for those looking for unusually large guestrooms, loads of ornate decor, and a mysterious history. Guest rooms are furnished in beautiful, period antiques and some have fridges. In the morning, guests enjoy a free full breakfast including sausage and eggs; in the evening, complimentary tea and cookies encourage guests to congregate in the common area to trade ghost stories. Around Halloween, this hotel becomes the subject of a popular ghost tour.

1590 Sutter St. (btw. Laguna and Webster sts.). ✆ **415/441-2828.** www.queenanne.com. 48 units. $109–$199 double; $145–$350 quad; $325–$459 suite for six. Extra person $10. Rates include continental breakfast, afternoon tea and sherry, morning newspaper. Parking $20. Bus: 2 or 3. **Amenities:** Concierge, airport shuttle service.

CIVIC CENTER/TENDERLOIN

This is another one of those locations where you get more bang for your buck. However, the area has a large homeless population, as well as drug addicts and dealers. But there is safety in numbers; with the Asian Art Museum, the opera, ballet, symphony, brand new SFJAZZ venue, and tons of up-and-coming bars all close by, you'll rarely find yourself alone.

Moderate

The Phoenix Hotel ★   Welcome to the unofficial rock and roll sleeping hall of fame. Stay here and you just may sleep in the same room as the Red Hot Chili Peppers, Moby, Pearl Jam, Joan Jett, and David Bowie. Rooms are colorful and noisy; all face the pool in the courtyard outside—a la "Melrose Place." Visiting entertainers, bands, and regular guests gather around the heated outdoor pool and fire pits. Breakfast, parking, and Wi-Fi are free. The lively bar and restaurant is also a big draw for guests and locals, despite the dicey neighborhood. Funky, mid-century furnishings, walls of vintage records, and sexy corners and booths recall a hip L.A. vibe.

601 Eddy St. (at Larkin St.). ✆ **415/776-1380.** www.thephoenixhotel.com. 44 units. $129–$369 double; $429–$609 suite. $20 for extra person. Rates include continental breakfast and free weekday passes to Kabuki Springs & Spa. Free parking. Bus: 47. Streetcar: F-Line. **Amenities:** Bar; concierge; heated outdoor pool.

Inexpensive

Sleep Over Sauce ★   Not quite a B&B, and much too hip to call itself a boutique hotel, Sleep Over Sauce is something all its own. The three brothers who run it call it an urban guesthouse for those seeking the comforts of home and friendly neighborhood living. It consists of eight cozy rooms (with comfortable beds and fresh bathrooms) and a living room complete with a fireplace over the award-winning restaurant Sauce. Located in the center of the city, the hotel makes a great base for visitors who want to see more than Fisherman's Wharf. Most of the city's performing arts venues, as well as the fabulous Asian Art Museum, are a short walk away. The Mission District, Japantown, Castro, and Haight-Ashbury neighborhoods can be reached by Muni in a few minutes, and the historic F-line will take guests to Union Square and Fisherman's Wharf. Don't look for a front desk, guests check in at the bar.

135 Gough St. (at Lily St.). ✆ **415/621-0896.** www.sleepsf.com. 8 units. From $155 double; $235 suite. Some dates have 2-night minimum. Parking: city parking garages within a few blocks. Bus: 21. Streetcar: F-Line. **Amenities:** Restaurant, bar, business center.

CASTRO

Most businesses here cater to LGBT customers, but everyone is welcome in this lively neighborhood. Though located a few miles from most of the tourist action, the Castro is centrally located for visiting local-favorites, such as the Mission and Hayes Valley, and public transportation makes for an easy ride straight to the visitor meccas of Union Square, Fisherman's Wharf, and the Ferry Building. Another perk of this area is that while most of the city is blanketed in fog, chances are it'll be sunny and warm(er) in this sheltered, walkable neighborhood.

Moderate

The Parker Guest House ★★★   Rated one of the city's top guesthouses by gay travel sites such as Spartacus and Purple Roofs, this lovely 1909 Edwardian B&B in the heart of the Castro is the perfect oasis to return to after a long day of sightseeing. Sip a glass of wine outside by the garden fountain at the daily complimentary social. Lounge by the fireplace, or, perhaps, in the library. Spacious rooms feature down comforters, terry robes, and period antiques. Located in San Francisco's sunniest neighborhood, it's an ideal launch pad for exploring the Mission, Hayes Valley, and Mid-Market neighborhoods. Do as the locals do and head to the favorite coffee shop Philz and Dolores Park a few blocks away.

520 Church St. (btw. 17th and 18th sts.). ✆ **415/621-3222.** www.parkerguesthouse.com. 21 units. From $169 double shared bathroom; $279 junior suite. Minimum stays on weekends and during events. Rates include extended continental breakfast and evening wine social. Self-parking $23. Bus: 22 or 33. Streetcar: J Church. **Amenities:** Steam room, gardens.

Inexpensive

Inn on Castro ★   If you prefer live like the locals live when traveling to a new city, this hotel is great option. Guests have two choices when it comes to sleeping arrangements. The first is one of the self-catered apartments, which sleeps four people comfortably and features a full kitchen. Mollie Stone's Grocery is just a short walk away as are some of the city's best eateries, like **Starbelly**. The second choice is a room in the full-service B&B, located in a restored Edwardian building filled with fresh flowers and original artwork. Contemporary furnishings make this old building feel modern and hip. Bathrooms are shared or private, depending on which room you choose. Guests of the B&B rooms enjoy a complimentary full breakfast each morning; the hosted afternoon brandy service is always a good way to unwind and socialize. Expect friendly and personal hospitality from the small, knowledgeable staff.

321 Castro St. (at Market St.). ℰ **415/861-0321.** www.innoncastro.com. 8 units, 2 w/bathroom across the hall; 6 apts. From $115 single w/shared bathroom; $135 w/private bathroom; $250 2-bedroom apartment w/full kitchen suitable for 4. Rates include full breakfast and evening brandy. Streetcar: F, K, L, or M lines.

The Willows Inn ★ If you don't mind sharing a bathroom and enjoy a friendly, social setting, the Willows is an excellent choice. Housed in an old Edwardian building in the heart of the Castro, this is a favorite among LGBT guests, but all are welcome. All have bentwood willow furnishings, antique dressers or armoires, and colorful cozy duvets. Though no rooms have a private bathroom, each has a vanity sink and some have chaise lounges or bay windows. Guests enjoy complimentary continental breakfast including eggs, juice, yogurt, fruit, and coffee. Evening cocktails are also hosted, encouraging guests to mingle and relax. Pick your price point or the room you want ahead of time so there are no surprises upon arrival.

710 14th St. (near Church and Market sts.). ℰ **415/431-4770.** www.willowssf.com. 12 units, all with shared bathroom. Room rates vary by size and number of guests, From $120 double; $170 triple; $205 quad. Rates include continental breakfast. Streetcar: F-Line.

HAIGHT–ASHBURY

San Francisco's summers of love are long gone, but open-minded folk wanting to escape the tourist scene and embrace eccentricity will dig the Haight.

Moderate

Stanyan Park Hotel ★ The main draw of this historic Victorian B&B located right across the street from the eastern entrance of Golden Gate Park is the location and classic San Francisco architecture. However, the property is old and shows heavy wear—think peeling paint and weathered furniture. Don't expect modern luxury or a ton of space (the rooms vary in size). Instead, set your sights on clean, cozy rooms decorated with Victorian furnishings. One- and two-bedroom apartments feature full kitchens, dining rooms, and living rooms.

750 Stanyan St. (at Waller St.). ℰ **415/751-1000.** www.stanyanpark.com. 36 units. From $175 double; $300 suite; $350 2-bedroom suite. Rollaway bed $20; cribs free. Rates include continental breakfast. Off-site parking: $20. **Amenties:** 24-hr. front desk; Wi-Fi (free). Bus: 6, 33, 43, or 71. Streetcar: N-line.

Inexpensive

Red Victorian Bed, Breakfast & Art ★★ Time travel back to the Summer of Love by staying at this famous, socially conscious B&B in the heart of Haight-Ashbury. The founder and current owner designed the 18 themed rooms to reflect the eclectic spirit of San Francisco. A tie-dye canopy and lava lamp decorate the Summer of Love room, while flower bedspreads and white wicker decor pay homage to the

Conservatory of Flowers in Golden Gate Park. Beware—the hotel is located near rowdy bars, so you'll hear a fair amount of street noise. While the rooms are small and the decor dated, if you're looking for an inn with hippie history and loads of groovy character, you've just found it.

1665 Haight St. (btw. Cole and Belvedere sts.). ℭ **415/864-1978.** www.redvic.com. 18 units, 4 w/private bathroom. From $89 double w/shared bathroom; $149 double w/private bathroom; $179 suite. Rates include continental breakfast. Lower rates for stays of 3 days or more. Bus: 6 or 71. **Amenities:** Cafe.

WHERE TO EAT

During the Gold Rush, immigrant miners hungry for a taste of home created a demand—and the supply—for small kitchens serving classic dishes from all over the globe. And just like that San Francisco's restaurant culture was born. Add year-round access to an unparalleled bounty of local organic produce, seafood, free-range meats, and wine, as well as a creative culinary scene, restaurant-obsessed residents, and a still-vibrant and diverse chef community and you've got one of the world's top foodie destinations.

With more than 3,500 restaurants within its seven square miles, San Francisco has more dining establishments per capita than any other U.S. city—and a heck of a lot of competition. While this guide barely scratches the surface of the culinary delights the city has to offer, we've included can't-miss favorites across a wide range of cuisines, price ranges, and neighborhoods. Some are brand new, yet already earning coveted foodie awards; others have been around forever for a reason. Some are white-tablecloth establishments that present their culinary masterpieces with warm formality, while others are so casual they practically toss you your food, a paper plate, and a napkin from out of the side of a truck. Regardless, it's impossible to get in and out of San Francisco without having some kind of gastronomic epiphany, or at least a few dining experiences that leave you wondering if you, in fact, left your stomach, as well as your heart, in San Francisco.

PRACTICAL INFORMATION

Although dining in San Francisco is usually a hassle-free experience, here are a few things to keep in mind:

- **If you want a table at the restaurants with the best reputations,** you probably need to **book 6 to 8 weeks in advance** for weekends, and a couple of weeks ahead for weekdays.
- **If you can't get a reservation** at your favorite restaurant, don't hesitate to put your name on a **waiting list** a few weeks in advance. I have received that call from some of the popular places; just make sure to call back quickly—they mean business.
- **If there's a long wait for a table, ask if you can order at the bar,** which is often faster and more fun.
- **Don't leave *anything* valuable in your car** while dining, particularly in or near high-crime areas such as the Mission, downtown, or—believe it or not—Fisherman's Wharf. (Thieves know tourists with nice cameras and trunks full of mementos are headed there.) Also, it's best to give the parking valet only the key to your car, *not* your hotel room.

The restaurants listed below are classified first by area, then by price, using the following categories: **Expensive,** dinner for $50 or more per person; **Moderate,** dinner from $35 per person; and **Inexpensive,** dinner less than $35 per person. These categories reflect prices for an appetizer, a main course, a dessert, and a glass of wine.

o **No smoking.** It is against the law to smoke in any restaurant in San Francisco, even if it has a separate bar or lounge area. You're welcome to smoke outside; make sure to stay 20 feet away from any entryway.

o **Plan on dining early.** This ain't New York. Most restaurants close their kitchens around 10pm.

o **If you're driving to a restaurant, add extra time to your itinerary for parking,** which can be an especially infuriating exercise in areas like the Mission, downtown, the Marina, and, well, pretty much everywhere. Expect to pay at least $12 to $15 for valet service, *if* the restaurant offers it.

o **If you have to find parking, check out sfpark.org** (more on p. 233).

5 FINANCIAL DISTRICT

Expensive

Kokkari ★★ GREEK/MEDITERRANEAN   A perfect choice for a date or large party, this upscale Mediterranean stalwart with cozy-chic environs never disappoints. Exposed wood, earthen pottery, soft lighting, an open kitchen, and a large rotisserie fireplace, slowly roasting some sort of beast each day, all give it a warm, chic Mediterranean feel. Reliably superb food completes the experience. Try Hellenic classics as *horiatiki* (traditional Greek salad), *dolmathes* (stuffed grape leaves), baked feta, *moussaka* (eggplant, potato, lamb, yogurt béchamel), or any dish with lamb. If you are into Greek coffee, ask your server to take you back by the kitchen and show you how the coffee is made in an *ibrik,* and slowly heated in hot sand, Mediterranean style. Best seat in the house for two is just to the right of the fireplace.

200 Jackson St. (at Front St.). ⓒ **415/981-0983.** www.kokkari.com. Main courses $17–$29 lunch, $22–$49 dinner. Mon–Fri 11:30am–5:30pm; bar menu only 2:30–5:30pm; Mon–Thurs 5:30–10pm; Fri 5:30–11pm; Sat 5–11pm, Sun 5–10pm. Valet parking (dinner only). Bus: 1, 12. All Market St. buses, light rail, and streetcars.

Quince ★★ CALIFORNIAN/ITALIAN   A love song to the region's exceptional ingredients, chef Michael Tusk's formula for success is straightforward: Make friends with the best famers, ranchers, and fishermen in the region, ensure they reserve the best of the best for you, then lovingly and simply combine them into superb, seasonally focused dishes. Tusk, who honed his skills at Chez Panisse (the iconic Bay Area restaurant that pioneered California's seasonal farm-table cooking style), takes this concept to the highest level, allowing ingredients to star on a plate without much distraction. Not surprisingly, the price for preciousness doesn't come cheaply. Diners have a choice of a five-course dinner menu ($130) or a nine-course tasting menu ($180 per person) that changes frequently. Wine pairings are also available for an additional $95. Many of the dishes are Italian in origin (like the squab cannelloni with wild nettle,

online resources FOR DINING

Want to book your reservations online? Go to **www.opentable.com,** where you can reserve seats in real time.

For local food blogs, Grub Street (www.grubstreet.com) posts daily updates, and Marcia Gagliardi's **Table-hopper** (www.tablehopper.com) posts smart, gourmand observations every Tuesday and Friday.

While Los Angeles has "It" celebrities, San Francisco has "It" restaurants. To see what's hot during your visit, check **SF Eater's Heatmap** (www.sf.eater.com/tags/heat-map), updated monthly by popularity.

For an epic culinary scavenger hunt, or simply more dining ideas, see **"7x7 Magazine's"** annual Big Eat list. At press time, **"The Big Eat 2014: 100 Things to Taste Before You Die,"** was online (www.7x7.com/eat-drink/big-eat-2014). The list shows photos of specific dishes to hunt for like chicken clay pot at **Slanted Door** (see below); Coffee-rubbed pork shoulder at **Range** (p. 94); Karnisio souvlaki at **Kokkari** (p. 74); California State Bird at **State Bird Provisions** (p. 90); and Whole Wheat Flour Carrot Cake at **Farallon** (p. 79). Also don't miss the annual Top 100 Restaurants list, according to the "San Francisco Chronicle," which will point you to a diverse selection of local flavors (www.sfchronicle.com).

If you really want to nosh like a tech-savvy local, download the **Foodspotting** mobile app (www.foodspotting.com), which lets you photograph and tag your favorite foods. Look for 7x7's "Big Eat" list (and other lists within the app), and tag their recommended items as you eat them. You can also search for dishes others have tagged at restaurants near you to see what looks appetizing.

For a collection of restaurant reviews and suggestions by bloggers, diners, and critics like "Zagat," "SF Weekly," and the "San Francisco Chronicle," check out **Urban Spoon** at www.urban spoon.com. Just watch the dates; while most are current, some reviews are 10 years old.

For food truck fans, your best bet is **Off the Grid,** a daily gathering of a half dozen or so trucks, usually from 11am to 2pm, and 5 to 9pm, occasionally with live music. Check www.offthegridsf.com/markets for information. Otherwise, **Roaming Hunger** (www.roaminghunger.com) lists locations of food trucks, based on Twitter feeds.

Vegetarians won't have trouble finding dishes on a typical menu here, and you'll find a couple of restaurants marked "vegetarian" throughout this chapter. For vegan eats, consult **Happy Cow** (www.happycow.net). Gluten-free is also big here, too.

spring onion, and porcini mushroom); though the meaty entrees also shine (dry-aged side of beef with salt-crusted formanova beet, bone marrow, and nasturtium is a menu stand out, as is the suckling pig featuring turnip and whey). Leave room for dessert—not to mention the international cheese cart with tastings from France, Italy, and California. For the sweet tooth, the ganache, with salted cocoa nib toffee, candied hazelnut, and buttermilk sherbet is sure to satisfy. For a lighter dining experience, check out the bar menu which offers la carte items.

470 Pacific Ave. (at Montgomery St.). © **415/775-8500.** www.quincerestaurant.com. Bar menu $12–$60. Mon–Sat 5:30–10pm. Valet parking $12. Bus: 1, 10, 12, or 30.

The Slanted Door ★★ VIETNAMESE Considered by many to be the best Vietnamese restaurant in America, the modern and slick Slanted Door has managed to

San Francisco Restaurants

Ace Wasabi Rock
  & Roll Sushi **5**
Acquerello **16**
AsiaSF **26**
Atelier Crenn **4**
Aziza **1**
B44 **22**
Benu **25**
Brindisi **22**
Buena Vista Café **8**
Burma Superstar **3**
Café Bastille **22**
Café Tiramisu **22**
The Crepe Café **10**
Farallon **19**
Forbes Island **9**
Gitane **21**
Greens **6**
Johnny Foley's
  Irish House **20**
La Folie **12**
Lemongrass Thai **12**
Nopa **29**

Pier 23 **11**
Plouf **22**
Restaurant
  Gary Danko **7**
Rich Table **28**
Sauce **22**

The Slanted Door **23**
SoMa StrEat Food
  Park **27**
Sons and Daughters **18**
SPQR **14**
State Bird Provisions **13**

Swan Oyster Depot **16**
Tacolicious **5**
Tommy's Joynt **15**
Ton Kiang **2**
U-Lee **17**
Waterbar **24**

5

WHERE TO EAT | Financial District

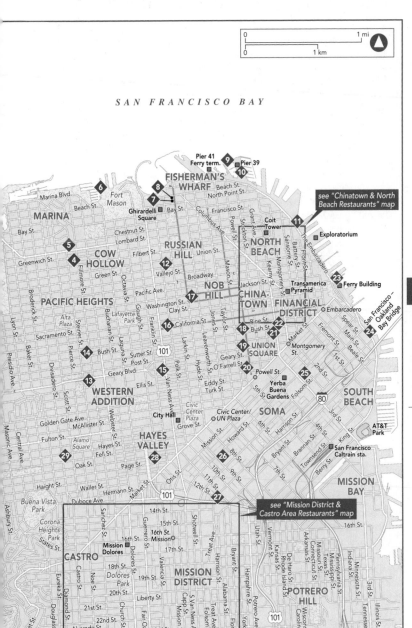

SAN FRANCISCO BAY

Pier 41
Ferry term.
Pier 39

FISHERMAN'S WHARF

see "Chinatown & North Beach Restaurants" map

Marina Blvd
Fort Mason
Beach St.
Ghirardelli Square
Bay St.
North Point St.
Beach St.
Francisco St.
Columbus Ave.
Coit Tower
Exploratorium

MARINA
Bay St.
Chestnut St.
Lombard St.
RUSSIAN HILL
NORTH BEACH
Battery St.
Sansome St.

Greenwich St.
COW HOLLOW
Filbert St.
Union St.
Grant Ave.
Kearny St.
Montgomery St.

Fillmore St.
Green St.
Vallejo St.
Broadway
NOB HILL
Jackson St.
Transamerica Pyramid
Ferry Building

PACIFIC HEIGHTS
Octavia St.
Gough St.
Pacific Ave.
Washington St.
Clay St.
CHINA-TOWN
FINANCIAL DISTRICT
Embarcadero
San Francisco – Oakland Bay Bridge

Alta Plaza
Lafayette Park
Buchanan St.
Larkin St.
Mason St.
Taylor St.
Jones St.
Leavenworth St.
California St.
Pine St.
Bush St.
Market St.
Spear St.
Main St.
Beale St.

Sacramento St.
Steiner St.
Pierce St.
Laguna St.
Franklin St.
Sutter St.
Post St.
Geary St.
UNION SQUARE
Montgomery St.
Fremont St.
1st St.

WESTERN ADDITION
Scott St.
Divisadero St.
Bush St.
Geary Blvd.
O'Farrell St.
Ellis St.
Eddy St.
Turk St.
Powell St.
Yerba Buena Gardens
Folsom St.
2nd St.
SOUTH BEACH
3rd St.
AT&T Park

City Hall
Civic Center Plaza
Civic Center/ UN Plaza
Grove St.
SOMA
Howard St.
6th St.
Harrison St.
4th St.
King St.
Townsend St.
Berry St.
San Francisco Caltrain sta.

HAYES VALLEY
Alamo Square
Hayes St.
Fell St.
Oak St.
Page St.
Mission St.
8th St.
9th St.
10th St.
11th St.
Bryant St.
Brannan St.
MISSION BAY

Haight St.
Waller St.
Hermann St.
Duboce Ave.
12th St.
see "Mission District & Castro Area Restaurants" map
16th St.

Buena Vista Park
Corona Heights Park
Sanchez St.
14th St.
15th St.
16th St.
16th St. Mission
Shotwell St.
Utah St.
Vermont St.
De Haro St.
Rhode Island St.
Connecticut St.
Arkansas St.
Missouri St.
Mississippi St.
Texas St.
Indiana St.
Minnesota St.
Pennsylvania St.
3rd St.

CASTRO
Castro St.
Noe St.
Mission Dolores
Dolores St.
Dolores Park
17th St.
18th St.
19th St.
20th St.
Valencia St.
Guerrero St.
Harrison St.
Alabama St.
Florida St.
Bryant St.
Hampshire St.
Potrero Ave.
York St.
POTRERO HILL
Wisconsin St.
Carolina St.
Tennessee St.

Eureka St.
Diamond St.
21st St.
Church St.
Liberty St.
22nd St.
Fair Oaks St.
Capp St.
S. Van Ness Ave.
Treat Ave.
Folsom St.
MISSION DISTRICT

Market St.
Douglass St.
Elizabeth St.
Alvarado St.
23rd St.
24th St.
24th St. Mission
NOE VALLEY

0 — 1 mi
0 — 1 km

5

WHERE TO EAT | Financial District

77

THE sun on your face AT BELDEN PLACE

San Francisco has long been lacking in the alfresco dining department, which may or may not have something to do with the Arctic summer fog. But **Belden Place**—an adorable little brick alley in the heart of the Financial District open only to foot traffic—is a little bit of Paris just off Pine Street. Restaurants line the alley sporting big umbrellas, tables, and chairs, and, when the weather is agreeable, diners linger long after the lunch hour.

A handful of cafes line the little alley and offer a variety of cuisines at moderate prices. There's **Cafe Bastille ★**, 22 Belden Place ((℃) **415/986-5673**), a classic French bistro with a boho basement that serves excellent crepes, mussels,

and French onion soup; it offers live jazz on Fridays. **Cafe Tiramisu ★**, 28 Belden Place ((℃) **415/421-7044**), is a stylish Italian hot spot, serving addictive risottos and gnocchi. **Plouf ★**, 40 Belden Place ((℃) **415/986-6491**), specializes in big bowls of mussels slathered in your choice of seven sauces, as well as fresh seafood. **B44 ★**, 44 Belden Place ((℃) **415/986-6287**), offers a little taste of Spain, with its revered paella and other seriously zesty Spanish dishes. **Brindisi ★**, 88 Belden Place ((℃) **415/593-8000**), dishes out small plates of Mediterranean fare. Finally, **Sauce ★**, 56 Belden Place ((℃) **415/397-8800**), is the place for large portions of American comfort food.

become one of the top must-trys when visiting the city by the bay. The draw? Gorgeously fresh and refined interpretations of Southeast Asian classics made from local, organic ingredients and served in a bustling, contemporary, vast and bright space in the Ferry Building overlooking the bay and twinkling Bay Bridge. Don't miss the grass-fed estancia shaking beef, crab with glass noodles, crispy imperial rolls, or pho—all conceived of by self-taught chef/owner, Charles Phan, the long-beloved darling of San Francisco's fickle restaurant scene. Celebrity fans, including Mick Jagger, Keith Richards, Quentin Tarantino, Luke Wilson, and Gwenyth Paltrow, have been known to sneak in for a bite.

1 Ferry Building (at the Embarcadero and Market). (℃) **415/861-8032.** www.slanteddoor.com. Lunch main courses $12–$36; dinner dishes $18–$45; fixed-price lunch $48 and dinner $53–$65 (parties of 7 or more only). Lunch Mon–Sat 11am–2:30pm Sun. Afternoon tea daily 2:30pm–4:30pm. 11:30am–3pm. Dinner daily 5:30am–10pm; bar only from 2:30–5:30pm. All Market St. buses, light rail, and streetcar.

Moderate

Barbacco Eno Trattoria ★★ ITALIAN   One of the most reliably satisfying dining experiences downtown, Barbacco shirks classic Italian restaurant trappings for sleek, modern, casual urban-surroundings and a menu that's simultaneously casual, affordable, and divine. Swedish chef Staffan Terje, who also oversees more formal and equally delicious neighboring Perbacco, is behind the robust menu featuring a slew of seafood, salumi, and vegetable antipasti; salads; pasta; bruschette; and a handful of entrees such as flat-iron steak or chicken under a brick. Like many restaurants in town, here the focus is in celebrating excellent ingredients, which means you'll get wonderfully pure preparations that receive just the right amount of embellishment.

220 California St. (btw. Davis and Drumm sts.). (℃) **415/955-1919.** www.barbaccosf.com. Lunch main courses $9–$16; dinner entrees $13–$19. Mon–Fri 11:30am–3pm and 5–10pm, Sat 5:30–10pm. All Market St. buses, light rail, and streetcar.

Bocadillos ★ SPANISH/BASQUE TAPAS   A communal table, exposed brick, and shared small tapas-style plates lend this small, casual, lively restaurant anchored in the Financial District a European ambiance. Basque favorites include Thai snapper ceviche with key lime and persimmon, quail with Moorish spices, bavette steak with chimichurri sauce, lamb burger with aioli and shallots, and patatas bravas with romesco sauce. For dessert, warm chocolate cake with banana ice cream is the house specialty. For a little privacy, try one of the bar tables or snag one of the few outdoor seats. Open for breakfast on weekdays.

710 Montgomery St. (at Washington St.). ℂ **415/982-2622.** www.bocasf.com. No reservations. Breakfast $5–$13; lunch and dinner tapas $7–$17. Mon–Fri 7am–10pm; Sat 5–10pm. Bus: 1 or 8X.

Tadich Grill ★ SEAFOOD   California was not even a state when Tadich Grill opened in 1849. It's the oldest, continuously run restaurant in San Francisco, owned by the Buich family since 1928. When you walk through the door, time stands still. From the dark wood, brass fixtures, long bar, and private booths, you get the feeling you are in an old boys club and expect to see deals being made under the haze of cigar smoke. If you can only try one dish here, know that people come from all over the world for Tadich's *cioppino:* a red stew chock full of scallops, clams, prawns, mussels, fish, and crab, served with garlic bread for dipping. Another specialty of the house is the Hangtown Fry, a mélange of eggs, bacon, and deep-fried oysters, scrambled together to make a dish the late Herb Caen—"Chronicle" journalist, unofficial mayor, and recipient of a Pulitzer Prize for being the "voice and conscience" of San Francisco—loved almost as much as the city itself. This special fry has been served continuously since the Gold Rush days, when miners who struck it rich would come in to enjoy one of the most expensive meals in the city. Finish your trip down memory lane with the simple rice pudding—the recipe has not changed in over 100 years.

240 California St. (btw. Battery and Front sts.). ℂ **415/391-1849.** www.tadichgrill.com. No reservations. Main courses $15–$38. Mon–Fri 11am–9:30pm; Sat 11:30am–9:30pm. All Market St. buses, light rail, and streetcars. BART: Embarcadero.

UNION SQUARE

Expensive

Farallon ★★ SEAFOOD   If you're looking for a seafood restaurant, this dramatically decorated, festive restaurant is one of your best bests. Even before looking at the menu, you'll get the point; Giant jellyfish lamps float overhead from the arched, mosaic ceiling, tentacles dangling, lighting the way to your table. Kelp columns in amber hues rise from the floor, amidst 8-foot sea urchins and a giant clamshell. The underwater theme is everywhere, but in the most stunning, artistic way. Owner/designer Pat Kuleto and owner/chef Mark Franz (who are also both behind seafood shrine Waterbar, p. 80) worked together to create a unique underwater fantasy in the former Elks Club building. Food sticks to the sea, too. Picks might range from petrale sole with caviar butter to grilled Georges bank diver scallops (a melt-in-your-mouth treat). But some offerings come from land, too, such as the petite filet of beef with red wine risotto in a pinot noir reduction. Desserts, like the bittersweet chocolate fudge bar or the salted peanut caramel sundae, also rate.

450 Post St. (at Powell St.). ℂ **415/956-6969.** www.farallonrestaurant.com. Reservations recommended. Main courses $28–$36. Dinner Sun 5–9:30pm, Mon–Thurs 5:30–9:30pm, Fri–Sat 5:30–10pm, Happy hour daily 4:30–7pm. Limited valet parking. Cable car: Powell–Mason or Powell–Hyde line. BART: Powell St.

Gitane ★ SPANISH   Always making the cool-restaurant lists, Gitane features a sensual, bordello-like interior and Andalusian cuisine, with offerings such as sausage-stuffed squid over black pasta; bacon "bonbons" of dates stuffed with Manchego and wrapped in smoked bacon; or the seafood *tajine*. For more casual atmosphere, head to the bar or the outdoor bistro tables. A final perk: the Bay Area's largest selections of sherry and gypsy cocktails, plus a fine collection of Spanish, Portuguese, and California wines.

6 Claude Ln (at Bush or Sutter). ℂ **415/788-6686.** www.gitanerestaurant.com. Reservations only through www.opentable.com. Main courses $22–$34, 5-course tasting menu $65, wine pairing $45, Taberna bar menu $8–$22. Mon–Wed 5:30–10:30pm, bar open until midnight, Thurs–Sat 5:30–11:30pm, bar open until 1am. Bus: 2, 30, 31, or 45. BART: Montgomery St.

Inexpensive

Johnny Foley's Irish House ★ IRISH PUB   Foley's is as well known for its surprisingly good pub food (bangers and mash, fish and chips, cottage pie and the like) as it is for its famous dueling pianos downstairs. It's the perfect place to head if you're needing the comfort of a home away from home. Truly: There are 16 types of beer on tap, sports on the telly, and a good kid's menu—what more would you need? Stop in, refresh, and get back out to the "grind" of heavy-duty sightseeing.

243 O'Farrell St. (at Cyril Magnin St.). ℂ **415/954-0777.** www.johnnyfoleys.com. Main Courses $15–$34. Daily 11:30am–1:30am (kitchen closes 10pm). Bus: 38. BART: Powell St.

SoMa

Expensive

Benu ★★ ASIAN FUSION   Housed in a heritage building in the heart of SoMa, a few minutes' walk from many of our cultural attractions and historic hotels and offering haute cuisine, Benu represents the changing face of fine dining in San Francisco. With no dress code, no tablecloths, and no stuffy servers, it is truly all about the food. And though you can order a la carte on some nights, the tasting menu is the way to go if you want to experience the two Michelin star–ranked chef Corey Lee's culinary wizardry (he's formerly of the famed French Laundry, see p. 215). Presented on custom-created porcelain designed specifically to show off the food, Lee's eclectic menu might include gorgeously sculpted choices like potato salad with anchovy; thousand-year-old quail egg with ginger and nasturtium; monkfish liver on brioche; or salt and pepper squid—none of which look like they sound. The faux shark fin soup with black truffle custard shows off Lee's ability to create daring combinations, as does the charcoal-grilled lamb belly with quinoa, pear, and sunflower. Plan to spend upwards of 3 hours basking in top quality food, wine, and service, in minimalist, serene surroundings.

22 Hawthorne St. (at Howard St.). ℂ **415/685-4860.** www.benusf.com. Tasting menu $180, wine pairing $150, a la carte (Tues–Thurs only) main courses $26–$42. Tues–Sat 5:30–9pm. Valet parking $15. All Market St. buses, light rail, and streetcars.

Waterbar ★ SEAFOOD   With a stunning view of the Bay Bridge, an outdoor patio, $1 oysters from 11:30am to 5:30pm daily, and a fab weekend brunch (the exotic Bloody Mary comes complete with smoked bacon and jumbo prawns), Waterbar delivers just about everything a San Francisco visitor could want—except, perhaps, for reasonable prices. Still, there's much to enjoy at this prime location, including a fun cocktail-bar scene and two floor-to-ceiling fish tank columns in the middle of the restaurant, filled with eels, fish, and other Pacific Ocean critters. Consistent with San Francisco's current zeitgeist, the menu offers a wide variety of fresh, ethically sourced, seasonal seafood such as squid and Alaskan halibut—and it even tells you the squid was caught aboard the "Seawave" near Monterey, and the halibut was hooked aboard the "St. John" in Homer, Alaska. Now that's ocean-to-table sustainability!

399 Embarcadero (at Harrison St.). © **415/284-9922.** www.waterbarsf.com. Main courses $34–$44. Daily 11:30am–2pm and 5:30–10pm. Valet parking. Bus: 1, 12, 14, or 41. BART: Embarcadero.

Moderate

AsiaSF ★ ASIAN/CALIFORNIAN   It doesn't get more wonderfully, if stereotypically, "San Francisco" than this dinner-and-show destination featuring an multicourse meal and world-famous transgender stars. A popular spot for bachelorette and birthday parties, dates, and curious tourists, this joint on a gritty stretch of SoMa gets you in and out with enough time to leisurely enjoy your meal and catch bar-top lip-sync performances and dancing by talents that are truly gifted at their craft. (Despite the high kicks and sashays on a miniscule space, owner, Skip Young, says only two girls have actually fallen off the bar in their 15-year history.) Truth be told, the meal isn't the draw here. But it really doesn't matter. It's plenty good enough and the performance more than makes up for any magic the kitchen lacks. For small groups, the *ménage a trois* menu gets you three dishes from a mouthwatering list, including sake steamed mussels, sesame steak salad, miso glazed king salmon served over black "forbidden" rice, truffled soba noodles, and "baby got back" ribs. It's a lot of fun and, believe it or not, kids are welcome at the first seating. *Note:* You must dine to see the show.

201 Ninth St. (at Howard St.). © **415/255-2742.** www.asiasf.com. Dinner packages $35–$69. Wed only (a la carte menu) with $25/person minimum. Sun, Wed, Thurs 7–10pm; Fri 7pm–2am; Sat 5pm–2am; cocktails and dancing until 2am on Fri–Sat. All Market St. buses, light rail, and streetcars. BART: Civic Center.

Inexpensive

SoMa StrEat Food Park ★★ FOOD TRUCKS   As the first permanent food truck plaza in San Francisco, SoMa StrEat Food Park established itself as one of the best places to sample a variety of outstanding foods. Here's how it works: each day 13 trucks roll in and serve lunch; some may stay on to serve dinner, others leave and their spot is given to a new truck. The only permanent truck is StrEat Brew, serving beer, wine, and sangria; and a $12 bottomless mimosa for the Sunday brunch crowd. With over 70 rotating vendors, with names like Curry Up Now, Seoul on Wheels, Adam's Grub Truck, and Chairman Bao, you are sure to find something you like, no matter when you show up. And this is not a roach coach scene at all. The food is high quality, the trucks are clean, music is playing, and there's covered seating, flatscreen TVs, restrooms, and free Wi-Fi. In fact, SoMa StrEat Food feels like one big party. With no tourist attractions close by, but easy public transportation access, this place is a destination in itself; come just to hang out and eat with the locals. Most vendors take credit cards; there's also an ATM on site.

428 11th St. (at Division St.). www.somastreatfoodpark.com. Main courses $5–$17. Mon–Fri 11am–3pm; Sat 11am–10pm; Sun 10am–5pm. Street parking. Bus: 9, 12, 27, or 47.

NOB HILL/RUSSIAN HILL

Expensive

Acquerello ★★★ CONTEMPORARY ITALIAN A perfect special-occasion restaurant, this hidden gem offers the city's most delicious, refined contemporary Italian fare in one of the most elegant and intimate settings. Don't let its obscure location off somewhat gritty Polk Street fool you. Inside, it's all luxury, from the surprisingly spacious, gorgeously adorned dining room (so you can actually hear your dinner companion) to the ever-attentive service to the Michelin-starred multicourse menu and wine list. Owners Giancarlo Paterlini and Chef Suzette Gresham-Tognetti have been here since 1989, and continue to ensure the most special experience (and don't miss the cheese cart). If there's an occasion to be celebrate and you want a quiet, memorable meal, this is your place.

1722 Sacramento St. (between Polk & Van Ness sts.) ✆ **415/567-5432.** www.acquerello.com. 3-course menu $85; 4-course menu $100; 5-course menu $115. Tues–Thurs 5:30–9:30pm, Fri–Sat 5:30–10pm. Street parking. Bus: 47, 49.

La Folie ★ FRENCH A fixture on the dining scene since 1988, this intimate, relaxed yet upscale restaurant is the prime pick if you're interested in a classic French meal. Chef/owner Roland Passat was born in the Rhône–Alpes in France and honed his craft at cooking school in Lyon; his food is anchored in French tradition, yet contemporary and seasonal and always quality, perhaps because unlike many celebrity chefs, this local legend is still in the kitchen every night. Diners choose between the three- ($85), four- ($95), and five-course ($105) menus which feature such indulgences as stunningly presented sautéed Burgundy snails in lemon butter and bone marrow gratin; lobster and mushroom risotto bathed in lobster broth with leeks; and duck breast coq au vin, served with rhubarb marmalade and duck liver mousse. As a final performance, do not miss the huckleberry baked Alaska, and the Edam cheese soufflé. Portions are generous, so if you're trying to decide how many courses to pick, you may want to go with the smaller choices.

2316 Polk St. (btw. Green and Union sts.). ✆ **415/776-5577.** www.lafolie.com. 3-course tasting menu $85; 4-course tasting menu $95; 5-course chef's tasting menu $105; vegetarian tasting menu $95. Mon–Sat 5:30–10:30pm. Valet parking. Bus: 12, 19, 27, 45, and 47.

Sons and Daughters ★★ AMERICAN Michelin-starred chefs Matt McNamara and Teague Moriarty source ingredients straight from their Los Gatos farm and keep their tiny Nob Hill restaurant full with the perfect combination of a cozy atmosphere and beautifully presented food that tastes as good as it looks. Its charm makes it a great place to celebrate a birthday or anniversary, sit by the fireplace, and enjoy an evening of culinary delights on the seasonal tasting menu. Recent luscious offerings included Rocky Point oysters; artichoke kale and Romesco cauliflower; Dixon lamb shoulder with spring nettles and fava beans; and blood orange and tarragon cheesecake. The staff is exceptionally friendly and approachable and they know the dishes well and are happy to accommodate any food allergies or dislikes. One last note: Don't even think of trying to park a car on the street around here. If you must drive, the Sutter/Stockton garage a block away is a good bet.

708 Bush St. (at Powell St.). ✆ **415/391-8311.** www.sonsanddaughterssf.com. Tasting menu $98; pairings $68. Wed–Sun 5–9:30pm. Bus: 1, 2, or 30. Cable Car: Powell–Hyde or Powell–Mason.

Moderate

Lemongrass Thai ★ THAI   The sweetest, most welcoming and humble Thai restaurant in town, Lemongrass is also delicious, which explains why it's been popular for 20 years. Chef/owner Toi Sawatdee, one of the hardest working women in the restaurant business, is in the kitchen every night, ensuring that every fresh, made-to-order dish is cooked to perfection. And trust me, they are. Even people who consider themselves Thai-food connoisseurs will find new favorites here, such as the must-try crispy rice salad, thanks to Toi's continued efforts to wow her regulars. A neighborhood spot through and through, it's a sweet peek into life along Russian Hill's Polk Street, which is a wonderful place to stroll or bar hop before or after the fact.

2348 Polk St. (btw. Green and Union sts.). ℭ **415/346-1818.** www.lemongrassthaisf.com. Main courses $8–$13. Sun–Thurs 11am–10pm, Fri–Sat 11am–10:30pm. Bus: 12, 19, 27, 45, and 47.

Swan Oyster Depot ★★ SEAFOOD   Historic Swan Oyster Depot—the city's most popular raw and seafood bar—opened in its current building in 1912, and little has changed since. Pull on a long, brass, fish-shaped door handle, step across the cracked mosaic floor, slide into one of the 18 barstools in the narrow room that has just enough space to accommodate the seats and bar, and get whisked back in time. There's no website, no computer system, no reservations on Open Table. You won't find over-the-top haute cuisine here, either. The winning recipe for as long as anyone can remember is beautifully simple: wonderfully fresh and barely adulterated seafood by a friendly member of the Sancimino Family—owners since 1946—at a worn, marble counter along with paper napkins to wipe the crab juice off your mug. Recipes are simple—think steamed, raw or fried seafood, the terrific cocktail sauce house-made, the prices very reasonable, and the service gruffly charming. Eating here is a fun, old-timey experience—and needs to be as there's usually an hour wait to get in! If you're starving and tired of waiting, you can call in a take-out order while standing in in line. Only cash and local checks accepted.

1517 Polk St. (btw. California and Sacramento sts.). ℭ **415/673-1101.** No reservations. Main courses $5–$45. Mon–Sat 10:30am–5:30pm. Bus: 1, 12, 19, 47, or 49. Cable Car: California.

Inexpensive

U-Lee ★★ CHINESE   The proverbial hole in the wall with no bells and whistles to jack up the price or distract you from the reliable menu, U-Lee offers some of the best Chinese food in the city for the cost of parking at other places. Locals in the know, and visitors lucky enough to find it, come back again and again for hot and sour soup, General Tsao chicken, beef with asparagus, and pork fried rice. U-Lee's is also known for succulent, juicy pot stickers the size of your fist. Portions are huge, so bring your appetite. And make sure to bring cash; it's all they accept. Because parking is almost impossible around here, take the cable car; it stops right outside.

1468 Hyde St. (btw. Washington and Jackson sts.). ℭ **415/771-9774.** www.u-leesf.com. No reservations. $2–$9 per dish. Tues–Sun 11am–9pm. Bus: 1, 12, 27, or 49. Cable Car: Powell–Hyde.

NORTH BEACH/TELEGRAPH HILL

Expensive

Coi ★★ CALIFORNIAN   Coi (pronounced "kwa"), meaning tranquil, this intimate beacon of refinery on bawdy Broadway offers one of the city's best and most famous iterations dedicated to haute cuisine with molecular gastronomy influence. A tiny spot divided into two wood-on-wood dining rooms that feel somewhere between a luxury double-wide and a modern cabin—in a good way—it's the place to experience the elegant, creative cooking of self-taught two-Michelin-star–ranked chef Daniel Patterson, whose attention to detail and strive for perfection is unparalleled. Each evening Coi offers only one tasting menu with 8 to 11 courses based on what is fresh and available. Selections might include grilled oyster seaweed bread, charcoal roasted beets with blackberry, Dungeness crab soup, salted marrow fat and arugula; a chilled yellow squash soup with saffron, lime and nasturtium; a gently steamed wild kind salmon, stuffed with morels, peas and sorrel; and whipped coconut olive oil, rhubarb and blood orange to finish. Brilliant wine pairings are an additional $105 per person.

373 Broadway (at Montgomery St.). © **415/393-9000.** www.coirestaurant.com. Nightly menu $150–$195. Tues–Sat 5:30–9:30pm. Valet parking. Bus: 1, 8, 10, or 12.

Moderate

Original Joe's ITALIAN   This San Francisco institution claims it has served everyone from "the head politician to the head prostitute"—presumably not at the same time, though you never know. First opened after the Great Depression by Tony Rodin in 1937, the restaurant is now run by his grandkids, John Duggan, and his sister, Elena, and they haven't changed it much. The menu still features a large selection of typical Italian comfort food in generous portion sizes, and at reasonable prices. By the way, this is not quite the original "Original Joes." That one was located in the Tenderloin from 1937 until it was destroyed by a fire in 2007. The current Original Joe's reopened in North Beach in 2012, but their loyal clientele followed and once you've had the Parmigiana here, you'll understand why.

601 Union Street (at Stockton St.). © **415/775-4877.** www.originaljoessf.com. Main courses $11–$44. Mon–Fri 11am–10pm, Sat–Sun 9am–10pm. Bus: 30, 41, or 45.

Inexpensive

Pier 23 ★ SEAFOOD   When the occasion calls for a casual, let-your-hair-down kind of place where you'll want to throw back a few cocktails, indulge in straightforward grub, and perhaps dance it up with tipsy locals after happy hour—all backed by an awesome view of the bay, this is where to go. Up front, the tables in the small, loud dining room are accessories to the long bar and band area, while out back—a favorite afternoon spot on sunny days—the patio flanked by the bay allows for salt-kissed alfresco dining. Ask the gravelly voiced hostess, Alicia, to seat you out back, then dig into heavenly fish and chips, or a juicy black angus burger, while watching the boats sail by. A hearty brunch is served on weekends, and features a variety of dishes like huevos rancheros, whole roasted Dungeness crab, and a smoked salmon plate. Even the little ones will be happy; the kid's menu offers all the usual faves—grilled cheese, chicken strips, and more.

Pier 23 (on Embarcadero). ©**415/362-5125.** www.pier23cafe.com. Main courses $12–$28. Weekdays 11:30am–10pm, Sat 10am–10pm, Sun 10am–9pm. Any Embarcadero light rail or streetcar.

FISHERMAN'S WHARF

Expensive

Forbes Island ★★ FRENCH   A truly one-of-a-kind experience, this "island" is actually a houseboat converted into a restaurant, complete with an elegant underwater

Chinatown & North Beach Restaurants

Barbacco Eno
  Trattoria **1**
Bocadillos **8**
Brandy Ho's
  Hunan Food **7**
Coi **11**
Great Eastern **4**
Hong Kong Clay Pot
  City Restaurant **3**

House of Nanking **6**
Hunan's Home **5**
Kokkari **9**
Original Joe's **12**
Quince **10**
R&G Lounge **2**
Tadich Grill **1**

CHINATOWN—SO MANY choices!

San Francisco's **Chinatown** has the largest Chinese population outside of China; so it follows that we have lots of Chinese restaurants. It's hard to know which place to try—some look clean and inviting, with bright colored photos of yummy delicacies posted outside; others have sun-faded menus peeling off of dirty windows—but looks can be deceiving. Most places in **Chinatown** fall into the inexpensive category—so how do you choose? We think the following restaurants stand out from the pack.

Brandy Ho's Hunan Food ★, 217 Columbus Ave. (✆ **415/788-7527;** www.brandyhos.com), is rightly known for its Three Delicacies—a main dish of scallop, shrimp, and chicken seasoned with ginger, garlic, and wine. Most dishes are served hot and spicy; just ask if you want the kitchen to tone it down.

Climb the steps at tiny **Hong Kong Clay Pot Restaurant** ★, 960 Grant Ave. (✆ **415/989-2638;** http://hongkongclay potrestaurant.webs.com), and try a signature clay pot filled with meat, seafood, or vegetables. Did you know the clay pots are soaked in water before cooking? When heated up, they release steam, making dishes that are extra moist and delicious. Yum!

R&G Lounge ★, 631 Kearny St. (✆ **415/982-7877;** www.rnglounge.com), is a very popular three-story restaurant with plenty of room for large and small parties; best on the menu are the salt and pepper crab, and R&G special beef.

Great Eastern ★, 649 Jackson St. (✆ **415/986-2500;** www.greateasternsf.com), specializes in dim sum, as well as fresh seafood pulled from tanks lining the walls—Prez Obama stopped in here for takeout.

At **House of Nanking** ★★, 919 Kearny St. (✆ **415/421-1429**), abrupt and borderline rude waiters—half the fun of Chinatown—serve vegetarian dishes as well as perfect sesame chicken. The fish soup is stellar too, though you have to ask for it specially, as it's not on the English–language menu.

Hunan Home's ★★, 622 Jackson St. (✆ **415/982-2844**), is known for their wicked hot and sour soup, and "Succulent Bread"—baked and then slightly deep fried. This is a locals' favorite.

dining room, beach, and climbable lighthouse, tied up beside the city's famous barking sea lions. As a lover of the uncommon, it's been one of my favorite places to take people for years. (I've even rented the place out for parties.) But not for the food, which is fine. The draw is the experience: Get to the dock, phone the restaurant to send their pontoon boat, take the 3-minute ride to the island, and explore the world that is Forbes Island. Thank master carpenter (and pontoon skipper) Forbes Kiddoo for this whimsical experience. In the late 1970s, Kiddoo spent 5 years building the 1,600-square-foot floating home. After adding a beach, boulders, and 40-foot palm trees, Kiddoo dropped anchor across the bay in Sausalito, and might have lived there forever had new houseboat regulations not forced him to shove off. After drifting around for a few years (pun intended), and adding a 40-foot lighthouse in 1998, the island was towed to Pier 39, a license was obtained, and San Francisco's first and only floating lighthouse restaurant was born. As well as two daily fresh fish dishes, the menu includes risotto, lamb chops, steaks and more. With a fire burning in the old fireplace, and the wood and brass interior, this underwater dining room is cozy, homey, and really cool. *Heads up:* Since you're dining on a vessel, a slight rocking occurs, but it's almost undistinguishable.

Free water shuttle is to the left of Pier 39 at "H" dock (the first dock to the left by the sidewalk). ℰ **415/951-4900.** www.forbesisland.com. Main courses $28–$39. Daily 5pm–close. Validated parking at Pier 39 garage. Bus: 47. All Embarcadero light rail and streetcars.

Restaurant Gary Danko ★★★ FRENCH   If there is one place to splurge in San Francisco, this is it. Fresh, sophisticated cuisine in an elegant, romantic atmosphere has earned Chef Danko prestigious awards, such as Michelin stars, a Five Star Mobil rating, and the James Beard Award for Best New Restaurant and Best Chef in California. Well-earned honors aside, the portions are generous, the service is unparalleled, and there's not a hint of pretention. There's a reason locals and visitors keep shelling out the cash for this modern San Francisco institution and it probably has much to do with the friendly, down-to-earth atmosphere that makes you feel as if you're dining on delicacies like caviar and lobster in a good friend's home—who just happens to be a culinary genius.

800 North Point Street (at Hyde St.). ℰ **415/749-2060.** www.garydanko.com. Main courses $28– $39. 3-course fixed-price menu $76; 4-course menu $96; 5-course menu $111; wine pairing $76. Daily 5:30–10pm. Valet parking. Bus: 30, 47, or 49. All Embarcadero light rail and streetcars. Cable car: Powell–Hyde.

Moderate

Buena Vista Cafe ★ AMERICAN   Serving breakfast all day, with a variety of fat burgers, sandwiches, salads, pasta, steaks, and crab cakes, and famed for its Irish coffees, a stop at the Buena Vista is a classic San Francisco activity for visitors—the cable car stops right outside. Buena Vista means "good view" in Spanish, and this classic certainly lives up to its name. Converted from a boarding house to a saloon in 1916, the setting was the perfect place for fishermen and dockworkers to take a break while watching the bay, literally, "for their ships to come in." When the fishing boats arrived, they could chug their drinks and quickly run down the hill to get back to work.

Grab an empty space at one of the large round communal tables by the window and laugh as 20-year veteran waitress Katherine flings napkins at you and scowls if, heaven forbid, you dare *not* order their famed Irish Coffee—a "national institution," for it was here, in 1952, that the first Irish coffee was crafted here by owner, Jack Koeppler, and Pulitzer Prize–winning travel writer Stanton Delaplane.

2765 Hyde St. (at Beach St.). ℰ **415/474-5044.** www.thebuenavista.com. Breakfast & lunch/ sandwiches $11.50–$15.50; dinner main courses $15–$22. Mon–Fri 9am–2am, weekends 8am–2am, no food or children after 9:30pm. Bus: 47. All Embarcadero light rail and streetcars. Cable Car: Powell–Hyde.

Inexpensive

Crepe Café ★ FRENCH   What started as a food cart in touristy Ghirardelli Square, has become a favorite in a permanent location on Pier 39. The cafe serves up all the usual crepe toppings, both sweet—sugar, Nutella, strawberries—and savory— ham, eggs, or chicken—but it also gets creative with unusual choices like pesto and avocado. People in the know take their crepes out the back door and find a seat on the wooden benches to watch chubby sea lions bark and fight for space on the docks.

Pier 39 (at Embarcadero). ℰ **415/318-1494.** Main courses $6–$10. Sun–Thurs 9am–9pm, Fri–Sat 9am–10pm. Bus: 47. All Embarcadero light rail and streetcars.

THE MARINA/PACIFIC HEIGHTS/COW HOLLOW

Expensive

Atelier Crenn ★★ FRENCH/CALIFORNIAN   An atelier is a French workshop, and Chef Dominique Crenn (of Luce fame) uses hers to create dishes that are so intricate and whimsical that it's wrenching to "ruin" them with that first bite. This is poetic culinaria at its best, complete with poetry for menus, and artsy plating with food served on slabs of bark, slate, and eucalyptus branches. With four menus per year to reflect each of the seasons, you essentially have two choices—five signature courses ($120) with wine pairing ($85), or the Chef's Grand Tasting Menu ($195) with wine pairing ($150); on Saturdays, only the Grand Tasting Menu is available. It's a unique concept, to be sure, but if you're game, you might just experience one of the most thought-provoking meals in your life.

3127 Fillmore St. (btw. Pixley and Filbert sts.). ℂ **415/440-0460.** www.ateliercrenn.com. 5-course menu $120, wine pairings $85; Chef's grand tasting menu $195, wine pairings $150. Bus: 22, 30, 41, 43, or 45.

Greens ★★ VEGETARIAN   Greens was, arguably, the first restaurant in the U.S. to take a gourmet approach to vegetarian food, both in its ambitious menu and its serene, all hand-carved wood decor and its oversized windows offering up one of the best water views in the city. (The restaurant is in a former warehouse at Fort Mason.) Its status remains untouched. Come here even if you're a devoted carnivore, the food is revelatory (truly, you won't miss the meat); and jumps continents with ease, offering terrific veggie takes on Moroccan, Mexican, and Italian foods. There's an extensive wine list and a "Greens to Go" menu if you'd like to take a picnic on the Marina Green.

Bldg. A, Fort Mason Center (across from Safeway). ℂ **415/771-6222.** www.greensrestaurant.com. Main courses $18–$24; Sat fixed-price dinner $56, wine pairings $33; Sun brunch $13–$18. Tues–Sat 11:45am–2:30pm; Sun 10:30am–2pm; Evenings 5:30–9pm. Greens To Go Mon–Thurs 8:30am–7pm; Fri–Sat 8:30am–5pm; Sun 9am–4pm. Bus: 28 or 30.

Moderate

Ace Wasabi Rock & Roll Sushi ★ SUSHI/JAPANESE   This hopping neighborhood restaurant frequented by a casual, younger set infuses affordable, creative sushi with moody brick-walled environs and '80s hits that makes you want to hang out for a while. Locals go for the tasty "Bowls of Bliss"—sushi favorites like sea urchin, tuna, and avocado, or eel and avocado atop sushi rice, all under $10—as well as standard nigiri, specialty rolls, and salads and cooked appetizers, such as whole grilled giant calamari, panko-fried chicken fingers with spicy garlic aioli, and grilled short ribs. Delicious, affordable—and fun. Weekday happy hour from 5:30 to 7pm is a great deal, too.

3339 Steiner St. (between Chestnut & Lombard sts.). ℂ **415/567-4903.** www.acewasabisf.com. Nigiri sushi $5–$7. Rolls $5–$14. Appetizers $8–$14.50. Mon–Thurs 5:30–10:30pm, Fri–Sat 5:30–11pm, Sun 5–10pm. Bus:

SPQR ★★ ITALIAN-INFLUENCED NORTHERN CALIFORNIAN   Of the many reasons to visit the charming upscale shopping stretch on upper Fillmore, this small, award-winning restaurant tops my list. Perpetually crowded, locals flock

family-friendly RESTAURANTS

Does it make you cringe to think about sitting at a restaurant with your child for 3+ hours for a multicourse farm-to-table culinary adventure when all your little ones really want is a quick bowl of buttered noodles?

Fear not. San Francisco is one of the best cities in the world to visit with children and we have lots of places to entertain and feed our hungry little guests.

Children love **Forbes Island** (p. 84) for some of the same reasons you do—because you have to take a water taxi to get there, you can climb up the lighthouse to spy on the barking sea lions, and you eat your dinner underwater. What's not to love?

Kids and adults can also be satisfied at **Ton Kiang** (p. 97), a dim sum restaurant where lazy susans in the center of the table can make accessing your pork bun extra fun, simple dishes like fried rice can be ordered off the menu, and when all else fails, there's always a big bowl of fresh fruit at the ready.

Farallon (p. 79), with its jellyfish lamps and kelp rising from the floor, is an underwater fantasy perfect for budding marine biologists; ordering from the a la carte menu means dinner does not have to be a 3-hour affair.

SoMa StrEat Food Park (p. 81) is a happening place to grab lunch with the kids, as 13 food trucks means there's bound to be something even the pickiest tot will like. Let them run free amongst the local dot-com geniuses lunching here. Who knows? Maybe they will make a few future connections.

Kids like getting up close to the sea creatures displayed in the **Swan Oyster Depot** (p. 83) window. Plus it's so small, loud, and crowded, if your child accidentally drops their bowl of chowder on the floor, no one will even notice.

One last thought for kids: Take them to one of our city's colorful Chinese restaurants—see **"Chinatown—So Many Choices"** on p. 86. My kids' favorite, partially because they can hop off the cable car right outside, is **U-Lee's** Chinese (p. 83). Order the potstickers, which are about the size of your fist (and $1 apiece), and they should be content.

here for the fine cooking of Executive Chef (and 2014 "Food & Wine" Best New Chef winner) Matthew Accarrino paired with the exceptional Italian wine list crafted by award-winning wine director and owner Shelley Lindgren. Order an array of plates to share—perhaps green asparagus and halibut cheek with brown butter and tarragon zabaglione or black cod, gulf prawn, tomato braised cannelini bean, salumi, and wild fennel shoot—and take advantage of the opportunity to sample three-ounce wine tastes so you can mix and match your way through a perfect San Francisco meal.

1911 Fillmore St. (between Bush and Pine sts.). ☏ **415/771-7779**. www.spqrsf.com. Main courses weekend lunch $24–$27; dinner $25–$36. Mon–Fri 5:30–10:30pm, Sat 11am–2:30pm and 5:30–10:30pm, Sun 11am–2:30pm and 5:30–10pm. Bus: 22.

Tacolicious ★ MEXICAN   This crowded, festive, and cramped spot is popular for its delicious gourmet tacos and strong cocktails. With high ceilings, modern lighting, warm green jewel tones on the walls, and nary a Mexican flag in sight, the only clue you've even entered a Mexican restaurant, and it's a big one, is the 120 types of tequila offered at the bar. To keep your girlish figure—and fit into the micro miniskirt that seems to be a customer uniform here—try the Marina Girl Salad, featuring avocado, cucumber, and cotija cheese. And where there are girls in miniskirts, you usually find sports figures—SF Giants pitcher Tim Lincecum is a regular, swears by the *carnitas,* and brings his Giants teammates by on occasion. We're guessing they go for the tacos, which are made with a variety of fillings including summer squash, filet mignon, and the house specialty, guajillo-braised beef short ribs. This place is so popular the owners have opened two more city locations in North Beach (1548 Stockton St.) and in the Mission (741 Valencia St.). No reservations.

2031 Chestnut St. (at Fillmore St.) ☏ **415/346-1966.** www.tacolicious.com. Main courses $10–$18. Thurs–Sat 11:30am–midnight; Sun–Wed 11:30am–1pm. Bus: 22, 30, or 43.

JAPANTOWN/WESTERN ADDITION

Moderate

Nopa ★★ AMERICAN A poster child for the current gestalt of the San Francisco restaurant scene, large and airy Nopa combines seasonal "urban rustic" and "organic wood-fired" cuisine made from local ingredients with high-ceilinged industrial-chic environs and a hopping bar scene. Make a reservation well in advance or wait to pounce on a barstool or seat at the big, first-come-first-serve communal table to enjoy artisan libatins, one of the city's best grass-fed burgers, and plenty of veggie-, meat-, and fishcentric dishes that celebrate the region's bounty and a successful use of restraint. Don't worry—the rather precious taste from the kitchen (perhaps a single radish with salt or some other tease) isn't indicative of the portions, which are hearty. Another reason to visit: Its Divisadero Street location exposes you to an up-and-coming stretch of the city rarely explored by tourists.

560 Divisadero St. (at Hayes St.) ☏ **415/864-8643.** www.nopasf.com. Mon–Fri 6pm–1am, Sat–Sun 11:30am–2:30pm and 6pm–1am. Main courses dinner $14–$27, main courses brunch $7–$16.

State Bird Provisions ★★★ CALIFORNIAN   The hottest destination since its December 2011 opening (and nearly impossible to get into thanks to online reservations that are never available), this American dim-sum restaurant snared a James Beard Award right out of the gate—a nearly unheard of occurrence. Chef Stuart Brioza's creative, fresh internationally influenced small plates are wheeled around on carts and carried on trays—just like at your favorite Chinese restaurant—and they are impossibly good. In the casual, friendly dining room with a shockingly tiny open kitchen, everything comes easily—perhaps too much so—as you need only point to what you want as it passes by and is described by enthusiastic staff. You may be presented with Nova Scotia oysters with spicy kohlrabi kraut and sesame seeds or croquettes created from rabbit and fontina cheese. Or you might order from their small menu of standards, which includes savory pancakes. Whatever the case, you're bound to have a meal to remember. Reservations are necessary up to 60 days in advance. If you don't have one, stand in line at 4:30pm, and wait for the doors to open at 5:30pm—you will eventually get seated; one third of the restaurant is set aside for walk-ins, including the chefs' counter where you may sit or stand, but get the best view of the cooks in action.

1529 Fillmore Street (at O'Farrell St.) ☏ **415/795-1272.** www.statebirdsf.com. Bites $3–$16. Mon–Thurs 5:30–10pm, Fri–Sat 5:30–11pm. Bus: 1, 22, or 38.

CIVIC CENTER/HAYES VALLEY

Expensive

Rich Table ★★ CALIFORNIAN   Though Rich Table lost the 2013 James Beard Award for Best New Restaurant to State Bird Provisions (p. 90), finishing second is not too shabby. And no wonder, as owners/chefs Evan and Sarah Rich have some serious cred behind them with years of combined experience at Michael Mina, Quince, and Coi. When they decided to launch their own restaurant, they wanted an open kitchen and California casual decor to make people feel they have been invited into their home. It works. Employees have a laidback, but attentive, style of service, fitting for the whole *mi-casa-su-casa* theme. The menu changes regularly depending on what's available and the whims of the chefs. The sardine chips are a house favorite (and one of "7x7" magazine's 100 bucket-list dishes), as are the dried porcini mushroom doughnuts served with raclette. If you are hungry for more than a bite, unique crowd pleasers are oxtail tagliatelle; lamb tartare with charred eggplant and cucumber; pork belly; and spaghetti with English peas, goat cheese, and mint.

199 Gough St. (at Oak St.). ✆ **415/355-9085**. www.richtablesf.com. Main courses $17–$30, chefs picks $80, wine pairings $55. Sun, Mon, Wed, Thurs 5:30–10pm, Fri–Sat 5:30–10:30pm. Bus: 5, 9, 38, 47, or 49. Any Market St. light rail or streetcar.

Inexpensive

Tommy's Joynt ★ AMERICAN   Vibrant murals outside and flea-market decor inside set the perfect scene for this ultracasual and utterly San Francisco cafeteria-style bar and restaurant serving heaping, affordable piles of comfort food. If you can tear your eyes away from the whimsical, old collection of bric-a-brac covering every square inch of this place, you'll be overwhelmed by the food options splayed across the heat lamp-warmed counter. Corned beef, buffalo stew, or roast beef...it's all here along with every heavy, delicious side you can imagine. And if you want to do some serious drinking, Tommy's offers a variety of almost 100 beers and ciders from over 30 different countries.

11011 Geary Blvd. (at Van Ness Ave.). ✆ **415/775-4216**. www.tommysjoynt.com. Main courses $6–$15; Daily 10am–1:40am. Parking: free hour with validation, $5 for 2 hours. Bus: 38 or 90.

MISSION DISTRICT

Expensive

Central Kitchen ★ CALIFORNIAN   This is the epitome of California-chic dining in the trendy Mission District, brought to you by Thomas McNaughton, of upscale pizzeria **flour + water** fame (another worthy dining option, it's at 2401 Harrison St.). Here, a covered garden patio provides alfresco dining space year round; and the open kitchen sets the tone for a laid back, relaxed feel. In that kitchen, McNaughton creates such delectables as hen roulade with confit of radish; raw Hamachi with kumquat, fennel, poppy seed and chili; black cod with artichoke; and beef tartare with oyster, buttermilk flatbread, frisee, and dill. The entrance is set back from the street, to the left of the McNaughton-owned market/cafe, Salumeria. Both share the 3000 address. Look up and left for the small, square CENTRAL KITCHEN sign.

3000 20th Street (at Florida St.). ✆ **415/826-7004**. www.centralkitchensf.com. Main courses $16–$27, tasting menu $95, pairings $55; cheese course $8; corkage fee $20. Mon–Thurs 5:30–10pm, Fri–Sat 5:30–11pm, Sun 5:30–9pm. Sunday brunch 10am–2:30pm. Bus: 22, 27, or 33.

Foreign Cinema ★★ CALIFORNIAN   One of the first hot spots during the late '90s dot-com boom is now a culinary (and still cool) stalwart in the Mission. Seasonal, fresh, and delicious food reigns on the plate—think oyster bar and internationally inspired dishes ranging from Hawaiian Kampachi crudo to five-spice duck breast. But it's the atmosphere of this large, bustling multidimensional spot that maintains this place's star status. Whether you eat at the industrial-chic inside or the atrium patio where foreign and indie flicks play on the side of a neighboring building, it feels plain cool to be here. And if you want to actually hear the film, you can turn to the little speaker box at each table.

2534 Mission St. (btw. 21st and 22nd sts.). ℂ **415/648-7600.** www.foreigncinema.com. Main courses $12–$31. Dinner Mon–Thurs 6–10pm; Fri–Sat 5:30–11pm; Sun 5:30–10pm; Weekend Brunch 11am–3pm; Bar opened until 2am nightly. Bus: 14.

Moderate

Blowfish Sushi ★ JAPANESE   The somewhat out-of-the-way location only adds to the allure of this destination Asian-fusion restaurant known for its deliciously creative Japanese dishes by Chef Ritsuo Tsuchida. His pyramid of tartare is case in point: a triangular edifice of tuna, salmon, and avocado, it arrives with a side of honey tartare and sweet garlic ginger soy sauce and house-made potato chips. To make his signature dish, the Ritsu Roll, Tsuchida quickly flash fries two types of tuna, avocado and masago, and serves it with a side of citrus ponzu sauce and Japanese Dijon aioli. The decor and ambience, with TV screens flashing anime, upbeat club music blasting, and cool artwork on the walls, are equally contemporary and jubilant.

2170 Bryant St. (btw. 19th and 20th sts.). ℂ **415/285-3848.** www.blowfishsushi.com. Main courses $17–$26. Lunch Mon–Fri 11:30am–2:30pm; dinner Mon 5–10pm; Tues 5:30–10pm; Wed–Thurs 5:30–10:30pm; Fri–Sat 5:30–11pm; Sun 5:30–10pm. Bus: 27 or 33.

Delfina ★★ ITALIAN   This super-urban, relatively casual neighborhood restaurant has been one of the city's top Italian restaurants for 15 years. James Beard Award–winning chef and owner/chef Craig Stoll is known for simple, rustic cuisine done right, while his wife, Annie, ensures the relaxed, knowledgeable service is equally pro. Yes, there are pastas here. But you'll find just as much satisfaction in other simple pleasures, such as roasted chicken with mushrooms and olive oil mashed potatoes or grilled octopus. An outdoor patio open from mid-March through October provides more space for diners who just can't get enough. More casual and less expensive is neighboring **Pizzeria Delfina** (3611 18th St.; ℂ **415/437-6800;** www.pizzeriadel finasf.com), and a second pizzeria is located at 2406 California St. in Pacific Heights (ℂ **415/440-1189).**

3621 18th St. (btw. Dolores and Guerrero sts.). ℂ **415/552-4055.** www.delfinasf.com. Main courses $17–$30. Mon–Thurs 5:30–10pm; Fri–Sat 5:30–11pm; Sun 5–10pm. Bus: 14 or 22. Streetcar: J.

Gracias Madre ★ VEGAN/MEXICAN   San Francisco is so famous for its Mexican food, no resident within city limits lacks opinion on where to find the best tacos or burrito. For vegans, this one often tops the list. Soft corn tacos laden with garlicky greens or grilled eggplant manage to be satisfying and surprisingly light—as well as fresh since many of the vegetables are grown at the restaurateur's own farm. Get here early, there's always a line out front. Organic beer, wine, and cocktails are also available.

2211 Mission St. (at 19th St.). ℂ **415/683-1346.** www.gracias-madre.com. Main courses $11–$16. Daily 11am–11pm; happy hour 3–6pm. Bus: 14 or 22.

Mission District & Castro Restaurants

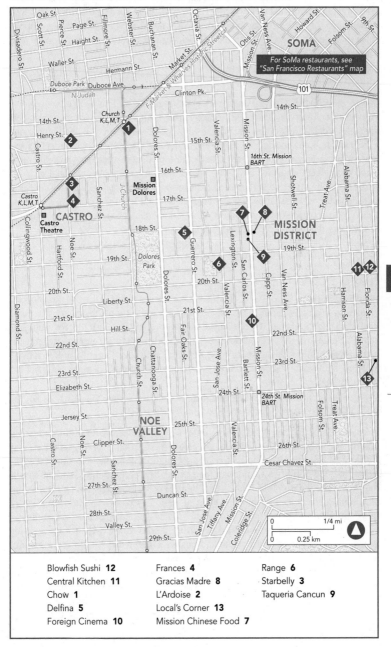

Blowfish Sushi **12**
Central Kitchen **11**
Chow **1**
Delfina **5**
Foreign Cinema **10**

Frances **4**
Gracias Madre **8**
L'Ardoise **2**
Local's Corner **13**
Mission Chinese Food **7**

Range **6**
Starbelly **3**
Taqueria Cancun **9**

Local's Corner ★ SEAFOOD   Local's Corner's is so small (and that goes for the seating area, too), it has room only for a convection oven, a few low-powered burners, and a circulator bath. That means the food here (mostly seafood) is often cooked at low temperatures, or served in raw preparations or tenderized via *sous vide* preparation, which provides a unique flavor profile and wonderfully tender textures. A kindly staff makes up for the cramped quarters.

2500 Bryant St. (at 23rd). © **415/800-7945.** www.localscornersf.com. Main courses $12–$25. Tues–Sat 8am–10pm; Sun 8am–2pm. Bus: 9, 10, 27, 33, 48, or 90.

Range ★★ AMERICAN   A near-perfect rendition of San Francisco's ever-popular seasonal new American restaurant, Range is two things at once: a somewhat quiet, urban-chic cocktail/bar dining area in the front and a rather noisy, boxy dining room in the back. In both spots you'll enjoy some of the city's finest food at excellent prices. From a spring greens soup that transforms the tops of root vegetables into the most luxurious, velvety, Indian-spiced soup (that's miraculously both light and rich) to glazed pork ribs enhanced with roasted cauliflower, pickled shallots, and mustard seed vinaigrette to red wine-braised short ribs done so right it'll bring tears to your eyes, you really can't go wrong here. Bonus: Its Mission District location puts you right in the center of the bar and cafe action.

842 Valencia St. (btw. 19th and 20th sts.). © **415/282-8283.** www.rangesf.com. Main courses $23–$27. Mon–Thurs 6pm–close, Fri–Sun 5:30pm–close. Bus: 14 or 22.

5 | Inexpensive

Mission Chinese Food ★ CHINESE   For many foodies, eating at now-famous James Beard Award–winning chef Dannie Bowien's walk-in-only restaurant is a rite of passage. While the Chinese food is indeed inventive (Kung Pao pastrami, for example), some (including myself) argue that it's overrated. Others can't get enough. Regardless, the cramped bustling dining space confusingly identified as "Lung Shan Restaurant" out front is affordably priced and always a fun time. Portions are large and great for sharing. BYOB.

2234 Mission St. (at 18th St.). © **415/863-2800.** www.missionchinesefood.com. Main courses $10–$18. Daily 11:30–3pm, 5–10:30pm, closed Wed. Bus: 14 or 22.

Taqueria Cancun ★★ MEXICAN   After a night on the town, visitors and locals looking for mouth-watering, cheap Mexican food walk, stagger, stumble, and shuffle into this tiny Mission *taqueria,* open nightly until the wee hours. Green, yellow, and red plastic cut-outs cover the ceiling; beer flags, guitars, and the Virgin Mary hang on bright yellow walls—the clientele is as decorated and colorful as the restaurant, and range from hipsters sporting seriously complex tattoos to slightly tipsy button-down finance guys. When you grab a table, chances are the last diner's yellow plastic food basket will still be sitting there—you'll wait a long time for someone to clear it; just take a seat and push it aside. If the line to order is long, don't worry, it moves quickly; this place is used to crowds. No wonder, the food is delicious; the Carne Asada Super Burrito for $6.50 is huge, juicy, and full of flavor; the steak charred to perfection. What a surprise—they only take cash. No reservations.

2288 Mission St. (btw. 18th and 19th sts.) © **415/252-9560.** Main courses $5–$9. Weekdays 9:30am–1:30am, Fri—Sat 9:30am–2:30am. Bus: 14 or 22.

ANYONE FOR sweet nothings?

After strolling across the Golden Gate Bridge, hiking up to Coit Tower, or walking through 6,000 years of history at the Asian Art Museum, you might feel the need for a sweet treat—here a are a few places sure to satisfy.

Bi-Rite Creamery and Bakeshop, 3692 18th St. (𝄐 **415/626-5600;** www.bi-ritecreamery.com) uses organic ingredients to create mouthwatering ice cream with flavors like roasted banana and toasted coconut.

The Candy Store, 1507 Vallejo St. (𝄐 **415/921-8000;** www.thecandystoresf.com), is a candy boutique featuring confections from around the world, and nostalgic, old-fashioned treats.

The Crepe Café (p. 87), Pier 39 on The Embarcadero (𝄐 **415/318-1494**). Push your nose up against the window to watch the workers make delicious dessert crepes loaded with Nutella, caramel, strawberries, bananas, and whipped cream.

Ghirardelli (p. 104), 900 North Point St. at Ghirardelli Square (𝄐 **415/474-3938;** www.ghirardelli.com), is an ice cream parlor and chocolate shop that's been serving up sweet treats for the last 160 years.

Miette, Ferry Building Marketplace Shop #10 (𝄐 **415/837-0300;** www.miette.com), is a pastry shop featuring pretty treats like Parisian macarons, chocolate eclairs, and lavender shortbread cookies.

The original **Swensen's Ice Cream,** 1999 Hyde St. (𝄐 **415/775-6818;** www.swensens.com), opened here in 1948—pure old school indulgence.

Tcho (p. 169), Pier 17 on The Embarcadero (𝄐 **415/963-5090;** www.tcho.com). Sign up online to take a chocolate factory tour, learn the history of chocolate, and taste artisan samples. Or, just show up and sample in this warehouse space.

THE CASTRO & NOE VALLEY

Expensive

Frances ★★ CALIFORNIAN With only 37 seats, this is a tiny neighborhood restaurant, with a tiny menu—and one big Michelin star—that consistently delivers a huge dining experience. Ever since its opening in 2009, Melissa Perello's baby has remained a top place in the city, known for an eclectic menu that might include choices as varied as squid ink linguini; or Sonoma duck breast with pumpkin seed *dukkah*, Japanese sweet potato, and blood orange. Don't miss the applewood-smoked bacon beignets—you dip them in crème, fresh with maple and chive. For dessert, the lumberjack cake—apple, kumquat, Medjool dates, and maple ice cream—is a crowd pleaser, as is the interesting idea of selling the house red and white wines for the bargain price of $1 an ounce. Make a reservation up to 60 days in advance, or walk in and sit at the bar.

3870 17th St. (at Pond St.) 𝄐 **415/621-3870.** www.frances-sf.com. Main courses $18–$29. Tues–Thurs and Sun 5–10pm; Fri–Sat 5–10:30pm. Bus: 22, 24, or 33. Any Market St. light rail or streetcar.

Moderate

L'Ardoise ★★ FRENCH When Dominique Crenn—of Atelier Crenn (p. 88) fame, smiles fondly and says she loves to drop in here for a late evening supper, you know this place is good—really good. Pronounced "lard wazz"—French for the large chalkboard listing the daily specials—this hidden Castro gem feels like an old Parisian bistro, with rich burgundy walls, plush carpet, heavy curtains, and dark wood. The mood is romantic, and the food a bit more special than usual. Escargots are served *en gueusaille*—in fried potato cups—with a garlic and parsley cream sauce. Favorite entrees are just as Gallic, think coq au vin in red wine sauce with potato puree, bacon and pearl onions; and roasted rack of lamb with *pomme frites*, garlic and parsley butter. Add a bottle from the selective wine list and a cheese plate to finish, and you have an evening that is *parfait*.

151 Noe St. (at Henry St.). ✆ **415/437-2600.** www.lardoisesf.com. Main courses $17–$39. Tues–Thurs 5:30–10pm; Fri–Sat 5–10:30pm. Bus: 24. Any Market St. light rail or streetcar.

Starbelly ★ CALIFORNIAN   American classics and a sweet, cafe atmosphere make this small, laid-back post with an outdoor patio a favorite. Burgers with house-cut fries, potpies, steaks, and a variety of thin-crust pizzas are complemented by microbrew beers, some imported from Belgium and Canada, others produced by local artisan breweries. Don't skip dessert: The salted caramel pot de crème with rosemary cornmeal cookies or warm toffee cake drenched in caramel sauce and served with Medjool dates and mascarpone cheese are anything but a second thought.

3583 16th St. (at Noe and Market sts.). ✆ **415/252-7500.** www.starbellysf.com. Main courses $11–$24. Mon–Thurs 11:30am–11pm; Fri 11:30am–midnight; Sat 10:30am–midnight; Sun 10:30am–11pm. Bus: 22. Any Market St. light rail or streetcar.

Inexpensive

Chow ★ AMERICAN   This perfect, casual San Francisco–style neighborhood restaurant with multiple locations is crowded, affordable, and features a slew of familiar comfort foods as well as a lot of wholesome options to satisfy every palate. Organic BLT sandwiches, Cobb salads, chicken noodle soup, spring pesto lasagna, grilled catch of the day, or beef pot roast…it's all represented here. The hearty weekend brunch is popular, as is the weekday breakfast. Beer and wine are available. There's usually a line to get in, but you can call the same day to put your name on the list; reservations are only accepted for groups of 8 or more.

215 Church St. (near Market St.). ✆ **415/552-2469.** www.chowfoodbar.com/church_location. Main courses $9–$16. Mon–Fri 8–11am; Sat–Sun brunch 8am–1pm; Lunch daily 11am–5pm; Sun–Thurs 5–11pm, Fri–Sat 5pm–midnight. Bus: 22 or 37. Any Market St. light rail or streetcar.

RICHMOND/SUNSET DISTRICTS

Yes, it's a haul from downtown to "the Avenues," but these spots are worth the trip.

Moderate

Aziza ★★ MOROCCAN   Warm, attractive, and out-of-the-way Aziza is one of the most highly regarded Moroccan restaurants in the country, as well as an all-around top city dining spot. Chef/owner Mourad Lahlou applies an elevated, contemporary, farm-fresh approach to classic dishes from his native Marrakesh. To sample this alchemist's gold, you have to try his traditional *basteeya* (a sweet and savory pot pie dish) made with duck confit instead of the usual chicken. And who else would think to add

Medjool date, celery, and parsley to lentil soup? Even the couscous is extra-tasty here, made with fig and urfa (a spicy Turkish pepper).

5800 Geary Blvd. (at 22nd Ave.). ℰ **415/752-2222.** www.aziza-sf.com. Tasting menu $95. Main courses $19–$29. Wed–Mon 5:30–10pm. Street and valet parking. Bus: 1, 28, or 38.

Inexpensive

Burma Superstar ★★ BURMESE Despite a no-reservations policy and a perpetual line to get in, this is one of my favorite restaurants because the authentic Burmese cuisine served here is just that good. So do what we do: Either arrive 15 minutes before the place opens to be seated first or leave your cell phone number with the host and browse the interesting shops on Clement Street until they give you a jingle. Once you're seated in the somewhat loud, upbeat dining room it'll be hard to determine what to choose, since many of the dishes, influenced by the cuisines of India, China, Laos, and Thailand, may sound very foreign. Trust me: It's all good. Don't miss the tea leaf salad or the fried yellow bean tofu appetizers—dishes you may swear you could live on—or try the clay-pot chicken, chili lamb with coconut rice, or any of the curries. If it's packed, and you don't want to wait the waiter may direct you to their sister restaurant down the street. It's not a bad choice. They have many of the same items and fantastic happy hour prices on their food for the first hour of opening.

309 Clement St. (at Fourth Ave.). ℰ **415/387-2147.** www.burmasuperstar.com. No reservations. Main courses $8–$16. Daily 11:30am–3:30pm; Sun–Thurs 5–10pm; Fri–Sat 5–10:30pm. Bus: 2, 38, or 44.

Ton Kiang ★★ CHINESE/DIM SUM If you love dim sum, two-story Ton Kiang is the best place to indulge. Visitors and locals line up early for the chance to take a seat and browse the passing trays of delish potstickers and dumplings filled with every imaginable combination of mushrooms, peas, spinach, cabbage, shrimp, scallops, pork, and crab. The *dai dze gao* (scallop and shrimp dumplings with cilantro), and *gao choygot* (green chives and shrimp dumpling) are so crunchy, light and perfect, you will inhale them and keep asking for more. If dim sum is not your style, the regular menu, filled with delicacies from southeastern China—including clay-pot casseroles and Peking duck—is always available. By the way, the hours on the website are incorrect; the hours below are correct.

5821 Geary Blvd. (btw. 22nd and 23rd aves.). ℰ **415/387-8273.** www.tonkiang.net. Dim sum $3–$7; main courses $10–$26. Mon–Thurs 10am–9:30pm; Fri 10am–10pm; Sat 9:30am–10pm; Sun 9am–9pm. Bus: 5 or 38.

5

WHERE TO EAT

Richmond/Sunset Districts

EXPLORING SAN FRANCISCO

San Francisco boasts panoramic vistas, distinct neighborhoods, outdoor activities to delight the most adventurous, and museums to engage the most curious. It's European charm meets cutting-edge technology meets laid-back California living. In other words, San Francisco offers something for everyone, whether your idea of exploring means history tours and museums or self-guided wandering. Spend time in world-famous tourist destinations or discover the city's lesser-known gems—either way you're bound to discover why millions of visitors leave their hearts in San Francisco.

A (Nearly) Citywide Attraction

Cable Cars ★★★   Although they may not be San Francisco's most practical means of transportation, cable cars are certainly the most beloved and are a must-have experience. Designated official moving historic landmarks by the National Park Service in 1964, they clank up and down the city's steep hills like mobile museum pieces, tirelessly hauling thousands of tourists each day to Fisherman's Wharf and elsewhere at the brisk pace of 9 miles per hour.

As the story goes, London-born engineer Andrew Hallidie was inspired to invent the cable cars after witnessing a heavily laden carriage pulled by a team of overworked horses, slip and roll backwards down a steep San Francisco slope, dragging the horses behind it. Hallidie resolved to build a mechanical contraption to replace horses, and in 1873, the first cable car made its maiden voyage from the top of Clay Street. Promptly ridiculed as "Hallidie's Folly," the cars were slow to gain acceptance. One early onlooker voiced the general opinion by exclaiming, "I don't believe it—the damned thing works!"

But indeed they do—and have for more than 100 years. The cars, each weighing about 6 tons, run along a steel cable enclosed under the street on a center rail. You can't see the cable unless you peer straight down into the crack, but you'll hear its characteristic hum and click-clacking sound whenever you're nearby. The cars move when the gripper (they don't call themselves drivers) pulls back a lever that closes a pincerlike "grip" on the cable. The speed of the car, therefore, is determined by the speed of the cable, which is a constant 9½ mph—never more, never less. The two types of cable cars in use hold a maximum of 90 and 100 passengers, and limits are rigidly enforced. The best view (and the most fun) is from a perch on the outer running boards—but hold on tightly, especially around corners.

Here's the secret to catching a ride on a cable car: Don't wait in line with all the tourists at the turnaround stops at the beginning and end of the lines. Walk a few blocks up the line (follow the tracks) and do as the locals do: Hop on when the car stops, hang on to a pole, and have your $6 ready to hand to the brakeman (hoping, of course, that he'll never ask). **Note:** On a really busy weekend, however, the cable cars often don't stop to pick up passengers en route because they're full, so you might have to stand in line at the turnarounds.

Hallidie's cable cars were imitated and used throughout the world, but all have been replaced by more efficient means of transportation. San Francisco planned to do so, too, but met with so much opposition that the cable cars' perpetuation was actually written into the city charter in 1955. The mandate cannot be revoked without the approval of a majority of the city's voters—a distant and doubtful prospect. San Francisco's three existing cable car lines form the world's only surviving system. Savvy travellers do like the locals do and catch the car a couple stops up from the origin to skip the often-long lines (sometimes a 2-hour wait in the summer). For more information on riding them, see "Getting Around By Public Transportation" in chapter 12 on (p. 228).

Powell–Hyde and Powell–Mason lines begin at the base of Powell and Market sts. California St. line begins at the foot of Market St. at the Embarcadero. $6 per ride.

FISHERMAN'S WHARF

More than 14 million tourists visit this world-famous historical site each year. Despite its name, it's been more Disney than Steinbeck for decades now, but for tourists, it's a spot with plenty to do and see along one of the city's famed postcard-perfect backdrops. Unless you come early in the morning to watch the few remaining fishing boats depart, you won't find many traces of the traditional waterfront life that once existed here. Originally called Meiggs' Wharf, this bustling strip of waterfront got its present moniker from generations of fishermen who used to dock their boats here. A small fleet of 30 or so fishing boats still set out from here, but now it's one long shopping and entertainment mall that stretches from Ghirardelli Square at the west end to Pier 39 at the east. Accommodating a total of 300 boats, two marinas flank Pier 39 and house the sightseeing ferry fleets, including departures to Alcatraz Island. The most famous residents of Fisherman's Wharf are the hundreds of **California sea lions** (p. 107) hanging out, barking on the docks at Pier 39.

Some folks love Fisherman's Wharf (my family falls into this category); others can't get far enough away from it. I suppose it has much to do with one's tolerance for kitsch. Among the most popular sites at the Wharf are the **Ripley's Believe It or Not! Museum** at 175 Jefferson St. (© **415/202-9850;** www.ripleysf.com) and the street performers who convene on the stage at Pier 39. In the summer of 2014 two more cheesy attractions opened at 145 Jefferson St.: **The San Francisco Dungeon** (http://sanfrancisco.thedungeons.com; no phone), where fully costumed character actors take visitors through 200 years of colorful San Francisco history with theatrical

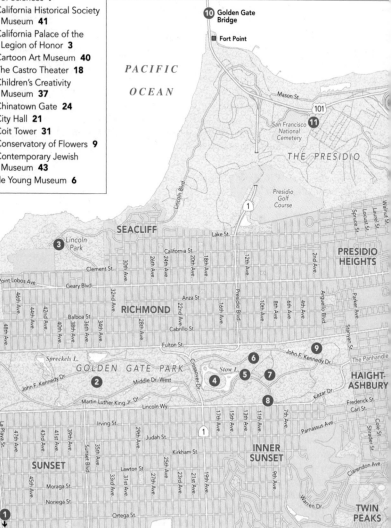

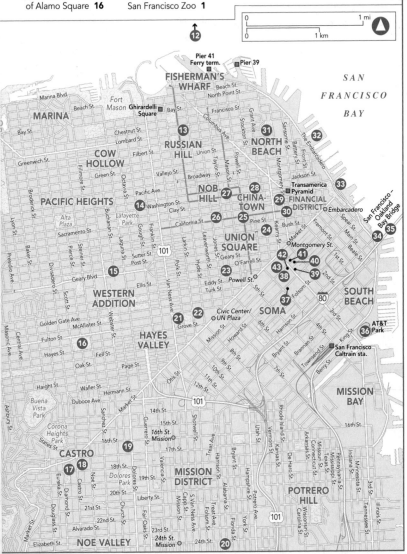

storytelling, special effects, and dramatic sets ($26 adult, $20 for kids 4–17, 3 and under free; daily 10am–7pm), and **Madame Tussauds** (www.madametussauds.com/SanFrancisco; no phone), the world-famous gallery of wax statues that features legends like Lady Gaga, Leonardo DiCaprio, and—get this—Mark Zuckerberg ($26 for adults, 20 for kids 4–17, 3 and under free; daily 10am–8pm).

However you feel about these sort of attractions, most agree that, for better or worse, Fisherman's Wharf has to be seen at least once in your lifetime. There are still some traces of old-school San Francisco character here to enjoy. In fact, nowadays more than ever, as the rest of the city is rapidly evolving with gentrification, the bric-a-brac shops, restaurants, and overall vibe of Fisherman's Wharf remain the same, making it the new old San Francisco. Even if you only drop by the neighborhood to see it, make sure to check out the convivial seafood street vendors who dish out piles of fresh Dungeness crab and sourdough bread bowls full of clam chowder from their steaming, stainless-steel carts. And, yes, you can hop on a boat and go fishing.

At Taylor St. and the Embarcadero. © **415/674-7503.** www.fishermanswharf.org. Bus: 30, 39, 47, or 82X. Streetcar: F. Cable car: Powell–Mason line to the last stop and walk to the wharf. If you're arriving by car, park on adjacent streets or on the wharf btw. Taylor and Jones sts. for $16 per day, $8 with validation from participating restaurants.

Alcatraz Island ★★★ HISTORIC SITE   If you can only do one tour while in San Francisco, make it Alcatraz. Probably the most famous prison in America, if not the world, this was where the worst of the worst criminals were marooned to suffer and freeze in the Bay. The building has barely changed at all from its days as a "grey-bar hotel." It's like walking through the past.

A bit of history: In 1775, Juan Manuel Ayala was the first European to set foot on the island. He named it after the many *alcatraces,* or pelicans that nested here. From the 1850s to 1933, Alcatraz served as a military fortress and prison. In 1934, the government converted the buildings of the military outpost into a maximum-security civilian penitentiary, one of the roughest places to be incarcerated in history. Inmates suffered psychologically and emotionally. The wind howled through the windows, the concrete was chilly and dank, and everything good and right in the world was perennially located at an unreachable distance. Given the sheer cliffs, treacherous tides and currents, and frigid water temperatures, it was believed to be totally escape-proof. Among the famous gangsters who occupied cellblocks A through D were Al Capone; Robert Stroud, the so-called Birdman of Alcatraz (an expert in ornithological diseases); Machine Gun Kelly; and Alvin "Creepy" Karpis, a member of Ma Barker's gang. It cost a fortune to keep them imprisoned here because all supplies, including water, had to be shipped in. In 1963, after an apparent escape in which no bodies were recovered, the government closed the prison. It moldered abandoned until 1969, when a group of Native Americans chartered a boat to the island and symbolically reclaimed the island for the Indian people. They occupied the island until 1971—the longest occupation of a federal facility by Native Americans to this day—but eventually were forcibly removed by the government. (See www.nps.gov/archive/alcatraz/indian.html for more information on the Native American occupation of Alcatraz.) The next year the island was given over to the National Park Service, natural habitats were restored, and the wildlife that was driven away during the prison years began to return. Today, you can see black-crested night herons and other seabirds here on a trail along the island's perimeter.

Fisherman's Wharf Attractions

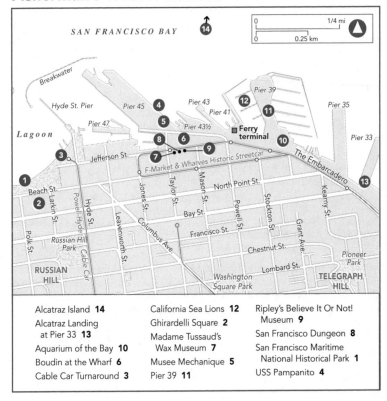

Alcatraz Island **14**	California Sea Lions **12**	Ripley's Believe It Or Not! Museum **9**
Alcatraz Landing at Pier 33 **13**	Ghirardelli Square **2**	San Francisco Dungeon **8**
Aquarium of the Bay **10**	Madame Tussaud's Wax Museum **7**	San Francisco Maritime National Historical Park **1**
Boudin at the Wharf **6**	Musee Mechanique **5**	USS Pampanito **4**
Cable Car Turnaround **3**	Pier 39 **11**	

Admission to the island includes a fascinating audio tour, "Doing Time: The Alcatraz Cellhouse Tour," narrated by actual former convicts, who are less grizzled than you might guess; the main voice pronounces "escape" as "excape," as someone's adorable Midwestern grandpa might. Don't be shy about pausing the recording with the STOP button, otherwise it rushes you along a bit too quickly. And don't be afraid to break away after your first pass through Broadway (the main corridor) so that you can explore the recreation yard. Wear comfortable shoes (the National Park Service notes that there are a lot of hills to climb) and take a heavy sweater or windbreaker, because even when the sun's out, it's cold and windy on Alcatraz. Although there is a beverage-and-snack bar on the ferry, the options are limited and expensive; you might want to bring your own snacks for the boat. Only water is allowed on the island.

Note: The excursion to Alcatraz is very popular and space is limited, so purchase tickets as far in advance as possible (up to 90 days) via the **Alcatraz Cruises** website at www.alcatrazcruises.com. You can also purchase tickets in person by visiting the Hornblower Alcatraz Landing ticket office at Pier 33. The first departure, called the "Early Bird," leaves at 9am, and ferries depart about every half-hour afterward until 4pm. Two night tours (highly recommended) are also available, offering a more intimate and wonderfully spooky experience.

For those who want to get a closer look at Alcatraz without going ashore, two boat-tour operators offer short circumnavigations of the island. (See "Self-Guided & Organized Tours" on p. 133 for complete information.)

Pier 33, Alcatraz Landing near Fisherman's Wharf. ☎ **415/981-7625.** www.alcatrazcruises.com. Admission (includes ferry trip and audio tour) $90 family ticket for 2 adults and 2 kids (not available for the night tour), $30 adults, $28 seniors 62+, $18 child 5–11, free 4 and under. Night tour prices slightly higher. Arrive at least 20 min. before departure time. Streetcar: F-Line.

Aquarium of the Bay AQUARIUM   Set streetside at Pier 39, this little, over-priced aquarium is a quick tour that you can turn to if you want to indulge the kids. With over 20,000 sea creatures swimming about, you'll see the usual eels, octopuses, and jellyfish; you can pat bat rays and leopard sharks at the touch pool, or check out the new otter exhibit. The highlight for most kids is the conveyor-belt floor that moves you along a clear tube through a 700,000-gallon tank while sharks, rays, and all sorts of fish swim frantically beside you and over your head. If you buy your tickets online, you'll save a few bucks.

Pier 39, the Embarcadero at Beach St. ☎ **415/623-5300.** www.aquariumofthebay.com. Aquarium admission $22 adults, $13 seniors (65+) and children 4–12, free for children 3 and under; family (2 adults, 2 children) package $64. Behind-the-scenes tours for an additional $12–$25 per person. Summer open daily 9am–8pm; fall/spring 10am–7pm (8pm weekends); winter 10am–6pm (7pm weekends). Closed Christmas. Parking: Pier 39 Garage across the street. Streetcar: F-Line.

Boudin at the Wharf ★ FACTORY TOUR   After more than 30 years of being simply a bread shop in the heart of Fisherman's Wharf, Boudin Bakery super-sized into this swank, 26,000-square-foot flagship baking emporium into a place to eat *and* learn. Nearly half a block long, it houses their demonstration bakery, museum, gourmet marketplace, cafe, espresso bar, *and* restaurant. You can see the bakery by guided tour, and you might want to: the Boudin (pronounced Bo-*deen*) family has been baking sourdough French bread in San Francisco since the gold rush, using the same simple recipe and original "mother dough" for more than 150 years. About 3,000 loaves a day are baked within the glass-walled bakery; visitors can watch the entire process from a 30-foot observation window along Jefferson Street or from a catwalk suspended directly over the bakery (which is fun). You'll smell it before you see it: the heavenly aroma emanating from the bread ovens is purposely blasted out onto the sidewalk.

Fisherman's Wharf 160 Jefferson St. (btw. Taylor and Mason sts.). ☎ **415/928-1849** or 510/219-1981 for more tour information. www.boudinbakery.com. Tours: Wed–Mon 11:30am–6pm; $3 for ages 12 and over, 11 and under tour free when accompanied by an adult. Bus and streetcar: All Embarcadero lines.

Ghirardelli Square ★   This National Historic Landmark property dates from 1864, when it served as a factory making Civil War uniforms, but it's best known as the former chocolate and spice factory of Domingo Ghirardelli (pronounced *Gear*-ar-dell-y), who purchased it in 1893. The factory has since been converted into an unimpressive three-level mall containing 30-plus stores and five dining establishments. Street performers entertain regularly in the West Plaza and fountain area. Incidentally, the **Ghirardelli Chocolate Company** ★ still makes chocolate, but its factory is in a lower-rent district in the East Bay. Still, if you have a sweet tooth, you won't be disappointed at the mall's fantastic (and expensive) old-fashioned soda fountain; their "world famous" hot fudge sundae is good, too. (Then again, have you ever had a bad

WHICH discount CARD SHOULD YOU BUY?

Several outfits in town will try to sell you a card that grants you discounts at a variety of attractions and restaurants; some throw in transportation, too. They really *do* give when they promise, but there's a problem with most of these cards: They usually include deals on stuff you'd never normally want to see or have time to cram in. Visiting extra attractions in an effort to make a "discount card" purchase pay off is a classic way to derail your vacation out of a sense of obligation.

Our advice? Don't buy a discount card without first mapping out the plans you have for your visit's days, because you will likely discover you'd spend more money obtaining the card than you'll make back in touring. Never buy a discount card, here or in any other city, on the spur of the moment.

That being said, some may pay off and those that allow you to skip the lines offer real value in terms of time saved. Here are the two we'd recommend you consider:

CityPass (www.citypass.com) is a 7-day Muni and cable car pass with unlimited rides. It also allots users 9 days to visit four (five if you opt for the de Young Museum and the Legion of Honor choice) top sights from a choice of eight—including Alcatraz and the Exploratorium. The attractions alone have a retail value of $148 for an adult, and the CityPASS costs $84. Throw in free Muni and cable cars for 7 days, and the savings add up. We think this is likely the better of the two options, as it only includes the sights most visitors want to see.

The **Go San Francisco Card** (www.smartdestinations.com) can be purchased for 1 to 7 days, and the price varies accordingly. It does not include Muni transportation, nor does it cover the Exploratorium. However, Alcatraz was recently added as an option *if* you buy a 3- or 5-day pass through Alcatraz itself (see website for details). For those interested in tours (including a tour of wine country) or traveling with children (it includes many sights that still interest them) it *might* be a worthwhile buy, especially if you can snag an additional 15% discount or the $10 off code for liking them on Facebook.

hot fudge sundae?) As if you need another excuse to laze the day away in this sweet spot, the square now boasts free Wi-Fi.

900 North Point St. (btw. Polk and Larkin sts.). www.ghirardellisq.com. Stores generally open daily 10am–9pm in summer; Sun–Fri 10am–6pm, Sat 10am–9pm rest of year. Chocolate store and ice cream parlor: © **415/474-3938.** www.ghirardelli.com. Sun–Thurs 10am–11pm, Fri–Sat 10am–midnight. Cable car: Powell–Hyde.

Musee Mechanique ★★ ARCADE   Less of a traditional museum and more a source of interactive amusement, this old-fashioned penny arcade (with some modern video games thrown in for good measure) has been one of my favorite places to go since I was a child. Once located at the Cliff House, this mechanical-minded warehouse of around 300 antique coin-operated penny arcade diversions is guaranteed fun. Because it's located among the pap of the Wharf, it's easy to confuse this one as a tourist trap, but in fact, the lack of an admission fee (you'll part only with whatever change you deposit into the machines of your choice) prove that's not the case. Most of the machines require a few quarters to reveal their Coney Island–era thrills, and almost all of the machines are representatives of a form of mechanical artistry rarely found in working condition anywhere. My favorite machines are the Opium Den, a morality tale in which a diorama of smoking layabouts comes alive with serpents and demons, and the Bimbo Box, in which seven monkey puppets respond to your loose change by playing the Tijana Brass. The Guillotine offers macabre fun; its doors open to reveal the bloodless beheading of a tiny doll. But the standout machine is creepy old Laffing Sal, a funhouse figure that roars with laughter (and horrifies small children) upon the dropping of a coin. Don't miss the black and white photo booths, which produce the old-fashioned, quality shots that make everyone look good. Ensuring guests have as much fun now as they did in the 1930s, when a guy named George Whitney was his generation's leading impresario of cheap entertainment, is descendent Daniel Zelinsky, an aficionado of such amusements, who can be found on hand every-day but Tuesday, repairing and polishing his beloved machines; he wears a badge reading "I work here."

Pier 45 at Taylor Street. ✆ **415/346-2000.** www.museemechanique.org. Free admission. Mon–Fri 10am–7pm, Sat–Sun 10am–8pm.

San Francisco Maritime National Historical Park ★ HISTORIC SITE/ MUSEUM

Since 1962, the Hyde Street Pier has been lined with one of the world's best collections of rare working boats, maintained by the National Park Service's San Francisco Maritime National Historic Park. They include the Glasgow-built *Balclutha,* a gorgeous 1886 three-mated sailing ship that, most famously, appeared in the classic Clark Gable movie "Mutiny on the Bounty"; the *Eureka,* an 1890 paddlewheel ferry-boat that was once the largest of its kind on earth; the *Hercules,* a 1907 tugboat that worked towing logs up the West Coast; and the lumber schooner *C.A. Thayer* from 1895. The *Alma,* built in 1891, was once one of many schooners that plied the water-ways of the Bay Area, but today, it's the only one left.

Although it's free to admire the boats from the dock, $5 will get you aboard the *Balclutha,* the *Eureka,* and the *Hercules* as much as you want for a week (NPS passes work to get you on for free). All of the vessels are designated National Historic Landmarks and it's worth seeing them, particularly the *Balclutha,* a 300-foot square-rigger cargo ship that moved goods like grain and coal between San Francisco, England, and New Zealand from 1886 to 1939. Especially interesting are the tiny crew bunk beds up front and the lavish Captain quarters farther back. In 1899, the wife of *Balclutha*'s Captain Durkee gave birth to a baby girl while aboard the ship; they named the little one India Frances as they were sailing between India and San Francisco at the time. For more tidbits of history, use your cell phone as an audio guide to the ships by calling ✆ **415/294-6754** and entering 1 of the 28 tour codes found at www.nps.gov/safr; click "plan your visit," "things to do," and then "cell phone audio tour."

Before heading to the boats, be sure to pop into the park's signature **Maritime Museum,** technically the **Aquatic Park Bathhouse Building**—on Beach Street at Polk Street, shaped like an Art Deco ship, and filled with sea-faring memorabilia; it's free to enter. Check out the maritime murals and seafaring memorabilia. Next stop is the **Visitor Center** (also free) at Hyde and Jefferson Streets for a look at "The Waterfront," a surprisingly impressive, informative, and interactive exhibit about San Francisco's waterfront history (really, even if you don't usually like history museums, you'll find this one compelling and so will your kids; allot a good 40 min. to explore). It provides a terrific "overture" before seeing the boats themselves. One more "floater," the USS *Pampanito* (see below), is also well worth a visit.

Visitor's Center: Hyde and Jefferson sts. (near Fisherman's Wharf). ✆ **415/447-5000.** www.nps. gov/safr. Free admission to Visitor's Center. Tickets to board ships $5, free for children 16 and

If the thought of walking up and down San Francisco's brutally steep streets has you sweating already, considering renting a talking **GoCar** ★ instead. The tiny yellow three-wheeled convertible cars are easy and fun to drive and they're cleverly guided by a talking GPS (Global Positioning System), which means that the car always knows where you are, even if you don't. The most popular computer-guided tour is a 2-hour loop around the Fisherman's Wharf area, out to the Marina District, through Golden Gate Park, and down Lombard Street, the "crookedest street in the world." As you drive, the talking car tells you where to turn and what landmarks you're passing. Even if you stop to check something out, as soon as you turn your GoCar back on, the tour picks up where it left off. Or you can just cruise around wherever

you want (but not across the Golden Gate Bridge). There's a lockable trunk for your things, and the small size makes parking a breeze. Keep in mind, this isn't a Ferrari—two adults on a long, steep hill may involve one of you walking (or pushing). You can rent a GoCar for 1 hour (standard GoCar: $54; Sport GoCar: $59), or for as long as you want (every hour after the first is $44/hr., prorated in 15-min. increments. If you have the car for 5 hours, you'll be charged the day rate of $200!). You'll have to wear a helmet, and you must be a licensed driver at least 18 years old. GoCar has two rental locations: at Fisherman's Wharf (431 Beach St.), and Union Square (321 Mason St.). For more information call ℂ **800/91-GOCAR** (46227) or 415/441-5695, or log onto their website at www.gocartours.com.

---

under. Visitor's Center and Hyde Street Pier: Daily 9:30am–5pm. Maritime Museum: Polk and Beach sts. ℂ**415/561-7100.** Free admission. Daily 10am–4pm. Bus: 19, 30, or 47. The park is open daily except for Thanksgiving, Christmas, and New Year's Day. Cable car: Powell–Hyde St. line to the last stop.

Pier 39 ★★ MALL/NATURE AREA   Pier 39 is a multilevel waterfront complex that makes up the eastern boundary of Fisherman's Wharf. Constructed on an abandoned cargo pier, it is, ostensibly, a re-creation of a turn-of-the-20th-century street scene, but don't expect a slice of old-time maritime life here: Today, Pier 39 is a bustling mall welcoming millions of visitors per year. You will find more than 90 stores (personal favorites include Lefty's, where you can buy things like left-handed scissors and coffee cups; Shell Cellar which carries nothing but shell stuff; and Candy Baron which offers barrels and barrels of candy, with adult-themed candy hidden at the back right), 14 full-service restaurants, a two-tiered Venetian carousel, the Aquarium of the Bay (p. 104), Magowan's Mirror Maze, bungee jumping, and a stage for street performers who juggle, ride unicycles, and tell corny jokes. Kids love Trish's Mini Donuts, where you can put your nose on the glass and watch a machine drop blobs of batter into boiling oil and make tiny, fat sugar-powdered rings.

Best of all, Pier 39 has the **California sea lions.** Decades ago, hundreds of them took up residence on the floating docks, attracted by herring (and free lodging). They can be seen most days sunbathing, barking, and belching in the marina—some nights you can hear them all the way from Washington Square. Weather permitting, naturalists from Aquarium of the Bay offer educational talks at Pier 39 daily from 11am–4pm (Memorial Day through mid-October) that teaches visitors about the range, habitat, and adaptability of the California sea lion.

Pier 39 is *the* place that some locals love to hate (present company excluded), but kids adore it. Considering Fisherman's Wharf, including Pier 39, is rated one of the top tourist attractions in the world, don't listen to the naysayers; go check it out for yourself—and grab a bag of donuts.

On the waterfront at the Embarcadero and Beach St. ✆ **415/705-5500.** www.pier39.com. Shops daily 10am–9pm, with extended hours during summer and on weekends. Restaurant hours vary. Parking: Pier 39 Garage across the street. 1 hour validated if dining at a full service restaurant. Bus: 8X, 39, or 47. Streetcar: F-Line.

USS Pampanito ★ HISTORIC SITE   This storied sub sank six Japanese ships during four tours of the Pacific in World War II. The vessel has been painstakingly restored to its 1945 condition by admirers, who also run a smart, war-themed gift shop on the dock alongside it. (Note that an interior visit is not recommended for the claustrophobic or the infirm.) Thanks to their efforts, she's still seaworthy, although sadly, the last time she was taken out into the ocean was for the filming of the abysmal 1996 Kelsey Grammer film, "Down Periscope." How glory fades . . . .

Pier 45, Fisherman's Wharf. ✆ **415/775-1943.** www.maritime.org. Admission $12 for ages 13 and older, $8 for seniors (62+) and students with ID, $6 for children 6 to 12, and free for children 5 and under. $3 for a self-guided tour. Open daily at 9am.

SoMa

Once little more than wide, desolate streets flanked by concrete warehouses, SoMa (South of Market) has become the city's cultural hub. With the Yerba Buena District at its core, SoMa boasts a large concentration of museums, centers for the arts, and nightclubs—and plays home base for the San Francisco Giants.

The Bay Lights ★ LIGHT SHOW   If you stand at the waterfront anywhere along the Embarcadero, your natural tendency will be to look left, towards our beautiful Golden Gate Bridge. If it's after sunset, look right—at the much-less-fussed-over Bay Bridge. To celebrate 75 years of connecting San Francisco to the East Bay, the bridge has been covered with the world's largest LED light sculpture that appear to dance on the bridge's cables. Open through March 2015, it's a sight that perfectly showcases San Francisco's blend of art and technology.

Each evening from dusk–2am through March 2015. www.thebaylights.org.

California Historical Society ★ MUSEUM   Established in 1871, and filled with a large collection of Californiana—including photos, documents, and fine art, this museum celebrates the diverse heritage that is California. Exhibits rotate, and have featured topics as varied as a celebration of the 75th birthday of the Golden Gate Bridge to local artists' impressions of homelessness. Check the website to see what is planned during your visit.

678 Mission St. (btw. Third and New Montgomery sts.). ✆ **415/357-1848.** www.california historicalsociety.org. Admission $5, free for children. North Baker Research Library Wed–Fri noon–5pm. Galleries Tues–Sun noon–5pm. Bus: 5, 9, 14, 30, or 45. Streetcar: F-Line or Metro to Montgomery St.

Cartoon Art Museum ★★ MUSEUM   This cool museum is exactly what it sounds like—a place to browse the works by seminal and well-known comic artists, particularly ones whose efforts primarily appeared on newsprint. It began in 1987 with an endowment from Charles M. Schulz, the "Peanuts" creator and since then, it's kept busy with up to seven changing exhibitions every year, and it has published 20 books (so far) on the neglected topic of cartoon history (the gift shop is excellent).

655 Mission St. (near 3rd St). ℰ **415/227-8666.** www.cartoonart.org. Admission $8 adults, $6 students and seniors, $4 kids 6–12; Tues–Sun 11am–5pm. Streetcar: F-Line.

Children's Creativity Museum ★ MUSEUM/AMUSEMENT CENTER   Also in Yerba Buena Gardens you'll find this innovative, hands-on multimedia, arts, and technology museum for children of all ages. Kids howl tunes to the karaoke machine, and make art projects from boxes and scraps of material. One of the most popular stations is the Claymation area where visitors make clay figures and learn all about stop-motion animation by making a quick movie, "Wallace and Gromit"–style. Next door is the fabulous 1906 carousel that once graced the city's bygone oceanside amusement park, Playland-at-the-Beach, plus there's a Children's Garden, a cafe, and a fun store.

221 Fourth St. (at Howard St.). ℰ **415/820-3320.** www.creativity.org. General admission $11; free for children 2 and under. Wed–Sun 10am–4pm. Carousel: Daily 10am–5pm. $4 per ride ($3 with paid museum admission). Bus: 14, 30, or 45. Streetcar: Powell or Montgomery.

Contemporary Jewish Museum ★ MUSEUM   Set in the heart of the Yerba Buena cultural hub, this museum is dedicated to the celebration of *L'Chaim* ("To Life"). Inside, under the skylights and soaring ceilings designed by celebrated architect Daniel Liebeskind, are displays of art, music, film, and literature that celebrate Jewish culture, history, and ideas. Past exhibit subjects have been as varied as Curious George, Gertrude Stein, and Allen Ginsberg. When you're ready for a culture break, nosh on bagels and lox, matzo ball soup, or pastrami on rye at the Wise Sons Jewish Deli.

736 Mission St. (btw. Third and Fourth sts.). ℰ **415/655-7800.** www.thecjm.org. Admission $12 adults, $10 seniors/students, 18 and under free. $5 for all Thurs after 5pm; free 1st Tues of the month. Fri–Tues 11am–5pm, Thurs 1–8pm. Closed Passover, July 4, Rosh Hashanah, Yom Kippur, Thanksgiving, and New Year's Day. Bus: 5, 9, 14, 15, 30, or 45. Streetcar: F-line or Metro to Montgomery St.

Pier 24 Photography ★★ MUSEUM   At over 90,000 square feet, this former warehouse-turned-museum is one of the largest galleries in the world devoted exclusively to photography and video. But even with this amount of space, the main worry here seems to be that it will get too crowded. So, in an eccentric move (hey, this is San Francisco, after all), the Pilara Foundation, which owns the institution, allows only 20 people in at a time. That means if you don't make advance reservations online, you might not get a place during one of the 2-hour visiting slots (entry is free). And that would be a shame, because its exhibits tend to be dazzling. In the past, they've featured iconic works by Diane Arbus, Man Ray, and Walker Evans—though you might never know those were the photographers: in an attempt to make the viewers' experience of the art more immediate and unfettered, the gallery posts no wall text whatsoever. Instead viewers can borrow a rather loosely organized gallery guide to lead them through the mazelike space. It's rather like an art scavenger hunt.

At Pier 24 (near Harrison St. and the Embarcadero). ℰ **415/512-7424.** www.pier24.org. Free admission, but advanced reservations are required. Mon–Thurs 10am–5pm. Streetcar: F-Line.

San Francisco Museum of Modern Art (SFMOMA) ★★★ MUSEUM   Closed until early 2016 for renovations and a major expansion, some of the

When asking for directions in San Francisco, be careful not to confuse numerical avenues with numerical streets. Numerical avenues (Third *Avenue* and so on) are in the Richmond and Sunset districts in the western part of the city. Numerical streets (Third *Street* and so on) are south of Market Street in the eastern and southern parts of the city. Get this wrong and you'll be an hour late for dinner.

SFMOMA's collections have been temporarily set up at the Contemporary Jewish Museum (p. 109), and the Legion of Honor (p. 131).

151 Third St. (2 blocks south of Market St., across from Yerba Buena Gardens). ℰ **415/357-4000.** www.sfmoma.org.

Yerba Buena Center for the Arts ★ ARTS COMPLEX   The **YBCA,** which opened in 1993, is part of the large outdoor complex that takes up a few city blocks across the street from SFMOMA, and sits atop the underground Moscone Convention Center. It's the city's cultural facility, similar to New York's Lincoln Center but far more fun on the outside. The Center's two buildings offer music, theater, dance, and visual arts programs and shows. James Stewart Polshek designed the 755-seat theater, and Fumihiko Maki designed the Galleries and Arts Forum, which features three galleries and a space designed especially for dance. As for the shows at the galleries, they're often slightly more risky—or even risqué (local cartoonist R. Crumb mounted an R-rated show here in 2007). As a testament to its quality, the museum also mounts traveling versions of shows for other museums. Bonus: For the cost of viewing their curated monthly series of video or film screenings that specializes in experimental film and documentaries, you can get into YBCA's galleries for free.

701 Mission St. ℰ **415/978-ARTS** (2787). www.ybca.org. Admission for gallery $10 adults; $8 seniors, teachers, and students; free children 5 and under. Free to all 1st Tues of each month. Thurs–Sat noon–8pm; Sun noon–6pm; 1st Tues of the month noon–8pm; closed major holidays. Contact YBCA for times and admission to theater. Bus: 14, 30, or 45. Streetcar: Powell or Montgomery.

Yerba Buena Gardens ★ GARDENS   This 5-acre patch of grass and gardens is the centerpiece of Yerba Buena's cultural activity, and a great place to relax in the grass on a sunny day. The most dramatic outdoor piece is an emotional mixed-media memorial to Martin Luther King, Jr. Created by sculptor Houston Conwill, poet Estella Majozo, and architect Joseph De Pace, it features 12 panels, each inscribed with quotations from King, sheltered behind a 50-foot-high waterfall. There are also several actual garden areas here, including a Butterfly Garden, the Sister Cities Garden (highlighting flowers from the city's 13 sister cities), and the East Garden, blending Eastern and Western styles. Don't miss the view from the upper terrace, where old and new San Francisco come together in a clash of styles that's fascinating. May through October, Yerba Buena Arts & Events puts on a series of free outdoor festivals featuring dance, music, poetry, and more by the San Francisco Ballet, Opera, Symphony, and others.

Located on 2 square city blocks bounded by Mission, Folsom, Third, and Fourth sts. www.yerba buenagardens.com. Free admission. Daily 6am–10pm. Contact Yerba Buena Arts & Events: ℰ **415/543-1718** or www.ybgf.org for details about the free outdoor festivals. Bus: 14, 30, or 45.

FiDi (FINANCIAL DISTRICT)

Though most of the buildings in the FiDi are filled with brokers and bankers, along the beautiful waterfront visitors will find a few of San Francisco's best attractions.

The Exploratorium ★★★ MUSEUM Relocated in 2013 from dark, dated quarters at the Palace of Fine Arts to hip, concrete and glass digs on Pier 15, the "world's greatest science museum"—according to "Scientific American" magazine—is cooler than ever. This hands-on museum is all about demonstrating scientific concepts in a sneaky enough way that kids think they're just playing. Instead they learn about the properties of motion by swinging a pendulum through sand or watch a chicken's heart beating through a microscope onto an egg yolk. (*Warning:* that exhibit may turn them off to scrambled eggs). With myriad rooms loaded with things to play with, you can spend an entire afternoon here—and may want to plan on it, as it tends to get crowded and you'll likely need to wait your turn to play with bubbles or discover how sound travels.

If kids need to refuel before going back to tormenting their siblings, the cafe has good sandwiches, chowder, cookies, muffins, and drinks. Also, if you're looking for something fun to do at night, there's an adults-only event every first Thursday evening of the month.

Pier 15 (on the Embarcadero). ✆ **415/528-4444.** www.exploratorium.edu. Admission $25 adults; $19 seniors (65+), youth 6–17, visitors with disabilities, and college students with ID; free for children 5 and under. Tues–Sun 10am–5pm, Wed also open 6–10pm (for 18+). Parking across the street for $10 per hour. Streetcar: F-Line.

Ferry Building Marketplace ★★★ HISTORIC SITE/MARKET Set inside a restored, history-rich ferry terminal, this shrine to gourmet living features many boutiques shops run by spectacular food vendors: fresh-baked bread, exotic mushrooms, fancy chocolates, killer hamburgers, and the best Japanese fast food you'll ever have—it's all here. A twice-weekly **farmers market** (p. 170) surrounding the building is one of the city's best local scenes, where everyone from chefs to hungry diners converge to indulge in cooked foods and load up on fresh produce for the week.

Ferry Bldg., the Embarcadero (at Market St.). ✆ **415/983-9030.** www.ferrybuildingmarketplace. com. Most stores daily 10am–6pm; restaurant hours vary. Bus: 2, 12, 14, 21, 66, or 71. Streetcar: F-Line. BART: Embarcadero. Farmer's Market Thurs and Sat 10am–2pm right on the Embarcadero outside the building.

Wells Fargo History Museum ★ MUSEUM Surprisingly, the Wells Fargo Museum paints a vivid portrait of early California life by using the company's once-vital stagecoaches as a centerpiece. For generations, the Wells Fargo wagon was the West Coast's primary lifeline; if you didn't want to or couldn't afford to use it (a ticket from Omaha to Sacramento was $300), then you'd be forced to take a long boat trip around Cape Horn. The curators have done a good job bringing the past to life by including biographies of some of the grizzled drivers of the 1800s, posting plenty of old ads, allowing visitors to climb aboard a nine-seat wagon, furnishing a reproduction of a "mug book" of highway robbers from the 1870s, and even putting together a sort of CSI: Stagecoach re-created investigation revealing how they'd catch thieves after the fact. Wells Fargo has lost a lot of its cache in American culture; the Western theme fascinated kids in the 1950s but faded soon after. This well-assembled, two-story museum (budget about 45 min.) helps restore some of that imagination again. There's a free audio tour, too, although everything is so well signed you won't need it.

420 Montgomery St. (at California St.). ℃ **415/396-2619.** www.wellsfargohistory.com. Free admission. Mon–Fri 9am–5pm. Closed bank holidays. Bus: Any to Market St. Cable car: California St. line. BART: Montgomery St.

NORTH BEACH/TELEGRAPH HILL

As one of the city's oldest neighborhoods and the birthplace of the Beat generation, the history of North Beach and Telegraph Hill is as rich as the Italian pastries found in the numerous shops along Columbus Avenue.

Coit Tower ★ HISTORIC SITE In a city known for its great views and vantage points, Coit Tower is one of the best. Located atop Telegraph Hill, just east of North Beach, the round stone tower offers panoramic views of the city and the bay. Completed in 1933, the tower is the legacy of Lillie Hitchcock Coit, a wealthy eccentric who left San Francisco a $125,000 bequest "for the purpose of adding beauty to the city I have always loved." Though many believe the tower is a fire hose–shaped homage to San Francisco firefighters (Coit had been saved from a fire as a child and became a lifelong fan and mascot for Knickerbocker Engine Co. #5), the tower is merely an expression of Coit's esteem; a memorial to firefighters lies down below in Washington Square Park. Inside the base of the tower are impressive and slightly controversial (by 1930s standards) murals entitled "Life in California" and "1934," which were completed under the Depression-era Public Works of Art Project. Depicting California agriculture, industry, and even the state's leftist leanings (check out the socialist references in the library and on the newsstands), the murals are the collaborative effort of more than 25 artists, many of whom had studied under Mexican muralist Diego Rivera. The only bummer: The narrow street leading to the tower is often clogged with tourist traffic. If you can, find a parking spot in North Beach and hoof it. The Filbert and Greenwich steps leading up to Telegraph Hill are one of the most beautiful walks in the city (p. 4).

Telegraph Hill. ℃ **415/362-0808.** Admission is free to enter; elevator ride to the top is $7 adults, $5 seniors (65+) and youth 12–17, $2 children 5–11. Daily 10am–5:30pm. Closes 4:30pm in winter. Closed major holidays. Parking: Don't even think about it. Bus: 39.

NOB HILL

When the cable car started operating in 1873, this hill became the city's exclusive residential area. Newly wealthy residents who had struck it rich in the gold rush and the railroad boom (and were known by names such as the "Big Four" and the "Bonanza kings") built their mansions here, but they were almost all destroyed by the 1906 earthquake and fire. The only two surviving buildings are the Flood Mansion, which serves today as the **Pacific Union Club,** and the **Fairmont San Francisco** (p. 59), which was under construction when the earthquake struck and was damaged but not destroyed. Today, the sites of former mansions hold the city's luxury hotels—the InterContinental **Mark Hopkins** (p. 58), the **Stanford Court** (p. 58), the **Huntington Hotel** (p. 58), and spectacular **Grace Cathedral** (see below), which stands on the Crocker mansion site. Nob Hill is worth a visit if only to stroll around delightful

Huntington Park with its cherubic fountain (a copy of the Tartarughe fountain in Rome), attend a Sunday service at the cathedral, visit the **Cable Car Museum** (below), or ooh and ahh your way around the Fairmont's spectacular lobby.

Cable Car Museum ★★ MUSEUM   Here, in this warehouse that combines a museum experience with a real inside look at the inner machinations of the system, four mighty winding machines work the underground cables that propel the entire system, and if there's a cable break, this is where engineers splice it back together using some seriously medieval-looking implements. From decks overlooking the roaring machines, you'll see the cables shoot in from the streets, wind around huge wheels, and be sent back underground to carry more tourists up the city hills. You'll find out how the whole system works, including a look at the gripping mechanism that every car extends below the street level. I find it remarkable to think that nearly every American city of size once had systems just like this, but now only San Francisco maintains this antique (1873) but highly functional technology.

Don't miss the chance to go downstairs, under the entrance to the building, where, in the darkness, you can peer at the whirring 8-foot sheaves that hoist in the cables from their various journeys around the city. Now and then, a real cable car will stall as it attempts to navigate the intersection outside, where drivers have to let go of one cable and snag another, and a worker will have to drive out in a cart and give it a nudge.

1201 Mason St. (at Washington St.). *℃* **415/474-1887**. www.cablecarmuseum.org. Free admission. Apr–Sept daily 10am–6pm; Oct–Mar daily 10am–5pm. Closed Thanksgiving, Christmas, and New Year's Day. Cable car: Both Powell St. lines.

Grace Cathedral ★ RELIGIOUS SITE   Although this Nob Hill cathedral, designed by architect Lewis P. Hobart, appears to be made of stone, it is in fact constructed of reinforced concrete beaten to achieve a stonelike effect. Construction began on the site of the Crocker mansion in 1928 but was not completed until 1964. Among the more interesting features of the building are its stained-glass windows, particularly those by the French Loire studios and Charles Connick, depicting such modern figures as Thurgood Marshall, Robert Frost, and Albert Einstein; the replicas of Ghiberti's bronze "Doors of Paradise" at the east end; the series of religious murals completed in the 1940s by Polish artist John De Rosen; and the 44-bell carillon.

Where Grace really stands out, however, is in the compassion of its congregation, in no finer display than in the Interfaith AIDS Memorial Chapel that's located to the right as you enter. Two weeks before his own death from the disease in 1990, pop artist Keith Haring completed a triptych altarpiece called "The Life of Christ." The final 600-pound work in bronze and white gold patina sits in the chapel's place of honor. The church has been respecting and praying for AIDS victims ever since 1986, back when most people in our government were sitting on their hands even while this city was being devastated. A segment of the famous AIDS Memorial Quilt is displayed above the chapel; it's rotated on a regular basis with new pieces.

Next door at the associated Diocesan House (1055 Taylor St.), there's a small and pleasant sculpture garden and, inside, often a free art or photography exhibition.

Along with its unique ambience, Grace lifts spirits with services, musical performances (including organ recitals and evensong, or evening prayer, on many Sundays). A lovely place to pray, meditate, or simply look at the beautiful building, doors are open every day to everyone.

1100 California St. (btw. Taylor and Jones sts.). *℃* **415/749-6300.** www.gracecathedral.org. Bus: 1 or 27. Cable Car: Powell–Hyde or Powell–Mason.

CHINATOWN

The first Chinese immigrants—fleeing famine and the Opium Wars—came to San Francisco in the early 1800s to work as laborers and seek a better life promised by the "Gold Mountain." By 1851, 25,000 Chinese people were working in California, and most had settled in San Francisco's Chinatown. For the majority, the reality of life in California did not live up to the promise. First employed as workers in the gold mines during the gold rush, they later built the railroads, working as little more than slaves and facing constant prejudice. Yet the community, segregated in the Chinatown ghetto, thrived. Growing prejudice led to the Chinese Exclusion Act of 1882, which halted all Chinese immigration for 10 years and severely limited it thereafter. The Chinese Exclusion Act was not repealed until 1943. Chinese people were also denied the opportunity to buy homes outside the Chinatown ghetto until the 1950s. Today, San Francisco's Chinatown—the oldest in North America—is the largest outside of Asia. Although frequented by tourists, the area continues to cater to Chinese shoppers, who crowd the vegetable and herb markets, restaurants, and shops. Tradition runs deep here, and if you're lucky, through an open window you might hear women mixing mah-jongg tiles as they play the centuries-old game. (*Be warned:* You're likely to hear and see lots of spitting around here, too—it's part of local tradition.)

With dragons at its base, the ornate, jade-roofed **Chinatown Gate** at Grant Avenue and Bush Street marks the entry to Chinatown. Red lanterns hang across the street and dragons slither up lampposts. The heart of the neighborhood is Portsmouth Square, where you'll find locals playing board games or just sitting quietly. On the beautifully renovated Waverly Place, a street where the Chinese celebratory colors of red, yellow, and green are much in evidence, you'll find three **Chinese temples:** Jeng Sen (Buddhist and Taoist) at no. 146, Tien Hou (Buddhist) at no. 125, and Norras (Buddhist) at no. 109. If you enter, do so quietly so that you do not disturb those in prayer. A block west of Grant Avenue, **Stockton Street,** from 1000 to 1200, is the community's main shopping street, lined with grocers, fishmongers, tea sellers, herbalists, noodle parlors, and restaurants. Here, too, is the Buddhist Kong Chow Temple, at no. 855, above the Chinatown post office. Explore at your leisure. For a Chinatown walking tour, see p. 140, and visit www.sanfranciscochinatown.com for more information.

Golden Gate Fortune Cookie Factory ★ FACTORY TOUR   Not much has changed at this tiny Chinatown storefront since it opened in 1963. Three women sit at a conveyer belt, folding messages into thousands of fortune cookies—20,000 a day—as the manager invariably calls out to tourists, beckoning them to stroll in, watch the cookies being made, and buy a bag of 40 for about $3. You can purchase regular fortunes, unfolded flat cookies without fortunes, or, if you bring your own fortunes, they can create custom cookies.

56 Ross Alley. ℰ **415/781-3956.** Free admission. Daily 9am–7pm. Photos are 50¢.

UNION SQUARE

The square itself is in the city block bounded by Stockton, Post, Powell, and Geary streets. It's San Francisco's Rodeo Drive—blocks and blocks of some of the best hotels, restaurants, and shops to keep the serious connoisseur happy for days. When you tire of consuming, or your credit cards max out, grab a latte—or a glass of wine—at one of the cafes in the square; sit outside, relax, and people watch—the show is free, and always entertaining.

Glide Memorial United Methodist Church ★★ RELIGIOUS SITE   Back in the 1960s, Glide Memorial's legendary pastor, Texas-born Cecil Williams, took over this 1931 church and began his famed, 90-minute "celebration" services. Williams has since retired the pastorship but he is usually on hand anyway, like a kindly high school principal, and his services are a little like a late night TV talk show, accompanied by a skilled six-piece jazz band (Leonard Bernstein was a fan, and Quincy Jones still is), backed by a 100-plus-voice choir (the Glide Ensemble, and man they're good). He's a solid American institution, counting Oprah Winfrey, Maya Angelou, and Robin Williams among his fans, and having appeared by himself in the Will Smith movie "The Pursuit of Happyness." His wife, Janice Mirikitani, a well-known city poet, has also been working at the church since 1969. Their messages, repeated throughout the service, are of diversity, compassion, ending racism, brotherhood, and acceptance, and it doesn't take long before the crowd is on its feet, clapping, swaying, and praying. The church operates 87 entities designed to help others in a city that desperately needs such outreach, from help with housing and health care to jobs training. Don't miss a service here; there's nothing else like it, and it's impossible to feel unwelcome. Services are at 9 and 11am, and don't show up with less than 15 minutes to spare or you will almost certainly have to participate by TV from a fellowship hall, and that would be a shame.

330 Ellis St. (at Taylor St.). ✆ **415/674-6000.** www.glide.org. Services Sun at 9 and 11am. Bus: 27. Streetcar: Powell. BART: Powell.

The Pacific Heritage Museum ★ MUSEUM   If Asian art is an interest for you, the grandiosely named Pacific Heritage Museum may have something modest to offer. Its several hushed rooms mount displays of artworks by Asian-descended artists, both living and dead, but for me, the most interesting aspect of the place is the basement exhibit, which uncovers the structure of the Subtreasury Building that stood in this spot from 1875 and was destroyed after the '06 quake. Of course, the palatial Asian Art Museum (p. 117) is the most elaborate repository in town for this sort of work, and shouldn't be missed.

608 Commercial St. (at Montgomery St.). ✆ **415/399-1124.** Free admission. Tues–Sat 10am–4pm. Bus: 1, 8X, or 12.

MISSION DISTRICT

This vibrant, cultural neighborhood gets its name from the oldest building in San Francisco, the haunting Mission Dolores (see below). Once inhabited almost entirely by Irish immigrants, the Mission District has long been the center of the city's Latino community. Although now they seem to be quickly being priced out by the young, well-to-do residents because the Mission, as gritty as it is, is by far the hippest place to live in San Francisco. It's an oblong area stretching roughly from 14th to 30th streets between Potrero Avenue on the east and Dolores Avenue on the west. The heart of the Latin community lies along 24th Street between Van Ness and Potrero avenues, where dozens of excellent ethnic restaurants, bakeries, bars, and specialty stores attract people from all over the city. The area surrounding 16th Street and Valencia Street is a hotbed for impressive—and often impressively cheap—vintage stores, artisan coffee shops, and restaurants and bars catering to the city's hipsters. While the area has been undergoing gentrification for years, the neighborhood can still be a little sketchy night, especially around BART stations located at 16th and 24th streets.

For insight into the community, visit **Precita Eyes Mural Arts Center,** 2981 24th St., between Harrison and Alabama streets (✆ **415/285-2287;** www.precitaeyes.org;), to take the 2-hour tour (Sat–Sun at 1:30pm), where you'll see a slide show covering the history of the murals that cover many walls in the area and the mural painting process. After the slide show, your guide will show you murals on a 6-block walk. Group tours are available during the week by appointment. The tour costs $20 adults, $10 seniors (65+) and college students, $6 youth (12–17), $3 under 12.

Another sign of cultural life in the neighborhood is the progressive **Theatre Rhinoceros** (www.therhino.org), in operation since 1977 (see p. 177).

Mission Dolores ★★ RELIGIOUS SITE   The history of this church, more formally known as Misíon San Francisco de Asís, is the history of the early city, and there is no other surviving building that is more intrinsic to the early days of the town's formation. The tale goes back to the storied summer of 1776, when this site, then an uninhabited grove, was selected for a mission in a network that ran up and down the coast. Its first Mass was celebrated under a temporary shelter. The current building dates from 1791 and is the oldest in town. For such a rich representative of a city that has lost so much of its history, this place is a rare glimpse into the not-so-distant past and the troubled origins of California. This adobe-walled building, with its 4-foot-thick walls and rear garden, is hushed and transporting, and a precious survivor from California's colonial days. It's also almost entirely original, having survived the 1906 quake by dint of good old-fashioned craftsmanship, and as you roam, you'll encounter gorgeous altars brought from Mexico during the days of the Founding Fathers. The trusses, lashed together with rawhide, are made of redwood, and in 1916, they were reinforced with steel.

Following the chapel and the sanctuary, the tour's path visits a modest museum in the back before proceeding outside. In its heyday, the mission was home to some 4,000 people, but of course, most of that land was long ago sold off; look for the diorama, built in 1939, for a clearer picture of how it was all laid out. The back garden contains the graves of California's first governor and the city's first mayor, as well as, shockingly, the bodies of at least 5,000 Indians who died "helping" (read: slaving for) the mission. Sad to say, while few people know about the mass extinction, the mission is famous for the one grave that isn't there: The headstone of Carlotta Valdes, which Kim Novak visits in the movie "Vertigo" (1958) was a prop. Around the same time (1952), the compound was named a Basilica, an honorary Church of the Pope, and in 1987, Pope John Paul II swung by for a visit.

16th St. (at Dolores St.). 🕐 **415/621-8203.** www.missiondolores.org. Suggested donation $5 adults, $3 seniors and children. May–Oct 9am–4:30pm; Nov–Apr 9am–4pm; Closed Thanksgiving, Easter, Christmas, and New Year's Day. Bus: 22. Streetcar: J.

Dolores Park ★★   If it's a sunny day and you want to hang with the locals, head to this hilly 16-acre park. Blanketed with lush green lawns and dotted with palm trees, a soccer field, tennis courts, a basketball court, a playground, and great views, it can be quite the scene of modern bohemia and it's a fantastic place to relax and take in good San Francisco vibes.

Bounded by Church, Dolores, 18th, and 20th sts. sfrecpark.org/destination/mission-dolores-park. Streetcar: J.

ALAMO SQUARE

The Painted Ladies of Alamo Square ★   San Francisco's collection of Victorian houses, known as the **Painted Ladies,** is one of the city's most famous assets. Most of the 14,000 extant structures date from the second half of the 19th century and are private residences. Spread throughout the city, many have been beauti-fully restored and ornately painted. The small area bordered by Divisadero Street on the west, Golden Gate Avenue on the north, Webster Street on the east, and Fell Street on the south—about 10 blocks west of the Civic Center—has one of the city's greatest concentrations of Painted Ladies. One of the most famous views of San Francisco—seen on postcards and posters all around the city—depicts sharp-edged Financial District skyscrapers behind a row of Victorians. This fantastic juxtaposition can be seen from Alamo Square, in the center of the historic district, at Fulton and Steiner streets. A **Victorian Homes Historical Walking Tour** (p. 134) is a great way to stroll past, and learn about, more than 200 restored Victorian beauties. For a peek inside, check out the **Haas-Lilienthal House.** Built in 1886, this home is filled with period pieces and depicts a slice of life back in a more genteel time. All visitors must take a docent-led tour, which lasts about an hour. Reservations are not required.

Haas-Lilienthal House, 2007 Franklin St. (at Washington St.). ℂ **415/441-3000.** www.sfheritage. org. 1-hr. guided tour $8 adults, $5 seniors and children 12 and under. Wed and Sat noon–3pm; Sun 11am–4pm. (**Note:** Some Saturdays the house is closed for private functions, so call to con-firm.) Bus: 1, 10, 12, or 47. Cable car: California.

CIVIC CENTER

Filled with dramatic Beaux Arts buildings, showy open spaces, one of the best muse-ums in the city, and a number of performing art venues, the Civic Center neighborhood has always made me think of a European city.

Asian Art Museum ★★ MUSEUM The largest collection of Asian art in the United States, this stellar museum boasts over 18,000 treasures from Asian countries as varied as China, Tibet, India, and The Middle East. With items spanning a 6,000-year history, it's also the largest museum of its kind in this hemisphere. The concept of a museum devoted solely to Asian culture began in 1960 when Chicago Industrialist, Avery Brundage, agreed to donate his personal collection of Asian art to the city of San Francisco. Over time, the collection outgrew its space in a wing of the de Young Museum, and Italian architect, Gae Aulenti (famed for the Musee d'Orsay in Paris and the Palazzo Grassi in Venice), was hired to convert San Francisco's former main library into a contemporary showcase. Skylights, glass, and concrete hold three stories of treasures sorted by country. To better understand what you're seeing, I highly recom-mend taking a free docent-led tour, on which you'll learn about the role of the elephant as the ancient SUV of India, the reason jade can't be chiseled, and, while looking at a Koran from the 14th century, find out what the word "Koran" means. A highlight: one of the only collections of Sikh art in the world. With items of different mediums—including furniture, statues, clothing, paintings, jewelry, and sculpture—the pieces are varied and intriguing, even for kids. The collections change regularly and there is usu-ally a visiting exhibition; the $5 audio tour is well worth the price. The museum store has handsome gifts for surprisingly good prices, and Café Asia serves a fabulous Asian chicken salad.

200 Larkin St. (btw. Fulton and McAllister sts.). ℂ **415/581-3500.** www.asianart.org. Admission $12 adults, $8 seniors, students (with college ID), youths 13–17, free for children 12 and under. Free 1st Sun of the month. Tues–Wed and Fri–Sun 10am–5pm; Thurs 10am–9pm. Closed Thanksgiving, Christmas, and New Year's Day. Bus: All Market St. buses. Streetcar: Civic Center.

City Hall ★★ HISTORIC SITE San Francisco's Beaux Arts City Hall was not built to be just another city hall. Having crumbled during the '06 quake, residents

6 | free CULTURE

To beef up attendance and give indigent folk like us travel writers a break, almost all of San Francisco's art galleries and museums are open free to the public 1 day of the month, and several never charge admission. You can use the following list to plan your week around the museums' free-day schedules; see the individual attraction listings in this chapter for more information on each museum.

FIRST TUESDAY

o Yerba Buena Center for the Arts (p. 110)
o de Young Museum (p. 123)
o Legion of Honor (p. 131)
o Contemporary Jewish Museum (p. 109)

FIRST SUNDAY

o Asian Art Museum (p. 117)

FREE RANDOM DAYS (CHECK INDIVIDUAL WEBSITES)

o Exploratorium (p. 111)
o California Academy of Sciences (p. 123)

ALWAYS FREE

o Cable Car Museum (p. 113)
o Glide Memorial United Methodist Church (p. 115)
o Musee Mechanique (p. 105)
o Maritime National Historical Park & Museum ($5 to board ships; p. 106)
o Wells Fargo History Museum (p. 111)

---

wanted to show the world that San Francisco was still an American powerhouse, so this current City Hall was designed (1915) to be as handsome, proud, and imposing as a government capital building. In fact, most visitors are shocked to learn that its mighty rotunda is *larger* than the one atop Congress in Washington, DC. (Only four domes are bigger: the Vatican, Florence's Duomo, St. Paul's in London, and Les Invalides in Paris). Should another horrible earthquake strike, a 1999 seismic retrofit saw to it that the structure can swing up to 27 inches in any direction; if you look closely at the stairs entering the building, you'll notice they don't actually touch the sidewalk because the entire building is on high-tech springs that had to be slipped, two by two, beneath a structure that already existed and was conducting daily business.

City Hall's most imposing attraction is indeed its fabulously ornate rotunda, a blend of marble (on the lower reaches) and painted plaster (high up), swept theatrically by a grand staircase where countless couples pose daily for their "just married" shots right after tying the knot (Fri is the busiest day for that). You've probably seen this staircase before. It featured in one of the final shots of "Raiders of the Lost Ark" (1981) as a stand-in for the U.S. Capitol. It was here, in 2004, that thousands of gay couples queued to sign up for their weddings; the first couple in line was an octogenarian lesbian couple that had been together for 51 years. Also, in 1954, Joe DiMaggio and Marilyn Monroe were married here and posed for photos on these steps. Not all the famous happenings at City Hall have been so hopeful. In 1978, the famous assassination of Mayor George Moscone and city Supervisor Harvey Milk occurred in two places on the second floor; the resulting trial, in which their killer got a light sentence because, as his lawyers argued, he was high on junk food (the so-called Twinkie Defense) became a lynchpin of outrage for the gay rights movement. In the rotunda, look up: Sculptures of Adam and Eve can be seen holding up the official seal of the city.

Across the hall at the top of the grand staircase, the sumptuous Chamber of the Board of Supervisors is worth a peek if it's open; its walls of Manchurian oak, plaster ceiling created to mimic wood, and doors hand-carved by French and Italian craftsmen make this one of the most opulent rooms in the city. Sunshine laws dictate that it must be open to the public unless in a special session, so pop in for a gander. Better yet, drop in during one of its colorful meetings.

Also check out the Light Court off the main rotunda on the ground floor, where you'll find the head of a statue of the Goddess of Progress; she was atop the prior City Hall, in fuller figure, but this is all that survives. The light bulb sockets in her hair were later additions. The well-done 45-minute tours (Mon–Fri at 10am, noon, and 2pm) are free. Reservations are not needed for groups less than eight people.

Civic Center 1 Dr. Carlton B. Goodlett Place (Polk St. btw. McAllister and Grove sts.). ⓒ **415/554-6139.** www.sfgov.org/cityhall. City Hall open to the public daily Mon–Fri 8am–8pm, closed major holidays. Parking: metered or CityPark lot across the street. Bart: Civic Center.

RUSSIAN HILL

This quiet residential area with stunning views of the bay is home to one of the best-known streets in the world.

Lombard Street ★ ICON   Known (erroneously) as the "crookedest street in the world," this whimsically winding block of Lombard Street between Hyde and Leavenworth streets draws thousands of visitors each year (much to the chagrin of neighborhood residents, most of whom would prefer to block off the street to tourists). The angle of the street is so steep that the road has to snake back and forth to make a descent possible. The brick-paved street zigzags around the residences' bright flower gardens, which explode with color during warmer months. This short stretch of Lombard Street is one-way, downhill, and fun to drive. Take the curves slowly and in low gear, and expect a wait during the weekend. Save your snapshots for the bottom where, if you're lucky, you can find a parking space and take a few quintessential pics. You can also take staircases (without curves) up or down on either side of the street. In truth, most locals don't understand what the fuss is all about. But it is a classic photo op. *Fun fact:* Vermont Street, between 20th and 22nd streets in Potrero Hill, is even more crooked, but not nearly as picturesque.

JAPANTOWN

More than 12,000 citizens of Japanese descent (1.5% of the city's population) live in San Francisco, or Soko, as the Japanese who first emigrated here often called it. After the earthquake in 1906, SoMa became a light industrial and warehouse area, and the largest Japanese concentration took root in the Western Addition between Van Ness Avenue and Fillmore Street, the site of today's Japantown, now over 100 years old. By 1940, it covered 30 blocks. In 1913, the Alien Land Law was passed, depriving Japanese Americans of the right to buy land. From 1924 to 1952, the United States banned Japanese immigration. During World War II, the U.S. government froze Japanese bank accounts, interned community leaders, and removed 112,000 Japanese Americans—two-thirds of them citizens—to camps in California, Utah, and Idaho. Japantown was emptied of Japanese people, and war workers took their place. Upon their release in 1945, the Japanese found their old neighborhood occupied. Most of them resettled in the Richmond and Sunset districts; some returned to Japantown, but it had shrunk to a mere 6 or so blocks.

If you're walking around San Francisco—especially Telegraph Hill or Russian Hill—and you suddenly hear lots of loud squawking and screeching overhead, look up. You're most likely witnessing a fly-by of the city's famous green flock of wild parrots. These are the scions of a colony that started out as a few wayward house pets—mostly cherry-headed Conures, which are indigenous to South America—who found each other, and bred. Years later they've become hundreds strong, traveling in chatty packs through the city (with a few parakeets along for the ride), and stopping to rest on tree branches and delight residents who have come to consider them part of the family. To learn just how special these birds are to the city, read the book "The Wild Parrots of Telegraph Hill," or see the heartwarming movie of the same name.

Today, the community's notable sights include the **Buddhist Church of San Francisco,** 1881 Pine St. at Octavia Street (www.bcsfweb.org); the **Konko-Kyo Church of San Francisco,** 1909 Bush St. (at Laguna St.); the **Sokoji–Soto Zen Buddhist Temple,** 1691 Laguna St. (at Sutter St.); **Nihonmachi Mall,** 1700 block of Buchanan Street between Sutter and Post streets, which contains two steel fountains by Ruth Asawa; and the **Japan Center** (see below) a Japanese-oriented shopping mall occupying 3 square blocks bounded by Post, Geary, Laguna, and Fillmore streets. At its center stands the five-tiered **Peace Pagoda,** designed by world-famous Japanese architect Yoshiro Taniguchi "to convey the friendship and goodwill of the Japanese to the people of the United States." Surrounding the pagoda, through a network of arcades, squares, and bridges, you can explore dozens of shops featuring everything from TVs and *tansu* chests to pearls, bonsai, and kimonos. **Kabuki Springs & Spa** (see the "Urban Renewal" box below) is one of the center's most famous tenants. But locals also head here for its numerous authentic restaurants, teahouses, shops, and the crazy-expensive Sundance multiplex movie theater. There is often live entertainment on summer weekends and during spring's cherry blossom festival, including Japanese music and dance performances, tea ceremonies, flower-arranging demonstrations, martial-arts presentations, and other cultural events. The **Japan Center** (© 415/922-7765) is open daily from 10am to midnight, although most shops close much earlier. To get there, take bus no. 2, or 3 (exit at Buchanan and Sutter sts.) or no. 22 or 38 (exit at the northeast corner of Geary Blvd. and Fillmore St.). For a complete list of Japantown events, shops, and restaurants, go to www.japantown.org.

HAIGHT–ASHBURY

Few of San Francisco's neighborhoods are as varied—or as famous—as Haight-Ashbury. Walk along Haight Street, and you'll encounter everything from drug-dazed drifters begging for change to an armada of the city's funky-trendy shops, clubs, and cafes. Turn anywhere off Haight, and instantly you're among the clean-cut, young urban professionals who can afford the steep rents in this hip 'hood. The result is an interesting mix of well-to-do professionals and well-screw-you aging flower children, former Dead-heads, homeless people, and throngs of tourists who try not to stare as they wander through this human zoo. Some find it depressing, others find it fascinating, but everyone agrees that it ain't what it was in the free-lovin' psychedelic Summer

Relaxation and rejuvenation are raised to an art form in the City by the Bay. Here are five spas you may want to try, for a massage, facial, or soak.

o **Kabuki Springs & Spa,** 1750 Geary Blvd. (☎ **415/922-6000;** www.kabukisprings.com), was once an authentic, traditional Japanese bathhouse. After the Joie de Vivre hotel group bought and renovated it, it became more of a Pan-Asian spa with a focus on wellness. Access to the deep ceramic communal tubs—at $25 per person—private baths, and shiatsu massages remain. The spa is open from 10am to 10pm daily; joining the baths is an array of massages and Ayurvedic treatments, body scrubs, wraps, and facials, which cost from $65 to $200.

o **Spa Radiance,** 3011 Fillmore St. (☎ **415/346-6281;** www.sparadiance.com), is an utterly San Francisco spa experience due to its unassuming Victorian surroundings and its wonderfully luxurious treatments such as facials, body treatments, massages, manicures, pedicures, Brazilian waxing,

spray-tanning, and makeup application by in-house artists.

o A more posh and modern experience is yours at **International Orange,** 2044 Fillmore St., second floor (☎ **415/563-5000;** www.internationalorange.com). The self-described spa yoga lounge offers just what it says in a chic white-on-white space on the boutique-shopping stretch of Fillmore Street. They've also got a great selection of clothing and face and body products, including one of my personal favorites, locally made In Fiore body balms.

o In the St. Regis Hotel, **Remède Spa,** 125 Third St. (☎ **415/284-4060;** www.remede.com), has two whole floors dedicated to melting away all your cares, worries, kinks, and knots. Expect wonderful massage, facials, manis and pedis, waxes, and more.

o A few doors down in the W Hotel is the city's outpost of New York's **Bliss Spa,** 181 Third St., fourth floor (☎ **877/862-5477;** www.blissworld.com). The hip version to St. Regis's chic, it offers a similar spa menu, including wedding specialties.

of Love. Is it still worth a visit? Not if you are here for a day or two, but it's certainly worth an excursion on longer trips, if only to visit the trend-setting vintage clothing stores on the street (p. 163).

THE CASTRO

Castro Street, between Market and 18th streets, is the center of what is widely considered the world's first, largest, and best-known gay community, as well as a lovely neighborhood teeming with shops, restaurants, bars, and other institutions that cater to the area's colorful residents. Among the landmarks on Castro are **Harvey Milk Plaza, The GLBT History Museum** (see below) and the **Castro Theatre** (www.castrotheatre.com), a 1930s movie palace with a Wurlitzer organ.

The gay community began to move here in the late 1960s and early 1970s from a neighborhood called Polk Gulch, which still has a number of gay-oriented bars and stores. Castro is one of the liveliest streets in the city and the perfect place to shop for gifts and revel in free-spiritedness. Go to www.mycastro.com for local events, and www.castromerchants.com for a list of specialty shops. Also, check out www.sanfrancisco.gaycities.com, another resource for local gay bars, restaurants, and events. www.nighttours.com/sanfrancisco has an interactive map listing gay clubs, saunas, cruise bars and, cruising areas.

The GLBT History Museum ★ MUSEUM   North America's first full-fledged gay history museum, set in a former storefront in the Castro, is tiny but formidable, and ultimately quite moving. Recent exhibits have included quirky recaps of 25 years of queer history, with profiles of the first lesbians to marry legally in California (including the pantsuits they wore); a section on the importance of gay bars for the community (illustrated by a marvelously decorative collection of matchbooks); an exhibit on the gay-rights movement (with Harvey Milk's sunglasses and the kitchen table he politicked at); and displays about gays in the military, hate crimes, AIDS, and gays of color, among other topics. The museum is not appropriate for children—"We want to show how the erotic pleasure can become political power," co-curator Amy Sueyoshi divulges—but should intrigue anyone with an interest in contemporary history.

4127 18th St. (btw. Castro and Collingwood sts.). ☏ **415-621-1107.** www.glbhistory.org. Admission $5, free the 1st Wed of each month. Mon and Wed–Sat 11am–7pm, Sun noon–5pm. Streetcar: F-Line.

GOLDEN GATE PARK ★★★

Everybody loves **Golden Gate Park**—people, dogs, birds, frogs, turtles, bison, trees, bushes, and flowers. Literally, everything feels unified here in San Francisco's enormous arboreal front yard. Conceived in the 1860s and 1870s, this great 1,017-acre landmark, which stretches inland from the Pacific coast, took shape in the 1880s and 1890s thanks to the skill and effort of John McLaren, a Scot who arrived in 1887 and began landscaping the park. When he embarked on the project, sand dunes and wind presented enormous challenges. But McLaren had developed a new strain of grass called "sea bent," which he planted to hold the sandy soil along the Firth of Forth back home, and he used it to anchor the soil here, too. Every year the ocean eroded the western fringe of the park, and ultimately he solved this problem, too, though it took him 40 years to build a natural wall, putting out bundles of sticks that the tides covered with sand. He also built the two windmills that stand on the western edge of the park to pump water for irrigation. Under his brilliant eye, the park took shape.

Today the park consists of hundreds of gardens and attractions connected by wooded paths and paved roads. While many worthy sites are clearly visible, there are infinite treasures that are harder to find, so pick up information at **McLaren Lodge and Park Headquarters** (at Stanyan and Fell sts.; ☏ **415/831-2700**) if you want to find the hidden gems. It's open daily 8am to 5pm and offers park maps for $3. Of the dozens of special gardens in the park, most recognized are **McLaren Memorial Rhododendron Dell,** the **Rose Garden, Botanical Gardens,** and, at the western edge of the park, a springtime array of thousands of tulips and daffodils around the **Dutch windmill.** In addition to the highlights described in this section, the park contains lots of recreational facilities: tennis courts; baseball, soccer, and polo fields; a golf course;

riding stables; and fly-casting pools. The Strawberry Hill boathouse handles boat rentals. The park is also the home of the **de Young Museum** (see below) Across from the de Young, you will find the **California Academy of Sciences** (also below).

To get around inside the park on weekends and public holidays, a free shuttle service is provided. For a complete list of maps, attractions, gardens, and events visit **www.golden-gate-park.com.** You can enter the park at Kezar Drive, an extension of Fell Street; bus riders can take no. 5, 28, 29, 33, 37 or 71.

Park Highlights

California Academy of Sciences ★★ MUSEUM   A Golden Gate Park tenant for over 150 years and treated to a stunning $500-million renovation completed in 2008, this fantastic family-friendly museum is a spectacular mélange of aquarium, planetarium, natural history museum, and more, with plenty of cool hands-on things for kids to do and see. The planetarium, access to which is included in admission, is the largest digital planetarium in the world. In the nature section, by the entrance, the main attraction is Claude, a formidable albino alligator. Up a circular ramp, four stories high, is a rainforest where brightly colored frogs play peek-a-boo while butterflies flit around your head. Below, an impressive collection of jellyfish glides its way around large, circular tanks. Topping it all off, literally, is a 2½-acre rooftop garden with 1.7 million plants and flowers. The only thing to complain about at the Academy of Science is the painfully steep entrance fee.

55 Concourse Dr., Golden Gate Park. ⓒ **415/379-8000.** www.calacademy.org. Admission $35 adults, $30 seniors (65+), youth 12–17, students (with ID), $25 children 4–11, free for children 3 and under. Free admission on random Sun, watch the website. Mon–Sat 9:30am–5pm; Sun 11am–5pm. Closed Thanksgiving and Christmas. Bus: 5, or 44. Streetcar: N-Judah.

Conservatory of Flowers ★★ CONSERVATORY   Opened to the public in 1879, this glorious Victorian glass structure is the oldest existing public conservatory in the Western Hemisphere. But it's not just a place of historic interest: the Conservatory is a cutting-edge horticultural destination with over 1,700 species of plants, including rare tropical flora of the Congo, Philippines, and beyond. In fact, this is one of only four public institutions in the U.S. to house a highland tropics exhibit. Its five galleries also host species from the lowland tropics, aquatic plants, the largest Dracula orchid collection in the world, and special exhibits. It doesn't take long to visit, but make a point of staying awhile; outside there are good sunny spots for people watching as well as paths leading to impressive gardens. If you're around during summer and fall, don't miss the Dahlia Garden to the right of the entrance in the center of what was once a carriage roundabout—it's an explosion of colorful Dr. Seuss–like blooms.

100 John F Kennedy Dr., Golden Gate Park ⓒ **415/831-2090.** www.conservatoryofflowers.org. Admission $8 adults; $5 youth (12-17), seniors (65+), and students with ID; $2 for children 5 to 11; and free for children 4 and under and for all visitors the 1st Tues of the month. Tues–Sun 10am–4:30pm.

de Young Museum ★★ MUSEUM   Founded in 1894 for the California Midwinter International Exposition, the de Young evolved from what was originally an eclectic collection of exotic oddities into a quality showcase of fine arts from around the world, many pieces of which were donated by the Rockefeller Family, and moved into a world-class custom-designed permanent home in 2005. Permanent displays featuring North American art, and works from Oceania and Africa, have helped make

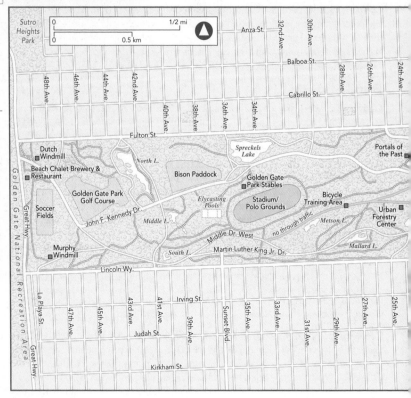

the de Young one of the most-visited fine arts museums in North America, and exciting temporary exhibits and evening wine and music events keep even locals coming back for more.

Be sure to climb the 144-foot tower to the observation floor for fantastic panoramic views of the city. As a bonus, your de Young admission ticket can be used for same day entrance at the Legion of Honor (p. 131).

50 Hagiwara Tea Garden Dr. (inside Golden Gate Park, 2 blocks from the park entrance at Eighth Ave. and Fulton). 📞 **415/750-3600.** https://deyoung.famsf.org. Admission adults $10, seniors (65+) $7, youths 13–17 and college students with ID $6, children 12 and under free. Free 1st Tues of the month. $2 discount for Muni riders with Fast Pass or transfer receipt. Tues–Sun 9:30am–5pm (Fri until 8:45pm [except Dec]). Closed New Year's Day, Thanksgiving, and Christmas. Bus: 5, 21, 44, or 71.

Japanese Tea Garden ★ GARDEN John McLaren, the man who began landscaping Golden Gate Park, hired Makoto Hagiwara, a wealthy Japanese landscape designer, to further develop this garden originally created for the 1894 Midwinter Exposition. It's a quiet, albeit crowded, place with cherry trees, shrubs, and bonsai crisscrossed by winding paths and high-arched bridges over pools of water. Focal points and places for contemplation include the massive bronze Buddha (cast in Japan

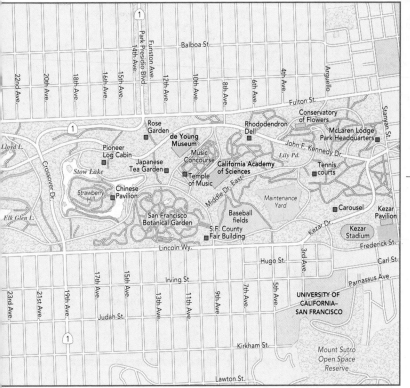

in 1790 and donated by the Gump family), the Buddhist wooden pagoda, and the Drum Bridge, which, reflected in the water, looks as though it completes a circle. It's fun to order some snacks and tea and enjoy them overlooking the grounds, although prices are a little expensive.

75 Hagiwara Tea Garden Dr. Golden Gate Park. ℂ **415/752-1171.** www.japaneseteagardensf. com. Daily 9am–6pm (4:45pm in winter months). Mon, Wed, Fri free admission before 10am, otherwise $7 adult, $5 senior (65+) and youth (12–17), $2 child (5–11), free 4 and under.

San Francisco Botanical Gardens at Strybing Arboretum ★ GARDEN
More than 8,000 plant species grow here on 55 acres, among them some ancient plants in a special "primitive garden," rare species, and a grove of California redwoods. Check the website for a variety of free docent-led tours.

1199 9th Ave., Golden Gate Park ℂ **415/661-1316** or visit www.strybing.org. Admission is $7 for adults, $5 for youth (12–17) and seniors (65+), $2 children (5–11), free 4 and under, $15 Family (2 adults and all children under 17). Daily 9am–6pm (5pm in winter).

Strawberry Hill/Stow Lake ★ NATURE AREA
One of the sweetest ways to spend a few hours, and a favorite with kids, is to come here, rent a boat, and cruise around the circular Stow Lake as painters create still lifes, joggers pass along the

ESPECIALLY FOR kids

San Francisco is one of the best cities in the world to visit with children. While some kids might want to visit our fine arts museums and cultural sights, for the rest of them we offer burping sea lions, an underwater restaurant, and a grumpy old man in Chinatown passing out fortune cookies and threats. The following attractions appeal to all kids:

o **Alcatraz Island** (p. 102)
o **Aquarium of the Bay** (p. 104)
o **Cable Car Museum** (p. 113)
o **Cable Cars** (p. 98)
o **California Academy of Sciences** (p. 123)
o **Chinatown Walk** (p. 140)
o **The Exploratorium** (p. 111)
o **Forbes Island Restaurant** (p. 84)
o **Ghirardelli Ice Cream** (p. 104)
o **Golden Gate Bridge** (p. 127)
o **Golden Gate Park** (p. 122)
o **Golden Gate Fortune Cookie Factory** (p. 114)
o **Fisherman's Wharf** (p. 99)

o **Maritime National Historical Park** (p. 106)
o **Metreon Entertainment Center** (p. 26)
o **Musee Mechanique** (p. 105)
o **Pier 39 and the California Sea Lions** (p. 107)
o **Ripley's Believe It or Not** (p. 99)
o **San Francisco Zoo** (p. 132)
o **Tcho Chocolate Factory Tour** (p. 169)
o **Uncle Gee in Chinatown** (p. 144)
o **Walt Disney Family Museum** (p. 128)
o **Yerba Buena Ice Skating, Bowling & Children's Creativity Center** (p. 110)

The website www.sfrecpark.org is an excellent resource for recreation centers, pool and parks; www.sfkids.org is another good resource for child-friendly activities.

grassy shoreline, ducks waddle around waiting to be fed, and turtles sunbathe on rocks and logs. Strawberry Hill, the 430-foot-high artificial island and highest point in the park, lies at the center of Stow Lake, and is a perfect picnic spot that boasts a bird's-eye view of San Francisco and the bay. It also has a waterfall and a peace pagoda. For the **Stow Lake Boathouse,** call ℭ **415/386-2531.** Boat rentals are available daily 10am to 4pm, weather permitting; you can rent a rowboats ($20/hour), pedal boats ($25/hour), and electric boats ($34/hour) with a $5 deposit, and there's a snack shop there, too.

50 Stow Lake Dr., Golden Gate Park. ℭ **415/386-2531.** www.stowlakeboathouse.com. Mon–Fri 10am–7pm, Sat–Sun 9am–7pm (weather permitting).

THE PRESIDIO

In October 1994, the Presidio passed from the U.S. Army to the National Park Service and became one of a handful of urban national parks that combines historical, architectural, and natural elements in one giant arboreal expanse. (It also contains a previously private golf course and a home for George Lucas's production company.) The 1,491-acre area incorporates a variety of terrain—coastal scrub, dunes, and prairie grasslands—that shelter many rare plants and more than 200 species of birds, some of which nest here.

This military outpost has a 220-year history, from its founding in September 1776 by the Spanish under José Joaquin Moraga to its closure in 1994. From 1822 to 1846, the property was in Mexican hands.

During the war with Mexico, U.S. forces occupied the fort, and in 1848, when California became part of the Union, it was formally transferred to the United States. When San Francisco suddenly became an important urban area during the gold rush, the U.S. government installed battalions of soldiers and built Fort Point to protect the entry to the harbor. It expanded the post during the Civil War and during the Indian Wars of the 1870s and 1880s. By the 1890s, the Presidio was no longer a frontier post but a major base for U.S. expansion into the Pacific. During the war with Spain in 1898, thousands of troops camped here in tent cities awaiting shipment to the Philippines, and the Army General Hospital treated the sick and wounded. By 1905, 12 coastal defense batteries were built along the headlands. In 1914, troops under the command of Gen. John Pershing left here to pursue Pancho Villa and his men.

The Presidio expanded during the 1920s, when Crissy Army Airfield (the first airfield on the West Coast) was established, but the major action was seen during World War II, after the attack on Pearl Harbor. Soldiers dug foxholes along nearby beaches, and the Presidio became the headquarters for the Western Defense Command. Some 1.75 million men were shipped out from nearby Fort Mason to fight in the Pacific; many returned to the Presidio's hospital, whose capacity peaked 1 year at 72,000 patients. In the 1950s, the Presidio served as the headquarters for the Sixth U.S. Army and a missile defense post, but its role slowly shrank. In 1972, it was included in new legislation establishing the Golden Gate National Recreation Area; in 1989, the Pentagon decided to close the post and transfer it to the National Park Service.

Today, the area encompasses more than 470 historic buildings, a scenic golf course, a national cemetery, the **Walt Disney Family Museum** (see below), several good restaurants, an inn, miles of hiking and biking trails, scenic overlooks, beaches, picnic sites, and a variety of terrain and natural habitats. The National Park Service offers docent and ranger-led tours, as well as a free shuttle called "PresidioGo." For more information, call the **Presidio Visitors Center** at ✆ **415/561-4323,** or visit www.nps. gov/prsf. Take bus no. 28, 29, or 43 to get there.

Golden Gate Bridge ★★★ ICON   Few cities possess an icon that so distinctly pronounces, "I'm here." New York has the Statue of Liberty, Sydney has its Opera House, but nothing makes you sigh "San Francisco" like the elegant profile of the stupendous **Golden Gate Bridge,** which links the city peninsula to the forests of Marin County.

It's not just an emblem. It was also an epic engineering feat that, when it was completed in 1937, changed the city from a clunky, ferry-dependent one to one of the motor age. President Franklin Roosevelt, in Washington, pushed a button and opened it to traffic, and what was then the world's longest suspension bridge went into service, as it has been reliably ever since (although now it's the second-longest in the country). It cost $35 million—less today than what it would cost to destroy it in an action movie, as so often happens. On the big day, cars paid 50¢, and pedestrians surrendered a nickel to thrill to the sight of deadly swirl of rushing currents far below. In an era when strides in steel and engineering measured a country's worth, this was a potent symbol of power.

The bridge is not named for its color—it's red, after all, not yellow—or even after the miners of old, but for the channel below, which was originally named by knowing sailors after the treacherous Golden Horn in Turkey. Depending on the weather or the ime of day, the stately bridge presents a different personality. That mutable color, known to its 38 ever-busy painters as "international orange," can appear salmon in daylight or clay red as the sun goes down. (It was originally going to be gunmetal grey, like the Bay Bridge, but folks fell in love with the red hue of the primer coat.) Wisely, the architects worked wonders in figuring out how to integrate the bridge with the landscape and not obliterate everything that led up to it, as usually happened in the 1930s. Consequently, getting a good snap of the thing isn't as easy as you'd think.

There's a pathway across the east side bridge for pedestrians (5am–9pm in summer, 5am–6pm in winter) that is on the best side for fantastic city views (the other side takes in the Pacific), but as you can imagine, it gets crowded on weekends. Unfortunately, the bridge isn't easy to reach on foot, as its entry on the San Francisco side is tangled up among the confusing and unfriendly roadways of the Presidio. The six-lane bridge, built to 1937 proportions, isn't the easiest or safest place to take photographs from your car, either, although plenty of tourists snarl traffic in the effort. Instead, planners constructed a viewing deck, complete with a restroom, at the bridge's northern end that is accessible no matter from which direction you're coming on the 101. I prefer using it on the way into town, because visitors from southbound traffic must use a walkway that goes underneath the bridge, giving them a unique second perspective of its structural underpinnings. Try to show up earlier in the day, when the sun is unlikely to ruin your shots. If you do go on the bridge, for an extra thrill, be in the middle when a boat goes underneath; freighters are exhilarating when seen from above, and the regular tourist sightseeing boats bob helplessly for an amusing moment as they turn around in the teeming waters; sometimes, you can hear their passengers shout in alarm.

A sad note: The bridge also has a dark side, as it is the site of a suicide every 1 or 2 weeks; see the documentary "The Bridge" for a troubling look at some of them.

Hwy. 101 N. www.goldengatebridge.org. $6 electronic toll when driving south, cash no longer accepted. Bridge-bound Golden Gate Transit buses (© **511**) depart hourly during the day for Marin County. No toll northbound.

The Walt Disney Family Museum ★ MUSEUM   While this museum features the expected collection of Walt Disney memorabilia, the museum is really more of a tribute to the life of the man behind the mouse. It takes a serious look at Walt Disney's personal life, including his childhood in Kansas City, his move to California with nothing but $40 in his pocket and a dream, and explains how he and his brother, Roy, decided to launch Disney Bros. Studio. The most moving room is the gallery filled with thoughts and condolences from around the world when Mickey's creator passed away in 1966. But it's not a downer, and children will enjoy the visit. How could they not with all of the character sketches on display, including the earliest known drawings of Mickey Mouse, and original art from feature films like "Fantasia" and "Dumbo"?

In the Presidio, Main Post, 104 Montgomery St. (at Sheridan Ave.). © **415/345-6800.** www.walt disney.org. Admission $20 adults, $15 for students with valid IDs and seniors 65 and over, $12 for children 6–17. Wed–Mon 10am–6pm. Bus: 28 or 43.

GOLDEN GATE NATIONAL RECREATION AREA

The largest urban park in the world, GGNRA makes New York's Central Park look like a putting green. It covers three counties along 28 miles of stunning, condo-free shoreline. Run by the National Park Service, the Recreation Area wraps around the northern

6

Golden Gate National Recreation Area

EXPLORING SAN FRANCISCO

and western edges of the city, and just about all of it is open to the public with no access fees. The Muni bus system provides transportation to the more popular sites, including Aquatic Park, Cliff House, Fort Mason, and Ocean Beach. For more information, contact the **National Park Service** (📞 **415/561-4700;** www.nps.gov/goga). For more detailed information on particular sites, see the "Getting Outside" section, later in this chapter.

Here is a brief rundown of the salient features of the park's peninsula section, starting at the northern section and moving westward around the coastline:

Aquatic Park, adjacent to the Hyde Street Pier, has a small swimming beach, although it's not that appealing (and darned cold).

Fort Mason Center, from Bay Street to the shoreline, comprises several buildings and piers used during World War II. Today they house museums, theaters, shops, and organizations, and **Greens** vegetarian restaurant (p. 88), which affords views of the Golden Gate Bridge. For information about Fort Mason events, call 📞 **415/345-7500** or visit www.fortmason.org. The park headquarters is also at Fort Mason.

Farther west along the bay at the northern end of Laguna Street is **Marina Green,** a favorite local spot for kite flying, jogging, and walking along the Promenade. The St. Francis Yacht Club is also here.

Next comes the 3½-mile paved **Golden Gate Promenade** ★, San Francisco's best and most scenic biking, jogging, and walking path. It runs along the shore past **Crissy Field** (www.crissyfield.org) and ends at Fort Point under the Golden Gate Bridge. Be sure to stop and watch the gonzo windsurfers and kite surfers, who catch major wind here, and admire the newly restored marshlands. **The Crissy Field Warming Hut Café and Bookstore** (📞 **415/561-4030**) is open daily from 9am to 5pm (9am–7pm summer weekends) and offers yummy, organic soups, salads, sandwiches, coffee drinks, and a good selection of outdoor-themed books and cards. Kids go crazy for **House of Air** (📞 **415/345-9675**; www.houseofair.com), a warehouse packed with trampolines, a dodge-ball court, and places to climb and jump off of. But be warned: there's a reason they make you sign a waiver and show an explicit video about safety and playing at your own risk; with a ton of kids wildly hopping about and bouncy surfaces, somebody's bound to get hurt—and plenty of them do.

Fort Point ★ (📞 **415/556-1693;** www.nps.gov/fopo) was built between 1853 and 1861 to protect the narrow entrance to the harbor. It was designed to house 500 soldiers manning 126 muzzle-loading cannons. By 1900, the fort's soldiers and obsolete guns had been removed, but the formidable brick edifice remains. Fort Point is open Friday to Sunday from 10am to 5pm (summer Thurs–Tues), and guided tours and cannon demonstrations are given at the site once or twice a day on open days, depending on the time of year.

Lincoln Boulevard sweeps around the western edge of the bay to **Baker Beach,** where the waves roll ashore—a fine spot for sunbathing, walking, or fishing. Hikers can follow the **California Coastal Trail** from Fort Point along this part of the coastline to Lands End (visit www.presidio.gov/explore/trails).

A short distance from Baker Beach, **China Beach** is a small cove where swimming is permitted. Changing rooms, showers, a sun deck, and restrooms are available.

A little farther around the coast is **Land's End** ★, looking out to Pyramid Rock. A lower and an upper trail offer hiking amid windswept cypresses and pines on the cliffs above the Pacific.

Still farther along the coast lie **Point Lobos,** the ruins of **Sutro Baths** (www.sutro baths.com), and the **Cliff House** (p. 137). The Cliff House which underwent major

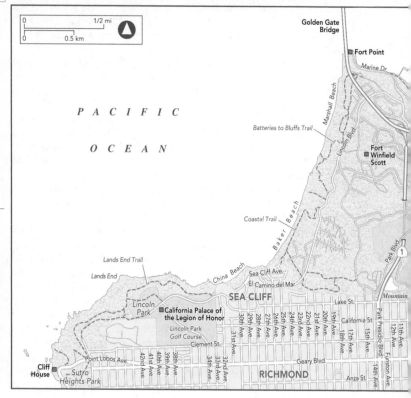

renovations in 2004, has been serving refreshments to visitors since 1863. It's famed for its views of Seal Rocks (a colony of sea lions and many marine birds) and the Pacific Ocean. Immediately northeast of Cliff House you'll find traces of the once-grand Sutro Baths. Built by mayor, Adolph Sutro, in 1896 as a bathing facility for the smelly masses without indoor plumbing, the baths turned into a swimming facility that was a major summer attraction accommodating up to 24,000 people. It burned down in 1966. See photos of the baths and a life-sized model in an antique Speedo inside the Cliff House.

A little farther inland at the western end of California Street is **Lincoln Park,** which contains a golf course and the spectacular **California Palace of the Legion of Honor Museum** (see below).

Though technically not inside the GGNRA, the **San Francisco Zoo** (p. 132) is located across the street where Sloat Boulevard meets the Great Highway.

At the southern end of Ocean Beach, 4 miles down the coast, is **Fort Funston** (© **415/561-4323**), where there's an easy loop trail across the cliffs. Here you can watch hang gliders take advantage of the high cliffs and strong winds. It's also one

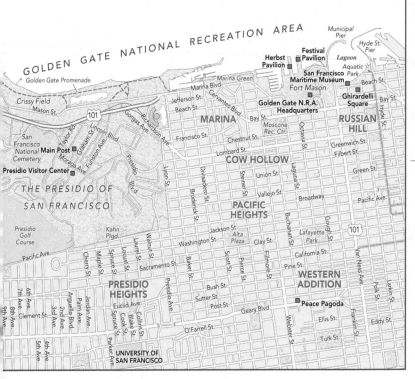

of the city's most popular dog parks. Check out the webcam at www.flyfunston.org/newwebcam.

Farther south along Route 280, **Sweeney Ridge** affords sweeping views of the coastline from the many trails that crisscross its 1,000 acres. From here the expedition led by Don Gaspar de Portolá first saw San Francisco Bay in 1769. It's in Pacifica; take Sneath Lane off Route 35 (Skyline Blvd.) in San Bruno.

The GGNRA extends into Marin County, where it encompasses the Marin Headlands, Muir Woods National Monument, and Olema Valley behind the Point Reyes National Seashore. See chapter 10 for information on Marin County and Muir Woods.

California Palace of the Legion of Honor ★★   The most beautiful museum in San Francisco sits perched high on the headlands with a stellar view of the Golden Gate Bridge. Built in 1924, in the Beaux Arts style, the Legion of Honor is a ¾ replica of the Palais de la Legion d'Honneur in Paris, and serves as a memorial to the 3,600 California soldiers who lost their lives fighting on the battlefields of France in World War I. Though the setting alone makes this beaut a must-visit, the collections and ever-changing exhibits of classical art and artifacts are sure to please fine arts connoisseur. Movie buffs might also recognize it as the setting for pivotal scenes in Alfred Hitchcock's "Vertigo." Filled with 4,000 years' worth of treasures, the focus is on ancient, and European, art and paintings, plus you'll find one of the largest collections of prints and drawings in the United States. Auguste Rodin's 1904 cast bronze sculpture "The Thinker" can be admired in the Court of Honor. Saturdays and Sundays at 4pm, visitors can hear Ernest Skinner's 1924 pipe organ reproducing the sounds of a full orchestra; it is considered one of the finest pipe organs in the world. As an added bonus, if you would like to see more fine arts treasures, your ticket is valid for same-day entrance to the de Young museum (p. 123) in Golden Gate Park.

100 34th St. (at Clement St.), Lincoln Park. ✆ **415/750-3600.** www.legionofhonor.famsf.org. Admission $10 adults, $7 seniors (65+), $6 youth 13-17 and students (with ID), free children 12 and under. Additional fees may apply for special exhibitions. Free admission 1st Tues of the month. Tues–Sun 9:30am–5:15pm. Closed Thanksgiving, Christmas, and New Year's Day. Bus: 1, 18, or 38.

San Francisco Zoo ★   Located between the Pacific Ocean and Lake Merced in the southwest corner of the city, the San Francisco Zoo, which once had a reputation for being a bit shoddy and out-of-date, has come a long way in recent years. Though grown-ups who are into wildlife will enjoy the visit, it's really aimed at kids, who get a kick out of attractions like the hands-on Children's Zoo, the flock of shockingly pink flamingos, the giant anaconda, the recently restored Carousel, and the ageless Little Puffer train.

Founded at its present site near the ocean in 1929, the zoo is spread over 100 acres and houses more than 930 animals, including some 245 species of mammals, birds, reptiles, amphibians, and invertebrates. Exhibit highlights include the **Lipman Family Lemur Forest,** a forest setting for five endangered species of lemurs from Madagascar; **Jones Family Gorilla World,** a tranquil haven for a family group of western lowland gorillas; **Koala Crossing,** which connects to the Australian Walkabout exhibit with its kangaroos, wallaroos, and emu; **Penguin Island,** home to a large breeding colony of Magellanic penguins; and the **Primate Discovery Center,** home to rare and endangered monkeys. **Puente al Sur (Bridge to the South)** has a pair of giant anteaters and some capybaras. The **Lion House** is home to rare Sumatran and Siberian tigers and African lions. **African Savanna** is a 3-acre mixed-species habitat with giraffes, zebras, antelopes, and birds. Check the website for a daily schedule of animal feeding times.

The 6-acre **Children's Zoo** offers kids and their families opportunities for close-up encounters with rare domestic breeds of goats, sheep, ponies, and horses in the Family Farm. Touch and feel small mammals, reptiles, and amphibians along the Nature Trail and gaze at eagles and hawks stationed on Hawk Hill. Don't miss a visit to the fascinating Insect Zoo or the Meerkat and Prairie Dog exhibit, where kids can crawl through tunnels and play in sand, just like these amazing burrowing species.

There's a coffee cart by the entrance as well as two decent cafes inside, definitely good enough for a bite with the kids (though the lines can be long and slightly confusing if you're handling food and kid duty at the same time).

Great Highway btw. Sloat Blvd. and Skyline Blvd. ✆ **415/753-7080.** www.sfzoo.org. Admission $17 adults, $14 for seniors (65+), $11 children 4–14, free for children 3 and under. San Francisco residents receive a discount. Daily 10am–5pm. Parking $8 weekdays, $10 weekends and holidays. Bus: 23 or 18. Streetcar: L from downtown Market St. to the end of the line.

SELF-GUIDED & ORGANIZED TOURS

The 49-Mile Scenic Drive ★★

This self-guided drive is an easy way to orient yourself and to grasp the beauty of San Francisco and its extraordinary location. Beginning in the city, it follows a rough circle around the bay and passes virtually all the best-known sights, from Chinatown to the Golden Gate Bridge, Ocean Beach, Seal Rocks, Golden Gate Park, and Twin Peaks. Originally designed for the benefit of visitors to San Francisco's 1939 and 1940 Golden Gate International Exposition, the route is marked by blue-and-white sea gull signs. Although it makes an excellent half-day tour, this 49-mile-long mini-excursion can easily take longer if you decide, for example, to stop to walk across the Golden Gate Bridge or to have tea in Golden Gate Park's Japanese Tea Garden.

If you are in the area, the **San Francisco Visitor Information Center** (www.san francisco.travel), at Powell and Market streets, distributes free route maps, which are handy since a few of the Scenic Drive marker signs are missing. Otherwise, you can download a great PDF map from their website. Try to avoid the downtown area during the weekday rush hours from 7 to 9am and 4 to 6pm.

Walking Tours

Do not miss the opportunity to take one of the 80-plus absolutely free walking tours offered in rotation by **San Francisco City Guides ★★★** (© 415/557-4266; www.sfcityguides.org), a simply terrific volunteer organization that runs up to a dozen tours a day, from 10am to 2pm, all around town. You don't need to make a reservation; just show up at the place and time listed online on its home page, where the weekly schedule is kept up-to-date by the group's single paid employee. Tours are free, but at the end your guide, who will be someone who loves and studies the city and wants to share that love, will pass around an envelope and hope for a few bucks. Some of the cooler tours include a walk through the historic Palace Hotel; City Scapes and Public places, on which you'll discover hidden rooftop gardens and little-known financial museums downtown; a retelling of the history of the Mission Dolores neighborhood, one of the city's most historic; and Gold Rush City, which takes in the stomping grounds of the original '49ers. Most of the city's great attractions, from Coit Tower to Fisherman's Wharf, will have a tour dedicated to their explication. Tours are probably the city's best bargain, and they're an inviting way to see some windswept places you may not want to go to alone, including along the walkway of the Golden Gate Bridge and the Fort Mason complex. Some 21,000 people a year take advantage of this terrific service, and frugal city buffs could easily fill their vacations with two or three a day.

Cruisin' the Castro (© 415/255-1821; www.cruisinthecastro.com; $30 adults, $25 children 5–12) is an informative historical tour of San Francisco's most famous gay quarter, concentrating on the contribution of the gay community to the city's political maturity, growth, and beauty. This fun and easy walking tour is for all ages, highlighting gay and lesbian history from 1849 to present. Stops include America's only Pink Triangle Park and Memorial, the original site of the AIDS Quilt Name Project, Harvey Milk's residence and photo shop, the Castro Theatre, and the Human Rights Campaign and Action Center. Tours run Monday through Saturday from 10am to noon and meet at the Rainbow Flag at the Harvey Milk Plaza on the corner of Castro and Market streets above the Castro Muni station. Reservations are required.

Segways are those weird-looking upright scooters you've probably seen on TV. The two-wheeled "human transporter" is an ingenious electric-powered transportation device that uses gyroscopes to emulate human balance. After the free 30-minute lesson, riding a Segway becomes intuitive: lean forward, go forward; lean back, go back; stand upright, stop. Simple. The **San Francisco Electric Tour Company** offers Segway-powered narrated 2-hour tours—choose from Wharf and Waterfront, Golden Gate Park, Chinatown–Little Italy–Wharf night tour, and, for advanced riders, the Hills and Crooked Streets tour. For $70 it's not a bad deal, and it's the closest you'll come to being a celebrity (*everyone* checks you out). **Note:** You must be at least 12 years old, weight between 100 and 250 lbs., and can't be pregnant to join the tour. No heels, sandals, or flip-flops. For more information, log onto www.sfelectrictour.com or call ☎ **415/474-3130.**

The **Haight-Ashbury Flower Power Walking Tour** (☎ 415/863-1621; www. haightashburytour.com; $20, free for kids 9 and under) explores hippie haunts with Pam and Bruce Brennan (aka "Hippy Gourmet"). You'll revisit the Grateful Dead's crash pad, Janis Joplin's house, and other reminders of the Summer of Love in 2½ short hours. Tours begin at 10:30am on Tuesdays and Saturdays, Thursdays at 2pm, and Fridays at 11am. Reservations are advised and you can buy tickets online.

To explore the less-touristy side, and get the hidden nooks and crannies of Chinatown, sign up with **Wok Wiz Chinatown Walking Tours & Cooking Center,** 250 King St., Ste. 268 (☎ 650/355-9657; www.wokwiz.com). Founded in 1984 by the late author and cooking instructor Shirley Fong-Torres, its guides today are all Chinatown natives, who speak fluent Cantonese, and are intimately acquainted with the neighborhood's history, folklore, culture, and food. Tours run daily from 10am to 1pm and include a seven-course dim sum lunch (a Chinese meal made up of many small plates of food). There's also a less expensive tour that does not include lunch. Since groups are generally held to a maximum of 15, reservations are essential. The tour (with lunch) costs $50 for adults and $35 for ages 6 to 10; without lunch, it's $35 and $25, respectively. Tickets can be purchased online. Wok Wiz also operates an **I Can't Believe I Ate My Way Through Chinatown** tour, which starts with breakfast, moves to a wok shop, and stops for various nibbles at a vegetarian restaurant, dim sum place, and a marketplace, before taking a break for a sumptuous authentic Cantonese luncheon. It's offered Saturdays, takes 3½ hours, and costs $90 per person ($50 for children 6–10), food included. The city mourns the loss of Shirley, who passed away in 2011.

Finally, for a tour of the areas where tour busses are forbidden, try Jay Gifford's **Victorian Homes Historical Walking Tour** (☎ 415/252-9485; www.victorianhome walk.com). As you might guess, the tour concentrates on architecture though Jay, a witty raconteur and San Francisco resident for more than 2 decades, also goes deeply into the city's history—particularly the periods just before and after the great earthquake and fire of 1906. You'll stroll through Japantown, Pacific Heights, and Cow Hollow. In the process, you'll see more than 200 meticulously restored Victorians, including the sites where "Mrs. Doubtfire" and "Party of Five" were filmed. Tours run daily at 11am rain or shine; cost is $25 per person (cash only).

Bike Tours

Several Fisherman's Wharf companies compete for biking business and frankly, there doesn't seem to be much difference between them, either in price or quality of the rental equipment. They are **Blazing Saddles Bike Rentals and Tours** (☎ **415/202-8888;** www.blazingsaddles.com), **Bay City Bike Rentals** (☎ **415/346-2453;** www.baycitybike.com), and **San Francisco Bike Rentals** (☎ **415/922-4537;** www.bikerentalsanfrancisco.com). The last one also has shops at the Ferry Building and in the Haight.

Along with rentals, the first two offer identical, guided bike tours over the Golden Gate Bridge, and down into Sausalito ($55 for adults, $35 for kids 11 and under on both). The guided portion of the tour ends in Sausalito, and you are then free to ride more, eat lunch, browse the shops, and take the ferry back at your leisure. (*Note:* the $11 ferry ride back to Pier 39 is not included in the price, but the two companies can sell you the ticket if you want one—or you can ride back!). Tours start at 10am and take about 3 hours; helmets, locks, maps, and a safety training class are all included.

Boat Tours

One of the best ways to look at San Francisco is from a boat bobbing on the bay, where you can take in views of the skyline and the dramatic topography. There are several cruises to choose from, and land/cruise options available online. Regardless of which you take, bring a jacket; it can be freezing cold on the bay.

Blue & Gold Fleet, Pier 39, Fisherman's Wharf (☎ **415/705-8200;** www.blueandgold fleet.com), offers a range of options including a 60-minute tour of the bay that follows along the historic waterfront, a 90-minute cruise around Alcatraz Island, and a "guaranteed to get soaked" bay adventure on the flame-covered RocketBoat. Prices for tours range from $28 for an adult on one of the cruises to $50 for a combo ticket of a cruise plus the RocketBoat. Ferries are available to Sausalito, Tiburon, and Angel Island for $17 to $22 roundtrip (adults), $10 to $14 (kids and seniors), free 5 and under.

The **Red & White Fleet,** established in 1892, departs daily from Pier 43½ (☎ **415/673-2900;** www.redandwhite.com), and offers a number of bay cruise tours including the 90-minute "Bridge 2 Bridge" ($36 adults, $24 kids 5–17, free 4 and under), 2-hour "California Twilight Tour" ($58 adults, $40 kids 5–17, free 4 and under), and "Golden Gate" ($28 adults, $18 kids 5–17, free 4 and under).

Bus Tours

San Francisco's public transportation system can be hard to master for newbies, so these Hop On/Hop Off tours fill a niche, especially for those looking to see just the major sites. A number of different combinations are offered by a number of different

Quack! Splash!

San Francisco Duck Tours—those weird-looking amphibian cars that drive around the city and then plunk into the bay for a water tour—have absolutely no historical importance or redeeming value. Oh well; judging by the grinning masses sitting inside blowing their duck whistles, no one seems to care. Try a tour on one, especially if you have kids in tow. 2766 Taylor St. (at Jefferson St.); ☎ **877/887-8225;** www.sanfrancisco ducks.com; $35 adults, $25 kids (4–17).

companies, but none is significantly better than the others. So before you book think about what you want to see: Do you want a funky old trolley or an open double-decker bus? A tour that crosses the Golden Gate Bridge and visits Sausalito? Look, too, at how many stops are en route and how often the busses start. In the off-season, that might be just twice a day, making a hop-on, hop-off tour more of a "stay on," so study the bus schedules before booking. Companies to compare include **Big Bus Tours** (www.bigbustours.com), **City Sightseeing San Francisco** (www.city-sightseeing.us), and the **San Francisco Sightseeing Company** (www.sanfranciscosightseeing.com). Prices vary depending on the tour. *Tip:* A second day of hopping on and off can often be added for only a few more dollars, though many people find 1 day on these buses is more than enough.

Air Tours

San Francisco Seaplane Tours (📞 **415/332-4843;** www.seaplane.com) is the Bay Area's only seaplane tour company, a good choice for thrill-seekers. For more than 60 years, this locally owned outfit has provided its customers bird's-eye views of the city, flying directly over San Francisco at an altitude of about 1,500 feet. Sights you'll see during the narrated excursions include the Golden Gate and Bay Bridges, Alcatraz, Tiburon, and Sausalito. Half the fun, however, is taking off and landing on the water (which is surprisingly smooth). Trips depart from Mill Valley; the company offers complimentary shuttle pickup at Pier 39. Prices range from $179 per person for the 30-minute Golden Gate Tour to $249 for the 40-minute Champagne Sunset Flight, which includes a bottle of bubbly and a cozy backseat for two, to $549, which includes a wine and cheese tasting and tour of a winery on the coast of Clear Lake 50 minutes to the North. Children's rates are available, and cameras most welcome. Call to reserve.

Equally thrilling (and perhaps more so if you've never been in a helicopter) is a tour of San Francisco and the bay via **San Francisco Helicopters.** The $175 ($135 child) Vista package includes free shuttle pickup from your hotel or Pier 39, and a 20-minute tour that takes you over the city, and past the Golden Gate and Bay Bridges, and Alcatraz Island. After takeoff, the pilot gives a narrated tour and answers questions while the background music adds a bit of Disney-ride quality to the experience. *Tip:* The view from the front seat is the best. Picnic lunch and sunset dinner packages are available as well. For more information or reservations, call 📞 **650/635-4500** or log onto www.sfhelicopters.com.

GETTING OUTSIDE

San Francisco is nature's city and thanks to the year-round mild weather, the residents are all about soaking up the great outdoors. Here are a few ways to enjoy the city's natural beauty.

BEACHES   Most days it's too chilly to hang out at the beach, but when the fog evaporates and the wind dies down, locals love to hit the sands. On any truly hot day, thousands flock to the beach to worship the sun, build sand castles, and throw a ball around. Without a wet suit, swimming is a fiercely cold endeavor and is not recommended. In any case, dip at your own risk—there are no lifeguards on duty and San Francisco's waters are cold and have strong undertows. On the South Bay, **Baker Beach** is ideal for picnicking, sunning, walking, or fishing against the backdrop of the Golden Gate (most fisherman do catch and release here, due to pollution in the Bay). **Ocean Beach,** at the end of Golden Gate Park, on the westernmost side of the city, is

A whale OF A TALE

Not many people outside of California know about the Farallon Islands, nor do many people get to visit up close. The entire Gulf of Farallones National Marine Sanctuary is off-limits to civilians, so visitors must gaze from the deck of a fishing or whale-watching boat if they want a peek firsthand.

This veteran eco-tourism company offers trips (starting at $125) out to the desolate outcropping of rock off the coast of San Francisco that is home to birds, sea lions, seals, dolphins, and the ever-present great white shark. Typically on the search for migrating gray, humpback, or blue whales, expeditions leave from Pier 39 at 8am sharp and pass underneath the majestic Golden Gate Bridge on the 27-mile trip out to the islands. A crew of trained naturalists accompany each voyage, and will stop at the first sign of water spouts on the 5- to 6-hour trips.

For more information on the different tours offered, call ☏ **415/331-6267** or visit www.sfbaywhalewatching.com.

San Francisco's largest beach—4 miles long. Just offshore, at the northern end of the beach, in front of Cliff House, are the jagged Seal Rocks, inhabited by various shorebirds and a large colony of barking sea lions (bring binoculars for a close-up view). To the left, Kelly's Cove is one of the more challenging surf spots in town. Ocean Beach is ideal for strolling or sunning, but don't swim here—tides are tricky, and each year bathers drown in the rough surf.

Stop by Ocean Beach bus terminal at the corner of Cabrillo and La Playa streets to learn about San Francisco's history in local artist Ray Beldner's whimsically historical sculpture garden. Then hike up the hill to explore **Cliff House** and the ruins of the **Sutro Baths.** These baths, once able to accommodate 24,000 bathers, were lost to fire in 1966.

BIKING   The San Francisco Parks and Recreation Department maintains two city-designated bike routes. One winds 7½ miles through Golden Gate Park to Lake Merced; the other traverses the city, starting in the south, and continues over the Golden Gate Bridge. These routes, however, are not just for bicyclists, who must exercise caution to avoid crashing into pedestrians. A bike map is available from the San Francisco Visitor Information Center, at Powell and Mason streets, for $3 (p. 245), and from bicycle shops all around town.

Ocean Beach has a public walk- and bikeway that stretches along 5 waterfront blocks of the Great Highway between Noriega and Santiago streets. It's an easy ride from Cliff House or Golden Gate Park.

Avenue Cyclery, 756 Stanyan St., at Waller Street, in the Haight (☏ **415/387-3155;** www.avenuecyclery.com), rents bikes for $8 per hour or $30 per day. It's open daily 10am to 6pm. For cruising Fisherman's Wharf and the Golden Gate Bridge, your best bet is **Blazing Saddles** (☏ **415/202-8888;** www.blazingsaddles.com), which has five locations around Fisherman's Wharf. Bike rentals start at $32 per day, and include maps, locks, and helmets; tandem bikes are available as well. They even have electric bikes if you don't have the energy to pedal but want to say you went biking. *Hint:* Reservations are not necessary, but if you reserve online you get a 10% discount.

BOATING   At the **Golden Gate Park Boathouse** (☏ **415/386-2531;** www.stowlake boathouse.com) on Stow Lake, the park's largest body of water, you can rent a boat by

Getting Outside

EXPLORING SAN FRANCISCO

When Eric Kipp, a certified yogi, conceptualized his wildly popular concept of Hiking Yoga, he aimed to bring tourists and locals alike out and about for some fresh air, intense cardio, and fantastic city views. Kipp's 90-minute urban treks, which take place several times a day, mostly on weekend days, depart from the clock tower at the Ferry Building and wind their way up to Coit Tower and around Telegraph Hill.

Participants enjoy intense and fast-paced hill hiking—this is no leisurely walk in the park—while stopping at four stations throughout the city for a series of yoga poses. For information or a schedule of hikes, call ✆ **415/261-3641** or visit www.hikingyoga.com. Reservations are required, and each session costs $20. Package deals for multiple hikes are available.

the hour and steer over to Strawberry Hill, a large, round island in the middle of the lake, for lunch. There's usually a line on weekends. The boathouse is open Monday to Friday 10am to 7pm, and weekends 9am to 7pm, weather permitting. Rowboats ($20/hour), pedal boats ($25/hour), and electric boats ($34/hour) are available with a $5 deposit.

CITY STAIR CLIMBING   Many health clubs have stair-climbing machines and step classes, but in San Francisco, you need only go outside. Several city stair climbs will give you not only a good workout, but seriously stunning neighborhood, city, and bay views as well. Check www.sisterbetty.org/stairways for a list of stairways—with photos—in locations all over the city.

GOLF   San Francisco has a few beautiful golf courses. One of the most lavish is the **Presidio Golf Course,** 300 Finley Rd. at the Arguello Gate (✆ **415/561-4653;** www.presidiogolf.com). Greens fees range from $49 (5pm start, no cart) to $145 (weekend morning with a cart) for non-residents. There are also two decent municipal courses in town. The 18-hole **Harding Park,** 99 Harding Rd. (at Skyline Blvd.; ✆ **415/664-4690;** www.tpc.com/tpc-harding-park-golf), charges greens fees of $155 Monday through Thursday, $175 Friday through Sunday. Opened in 1925, and home to the Charles Schwab Cup Championship, it was completely overhauled in 2002, and the new Harding has been getting rave reviews ever since. In 2004, it was named by "Golf" magazine as the number-two best municipal golf course in America; in 2009 it hosted the President's Cup. The course, which skirts the shores of Lake Merced, is a 6,743-yard, par-72. You can also play the easier Fleming 9 Course at the same location. The 18-hole **Lincoln Park Golf Course,** 300 34th Ave. (at Clement St.; ✆ **415/221-9911;** www.lincolnparkgc.com), charges greens fees of $38 per person Monday through Thursday, $42 Friday through Sunday, with rates decreasing after 3pm. It's San Francisco's prettiest municipal course, with terrific views and fairways lined with Monterey cypress and pine trees. The 5,181-yard layout plays to par 68, and the 17th hole has a glistening ocean view. This is the oldest course in the city and one of the oldest in the West. It's open daily at daybreak.

PARKS   In addition to **Golden Gate Park** (p. 122) and the **Golden Gate National Recreation Area** (p. 127), San Francisco boasts more than 2,000 acres of parkland, most of which is perfect for picnicking or throwing around a Frisbee.

Smaller city parks include **Buena Vista Park** (Haight St. btw. Baker and Central sts.), which affords fine views of the Golden Gate Bridge and the area around it and is also a favored lounging ground for gay trysts; **Ina Coolbrith Park** (Taylor St. btw. Vallejo and Green sts.), offering views of the Bay Bridge and Alcatraz; and **Sigmund Stern Grove** (19th Ave. and Sloat Blvd.) in the Sunset District, which is the site of a famous free summer music festival.

One of my personal favorites is **Lincoln Park,** a 270-acre green space on the northwestern side of the city at Clement Street and 34th Avenue. The Legion of Honor is here (p. 131), as is a scenic 18-hole municipal golf course (see "Golf," above). But the best things about this park are the 200-foot cliffs that overlook the Golden Gate Bridge and San Francisco Bay. To get to the park, take bus no. 38 from Union Square to 33rd and Geary streets, and then walk a few blocks.

RUNNING The **Bay to Breakers Foot Race** ★ (© **415/864-3432;** www.baytobreakers.com) is an annual 7½-mile run from downtown to Ocean Beach. About 80,000 entrants take part in it, and it's one of San Francisco's trademark events. Costumed participants and hordes of spectators add to the fun. The event is held on the third Sunday of May.

The **San Francisco Marathon** takes place annually at the end of July or first weekend in August. For more information, call © **888/958-6668** or visit www.thesfmarathon.com.

Great **jogging paths** include the entire expanse of Golden Gate Park, the shoreline along the Marina, and the Embarcadero.

TENNIS The **San Francisco Parks and Recreation Department** maintains more than 132 courts throughout the city. Almost all are available free, on a first-come, first-served basis. For an interactive map with addresses, directions, parking, and restroom information, check out www.sfrecpark.org/recprogram/tennis-program. An additional 21 courts are available in **Golden Gate Park,** which cost around $5 for 90 minutes. Check the website for details on rules for reserving courts (www.golden-gate-park.com/tennis.html).

WALKING & HIKING The **Golden Gate National Recreation Area** offers plenty of opportunities. One incredible walk (or bike ride) is along the Golden Gate Promenade, from Aquatic Park to the Golden Gate Bridge. The 3½-mile paved trail heads along the northern edge of the Presidio out to Fort Point, passing the marina, Crissy Field's restored wetlands, a small beach, and plenty of athletic locals. You can also hike the Coastal Trail all the way from the Fort Point area to Cliff House. The park service maintains several other trails in the city. For more information or to pick up a map of the Golden Gate National Recreation Area, stop by the park service headquarters at Fort Mason; enter on Franklin Street (© **415/561-4700**). A number of PDF maps are available at www.nps.gov/goga/planyourvisit/maps/htm.

Although most people drive to this spectacular vantage point, a more rejuvenating way to experience **Twin Peaks** is to walk up from the back roads of U.C. Medical Center (off Parnassus Ave.) or from either of the two roads that lead to the top (off Woodside or Clarendon aves.). The best time to trek is early morning, when the city is quiet, the air is crisp, and sightseers haven't crowded the parking lot. Keep an eye out for cars, however, because there's no real hiking trail, and be sure to walk beyond the lot and up to the highest vantage point.

CITY STROLLS

Despite its notorious hills, San Francisco has a reputation for being a walking city. Perhaps it's because around every corner, there's a panoramic view that rewards those who tackle the steep slopes. Plus, as a city that boasts the most restaurants per capita in the country, we need all the walking we can get to work off the ongoing gastro indulgences. Regardless, the best way to soak up the distinct personalities of each neighborhood is to hoof it—you'll get a better sense of the geography and topography and an intimate understanding of why San Francisco regularly tops "Best City" lists. The following introductory city strolls boast the best views and most interesting streets. While they won't divulge all of the town's beloved nooks and crannies, they'll certainly inspire you to seek more of them out.

WALKING TOUR 1: CHINATOWN: HISTORY, CULTURE, DIM SUM & THEN SOME

START:	**Corner of Grant Avenue and Bush Street.**
PUBLIC TRANSPORTATION:	**Bus no. 2, 3, 9X, 30, 38, 45, or 76.**
FINISH:	**Commercial Street between Montgomery and Kearny streets.**
TIME:	**2 hours, not including museum or shopping stops.**
BEST TIMES:	**Daylight hours, when the streets are most active.**
WORST TIMES:	**Early or late in the day, because shops are closed and no one is milling around.**
HILLS THAT COULD KILL:	**None.**

This tiny section of San Francisco, bounded loosely by Broadway and by Stockton, Kearny, and Bush streets, is said to harbor one of the largest Chinese populations outside Asia. Daily proof is the crowds of Chinese residents who flock to the herbal stores, vegetable markets, restaurants, and businesses. Chinatown, specifically Portsmouth Square, also marks the original spot of the city center. On this walk, you'll learn why Chinatown remains intriguing to all who wind through its narrow, crowded streets, and how its origins are responsible for the city as we know it.

Chinatown & North Beach Walking Tours

CHINATOWN

1 Chinatown Gateway Arch
2 Grant Ave
3 St. Mary's Square
4 Old St. Mary's Cathedral
5 Canton Bazaar
6 Bank of America
7 Chinatown Kite Shop
8 The Wok Shop
9 Original Street of "American" California
10 United Commercial Bank
11 Washington Bakery
12 Vital Tea Leaf and Uncle Gee
13 Ross Alley
14 Golden Gate Fortune Cookie Company
15 Great China Herb Co.
16 Stockton Street
17 Chinese Historical Society of America
18 Waverly Place
19 Portsmouth Square
20 Chinese Culture Center
21 Joshua Norton's Home
22 R&G Lounge

NORTH BEACH

1 Transamerica Pyramid
2 The Montgomery Block
3 Original Transamerica Building
4 Golden Era Building
5 400 Block of Jackson Square
6 Columbus Tower
7 1010 Montgomery Street
8 Broadway
9 The Beat Museum
10 hungry i
11 Former Site of Condor Club
12 City Lights Booksellers & Publishers
13 Vesuvio
14 Spec's Twelve Adler Museum Cafe
15 Caffe Trieste
16 Molinari Delicatessen
17 Biordi Art Imports
18 Club Fugazi
19 O'Reilly's Irish Pub
20 Washington Square

To begin the tour, make your way to the corner of Bush Street and Grant Avenue, 4 blocks from Union Square and all the downtown buses, where you can't miss the:

1 Chinatown Gateway Arch

Many Chinese villages have their own gateways, and bowing to tradition, so do many Chinatowns around the world. This one, to me, is very much an emblem of San Francisco's Chinatown. That's because it's not even Chinese, but Pan-Asian. It was a gift from modern-day Taiwan.

Once you cross the threshold, you'll be at the beginning of Chinatown's portion of:

2 Grant Avenue

This is a mecca for tourists who wander in and out of gift shops that offer a variety of junk interspersed with quality imports.

But all of this is today's Chinatown. Before rampant landfilling, this area was closer to the wharves, and Chinese residents could easily get back and forth from here to work on the docks. In 1849, there were only 54 Chinese here, but by 1876, there were 116,000 in the state. They mined for treasure. They broke their backs building the railroad. For their pains, they were despised, overtaxed, and excluded. In the late 1800s, this area would have been teeming with prostitutes, many young teens who were brought here as virtual slaves. As for the men, the so-called "coolies"—a bastardized word derived from the Chinese words for "rent" and "muscle—they had slightly more protection in the form of benevolent societies, where acclimated Chinese helped them negotiate for jobs. But to boom-ing San Francisco industry, these men were just as disposable as the girls.

The great earthquake of 1906 changed everything. The whole district was wiped out. The rebuilt Chinatown was more civilized than the old one, full of benevolent societies and churches rather than opium dens and saloons—although the buildings were still mostly owned by Western men, not Chinese. A local businessman named Look Tin Eli recognized that the squalor of the old China-town gave his neighbors an image problem, so he arranged to make buildings more tourist-friendly, decorating them with false pagodas and sloping roofs. At a time when the vast majority of Americans never left their home country, coming here felt like venturing to the Orient. The ruse worked, and today, Chinatown retains both its stage-set appearance and its fascination for visitors.

Tear yourself away from the shops and turn right at the corner of Pine Street. Cross to the other side of Pine and on your left you'll come to:

3 St. Mary's Square

The 14-foot metal-and-granite statue of Dr. Sun Yat-sen, the founder of the Republic of China, was the work of sculptor Beniamino Bufano, whose lifelong dream according to the "New York Times," was to carve the face of U.S. President Franklin Delano Roosevelt on Mount Rushmore. Let's hope getting to create this likeness of the heroic Sun Yat-sen (he led the rebellion that ended the reign of the Qing Dynasty) was a happy second prize for him. It's appropriate the statue is here: during Sun Yat-sen's exile in San Francisco (before the revolution in 1916), he often whiled away the hours in this square. Visit early in the morning and you may see locals practicing tai chi here.

Walk to the other end of the square, toward California Street, turn left, cross California Street at Grant Street, and you'll be standing in front of:

4 Old St. Mary's Cathedral

Here stands the state's first building purpose-built to be a cathedral, which it was from 1854 to 1894. Because the city began with such meager resources and fires were rampant, the oldest churches here are not the prettiest. The interior of this one is no exception, mostly because it was gutted by two catastrophic blazes—one being the Great Earthquake on 1906. The shell of the building is original, but the inside dates to the days of Donna Reed. It was here, in 1902, that America's first mission for indigent Chinese immigrants was established; food was served, English taught, and charity otherwise available for anyone who was suffering in the New World.

Step inside to find a written history of the church and turn-of-the-20th-century photos of San Francisco.

Upon leaving the church, take a right, walk to the corner of Grant Avenue and California Street, and go right on Grant. Here you'll find a shop called:

5 Canton Bazaar

Of the knickknack and import shops lining Grant Avenue, this one (at no. 616) has the most comprehensive selection, including a boatload of Mao memorabilia for fans of kitsch.

Continue in the same direction on Grant Avenue and cross Sacramento Street to the northwest corner of Sacramento and Grant. You'll be at the doorstep of the:

6 Bank of America

Look up: even chain banks use traditional Chinese architectural style here. Notice the dragons subtly portrayed on many parts of the building.

Head in the same direction (north) on Grant Avenue to 717 Grant Ave.:

7 Chinatown Kite Shop

A popular neighborhood fixture, owned by the same family since 1969, the Kite Shop offers an assortment of flying objects, including lovely fish kites, nylon or cotton windsock kites, hand-painted Chinese paper kites, wood-and-paper biplanes, pentagonal kites, and even design-it-yourself options.

Cross Grant Avenue to 718 Grant Ave.:

8 The Wok Shop

Here's where you can purchase just about any cleaver, wok, cookbook, or vessel you might need for Chinese-style cooking in your own kitchen.

When you exit the shop, go right. Walk past Commercial Street and you'll arrive at the corner of Grant Avenue and Clay Street; cross Clay and you'll be standing on the:

9 Original Street of "American" California

Here an English seaman named William Richardson set up the first tent in 1835, making it the first place that an Anglo set up base in California.

Continue north on Grant Avenue to Washington Street. Turn right and at 743 Washington St. you will be standing in front of the former Bank of Canton, now known as the:

10 United Commercial Bank

This building boasts the oldest (from 1909) Asian-style edifice in Chinatown. After the earthquake, the city fathers were contemplating moving Chinatown to the outskirts of the city. The construction of this three-tiered pagoda-style building (it once housed the China Telephone Exchange) convinced these powerful men that the neighborhood had the potential to lure tourists and so Chinatown remained where it was.

You're probably thirsty by now, so follow Washington Street a few doors down (east); on your right-hand side, at 733 Washington St., you will come upon:

11 Washington Bakery & Restaurant ☕

No need to have a full meal here—the service can be abrupt. Do stop in, however, for a little potable adventure: snow red beans with ice cream. The sugary-sweet drink mixed with whole beans and ice cream is not something you're likely to have tried elsewhere, and it happens to be quite tasty.

Head back to Grant Avenue, cross Washington Street, and follow the east side of street 2 blocks to 1044 Gran Avenue:

12 Vital Tea Leaf

Stop here for tea and Gee—Uncle Gee, that is. The grouchy owner, who stands on the sidewalk luring passersby in with good-natured insults and jokey threats (along with the occasional fortune cookie) will introduce you to dozens of varieties of tea. And yes, tastings are part of the experience. You'll come in a stranger, but you leave feeling like part of the family (I promise).

Leave Vital Tea Leaf, make a left, cross Jackson Street and cross Grant Street, walk to Ross Alley, make a left into the alley:

13 Ross Alley

These alleys, in the bad old days, were rife with gambling, brothels, drug dealing, and worse. Duncombe Alley, off Pacific, was famous for its opium dens. St. Louis alley, also off Pacific, was known for its slave market, where naked girls were auctioned off to pimps. It's all so hard to picture today, but thankfully, it's over. So have a cookie (see below).

As you follow the alley south, on the left side of the street, at no. 56, you'll encounter the:

14 Golden Gate Fortune Cookie Company

This store is worth a stop if only for the glimpse of workaday Chinatown that is so rarely afforded to outsiders. It's little more than a tiny place where three women sit at a conveyer belt, folding messages into warm cookies as the manager invariably calls out to tourists, beckoning them to buy a big bag of the fortune-telling treats and come in and try a sample. You can purchase regular fortunes, unfolded flat cookies without fortunes, or, if you bring your own fortunes, make custom cookies. Photos inside the factory cost 50¢.

As you exit the alley, cross Washington Street, take a right heading west on Washington, and you're in front of the:

15 Great China Herb Co.

Herbs and roots and mysterious powders—oh my! For centuries, the Chinese have come to shops like this one to cure all types of ailments, plus ensure good health and a long life. Thankfully, unlike owners in many similar area shops, Mr. and Mrs. Ho speak English, so you will not be met with a blank stare when you inquire what exactly is in each box, bag, or jar arranged along dozens of shelves. And the answers should be truly fascinating. A wonderful place to browse.

Take a left upon leaving the store and walk to:

16 Stockton Street

This is my favorite part of Chinatown, and the part that most closely resembles a typical urban street in an older Chinese city, with sidewalk produce stands, fish markets, and bakeries. Some of the greasy spoons display the roasted meats of the day in their windows, head and all—the sight repulses some Westerners, but many Chinese customers know how to tell at a glance whether the quality of the inventory is high today. You'll also notice that the signs in the shop windows aren't in English as often as they are on Grant Avenue; that's because this is an active shopping street for everyday sundries, particularly for older Chinese-born residents.

Take your time and wander into the groceries to see what non-endemic produce is for sale. You'll find durian, starfruit, lychee, and other fruits you won't find at your local Winn-Dixie, and you'll have to swim through crowds of Asian folks to get to them. Happily, shopkeepers, though displaying a businesslike manner, are generally willing to explain any product for which you can't read the label.

One noteworthy part of this area's history is **Cameron House** (actually up the hill at 920 Sacramento St., near Stockton St.), which was named after Donaldina Cameron (1869–1968). Called Lo Mo, or "the Mother," by the Chinese, she spent her life trying to free Chinese women who came to America in hopes of marrying well but who found themselves forced into prostitution and slavery. Today, the house still helps women free themselves from domestic violence.

At 1068 Stockton St. you'll find **AA Bakery & Café,** an extremely colorful bakery with Golden Gate Bridge–shaped cakes, bright green and pink snacks, moon cakes, and a flow of Chinese diners catching up over pastries. **Gourmet Delight B.B.Q.** (1045 Stockton St.) is another recommended stop; here, barbecued duck and pork hang alongside steamed pig feet and chicken feet. Everything's to go, so if you grab a snack, don't forget napkins. Head farther north along the street and you'll see live fish and fowl awaiting their fate as the day's dinner.

Meander south on Stockton Street to Clay Street and turn west (right) onto Clay. Continue to 965 Clay St., being sure to plan your visit during the museum's open hours (see below):

17 Chinese Historical Society of America Museum

Founded in 1963, this museum (© **415/391-1188**) has a small but fascinating collection illuminating the role of Chinese immigrants in American history, particularly in San Francisco and the rest of California.

Artifacts on display—and they're more interesting to see than they are to read about—include a shrimp-cleaning machine, 19th-century clothing and slippers of the Chinese pioneers, Chinese herbs and scales, historic hand-carved and painted shop signs, and a series of photographs that document the development of Chinese culture in America. The museum is open Tuesday through Friday from noon to 5pm and Saturday and Sunday from noon to 4pm. Admission is $5 for adults, $3 for college students with ID and seniors, and $2 for kids 6 to 17.

Retrace your steps, heading east on Clay Street back toward Grant Avenue. Turn left onto:

18 Waverly Place

Also known as "the Street of Painted Balconies," Waverly Place is probably Chinatown's most popular side street or alleyway because of its colorful balconies and architectural details—a sort of Chinese-style New Orleans street. At 125 Waverley, you'll find the **Tin Hou Temple.** Founded in 1852, it's the oldest Chinese temple in America. Visitors are welcome, although it's polite to remove your shoes when you go inside to inspect its carvings, traditional architectural details, and altar, portions of which survived the 1906 blaze; it's also customary to leave a few dollars in a red envelope found on the front table. The temple, serene and wafting with incense, is on the top floor and there's no elevator. (By the way, this kind of house of worship isn't so common here; there are more Chinese Christians in Chinatown than there are Buddhists.)

Once you've finished exploring Waverly Place, walk east on Clay Street, past Grant Avenue, and continue until you come upon the block-wide urban playground that is also the most important site in San Francisco's history.

19 Portsmouth Square

This very spot was the center of the region's first township, which was called Yerba Buena before it was renamed San Francisco in 1847. Around 1846, before any semblance of a city had taken shape, this plaza lay at the foot of the bay's eastern shoreline. There were fewer than 50 non–Native American residents in the settlement, no substantial buildings to speak of, and the few boats that pulled into the cove did so less than a block from where you're standing.

In 1846, when California was claimed as a U.S. territory, the marines who landed here named the square after their ship, the USS *Portsmouth.* (Today a bronze plaque marks the spot where they raised the U.S. flag.)

Yerba Buena remained a modest township until the gold rush of 1849 when, over the next 2 years, the population grew from under 1,000 to over 19,000, as gold seekers from around the world made their way here. When the square became too crowded, long wharves were constructed to support new buildings above the bay. Eventually, the entire area became landfill. That was almost 150 years ago, but today the square still serves as an important meeting place for neighborhood Chinese—a sort of communal outdoor living room.

Throughout the day, the square is heavily trafficked by children and—in large part—by elderly men, who gamble over Chinese cards and play chess. If you arrive early in the morning, you might come across people practicing tai chi.

It is said that Robert Louis Stevenson used to love to sit on a bench here and watch life go by. (At the northeast corner of the square, you'll find a monument to his memory, consisting of a model of the *Hispaniola,* the ship in Stevenson's novel "Treasure Island," and an excerpt from his "Christmas Sermon.")

Once you've had your fill of the square, exit to the east at Kearny Street. Directly across the street, at 750 Kearny St., is the Holiday Inn. Cross the street, enter the hotel, and take the elevator to the third floor, where you'll find the:

20 Chinese Culture Center

This center is oriented toward both the community and tourists, offering display cases of Chinese art and a gallery with rotating exhibits of Asian art and writings that are often worth a look. The center is open Tuesday through Friday from 9:30 to 4pm, Saturday 10am to 4pm.

When you leave the Holiday Inn, take a left on Kearny Street and go 3 short blocks to Commercial Street. Take a left onto Commercial and note that you are standing on the street once known as the site of:

21 Joshua A. Norton's Home

Every town has its eccentric local celebrities, and San Francisco likely has had more than its share. But few are as fondly remembered as "Emperor Joshua Norton."

Norton was born around 1815 in the British Isles and sailed as a young man to South Africa, where he served as a colonial rifleman. He came to San Francisco in 1849 with $40,000 and proceeded to double and triple his fortune in real estate. Unfortunately for him, he next chose to go into the rice business. While Norton was busy cornering the market and forcing prices up, several ships loaded with rice arrived unexpectedly in San Francisco's harbor. With rice market was suddenly flooded, Norton was forced into bankruptcy. He left San Francisco for about 3 years and must have experienced a breakdown (or revelation) of some sort, for upon his return, Norton thought he was an emperor. In fact, he called himself: "Emperor of the United States and Protector of Mexico," and used to walk around the streets in an old brass-buttoned military uniform, sporting a hat with a "dusty plume."

He lived in a fantasy world, but instead of ostracizing him, San Franciscans embraced him and gave him free meals. When Emperor Norton died in 1880 (while sleeping at the corner of California St. and Grant Ave.), approximately 10,000 people passed by his coffin, which was bought with money raised at the Pacific Union Club, and more than 30,000 people participated in the funeral procession.

From here, if you've still got an appetite, you should go directly to 631 Kearny St. (at Clay St.), home of the R&G Lounge.

22 R&G Lounge 🍴

The R&G Lounge is a sure thing for tasty $5 rice-plate specials, chicken with black-bean sauce, and gorgeously tender and tangy R&G Special Beef.

Otherwise, you might want to backtrack on Commercial Street to Grant Avenue, take a left, and follow Grant back to Bush Street, the entrance to Chinatown. You'll be at the beginning of the Union Square area, where you can catch any number of buses (especially on Market St.) or cable cars, or do a little shopping. Or you might backtrack to Grant, take a right (north), and follow Grant to the end. You'll be at Broadway and Columbus, the beginning of North Beach, where you can venture onward for our North Beach tour (see below).

WALKING TOUR 2: GETTING TO KNOW NORTH BEACH

START: **Intersection of Montgomery Street, Columbus Avenue, and Washington Street.**

PUBLIC TRANSPORTATION: **Bus no. 10, 12, 30X, or 41.**

FINISH:	**Washington Square.**
TIME:	**3 hours, including a stop for lunch.**
BEST TIMES:	**Monday through Saturday between 11am and 4pm.**
WORST TIMES:	**Sunday, when shops are closed.**
HILLS THAT COULD KILL:	**The Montgomery Street hill from Broadway to Vallejo streets; otherwise, this is an easy walk.**

Along with Chinatown, North Beach is one of the city's oldest neighborhoods. In the 1800s, one of its main thoroughfares, Pacific Avenue, was considered to be the spine of the notorious Barbary Coast area. Think of a wooden shantytown leading down to a bustling, curved wharf. Over time, the settlement grew, but it always retained its male-heavy population and its rough profile. Respectable men with families didn't come out West to seek their fortunes during the Gold Rush; that was the province of drifters, opportunists, and poor laborers. And San Francisco was founded by these men.

North Beach (especially Pacific Avenue) was a den of sin, pleasure, and crime. Routinely, young men on a night of carousing at the saloons and opium dens would pass out and wake up the next day on a ship already well out to sea, where they'd be forced to join the crew for months on end until they'd be able to return home. This impression-by-kidnapping method was called being "shanghaied," it often involved drugs slipped surreptitiously into beer, and it was so common that the police barely kept track of incidents. The brilliant underworld journalist Herbert Asbury, famous today for his book "Gangs of New York," wrote in his "Barbary Coast" that the period was "the nearest approach to criminal anarchy that an American city has yet experienced."

Because of the fire, the Barbary Coast is now gone and barely a plank of the original place remains. The land is also no longer on the coast, thanks to subsequent landfilling. But the Barbary Coast's 70-odd year reign gave San Francisco its reputation as a devil-may-care town of hedonistic inclinations, a reputation it no longer deserves but which persists among people who have never actually visited.

North Beach became the city's Italian district when Italian immigrants moved "uphill" in the early 1870s, crossing Broadway from the Jackson Square area and settling in. They quickly established restaurants, cafes, bakeries, and other businesses familiar to them from their homeland.

The "Beat Generation" helped put North Beach on the map, with the likes of Jack Kerouac and Allen Ginsberg holding court in the area's cafes during the 1950s. Although most of the original Beat poets are gone, their spirit lives on in North Beach, which is still a haven for bohemian artists and writers. The neighborhood, thankfully, retains its Italian village feel; it's a place where residents from all walks of life enjoy taking time for conversation over pastries and frothy cappuccinos.

If there's one landmark you can't miss, it's the familiar building on the corner of Montgomery Street and Columbus Avenue (take bus 30X or 41 to get there):

1 Transamerica Pyramid

Petitions and protests greeted the plan to build this unusual skyscraper, but once it was completed it immediately became a beloved fixture of the skyline. Noted for its spire (which rises 212 ft. above the top floor) and its "wings" (which begin at the 29th floor and stop at the spire), this pyramid is San Francisco's tallest building. You might want to take a peek at one of the rotating art exhibits in the lobby or go around to the right and into half-acre Redwood Park, which is part of the Transamerica Center.

The Transamerica Pyramid occupies part of the 600 block of Montgomery Street, which once held a historic building called:

2 The Montgomery Block

Originally four stories high, the Montgomery Block was the tallest building in the West when it was built in 1853. San Franciscans called it "Halleck's Folly" because it was built on a raft of redwood logs that had been bolted together and floated at the edge of the ocean (which was right at Montgomery St. at that time). The building was demolished in 1959 but is remembered as the power center of old San Francisco. Its tenants included artists and writers of all kinds, among them Jack London, George Sterling, Ambrose Bierce, Bret Harte, and Mark Twain. This is a picturesque area, but there's no particular spot to direct you to. It's worth looking around, however, if only for the block's historical importance.

From the southeast corner of Montgomery and Washington streets, look across Washington to the corner of Columbus Avenue to 4 Columbus Ave which is the:

3 Original Transamerica Building

A Beaux Arts flatiron-shaped building covered in terra cotta, this old-fashioned beauty was built in 1909 as a bank. Today, the building houses a Church of Scientology.

Cross Washington Street and continue north on Montgomery Street to no. 730:

4 Golden Era Building

Erected around 1852, this San Francisco historic landmark building is named after the literary magazine "The Golden Era," which was published here. Some of the young writers who worked on the magazine were known as "the Bohemians"; they included Samuel Clemens (better known as Mark Twain) and Bret Harte (who began as a typesetter here). Backtrack a few dozen feet and stop for a minute to admire the exterior of the annex, at no. 722, which, after years of neglect and lawsuits, has finally been stabilized and is going to be developed. The Belli Annex, as it is currently known, is registered as a historic landmark.

Continue north on Washington Street and take the first right onto Jackson Street. Continue until you hit the:

5 400 Block of Jackson Square

Here's where you'll find some of the only commercial buildings to survive the 1906 earthquake and fire. The building at 415 Jackson St. (ca. 1853) served as headquarters for the Ghirardelli chocolate company from 1855 to 1894. The Hotaling Building (no. 451) was built in 1866 and features pediments of cast iron applied over the brick walls. At no. 441 is another of the buildings that survived the disaster of 1906. Constructed between 1850 and 1852 with ship masts for interior supporting columns, it served as the French Consulate from 1865 to 1876.

Cross the street and backtrack on Jackson Street. Continue toward the intersection of Columbus Avenue and Jackson Street. Turn right on Columbus and look across the street for the small triangular building at the junction of Kearny Street and Columbus Avenue, Columbus Tower (also known as the Sentinel Building).

6 Columbus Tower

Also known as the Sentinel Building, it survived the Quake by virtue of being under construction at the time. The Kingston Trio owned it in the 1960s, when it went to seed; at the time, the basement contained a recording studio where the Grateful Dead recorded its second album. The movie director Francis Ford Coppola owns the building now; upstairs are the offices for the production company he started (now co-owned by his son Roman and his daughter, "Lost in Translation" director, Sofia). Downstairs, he sells his Napa and Sonoma county wines and there's also a little slightly overpriced but good European-style bistro, Café Zoetrope.

Continue north on Columbus Avenue and then turn right on Pacific Avenue. After you cross Montgomery Street, you'll find brick-lined Osgood Place on the left. A registered historic landmark, it is one of the few quiet—and car-free—little alleyways left in the city. Stroll up Osgood and go left on Broadway to:

7 1010 Montgomery St.

This is where Allen Ginsberg lived when he wrote his legendary poem, "Howl," first performed on October 13, 1955, in a converted auto-repair shop at the corner of Fillmore and Union streets. By the time Ginsberg finished reading, he was crying and the audience was going wild. Jack Kerouac proclaimed, "Ginsberg, this poem will make you famous in San Francisco." He underestimated the poem's impact, obviously.

Now head back to:

8 Broadway

The old Barbary Coast frolic hasn't completely died out—it limps along here, along Broadway between Columbus and Montgomery Street, where a fleet of stores and go-go houses continue to attract men at all hours. Strange to think of a porno-shop block as having a long and established heritage, but this one does.

Keep walking west on Broadway and a little farther up is the current location of the:

9 The Beat Museum

You can purchase "Howl" and other Beat works and memorabilia at this museum, which has among its collections a $450 first edition of "On the Road" and a replica of Kerouac's 1949 Hudson. The car was featured in Walter Salles "On the Road" film adaptation (2012) and is on permanent loan from the director. Tickets to the museum within the store are $8 ($5 students and seniors).

Continue along Broadway to:

10 hungry i

Now a seedy strip club (at 546 Broadway), the original hungry i (at 599 Jackson St., which is under construction for senior housing) was owned and operated by the vociferous "Big Daddy" Nordstrom. If you had been here while Enrico

Banducci was in charge, you would have found only a plain room with an exposed brick wall and director's chairs around small tables. A who's who of nightclub entertainers performed at the original hungry i, including Lenny Bruce, Billie Holiday (who sang "Strange Fruit" there), Bill Cosby, Richard Pryor, Woody Allen, and Barbra Streisand.

At the corner of Broadway and Columbus Avenue, you will see the:

11 Former Site of the Condor Club

The city's topless scene got its start in 1964 in this tan building with green cornice and a lower floor of arched brick. The owner, looking for something to liven up his club, asked the chief of police if his waitresses could loosen their bikini tops. They did, and toplessness wasn't far behind. The mayor at the time tolerated it by saying "fun is part of our city's heritage." Within days, every club in the vicinity had also gone topless.

But the person who gets the most credit, to this day, is the copiously chested Carol Doda, who danced a dozen shows nightly at the Condor and was profiled in Tom Wolfe's "The Pump House Gang." Only around 20 at the time, Doda is still a fixture on the San Francisco scene, now as a chanteuse and the owner of a store in the Marina district (at 1850 Union St.). What does she sell? Bras.

Note the bronze plaque claiming the Condor Club as BIRTHPLACE OF THE WORLD'S FIRST TOPLESS & BOTTOMLESS ENTERTAINMENT.

When you leave the Condor Sports Bar, cross to the south side of Broadway. Note the mural of jazz musicians painted on the entire side of the building directly across Columbus Avenue. Diagonally across the intersection from the Condor Sports Bar is:

12 City Lights Booksellers & Publishers

Founded in 1953, this is one of the best and most historic bookstores in the country, a triangular building stuffed with volumes, particularly hard-to-find ones by fledgling presses. Back in the 1950s, its owner, Lawrence Ferlinghetti, decided that good books didn't have to be expensive, and he set about publishing new writers who he thought deserved to be read. One of his choices was "Howl and Other Poems" by Allen Ginsberg. The book's homoerotic overtones scandalized some, and the resulting obscenity trial (which the poet won) made Ferlinghetti's bookstore nationally famous among both literary types and civil liberties defenders. By the 1960s, the Beat writers, a restless lot, had moved on, mostly taking their jazz-and-poetry evenings with them, but North Beach was indelibly stamped with their reputation.

Upon exiting City Lights bookstore, turn right, cross aptly named Jack Kerouac Street, and stop at 255 Columbus Ave., where you'll find:

13 Vesuvio

Because of its proximity to City Lights bookstore, this bar became a favorite hangout of the Beats. Dylan Thomas used to drink here, as did Jack Kerouac, Ferlinghetti, and Ginsberg. The building dates from 1913, but maintains the same quirky decor it had during the beat era. It is an excellent example of pressed-tin architecture.

Facing Vesuvio across Columbus Avenue is another favorite spot of the Beat Generation:

14 Spec's Twelve Adler Museum Cafe

Located at 12 Saroyan Place, this is one of the city's funkiest bars, a small, dimly lit watering hole with ceiling-hung maritime flags and exposed brick walls crammed with memorabilia. Within the bar is a mini-museum that consists of a few glass cases filled with mementos brought by seamen who frequented the pub from the '40s and onward.

From here, walk back up Columbus Avenue across Broadway to Grant Avenue. Turn right on Grant and continue until you come to Vallejo Street. At 601 Vallejo St. (at Grant Ave.) is:

15 Caffe Trieste

Generally acknowledged to be the king of the North Beach cafés, Trieste makes a mean espresso—in fact, it claims to have served the first one in the neighborhood back in the 1950s when it opened. Its paneled dining area is the kind of place where you're encouraged to linger for hours, and many do. Some of the Beats hung here, shaking off their hangovers, and Francis Ford Coppola is said to have fashioned the screenplay to his "The Godfather" at the tables.

Look across Columbus where you'll see the famed:

16 Molinari Delicatessen

This deli, located at 373 Columbus Ave., has been selling its pungent, air-dried salamis since 1896. Ravioli and tortellini are made in the back of the shop, but it's the sandwiches and the mouthwatering selection of cold salads, cheeses, and marinades up front that captures the attention of most folks. One Italian sub is big enough for two hearty appetites.

Continue in the same direction on Columbus until you reach 412, home of:

17 Biordi Art Imports

This store has carried imported hand-painted majolica pottery from the hill towns of central Italy for more than 50 years. Some of the colorful patterns date from the 14th century. Biordi handpicks its artisans, and its catalog includes biographies of those who are currently represented.

Walk north to the lively intersection of Columbus and Green St. and go left to no. 678, the home of:

18 Club Fugazi

For many years, Fugazi Hall has been staging the zany and whimsical musical revue "Beach Blanket Babylon." The show evolved from Steve Silver's Rent-a-Freak service, which consisted of a group of partygoers who would attend parties dressed as any number of characters in outrageous costumes. The fun caught on and soon became "Beach Blanket Babylon," now the longest-running musical revue in the nation.

If you love comedy and enormous hats, you'll love this show. I don't want to spoil it for you by telling you what it's about, but if you get tickets and they're in an unreserved-seat section, you should arrive fairly early because you'll be seated around small cocktail tables on a first-come, first-served basis. (Two sections have reserved seating, four don't, and all of them frequently sell out weeks in advance; however, sometimes it is possible to get tickets at the last minute on weekdays.) You'll want to be as close to the stage as possible. This supercharged show (p. 178 for more information) is definitely worth the price of admission.

19 O'Reilly's Irish Pub 🍺

Head back the way you came on Green Street. Before you get to Columbus Avenue, you'll see this pub, at 622 Green St., a homey watering hole that dishes out good, hearty Irish food and a fine selection of beers (including Guinness, of course) that are best enjoyed at one of the sidewalk tables. Always a conversation piece is the mural of Irish authors peering from the back wall. How many can you name?

As you exit O'Reilly's, turn left, cross Columbus Avenue, and then take a left onto Columbus. Proceed 1 block northwest to:

20 Washington Square

The Romanesque church on its northern side, Saints Peter and Paul Church (1924), is most often cited as the background of some shots of Marilyn Monroe and Joe Dimaggio (who grew up about a block from here) after their wedding in 1954. (They actually got married at City Hall—the images were just for publicity.) In true literary North Beach style, the Italian motto on the façade quotes not the Bible but Dante's "Paradise," from "The Divine Comedy." About a third of the congregation these days is of Chinese extraction.

The statue of Ben Franklin in the square—why are there so few statues of Ben in America, by the way?—was a gift (1879) from a dentist named Henry Cogswell, who made a mint in the gold rush. An avid teetotaler, he built such statues, fitted with fountains, across the country in an effort to get people to drink water instead of beer or liquor. North Beach was lucky; usually, the statue was of him, glass of water proffered in an outstretched hand.

So where's the beach of North Beach? Gone. When sailors first got here, the shoreline was actually around Taylor Street, 2 blocks west. So deep beneath your feet, North Beach's beach, now dry, still lies. Landfill erased it, but the name stuck.

Your walking tour is over, but your tour of North Beach can be just beginning, if you like, for this park is its unofficial heart, and there are dozens of shops, bakeries, and restaurants in the blocks around here. Enjoy!

WALKING TOUR 3: **RUSSIAN HILL & FORT MASON**

START:	**Hyde St. and Union St.**
PUBLIC TRANSPORTATION:	**Bus no.45, 41 Cable Car: Powell-Hyde line.**
FINISH:	**Fort Mason Center.**
TIME:	**1.5 hours**
BEST TIMES:	**Friday afternoons for Off the Grid, Sunday mornings for Farmer's Market or anytime of day.**
WORST TIMES:	**Nighttime.**
HILLS THAT COULD KILL:	**Hyde S. has a slight incline. This route is mostly downhill, however.**

Gorgeous views of the bay, history, good food, and pleasant parks converge on this walking tour. Hyde Street is a charming, tree-lined street with a cable car line, vistas, classic Victorian architecture, and cute shops and restaurants. From there, this tour will wind you through lesser-known city parks and gardens to the historic and lively Fort Mason.

1 Swenson's Ice Cream Shop

There's nothing like starting off a walk with a little ice cream nourishment. Hop off the Powell–Hyde cable car or start this tour on the corner of Hyde and Union streets at the original Swenson's. Established in 1948, Swenson's is now in 10 countries worldwide, but this quaint shop is the original and still a local favorite. A cone of the Gold Rush flavor is fitting for the sites ahead.

Continue up Hyde St. to Lombard St.

2 Lombard Street

You've no doubt seen this tourist attraction on San Francisco postcards. The whimsically winding block of Lombard Street between Hyde and Leavenworth streets draws thousands of visitors each year. The angle of the street is so steep that the road has to wind back and forth around the residences' bright flower gardens. While its moniker, "the crookedest street in the world," isn't exactly accurate, the view makes for a classic San Francisco photo-op. From here you can also see Alcatraz and Coit Tower.

Walk west down Lombard Street to Larkin Street.

3 Alice Marble & George Sterling Park

At the corner of Lombard and Larkin streets is a charming, secret garden, named for George Sterling, the unofficial poet laureate of San Francisco and an instrumental figure in establishing the city's bohemian culture in the early 20th century. At the entrance, a plaque commemorates one of the many poems he wrote about the "cool, grey city of love." The park boasts benches and paths and spectacular views of the Golden Gate Bridge. Just above the park is the Alice Marble Tennis and Basketball Courts. Here, locals play ball while trying not to get distracted by the incredible 360-degree views. See Alcatraz and Coit Tower to the east, the Golden Gate Bridge and Marin County to the north, and the sloping European-esque neighborhoods of Pacific Heights and the Marina to the west.

Head northeast on Larkin St. At Francisco St., take the stairs down to Bay St. On the way, notice Aquatic Park and Fisherman's Wharf to your right and Ghirardelli Square straight in front. Turn left on Bay St. and continue on until:

4 Fort Mason

At the corner of Bay and Van Ness streets is one of the entrances of Fort Mason, one of the oldest military posts in San Francisco and a National Historic Landmark since 1985. Between Marina Green to the west and Aquatic Park to east, Fort Mason has been an important part of San Francisco history since the Spanish first settled the area in 1797. Since then it's been the site of a fatal duel, where generals governed the city as the earthquake and fire threatened unrest, and was an important military outpost since the Civil War. If you're interested in military history, check out the signs along this tour route for more highlights or join one of the regular tours offered by San Francisco City Guides (p. 133), which provides extensive information about the area in about an hour. Today, the lower part fronting the waterfront is a cultural hub, home to the Greens Restaurant

Russian Hill & Fort Mason Tour

SAN FRANCISCO BAY

Municipal Pier

Hyde St. Pier

Pier 45

Pier 47

Stairs

Aquatic Park

Jefferson St.

FISHERMAN'S WHARF

Taylor St.

finish here

Maritime Museum

Beach St.

North Point St.

Fort Mason

Ghirardelli Square

Bay St.

Columbus Ave.

Powell-Hyde Cable Car

Bay St.

Russian Hill Park

Francisco St.

North Point St.

MARINA

Bay St.

Chestnut St.

Moscone Recreation Center

Francisco St.

Larkin St.

Lombard St.

Octavia St.

Laguna St.

Gough St.

Franklin St.

Van Ness Ave.

Polk St.

Greenwich St.

Lombard St.

Filbert St.

Jones St.

RUSSIAN HILL

Hyde St.

Union St.

Leavenworth St.

start here

Green St.

Vallejo St.

Broadway

1 Swenson's Ice Cream Shop
2 Lombard Street
3 Alice Marble & George Sterling Park
4 Fort Mason
5 McDowell Hall

6 Haskell House
7 West Battery Park
8 Community Garden
9 The Great Meadow
10 Off the Grid & Fort Mason Farmer's Market

(p. 88), San Francisco Museum of Modern Art Artists Gallery, and BATS Improv Theater (p. 178), while the upper green (The Great Meadow) is one of San Francisco's most scenic parks.

Enter Fort Mason on the corner of Bay and Van Ness sts. Walk straight to come to the first historic building:

5 McDowell Hall

Built in 1855, Commanding Generals of the Army's Western Headquarters often ruled San Francisco from these officers' quarters during times of unrest, such as just following the great Earthquake. Today the building is used as a U.S. Army Officer's club and is a favorite location for weddings thanks to unobstructed views of the embarcadero and bay.

6 Haskell House

By the 1850s the California Gold Rush attracted U.S. residents from both the North and South, bringing with them the politics and issues of the day. As the civil war raged across the country, Fort Mason was home to smaller battles around the issue of slavery. One such example is the fatal duel that took place at the site of this residence. Anti-slavery U.S. Senator David Broderick died here after his duel with Justice David S. Terry who wanted to extend slavery to California. Though the politically connected Leonidas Haskell built the house as a private residence, the government confiscated the building in 1863, allowing it to play host to a succession of military men. These days, it's rumored that Haskell, who spent the remainder of his life unsuccessfully trying to get his house back from the government, and others, haunt the storied walls.

Continue down the path with the Haskell House on your right. You'll notice gorgeous private residences with some of the best real estate in the country. Along the left, the building with the long porch is the site of Fort Mason's first hospital.

7 West Battery Park
Come to a quiet garden and picnic area right on the edge of the bluff, jutting out over the bay. On a clear day, Alcatraz will seem close enough to touch, and this is a great lookout to watch the sailboats while enjoying a picnic among fragrant Bay Trees. This area was established to protect against an attack from Confederate soldiers during the Civil War, but the guns never saw any battle action. One still exists, pointing toward Marin County.

8 Community Garden
In front of the Fort Mason Hostel lays the serene community garden, established in 1976. Today there are 125 plots where members toil away at native and exotic plants. The garden is so popular, there's a 9-year waitlist, but it's open to the public for visits and meditation.

9 The Great Meadow
Just beyond the Community Garden is the Great Meadow, with five palm trees in the center. Here San Francisco residents sought refuge after the 1906 Earthquake and watched the city burn around them. Today the elevated green puts you at eye-level with the buildings built into the surrounding hillside and offers spectacular views of the Golden Gate Bridge, Marina, and the Palace of Fine Arts. Recently dubbed "Frat Mason," you'll find the city's young, tank-top–clad professionals taking over the park on warm weekend days for not-so-legal boozy picnics and lawn games, loosely monitored by police on horseback. The meadow is a great place to picnic among 360-degree views.

10 Off the Grid and Fort Mason Farmer's Market
Off the Grid is the city's roaming epicurean extravaganza. Every Friday, from 5 to 11pm, in March through October, food trucks set up shop in the Fort Mason parking lot (below the green at Bay and Marina boulevards, though it's also accessible by taking the steps on the northwest side of the park). The trucks converge to create a unique night market, featuring inventive cuisine, live music, and arts and crafts. If you find yourself in the area during Off the Grid, it's worth taking your time to sample flavors from all over the world. Some of the city's best restaurants and most popular food movements (like Mexican-Indian fusion) started here. The same location sees a lively Farmer's Market every Sunday (9:30am– 1pm), where you start your day the San Francisco way with fresh coffee, produce, and local goods from nearby farms.

From here you can continue along the shoreline to pass through the beautiful Marina Green and restored waterfront marshlands that lead to the base of the

Golden Gate Bridge, walk up to Chestnut Street for some shopping and dining, or head to your next San Francisco adventure.

WALKING TOUR 4: HEADING THROUGH THE OH-SO-HIP MISSION DISTRICT

START:	**24th St. and Harrison St.**
PUBLIC TRANSPORTATION:	**Bus no. 47, 12, BART to 24th St.**
FINISH:	**Valencia St. and 18th St.**
TIME:	**2 hours**
BEST TIMES:	**Weekend afternoons**
WORST TIMES:	**Nighttime.**
HILLS THAT COULD KILL:	**None.**

In recent years the Mission's Latino culture has given way to hipsters who have commandeered the gritty urban area and its plethora of late-night burrito joints (some of which are the best north of the Mexico). Now, colorful produce markets, *taquerias,* and dollar stores stand alongside hipper-than-hip bars serving drinks you need a dictionary and a culinary degree to understand. If you like a little culture, history, and loads of eccentricity with your boutique shopping and imbibing, this stroll is for you!

Start at 24th and Harrison streets, the heart of the Mission's Latin neighborhood.

1 24th Street

Here you'll immediately see evidence of the neighborhood's Mexican character: street musicians in cowboy hats and mariachi outfits, storefronts overflowing with Catholic trinkets, Mexican music blaring from shop fronts and car stereos, and shop signs written only in Spanish.

Walk half a block west to come to your first destination. Turn left down Balmy Alley.

2 Balmy Alley Murals

One of the things that makes the Mission District so colorful—literally and figuratively—is its street art and hundreds of murals. Some of the area's oldest murals are along Balmy Alley, a block-long corridor between Harrison and Folsom streets. The murals started in the '80s, as a response to the political and social abuses happening in Central America. And many continue to be restored so they may remain today.

Return to 24th Street and continue walking west less than a block to come to:

3 Philz Coffee

Coffee is the new religion of the neighborhood, so if you need a pick-me-up head into Philz on 24th Street and Folsom St. Here, there's not a blended drink in sight, beans have their own histories, and each coffee is made one cup at a time—which can take up to 10 minutes, but you will taste a difference. For the coffee lover, a trip to Philz is like a visit to the holy land. And for the java novice, you may never be able to sip instant (or Starbucks) coffee again. The friendly baristas will suggest the coffee or tea right for you based on your preferences.

Continue down 24th Street until you get to Valencia Street.

4 Valencia Street

While Mission Street and 24th Street retain much of the area's Latin roots, Valencia is the area's hipster hub. Wander in and out of funky, vintage clothing and housewares stores. Pop into the lively bars (many of which are featured in our Nightlife chapter, beginning on p. 175) if you need a people-watching break.

Turn right on Valencia to walk north on the west side of the street until you come to:

5 826 Valencia

On the surface, this storefront is the nation's only pirate store. And it is in fact packed with fun nautical knickknacks and clothing. But it's much more than a captivating store. Famed author Dave Eggers started this writing center to help local students with their reading and writing skills. Because of zoning issues the space needs to operate as a store, which makes for an imaginative setting for the tutoring and classes that take place daily in the back. While the writing center's mission is to enrich the lives of inner-city youths, many of the city's up-and-coming writers find a community here among the literary-minded volunteers. Check the pamphlets at the front of the store for any upcoming readings and meet-ups for the city's bohemian, literary set.

Your next destination is just a few stops away at 824 Valencia.

7 Paxton Gate

It wouldn't be the Mission without eccentricities to marvel at and this gardening store is a prime example. Treasures and oddities inspired by science, taxidermy, and plants fill this mind-bending boutique. If you're in the market for a succulent plant or an animal skull, this is your one-stop shop.

Continue down Valencia Street 1 more block and turn left on 18th Street. On the south side of the street between Valencia Street and Guerrero Street you'll see:

8 The Maestrapeace Mural on the Women's Building

San Francisco has a ton of street art, but this mural is the city's largest and most colorful, spanning two sides of the Women's Building. Painted in 1994, the mural is the work of seven multigenerational and multicultural female artists. The vibrant painting pays homage to women and includes such female icons as Georgia O'Keeffe, Audre Lorde, Quan Yi, Yemeyah, and Coyoxauqui. Go inside the building to purchase postcards and shirts inspired by the wall.

18th Street is one of the hottest food streets in the city. In just a 2-block stretch you'll come to a few great noshing opportunities:

9 Tartine

This bakery is a San Francisco (and world!) favorite and it has the lines to prove it. People queue around the block to taste the award-winning cakes, tarts, croissants, and sandwiches. Pastry chefs and married couple Chad Robertson and Elisabeth Prueitt are at the helm of this beloved establishment, earning themselves the James Beard Award for Outstanding Pastry Chef. If you can stand the wait, you'll be rewarded with not only delicious baked goods, but also bragging rights that you've tasted what some consider the best bread in the world.

Mission District Tour

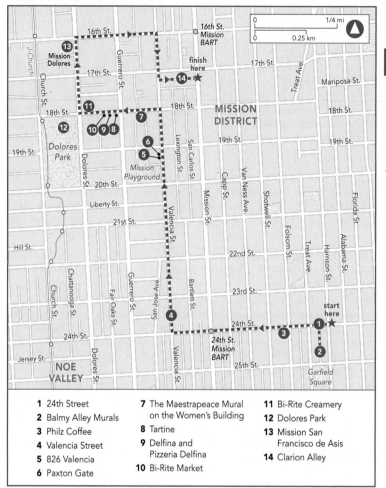

1 24th Street
2 Balmy Alley Murals
3 Philz Coffee
4 Valencia Street
5 826 Valencia
6 Paxton Gate
7 The Maestrapeace Mural on the Women's Building
8 Tartine
9 Delfina and Pizzeria Delfina
10 Bi-Rite Market
11 Bi-Rite Creamery
12 Dolores Park
13 Mission San Francisco de Asis
14 Clarion Alley

If it's a full meal you're after, walk west about a block. On the left side of the street, just past Guerrero St. you'll see:

10 Delfina & Pizzeria Delfina

One of San Francisco's most famous restaurants, hip and relaxed Delfina is the place to go for James Beard Award–winning Italian fare served San Francisco–style (by a polished, professional hipster staff in industrial-chic environs). Run by chef Craig Stoll and his wife, Annie, who is one of the best front-of-house managers around, it has a neighboring pizzeria, which inspired two other locations serving upscale thin-crust pizzas and other deliciously simple provisions.

If the wait is too long at Delfina or you're hoping to enjoy a meal alfresco (there's a great picnicking destination in just two stops), head into Bi-Rite Market half a block away.

11 Bi-Rite Market

While this little grocery store is no bigger than most 7-Elevens, meandering through its crowded aisles is like getting a crash course in the bounty that Northern California has to offer. Everything is locally sourced, from the fancy cheese and cured meats to the colorful selection of fruits, veggies, and fresh flowers. There's also a wide selection of prepared food, made fresh daily, and a selection of ice cream from their famous creamery a couple doors down. Expect to spend a pretty penny here on groceries (a chocolate bar can go for upwards of $10), but if you're a serious foodie, this shop is a worthy stop.

12 Bi-Rite Creamery

If the sidewalk looks crowded to you, a pop star isn't in town—that's just the line for the world-famous ice cream stand on the corner of 18th and Dolores streets. The legendary creamery makes small batches of soft serve and regular ice cream in bewildering, yet delicious flavors. Balsamic strawberry, toasted coconut, and Earl Grey are a few favorites. Prepare to share in order to sample as much as you can or splurge on one of the creative sundaes or splits.

On the corner of 18th and Dolores streets is one of the entrances to San Francisco's popular Dolores Park:

13 Dolores Park

If San Francisco was a high school, Dolores Park would be the cafeteria—who you are largely dictates where you hang out. It's sort of like a microcosm of the city's young people, making for an entertaining scene. In the Southwest corner, you have what's affectionately referred to as "Gay Beach," where ripped, topless men congregate until the last rays of sun dip behind the hills to the west. As the park slopes down, the families of Noe Valley bring their strollers to the playground. And as you move North, the scene gets younger and rowdier, with spontaneous DJ parties, boozy lawn games, and even costumed theme parties—there's always an occasion in San Francisco! Don't be surprised if you're offered "special truffles" (hint: they're marijuana laced) or other not-so-legal substances.

If you want to take in great views of the city skyline and enjoy a rest, head to the Southwest corner at Church and 22nd streets. Otherwise turn right and walk on the west side of palm tree–lined Dolores Street until you come to:

14 Mission San Francisco de Asís

The white building next to the cathedral is the city's oldest structure, dating back to 1791, and is one of few structures not destroyed in the 1906 earthquake. The mission offers a rare glimpse into the origins of the city, and the troubled colonial history of California in general. Take a self-guided tour, starting at the gift shop and through the cemetery where scenes from Alfred Hitchcock's "Vertigo" were filmed. Spend a few minutes at the modest museum for a refresher course on California's mission history.

Walk east down 16th Street where bars and tiny, expensive boutiques reign supreme (see the Nightlife chapter and Shopping chapter for a couple recommendations in the area), otherwise walk until you return to Valencia St. and turn right. Walk 2½ blocks on the east side of the street to come to:

15 Clarion Alley

One of the best examples of buildings acting as canvasses is Clarion Alley, bounded by Mission and Valencia streets and 17th and 18th streets. Every square inch of the alleyway is covered in art, thanks to the Clarion Alley Mural Project (CAMP), which was established in 1992. The group has worked with a diverse group of artists from folk art painters to impressionists to graffiti artists to transform the street into a gallery. Many of the masterpieces contain activist messages that speak to the area's extensive history as a center of social consciousness.

Now that you've got a feel for the neighborhood, surely there are some places you want to revisit or explore further. You can easily do that, or hop on the underground metro and BART station at 24th Street and Mission Street to get you downtown or anywhere else you'd like to go.

SHOPPING

S an Francisco is a little like a consignment shop itself—if you look in the corners and do a little digging, you're bound to find treasures. As diverse as the clientele itself, shopping options represent every style, era, fetish, and financial status here—not in sprawling shopping malls, but scattered throughout the city in the unique neighborhood boutiques. Whether it's a pair of Jimmy Choo shoes, a Chanel knockoff, or Chinese herbal medicine you're looking for, San Francisco's got it. Just pick a shopping neighborhood, wear some sensible shoes, and you're sure to end up with at least a few take-home treasures.

THE SHOPPING SCENE
Major Shopping Areas

San Francisco has many shopping areas, but here's where you'll find most of the action.

UNION SQUARE & ENVIRONS San Francisco's most congested and popular shopping mecca is centered on Union Square and bordered by Bush, Taylor, Market, and Montgomery streets. Most of the big department stores and many high-end specialty shops are here, including **Bloomingdales** (at 4th and Market sts.), **Brooks Brothers** (Post St. at Grant Ave.), **Macy's** (at Stockton and O'Farrell), **Neiman Marcus** (at Stockton and Geary), and **Nordstrom** (Market at 5th sts.). Be sure to venture to Grant Avenue, Post and Sutter streets, and Maiden Lane. This area is a hub for public transportation; all Market Street and several other buses run here, as do the Powell–Hyde and Powell–Mason cable car lines. You can also take the Muni streetcar to the Powell Street station.

CHINATOWN When you pass through the gate to Chinatown on Grant Avenue, say goodbye to the world of fashion and hello to a swarm of cheap tourist shops selling everything from linen and jade to plastic toys and $2 slippers. But that's not all Chinatown has to offer. The real gems are tucked away on side streets or are small, one-person shops selling Chinese herbs, original art, and jewelry. Grant Avenue is the area's main thoroughfare, and the side streets between Bush Street and Columbus Avenue are full of restaurants, markets, and eclectic shops. Stockton Street is best for food shopping (including live fowl and fish) and walking is the way to get around, because traffic through this area is slow and parking is next to impossible. Most stores in Chinatown are open longer hours than in the rest of the city (see box), from about 10am to 10pm. Take bus no. 1, 9X, 15, 30, 41, or 45.

JACKSON SQUARE A historic district just north of the Financial District's Embarcadero Center, this is the place to go for the top names in fine furniture and fine art. More than a dozen dealers on the 2 blocks between Columbus and Sansome streets specialize in European furnishings from the 17th to the 19th centuries. And here you'll encounter earlier than usual with most shops only open Monday through Friday from 9am to 5pm and Saturday from 11am to 4pm. Bus: 1, 3, 8, or 10.

UNION STREET   Union Street, from Fillmore Street to Van Ness Avenue, caters to the upper-middle-class crowd. It's a great place to stroll, window-shop the plethora of boutiques, try the cafes and restaurants, and watch the beautiful people parade by. Take bus no. 22, 41, 45, 47, 49, or 76.

CHESTNUT STREET   Parallel and a few blocks north, Chestnut Street is a younger version of Union Street. It holds plenty of shopping and dining choices, and an ever-tanned, superfit population of postgraduate singles who hang around cafes and scope each other out. Take bus no. 22, 28, 30, 43, or 76.

FILLMORE STREET   Some of the best boutique clothing shopping in town is packed into 5 blocks of Fillmore Street in Pacific Heights. From Jackson to Sutter streets, Fillmore is the perfect place to grab a bite and peruse the high-priced boutiques, crafts shops, and contemporary housewares stores. (Don't miss Zinc Details; p. 172.) Take bus no. 1, 2, 3, 4, 12, 22, or 24.

HAIGHT STREET   Green hair, spiked hair, no hair, or mohair—even the hippies look conservative next to Haight Street's dramatic fashionistas. The shopping in the 6 blocks of upper Haight Street between Central Avenue and Stanyan Street reflects its clientele. It offers everything from incense and European and American street styles to furniture and antique clothing. Bus nos. 6, 7, 66, and 71 run the length of Haight Street, and nos. 33 and 43 run through upper Haight Street. The Muni streetcar N-line stops at Waller Street and Cole Street.

SoMa   Although this area isn't suitable for strolling, you'll find almost all the discount shopping in warehouse spaces south of Market. You can pick up a discount-shopping guide at most major hotels. Many bus lines pass through this area.

HAYES VALLEY   While most neighborhoods cater to more conservative or trendy shoppers, the few blocks of lower Hayes Street, between Octavia and Gough streets, celebrate all things vintage, chic, artistic, and contemporary. It's definitely the most interesting shopping area in town, with furniture and glass stores, modern furniture shops, trendy shoe stores, and men's and women's clothiers. You can find lots of great

---

Just the Facts: Hours, Taxes & Shipping

Store hours are generally Monday through Saturday from 10am to 6pm and Sunday from noon to 5pm. Most department stores stay open later, as do shops around Fisherman's Wharf, the most heavily visited area (by tourists).

Sales tax in San Francisco is 9.5%, which is added on at the register. If you live out of state and buy an expensive item, you might want to have the store ship it home for you. You'll have to pay for shipping, but you'll escape paying the sales tax. Most of the city's shops can wrap your purchase and ship it anywhere in the world. If they can't, you can send it yourself, either through **UPS** (© 800/742-5877), **FedEx** (© 800/463-3339), or the U.S. Postal Service.

antiques shops south on Octavia Street and on nearby Market Street. Take bus no. 16AX, 16BX, or 21.

THE MISSION   Where Mexican wrestler masks meet new-age apothecaries meet trendy boutiques, the Mission offers an eclectic mix perfect for some entertaining browsing. In just the last few years a treasure trove of fashionable and funky stores have popped up on 16th and 17th streets in the Mission, as well as along Valencia Avenue. Find Mexican trinkets, Dia de los Muertos (Day of the Dead) paraphernalia, designer lotions and herbal remedies, trendy fashions, locally designed jewelry, funky art and home decor, and even taxidermy—all in the same quarter-mile stretch. Bus: 12, 14, 22, or 49.

SHOPPING A TO Z

Antiques

Bonhams   Part of a world-renowned chain of auction houses, the goodies here are international, ranging from exquisite ancient Japanese screens to Hopi pottery to art deco jewelry and more. Open Monday through Friday, 9am to 5pm. 220 San Bruno Ave. (at 16th St.). ✆ **800/223-2854** or 415/861-7500. www.bonhams.com.

Therien & Co.   Once a showroom primarily for Scandinavian, French, and eastern European antiques, in the past few years they've expanded to include Mid-century Modern furniture, as well. You'll find both the real thing and replicas here, as well as made-to-order furniture. Monday through Friday, 10am to 5pm. 411 Vermont St. (at 17th St.). ✆ **415/956-8850.** www.therien.com.

Art

For the latest on what artists are showing at the town's galleries, go online to www. sfbayareagalleryguide.com.

Catharine Clark Gallery   Here the majority of the exhibits focus on local artists in video and media art. The beloved contemporary gallery moved from downtown to Potrero Hill for more space, so would-be buyers are able to see even more work by California's up-and-coming artists. Shows change every 6 weeks. Open Tuesday through Saturday, 11am to 6pm. Utah St. (btw. 15th and 16th sts.). ✆ **415/399-1439.** www.cclarkgallery.com.

Fraenkel Gallery   Photography is the focus here; world-class artists from around the globe are featured in shows that change every 2 months. Open Tuesday through Friday 10:30am to 5:30pm and Saturday 11am to 5pm. 49 Geary St. (btw. Grant Ave. and Kearny St.), 4th floor. ✆ **415/981-2661.** www.fraenkelgallery.com.

Hang   Only Bay Area artists are exhibited at Hang, and since many are at the beginning of their careers, prices for pieces tend to be more affordable than at other galleries. Open Monday through Saturday 10 am to 6pm and Sunday noon to 5pm. 567 Sutter St. ✆ **415/434-4264.** www.hangart.com.

Meyerovich Gallery   A blue chip gallery, Meyervoich concentrates on selling the works of such modern masters as Chagall, Matisse, Miró, and Picasso. A Contemporary Gallery, across the hall, features works by Lichtenstein, Stella, Motherwell, and Hockney. Open Monday through Friday 10:30am to 6:30pm and Saturday 10:30am to 5pm. 251 Post St. (at Stockton St.), 4th floor. ✆ **415/421-7171.** www.meyerovich.com.

Books

Adobe Books & Arts Cooperative Yes, they sell books, both new and used at great prices, but to call this beloved Mission District institution just a bookstore would be selling it short. It's also a haven for emerging musicians and artists and a sort of salon for the city's eccentrics. Charming corners to read, art rooms, and regular cheese and wine receptions make this store both a vintage-book shopping destination and a cultural hub. Open Monday through Friday noon to 8pm and Saturday and Sunday 11am to 8pm. 3130 24th St. (between Folsom and South Van Ness Sts.) ℂ **415/864-3936.** www.adobebooks.com.

Argonaut Book Shop When Alfred Hitchcock walked into this book store while filming the movie "Vertigo," he said something to the effect of "This is exactly what a book store should look like," and promptly recreated every detail of the store on his movie set in Hollywood. This antiquarian book shop specializes in California history, American West, rare books, as well as maps, prints, and photographs. Open Monday through Friday 9am to 5pm and Saturday from 10 am to 4pm. 1786 Sutter St. (at Jones St.). ℂ **415/474-9067.** www.argonautbookshop.com.

Book Passage Run by the ebullient Elaine Petrocceli, this bookstore in the Ferry Building may be small but its wonderfully well curated, meaning you're sure to find something entertaining to read here. Book Passage is also known for its excellent author events and writer's conferences, both in San Francisco, and in its main store in Corte Madera. It's open from 9am to 8pm Monday through Friday, 9am to 7pm on weekends. Ferry Building Marketplace (at the Embarcadero and Market St.). ℂ **415/835-1020.** www.bookpassage.com.

Books Inc. Holding the title "The West's Oldest Independent Bookseller," Books Inc., established in 1857, is living proof that an indie book seller can adapt, survive, and even prosper, despite Gold Rush busts and booms, numerous earthquakes, The Great Depression, fires, death, bankruptcy, and, most important (and probably toughest of all), the rapidly changing bookselling climate. Owners Margie and Michael Tucker have created a warm, inviting environment, hosting book clubs, author events, and travel lit groups—everyone is welcome to attend. The chain has four city locations, as well as two **Compass Books** at San Francisco International Airport. Hours vary by store, but most open and 10am and close no earlier than 7pm, seven days a week (with the Castro store open until 10pm nightly). Marina: 2251 Chestnut St. (btw. Scott and Pierce Sts.). ℂ **415/931-3633.** Castro: 2275 Market St. (at 16th St.). ℂ **415/864-6777.** Presidio Heights: 3515 California St. (at Locust St.) ℂ **415/221-3666.** Opera Plaza: 601 Van Ness (btw. Turk St. and Golden Gate Ave.) ℂ **415/776-1111.** SFO Airport: Terminals 2 and 3. www.booksinc.net.

The Booksmith A true gem, with erudite, handwritten recommendations for books dotting the shelves. This Haight store may not be huge, but it's smartly curated and has more than 1,000 different magazines on sale. Open Monday through Saturday 10am to 10pm and Sunday 10am to 8pm. 1644 Haight St. (btw. Clayton and Cole sts.). ℂ **800/493-7323** or 415/863-8688. www.booksmith.com.

City Lights Booksellers & Publishers The city's iconic bookstore—once owned by Lawrence Ferlinghetti, the renowned Beat Generation poet—is still going strong. The three-level store is particularly good for art, poetry, and political paperbacks, though it also carries more mainstream books. Open daily 10am to midnight. 261 Columbus Ave. (at Broadway). ℂ **415/362-8193.** www.citylights.com.

Green Apple Books   A massive purveyor of both new and used books—the store boasts more than 160,000 tomes!—it's an excellent resource for those seeking special books, like modern first editions; and rare graphic comics. We also have to give kudos to the knowledgeable and friendly staff, who will help you find whatever you need *Note:* There's a separate music, fiction, and DVD annex next door. Hours are 10am to 10:30pm Sunday through Friday, until 11:30pm on Saturday. 506 Clement St. (at Sixth Ave.). ℂ **415/387-2272.** www.greenapplebooks.com.

Cigars

Occidental Cigar Club   Hinton Rowan Harper, an 1800s Gold Rush–era writer, once remarked he'd seen "the purest liquor, the best segars (sic), the finest tobacco, the prettiest courtezans (sic)" and it was his "unbiased opinion that California can and does furnish the best bad things that are available in America." I haven't seen any courtesans here, but if you are looking for a fine stogie with a tumbler of rare scotch, and a legal smoking room to enjoy your treasures, step inside. Though the name implies it is a private club, Occidental is open to the public. A varied selection of premium cigars make good souvenirs to remember your time in the Sin City of the West. Open daily noon to 1am. 471 Pine St. (at Kearney St). ℂ **415/834-0485.** www.occidentalcigarclub.com.

Vendetta Men's Apparel & Vintage Cuban Cigars   Vendetta's motto is "living well is the best revenge" and owner, Bruce Rothenberg, is all about the finer things in life. This is more than evident at his shop in Nob Hill's Fairmont Hotel, where he sells high quality items like fine Italian caps and Persol sunglasses. But Bruce's real specialty, his baby if you will, are the pre-embargo Cuban cigars he lovingly sells to customers with the reluctance of someone selling his offspring. He knows the history of these babies, dating from 1947 to 1962, and assures that, like a fine wine, they only get better—more complex and more character—with age. As one of the only (if not the only) stores in the country selling Cubans, you will pay the price for one of these rare stogies—cigars range from $125 to $250 apiece. Bruce has added a separate smoking room with a cushy sofa for a few guests to light up and enjoy their purchases. Don't worry, if the Cubans are a little out of your price range, he carries Dominican and Nicaraguan cigars for a fraction of the price. Open Tuesday through Saturday, noon through 7pm. Fairmont Hotel, 950 Mason (btw. California and Sacramento sts.). ℂ **415/397-7755.** www.vendettablu.com.

Fashion

MEN'S FASHIONS

Cable Car Clothiers   Since 1939, this gentleman's store has been helping San Francisco's elite look their most dashing. Selling everything from three-button suits to fedoras to pocket squares, they source the best from around the world for their clientele and that even goes for the more esoteric buys, like wool hosiery from France and cotton underwear from Switzerland. Open Monday through Friday 9:30am to 6pm, Saturday, 11am to 5pm. 200 Bush St. (at Sansome St.). ℂ **415/397-4740.** www.cablecar clothiers.com.

Citizen Clothing   Ben Sherman, Jack Spade, Fred Perry are just a few of the swanky brands this Castro shop carries to keep the neighborhood fellows looking dapper. Topnotch service is another hallmark of the store. Open Sunday through Thursday 11am to 7pm. Friday and Saturday 10am to 8pm. 536 Castro St. (btw. 18th and 19th sts.). ℂ **415/575-3560.** www.citizensf.co.

UNISEX

A-B Fits   The solution for those who've given up finding a flattering pair of jeans, this North Beach boutique specializes in finding denim that, well, fits. Doing so requires a broad range of options and a dedicated staff. Luckily, A-B Fits has both—the shop carries over 100 styles of jeans and the salespeople are true experts at their highly specialized trade. Open Tuesday through Saturday 11:30am to 6:30pm and Sunday from noon to 6pm. 1519 Grant Ave. (at Union and Filbert sts.). ℰ **415/982-5726.** www.abfits.com.

Goorin Brothers   Fabulous hats, for both men and women, are the stock in trade of this three-store chain. You'll find funky straw fedoras here (made by local artists), modern cloth cloches in all colors, porkpie hats, cowboy hats, and wide-brimmed hats perfect for fashionable garden parties (or gardening). Open Sunday to Thursday 10am to 7pm and Friday and Saturday 10am to 8pm on Haight Street; Sunday to Thursday 11am to 8pm and Friday and Saturday 10am to 9pm in North Beach; and daily 11am to 7pm on Stockton Street. 1612 Stockton St., 111 Geary St., and 1446 Haight St. ℰ **415/426-9450.** www.goorin.com.

Jeremys   Fashionistas flock to Jeremys because they can scoop up top-of-the-line name brand clothing at bargain-basement prices. Jeremys fills its shelves with shirts, dresses, trousers, you name it, that were either used in window displays at big department stores, were created as samples, or are overstocks. So these are not second-hand clothes or cheap knock-offs, but the real thing, just for far less than you'd usually pay. This place is a true treasure trove. Open Monday to Wednesday and Friday to Saturday 11am to 6pm; Thursday 11am to 8pm; Sunday noon to 6pm. 2 S. Park (btw. Bryant and Brannan sts. at Second St.). ℰ **415/882-4929.** www.jeremys.com.

MAC   Nope, not the makeup store. The name stands for Modern Appealing Clothing, and that about sums up what's being sold here. The owners source attractive and (sometimes) unusual pieces from around the world—Belgium's Dries Van Noten and Martin Margiela, New York's John Bartlett to name a few—and then helps customers arrange them into drop-dead gorgeous outfits. And happily, prices are *slightly* kinder at MAC than they are in the other trendy shops of the area. Open Monday through Saturday 11am to 7pm and Sunday noon to 6pm in Hayes Valley. Open Tuesday to Saturday 11am to 7pm and Sunday noon to 6pm Sunday in the Dogpatch. 387 Grove St. (at Gough St.). or 1003 Minnesota St. (at 22nd St.) ℰ **415/863-3011.**

Marine Layer   Comfort is Marine Layer's *raison d'etre.* The firm makes basic tops that are great for layering—T's, polos, button downs, cardigans, and hoodies—and feel already broken in. They do this by using a special blend of pima cotton and micro modal. And best of all, their products are made in the USA. (unlike most of the clothing we buy in this country). Open daily 10am to 7pm. 2209 Chestnut St. and 498 Hayes St. ℰ **415/346-2400.** www.marinelayer.com.

Wilkes Bashford   The couture boutique that first introduced Armani to the U.S. underwent a total facelift in 2012, making this elegant temple of commerce even more hoity toity. The fashions are primarily from France and Italy, and services include custom fittings on-site, free wine and coffee, and the advice of a staff of expert stylists. *Tip:* If you just can't stomach paying $6,000 for a blouse, shop here in February when the warehouse sale is held, and prices drop by a hair. Open Monday through Saturday 10am to 6pm. 375 Sutter St. (at Stockton St.). ℰ **415/986-4380.** www.wilkesbashford.com.

WOMEN'S FASHIONS

Bell Jar   Bell Jar is the type of boutique that makes you want to move in. From essentials like luxe lotions and chic dresses to things you didn't even know you needed (like a vintage set of tarot cards and artful glass bottles), this store is home to "gorgeous little things"—just as its sign promises. Go here if you're looking for precious gifts and treasures that are authentically "San Francisco," yet don't have a bridge or Alcatraz printed on them. Open Monday through Saturday noon to 7pm and Sunday noon to 6pm. 3187 16th St. (between Valencia St. and Guerrero St.) © **415/626-1749.** http://belljarsf.com.

440 Brannan Studio Showroom   In this massive factory space, local designers sell limited edition lines to the public; you'll sometimes see one stitching a hem or constructing a jacket in the back. In business since 1998, the Studio's been an incubator for a number of talented San Francisco designers. While it does carry menswear, the vast majority of these unique, and often really fun and funky creations, are for women. Open Monday to Saturday 11am to 7pm. 440 Brannon St. (near Zoe St.). © **415/957-1411.** www.440Brannan.com.

emily lee   Not everyone is 22 and a size 2. For those who like to look stylish, but have bodies that are, well, like the majority of our bodies, emily lee offers artsy, generously cut duds that make most everyone look good. Among the designers sold here: Blanque, Eileen Fisher, Flax, Ivan Grundahl, and Three Dots. Open Monday through Friday 10am to 6pm, Saturdays 9:30am to 5:30pm. 3509 California St. (at Locust St.). © **415/751-3443.**

RAG   RAG stands for Residents Apparel Gallery, and it's a co-op shop for 55 new to newish designers to showcase their trousers, blouses, T-shirts, and dresses. Prices are low; fashions are forward, youthful, and of-the-moment. Daily 11:30am to 7pm. 541 Octavia St. (btw. Hayes and Grove sts.). © **415/621-7718.** www.ragsf.com.

Sunhee Moon   Clothing for the "modern day Audrey Hepburn" is the goal of local designer SunHee Moon, and with her eye for color and fit, I'd say she's succeeding. Her dresses, which come in a variety of streamlined shapes and exuberant colors, will likely become a staple of your wardrobe. Moon creates equally flattering separates: sleek pants, tailored and/or draped tops, and quirkily patterned skirts. And prices, while not low, are more than reasonable for clothing this sturdy, yet chic. Open Monday through Friday noon to 7pm and weekends noon to 6pm. 3167 13th St. and 1833 Fillmore St. © **415/928-1800.** www.sunheemoon.com.

Therapy   At this fast-fashion boutique, the merchandise ranges from the latest garb to housewares to novelty items and the prices are just reasonable enough to be dangerous. As in, you'll come in for a small splurge on, say, a scented candle, and you'll be tempted to leave with a new pair of Toms, a locally designed dress, a chunky infinity scarf, and a hat. Find local designers alongside hipster-favorite brands, like Obey and Hobo. Also a great place for playful gifts and quirky cards and books for those who suspect gifts upon your return home. Considering a little retail therapy can save you hundreds on the real thing, a trip to either of the Mission District (Mon–Thurs 11am–9pm, Fri–Sat 10:30am–10pm, and Sun 11am–8pm) or North Beach (Mon–Thurs 11:30am–7:30pm, Fri–Sat 11am–9pm, and Sun 11am–9pm) locations may be worth it. 545 Valencia St. (btw. 17th and 18th sts.). © **415/865-0981.** 1445 Grant Ave. (btw. Green and Union sts.) © **415/781-8899.** www.shopattherapy.com.

Consignment and Vintage Stores

Good Byes The style-conscious citizens of San Francisco consign their cast-offs to this shop, meaning the quality of the goods is high, but the prices often surprisingly low (we've seen $350 pre-owned shoes going for just $35 here). Menswear is the focus at this store; womenswear is in a separate boutique across the street. Open Monday through Saturday 10am to 6pm, Thursday 10pm to 8pm, and Sunday 10am to 5pm. 3464 Sacramento St. and 3483 Sacramento St. (btw. Laurel and Walnut sts.). ✆ **415/346-6388** (men's) and 415/674-0151 (women's). www.goodbyessf.com.

La Rosa Specializing in clothes from the 1940s through the 1960s, this long-established store (founded in 1978) has a lot of great buys for folks who enjoy vintage fashions. Rumor has it that Dita Von Teese shops here regularly. Their sister store, **Held Over** (1543 Haight St., near Ashbury; ✆ **415/864-0818**) features less expensive and more modern duds (some are sold for $12 per pound!). Both open daily 11am to 7pm. 1711 Haight St. (at Cole St.). ✆ **415/668-3744.**

Food

Cowgirl Creamery Cheese Shop Arguably one of the farms that pioneered the artisanal cheese craze, the small-production Cowgirl Creamery has its head-quarters up in Point Reyes. Their city outpost is located in the Ferry Building Marketplace and offers all their signature cheeses—robust Red Hawk to smooth, creamy Mt. Tam. Open Monday through Friday 10am to 7pm, Saturday 8am to 6pm, Sunday 11am to 6pm. Ferry Building Marketplace, no. 17. ✆ **415/362-9354.** www.cowgirlcreamery.com.

Molinari Delicatessen You can't help but take your camera out when you walk into this North Beach institution dating back to 1896. It's a food sensory overload. Everywhere you look, shelves, counters, and rafters are filled with jars of colorful sauces, olive oils, cheeses, and imported wines. Did I mention the salami? All sizes of red and white salamis hang from strings, creating a savory curtain. Molinari's is the perfect place to grab a thick meat-stuffed sandwich and picnic supplies; I recommend taking your feast to Washington Square Park two blocks away at Columbus and Union Streets. Open Monday through Friday 8am to 6pm and Saturday 7:30am to 5:30pm. 373 Columbus St. (at Vallejo St.). ✆ **415/421-2337.**

Tcho Chocolate Tcho is far more than just another candy store. It offers free, 1-hour factory tours (online reservations required) which include serious sampling. You'll also learn about the widespread problem of slavery in the chocolate biz. Who knew? If you don't do the tour, drop in for a sweet treat. Now, if they could just take out the calories. Open Monday through Friday 9am to 5:30pm, 10am to 5:30pm on weekends. Pier 17. ✆ **415/981-0189.** www.tcho.com. Tours daily 10:30am and 2pm; no children under 8 allowed. Open Mon–Fri 9am–5:30pm; Sat–Sun 10am–5:30pm. Bus: 2, 12, 14, 21, 66, or 71. Streetcar: F-Line. BART: Pier 17 Embarcadero.

Z. Cioccolato This sweet-tooth wonderland offers 40 flavors of fresh fudge, plus saltwater taffy, classic brands of candies of all sorts, and such novelty items as candy bras or G-strings. A decadent North Beach store that's sure to satisfy. Open Monday through Wednesday 10am to 10pm, Thursday and Sunday 10am to 11pm and Friday through Saturday 10am to midnight. 474 Columbus Ave (at Green St.). ✆ **415/395-9116.** www.zcioccolato.com.

AMAZING grazing: THE FERRY BUILDING

As much a sightseeing attraction as a place to buy and consume food, the **Ferry Building Marketplace** and its corollary **Farmers' Market** (one of the most highly acclaimed farmers' markets in the United States) are tangible proof that people who live in San Francisco lead tastier lives than the rest of the nation (sorry, but it's true!). The produce looks like it was taken from a still-life painting (it's organic and sourced from small family farms), the meats and fish are super-fresh and the quality and variety of specialty goods—many of which you may never have encountered before (who knew balsamic vinegar is sometimes clear!)—will blow your mind.

Saturday morning is the best time to stop by, as the farmer's market is in its full glory, playing host to local meat ranchers, artisan cheese makers, bread bakers, specialty food purveyors, and farmers. Some are picked for the 10:30am **Meet the Farmer** event, a half-hour interview created to give the audience in-depth information about how and where their food is produced. At 11am, Bay Area chefs give cooking demonstrations using ingredients purchased that morning from the market. (And yes, tastings are given out, as are recipes.) Several local restaurants also have food stalls selling their cuisine—including breakfast items—so don't eat before you arrive.

The Marketplace is open daily and features Northern California's best gourmet food outlets including Cowgirl Creamery's Artisan Cheese Shop, Recchiuti Confections (amazing chocolate), Acme Breads, Hog Island Oysters, famed Vietnamese restaurant the Slanted Door, Imperial Tea Court (where you'll be taught the traditional Chinese way to steep and sip your tea), and a myriad of other restaurants, delis, gourmet coffee shops, specialty foods, and wine bars.

The Ferry Building Marketplace is open Monday through Friday from 10am to 6pm, Saturday from 9am to 6pm, and Sunday from 11am to 5pm. The Farmers' Market takes place year-round, rain or shine, every Tuesday and Thursday from 10am to 2pm and Saturday 8am to 2pm. The Ferry Building is located on the Embarcadero at the foot of Market Street (about a 15-min. walk from Fisherman's Wharf). Call ✆ **415/693-0996** for more information or log onto www.ferryplaza farmersmarket.com or www.ferrybuilding marketplace.com.

Gifts

Art of China   Since 1974, this shop has been selling refined Chinese exports, so no plastic here! Instead you'll find genuine collectibles, from elegant hand-carved Chinese figurines to cloisonné, porcelain vases, and decorative items (and jewelry) created from ivory, quartz, and jade. Hours vary. 839–843 Grant Ave. (btw. Clay and Washington sts.). ✆ **415/981-1602.** www.artsofchinasf.com.

Cost Plus World Market   It sometimes feels like the entire world is on sale at this Fisherman's Wharf store (it's right at the cable car turnaround). You'll find biscuits from Australia and inlaid stools from India, artisanal beers from across the U.S. (they let you build your own six-pack so you can do a tasting), funky shower curtains, you name it! They have it here, usually in a foreign brand you haven't seen before and at a price that's more than fair. World Market is open Monday to Friday 10am to 9pm; Saturday 9am to 9pm. 2552 Taylor St. (btw. North Point and Bay sts.). ✆ **415/928-6200.** www.worldmarket.com.

Dandelion   Paperweights and trivets, bookends and multi-colored garden trowels, 90 different teapots—these are just some of the pretty and well-designed goods on sale at local favorite Dandelion, many imported from India and Japan. If you can't find a gift here, well, you've got extraordinarily finicky friends. The store is closed Sunday and Monday, except during November and December, when it's open daily. Hours are 10am to 6pm. 55 Potrero Ave. (at Alameda St.). ℂ **415/436-9200.** www. dandelionsf.com.

Good Vibrations   This female-oriented sex-toy shop is more straightforward and empowering than seedy thanks to the open, nonjudgemental attitude of the staff (who own the place, incidentally; this is a woman-owned, worker-owned co-operative). If you're not in the market for any new gadgets, you can always stop by to see the on-site vibrator museum. 603 Valencia St. (at 17th St.). ℂ **415/522-5460** or 800/BUY-VIBE (289-8423) for mail order. A 2nd location is at 1620 Polk St., at Sacramento St. (ℂ **415/345-0400**), and a 3rd is at 2504 San Pablo Ave., Berkeley (ℂ **510/841-8987**). www.goodvibes.com.

Gump's   Those who need a special item for a special event come here, and have been doing so since 1861 when the boutique department store was founded. The service is legendary, many items can't be found anywhere else, and Gump's carries everything from jewelry to vases to Asian antiques. A particularly popular choice for wedding registries. the store also has an unusually good and large collection of Christmas ornaments. Monday through Saturday 10am to 6pm, Sunday noon to 5pm. 135 Post St. (btw. Kearny St. and Grant Ave.). ℂ **800/766-7628** or 415/982-1616. www.gumps.com.

Nest   It's hard to categorize Nest as it carries everything from throws and handmade quilts to flowing boho dresses and sleepwear. What ties it all together is the impeccable taste of the owner, and the fact that you won't find a lot of these items anywhere else. This one's fun to just browse, even if the prices stop you from buying. Open Monday to Friday 10:30am to 6:30pm, Saturday 10:30 to 6pm, and Sunday 11am to 6pm. 2300 Fillmore St. (at Clay St.). ℂ **415/292-6199.** www.nestsf.com.

New People World   More than just a store, New People World is a $15-million complex dedicated to modern Japanese culture, both its zen side and its over-the-top, *anime* wackiness. In the basement is a THX-certified theater to showcase Japanese cinema; the other floors (there are five altogether) feature a nail salon, a crumpet and tea shop, a boutique dedicated to cute gadget cases, two clothing stores, and the SuperFrog art gallery. But back to those fashion stores, because they carry items you likely won't find anywhere else in North America. Like Lolita clothes (dresses for grown women that are made to look like outfits a toddler would wear; don't ask) and Sou Sou shoes, which are the classic, form-fitting Japanese shoes that come with an indent between the big toe and the rest of the toes (and here are done in all sorts of wacky, modern patterns). Open Monday to Saturday noon to 7pm and Sunday noon to 6pm. 1746 Post St. (btw. Buchanan St. and Webster St.). No phone. www.newpeopleworld.com.

Housewares/Furnishings

Alessi   Functional yet whimsical—that about describes the kitchen utensils of Italian designer Alberto Alessi (love his spiderlike lemon squeezer), and this is his North American flagship. It's a great place to find a gift, though most end up getting something for themselves, too, like a silver beaver shaped pencil sharpener or one of their oh-so-cute kettles. Open Monday to Saturday 10am to 6pm. 424 Sutter St. (at Stockton St.). ℂ **415/434-0403.** www.alessi.com.

Biordi Art Imports   Exquisite Italian majolica pottery is the lure here. Some use it to eat off of, but it's so pretty my guess is most buyers take those plates, bowls, and other items and stick them on the wall for decoration. The owner has been importing these hand-painted collectibles since 1946. Open Monday to Friday 11am to 5pm and Saturday 9:30 to 5pm. 412 Columbus Ave. (at Vallejo St.). ✆ **415/392-8096.** www.biordi.com.

Propeller   For ultra-contemporary furniture and accessories, often by up-and-coming designers from around California and the globe, head to this stylish shop. Perpetually voted as a top shop by locals, its success is due to owner Lorn Dittfeld, who handpicks pieces, promising that they are "built and offered by people with a stake in your happiness." Open Monday to Saturday 11am to 7pm and Sunday noon to 5pm. 555 Hayes St. (btw. Laguna and Octavia sts.). ✆ **415/701-7767.** www.propeller modern.com.

The Wok Shop   Every implement ever created for Chinese cooking is available in a store that goes well beyond woks. Cleavers, circular chopping blocks, dishes, oyster knives, bamboo steamers, strainers, aprons, linens, and baskets . . . they're all here at great prices and all imported from China. Open Monday to Thursday 11am to 10pm, Friday and Saturday 11:30am to 10:30pm, and Sunday 4pm to 10pm. 718 Grant Ave. (at Clay St.). ✆ **415/989-3797.** www.wokshop.com.

Zinc Details   This high-style furniture and accessories store just about defines the San Francisco aesthetic, with alternately hip, colorful, and quirky pieces to dress up any home. While many of the furniture comes from international brands like Knoll, a portion are made specifically for the store. Open Monday to Saturday 11am to 7pm and Sunday from noon to 6pm. 1905 Fillmore St. (btw. Bush and Pine sts.). ✆ **415/776-2100.** www.zincdetails.com.

Jewelry

Dianne's Old & New Estates   A preferred pick for vintage engagement rings, this family-owned shop has baubles for all tastes, from fine antique jewels to contemporary pieces. It also has a very forgiving payment policy: you can buy jewelry on layaway here and pay no interest for the first 12 months. Open Monday to Saturday 11am to 6pm and Sunday 11am to 5pm. 2181A Union St. (at Fillmore St.). ✆ **888/346-7525** or 415/346-7525. www.diannesestatejewelry.com.

Love and Luxe   There's jewelry and then there's wearable art. The highly curated conversation-starters at this Mission District art gallery and jewelry atelier are the latter. A tad on the edgy side, necklaces, rings, earrings, and accessories at this charming boutique are all handmade by a rotating crop of emerging artists, giving you a sense of the local aesthetic. Guaranteed you'll find a few off-beat, beautiful pieces to commemorate your trip, but even if you're not in the market for anything in particular, this store is still worth the browse. Open Wednesday and Thursday noon to 6pm, Friday and Saturday 11am to 7pm, and Sunday noon to 5pm. 1169 Valencia St. (btw. 22nd and 23rd sts.). ✆ **415/648-7781.** http://loveandluxesf.com.

Union Street Goldsmith   Locally made contemporary jewelry is the focus here, and many of the pieces feature vibrantly colorful stones. The staff will also create custom designs upon request. Open Monday through Saturday 11am to 5:30pm and Sunday from noon to 4:30pm. 1909 Union St. (at Laguna St.). ✆ **415/776-8048.** www.union streetgoldsmith.com.

Pirate Supplies

826 Valencia/Pirate Supply Store   When "A Heartbreaking Work of Staggering Genius" author Dave Eggers wanted to set up a literary salon to inspire young people to write, the city said his space was zoned for retail. Naturally, he opened a pirate supply store as a sort of front for the tutoring, mentoring, and writing that goes on just beyond the displays of maritime knickknacks. Pick up a bottle of "Scurvy be Gone" or tattoo remover. Stock up on eye patches or glass eyes. When you order your custom hook, make sure to specify whether it is for the right or left hand. All proceeds from the store support up-and-coming young writers who hone their craft in the classroom in the back. Open daily from noon to 6pm. 826 Valencia St. (btw. 19th St. and Cunningham Lane). ℂ **415/642-5905.** www.826valencia.org.

Shoes

Bulo   Fashion-forward footwear from designers like Donald J. Pliner, Yuko Imanishi, and Bed Stu draws shoppers to this small, hip store. In addition to shoes, Bulo sells belts, socks, wallets, jewelry, and shoe care products. Open Monday through Saturday 11am to 7pm and Sunday from noon to 6pm. 418 Hayes St. ℂ **415/255-4939.** www.bulo shoes.com.

Paolo Shoes   Paolo is short for Paulo Iantorno, the owner who designs the store's colorful wedges and towering stilettos for women and funky purple suede ankle boots for men—and then sends his designs to Italy to be handcrafted. But what might make these shoes so unique is they're not only creative and colorful, they're actually comfortable—even the pumps! Open Monday through Saturday 11am to 7pm and Sunday from noon to 6pm. 524 Hayes St. ℂ **415/552-4580.** A 2nd location is at 2000 Fillmore St. (ℂ 415/771-1944). www.paoloshoes.com.

Toys

The Chinatown Kite Shop   This delightful Chinatown classic sells all sorts of kites from ones you design yourself to color-saturated fish kites, windsocks, hand-painted Chinese paper kites, wood-and-paper biplanes, pentagonal kites, and more. All of it makes great souvenirs and decorations. Open daily from 10am to 7:30pm. 717 Grant Ave. (btw. Clay and Sacramento sts.). ℂ **415/989-5182.** www.chinatownkite.com.

Travel Goods

Flight 001   The store for jetsetters, it sells you the coolest of luggage tags, TSA-friendly manicure sets, sleek travel pillows, and all sorts of other gadgets that will make your flight home that much more comfortable and/or fun. Open Monday through Saturday 11am to 7pm and Sunday from 11am to 6pm. 525 Hayes St. (btw. Laguna and Octavia sts.). ℂ **415/487-1001.** A 2nd location is out in Berkeley at 1774 4th St. (ℂ 510/526-1001). www.flight001.com.

Wine & Sake

True Sake   Some 150 different brands of sake are available at this specialty store, many of which, owner Beau Timken claims, are available at no other retail store in the U.S. Don't be intimidated if you know nothing about sake: the informed staff will help you make the best decision to suit your tastes and won't just push the pricier varieties (in fact, many of the bottles here are surprisingly affordable). Open Monday through

shopping CENTERS & COMPLEXES

Crocker Galleria Modeled after Milan's Galleria Vittorio Emanuele, this glass-domed, three-level pavilion, about 3 blocks east of Union Square, features around 40 high-end shops with expensive and classic designer creations. Fashions include Aricie lingerie, Gianni Versace, and Polo/Ralph Lauren. Closed Sunday. 50 Post St. (at Kearny St.). ℂ 415/393-1505. http://thecrocker galleria.com/shop/.

Ghirardelli Square This former chocolate factory is one of the city's quaintest shopping malls and most popular landmarks. Though now dotted with tourist-centric shops, and is best known as the former chocolate and spice factory of Domingo Ghirardelli (say "*Gear*-ar-dell-y"), it actually dates back to 1864, when it served as a factory making Civil War uniforms. A clock tower, an exact replica of the one at France's Château de Blois, crowns the complex. Inside the tower, on the mall's plaza level, is its most popular attraction—the fun yet pricey Ghirardelli soda fountain. It still makes and sells small amounts of chocolate, but the big draw is the old-fashioned ice-cream parlor. Stores range from a children's club to a perfumery, cards and stationery to a doggie boutique. The main plaza shops' and restaurants' hours are 10am to 6pm Sunday through Thursday and 10am to 9pm Friday and Saturday, with extended hours during the summer, and the

square has free Wi-Fi. 900 North Point St. (at Polk St.). ℂ 415/775-5500. www.ghirardellisq.com.

Pier 39 To residents Pier 39 is an expensive spot where out-of-towners buy souvenirs and greasy fast food. But it does have some redeeming qualities—fresh crab (when in season), stunning views, playful sea lions, fun street performers, and plenty of fun for the kids. If you want to get to know the real San Francisco, skip the cheesy T-shirt shops and limit your time here to one afternoon, if that. Located at Beach St. and the Embarcadero.

Westfield San Francisco Centre This ritzy 1.5-million-square-foot urban shopping center is one of the few vertical malls (multilevel rather than sprawling) in the United States. Its most attractive feature is a spectacular atrium with a century-old dome that's 102 feet wide and three stories high. Along with Nordstrom (p. 162) and Bloomingdale's (p. 162) department stores and a Century Theatres multiplex, there are more than 170 specialty stores, including Abercrombie & Fitch, Zara, H&M, bebe, Juicy Couture, J. Crew, and Movado. The bottom level is sprinkled with probably the best food-court fare you've ever had (don't miss the amazing array of grab-and-go eats at Bristol Farms grocery store). 865 Market St. (at Fifth St.). ℂ 415/512-6776. www.west field.com/sanfrancisco.

Friday from noon to 7pm, Saturday 11am to 7pm, and Sunday noon to 6pm. 560 Hayes St. (btw. Laguna and Octavia sts.). ℂ 415/355-9555. www.truesake.com.

Wine Club San Francisco The Wine Club is a discount warehouse that offers excellent prices on more than 1,200 domestic and foreign wines. If you can't find your favorite on sale, the well-informed staff should be able to find you a similar tipple. Open Monday through Saturday from 10am to 7pm and Sunday from 10am to 6pm. 953 Harrison St. (btw. Fifth and Sixth sts.). ℂ 415/512-9086. www.thewineclub.com.

NIGHTLIFE

San Francisco's nightlife is as varied and colorful as the clientele, and each neighborhood offers a different vibe, which means there's something for everyone, but there isn't one place that offers a quintessential experience. Whether you linger downtown or head to the various corners of the city, there's always something going on. The best part? Unlike Los Angeles or New York, you won't pay outrageous cover charges to be a part of the scene. For up-to-the-minute nightlife information, turn to the "San Francisco Weekly" (www.sfweekly.com) and the "San Francisco Bay Guardian" (www.sfbg.com), both of which run comprehensive listings. They are available for free at bars and restaurants and from street-corner boxes all around the city. "Where" (www.wheresf.com), a free tourist-oriented monthly, also lists programs and performance times; it's available in most of the city's finer hotels. The Sunday edition of the "San Francisco Chronicle" features a "Datebook" section, printed on pink paper, with information on and listings of the week's events. If you have Internet access, it's a good idea to check out www.citysearch.com, www.sfstation.com, or www.7x7.com for the latest in bars, clubs, and events. And if you want to secure seats at a hot-ticket event, either buy well in advance or contact the concierge of your hotel and see if they can swing something for you.

Tix Bay Area (also known as **TIX;** ☎ **415/430-1140;** www.tixbayarea.org) sells half-price tickets on the day of performances and full-price tickets in advance to select Bay Area cultural and sporting events. TIX is also a Ticketmaster outlet and sells Gray Line tours and transportation passes. Tickets are primarily sold in person with some half-price tickets available on their website. To find out which shows have half-price tickets, call the TIX info line or check out their website. A service charge, ranging from $1.75 to $6, is levied on each ticket, based on its full price. You can pay with cash, traveler's checks, Visa, MasterCard, American Express, or Discover with photo ID. TIX, located on Powell Street between Geary and Post streets, is open Tuesday through Friday from 11am to 6pm, Saturday from 10am to 6pm, and Sunday from 10am to 3pm. *Note:* Half-price tickets go on sale at 11am the day of the performance.

You can also get tickets to most theater and dance events through **City Box Office,** 180 Redwood St., Ste. 100, between Golden Gate and McAllister streets off Van Ness Avenue weekdays from 9:30am to 5pm and Saturdays noon to 4pm. (☎ **415/392-4400;** www.cityboxoffice.com). MasterCard and Visa are accepted.

Tickets.com (✆ 800/225-2277; www.tickets.com) sells computer-generated tickets (with a hefty service charge of $3–$19 per ticket!) to concerts, sporting events, plays, and special events. **Ticketmaster** (✆ 415/421-TIXS [8497]; www.ticketmaster.com) also offers advance ticket purchases (also with a service charge).

For information on local theater, check out **www.theatrebayarea.org**. For information on major league baseball, pro basketball and pro football, and "Professional Sports Teams," see p. 188.

And don't forget that this isn't New York: Bars close at 2am, so get an early start if you want a full night on the town here.

THE PERFORMING ARTS

San Francisco Performances ★★ (www.performances.org), has brought acclaimed artists to the Bay Area since 1979. Shows run the gamut from chamber music to dance to jazz and are held in several venues, including the Herbst Theater and the Yerba Buena Center for the Arts. The season runs from late September to June. Tickets cost from $15 to $96 and are available through **City Box Office** (✆ 415/392-4400) or through the San Francisco Performances website.

Classical Music and Opera

San Francisco Opera ★★★   The second largest opera company on the continent, this opera company is also one of the most courageous: along with presenting the classics, in lavish, huge productions, the SFO commissions new works each year. Sometimes these fresh operas can be quite controversial, such as the fall of 2013 adaptation of the Stephen King novel "Dolores Claiborne" by American composer Tobias Picker. All productions have English supertitles. The performance schedule is a bit of an odd one, with the season starting in September and lasting 14 weeks. It then takes a break for a few months before starting again in June for 2 months. It's usually possible to get the less coveted seats as late as the day of performance (though prime seats can go months in advance). War Memorial Opera House, 301. Van Ness Ave. (at Grove St.). ✆ **415/864-3330** (box office). www.sfopera.com. Tickets $25–$380; standing room $10 cash only; student rush $27; active military and seniors $32.

San Francisco Symphony ★★★   Michael Tilson Thomas is perhaps the most celebrated living American conductor and he holds the baton here. Thanks in part to his leadership, the roster is full of world-class soloists, world-premier pieces and high-quality performances. Davies Symphony Hall, 201 Van Ness Ave. (at Grove St.). ✆ **415/864-6000** (box office). www.sfsymphony.org. Tickets $15–$156; rush tickets on select performances $20.

Free Opera

Every year, the **San Francisco Opera** stages a number of free performances, beginning with Opera in the Park every September to kick off the season. They follow it with occasional free performances throughout the city as part of the Brown Bag Opera program. Schedule details can be found on the company's website at **www.sfopera.com**.

Theater

American Conservatory Theater (A.C.T.) ★★★ This is, quite simply, one of the best theater companies in the U.S., with peerless acting, design and show-selecting chops. Since its debut in 1967 a number of big names have "trod the boards" here, including Annette Bening, Denzel Washington, Danny Glover, and Nicolas Cage. The A.C.T. season runs September through July and features both classic and contemporary plays. Its home is the stupendously beautiful (and viewer-friendly) **Geary Theater,** built in 1910. It's a national historic landmark. Performing at the Geary Theater, 415 Geary St. (at Mason St.). *C* **415/749-2ACT** (2228). www.act-sf.org. Tickets $20–$140.

Berkeley Repertory Theater ★★★ Across the bay, this theater was founded in 1968 and has been mopping up awards ever since. It rivals A.C.T. in the quality of its shows, though sometimes skews a bit more avant garde. Contemporary plays are offered throughout the year, usually Wednesday through Sunday. 2025 Addison St. Berkeley. *C* **510/647-2900.** www.berkeleyrep.org. Tickets $55–$81.

The Magic Theatre ★★ Sam Shepard was a longtime artist-in-residence at the Magic, premiering his plays "Fool for Love" and "True West" here. That should give you an idea of the quality of work (it's usually quite high). The company has been performing since 1967. Performing at Building D, Fort Mason Center, 2 Marina Blvd. (at Buchanan St.). *C* **415/441-8822.** www.magictheatre.org. Tickets $20–$60; discounts for students, educators, and seniors.

San Francisco Playhouse ★ The city's oldest off-Broadway company is located in the intimate upstairs theater of a charming old theater-district hotel. Located a quick stroll away from Union Square hotels, it's a wonderful way to enjoy some San Francisco culture without having to leave the downtown area. 450 Post St., in Kensington Park Hotel (btw. Powell & Mason sts.). *C* **415/677-9596.** www.sfplayhouse.org. Tickets $30–$100.

Theatre Rhinoceros ★ Founded in 1977, this was America's first theater created to address LGBT themes and stories. It's still going strong. The theater is 1 block east of the 16th Street/Mission BART station. 2926 16th St. *C* **866/811-4111.** www.therhino.org. Tickets $15–$30.

Dance

Top traveling troupes like the Joffrey Ballet and American Ballet Theatre make regular appearances in San Francisco. Primary modern dance spaces include **Yerba Buena Center for the Arts,** 701 Mission St. (*C* **415/978-2787;** www.ybca.org); the **Cowell Theater,** at Fort Mason Center, Marina Boulevard at Buchanan Street (*C* **415/345-7575;** www.fortmason.org); and the **ODC Theatre,** 3153 17th St., at Shotwell Street in the Mission District (*C* **415/863-9834;** www.odcdance.org). Check the local papers for schedules or contact the theater box offices for more information.

San Francisco Ballet ★★★ This venerable company (founded in 1933), is the oldest professional ballet company in the United States and is still regarded as one of the country's finest. Along with its beloved "Nutcracker," it performs a varied repertoire of full-length contemporary and classic ballets. The season generally runs February through May, with "Nutcracker" performances in December. War Memorial Opera House, 301 Van Ness Ave. (at Grove St.). *C* **415/865-2000** for tickets and information. www.sfballet.org. Tickets $18–$355.

COMEDY & CABARET

BATS Improv ★   Born out of the improvisational comedy craze that swept the U.S. in the '80s, BATS Improv is the longest-running improv theater in Northern California, and every weekend it serves up new plays, competitions, and even musicals. The award-winning theater focuses on "long form" improv, which means shows are geared towards creating a coherent story line, rather than just 2 minute bursts of weirdness (though the audience is encouraged to yell out ideas throughout the performance). On some nights, teams compete for trophies and bragging rights. Main Company shows are Fridays and Saturdays at 8pm; student performance ensemble shows are Sundays; the times vary each week. Reservations and discount tickets available through their website. Remaining tickets are sold at the box office the night of the show. Performing at Bayfront Theatre at the Fort Mason Center, Building B no. 350, 3rd floor. ✆ **415/474-6776**. www.improv.org. Tickets $5–$22.

Beach Blanket Babylon ★★★   The longest-running musical revue in America, and by far one of the most "San Francisco" things to do, this beloved cabaret-style show—playing since 1974—is a riveting 90-or-so minutes of hilarious and outrageous costumes, bawdy humor, campy sexual flirtation, and political and cultural commentary.

The show's name doesn't describe what you'll see, except possibly the "Babylon" part; it's left over from its debut incarnation, when the theater was filled with sand and audience members had their hands slapped with Coppertone lotion. Some 12,000 performances and 4.8 million tickets later, the show's toothless political commentary and mild sexual innuendo hit just the right spot for a hilarious evening out. Everything about it is pleasingly silly, from the silly plots to the songs (mostly radio standards in 1-minute bursts) and the impersonations (Kim and Kanye made a recent appearance).

The show's main claim to fame, besides its longevity, are the huge wigs and hats, which are as tall as the proscenium will allow. The climactic bonnet, an illuminated and mechanized city skyline, requires a hidden scaffolding to support. There's a family friendly option on Sunday afternoons, but the content is still mildly eyebrow-raising. Performances are Wednesday and Thursday at 8pm, Friday and Saturday at 6:30 and 9:30pm, and Sunday at 2 and 5pm; check the website for additional Tuesday shows in July. Club Fugazi, 678 Beach Blanket Babylon Blvd. (Green St. at Powell St.). ✆ **415/421-4222**. www.beachblanketbabylon.com. Tickets $25–$130. Bus: 9X, 20, 30, or 45. Cable car: Powell–Mason.

Cobb's Comedy Club ★★   Some of the hottest names in comedy—Louis CK, Sarah Silverman, Dave Chapelle—as well as up-and-coming local comics have been performing at Cobb's since 1984. With cabaret seating and higher stools along the back bar, there's not a bad seat in the house. Cover varies by act and there's a two-drink minimum (the drinks, alas, are weaker than the line-ups). Shows are held Wednesday, Thursday, and Sunday at 8pm, Friday and Saturday at 8 and 10:15pm. 915 Columbus Ave. (at Lombard St.). ✆ **415/928-4320**. www.cobbscomedyclub.com. Cover $15–$60. 2-beverage minimum.

Martuni's Piano Bar ★★   Open 7 nights a week, this friendly watering hole is the best place in the city to catch casual cabaret–style performances from talented singers and piano players. Patrons range in age from 20s to 60s, but everyone enjoys the strong drinks and convivial atmosphere. Come for the performance or join in yourself with piano karaoke on Monday nights. 4 Valencia St. (at Market St.). ℗ **415/241-0205.** Cover and hours vary.

Punch Line Comedy Club ★   As San Francisco's longest-running comedy club, Punch Line has played host to celebrity comics such as Ellen Degeneres and Robin Williams, and continues to bring established and emerging stars to its stage, which features a mural of San Francisco as a backdrop. Showcase night is Sunday, when 15 local comics take the mic to try out new material. Doors open at 7pm and shows are Sunday to Thursday at 8pm, Friday and Saturday at 8 and 10pm (18 and over; 2-drink minimum). 444 Battery St. (btw. Washington and Clay sts.), Plaza level. ℗ **415/397-4337** or 415/397-7573 (recorded information). www.punchlinecomedyclub.com. Cover Tues–Thurs $16; Fri–Sat $20; Sun $13. Prices are subject to change for more popular comics, maxing out at $45.

THE CLUB & MUSIC SCENE

The greatest legacy from the 1960s is the city's continued tradition of live entertainment and music, which explains the great variety of clubs and music enjoyed by San Francisco. The hippest dance places are south of Market Street (SoMa), in former warehouses; the artsy bohemian scene centers are in the Mission; and the most popular cafe culture is still in North Beach.

Drinks at most bars, clubs, and cafes follow most big-city prices, ranging from about $7 to $14, unless otherwise noted.

Rock, Jazz, Blues and Dance Clubs

In addition to the following listings, see "Dance Clubs," below, for (usually) live, danceable rock.

Bimbo's 365 Club ★★   Family-owned-and-operated since 1931, this intimate retro-stylish performance venue still manages to be hip, with its wide variety of fresh musical acts (I saw Beck here recently), while maintaining its old dance-hall feel. Lavish art deco details, cabaret seating, and lush curtains transport patrons to a bygone era, while the large dance floor in front of the stage plays host to the city's young revelers and those who want to relive their glory days. Grab tickets in advance at the box office, which is open Monday through Friday (10am–4pm). 1025 Columbus Ave. (at Chestnut St.). ℗ **415/474-0365.** www.bimbos365club.com.

The Boom Boom Room ★★   To get a sense of what San Francisco was like when Fillmore Street was the most important scene for West Coast blues, head to this little venue that packs a big sound. Opened by the venerated Mississippi bluesman John Lee Hooker, in the last years of his life, it wasn't just his business but his hangout. Today, though it still maintains street cred as a blues hall, it plays host to root music as well, ranging from New Orleans funk to trance jazz. The monthly Soul Train Revival draws a big crowd of weekday warriors who want to shake it on a Wednesday. Open Tuesday through Sunday until 2am. 1601 Fillmore St. (at Geary Blvd.). ℗ **415/673-8000.** www.boomboomblues.com. Cover varies from free to $15.

Bottom of the Hill ★   One of the few places in town to offer a ton of all-ages shows, it's the savvy programming (and excellent sound system) here that brings in the crowds. You'll hear everything from indie punk to rockabilly to hard funk, and all of it top-notch. Doors open nightly around 8:30pm; bar closes a tad before 2am. Kitchen open until midnight most nights. 1233 17th St. (at Missouri St.). ℗ **415/621-4455.** www.bottomofthehill.com. Cover $8–$50.

9

NIGHTLIFE

The Club & Music Scene

The Chapel ★★ Named 2013's best new live venue by "SF Weekly," this bar/restaurant/venue is a great place to catch dinner and a show in the Mission District. You don't even need to change locations! The venue's sister restaurant, The Vestry, housed in the same complex, serves upscale comfort food in a loud, lively setting—a contrast to its gothic Church theme. After enjoying cocktails and food at the rustic wood tables or on the back twinkle-lit patio, head into the venue in a separate room, which as its name suggests, is shaped like a cathedral. Make your way to the front see the band in action, or head to the mezzanine to get a bird's-eye view and an up-close look at the arched ceiling. There are two bars in the venue area, but it's just as easy to refill drinks in the restaurant area, where the lines are generally shorter. Indie punk rock acts as well as 19-piece orchestras and everything in between have been on the bill. Check the website for bookings. 777 Valencia St. ✆ **415/551-5157.** www.thechapelsf.com. Cover varies by act $10–$30.

DNA Lounge ★ If you're after a wild nightclub scene, DNA Lounge, host of the famous mash-up party Bootie SF, is where it's at. While Bootie is now in several cities around the country, San Francisco is where it originated and it continues to be voted Best Dance Club and Best Theme Night year after year. There's not much ambience to speak of, except what's created from the DJ booth, but when last call is ringing in the rest of the city, this party is just getting started. (Just don't expect to buy more drinks after 2am). 375 Eleventh St. (btw. Folsom and Harrison sts.) ✆ **415/626-1409.** dnalounge.com. Cover $10 before 10pm; $15 after.

The Fillmore ★ Though concert halls around the nation are now called the Fillmore, this is the original, and it's a treasure of San Francisco history. In the 1960s it was the heartbeat of San Francisco counter-culture, where legendary promoter Bill Graham booked the Grateful Dead, Jefferson Airplane, Janis Joplin, and Led Zeppelin. While it's no longer a crucible of what's next, it's still an excellent place to see a show and small enough (1,250 capacity for most shows) that you can stand in the back, near the bar, and still be satisfied. 1805 Geary Blvd. (at Fillmore St.). ✆ **415/346-6000.** www.thefillmore.com. Tickets $23–$62.

Great American Music Hall ★★ Acts and audiences alike dig this saloonlike ballroom, that recalls San Francisco's scandalous past. Opened by a crooked politician as Blanco's Café, the elegant bordello catered to the hedonism of the emerging metro. Now if only the frescoed ceilings, baroque details, ornate balconies, and marble columns could talk…. Over the years, acts who have played here have ranged from Duke Ellington and Sarah Vaughan to Arctic Monkeys, the Radiators, and She Wants Revenge. All shows are all ages 6 and up so you can bring your family, too. Purchase tickets online or over the phone (✆ **888/233-0449**) for a $4 to $5 service fee. Or download a form from the website and fax it to ✆ **415/885-5075** with your Visa or MasterCard info; there is a service fee of $2 per ticket. Stop by the box office to purchase tickets directly the night of the performance for no charge (assuming the show isn't sold out), or buy them online at www.gamhtickets.com or Tickets.com (✆ **800/225-2277**). 859 O'Farrell St. (btw. Polk and Larkin sts.). ✆ **415/885-0750.** www.musichallsf.com. Ticket prices and starting times vary; call or check website for individual show information.

SFJAZZ ★ As the only structure in the country built just for jazz, this $64-million building, which debuted in 2013, is a must-visit for music fans. The lineup consists mostly of jazz, though everything from gospel brunches to Ethiopian blues bands has

DRINKING & SMOKING laws

The drinking age is 21 in California, and bartenders can ask for a valid photo ID, no matter how old you look. Some clubs demand identification at the door, so it's a good idea to carry it at all times. Once you get through the door, however, forget about cigarettes—smoking is banned in all California bars. The law is generally enforced and though San Francisco's police department has not made bar raids a priority, people caught smoking in bars can be—and occasionally are—ticketed and fined. Music clubs strictly enforce the law and will ask you to leave if you light up. Also, last call for alcohol usually rings out at around 1:30am, since state laws prohibit the sale of alcohol from 2 to 6am every morning. A very important word of warning: Driving under the influence of alcohol is a serious crime in California, with jail time for the first offense. You are likely to be legally intoxicated (.08% blood alcohol) if you have had as little as one alcoholic drink an hour. When in doubt, take a taxi.

been on the bill. Start with dinner and drinks at the full-service café by Charles Phan of Slanted Door (p. 75) fame in the lobby, where there is sometimes live music. The main hall has circular stadium seating so there is no bad seats in the house. Last minute tickets are often available. 201 Franklin St. (at Fell St.). © **866/920-5299.** www.sfjazz.org. Tickets $5–$200. Bart: Civic Center.

Yoshi's Jazz Club ★★   Rarely does jazz get such a grand setting (28,000-square feet!) as at this club. The front is a festive restaurant, which becomes a nightclub venue on occasion. The back is specifically for concerts—although with light nibbles—and regularly features known entertainment. Expect a sophisticated, music-aficionado crowd. 1330 Fillmore St. (at Eddy St.). © **415/655-5600.** www.yoshis.com.

THE BAR SCENE

Finding your kind of bar in San Francisco has a lot to do with which district it's in. The following is a general description of what types of bars you're likely to find throughout the city:

- **Marina/Cow Hollow** bars attract a yuppie post-collegiate crowd that often gets very rowdy.
- Young, trendy hipsters who would turn their noses up at the Marina frequent the **Mission District** haunts. Look out for plaid, skinny jeans, and beanies.
- **Haight-Ashbury** caters to eclectic neighborhood cocktailers and beer-lovers.
- The **Tenderloin,** though still dangerous at night (take a taxi), is now a hot spot for serious mixologists and has its fair share of dark, cozy dives.
- Tourists mix with conventioneers at **downtown** pubs.
- **North Beach** serves all types, mostly tourists and post-collegiate crowds.
- **Russian Hill**'s Polk Street has become the new Marina/Cow Hollow scene.
- The **Castro** caters to gay locals and tourists.
- **SoMa** offers an eclectic mix from sports bars to DJ lounges.

The following is a list of a few of San Francisco's more interesting bars. Unless otherwise noted, these bars do not have cover charges.

SoMa, Downtown, Tenderloin & FiDi

Bar Agricole ★★★ In mixology circles, the name Thad Vogler carries major weight. He's the drink master behind this chic, sleek bar. There's not a hint of the oft-used vintage decor here—clean, industrial lines and reclaimed wood create the sophisticated, modern atmosphere. The heated outdoor patio is also a rare draw. As for the cocktails, they're created from hard-to-source small batch liquors; the bar food is darn good too, a mix of Northern European and Californian cuisine. 355 11th St. (near Folsom St.). ✆ **415/355-9400.** www.baragricole.com. Mon–Thurs 6–10pm, Fri–Sat 5:30–11pm, Sun 11am–2pm.

Bourbon & Branch ★★★ Meet San Francisco's modern day speakeasy, right down to the password you have to give at the door to get in. The folks behind Bourbon & Branch are determined to create an authentic prohibition-era atmosphere, which means only those who have reservations are admitted, and cell phone use is strictly forbidden. Those who get in the unmarked door (look for the address) choose from an extensive and creative cocktail list, sitting in one of the sexiest lounges in town. There's even a speakeasy within the speakeasy (even harder to get into!) called Wilson & Wilson, which offers a $30 tasting flight of cocktails. 501 Jones St. (at O'Farrell St.). ✆ **415/346-1735.** www.bourbonandbranch.com. Daily 6pm–2am.

Burrit Room ★★ If you want a prohibition-era cocktail without the fussiness and exclusivity of Bourbon & Branch, pop into this stylish, upstairs Union Square bar in the Mystic Hotel. Some of the city's best bartenders, clad in suspenders and vests, serve up classic and new-age cocktails without a hint of pretention. There's live jazz every night and a film-noir aesthetic provide a sexy, vintage vibe. Delicious (and substantial) bar bites add to the lure. 417 Stockton St. (between Sutter St. and Bush St.). ✆ **415/400-0555.** Daily 5pm–1am.

Edinburgh Castle ★ An oldie but a goodie (founded in 1958), this Scottish pub has the finest selection of single-malt scotches in the city as well as a number of unusual British ales on tap. Beloved of ex-pats (and Britophiles), the decor is filled with U.K. brit-a-brac, and the bar menu, naturally, includes fish and chips. Enjoy a pool table, a smoking room with an old piano, large wooden booths, and a balcony area that's great for people watching. Friday and Saturday nights, this divey, no-fuss pub hosts DJs and the crowd gets younger and more rowdy. 950 Geary St. (btw. Polk and Larkin sts.). ✆ **415/885-4074.** www.castlenews.com. Mon–Fri 5pm–2am, Sat–Sun 1pm–2am.

Local Edition ★★★ Housed in the bowels of the historic Hearst Building on Market Street, this subterranean bar pays homage to San Francisco's newspaper history, as well as it current mixology craze with contemporary and classic craft cocktails. Inspired by the newspaper business of the '50s and '60s, vintage presses, typewriters and archived clippings from San Francisco periodicals provide most of the décor and guests sit in rolling desk chairs from the *"Mad Men"* era. While it's a relatively new establishment in the Financial District, it's the type of place famed newspaper columnist Herb Caen likely would have headed for a drink after filing his weekly column at the "San Francisco Chronicle" around the corner. The bar attracts an after-work crowd, and often gets crowded on weekdays around happy hour. Make a reservation for a table or try your luck at the bar. 691 Market St (on the corner of 3rd St.) ✆ **415/795-1375.** www.localeditionsf.com. Mon–Fri 5pm–2am; Sat 7pm–2am.

Smuggler's Cove ★★ Behind the non-descript exterior on thoroughfare Gough Street, lies this piratey tiki bar of Disneyland proportions, that also happens to be one of the world's best bars. The space is transformed into a vintage pirate ship a la "Pirates of the Caribbean," complete with a roped off balcony area that resembles a ship's crow's nest. Exotic Caribbean cocktails, prohibition-era Havana libations, and more then 400 rare rums ensure you'll taste something you've never had before. And with its fair share of flaming cocktails and punch bowls, the cocktails are serious, but the atmosphere is not. The space is small so expect a line on Friday and Saturday nights. 650 Gough St. (at McAllister St.). *C* **415/869-1900.** www.smugglerscovesf.com. Daily 5pm–1:15am.

Terroir Natural Wine Merchant ★★★ With its rustic wooden beams and a library loft—not to mention a selection of wines to rival any Napa or Sonoma store—this is the oenophile's Shangri-la. Sit at the bar and get an education about the art, science, and soul of the winemaking process. Owners Luke, Billy, and Dagan will be happy to tell you everything you ever wanted to know about wine. Not in the mood for a lesson and prefer to simply relax? Head upstairs to the lounge and flip through a book, or play a game (board games are available), while you savor the nectar of the gods. Add in cheese and charcuterie and you probably won't want to return to your hotel. 1116 Folsom St. (btw. 7th and 8th sts.). *C* **415/558-9946.** www.terroirsf.com. Mon–Thurs 2pm–midnight, Fri–Sat noon–2am, Sun 2–9pm.

Fisherman's Wharf, Russian Hill, Nob Hill & North Beach

Buena Vista Café ★ It's considered a modern tradition to visit Buena Vista Cafe to order a $7.25 Irish Coffee (it was conceived here in 1952 by a local travel writer). This punch-packing quaff lures hordes of tourists before they wobble toward the cable car turnaround across the street. You may not want to hear how the bartender gets the cream to float—it's aged for 2 days before use. Some 2,000 are served each day in high season, which means you will probably have to wait for a table on a weekend afternoon (better, probably, to come at night; it's open until 2am). These beverages are indeed delicious, and the spublike setting is classic without being snooty. 2765 Hyde St. (at Beach St.). *C* **415/474-5044.** www.thebuenavista.com. Daily 9am–2am.

The Saloon ★ A true dive, this is supposedly the oldest bar in the city and it certainly looks (and smells) like it. Floors are but worn planks, staff are grizzled and hairy, and the story goes that this place managed to survive the conflagration of 1906 by offering the firefighters free booze. There's live music every night—mostly blues and jazz. Don't come expecting a cruisey scene; come for down-and-dirty music and cheap whiskey. 1232 Grant Ave. (at Columbus St.). *C* **415/989-7666.** Music cover $5–$15 Fri–Sat. Daily noon–2am.

The Tonga Room & Hurricane Bar ★★ This sublime, vast, one-of-a-kind bar and restaurant is the pinnacle of fabulous classic San Francisco kitsch. Every half-hour in this dim, Polynesian-themed fantasia, decorated with rocks and 12-foot tikis, lightening strikes, thunder rolls in, and rain falls above the pond in the middle of it all (once the hotel's indoor pool). If you're lucky, you'll be here late enough to see the band playing on a raft right in the middle of the thing. Yes, it's gimmicky and yes, you'll pay a lot for a cocktail here, but it's pure fun anyway. During happy hour (Wed–Fri 5–7pm), there's a list of strong, tropical drinks sold at a discount, and if you throw down just $10 you get unleashed on a heat-lamp-lit buffet of egg rolls and other grub, served beneath the rigging on the deck of an imaginary ship. There's a full menu, too, but people tend to take advantage of that later in the night. In the Fairmont Hotel, 950 Mason St. (at California St.). ✆ **415/772-5278.** www.tongaroom.com. Wed–Thurs and Sun 5–11:30pm, Fri–Sat 5pm–12:30am.

Vesuvio ★★★   You haven't fully experienced San Francisco's literary history without a trip to this famous, trinket-stuffed watering hole. It was opened in 1948, just in time to catch all the dissolute Beat writers as they staggered in and out of City Lights, located directly across Jack Kerouac Alley from its front door. In fact, this is where Kerouac and other Beat writers nursed their alcoholism and creative endeavors. Snag a table in the cozy, secluded balcony area, overlooking the bar, providing a prime people-watching view. 255 Columbus Ave. (at Broadway). ✆ **415/362-3370.** www.vesuvio.com. Daily 6am–2am.

The Marina, Cow Hollow

Nectar Wine Lounge ★   Few places in the city, or in North America for that matter, have as copious a menu when it comes to wine: 50 are available by the glass (from all around the globe) and a good 800 by the bottle. Just as impressive is the handsome crowd this hip, industrial-chic watering hole draws. It's a nice place to linger. 3330 Steiner St. (at Chestnut St.). ✆ **415/345-1377.** www.nectarwinelounge.com. Mon–Wed 5–10:30pm, Thurs–Sat 5pm–midnight, Sun 5–10pm.

Perry's ★   Made famous by "Tales of the City," this is not the crazy pick-up scene it was in the book. Still, locals and visitors alike enjoy chilling at the dark mahogany bar. An attached dining room offers up all sorts of simple food (think burgers or grilled fish) should you be feeling peckish. 1944 Union St. (at Laguna St.) ✆ **415/922-9022.** www.perryssf.com. Mon–Wed 7:30am–10pm, Thurs–Sat 7:30am–11pm, Sun 8:30am–10pm.

Press Club ★   Come here if you can't get to the Wine Country this trip but still want a wine-tasting experience. Calling itself "urban wine tasting bar" the huge space features eight separate bars which are often manned by reps from regional Northern California wineries (the list of wineries rotates and these sellers are always happy to ship home cases for you, should you enjoy your glass). Gourmet small bites (including Cowgirl Creamery cheese plates), elbow room, and a mellow soundtrack make the Press Club quite popular among the 35-plus crowd. 20 Yerba Buena Lane (near Market St.). ✆ **415/744-5000.** www.pressclubsf.com. Mon–Thurs 4–11pm, Fri–Sat 2pm–midnight, Sun 2–9pm.

Tipsy Pig ★   This cozy (and noisy) gastropub is a great starting point for a Chestnut Street bar crawl. The heated back garden patio, leather booths in the front window, and famous Strawberry Fields cocktails lure a crowd of all ages. For a neighborhood with the reputation of being a bit frat-tastic, this bar is diverse enough to resist the stereotype (most of the time), while still embracing the lively, convivial atmosphere the Marina is known for. The food is good too, if you need something to soak up the heavy pours. In fact, "San Francisco Chronicle" food critic Michael Bauer included it in his list of top 100 restaurants in the Bay Area. Plus it has a dedicated kid's menu for family-friendly imbibing. 2231 Chestnut St. (between Pierce St. and Scott St.) ✆ **415/292-2300.** www.thetipsypigsf.com. Mon–Thurs 5pm–2am, Fri–Sun 11am–2am.

The Mission

Elbo Room ★   If you're not sure if you want a dive, lounge, or dance floor, Elbo Room offers all three in one playful two-story saloon. Cozy up with no-fuss well cocktails or a PBR-and-shot deal in one of the big booths, try your luck at a classic

cocktails WITH A VIEW

Harry Denton's Starlight Room ★★★
There are few better places to raise a stylish drink with an unspoiled panorama of one of the world's greatest cities. Most stay for dinner and dancing, but it's possible to simply come and enjoy a drink at the bar (though on nights that there's live music, you'll pay a cover charge). *Tip:* Come dressed to impress (no casual jeans, open-toed shoes for men, or sneakers), or you'll be turned away at the door. Atop the Sir Francis Drake Hotel, 450 Powell St., btw Post and Sutter St., 21st floor. *(* 415/395-8595. www.harrydenton. com. Cover $10. Tues–Thurs 6pm–midnight, Fri–Sat 6pm–1:30am, Sun 11am–3:30pm.

Top of the Mark ★★★ A 19th-floor bar doesn't sound like much, but considering in this case it's in a building that's already atop Nob Hill, and adding the fact that it's one of the most famous bars in the country, both the view and the mood are high. Floor-to-ceiling windows take in the kind of panorama that makes people want to move to this city: Golden Gate Bridge, Coit Tower, Alcatraz, and beyond, all in a smart, swanky setting. The operators regularly close the space for private parties, so call ahead to make sure it's open. From Tuesday to Saturday, musical acts are booked—mostly jazz or other styles that make nice background—and covers are surprisingly cheap. Dinner is pricey, so we'd recommend just coming by for the tipple. In the Mark Hopkins InterContinental, 1 Nob Hill Place (btw. California and Mason sts.). *(* 415/616-6199. www.topofthemark.com. Cover $15. Mon–Thurs and Sun 5pm–midnight, Fri–Sat 4pm–1am.

arcade game in the back, or head upstairs to dance to a live show or DJ set in an intimate setting. The vibe is pure fun, right down to the photo booth. It can get crowded and the bartenders are all business, so know your poison when you catch their attention. 647 Valencia St. *(* **415/552-7788.** www.elbo.com. Open daily 5pm–2am.

El Rio ★ If you head just a few blocks farther south from the most hopping stretch of Mission area bars, you'll come to this gem that bills itself as a neighborhood bar with "heck of a lot to offer." And it delivers: there's a garden patio, space for regular live shows, juke box, pool table, shuffle board, and some of the best happy hour deals in the city—$1 beers for 7 hours every day. Come here to mingle with friendly locals who care more about neighborhood community than the latest trendy scene. Cash only. 3158 Mission St. (at Caesar Chavez). *(* **415/282-3325.** www.elriosf.com. Daily 1pm–2am.

Southern Pacific Brewing Company ★★ In a city of narrow, hole-in-the-wall bars, it's rare for beer to get such a grand setting. Two floors, a front patio, and 10,000 square feet doesn't necessarily mean it won't be crowded, but your chances of snagging a table near one of the twinkle-light-lit trees inside the warehouse space are pretty good. Sip on unique, small-batch brews made in-house or a curated selection of interesting guest beers. Beer-inspired pub fare almost steals the show—the Brussels sprouts and sage fries are to-die-for! 620 Treat Ave. (between 18th St. and 19th St.) *(* **415/341-0152.** www.southernpacificbrewing.com. Sun–Wed 11am–midnight. Thurs–Sat 11am–2am.

Zeitgeist ★★ It used to be a rough biker bar, but you'll like see more fixed-gear bicycles locked up front than Harleys these days. Zeitgeist serves more than 20 types

Dog Patch, the gritty, industrial, historic, and increasingly popular artistic and industrial hub south of AT&T ballpark, is San Francisco's most exciting up-and-coming neighborhood, and **Third Rail** ★★, at 628 20th St. (btw. 3rd St. and Illinois sts.; ✆ **415/252-7966;** www.thirdrailbarsf.com), is the ultimate example of why. The railroad theme, simple industrial design, and relaxed atmosphere pay homage to the area's history, while the unusual craft cocktails embrace the city's artisanal cocktail trend. At the helm is the team behind longtime Mission favorite Range (p. 94), bringing with them both cocktail chops and a jerky bar. Instead of nuts, nosh on homemade dried meats by the ounce while sipping creative cocktails, like the Mt. Tam, named for the local gin used in the refreshing concoction. It smells and tastes like the moist pine needles (in a good way!) from the nearby mountain. Other libations, like the Fireside Sour and Bone Machine experiment with texture and lesser-used liquors. Tell the bartenders what kind of flavors you like, and they'll skillfully deliver without a hint of pretention. Open daily 3pm to 2am.

of German beer, most of them dead cheap, making the dive a favorite among the Mission's hipster crowd. Come in good weather if you can, because the mellow beer-garden vibe is half the appeal. Zietgeist's Bloody Mary is the best in the city. Cash only. 199 Valencia St. (at Duboce Ave.). ✆ **415/255-7505.** Daily 9am–2am.

The Haight–Ashbury

Alembic ★★★   The highly curated drink menu at this Haight Street bar is divided into two parts: one pays homage to the classic cocktail canon and the other offers inventive, new-school concoctions you can't get anywhere else. Gin lovers who need a pick-me-up will love the "Nine Volt"—gin mixed with green tea and mint makes for a refreshing buzz, while the white Szechuan pepper leaves a slightly tingly mouth-feel. Another creative favorite is "Vasco de Gama," which blends Islay Scotch and Buffalo Trace bourbon with an apple syrup spiked with garam masala spices. The heavily tattooed bartenders do well by such classics as Manhattans and Old Fashioneds, too. The surprisingly good bar food has made name for itself, prompting the owners to expand the kitchen and seating space next door. The menu is in flux and relies on seasonality but the house-cured salmon and bone marrow are main-stay musts! 1725 Haight (at Cole St.). ✆ **415/660-0822.** www.alembicbar.com. Daily noon–2am.

The Ice Cream Bar ★★   Mixology and nostalgia collide in this 1930s-style soda fountain. Add in locally sourced, organic ingredients and you've got a quintessential San Francisco establishment—and perhaps the only "bar" that can satisfy both kids and adults in one delightfully retro space. While kids can choose from the unique ice cream flavors, sundaes, and floats made in-house daily, adults can imbibe on adult-sweet treats, like Dublin Honey, which is a float made with Guinness and port. For those not into sweets, they also serve a wide selection of beer, wines, and artisanal cocktails (made with liquors and syrups that the staff infuses on site), plus dessert and food items. 815 Cole St. (btw. Frederick and Carl sts.). ✆ **415/742-4932.** www.icecreambarsf.com. Sun–Thurs noon–10pm, Fri–Sat noon–11pm.

Madrone Art Bar ★★   San Francisco's bar scene can be a bit quiet during the work week, but that's not the case at this favorite in the Lower Haight area, where a rotating crop of DJs and bands draw crowds every night of the week. Monday nights are the new Saturday with cult-favorite theme night, Motown Monday. People line up around the block to dance to retro mash-ups among paintings from local artists. Come early and you could even enjoy a pre-dancing neck-and-shoulder massage. Cash only. 500 Divisadero St. (at Fell St.) ✆ **415/241-0202.** www.madroneartbar.com.

GAY & LESBIAN BARS & CLUBS

Check the free weeklies such as the "San Francisco Bay Guardian" and "San Francisco Weekly" for listings of events and happenings around town. The "Bay Area Reporter" is a gay paper with comprehensive listings, including a weekly community calendar. All these papers are free and distributed weekly on Wednesday or Thursday, and can be found stacked at the corners of 18th and Castro streets and Ninth and Harrison streets, as well as in bars, bookshops, and other stores around town. See "LGBT Travelers," in chapter 12 for further details on gay-themed guides. Also check out the rather homely but very informative site "Queer Things to Do in the San Francisco Bay Area" at www.sfqueer.com, or www.gaywired.com for more gay happenings.

Badlands ★   The barely legal Abercrombie crowd comes here to dance under the giant disco ball and throw back happy hour two-for-one cocktails, from 3 to 8pm Monday through Saturday. Videos blast the music played by the DJ while lights flash. It's one noisy, energetic party filled with a crowd that wants to meet and greet. 4121 18th St. (at Castro). ✆ **415/626-9320.** www.badlands-sf.com.

Diva's Nightclub and Bar ★★   Located in the Tenderloin, all is not as it appears at this transgender-friendly dance and drag bar. Want to go back to school? Naughty schoolgirls appear each Wednesday at 10pm. The Diva Darlings take center stage each Thursday at 10pm. With dance floors, regular shows, and numerous bars, this three-story club filled with beautiful girlz can best be described as a party palace. 1081 Post St. (btw Polk and Larkin Sts.). ✆ **415/928-6006.** www.divassf.com. Open 6am–2am.

440 Castro ★★   A warm and fuzzy bear bar for the Levi's and leather crowd, most cruise between the video bar downstairs to the dark intimate bar up a few stairs in the back. Always popular, Monday is Underwear Night; Tuesday features $2 beers all day and night. No matter the day, drinks are always strong and cheap. Regular contests like the Battle of the Bulge, are a great way to meet new friends. 440 Castro St. (btw 17th and 18th). ✆ **415/621-8732.** www.the440.com. Open daily until 2am.

The Lexington Club ★★★   San Francisco's premier lesbian bar features a full roster of events, an always-busy pool table, cheap drinks and a chill atmosphere. For those on the prowl, it's also commended for having an "eye candy" clientele (and bartenders). 3464 19th St. (btw. Lexington and Valencia sts.). ✆ **415/863-2052.** www.lexington club.com. Daily 3pm–2am.

Brunch Is A Drag

Harry Denton's Starlight Room (p. 185) hosts a weekly **Sunday's a Drag** brunch performance, where divas perform female impersonation acts and lip-sync Broadway tunes. The "brunch with an attitude" has two seatings every Sunday at noon and 2:30pm. The price of brunch is $45 per person, which includes enter-tainment, brunch, coffee, tea, and fresh juices.

The Lookout ★   With two walls of glass and a massive deck looking down on the heart of the Castro, this karaoke bar is a good place to dance and belt out your best rendition of "I Will Survive." Nightly DJs and a weekly drag show add to the excitement. If you get hungry, you don't have to lose your spot in line for the karaoke machine; the Lookout serves surprisingly good food. 3600 16th St. (at Market St.). ✆ **415/431-0306.** www.lookoutsf.com. Open daily until 2am. Kitchen until 9:30pm, closed on Tues.

Twin Peaks Tavern ★★   Known locally as the gay "Cheers," Twin Peaks was the first gay bar in the country to unblock the floor to ceiling windows and let the world see just what was going on inside. It sits at the corner of Market and Castro, the true heart of the gay community. In a culture that often worships youth and beauty, Twin Peaks is an oldie but goodie—and tends to attract an older crowd. The 1880s building survived the earthquake and recently gained historic landmark status. 401 Castro St. (at Market St.). ✆ **415/864-9470.** www.twinpeakstavern.com. Hours vary, so call.

PROFESSIONAL SPORTS TEAMS

The Bay Area's sports scene isn't just about the Giants; it includes several major professional franchises. Check the local newspapers' sports sections and team websites for daily listings of local events. Along with each teams' website, www.tickets.com and www.stubhub.com are two good places to hunt for tickets.

AT&T Park ★★   If you're a baseball fan, you'll definitely want to schedule a visit to the magnificent AT&T Park, home of the San Francisco Giants and hailed by the media as one of the finest ballparks in America. From April through October, an often sellout crowd of 40,800 fans packs the $319-million ballpark—which has prime views of San Francisco Bay—and roots for the National League's Giants.

During the season, regular tickets to see the team play can be expensive and hard to come by (see the website). Bleacher and standing room only seats are a cheaper option. If you can't get bleacher seats, you can always join the "knothole gang" at the Portwalk (located behind right field) to catch a free glimpse of the game through cutout portholes into the ballpark. In the spirit of sharing, Portwalk peekers are encouraged to take in only an inning or two before giving way to fellow fans.

One guaranteed way to get into the ballpark is to take a **guided tour of AT&T Park** and go behind the scenes where you'll see the press box, the dugout, the visitor's clubhouse, a luxury suite, and more. All tours run daily (except most game days) at 10:30am and 12:30pm. Ticket prices are $20 for adults, $15 for seniors (55+), $10 for kids 3 to 12, free for active military (with ID). To buy tickets online log onto the website, click on "AT&T Park" at the bottom and then select "AT&T Park Tours." At the southeast corner of SoMa at the south end of the Embarcadero (bounded by King, Second, and Third sts.). ✆ **415/972-2000.** www.sfgiants.com. Bus: 10, 30, 45, or 47. Metro: N-line.

Major League Baseball

The American League's **Oakland Athletics** (www.athletics.mlb.com) play across the bay in Oakland at the Coliseum, Hegenberger Road exit from I-880. The stadium holds over 50,000 spectators and is accessible through BART's Coliseum station.

Pro Basketball

For now, the **Golden State Warriors** (www.nba.com/warriors) play at the ORACLE Arena, a 19,200-seat facility at 7000 Coliseum Way in Oakland. In 2017, they plan to move to new waterfront digs in the city close to AT&T Park in 2017. The season runs November through April, and most games start at 7:30pm.

Pro Football

The **San Francisco 49ers** (www.sf49ers.com) moved to their new Levi's Stadium in Santa Clara, where the 2016 Super Bowl will be held. Football season runs August through December. Tickets are generally sold out, but are available at higher prices through ticket agents beforehand. The 49ers' arch enemies, the **Oakland Raiders** (www.raiders.com), play at the Oakland-Alameda Coliseum, off the I-880 freeway (Nimitz).

DAY TRIPS FROM SAN FRANCISCO

One of the best things about the City by the Bay is its proximity to breathtaking natural beauty and vibrant, diverse, neighboring communities. In less than 30 minutes from San Francisco, you can feel on the edge of the world at the cliffs of the Marin Headlands, look up the trunk of a 600-year-old Redwood, or explore the scenic waterfronts of Sausalito and Tiburon. And to the east, Oakland and Berkeley are destinations in their own right for their fantastic restaurants burgeoning art scenes. Plus, if the fog's got you shivering, any of these locations are worth the trip just to warm up! Whether you use public transportation, rent a car for the day, or take a guided tour, here are some great ways to spend a day out of the city.

10 | BERKELEY

10 miles NE of San Francisco

While Berkeley has lost some of the counter-culture cache that made it famous in the 1960s, it's still fun to visit the iconic University of California at Berkeley and its surrounding town. Despite the media portrayal, the university is more academic than psychedelic with 22 Nobel Prize winners over the years (8 are active staff). Today, there's still some hippie idealism in the air, but gone are the days of free love and violent protests. The Summer of Love is present only in tie-dye and paraphernalia shops and like elsewhere in the Bay Area gentrification is reshaping Berkeley's vibe. As San Francisco's rent and property prices soar out of the reasonable range, young people, artists, and everyone with less than a small fortune are seeking shelter elsewhere, and Berkeley is one of the top picks—although Oakland is gaining popularity—a lively city teeming with all types of people, a beautiful college campus, vast parks, great shopping, and some incredibly deliciously affordable restaurants.

Getting There

The Berkeley **Bay Area Rapid Transit (BART)** station is 2 blocks from the university. The fare from San Francisco is less than $3.90 one-way. Call ℂ 511 or visit www.bart.gov for detailed trip information and fares.

If you are coming **by car** from San Francisco, take the Bay Bridge. Follow I-80 east to the University Avenue exit, and follow University Avenue until you hit the campus. Parking is tight, so either leave your car at the Sather Gate parking lot at Telegraph Avenue and Durant Street, or expect to fight for a spot.

What to See & Do

Prospective students, history buffs, or anyone interested in learning about the town's most profound cultural influence should take advantage of the free campus tours (reservations required), which depart Monday through Saturday at 10am, and Sunday at 1pm from the **Visitor Services center,** 101 Sproul Hall (© **510/642-5215;** www.berkeley.edu/visitors), The student-led tours are heavily used by prospective scholars, so in springtime your group may swell to 200 and your guide may dwell rather tediously on the school's rivalry with Stanford, but everyone is welcome, and you'll get heaps of fascinating historical information about the educational institution that fomented some of the strongest protests of the 1960s and 1970s. There are tons of milestones that Cal is responsible for, including the discovery of vitamins B, E, and K, plutonium, uranium 238, and the stumpy London plane tree, a hybrid that you'll only see here and in San Francisco.

A noteworthy building you'd only have access to on the tour (or with a student ID) is **Le Conte Hall,** where the first atom splitters did their work. (Keep your eyes peeled for parking signs that read, in total seriousness, RESERVED FOR NL—meaning Nobel Laureate; you know the parking situation is grim if you need a Nobel Prize to get a space.) The **Doe & Moffitt Library** doesn't allow public access to the 10 million books in its stacks, but its lobby areas, lined with glass cases filled with priceless manuscripts, is open to all. In a reading room upstairs, you'll also find Emanuel Leutze's 1854 "Washington Rallying the Troops at Monmouth," which was intended to be a companion piece to his "Washington Crossing the Delaware" (now at New York's Met). Your tour will end with a discussion of the messy student protests for freedom of speech, in 1969, that resulted in the death of a student protester.

UC Berkeley has two noteworthy museums. The first is the hands-on, kid-friendly **Lawrence Hall of Science ★** (east of campus at 1 Centennial Drive, © **510/642-5132;** www.lawrencehallofscience.org). Open daily from 10am to 5pm. Admission is $17 for adults; $14 for seniors 62 and over, students, and children 7 to 18; $11 for children 3 to 6; and free for kids 2 and under. The second is the **UC Berkeley Art Museum ★**, 2626 Bancroft Way, between College and Telegraph avenues (© **510/642-0808;** www.bampfa.berkeley.edu), which features paintings, a sculpture garden, a library, and a film study center. It's open Wednesday through Sunday from 11am to 5pm. Admission is $10 for adults; $7 for seniors, non–UCB students, visitors with disabilities, and children 17 and under; and $6 for UCB students.

Cal also boasts the **William Randolph Hearst Greek Theater**, an 8,500-seat outdoor amphitheater, that's been host to the greatest talent and celebrities of the last century, from Elvis to the Grateful Dead to the Dalai Lama. Chances are there's a fantastic show during your visit, where you'll take in the amazing acoustics while enjoying views of the entire bay and San Francisco skyline. There's not a bad seat in the house, but you may want to pay for reserved seating unless you plan to get there early to claim a spot on the lawn. Check the website for the calendar or call the box office (© **510/642-9988;** https://commerce.cpsma.berkeley.edu/CPPresents/calendar) for more information.

PARKS

Golden Gate Park might have the name recognition, but Berkeley has some of the most extensive and beautiful parks around. Plus you can count on temperatures being 10 to 20 degrees warmer than San Francisco. If you want to wear the kids out or enjoy hiking, swimming, sniffing roses, or just getting a breath of California air, head for

Tilden Park ★, where you'll find plenty of flora and fauna, hiking trails, an old steam train and merry-go-round, a farm and nature area for kids, and a chilly tree-encircled lake. The East Bay's public transit system, **AC Transit** (✆ **511;** www.actransit.org), runs the air-conditioned no. 67 bus line around the edge of the park on weekdays and all the way to the Tilden Visitors Center on Saturdays and Sundays. Call ✆ **888/327-2757** or see www.ebparks.org for further information.

Shopping

For boutique shopping, head to **College Avenue** from Dwight Way to the Oakland border. Eclectic boutiques, antiques shops, book stores, and restaurants line this street, making it a favorite among students and locals. The other, more upscale option is **Fourth Street,** in west Berkeley, 2 blocks north of the University Avenue exit. This shopping strip is the perfect place to go on a sunny morning. Grab a cup of java and outstanding pancakes and scones at **Bette's Ocean View Diner,** 1807 Fourth St. (✆ **510/644-3932**). Read the paper at a patio table, and then hit the **Crate & Barrel Outlet,** 1785 Fourth St., between Hearst and Virginia streets (✆ **510/528-5500**). Prices are 30 percent to 70 percent off retail. It's open daily from 10am to 7pm. This area also boasts small, wonderful stores crammed with imported and locally made housewares.

Where to Eat

The East Bay boasts the foodie scene of San Francisco, only with often-better prices, a focus on ethnic food, more parking and generally larger spaces, which means less wait time for a table. If you want to dine student-style, eat on campus Monday through Friday. Buy something at a sidewalk stand or in the building directly behind the Student Union. All the university eateries have both indoor and outdoor seating. Telegraph Avenue has an array of small ethnic restaurants, cafes, and sandwich shops. Follow the students: If the place is crowded, it's good, super cheap, or both.

You can't get more "Bay Area" than opting for a farm-to-table dining experience. Go for the restaurant that shaped an entire generation of chefs with Alice Waters's **Chez Panisse ★★★** at 1517 Shattuck Ave. (✆ **510/548-5525** for restaurant and ✆ **510/548-5049** for café; www.chezpanisse.com); try to reserve a few weeks ahead. Carnivores will love **Café Rouge** (1782 Fourth St., ✆ **510/525-1440;** www.caferouge. net), the Mediterranean darling of chef-owner, Marsha McBride, formerly of Zuni Café.

OAKLAND

10 miles E of San Francisco

Despite its areas with ongoing and infamous gang violence, sprawling Oakland is quickly eschewing its bad rap as one of the country's most dangerous cities for the reputation of being one of the hippest. In fact, after Brooklyn, it has more resident artists per capita than any other US city, making it a mecca for young, socially conscious individuals who are fleeing San Francisco's increasingly sterile and exclusive tech scene. While Oakland still has grit in spades and some areas are to be avoided, there are also charming shopping areas, well-heeled hillside enclaves, temperate weather, and enough attractions and to make it a destination in its own right.

But this is not the city's first coming. Originally little more than a cluster of ranches and farms, Oakland exploded in size and stature practically overnight, when the last

San Francisco Bay Area

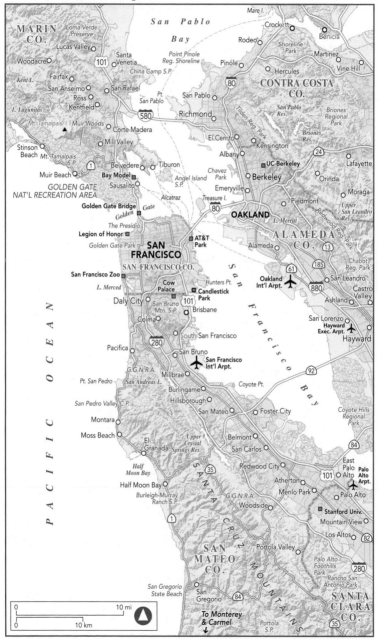

mile of transcontinental railroad track was laid down. Major shipping ports soon followed and, to this day, Oakland remains one of the busiest industrial ports on the West Coast. The price for economic success, however, has been Oakland's lowbrow reputation as a predominantly working-class city; it is forever in the shadow of chic San Francisco. Still, now that the City by the Bay is so crowded and undisputedly one of the most expensive places to live in the country, "Oaktown" is in the midst of a renaissance, and its future continues to look bright. A 2012 "New York Times" article ranked Oakland the fifth most desirable destination to visit in the *world,* just above Tokyo. Rent a sailboat on Lake Merritt, go to the retro toddler-attracting amusement park that is Fairyland, stroll along the waterfront, see a show at the Paramount Theatre, explore the fantastic Oakland Museum—they're all great reasons to hop the bay and spend a fog-free day exploring one of California's largest and most ethnically diverse cities.

Getting There

BART (*©* **511;** www.bart.gov) connects San Francisco and Oakland through one of the longest underwater transit tunnels in the world. Fares range from $3 to $4 one-way, depending on your station of origin; children 4 and under ride free. BART trains operate Monday through Friday 4am to midnight, Saturday from 6am to midnight, and Sunday from 8am to midnight. Exit at the 12th Street station for downtown Oakland.

By car from San Francisco, take I-80 across the San Francisco–Oakland Bay Bridge and follow signs to downtown Oakland. Exit at Grand Avenue South for the Lake Merritt area. *Note:* Make sure you have a map of Oakland or GPS device—you do not want to get lost in Oakland and end up in a bad neighborhood.

For a calendar of events in Oakland, contact the **Oakland Convention and Visitors Bureau,** at 463 11th St. (*©* **510/839-9000;** www.oaklandcvb.com). The city sponsors eight free-guided tours (Wed and Sat at 10am), including African-American Heritage. Call *©* **510/238-3234** or visit www2.oaklandnet.com, and click on "free walking tours" found at the bottom left.

Downtown Oakland lies between Grand Avenue on the north, I-980 on the west, Inner Harbor on the south, and Lake Merritt on the east. Between these landmarks are three BART stations (12th St., 19th St., and Lake Merritt), City Hall, the Oakland Museum, Jack London Square, and several other sights.

What to See & Do

Lake Merritt is one of Oakland's prime tourist attractions and is a favorite among locals. The tidal lagoon, 3½ miles in circumference, was bridged and dammed in the 1860s and is now a wildlife refuge that is home to flocks of migrating ducks, herons, and geese. For a romantic, pre-dinner stroll, catch a sunset at the lake and watch as the "Necklace of Lights," the 126 lampposts and a 3,400 bulbs that encircle the lake, dance on the water. Just don't linger too long after dark as it becomes less safe the later it gets. The 122-acre **Lakeside Park** (www2.oaklandnet.com), a popular place to picnic, feed the ducks, and escape the fog, surrounds the lake on three sides. To get out on the water, you can rent a boat from **Lake Merritt Boating Center ★** (*©* **510/238-2196**), in Lakeside Park along the north shore. Or, perhaps, take a gondola ride with **Gondola Servizio** (*©* **510/663-6603;** www.gondolaservizio.com). Experienced gondoliers will serenade you, June through October, as you glide across the lake. The clear skies, sparkling lights, city views, and old-world gondolas make for a romantic excursion.

Prices start at $60 for the first couple and $10 for each additional person, depending on the time and gondola style. Also along Lake Merritt's expansive shores is the fantastic, simple pleasure that is **Fairyland ★** (699 Bellevue Ave.; © **510/452-2259**; www.fairyland.com). Before Disneyland or any other childhood fantasy park, there was this "storybook theme park." Founded in 1950 and featuring fairytale sets, farm animals, and live entertainment, it's an interactive flashback to a simpler time, complete with live puppet shows, tiny toddler rides, the ability to walk into a (fake) whale's mouth, play structures, picnic areas, and fun interactive fairytale sets with recorded storytelling boxes that work at the turn of a plastic key you can buy onsite. This spot is so child-focused that adults can't get in without one. So bring a child and a sense of sweet, relaxed adventure to this mellow, charming spot.

Also worth visiting is the Oakland's **Paramount Theatre ★**, 2025 Broadway (© **510/893-2300**; www.paramounttheatre.com), an outstanding National Historic Landmark and example of Art Deco architecture and decor. Built in 1931 and authentically restored in 1973, its intricately carved walls, plush carpet, beveled mirrors, and gilded details will transport you to Hollywood's Golden Era. As the city's main performing-arts center, it plays host to big-name performers like Smokey Robinson and Alicia Keys, but is just as popular for its old movie nights, where guests can see a classic film, complete with a pre-show organ serenade, for a mere $6. Guided tours of the 3,000-seat theater are given the first and third Saturday of each month, excluding holidays. No reservations are necessary; just show up at 10am at the box office entrance on 21st Street at Broadway. The tour lasts 2 hours, cameras are allowed, and admission is $5. Children must be at least 10 years old.

The **Oakland Museum of California,** 1000 Oak St. (© **510/318-8400**; www.museumca.org) is a favorite with Bay Area fourth graders studying the history of our fair state. While the Galleries of Art and Natural Science feature the expected paintings and specimens, I particularly like the Gallery of History, which focuses on "Coming to California," with interesting displays of Native American baskets, the Spanish influence, and, of course, the Gold Rush. While the SFMOMA is closed for expansion, important works from the likes of Frida Kahlo, Diego Rivera, and Ansel Adams will be displayed through April 15, 2015 in the "Fertile Ground: Art and Community in California" exhibit. Admission is $15 for adults, $10 seniors and students, $6 youth, free ages 8 and under. The museum is open Wednesday through Sunday 11am to 5pm, Friday until 9pm.

To experience the avant-garde and burgeoning Bay Area art scene as the locals do, check out Oakland's **Art Murmur**, a free monthly gallery stroll in which the galleries and multi-use venues are open to the public for artist receptions (http://oaklandart murmur.org). Wander in and out of exhibits while enjoying a lively street festival complete with food trucks, live music, and spontaneous dance circles on Telegraph Avenue between Grand and 27th streets on the first Friday of every month from 5 to 9pm.

If you take pleasure in strolling sailboat-filled wharves or are a die-hard fan of Jack London, you'll likely enjoy a visit to **Jack London Square ★** (© **510/645-9292**; www.jacklondonsquare.com), the waterfront area where the famous author spent most of his youth. The square fronts the harbor, and at press time was undergoing a $400 million revival, which will bring, among other things, restaurants, entertainment, shops, a farmers' market, and a hotel to the property. In the center of the square is a small model of the Yukon cabin in which Jack London lived while prospecting in the Klondike during the gold rush of 1897. In the middle of Jack London Square is a more

FDR's floating WHITE HOUSE

For those interested in naval history and presidential trivia, this tour is a must-do. The 165-foot presidential yacht, the USS *Potomac*, President Franklin D. Roosevelt's beloved "Floating White House" is open to the public thanks to the work of hundreds of dedicated volunteers. It took 12 years and $5 million to restore the yacht, but now visitors can be steeped in World War II history while cruising the San Francisco Bay or learn little-known facts about FDR during dockside tours while taking in sweeping views of the city's skyline. The dockside tours are available Wednesday, Friday, and Sunday from 11am to 3pm mid-January through mid-December. Admission is $10, $8 for seniors age 60 and over, and free for children age 12 and under. See the website for information about various historic cruises.

Hours and cruise schedules are subject to change, so be sure to call the Potomac Visitor Center before arriving. Tickets for the Dockside Tour can be purchased at the Visitor Center upon arrival; tickets for the History Cruise can be purchased in advance via **Ticketweb** (℗ **866/777-8932;** www.ticketweb.com) or by calling the **Potomac Visitor Center** (℗ **510/627-1215;** www.uss potomac.org). The Visitor Center is located at 540 Water St., at the corner of Clay and Water streets adjacent to the FDR Pier at the north end of Jack London Square.

authentic memorial, **Heinold's First and Last Chance Saloon** (℗ **510/839-6761;** www.heinoldsfirstandlastchance.com), a funky, friendly little bar and historic landmark. Here a clock remains frozen at the exact time the 1906 earthquake shook this little dive, forever making the bar slant at 10 degrees. Watch your step, too, because the 'quake warped the floors, adding even more eccentricity to this topsy-turvy establishment. This is where London did some of his writing and most of his drinking. Jack London Square is at Broadway and Embarcadero. Take I-880 to Broadway, turn south, and drive to the end. Or you can ride BART to the 12th Street station and then walk south along Broadway (about half a mile). Or take bus no. 72R or 72M to the foot of Broadway.

Where to Eat

Oakland may come in a distant second to San Francisco's property values and crime statistics, but there's no compromising when it comes to food. One place guaranteed to please is Daniel Patterson's **Plum ★★** (2214 Broadway; ℗ **510/444-7586;** www. plumoakland.com). With simple menus, reasonable prices, and vegetable-heavy delicious food, it's been a hit since its 2010 opening. I always end up dining at the bar at **Wood Tavern ★**, 6317 College Ave. (℗ **510/654-6607),** a contemporary and convivial spot known for its great selection of wines by the glass and contemporary American food (think seasonal, farm-fresh cooking). Vegetarians won't find tons of offerings on the menu, but don't let that dissuade you; when asked, the chefs will put together spectacular animal-free ensembles. Another favorite is **Yoshi's Jazz Club & Japanese Restaurant ★**, 510 Embarcadero West (℗ **510/238-9200;** www.yoshis.com), a longtime destination in Jack London Square where you can watch legendary jazz musicians perform live in a proper nightclub while noshing on sushi. Like its sister Berkeley, Oakland also has a slew of wonderful, spectacularly affordable ethnic restaurants dotting its streets.

ANGEL ISLAND ★ & TIBURON ★

8 miles N of San Francisco

A California State Park, **Angel Island** is the largest of San Francisco Bay's three islets (the others are Alcatraz and Yerba Buena). The island has been, at various times, a prison, a quarantine station for immigrants, a missile base, and even a favorite site for duels. Nowadays, its dark past exists only in the ghosts rumored to haunt the former military buildings. The island is now the domain of visitors who are looking for 360-degree views of the bay, sunshine, trails, grassy picnic grounds, and a scenic beach. Hike, bike, take a tour, or just relax on this picturesque, car-free island.

Uberwealthy **Tiburon,** situated on a peninsula of the same name, is a living post-card, almost too beautiful to be real. It looks like a cross between a seacoast town and a Hollywood Western set, as Main Street has been preserved to reflect its roots as a Gold Rush train town. The boutiques, souvenir stores, art galleries, and dockside restaurants flanking its one tiny main shopping street at the water's edge are housed in color-splashed, turn-of-the-century converted boathouses. Despite its historic facade, Tiburon is, in reality, a sleepy, luxurious stretch of yacht-club suburbia. Palatial, multimillion-dollar homes perch on the hills, overlooking the proud yachts and sail-boats below. The view from the waterfront of San Francisco's skyline and the islands in the bay explain why residents happily pay the precious price to live here.

Getting There

Ferries of the **Blue & Gold Fleet** (✆ 415/705-5555; www.blueandgoldfleet.com) from Pier 41 (Fisherman's Wharf; buy your ticket here or online) travel to both Angel Island and Tiburon. Boats run on a seasonal schedule; phone or look online for departure information. The round-trip fare to Angel Island is $17 for adults, $9.50 for seniors (65+) and kids (5-12), and free for kids 5 and under when traveling with an adult. The fare includes state park fees. A one-way ticket to Tiburon is $11 for adults, $6.75 for seniors (65+) and kids (5-12), and free for kids 5 and under.

By car from San Francisco, take U.S. 101 to the Tiburon/Hwy. 131 exit and then follow Tiburon Boulevard all the way downtown, a 40-minute drive from San Francisco. Good luck finding a parking spot in Tiburon; try the lot behind the **Tiburon Playhouse** movie theater at 40 Main St. Catch the **Tiburon–Angel Island Ferry** (✆ 415/435-2131; www.angelislandferry.com) to Angel Island from the dock at Tiburon Boulevard and Main Street. The 15-minute round-trip costs $13.50 for adults, $11.50 for children 6 to 11, $3.50 for kids 3 to 5, and $1 for bikes. One child 2 or under is admitted free of charge with each paying adult (after that it's $3.50 each). Boats run on a seasonal schedule, but usually depart hourly from 10am to 5pm on weekends, with a more limited schedule on weekdays. Call ahead or look online for departure information. Tickets can only be purchased when boarding and include state park fees.

What to See & Do on Angel Island

Passengers disembark from the ferry at **Ayala Cove,** a small marina abutting a huge lawn area equipped with tables, benches, barbecue pits, and restrooms. During the summer season, there's also a small store, a gift shop, the Cove Cafe (with surprisingly good grub), and an overpriced mountain-bike rental shop at Ayala Cove.

Angel Island's 12 miles of hiking and bike trails include the **Perimeter Road,** a paved path that circles the island and offers breathtaking views of San Francisco, the Marin Headlands, the Golden Gate and Bay Bridges. The perimeter path is bike friendly for all levels, with only slight inclines and clear markers. For more experienced riders, an interior path offers a more strenuous mountain biking experience. The Perimeter Road winds past World War II military barracks, former gun emplacements, and other historic government buildings that recall the island's storied and dark pasts; several turnoffs lead to the top of Mount Livermore, 776 feet above the bay. Sometimes referred to as the "Ellis Island of the West," Angel Island was used as a holding area for detained Chinese immigrants awaiting admission papers from 1910 to 1940. You can still see faded Chinese characters on some of the walls of the barracks where the immigrants were held, sometimes for months.

Besides walking and biking, there are a number of other ways to get around the island, all of which can be booked at www.angelisland.com. Schedules vary depending on the time of year. The 1-hour audio-enhanced open-air **Tram Tour** costs $15 for adults, $14 for seniors, $10 for children 5 to 11, and is free for children 4 and under. The Tram will stop at vistas and riders can get off for photo ops. A guided 2-hour **Segway Tour** costs $68 per person, and is only available for those 16 years and up. Long pants are recommended; closed shoes are mandatory. A guided 2-hour **Electric Scooter Tours** is available for $50 (again for 16 and up). For more information about activities on Angel Island, visit **www.angelisland.com.**

For a more adventurous way to see the entire circumference of the island and take in the surrounding panoramas from a unique vantage point, try a guided **sea-kayak tour ★**, available for all ages. The 2½-hour trips combine the thrill of paddling stable, two-person kayaks with an informative, naturalist-led tour around the island (conditions permitting). All equipment is provided (including a wetsuit, if needed), and no experience is necessary. Rates run $75 per person. For more information, contact the Sausalito-based **Sea Trek** (✆ **415/488-1000**; www.seatrek.com). *Note:* Tours depart from Ayala Cove on Angel Island, not Sausalito.

What to See & Do in Tiburon

The main thing to do in tiny Tiburon is stroll along the waterfront, pop into its handful of stores, and spend an easy $50 on drinks and appetizers before heading back to the city. With fudge samples, edible Lego bricks, and every imaginable sweet you'd expect to find in Willy Wonka's factory, kids will love **The Candy Store on Main Street** at 7 Main St. (✆ **415/435-0434;** www.candystoretiburon.com).

Where to Eat in Tiburon

It's rare that a restaurant with such a tourist-friendly view has delicious food to boot but pricy **Guaymas ★★★** (5 Main St.; ✆ **415/435-6300;** www.guaymasrestaurant.com) delivers on both fronts, which is why it remains a favorite among this discerning community. Sit outside mere feet away from bobbing sailboats and indulge in margaritas, guacamole, ceviche, and a number of authentic Mexican dishes from various regions. Add on a stunning panoramic view of the city, and the damage the drinks do to your wallet might be the only reason to leave. On a sunny day, you'll find San Francisco's brunch-time warriors flocking in droves to **Sam's Anchor Cafe ★★** (27 Main St.; ✆ **415/435-4527;** www.samscafe.com) a few doors away. Same stunning view, an even bigger outdoor patio, brunch, and top-quality burgers, bloody Marys, and beer draw crowds of twenty- and thirtysomethings who linger at the sundrenched tables and get good and tipsy before biking or ferrying their way back into the fog. It gets crowded on nice days so it's worth getting there early for prime seating.

SAUSALITO ★

5 miles N of San Francisco

The picturesque, European-feeling Sausalito is the first town you'll meet once you cross the Golden Gate Bridge. With houses scaling the hillside, fewer than 8,000 residents, and a quaint waterfront, Sausalito feels rather like St. Tropez on the French Riviera (minus the beach) and the hotter climes. Next to the pricey bayside restaurants, antiques shops, and galleries, are hamburger joints, ice-cream shops, and souvenir shops where it's Christmas all year round. Sausalito's main strip is Bridgeway, which runs along the water; on a clear day the views of San Francisco far across the bay are spectacular. After admiring the view, those in the know make a quick detour to Caledonia Street, 1 block inland; not only is it less congested, but it also has a better selection of cafes and shops. Since the town is all along the waterfront and only stretches a few blocks, it's best explored on foot.

Getting There

The **Golden Gate Ferry Service** fleet, Ferry Building (© **415/923-2000;** www.golden gate.org), operates between the San Francisco Ferry Building, at the foot of Market Street, and downtown Sausalito. Service is frequent, running at reasonable intervals every day of the year except January 1, Thanksgiving, and December 25. Check the website for an exact schedule. The ride takes a half-hour, and one-way fares are $10.25 for adults; $5 for youth (ages 6–18), seniors (65+), and passengers with disabilities; children 5 and under ride free (limit 2 children per full-fare adult).

Ferries of the **Blue & Gold Fleet** (© **415/705-5555;** www.blueandgoldfleet.com) leave from Pier 41 (Fisherman's Wharf); the one-way cost is $11 for adults, $6.75 for kids 5 to 12, free for 4 and under. Boats run on a seasonal schedule; phone or log onto their website for departure information.

By car from San Francisco, take U.S. 101 N. and then take the first right after the Golden Gate Bridge (Alexander exit). Alexander becomes Bridgeway in Sausalito. But before that, consider taking a quick detour for a memorable photo-op at the Headlands. Once you cross the Golden Gate Bridge take the first exit and merge onto Alexander Avenue. Drive under Highway 101 and turn right onto Conzelman Road right before the ramp heading back to San Francisco. From here, you can pull over along the shoulder (you may have to wait for parking) to get a dramatic vantage point of the red bridge jetting out from tumultuous waters. Drive further and you'll glimpse the rolling hills of the Marin Headlands and the secluded Rodeo Beach to the right. You might be tempted to keep driving on this dramatic, winding road high above the city behind you. If you do, you'll eventually get to Point Bonita Lighthouse, the opposite direction of Sausalito but a wonderfully scenic, undeveloped diversion.

What to See & Do

Above all else, Sausalito has scenery and sunshine, for once you cross the Golden Gate Bridge, you're usually out of the San Francisco fog patch and under blue California sky—with more comforting climate to boot. Houses cling to the town's steep hills, overlooking a colony of sailboats below. Most of the tourist action, which is almost singularly limited to window-shopping and eating, takes place at sea level on Bridgeway. Sausalito is a mecca for shoppers seeking souvenirs, kitschy clothes and footwear, and arts and crafts. Many of the town's shops are in the alleys, malls, and second-floor boutiques reached by steep, narrow staircases on and off Bridgeway. Caledonia Street, which runs parallel to Bridgeway 1 block inland, is home to more shops.

Younger children (up to 8 years old) will love the **Bay Area Discovery Museum ★★,** East Fort Baker, 557 McReynolds Rd. (© **415/339-3900;** www.bay kidsmuseum.org; admission $11; 9am–5pm Tues–Sun, except holidays). Set upon 7½ acres at Fort Baker, close to the base of the Golden Gate Bridge, this indoor-outdoor hands-on learning and play center is like San Francisco's science-based Exploratorium for younger kids, complete with a pirate ship to climb on, art studios, interactive science exhibits, and a room devoted to trains. If you need to occupy young, active minds and want to experience a gorgeous setting yourself, this is the place to spend a few hours. There is a modest, but expensive cafe on-site serving wholesome sandwiches, soups, and salads. If you don't want to pay a premium for basic provisions, bring your own snacks or lunch and eat at one of the picnic tables.

For science-minded folks fascinated by the Bay Area's complex geography, visit the wholly original **Bay Model Visitors Center,** 2100 Bridgeway (© **415/332-3871;** www.spn.usace.army.mil/missions/recreation/baymodelvisitorcenter.aspx; free admission; typically open Tues–Sun 10am–4pm). It's a hangarlike space filled with a working, wet model of the entire Bay Area. Built in 1957 by the U.S. Army Corps of Engineers to help scientists understand the complex patterns of the water currents and the tides, it's capable of duplicating, at a smaller time scale, the way the tides flow in the Bay. Buildings aren't represented, but major landmarks such as bridges are identifiable as you walk around the space, which is about the size of two football fields, or 1.5 acres. Water, which is shallow throughout, is studded with some 250,000 copper tabs that help recreate known current patterns.

The facility, the only one of its kind in the world, hasn't been used for research since 2000, leaving it to educate school groups about Bay conservation. A visit is quite relaxing; many days, you'll be one of the only guests there, and the only sounds in the enormous room will be the faint sound of the water pumps. The model sits on the site of an important World War II shipbuilding yard, called Marinship ("ma-RINN-ship"), and tucked away to the left of the exit (don't miss it); it's a terrific exhibit, full or artifacts and a video, that chronicles the yard, where an astonishing 93 ships were built in 3½ wartime years.

Nearby, you'll find one of my favorite things to do in Marin—head to **Sea Trek Kayak** at Richardson Bay (© **415/488-1000;** www.seatrek.com), rent a kayak or standup paddleboard, and get out on the calm waters. Don't worry if you've never been in a kayak before or don't have the right attire; these are unsinkable and virtually untippable, and Sea Trek provides waterproof gear you can slip over your clothes, and the experience is unbeatable. Rent a single-person kayak or a double and paddle your way around the shoreline to get up close and personal with dozens of sea lions and harbor seals, Sausalito's charming and famously bohemian houseboat communities, and shorebirds. Afterward, a walk through the parking lot leads to my favorite lunch spot in Marin—**Le Garage** (see below).

Where to Eat

Poggio ★, 777 Bridgeway (© **415/332-7771**; www.poggiotrattoria.com), is an upscale-casual Italian place, with perfect-for-people-watching outdoor seating in the

If your trip allows for a night away from city noise, Sausalito's Fort Baker boasts one of the most charming getaways in the country in an unforgettable, soothing setting. Called **Cavallo Point Lodge** (601 Murray Circle, Fort Baker; 🕾 **415/339-4700;** www.cavallopoint.com; $309–$429 standard suite; $600 for two-bedroom suite, which sleeps 6), it's located in the fort's former general's quarters that flank the center green have been restored to offer historic lodging at the base of the Golden Gate Bridge, just 10 minutes from the city. Each room has postcard-perfect views of the famous red arches, San Francisco's Marina district, or the rolling hills of the Marin Headlands. The resort's partnership with Lexus means U.S. residents staying at the hotel can borrow a luxury sedan to explore the surrounding areas and city. Even if you can't stay the night, this historic slice of paradise is worth a visit. Have a meal at Murray Circle or Farley Bar, where you can enjoy Californian cuisine on the plush porch seating while soaking up the view. Or snag a rocking chair, the perfect place to enjoy the hosted wine and appetizer hour every evening. Take a cooking class in the sunny working kitchen where local chefs teach guests how to use the organic bounty of the area. Or for a daily fee, enjoy use of the meditation pool, sauna, and Jacuzzi at the hotel's spa.

heart of Sausalito, across the street from the ferry dock. A few blocks away, **Sushi Ran ★★**, 107 Caledonia St. (🕾 **415/332-3620**; www.sushiran.com), is one of the best (although shockingly priced) spots for sushi in the Bay Area. A funkier, cheaper option is **Salsalito Taco Shop** 1115 Bridgeway (🕾 **415/331-5595;** www.salsalitotacoshop. com), where the fish tacos and house-made chips are delicious. **Bar Bocce ★**, 1250 Bridgeway (🕾 **415/331-0555;** www.barbocce.com), the hippest spot on the waterfront, draws young crowds from San Francisco on nice days. As its name suggests, you can play bocce ball while sipping your drink (there's not a full bar, but the sangria is yummy). With outdoor seating featuring cushioned benches wrapped around fire pits, and a tiny sandy beach for the kids a few feet away, this is the perfect place to relax and refresh. My all time favorite spot, however, is **Le Garage** (85 Liberty Ship Way #109; 🕾 **415/332-5625**), a marina-front French bistro with indoor and outdoor seating. The fresh, reliable fare is served up with a hearty side of atmosphere and relaxed tranquility. Don't miss the grass-fed burger with perfect fries and aioli, mussels in white wine sauce, or the shrimp or lobster salad. Though off the beaten path, it's an easy stroll from the ferry landing, and you can also drive and park in the restaurant's designated parking lot.

MARIN ★, MUIR WOODS ★★ & MOUNT TAMALPAIS ★★

N of the Golden Gate Bridge

Don't be fooled by the several tours available for these spots; these day trips are an easy drive. A family of four will save a fortune—and see a lot more—by simply hiring a rental car for about $90 for the day.

Muir Woods

While the rest of Marin County's redwood forests were being devoured to feed San Francisco's turn-of-the-20th-century building spree, Muir Woods, in a remote ravine on the flanks of Mount Tamalpais, escaped destruction in favor of easier pickings.

Although the magnificent California redwoods have been successfully transplanted to five continents, their homeland is a 500-mile strip along the mountainous coast of southwestern Oregon and Northern California. The coast redwood, or *Sequoia sempervirens,* is one of the tallest living things known to man; the largest known specimen in the Redwood National Forest towers 368 feet. It has an even larger relative, the *Sequoiadendron giganteum* of the California Sierra Nevada, but the coastal variety is stunning enough. Soaring toward the sky like a wooden cathedral, Muir Woods is unlike any other forest in the world; visiting here is an experience you won't soon forget.

Teddy Roosevelt consecrated this park as a National Monument in 1908. In the 1800s, redwoods were so plentiful here that people thought they'd never run out, and pretty much every single building in San Francisco and beyond was built of the trees. You could argue that the trees got their revenge on the city, when anything made of them went up in smoke in the fire after the earthquake. Today, Muir Woods is one of the last groves of the trees in the area.

Granted, Muir Woods is tiny compared to the Redwood National Forest farther north, but you can still get a pretty good idea of what it must have been like when these giants dominated the entire coastal region. What is truly amazing is that they exist a mere 6 miles (as the crow flies) from San Francisco—close enough, unfortunately, that tour buses arrive in droves on the weekends. You can avoid the masses by hiking up the **Ocean View Trail,** turning left on **Lost Trail,** and returning on the **Fern Creek Trail.** The moderately challenging hike shows off the woods' best sides and leaves the lazy-butts behind.

To reach Muir Woods from San Francisco, cross the Golden Gate Bridge heading north on Hwy. 101, taking the Stinson Beach/Hwy. 1 exit heading west, and follow the signs (and the traffic). The park is open daily from 8am to sunset, and the admission fee is $7 per person 16 and over. Check the website for "fee free" days. There's also a small gift shop, educational displays, and ranger talks. For more information, call the **National Parks Service at Muir Woods** (☏ **415/388-2596**; www.nps.gov/muwo).

Mount Tamalpais

Though Mount Tam—as the locals call it—is just barely tall enough to be considered a mountain, it doesn't keep residents from lovingly referring to it as "the sleeping lady" for the way the peak and surrounding foothills resemble feminine curves. While sunny most days, it's equally alluring to watch the fog from the West wrap the lady in a blanket most evenings. Mount Tam's trails, peaks, and vistas are the Bay Area's favorite outdoor playground, and it's a mission of most active residents to discover their favorite secret trails and overlooks. You don't need inside knowledge, however, to appreciate the scenic beauty. The main trails—mostly fire roads—see a lot of foot and bicycle traffic on weekends, particularly on clear, sunny days when you can see a 100 miles in all directions, from the foothills of the Sierra to the western horizon. It's a great place to escape the city for a leisurely hike and to soak in towering redwood groves and breathtaking views of the bay. Follow the windy roads to the west and you'll ultimately end at **Stinson Beach**, a dreamy, quiet coastal community with downhome residents, multimillion-dollar beachfront second homes, and a beautiful, expansive sandy shoreline.

To get to Mount Tamalpais by car, cross the Golden Gate Bridge heading north on Hwy. 101, and take the Stinson Beach/Hwy. 1 exit. Follow the signs up the shoreline highway for about 2½ miles, turn onto Pantoll Road, and continue for about a mile to Ridgecrest Boulevard. Ridgecrest winds to a parking lot below East Peak. From there, it's a 15-minute hike up to the top, where you'll find a visitor center with a small exhibit and a video, plus a helpful staff. Visitor center admission is free; it is open weekends 11am to 4pm. Park hours are 7am to sunset year round. For a list of guided hikes, see **www.friendsofmttam.org.** You are welcome to hike in the area on your own; it is safe, great for little ones, and the trails are well marked.

Where to Eat

Right off Highway 101 at the turnoff to begin the climb to Mount Tam and beyond is **Buckeye Roadhouse** ★ (15 Shoreline Hwy, Mill Valley; ℂ **415/331-2600**), an extremely popular, historic, and somewhat pricy restaurant serving updated versions of familiar comfort foods in an atmospheric lodgelike setting. I can be found here once a week, eating at the festive bar, chatting with knowledgeable head bartender Jeff, and throwing back oysters bingo (Try them!), chili-lime brick chicken, and cucumber martinis. Because they serve continuously from lunch through dinner, this could be the perfect stopover on your way in or out of the area. Note that if you come during prime dining time without a reservation, you're likely to have a long wait. High up on the mountain, The **Mountain Home Inn** ★, 810 Panoramic Hwy., Mill Valley (ℂ **415/381-9000;** www.mtnhomeinn.com) offers a swell brunch and panoramic views from their outdoor deck.

If you make it over Mount Tam, just past Muir Woods, look for the **Pelican Inn,** 10 Pacific Way, Muir Beach (ℂ **415-383-6000;** www.pelicaninn.com). Built in 1979 to resemble a 16th-century English cottage, this is the perfect place to grab a beer at the old-fashioned bar—dartboard and all—and sprawl out on the lawn for lunch after a hike.

WINE COUNTRY

The rolling green hills and pocket ponds of this region are so beautiful they could be considered draw enough, but of course, the main reason one comes here is unparalleled access to enjoy world-class food and drink surrounded by pastoral splendor. There's no doubt the Wine Country is all about the Good Life—so much so that you may find yourself developing a desire to drop everything and move here to stomp grapes. Use this chapter as a quick primer for a weekend or day trip into a world that you are sure to fall in love with.

A QUICK LAY OF THE LAND

Picture the whole area as a long, uppercase U in which the two top tongs are pinched together around a light mountain range. On the "left," or western, tong of the U is vast and widespread Sonoma County, where the principal north-south road is U.S. 101, which goes straight to the Golden Gate; while in Napa County, the eastern half, it's the more congested 128. In Napa County, the main road is 29, which, especially around rush hour, can be slow going.

At the bottom of the U, the town of Sonoma is connected to the town of Napa, which is 30 minutes east, by a long stretch of rural Highway 121/12. That's also where Highway 37 links Napa County to Highway 101, as well as to the town of Vallejo (no need to stop there, trust us) and I-80; either road can take you back to the city, although the 101 is probably faster.

North from Napa, the principal towns, which gradually grow smaller and quainter, are **Yountville, Oakville, St. Helena** (all adorable), and finally the Main Street town of **Calistoga** (known for hot springs). Not far north from that, 29 turns into 128 and links up with **Geyserville**, at the tippy top of the Sonoma wine region.

From there, heading south through Sonoma County, you hopscotch between populous towns and quiet hamlets. First is **Healdsburg** (a swanky-sweet weekenders' town square good for strolling), and **Santa Rosa** (bigger and with cheaper motels, but no wineries to speak of within it, though there is an airport here). Route 12, also known as Sonoma Highway, branches off to the east there, taking you through **Kenwood** and the charming town of **Glen Ellen**, and finally **Sonoma,** the county's historic seat. West and southwest of Santa Rosa along 116 are the towns of **Sebastopol** and **Forestville,** and finally, **Guerneville,** where the thick redwood forests begin in what's called the Russian River Valley. The vibe here is more laid-back, and in summer, the big pastimes are canoeing and swimming. Guerneville is also a well-known gay resort town, particularly in summer, although you won't find that it rages often with parties; the

Wine Country

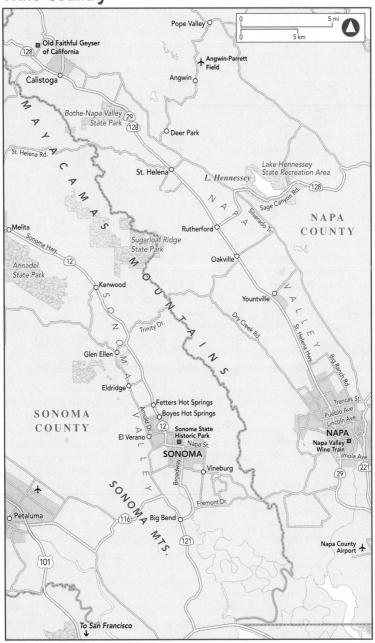

Pope Valley

0   5 mi
0   5 km

Old Faithful Geyser of California
(128)

Calistoga

Angwin-Parrett Field

Angwin

MAYACAMAS

Bothe-Napa Valley State Park
(29)
(128)

Deer Park

St. Helena Rd.

St. Helena

L. Hennessey

Lake Hennessey State Recreation Area

Sage Canyon Rd.
(128)

Melita

Sonoma Hwy.

Annadel State Park

Sugarloaf Ridge State Park

NAPA

Silverado Tr.

NAPA COUNTY

(12)

Rutherford

Kenwood

Oakville

VALLEY

Trinity Dr.

Yountville

St. Helena Hwy.

Dry Creek Rd.

MOUNTAINS

Glen Ellen

Big Ranch Rd.

Eldridge

MAYACAMAS

VALLEY

Fetters Hot Springs
Boyes Hot Springs

Trancas St.
Pueblo Ave.
Lincoln Ave.

Arnold Dr.

El Verano
(12)

Sonoma State Historic Park
Napa St.

SONOMA

NAPA

Napa Valley Wine Train

SONOMA COUNTY

Broadway

SONOMA

Vineburg

Imola Ave.
(221)
(29)

Petaluma

SONOMA MTS.

Fremont Dr.

(116)

Big Bend

(121)

Napa County Airport

(101)

To San Francisco

deciding BETWEEN NAPA OR SONOMA

Choosing which area to visit is a tough call, but the choice can be easily made if you consider the strong suits of each. If world-famous restaurants, super luxury accommodations or funky hot springs, and larger well-known brand-name wineries with elaborate facilities and tours sound good to you, aim for Napa. You can stay in the town of Napa, Calistoga, or anywhere in between—getting across the valley takes about 45 minutes, so it really doesn't matter. If I were you, I'd plan my accommodations around where I want to dine. Yes, you'll need to hop in and out of the car all day while wine tasting. (Hire a car service or designate a driver; there's no public transportation here.) But trust me: There's nothing worse than gorging yourself silly on a memorable meal and too much wine, and finding yourself a half-hour's drive from your hotel.

Sonoma County, on the other hand, is the more pastoral, laid-back, wholesome-feeling escape. It's where you'll find more family-owned wineries where the winemakers themselves are pouring the day's drink. More expansive with charming rural little roads leading to the next great wine tasting experience, it's less congested, more spread out, and has the most attractive square around (in Healdsburg). That's not to say you won't find luxury and hot springs here, too. Famed Sonoma Mission Inn (p. 218) is case in point. There are also noteworthy dining excursions and an abundance of exceptional wines. Should Sonoma be your pick, I highly recommend you choose between spending your time in Sonoma Valley (cute shopping and dining square in the town of Sonoma, a handful of great wineries, including some historic ones) or Northern Sonoma (vast, with Healdsburg as its epicenter, a plethora of wonderful wine regions scattered over winding roads flanked by overgrowth, and fun outdoor activities such as canoeing along the Russian River).

Maybe it's not so easy to choose. But the good news is, you really can't go wrong.

visitors tend to be a bit more middle-aged and settled. (For a resource on gay friendly and specific resorts and restaurants, go to www.gayrussianriver.com.

The character of the two counties varies slightly. While Napa is mostly verdant farmland and some small towns, Sonoma has a few larger communities (Santa Rosa) and its topography is much more varied. There's rolling hills and farms in the east, which gives way to deliciously damp redwood forests in the middle west, to wild and undeveloped seashore. (Remember Hitchcock's *The Birds*? It was shot in Bodega Bay, on the Sonoma Coast. It's still just as rustic now, although it's about 30 minutes' drive through forests from what we consider Wine Country.)

It really doesn't matter which area you choose to make home base. They're all spectacular. But Sonoma and Napa combined cover a heck of a lot of real estate, so you'd be wise to select and explore either Napa Valley, Sonoma Valley, or Northern Sonoma. To do them all justice, you'd need at least 2 weeks!

WHEN TO GO

Because the area is a major draw from the cities in the Bay Area, you'll find that crowds build when people are normally vacationing. Summertime is ludicrously busy, and the season's lines of cars and endless traffic on the counties' two-lane roads can truly try the patience. Still, the scenery is gorgeous then, with the grapes sprouting on the vine; and it's also the season for garden tours. The grapes are harvested and squeezed in the fall, and, alas, this time can also be maddening, because people flock here to witness some of the rare action involved in harvest and the resulting winemaking. I'm a fan of visiting in winter: Tourists tend to stay away then so you'll get much more attention and education from the vintners, hotel prices (notoriously expensive) are way down, and it's easier to get restaurant reservations. Plus, with the nip of winter, the dormant grape-vines, and twinkle lights illuminating various nooks and crannies, it's extremely romantic. Spring is a close second, because the area bursts with the green and yellow of mustard flowers. It's never terribly cold—wine country everywhere, by definition, is mostly mild, because that's what makes it good for grape growing.

NAPA VALLEY

Just 55 miles north of San Francisco, 35-mile-long Napa Valley comprises a string of small towns surrounded by vineyards, all of which rely on tourism for the majority of their livelihoods. At its southern end, the town of Napa is the most cosmopolitan. With no vineyards in sight, a walkable downtown that's currently undergoing major renova-tions, and a continually growing number of restaurants and hotels, the once lesser-than urban area has become hotbed for wine country fun. To the north, off thoroughfare Highway 29, the tiny town of Yountville is home to one of the most well-traveled foodie strips in the country (thanks to restaurants by Thomas Keller, Michael Chiarello, and more). Oakville and Rutherford are primarily known for the wineries that reside there, while St. Helena has charming shopping and dining along its tiny Main Street. Further north still is Calistoga, where a cluster of hot springs, motels, B&Bs, shops, and a very relaxed vibe draw laid-back tourists. No matter where you stay, you'll be minutes from dozens of wineries worth a visit.

Napa Wineries

With some 300 wineries, the fact is that you could tour Napa's wineries for months. So don't approach winery circuits the way you might the great museums of Paris or the rides at Disneyland. You can't hit everything, so don't even try. The key is to find places that deliver the experience you want, whether it's a specific wine varietal, a style, dramatic architecture, or a killer view. No matter where you choose to go, you can trust that in this competitive, expensive region, you're not going to be served swill, so relax about tasting. Besides, I've always found that during the course of a fun adventure, almost any wine tastes amazing. Rather than provide a laundry list of Napa's offerings, in the pages that follow I highlight the wineries that possess a little something extra—a terrific view, an unusual or rich history, an outstanding art collec-tion, or a particularly noteworthy tour. Still, there are more delicious experiences to be had here in Napa, so don't hesitate to ask your well-traveled friends, hotel concierge, or people you meet along the way for wineries they might recommend.

To make planning an itinerary easy on yourself, get the downloadable maps from www.napavalley.org, the site run by the Napa Valley Conference and Visitors Bureau. If you are unable to download maps before you arrive, don't fret, because they're distributed widely and for free, and there's no doubt your hotel or B&B has more maps than you'll know what to do with. Then check out the opening hours and tour times, scheduling advance tours if required, and chart a path that doesn't require a lot of backtracking. Otherwise, you'll spend more time in the car than the tasting room.

HOW TO WINE taste

It doesn't really matter if you don't know the difference between chardonnay and cabernet; trust me, no one cares. But if you want to learn about how to wine taste, California's wine country is the perfect classroom, and provided the tasting room you're visiting isn't slammed with visitors, the hosts will certainly show you exactly how to taste. But if you're left to your own devices, follow these tips:

Look: It may seem pompous to raise your glass in the air toward the light, but go ahead—then tip it to the side, and admire the wine's color. You can actually tell a lot about the wine by its color, including the varietal, whether it's a "young" or an "aged" wine. or how it was fermented. It takes time to understand exactly what to look for, but if you follow this practice for the wines you taste, you might just begin noticing distinctions between varietals and vintages.

Swirl: Gently swirl the contents of your wineglass. This process will aerate the wine and allow you to smell it better. It also creates an opportunity to learn more about the wine. It's "legs" or drips down the side of the glass can indicate whether the wine is fuller (stronger in flavor) or lighter (more delicate).

Smell: Stick your nose in the tilted glass and take a good whiff. Make up words to describe what you smell: barnyard, strawberries, cotton candy, whatever. Wines have distinctive aromas, and with practice you can begin to identify, but I've found the power of suggestion plays an equal hand and no matter whether you smell pineapple and stone fruit or plain old wine, it's still fun to play the guessing game.

Sip: This part is pretty straightforward, but do it like the pros: Take small sips and breathe a little air into your mouth while the wine's in there to further aerate it and spread the flavor across your palate.

Spit: Your choice, of course, but wineries keep a little spittoon on the bar that's for your use. I hate this part, even though I spit fairly often, because it requires some finessing to do it right. Otherwise, you'll be like me with a little steam of wine dripping down your chin. Still, it's another thing that's fun to try.

Pace Yourself: Plenty of people saddle up to the bar and gulp down every last drop of every last wine—and you're welcome to do the same (provided you're not driving, of course). But know that even small sips at three or four wineries can add up to a sudden need to splay out on the back seat of your car for an impromptu siesta. So, if you want to have fun and make it to the dinner hour, slow it down.

Castello di Amorosa Winery ★★ The exuberant, over-the-top European pretensions of some of the area's landlords is on no more immoderate display than at this sublime, 121,000-square-foot medieval-style castle (completed in 2007). With its basement dungeon outfitted with antique torture devices, 72-foot-long Great Hall with a 22-foot-high coffered ceiling, and 107 guest rooms, Castello di Amorosa gets it's a reputation more for being a tourist attraction than for its quality wines, which are only sold here. The $19 entry fee includes a tasting of five wines; for $29 you taste of six wines, including some reserves. Visitors under 21 pay $9. Combined tours and tastings (1 hr., 45 min.) go for $34 per person (reservations required). Owner Daryl Sattui also runs the V. Sattui Winery in St. Helena, which regularly overflows with picnickers.

4045 North Saint Helena Highway, Calistoga. ℭ **707/967-6272.** www.castellodiamorosa.com. Daily Mar–Oct 9:30am–6pm, Nov–Feb 9:30am–5pm.

Chateau Montelena ★   One of the wineries that put Napa Valley on the global map, this pastoral estate won a top honor among white wines at the Judgment of Paris in 1976, and continues to hold its head high today. The basic tasting is $20 for four wines, but this will be credited with a $100 purchase. If you're deeply interested, set aside 45 minutes for its Library Wine Tasting (11:30am and 1:30pm; $50; reservation required). This isn't a place well laid out for hordes of casual gawkers, even if the ivy-covered stone castlelike winery building (1882) is pretty and the Chinese garden and 5-acre pond, Jade Lake, make for a lovely place to sit for a few minutes. The people pouring here (they're in the modern ranch-style building) know their wine, and they're still proud of the victory that put Napa on the serious wine drinker's map. In fact, if you've seen the movie "Bottle Shock" (2008), a retelling of the Judgment of Paris, this is the central winery in that story. Look carefully for the easy-to-miss driveway; as you're driving to the winery, if the road you're on starts giving way to hairpins and ever-climbing altitude, you've gone too far, and you're on a mountain pass.

1429 Tubbs Lane, Calistoga. ℭ **707/942-5105.** www.montelena.com. Daily 9:30am–4pm.

Chandon ★★   Founded in 1973 by French champagne house Moët et Chandon, this gorgeous, well-manicured sparkling wine producer is the place to go if you want to join revelers basking on the sunny patio with bottles of bubbly and gourmet snacks. Tours of the sparkling wine making process are comprehensive and fun, but what makes this place pop is the scene—unlike other tasting rooms, this one is designed to encourage you to kick back and stay awhile. And people happily do. A formal Michelin star–awarded, French-inspired restaurant is also located here.

1 California Dr. (at Hwy. 29), Yountville. ℭ **707/944-2280.** www.chandon.com. Daily 10am–5pm; hours vary by season, so call to confirm. Call or check website for free tour schedules and seasonal hours.

Domaine Charbay Winery & Distillery   After you finally reach this mountain-top hideaway, affectionately called "the Still on the Hill," you immediately get the sense that something special is going on here. Owner Miles Karakasevic considers himself more of a perfume maker than a 12th-generation master distiller, and it's easy to see why. The tiny distillery is crammed with bottles of his latest fragrant potions, such as brandy, whole-fruit-flavor-infused vodkas, grappa, and pastis. He's also become known for other elixirs: black walnut liqueur, apple brandy, a line of ports, several cabernet sauvignons, and the charter product—Charbay (pronounced Shar-*bay*)—a brandy liqueur blended with chardonnay. The low-key tour—which costs $20 per person, is private and exclusive, and includes tastes of premade cocktails—centers on a small, 25-gallon copper alembic still and the distilling process.

4001 Spring Mountain Rd. (5 miles west of Hwy. 29), St. Helena. ℭ **800/634-7845** or 707/963-9327. www.charbay.com. Tues–Sat 10am–4pm by appointment. Closed holidays.

The Hess Collection ★★★   A top choice for art lovers, here wine is served in a ground-floor tasting room and an expertly curated selection of modern art, collected by Swiss owner Donald Hess (who regularly loans his works to top museums), is displayed in a spacious two-level gallery. Hess grants his support to 20 living artists, saying he'll reassess when they either die or become "well established." Since he chose both Robert Motherwell (displayed here) and Francis Bacon, it's fair to say the guy's got an eye. The art he has is here arresting, the front garden is picture perfect, and the drive up the winding roads to get here is fun, too.

4411 Redwood Rd., Napa. ℭ **707/255-1144.** www.hesscollection.com. Tours and tasting $30–$85 per person. Visitor Center and gallery 10am–5:30pm; winery and vineyard tours 10:30am–3:30pm.

Quixote ★★   This hidden, hillside property owned by longtime industry power player Carl Doumani is the only U.S. structure designed by late great European artist Friedensreich Hundertwasser. Whimsical and captivating even to those who know nothing about design, it's a structural fantasy world with undulating lines, a gilded onion dome, and a fearless use of color. During the $25-per-person reservation-only sit-down tasting, visitors can fill their agape mouths with tastes of the winery's current releases. If you're interested in visiting, reserve in advance; Due to zoning laws, this spectacular and truly one-of-a-kind Stags' Leap District winery welcomes up to eight guests per day, all of whom are likely to find themselves as awestruck by the architecture as they are by the powerful petite syrahs and cabernet sauvignons.

6126 Silverado Trail, Napa. ✆ **707/944-2659.** www.quixotewinery.com. Tastings by appointment only Tues–Sun 10am–4pm.

Robert Mondavi ★★   This Mission-style winery with varied and very informative tours was started by the acknowledged pioneer of modern-day California winemaking of the same name who died at 94 in 2008. As you drive up to the polished and expansive grounds, you're greeted by a handsome bronze-and-glass-mosaic statue of St. Francis by Beniamino Bufano, and from there, the Mission-style buildings open up into a view of the vineyards and the hills beyond. Check into the Visitors Center, to the left, for a highlight history of the winery and to arrange a tour. The Discovery Tour lasts 30 minutes and is offered every weekend in the summer. The cost is $15 for two tastings and kids are welcome (under 13 tour free). The year-round 75-minute Signature Tour features a sit-down guided wine tasting (3 tastes) and costs $30 per person. You'll stroll the vineyards and the cellars; children are welcome but must be at least 13 years old to attend. After your tour, stroll around the grounds; you'll encounter a collection of more chunky Bufano works. (Benny Bufano was famous for chopping off his trigger finger and mailing it to President Woodrow Wilson rather than fight in World War I. His digital protest didn't seem to affect the power of his art.) The tasting rooms generally offer about 10 wines that are exclusive to the winery, and the Vineyard Room charges $20 for 4 tastings of Appellation wines. All summer long, the winery hosts outdoor concerts on its grounds, something it's been doing since 1969, 3 years after Mondavi kicked off Napa's post-Prohibition rise. Don't miss a chance to attend a concert if you can; with wine flowing and people picnicking and dancing to the music of extremely famous names, it's Napa Valley living at its best.

Highway 29, Oakville. ✆ **888/766-6328.** www.robertmondaviwinery.com. Daily 10am–5pm; closed holidays.

Schramsberg ★★   This 217-acre sparkling wine estate, a landmark once frequented by Robert Louis Stevenson and the second-oldest property in Napa Valley, is one of the valley's all-time best places to explore. Schramsberg is the label that presidents serve when toasting dignitaries from around the globe, and there's plenty of historical memorabilia in the winery's front room to prove it. But the real mystique begins when you enter the sparkling wine caves, which wind 2 miles (reputedly the longest in North America) and were partly hand-carved by Chinese laborers in the 1800s. The caves have an authentic Tom Sawyer ambience, complete with dangling cobwebs and seemingly endless passageways; you can't help but feel you're on an adventure. The comprehensive, unintimidating tour ends in a charming, cozy tasting room, where you'll sample four surprisingly varied selections of their high-end bubbly. At $50 per person, tasting is mighty pricey, but many feel its money well spent. Note that tastings are offered only to those who take the free tour, and you must make reservations in advance.

1400 Schramsberg Rd. (off Hwy. 29), Calistoga. ✆ **707/942-2414.** www.schramsberg.com. Daily 10am–4pm, with 5 scheduled tours. Tours and tastings by appointment only.

Shafer Vineyards ★★   An intimate and educational tour and tasting experience is the reason to make an appointment at this low-key family-owned winery. Founded by John and Doug Shafer, they, along with winemaker Elias Fernandez, use sustainable farming and solar energy to make truly outstanding wines. But more important, you'll be hard pressed to find a more relaxed, personal tour and tasting. The $55-per-person price is steep, but for wine lovers, the 1½-hour experience is worth it. These are popular tours so book at least a month in advance.

6154 Silverado Trail, Napa. ✆ **707/944-2877.** www.shafervineyards.com. By appointment only Mon–Fri 9am and 4pm; closed weekends and holidays.

Sterling Vineyards ★   The highlight of this winery is a ride on its aerial tram ($28; $10 ages 4 to 21; free under 4), which takes you to and through some fantastic views over the area. The main building sits on a hill some 300 feet above the valley floor and the parking lot. Obviously, to visit it completely, you'll need to budget plenty of time and go on a clear day. You've got to pay the fee even if you don't want to ride the tram, but the price also includes a tour (self-guided, not narrated) and a five-wine tasting at your own table. Interesting side note: The bells in the tower used to hang in St. Dunstan's of Fleet Street London, which was destroyed in World War II. There are not a lot of places where kids will be welcomed or engaged in the wine country, but because of the tram, I'd take hard-to-please kids here. Picnicking is allowed.

1111 Dunaweal Lane, Calistoga. ✆ **800/726-6136.** www.sterlingvineyards.com. Mon–Fri 10:30am– 4:30pm, Sat–Sun 10am–5pm.

Napa Beyond the Wineries

Don't bother with the touristy wine train that traverses Napa County; it's a trap on which you're required to eat their mediocre food, and you can't get off and on as you wish (and as would actually be useful).

diRosa Preserve ★   Some 2,200 works of art are kept on 900 stunning acres, centering on a 35-acre pond. The works here are delightfully fractured, wild, *avant garde* experiments, many of the kinetic variety and every one of them by Bay Area hands and minds. Three tours offer three levels of access to the grounds. Unless you really must see everything, the $12 "Introductory" version, a 90-minute overview of the highlights, including the Historic Residence and the core of the collection, will do almost everyone. Pay $3 more, and you can enjoy all of the above as well as extended viewing in the Gatehouse Gallery on a 2-hour tour. Better yet, for a suggested donation of $5 you can enjoy the manageable rotating selection of art in the Gatehouse Gallery without a tour of the grounds, pretty as they are. Students of landscaping and architecture won't want to miss it, and nor will fans of eccentric contemporary art. Others may leave scratching their heads. But no one departs without sighing over the greenery at least once. 5200 Carneros Highway/121, Napa. ✆ **707/226-5991.** www.dirosaart.org. Wed–Sun 10am–4pm. Closed holidays. Children 12 and under are free.

Where to Stay

Accommodations in Napa Valley run the gamut—from standard motels and floral-and-lace Victorian-style B&Bs to world-class luxury retreats—and all are easily accessible

mud BATHS

In the 1800s, the big draw in this region wasn't wine, but hot mud baths. The Quake of 1906 shifted the location of many of the springs, wiping out most of the wells that then existed in Sonoma County as well, so that today, the best place to participate in a geothermal treatment is in Calistoga in Napa County. Like bungee jumping or hot-air ballooning, it's a once-in-a-lifetime vacation treat

Most places mix the mud and hot springs water (which is a little over 100 degrees) with clay, peat, and volcanic ash from nearby St. Helena volcano, which may stain some swimsuits, so don't wear your best one, or, like most people, don't wear anything at all. These treatments used to be touted as an excellent treatment for arthritis, but modern marketing laws being what they are, they're now meant mostly as stress relievers (though supporting scientific studies show that arthritis suffers may, in fact, find some relief).

The following day spas all include mud baths—the most "local" of the treatment—and other treatments such as massage and hydrotherapy (check their websites for full menus). Some mud baths are thick, others soupy; some start as mineral-water baths before having ash mixed in (to prove it's fresh, I suppose), and others offer a pre-mixed tub before you begin. The style doesn't matter but make sure the spa you visit uses mineral water, which means it's been drawn hot from the earth.

Dr. Wilkinson's Hot Springs Resort (1507 Lincoln Ave., Calistoga; ✆ 707/942-4102; www.drwilkinson. com), set in a delightfully 1950s motel complex, has been a player in Calistoga for generations and offers a range of treatments, but it's basic in the classically medicinal sense that spas once had. The mud bath as described above is $89 and takes a little over an hour.

Golden Haven (1713 Lake St., Calistoga; ✆ 707/942-8000; www.goldenhaven. com), with its couples-sized tubs, is popular with honeymooners. A treatment costs $89 per person ($72 Mon–Thurs in winter).

Lavender Hill Spa (1015 Foothill Blvd., Calistoga; ✆ 707/942-4495; www.laven derhillspa.com) does everything with Asian flair and extras (like a Thai Bath uses milk, the mud bath, kelp), and its mud is thinner than at other spas. One-hour treatments are $95 per person.

Lincoln Avenue Spa (1339 Lincoln Ave., Calistoga; ✆ 707/942-2950; www.lincolnavenuespa.com) might be the choice for severe claustrophobes, since they won't have to get into the thick, mucky baths that alarm some people. Instead, they apply mud onto themselves in a private room—with a loved one, if desired—followed by time in a less-constricting steam capsule. That's $79 per person, or $149 for two.

from the main highway that stretches across the valley and leads to its attractions. Most of the romantically pastoral options (think hidden hillside spots with vineyard views or quaint small-town charmers) are found on the outskirts of historic St. Helena, which has the best walking/shopping street (at least for now; my bet is Napa will soon surpass it), and the equally storied, but more laid-back and affordable than hot springs–heavy Calistoga, which also boasts some of the region's most affordable options. The few commercial blocks of pastoral Yountville have become a destination in itself thanks to a number of famous restaurants (including world-renowned French Laundry) as well as a handful of high-end hotels and middle-end B&Bs. The most "reasonably priced" (a relative term in this high-priced area) choices are the B&Bs, small hotels, and national chain options in downtown Napa, the closest thing you'll find to a city in these parts, which also happens to be very up-and-coming with restaurants. No matter where you stay, you're just a few minutes—or less—away from world-class wineries.

EXPENSIVE

Calistoga Ranch ★★★   One of the most luxurious retreats in the region, this resort set on an eastern mountainside on 157 pristine hidden-canyon acres is dotted with freestanding accommodations along hilly pathways that accommodate only foot and golf-cart traffic. As the area's newest uberluxe address, its rooms are also the most tricked out—and all are steps away from swimming in the natural thermal pool (which, has a nearby children's pool), pampering at the gorgeous, state-of-the-art indoor-outdoor spa, free yoga and painting classes, and dining at the lakeside restaurant (open only to guests; it's fine but not great). Completing the world-class experience are Mercedes Benzes or and bicycles for use, free of charge.

580 Lommel Rd., Calistoga. ✆ **707/254-2800.** www.calistogaranch.com. 46 cottages. $450–$4,000 double. **Amenities:** Restaurant; concierge; gym; Jacuzzi; large heated outdoor pool; room service; outdoor rain showers, spa; Wi-Fi (free).

MODERATE

Cedar Gables Inn ★★   In 1892, Edward S. Churchill commissioned the noted British architect Ernest Coxhead to create this magnificent, 10,000-square-foot Tudor mansion as a wedding present for his engaged son, which now attracts honeymooning couples visiting the area. Rooms are romantic, too, especially the four that have fireplaces (five have whirlpool tubs and all come with a bottle of complimentary port). Guests can mingle in the evening in front of the roaring fireplace in the lower "English tavern" for wine and cheese and at breakfast in the mornings, which is a sumptuous three-course feast.

486 Coombs St. (at Oak St.), Napa. ✆ **800/309-7969** or 707/224-7969. www.cedargablesinn.com. 9 units. $189–$329 double. Rates include full breakfast, evening wine and cheese, and port. From Hwy. 29 N., exit onto First St. and follow signs to downtown; turn right onto Jefferson St. and left on Oak St.; house is on the corner. **Amenities:** Free local calls and Wi-Fi.

Chanric Inn ★★★   Art-filled decor, tons of thoughtful touches, an outdoor pool and hot tub, and hosts who ensure your every wish is granted make this a fantastic choice in Calistoga. Each morning, hot coffee and biscotti sit outside guest room doors, which is followed by a gourmet three-course breakfast. Later in the day, guests are treated to hors d'oeuvres, wine, and a champagne nightcap.

1805 Foothill Blvd., Calistoga. ✆ **877/281-3671** or 707/942-4535. www.thechanric.com. 6 units. $229–$499 double. Rates include breakfast. **Amenities:** Wi-Fi (free).

INEXPENSIVE

Best Western Plus Elm House Inn ★★   One of the best values in Napa, this bargain escape's rooms are spacious and attractive, the service gracious, and there are all sorts of extras, including a good breakfast and freshly baked cookies in the afternoon, lovely landscaping, a hot tub on the patio, and experts behind the desk (they're helpful in setting up wine tasting itineraries for first timers). The hotel is within walking distance of Napa's downtown center and close to Hwy. 29, the region's thoroughfare; wineries are mere minutes away.

800 California Blvd., Napa. ✆ **888/849-1997** or 707/255-1831. www.bestwestern.com. 22 units. $129–$279 double. Rates include full breakfast and evening cookies. From Hwy. 29 north, take the First St. exit, take a right onto California Blvd., and the hotel is on the corner of Second St. and California Blvd. **Amenities:** Free phone calls; hot tub; laundry facilities; Wi-Fi (free).

Dr. Wilkinson's Hot Springs Resort ★   An institution among the Calistoga spas, your money here buys you a simple, immaculately clean and comfy room (some with kitchenettes) along with access to multiple hot-spring pools. Buildings are distinctly 1950s motel (standard room sizes, walls made of era brick tile, and an Americana-style neon sign out front), the resort has gone to extra lengths to renovate the rooms to a more refreshed standard (think flatscreen TVs, iPod docking stations, nice textiles). The patios and outdoor courtyards are well-groomed, fitting places to unwind before exploring the shops and food along Lincoln Avenue. If you stay here, you can avail yourself of a standard pool plus a pair (indoor and outdoor) of pools fed by mineral water. Then, of course, there's this place's famously medicinal mud bath spa (p. 212). The resort also maintains a few multi-room cottages nearby, which are terrific for families and well priced.

1507 Lincoln Ave. (Calif. 29, btw. Fairway and Stevenson aves.), Calistoga. ☎ **707/942-4102.** www.drwilkinson.com. 42 units. $165–$310 double; $164–$670 cottages. **Amenities:** Jacuzzi; 3 pools; spa; Wi-Fi in lobby (free).

Maison Fleurie ★★   This charming inn comprises three, ivy-covered houses, so the digs vary greatly depending on whether you're in the Provencal-style main house, in the carriage house, or the bakery-turned-guesthouse. If having a private balcony, patio, or Jacuzzi tub is important, be sure to read the website descriptions carefully; what all rooms have in common is their cozy looks, comfortable beds, and private bathrooms. The lovingly tended grounds include a pool and a hot tub. A generous breakfast starts the day; end it in style with afternoon hors d'oeuvres and wine (also complimentary).

6529 Yount St. (btw. Washington St. and Yountville Cross Rd.), Yountville. ☎ **800/788-0369** or 707/944-2056. www.maisonfleurienapa.com. 13 units. $149–$285 double. Rates include full breakfast and afternoon hors d'oeuvres and wine. **Amenities:** Free use of bikes; Jacuzzi; heated outdoor pool, Wi-Fi (free).

Roman Spa Hot Springs Resort ★   It's clean, not pricey for a double, and well located (just a block off Calistoga's main street), so try not to worry that there's nothing "Roman," or even remotely chic about this place? There are three mineral pools onsite (one's an outdoor whirlpool), and mud baths and massage are available. The two-bedroom units (with full kitchens) are good for families.

1300 Washington St., Calistoga. ☎ **800/914-8957** or 707/942-4441. www.romanspahotsprings. com. 60 units. $169–$650. **Amenities:** 3 mineral pools; sauna; spa.

Where to Eat

Napa Valley's restaurants draw as much attention to the valley as its award-winning wineries. Nowhere else in the state are kitchens as deft at mixing fresh seasonal, local, organic produce into edible magic, which means that menus change constantly to reflect the best available ingredients. Add that to a great bottle of wine and stunning views, and you have one heck of an eating experience. Here are some picks, from an affordable diner to once-in-a-lifetime culinary experience, and everything in between.

Ad Hoc ★★ INTERNATIONAL   For those who'd like to try star chef Thomas Keller's cuisine (see French Laundry review, below), but also pay rent this month, Ad Hoc is the solution. Most famous for its fried chicken dinners (served only on Mon), the restaurant offers a daily changing, prix fixe menu, which is served family style and ranges across the globe for its inspirations. One day you might get jambalaya and on another day the menu will feature falafel, the one constant being the high quality of both the ingredients and the cooking.

6475 Washington St., Yountville, Napa Valley. © **707/944-2487.** www.adhocrestaurant.com. Thurs–Mon 5–10pm, Sun 10am–1pm. Prixe fixe $52.

Angèle ★★ COUNTRY FRENCH   Whether you're seated in the cozy dining room or on the riverfront patio, you can count on Angèle to deliver a delicious downtown Napa experience. It's not that its design should be a case study on how to do a restaurant right (though it is), or that the seasonally inspired menu holds on to local favorites like crispy roast chicken while continuing to elevate familiar French fare (It does). It's all of it put together—alongside the pro hospitality of owner Bettina Rouas, who is almost always on hand. Add a bottle of wine and you've got the makings of a beautiful friendship.

540 Main St. (in the Hatt Building). © **707/252-8115.** www.angelerestaurant.com. Reservations recommended. Main courses $18–$32. Sun–Thurs 11:30am–9pm; Fri–Sat 11:30am–10pm.

BarBersQ ★ BARBECUE   When you just can't stomach another precious salad or truffle-covered something, come here for down-home, genuine Memphis-style BBQ. Ribs, brisket, beans and ham, fried chicken—yup, it's a carnivores paradise, though this being Napa, anything that once grew in the ground will be locally sourced. Top it all off with addictive chocolate bourbon pecan pie, or Key lime pie—if you can.

3900 D Bel Aire Plaza, Napa. © **707/224-6600.** www.barbersq.com. Main courses $8–$30. Sun–Thurs 11:30am–8:30pm; Fri–Sat 11:30am–9pm.

Bottega Ristorante ★★ ITALIAN   Emmy-winning TV host Michael Chiarello was a chef first, and here he goes back to his roots. As with the many other restaurants in the area, the ingredients are proudly locavore, but here the cooking is decidedly Italian. When the weather's chilly, there are few more pleasant places to linger than in front of the fireplace in Bottega's dining room, with a glass of local red in your hand and a perfectly plated pasta within your fork's reach.

6525 Washington St, Yountville, Napa Valley. © **707/945-1050.** www.botteganapavalley.com. Main entrees $15–$25 at lunch, more at dinner. Mon–Thurs 11:30am–2:30pm and 5:30–9:00pm, Sat–Sun 11:30am–3pm and Fri–Sat 5:30–9:30pm Sun 5–9pm.

The French Laundry ★★★ FRENCH   Repeatedly recognized as one of the best restaurants in the world by pretty much everyone for well over a decade, a visit to famed chef Thomas Keller's original flagship culinary shrine is about as far away from your average dining experience as you can get. A multicourse affair that literally takes hours to complete, it consists of plate after plate of bite-size edible works of art. Some hinted at on the menu, many others arriving unexpectedly, all courses are presented to guests and finished at each table in unison by an impossibly well-trained staff that commands attention throughout the meal with their elaborate explanations of what you're about to eat. It's A-list dining theater done right, from the dramatic and astonishing flavors on the plate to the stellar performances of the staff. Alas, it's hard to leave here without feeling about as overfed as a goose destined to become foie gras. But that doesn't stop French Laundry from being on every foodie's bucket list.

6640 Washington St., Yountville. www.frenchlaundry.com. © **704/944-2380.** Tasting menu $295. Daily lunch Fri–Sun 11am–1pm, dinner 5:30–9:15pm.

Gott's Roadside ★   The original drive-in that spawned the popular outpost in San Francisco's Ferry Building, Gott's does classic comfort food with clean ingredients, served in an old-style counter-service setting. Formerly called Taylor's Refresher, it's been slinging burgers since 1949 and looks it. But looks can be deceiving. Though there are classic burgers and fries on the menu, you'll also find gourmet salads and fish sandwiches, all of it pricey for what it is. Don't skip the lusciously thick milkshakes, served with both spoon and straw. Beware if it's cold or rainy, because every seat is outdoors and not every one is sheltered. A third branch, pressed from the same mold, exists at the Oxbow Market in central Napa.

933 Main St., St. Helena. © **707/963-3486.** www.gotts.com. Main courses $7–$15. Open daily 7am–9pm. Summer hours 7am–10pm.

Morimoto ★★ JAPANESE   Continuing the Napa parade of chefs you watch on TV, this shockingly large, industrial-chic restaurant is the offering of Masahiru Morimoto of "Iron Chef" fame. No mere vanity project, Morimoto has called this his flagship, and the food certainly is worthy of that moniker, though it can be hard to decide what to order (the menu is *very* extensive). Some specials include tofu made fresh at tableside, creative sushi offerings and salads crafted from ingredients that are freshly picked on nearby farms. I tend to have the best experience ordering from the appetizers. Along with 200 sakes, Morimoto serves a fine selection of wines from nearby vineyards.

610 Main St., Napa. © **707/252-1600.** www.morimotonapa.com. Main dishes $13–$80. Sun–Thurs 11:30am–2:30pm and 5–midnight, Fri–Sat 11:30am–2:30pm and 5pm–1am.

Terra/Bar Terra ★★ CONTEMPORARY AMERICAN   Casual or dressy dining—you choose at this two-in-one restaurant. One side (Bar Terra) houses a relaxed bar with terrific (and unusual) eats, while the original Terra showcases James Beard Award–winning chef Hiro Sone's awe-inspiring ability to master and borrow from French, Italian, and Japanese cooking traditions and make them his own. Crudo, pasta, fish, steak, it's all done perfectly here. Cocktails are made from fruits and herbs grown in the owners' garden. Desserts are also primo, so save room.

1345 Railroad Ave. (btw. Adams and Hunt sts.), St. Helena. © **707/963-8931.** www.terrarestaurant. com. Reservations recommended. Bar: Plates $6–$25. Dining room: 4-course $78; 5-course $93; 6-course $105; chef's menu changes nightly. Mon & Wed–Fri 6–9pm, 6–9:30pm Sat–Sun. Closed 2 weeks in early Jan.

SONOMA VALLEY

A less developed contrast to Napa, Sonoma's unpretentious gaggle of ordinary towns, ranches, and wineries result in a genuine backcountry ambience—and a lower density of wineries, restaurants, and hotels. But that doesn't mean there isn't plenty to do and see. Low-key wine tastings are held at the small, family-owned wineries scattered along the quiet woodsy roads of this 17-mile-long, 7-mile-wide valley bordered by two mountain ranges: the Mayacamas to the east and the Sonomas to the west.

Sonoma Valley Wineries

Unlike Northern Sonoma, Sonoma Valley is relatively condensed, with a small cluster of wineries surrounding Sonoma's town square, and a string of additional stops off the highway as you head south or north along the main highway. While planning your route, get a copy of the Official Visitors Map put out by Sonoma County Tourism Bureau (© **800/576-6662;** www.sonomacounty.com); online you can order a variety of information to be sent to you.

Benziger Family Winery ★★ Benziger offers one of the better tours: a $40 tram run that concludes with four tastings. This all-organic, sustainable winery is doing things right, and it's fun to see how they go about making good wine without despoiling the land. In winter, sheep wander the property, eating the grass around the vines. (When grapes are growing, said our guide, "They can't be trusted.") All organic waste is recycled, and the winery even runs an "insectary" where beneficial bugs are encouraged to breed. The tram tour whisks you about to show the general layout of the property, which occupies a microclimate specific to its valley, and takes you into wine caves that are some 70 feet under the hillside. You'll also hear about the cooperage (barrel making), although you won't see a demonstration. All in all, it's one of the most well-rounded tours on the market, and something about the family-run facility, or maybe its idealism, doesn't make you feel like you're being herded from site to site.

1883 London Ranch Rd., Glen Ellen. ℂ **888/490-2739.** www.benziger.com. Daily 10am–5pm.

Gundlach Bundschu Winery ★★ This is the quintessential Sonoma winery— relaxed and playful, yet wine obsessed. It's the oldest continually running family-owned and -operated winery in California, plus it's got great wines to try and the best picnic grounds in the valley. (Hike to the top of Towles' Hill for a sensational view.) Fantastic additional activities (Midsummer Mozart Festival, film fests) give even more reason to find out what's going on at GB.

2000 Denmark St. (off Eighth St. E.), Sonoma. ℂ **707/938-5277.** www.gunbun.com. Daily 11am– 4:30pm. Tours last 1 hr. and are by appointment only. Groups of 8 or more should make an appointment.

Kaz Vineyard & Winery ★★★ It looks like some guy's house because it is: Richard "Kaz" Kasmier makes only 60 barrels a year, but he does it with care and with 10 times fewer sulfites as his competitors. Some say that you really need more sulfites to balance the flavor out, but the many people who are made ill by sulfite-heavy wines will find his efforts useful. His winery is very family oriented; the swing set on his property is for his grandkids, but he encourages any visiting shorty to play on it, and to feed the fish in the koi pond out back. Kaz doesn't take the area's pretentiousness very seriously; when I first called to ask if his winery was open to visitors, I was told, "Yes, but only if you're the *right kind* of visitor." They were kidding, of course, a dry wit made even clearer by the amusing names of his wines: Say "Rah," Red Said Fred, and Moo Vedra among them. Tastings are $5 for five wines or ports. You'll find it a little down the turn-off from Route 12 where you'll also find Landmark Vineyards.

233 Adobe Canyon Rd., Kenwood. ℂ **877/833-2536.** Tastings $2–$12. www.kazwinery.com. Fri– Mon 11am–5pm, Tues–Wed by appointment.

Robledo Family Winery ★★★ This quiet winery is one of the great personal success stories of the area. The family patriarch came to America from Michuacuan, Mexico, in 1968 and worked as a laborer for the Christian Brothers, respected winemakers, before working his way up, bit by bit, to finally owning his own spread. There are "live barrels" in the tasting room, which means they're full of aging wine, and the smell throughout the former dairy barn is marvelous. They don't do tours, but because one of Mr. Robledo's kids is usually on duty and there aren't many tourists that come through, you're bound to have a truly interesting and possibly inspiring conversation. Tastings are $10 for six wines, and bottles, which you can't buy anywhere else, start at $22. This winery received a huge honor in early 2008 when Mexican president Felipe

Calderón, on the first visit to the region by any Mexican president ever, chose Robledo and no other winery for an appearance. He, too, is from Michuacuan.

21901 Bonness Rd. ✆ **707/939-6903.** www.robledofamilywinery.com. Mon–Sat 10am–5pm, Sun 11am–4pm.

Sonoma Beyond the Wineries

Jack London State Historic Park ★   The famous writer's ashes are buried at this historic park, where he spent his final years and where his wife stayed on afterward. London's study, in the cottage, contains some artwork from his stories and items he picked up on his travels. Elsewhere on the property is a ruin of a magnificent house he tried to build—it burned down before it was done. There's an easy half-mile trail through the bucolic surroundings. On weekends, docents show up at 11am, 1pm, 2pm, and 3pm to give tours. 2400 London Ranch Rd., Glen Ellen. ✆ **707/938-5216.** www.jacklondonpark.com. Daily 9:30am–5pm, cottage noon–4pm on weekends; $10 per vehicle.

Sonoma Valley Historical Society ★   Just north of Sonoma Plaza, this often overlooked museum is stuffed with intriguing artifacts, such as painted stage curtain from the long-gone Union Hotel (now a modern bank on the southwest of the square), complete with era ads painted onto it; it was found rolled up in a barn. The women in charge of the place are generous and excited; ask to hear the 1850s Swiss music box and they'll tune it up for you. Not all the exhibits in this museum are labeled so just ask questions—they love telling tales here. 270 First Street West, Sonoma. ✆ **707/938-1762.** www.depotparkmuseum.org. Fri–Sun 1–4pm.

Where to Stay

The biggest choice you need to make when considering where to shack up is whether to stay in downtown Sonoma, which allows for easy access to its walkable shopping and dining square, or anywhere else in the valley, which promises more rural small-town surroundings and guaranteed time in the car to get to any activities. Regardless, you're destined to spend time behind the wheel, as the wineries and attractions are scattered. Keep in mind that during the peak season and on weekends, most B&Bs and hotels require a minimum 2-night stay. Of course, that's assuming you can find a vacancy; make reservations as far in advance as possible. If you are having trouble finding a room, call the **Sonoma Valley Visitors Bureau** (✆ **866/996-1090** or 707/996-1090; www.sonomavalley.com). The staff will try to refer you to a lodging that has a room to spare, but won't make reservations for you. Another option is the **Bed and Breakfast Association of Sonoma Valley** (✆ **800/969-4667**), which can refer you to a B&B that belongs to the association. You can also find updated information on their website, **www.sonomabb.com**.

EXPENSIVE

Fairmont Sonoma Mission Inn & Spa ★★   Located on 12 meticulously groomed acres, this is the only world-class resort in Sonoma. Known for its glamorous old-world looks—it's a stunning three-story replica of a California mission, built in 1927 and painted pink, plus newer wings with luxury rooms and suites—it's even more famous for its unparalleled spa facilities. Along with naturally heated artesian mineral pools and whirlpools, it features beautiful indoor pools, a great gym, plus access to golf, tennis, and excellent white-tablecloth dining. Rooms are elegant, and many have fireplaces.

100 Boyes Blvd. ✆ **800/441-1414** or 707/938-9000. www.fairmont.com/sonoma. 226 units. $259–$1,079 double. Rates include free wine tasting (4:30–5:30pm) and free bottle of wine upon arrival.

Valet parking is free for day use (spa-goers) and $25 for overnight guests. Amenities: 2 restaurants; babysitting; bike rental; concierge; golf course; health club and spa; Jacuzzi; 3 large, heated outdoor pools; room service; sauna; Wi-Fi ($14/day).

Kenwood Inn & Spa ★★   You'll feel like you've landed in Italy when you drive up to this boutique Tuscan-inspired resort with it honey-colored villas, its flower-filled flagstone courtyard, and splendid views of vineyard-covered hills. The rooms are just as Italianate, swathed in imported tapestries and velvets, and filled with custom-made furniture, shipped in from across the pond. Plus each gets a fireplace, balcony (except those on the ground floor), and spa tub. The lack of TVs is intentional; this is a place to slow down and be in the moment. As for the included breakfast, get ready to skip lunch. You won't need it after the three-course feast that's served here.

10400 Sonoma Hwy., Kenwood. 🕾 **800/353-6966** or 707/833-1293. www.kenwoodinn.com. 29 units. $325–$500 double. $35 resort fee includes gourmet breakfast, turndown service, daily newspaper, day pass to Parkpoint Health Club, and port wine in the evenings. Rates include gourmet breakfast. 2-night minimum on weekends. No pets allowed. Children 17 and under not accepted. **Amenities:** Concierge; 2 outdoor hot tubs; heated outdoor pool; indoor soaking tub; full-service spa, free high-speed Internet.

MODERATE

Beltane Ranch ★★★   This century-old, plantation style working ranch just about defines the word bucolic. And you can throw "charming" in there for good measure. The rooms are spacious and filled with well-chosen antiques, each with its own sitting area. The 105-acre estate is laced with hiking trails and gardens and it boasts a good tennis court, for those who want to work up a sweat. Breakfast is included and it's superb, the eggs are produced right on the ranch. Guests have a tough time leaving Beltane's expansive wrap-around porch; it's the perfect place to while away the afternoon-into-evening, glass of vino in hand. *Tip:* Request one of the upstairs rooms for the best views.

11775 Sonoma Hwy./Hwy. 12, Glen Ellen. 🕾 **707/996-6501.** www.beltaneranch.com. 5 units, 1 cottage. $160–$285 double. Rates include full breakfast. **Amenities:** Tennis court; walking trails, Wi-Fi (free).

Sonoma's Best Guest Cottages ★★   These adorable little houses were once grubby workmen's cottages for field hands. Today, they've been upgraded to become terrific mini-homes for tourists. Candy colored and sweet, they're equipped with kitchens, living rooms, big bathrooms, wide-plank wood floors, and outdoor sitting areas. Their location 2 miles east of Sonoma town makes for an ideal home base to explore both counties. Though they're meant as cozy retreats for two, you might be able to squeeze a tot or two in with you, and the maintenance standards couldn't be higher. Bonus: their small on-premise market café offers local cheeses, wines, coffee, and sandwiches and salads.

1190 East Napa St., Sonoma. 🕾 **800/291-8962** or 707/933-0340. www.sonomasbestcottages.com. $179–$299 cottage. 4 units. **Amenities:** Private garden; full kitchen; BBQ grill on request; Wi-Fi (free).

INEXPENSIVE

Sonoma Creek Inn ★   An excellent value for the price, the Sonoma Creek Inn is sweetly decorated (colorful bedspreads, fun lampshades, the odd tile mosaic in the wall) and fitted with flat-screen TVs and in-room coffeemakers). The property is clean and the staff friendly. Rooms are a tad more spacious than they are at other converted motels that are a bit older, and an extra $20 buys you a balcony or a pleasant walled patio with your own fountain—a nice touch. Boyes Boulevard is a little noisy (well, for Sonoma), and the neighborhood is strictly farm community—meaning it needs some grooming but is safe—and you'll have to drive a minute or two to get anywhere else in town. Check the website's special offers.

239 Boyes Blvd., Sonoma. ⓒ **888/712-1289** or 707/939-9463. www.sonomacreekinn.com. 16 units. $105–$205. Free parking. **Amenities:** Concierge services; free phone calls within the US and Canada; wine-tasting passes; Wi-Fi (free).

Where to Eat

Fremont Diner ★ DINER   This adorable, roadside diner with an old-fashioned aesthetics and homey, hearty cooking has Bay Area foodies making a special trip. Come here for fluffy omelets, serious coffee, brisket hash, fried chicken, pies, and milkshakes so thick they need a spoon. When the weather's nice, people eat outside, though the real character is indoors here.

2660 Fremont Dr., Sonoma. ⓒ **707/938-7370.** www.thefremontdiner.com. Main courses $4–$12. Mon–Wed 8am–3pm, Thurs–Sun 8am–9pm.

Girl and Fig ★★ PROVENCAL   One of the longest-running Sonoma favorites for top-quality food, this restaurant's "girl" is owner Sondra Bernstein, the chef/proprietress behind this acclaimed venture who's known for her charcuterie platters and her talent at mixing the cuisine of Provencal with local Sonoma ingredients. It's a delightful place to dine, but if you don't make it here know that you can now buy some of Bernstein's jams and chutneys (and yes, some are made with figs) at stores around the area; they make a great gift. On warm days and eves, the patio seating is special, and the wine list is always a treat.

110 W. Spain St., Sonoma. ⓒ **707/938-3634.** www.thegirlandfig.com. Main courses $17–$26. Daily 11:30am–10pm.

La Bamba ★★   A true locals spot, this taco truck with extremely tasty grub caters to many of the people working the land—the ones who prune the vines and make the wine happen and are, for the most part, immigrants from Mexico, Colombia, and other Latin countries. For real, local flavor, grab a meal here; tacos are just $1.50 each and fillings change daily (though you can usually get the delish *pastor* tacos).

Usually parked at 487 First St., Sonoma. Daily noon–midnight. No phone.

Northern Sonoma Wineries

Northern Sonoma is expansive, with a variety of appellations to explore, including many well-known areas such as Dry Creek Valley, Alexander Valley, and Russian River Valley. Each area has at least one cluster of wineries, and getting from one appellation to another along the rural roads is part of the fun—provided you have a designated driver. Alas, there's no way for us to include all the wineries worth visiting, but the following selection will get you started. Once you head out, you're bound to stumble upon many more.

Armida ★★★   People come from miles around to sit out on its generous wooden deck overlooking a manmade reedy pond, sip wine, share food they've brought, and enjoy great photo ops. Choose to settle in the sun or in the shade and hang out for as long as you like. The winery just asks that you only drink their wine on property. (If you don't, as they explain it, "it upsets our dog.") The tasting center, for its part, is relaxed and non-aggressive, and the winemakers don't take the scene too seriously;

one of its wines is called PoiZin (as in "the wine to die for") and the wine club is called Wino. Six specialty wines (usually 3 red, 3 white) can be sampled for $10—the fee is waived if you spend $25. It's a warm-hearted place without a slice of pretension, but with very good vino.

2201 Westside Rd., Healdsburg. ℰ **707/433-2222.** www.armida.com. Daily 11am–5pm. Closed holidays.

Bella Vineyards & Wine Caves ★★   The arched doors built into the hillside and visible from the parking lot is the entrance to one of the coolest tasting areas you'll ever visit. Zins and Rhône varietals are poured here, in a cave complete with cafe tables and impossibly chic ambiance. Tastes go for $10.

9711 W. Dry Creek Rd., Healdsburg. ℰ **866/572-3552** or 707/473-9171. www.bellawinery.com. Daily 11am–4:30pm. Appointment necessary for groups of 8 or more.

Ferrari-Carano Vineyards & Winery ★   One of the more big-business wineries in the area is also the place to ogle the most incredible gardens and views. In spring, wisteria is bursting with blooms and thousands of tulips brighten the already-gorgeous grounds. A formal Asian garden features rhododendron, Japanese arched bridges, boxwood, maples, magnolia, and roses. Tours are offered once daily, at 10am Monday through Saturday, and they require reservations. The $5 tasting charge for four current releases is refunded with a $25 purchase. A reserve tasting, offered in their Enoteca Lounge, is $15.

8761 Dry Creek Rd., Healdsburg. ℰ **707/433-6700.** www.ferrari-carano.com. Daily 10am–5pm. Tours Mon–Sat 10am with a reservation. From Hwy. 101, take Dry Creek Rd. exit headed west and go 9 miles.

Francis Ford Coppola Winery ★★   The winery owned by the legendary director is, not surprisingly, perfectly directed, from its wine tours to its movie memorabilia to its utterly chic and fun (but crazy expensive) swimming pool. You'll find a glass case full of his film-making awards, including the Oscars he won for "The Godfather.") You'll also see a giant bamboo cage used as a prop in "Apocalypse Now." The 45-minute tour (daily at 11:30am, 1pm, and 2:30pm) is a good deal; for $20, you see the vineyard, learn about the vintner's grape philosophy, pop into the barrel room where you taste wine right out of barrels, and wind up with a sampling of some reserve wines. Even without the tour, tastings are free (for two pours). This is also one of the few wineries where you'll find picnic tables that are actually in the vineyards. Though it seems out of place, the pool and cafe area is a genius idea and a fantastic place to spend the day if your hotel doesn't have a pool. You'll pay dearly for the limited access ($30 for ages 13 and up for the day, $15 ages 3–12), lounge chairs and use of your own dressing room ("cabine") are extra. But when the thermostat rises and your server delivers yet another perfect iced cocktail and a crisp salad as you linger under the shade of an oversized umbrella, you might think it's worth every penny.

300 Via Archimedes, Geyserville. ℰ **707/857-1400.** www.francisfordcoppolawinery.com. Daily 11am–6pm.

Korbel ★★★   One of the best historical tours is at the home of the best-selling sparkling wine maker in America that, for reasons that are still not entirely clear, claims it is permitted to call itself a champagne maker (usually only wineries in the Champagne region of France may do so). Korbel was started here in 1882 by a Czech cigar box maker who got in trouble back home for political unrest. His mom snuck him out of prison by smuggling civilian clothes under her skirts during a visit. That story is interesting enough, but the place is full of stuff like that. For example, the cleared area in front of the work buildings was once the site of the train line to San Francisco, 70 miles south, and 50-minute tours of the property start in the old railway station. Call them whistle-stop tours, then: The old winery is now a history center, with lots of period winemaking implements and photographs, including some fascinating snaps of the property when it was full of redwood stumps. (They called Guerneville "Stumptown" then. There are none left.) Guides keep things witty and fresh; you'll learn a lot about the tools and the process of champagne-making wrapped in a mini-history of the area. Free tours (includes four tastings) run daily on the hour from 11am to 3pm in winter, or every 45 minutes in summer, from 11am to 3pm. From mid-April to mid-October, Tuesday to Sunday at 1pm and 3pm, there's also an impressive rose garden tour for more than 250 varieties of roses, many of them antiques planted by the first Czech immigrants. Interestingly, although 1.3 million cases a year are made here, there are only eight people working in the factory, which probably means your tour will outnumber them.

13250 River Rd., Guerneville. ℗ **707/824-7000.** www.korbel.com. Shop/Tasting room open daily 10am–4:30pm.

Preston of Dry Creek ★★   One of the loveliest wineries to visit in Sonoma, this spacious, bucolic spot overflows with charm, from its wisteria-shaded picnic tables to its a bocce court to its farmhouse tasting room. Follow the neon sign's instruction and "drink zin," but also dabble in the Rhone varietals—and the seasonal produce and bread made on location from the farm store. A $10 tasting, refundable with purchase, is a small price to pay for the fun you'll have here. Note: No groups over eight.

9282 W. Dry Creek Rd. (about 1 mile west of Yoakim Bridge Rd.), Healdsburg. ℗ **707/433-3372.** www.prestonofdrycreek.com. Daily 11am–4:30pm.

Northern Sonoma Beyond the Wineries

Armstrong Redwoods State Reserve ★★   The 805-acre reserve, 2 miles north of Guerneville, is a place of peace, silence, and very big redwood trees—some of them are more than 300 feet tall and at least 1,400 years old. The moistness of the air means that when the sunlight does manage to break through the density of the ecosystem, it can draw steam off the bark of the mighty trees, creating a seriously beautiful environment. Save the entrance fee by parking at the visitor's center and walking in. There are a few trails, but overall, it's not busy, so it's often pin-drop quiet. ℗ **707/869-2015.** www.parks.ca.gov/?page_id=450. 8am–1hr. after sunset; $8 per vehicle.

Luther Burbank Home & Gardens ★   Horticulturalists will be drawn here. The name doesn't ring a bell for most, but gardeners revere Burbank for developing more than 800 new varieties of plants, particularly roses. His former home is now a national historic landmark and the surrounding acre of land, free and open until sunset, is still tended and contains many of his creations. Santa Rosa Avenue at Sonoma Avenue, Santa Rosa. ℗ **707/524-5445.** www.lutherburbank.org.

Where to Stay in Northern Sonoma

Accommodations run the gamut here, although, like Napa, you won't find lots of large brand-name hotels. Santa Rosa, the most densely populated area, also has the most

A PAEAN TO peanuts

Fans of the "Peanuts" comics and TV shows should try to spend a few hours in happy absorption at the surprisingly lavish **Charles M. Schulz Museum and Research Center ★★★** (ⓒ **707/579-4452;** www.schulzmuseum.org), at 2301 Hardies Lane in Santa Rosa. Sparky, as he was called, made ungodly amounts of money off the licensing of his creations, and so his estate has the financial wherewithal to burnish his reputation at this two-story facility, which would be worthy of any major artist.

There's lots to see and do at this two-level gallery-cum-library. Of course, there's tons of strips from the entire run of the series—always the original, never copies—and biographical information about Sparky, who died in 2000 (this place opened in 2002). Even more interesting are the many tributes to the strip by other artists, such as a life-sized Snoopy made of Baccarat crystal, Christo's "Wrapped Snoopy House," and a wall mosaic of 3,588 tiles by Yoshitero Otari. The museum preserves Schulz's work room, with its worn drawing board, bottles of Higgins ink, and an unremarkable book selection. Also fun is the non-stop slate of showings of classic TV specials and movies in a screening room. (Kids will particularly enjoy that as well as the play area outside.)

The museum is open 11am to 5pm weekdays, 10am to 5pm weekends, and is closed on Tuesdays except in the summer. Admission is $10 for adults and $5 for youth, seniors, and students.

choices, ranging from B&Bs to motels to hotels, though it's not exactly in the middle of the vineyard action. If you want to immerse yourself in a community with true wine country flair, Healdsburg is the best choice. They have a variety of places to stay, including the region's swankest boutique hotels. More laid-back is Russian River, which doubles as a summer getaway for visitors who want to spend their days playing in or lounging by the lazy river. In between are many sweet towns and wooded enclaves offering places to lay your head. No matter where you stay, you're sure to venture to other areas in search of the next great wine-tasting experience, so be sure to look at a map and your hotel's proximity to the attractions you want to visit if you care to limit your time in the car.

EXPENSIVE

Honor Mansion ★★★ Heading to wine country for your honeymoon? This is where you'll want to stay, and it truly is a mansion. With the exception of the Angel Oak room (which features a schmaltzy, off-putting mural of cherubim), the decor here is to die for, with each room decorated different, and featuring such luxe furnishings as sleigh or wrought-iron beds, hand-carved wooden dressers, gazillion thread-count linens, wood burning fireplaces, and private patios (some rooms have two!). Every morning, coffee and biscotti arrive at your door at a pre-requested time; that's followed by a sumptuous buffet breakfast in the main house (guest choose from rooms in that house and free standing cottages, including one swank one that's at the bottom of a historic water tower, with an outdoor spa tub on the roof). On-site: a 40-foot lap pool, tennis and basketball courts, a PGA-certified putting green, two competition bocce ball courts, croquet courts, and a quarter acre of zinfandel vines. Sorry, to keep the romantic atmosphere intact, kids under 16 are not welcome.

891 Grove St., Healdsburg. ℂ **800-554-4667** or 703/433-4277. www.honormansion.com. $240–$700 double. Rate includes buffet breakfast, evening wine and cheese, free parking. **Amenities:** Pool, tennis courts, basketball courts.

MODERATE

Creekside Inn and Resort ★★   I like staying in the Russian River Valley, primarily because I find the thick redwood forests so soothing and at odds with the open farmland I experience all day. The Creekside is a complex of apartments of varying sizes, all built on stilts above the forest floor. There are two options: an individually themed and designed bed and breakfast room (the waffles you'll get are marvelous and the rooms are adorable), and cottages with full kitchens (most have gas fireplaces, and all have private decks and screened in porches). The staff here is genuinely friendly and laid-back, and there's also a pool. The pubs and coffee cafes of downtown Guerneville are a short walk away over a pedestrian bridge.

16180 Neeley Rd., Guerneville. ℂ **707/869-3623.** www.creeksideinn.com. 15 units. $98–$185 double, though many of the pricier cabins (up to $270) will easily house 6 people. **Amenities:** Pool; Wi-Fi (free).

INEXPENSIVE

Travelodge Healdsburg ★   While this motel is in a not-so-sexy industrial part of town, its rates flat-out rock and its rooms do the job. You'll be happy if all you want is a clean room in an expensive area and easy access to the region's bucolic charms, which are less than 3 minutes away.

178 Dry Creek Rd., Healdsburg. ℂ **800/499-0103** or 707/433-0101. www.travelodge.com. $76–$150 double. Free parking. **Amenities:** Wi-Fi (free).

Where to Eat in Northern Sonoma

While there are plenty of restaurants around Sonoma Valley and Santa Rosa, Healdsburg has the highest concentration of outstanding restaurants. Because most of them surround the square, you can easily indulge and then take a stroll to window shop and get a feel for local life.

MODERATE

Willi's Seafood & Raw Bar ★ SEAFOOD/LATIN-INSPIRED AMERICAN There's something for everyone at this festive, modern, longtime hot spot; the menu is large and diverse, comprising numerous small plates. You'll also find dozens of local wines available by the glass, carafe, and full bottle. Outdoor seating is prime during summer evenings, while inside provides much needed respite when the thermostat reaches for the cloudless skies.

403 Healdsburg Ave. (at North St.). ℂ **707/433-9191.** www.willisseafood.net. Small plates $10–$15. Sun–Thurs 11:30am–9pm; Fri–Sat 11:30am–10pm.

Zin Restaurant & Wine Bar ★★ AMERICAN   Seasonal cooking using local ingredients and a stellar local wine list have always been the focus of this cozy local favorite. Long before farm-to-table became the rage, Zin was already focused on local and homemade, making everything, including bread and cured meats made on premises, and harvesting honey and eggs from their very own farm. Accompanying the internationally influenced menu is a fantastic wines-by-the-glass list, as well as a robust by-the-bottle selection.

344 Center St., Healdsburg. ℂ **707/473-0946.** www.zinrestaurant.com. Main courses $18–$31. Daily 5:30–9pm; slower nights close earlier.

INEXPENSIVE

Jimtown Store ★★ DELI   A gourmet country store with loads of charm, this is the place to stop for fantastic boxed lunches, gourmet picnic grub, and fun trinkets. A small seating area helps when you realize that what you've just ordered looks so good, you can't wait another minute to try it.

6706 State Hwy. 128, Healdsburg. ℂ **707/433-1212.** www.jimtown.com. Box lunches $12–$16. Mon–Fri 7am–5pm; Sat–Sun 7:30am–5pm; closes earlier during winter.

PLANNING YOUR TRIP TO SAN FRANCISCO

As with any trip, a little preparation is essential before you start your journey. This chapter provides a variety of planning tools, including information on how to get there, how to get around within the city once there, and when to visit. And then, in a mainly alphabetical listing, we deal with the dozens of miscellaneous resources and organizations that you can turn to for even more trip-planning assistance.

GETTING THERE

By Plane

The northern Bay Area has two major airports: San Francisco International and Oakland International.

San Francisco International Airport   Almost four dozen major scheduled carriers serve **San Francisco International Airport** (**SFO;** www.flysfo.com), 14 miles directly south of downtown on U.S. 101. Drive time to downtown during rush hour is about 40 minutes; at other times, it's about 20 to 25 minutes. You can also ride BART from the airport to downtown and the East Bay.

Oakland International Airport   About 5 miles south of downtown Oakland, at the Hegenberger Road exit of Calif. 17 (U.S. 880; if coming from south, take 98th Ave.), **Oakland International Airport** (**OAK;** www.oaklandairport.com) primarily serves passengers with East Bay destinations. Some San Franciscans prefer this less-crowded, more accessible airport, although it takes about a half-hour to get there from downtown San Francisco (traffic permitting). The airport is also accessible by BART via a shuttle bus.

ARRIVING AT THE AIRPORT

Immigration & Customs Clearance   International visitors arriving by air, no matter what the port of entry, should cultivate patience and resignation before setting foot on U.S. soil. U.S. airports have considerably beefed up security clearances in the years since the terrorist attacks of September 11, 2001, and clearing Customs and Immigration can take as long as 2 hours.

GETTING INTO TOWN FROM THE SAN FRANCISCO AIRPORT

Traffic Alert

Call ✆ **511** or visit www.511.org for up-to-the-minute information about public transportation and traffic.

One of the fastest and cheapest way to get from SFO to the city is to take **BART** (Bay Area Rapid Transit; ✆ **415/989-2278;** www.bart.gov), which offers numerous stops within downtown San Francisco. This route, which takes about 35 minutes, avoids traffic on the way and costs a heck of a lot less than taxis or shuttles. A BART ticket costs $8.65 ($3.20 youth/senior) for a one-way ride from SFO to the Embarcadero stop. Just jump on the airport's free shuttle bus to the international terminal, enter the BART station there, and you're on your way to San Francisco. Trains leave approximately every 15 minutes.

A **cab** from SFO to Fisherman's Wharf costs about $60, plus tip, and takes around 30 minutes, traffic permitting.

SuperShuttle (✆ **800/BLUE-VAN** [258-3826], or 415/558-8500; www.super shuttle.com) is a private shuttle company that offers door-to-door airport service, in which you share a van with a few other passengers. They will take you anywhere in the city, charging $17 per person to a residence or business. On the return trip, add $10 to $17 for each additional person depending on whether you're traveling from a hotel or a residence. The shuttle stops at least every 20 minutes, sometimes sooner, and picks up passengers from the marked areas outside the terminals' upper levels. Reservations are required for the return trip to the airport only and should be made one day before departure. Remember, if it is summertime, or holiday season, you need to be at the airport a good 2 hours before your flight (3 hours for international flights), as TSA security lines can be long. Keep in mind that you could be the first one on and the last one off, so this trip could take a while. For $75, you can either charter the entire van for up to seven people or reserve an **ExecuCar** private sedan ($65) for up to three people. For more info on the ExecuCar, call ✆ **800/410-4444,** or make a reservation at www.execucar.com.

The San Mateo County Transit system, **SamTrans** (✆ **800/660-4287** in Northern California, or 650/508-6200; www.samtrans.com), runs two buses between SFO and the Transbay Terminal at First and Mission streets. Bus no. 292 costs $2 and makes the trip in about an hour. The KX Express bus costs $5 and takes just 35 minutes, but permits only one carry-on bag. Both buses run daily.

GETTING INTO TOWN FROM OAKLAND INTERNATIONAL AIRPORT

A **cab** from OAK to Fisherman's Wharf costs about $70, plus tip, and takes around 40 minutes, traffic permitting.

The cheapest way to reach downtown San Francisco is to take the shuttle bus from the Oakland Airport to **BART** (Bay Area Rapid Transit; ✆ **510/464-6000;** www.bart. gov). The AirBART shuttle bus runs about every 10 minutes Monday to Saturday from 5am to midnight (Sun 8am–midnight). It makes pickups in between Terminals 1 and 2 near the ground transportation sign. Tickets must be purchased at the Oakland Airport's vending machines prior to boarding. The cost is $3 ($1 children/seniors) for the 10-minute ride to BART's Coliseum station in Oakland. BART fares vary, depending on your destination; the trip to the Embarcadero costs $4.05 ($1.50 children/seniors) and takes 15 minutes once you're on board. The entire excursion should take around 45 minutes.

By Car

San Francisco is easily accessible by major highways: I-5, from the north, and U.S. 101, which cuts south-north through the peninsula from San Jose and across the Golden Gate Bridge to points north. If you drive from Los Angeles, you can take the longer coastal route (437 miles and 11 hr.) or the inland route (389 miles and 8 hr.). From Mendocino, it's 156 miles and 4 hours; from Sacramento, 88 miles and 1½ hours; from Yosemite, 210 miles and 4 hours.

If you are driving and aren't already a member, it's worth joining the **American Automobile Association** (AAA; ℂ **800/922-8228;** www.csaa.com). Memberships start as low as $57 per year, and provide roadside and other services, including massive hotel discounts, to motorists. **Amoco Motor Club** (ℂ **800/334-3300;** www.bpmotor club.com) is another recommended choice.

By Train

Traveling by train takes a long time and usually costs as much as, or more than, flying. Still, if you want to take a leisurely ride across America, rail may be a good option.

San Francisco–bound **Amtrak** (ℂ **800/872-7245;** www.amtrak.com) trains leave from New York and cross the country via Chicago. The journey takes about 3½ days, and seats sell quickly. At press time, the lowest one-way fare costs $437 from New York and $228 from Chicago. Round-trip tickets from Los Angeles start at $59 and involve two buses and a train. All trains arrive in Emeryville, just north of Oakland, and connect with regularly scheduled buses to San Francisco's Ferry Building and the Caltrain station in downtown San Francisco.

Caltrain (ℂ **800/660-4287;** www.caltrain.com) operates train service between San Francisco and the towns of the peninsula. The city depot is at 700 Fourth St., at Townsend Street.

GETTING AROUND

You can call ℂ **511** for current transportation and traffic information. The best way to figure out how to get around San Francisco is www.511.org. Input your current and desired addresses, and the site will give you all your transportation options, including fares, what type of transportation, and when the next bus, for example, will be at your stop. For more "Getting Around" advice, see p. 21.

Hint: The **historic F-Line** streetcar runs from the Castro to Fisherman's Wharf, with stops a block or two from the Mission District, Civic Center, Union Square, SoMa, Ferry Building, Exploratorium, Coit Tower, North Beach, and Pier 39—in other words, most of the places you want to visit.

By Public Transportation

The **San Francisco Municipal Transportation Agency,** 1 S. Van Ness Ave., better known as "Muni" (ℂ **415/673-6864;** www.sfmta.com), operates the city's cable cars, buses, and streetcars. Together, these three services crisscross the entire city. Fares for buses and streetcars are $2 for adults, 75¢ for seniors 65 and over, children

Muni discount passes, called **Passports** (www.sfmta.com), entitle holders to unlimited rides on buses, streetcars, and cable cars. A Passport costs $15 for 1 day, $23 for 3 days, and $29 for 7 consecutive days. There is no discount for children or seniors. Passports are sold at a number of locations throughout the city listed on the website. Another option is buying a **CityPASS** (www.citypass.com; $86 adults, $64 kids 5–11), which entitles you to unlimited Muni rides for 7 days, and includes admission to four (or five, depending on which you choose) attractions for 9 days. These passes are sold online, or at any of the CityPASS attractions.

5 to 17, and riders with disabilities. Cable cars, which run from 6:30am to 12:50am, cost a whopping $6 for all people 6 and over ($3 for seniors and riders with disabilities before 7am or after 9pm). Needless to say, they're packed primarily with tourists. Exact change is required on all vehicles except cable cars. Fares are subject to change. If you're standing waiting for Muni and have wireless Web access (or from any computer), check www.nextmuni.com to get up-to-the-minute information about when the next bus or streetcar is coming. Muni's NextBus uses satellite technology and advanced computer modeling to track vehicles on their routes. Each vehicle is fitted with a satellite tracking system, so the information is constantly updated.

For detailed route information, click "Muni Route Maps" on the website at www.sfmta.com/maps. Each route has its own map, and when you click on the map, you will see live-time details of where the buses are at that moment—you can even watch them slowly crawl across your computer screen as the move. For a big picture look at all Muni routes, click on "Muni System Maps."

CABLE CAR   San Francisco's cable cars might not be the most practical means of transport, but the rolling historic landmarks are a fun ride. The three lines are concentrated in the downtown area. The most scenic, and exciting, is the **Powell–Hyde line,** which follows a zigzag route from the corner of Powell and Market streets, over both Nob Hill and Russian Hill, to a turntable at gas-lit Victorian Square in front of Aquatic Park. The **Powell–Mason line** starts at the same intersection and climbs Nob Hill before descending to Bay Street, just 3 blocks from Fisherman's Wharf. The least scenic is the **California Street line,** which begins at the foot of Market Street and runs a straight course through Chinatown and over Nob Hill to Van Ness Avenue. All riders must exit at the last stop and wait in line for the return trip. The cable car system operates from approximately 6:30am to midnight, and each ride costs $6.

BUS   Buses reach almost every corner of San Francisco and beyond—they even travel over the bridges to Marin County and Oakland. Overhead electric cables power some buses; others use conventional gas engines. All are numbered and display their destinations on the front. Signs, curb markings, and yellow bands on adjacent utility poles designate stops, and most bus shelters exhibit Muni's transportation map and schedule. Many buses travel along Market Street or pass near Union Square and run from about 6am to midnight. After midnight, there is infrequent all-night "Owl" service. For safety, avoid taking buses late at night.

Popular tourist routes include bus number 71, which run to Golden Gate Park; 41 and 45, which travel along Union Street; and 30, which runs between Union Square, Chinatown, Ghirardelli Square, and the Marina District. A bus ride costs $2 for adults and 75¢ for seniors 66 and over, children 5 to 17, and riders with disabilities.

STREETCAR   Six of Muni's seven streetcar lines, designated J, K, L, M, N, and T, run underground downtown and on the streets in the outer neighborhoods. The sleek rail cars make the same stops as BART (see below) along Market Street, including Embarcadero Station (in the Financial District), Montgomery and Powell streets (both near Union Square), and the Civic Center (near City Hall). Past the Civic Center, the routes branch off: The J line takes you to Mission Dolores; the K, L, and M lines run to Castro Street; and the N line parallels Golden Gate Park and extends all the way to the Embarcadero and AT&T Park. The T-Third Street car runs to AT&T Park and the San Francisco Caltrain station and then continues south along Third Street.

Streetcars run about every 15 minutes, more frequently during rush hours. They operate Monday through Friday from 5am to 12:15am, Saturday from 6am to approximately 12:15am, and Sunday from approximately 8am to 12:20am. The L and N lines operate 24 hours a day, 7 days a week, but late at night, regular buses trace the L and N routes, which are normally underground, from atop the city streets. Because the operation is part of Muni, the fares are the same as for buses, and passes are accepted.

The most recent line to this system is not a newcomer at all, but is, in fact, an encore performance of rejuvenated 1930s streetcars from all over the world. The beautiful, retro multicolored F-Market and Wharves streetcar runs from 17th and Castro streets to the Embarcadero; every other streetcar continues to Jones and Beach streets in Fisherman's Wharf. This is a quick, charming, and tourist-friendly way to get up- and downtown without any hassle.

BART   BART, an acronym for **Bay Area Rapid Transit** (✆ **415/989-2278;** www.bart.gov), is a futuristic-looking, high-speed rail network that connects San Francisco (starting just south of the airport) with the East Bay—Oakland, Richmond, Concord, Pittsburg, and Fremont. Four stations are on Market Street (see "Streetcar," above). One-way fares range from $1.85 to $11, depending on how far you go. Machines in the stations dispense tickets that are magnetically encoded with a dollar amount. Computerized exits automatically deduct the correct fare. Children 4 and under ride free. Trains run every 15 to 20 minutes, Monday through Friday from 4am to midnight, Saturday from 6am to midnight, and Sunday from 8am to midnight. In keeping with its futuristic look, BART now offers online trip planners that you can download to your smartphone or tablet. The 33-mile BART extension extends all the way to San Francisco International Airport; see p. 227 for more information.

By Taxi

This isn't New York, so don't expect a taxi to appear whenever you need one—if at all. If you're downtown during rush hour or leaving a major hotel, it won't be hard to hail a cab; just look for the lighted sign on the roof that indicates the vehicle is free. Otherwise, it's a good idea to call one of the following companies to arrange a ride; even then, there's been more than one time when the cab never came for us. What to do? Call back if your cab is late and insist on attention, but don't expect prompt results on weekends, no matter how nicely you ask. The companies are **Nation and Veteran's Cab** (☎ 415/552-1300), **Luxor Cabs** (☎ 415/282-4141), **De Soto Cab** (☎ 415/970-1300), **Green Cab** (☎ 415/626-4733), **Metro Cab** (☎ 415/920-0700, and **Yellow Cab** (☎ 415/626-2345). For an estimate of fares, including an allowance for traffic, visit www.taxifarefinder.com.

To combat the woeful lack of taxis, San Francisco has been an early adopter of ride-sharing technologies, such as Lyft and Uber. Even the taxis have gotten on board, drastically reducing the hassle of scoring a ride. Download a number of apps (the most popular at press time were **Uber, Lyft,** and **Sidecar**) onto your smartphone. From the app you can request a taxi, town car, or someone's personal ride from wherever you are and a car will come pick you up, usually within minutes. If you go with personal car, a friendly, registered driver will pick you up in his or her own car. Often, these drivers are young locals trying to make a little extra money by driving people around in their free time and are eager to make conversation. You enter your credit card information into the secure app and tip is included, so you don't need to carry cash. While ordering a black town car will cost more, the price of ordering a taxi or riding in someone's personal car is about the same price as hailing a cab.

By Car

You don't need a car to explore downtown San Francisco. In fact, with the city becoming more crowded by the minute, a car can be your worst nightmare—you're likely to end up stuck in traffic with lots of aggressive and frustrated drivers, pay upwards of $50 a day to park (plus a whopping new 14% parking lot tax), and spend a good portion of your vacation looking for a parking space. Don't bother. However, if you want to venture outside the city, driving is the best way to go. If you want to take a daytrip to Napa or Muir Woods, picking up a car in the city early in the morning, and returning it that evening, will save a fortune for a family of four.

Before heading outside the city, especially in winter, call ☎ **800/427-ROAD (7623)** for California **road conditions.** You can also call ☎ **511** for current traffic information.

CAR RENTALS All the major rental companies operate in the city and have desks at the airports. You could usually get a compact car at the airport for a week starting at $215, including all taxes and other charges, but prices change dramatically when you rent on a daily basis and depending on the agency you use.

Some of the national car-rental companies operating in San Francisco include **Alamo** (☎ 800/327-9633; www.alamo.com), **Avis** (☎ 800/331-1212; www.avis.com), **Budget** (☎ 800/527-0700; www.budget.com), **Dollar** (☎ 800/800-4000; www.dollar.com), **Enterprise** (☎ 800/325-8007; www.enterprise.com), **Hertz** (☎ 800/654-3131; www.hertz.com), **National** (☎ 800/227-7368; www.nationalcar.com), and **Thrifty** (☎ 800/367-2277; www.thrifty.com).

Car-rental rates vary even more than airline fares. Prices depend on the size of the car, where and when you pick it up and drop it off, the length of the rental period, where and how far you drive it, whether you buy insurance, and a host of other factors. A few key questions can save you hundreds of dollars, but you have to ask—reservations agents don't often volunteer money-saving information:

- Are weekend rates lower than weekday rates? Ask if the rate is the same for pickup Friday morning, for instance, as it is for Thursday night. Reservations agents won't volunteer this information, so don't be shy about asking.

Safe Driving

Keep in mind the following handy driving tips:

- California law requires that drivers and passengers all wear seat belts.
- You can turn right at a red light (unless otherwise indicated), after yielding to traffic and pedestrians, and after coming to a complete stop.
- Cable cars always have the right of way, as do pedestrians at intersections and crosswalks.

- Pay attention to signs and arrows on the streets and roadways, or you might suddenly find yourself in a lane that requires exiting or turning when you want to go straight. What's more, San Francisco's many one-way streets can drive you in circles, but most road maps of the city indicate which way traffic flows.

- Does the agency assess a drop-off charge if you don't return the car to the same location where you picked it up?
- Are special promotional rates available? If you see an advertised price in your local newspaper, be sure to ask for that specific rate; otherwise, you could be charged the standard rate. Terms change constantly.
- Are discounts available for members of AARP, AAA, frequent-flier programs, or trade unions? If you belong to any of these organizations, you may be entitled to discounts of up to 30%.
- How much tax will be added to the rental bill? Will there be local tax and state tax?
- How much does the rental company charge to refill your gas tank if you return with the tank less than full? Most rental companies claim their prices are "competitive," but fuel is almost always cheaper in town, so you should try to allow enough time to refuel the car before returning it.

Some companies offer "refueling packages," in which you pay for an entire tank of gas upfront. The cost is usually fairly competitive with local prices, but you don't get credit for any gas remaining in the tank. If a stop at a gas station on the way to the airport will make you miss your plane, then by all means take advantage of the fuel purchase option. Otherwise, skip it.

Most agencies enforce a minimum-age requirement—usually 25. Some also have a maximum-age limit. If you're concerned that these limits might affect you, ask about rental requirements at the time of booking to avoid problems later.

Make sure you're insured. Hasty assumptions about your personal auto insurance or a rental agency's additional coverage could end up costing you tens of thousands of dollars, even if you are involved in an accident that is clearly the fault of another driver.

If you already have your own car insurance, you are most likely covered in the United States for loss of or damage to a rental car and liability in case of injury to any other party involved in an accident. Be sure to check your policy before you spend extra money (around $10 or more per day) on the **collision damage waiver (CDW)** offered by all agencies.

Most major credit cards (especially gold and platinum cards) provide some degree of coverage as well—if they were used to pay for the rental. Terms vary widely, however, so be sure to call your credit card company directly before you rent and rely on the card for coverage. If you are uninsured, your credit card may provide primary coverage as long as you decline the rental agency's insurance. If you already have insurance, your credit card may provide secondary coverage, which basically covers your deductible. However, note that *credit cards will not cover liability,* which is the cost of injury to an outside party and/or damage to an outside party's vehicle. If you do not hold an insurance policy, you should seriously consider buying additional liability insurance from your rental company, even if you decline the CDW.

International visitors should note that insurance and taxes are almost never included in quoted rental car rates in the U.S. Be sure to ask your rental agency about additional fees for these. They can add a significant cost to your rental car.

If you're visiting from abroad and plan to rent a car in the United States, keep in mind that foreign driver's licenses are usually recognized in the U.S., but you may want to consider obtaining an international driver's license.

PARKING   If you want to have a relaxing vacation, don't even attempt to find street parking on Nob Hill, in North Beach, in Chinatown, by Fisherman's Wharf, or on Telegraph Hill. Park in a garage or take a cab or a bus. If you do find street parking, pay attention to street signs that explain when you can park and for how long. Be especially careful not to park in zones that are tow areas during rush hours. And be forewarned, San Francisco has a 14% parking tax.

Curb colors also indicate parking regulations. *Red* means no stopping or parking, *blue* is reserved for drivers with disabilities who have a disabled plate or placard, *white* means there's a 5-minute limit and the driver must stay in the vehicle, *green* indicates a 10-minute limit, and *yellow* and *yellow-and-black* curbs are for stopping to load or unload passengers or luggage only. Also, don't park at a bus stop or in front of a fire hydrant, and watch out for street-cleaning signs. If you violate the law, you might get a hefty ticket or your car might be towed; to get your car back, you'll have to get a release from the nearest district police department and then go to the towing company to pick up the vehicle.

When parking on a hill, apply the hand brake, put the car in gear, and *curb your wheels*—toward the curb when facing downhill, away from the curb when facing uphill. Curbing your wheels not only prevents a possible "runaway" but also keeps you from getting a ticket—an expensive fine that is aggressively enforced.

In a high-tech city like San Francisco, it only follows there would be a way to use your computer or smartphone when parking a car. **Sfpark.org** is an award-winning website (a phone app is available too) that collects and displays real-time information about available parking in the city, in an effort to stop people from driving in circles and polluting our city while hunting for a spot. You can look at a map of the city parking garages, get addresses, directions, hourly prices, and even see how many spots are available inside each garage. If you hit the green "pricing" key, it will show dark green for more expensive garages and light green for the less expensive places. For metered street parking, the map will show red in areas of limited street parking, navy for some availability, and light turquoise for good availability. For both garage and metered parking, prices are regularly adjusted up or down monthly, depending on demand.

By Ferry

TO/FROM SAUSALITO OR LARKSPUR   The **Golden Gate Ferry Service** fleet (*C* **415/455-2000;** www.goldengateferry.org) shuttles passengers daily between the

San Francisco Ferry Building, at the foot of Market Street, and downtown Sausalito and Larkspur. Service is frequent, departing at reasonable intervals every day of the year except January 1, Thanksgiving Day, and December 25. Phone or check the website for an exact schedule. The ride to Sausalito or Larkspur takes about half an hour. One-way fares to Sausalito are $10.25 for adults, $5 for seniors (65+), passengers with disabilities, and youth (6–18). One-way fares to Larkspur are $9.50 for adults, $4.75 for seniors (65+), passengers with disabilities, and youth (6-18). Children 5 and under travel free when accompanied by a full-fare paying adult (limit 2 kids per adult).

Ferries of the **Blue & Gold Fleet** (𝄇 **415/773-1188** for recorded info; for tickets and schedules, visit www.blueandgoldfleet.com) provide round-trip service to downtown Sausalito, Tiburon, and Angel Island. For Sausalito and Tiburon, the one-way fare is $11 for adults, $6.75 for kids (5–11) and seniors (65+). The Angel Island one-way fare is $8.50 for adults, $4.75 for children (6–12) and seniors (65+). Boats run on a seasonal schedule, so check the website for details. Boats leave from Pier 41, and tickets can be purchased at the pier.

FAST FACTS: SAN FRANCISCO

Area Codes   The area code for San Francisco is **415;** for Oakland, Berkeley, and much of the East Bay, **510;** for the peninsula, generally **650.** Napa and Sonoma are **707.** Most phone numbers in this book are in San Francisco's 415 area code, but there's no need to dial it if you're within the city limits.

ATMs   In the land of shopping malls and immediate gratification, there's an ATM on almost every block—often droves of them. In fact, finding a place to withdraw cash is one of the easiest tasks you'll partake in while visiting San Francisco.

Nationwide, the easiest and best way to get cash away from home is from an ATM (automated teller machine), sometimes referred to as a "cash machine" or "cashpoint." The **Cirrus** (𝄇 **800/424-7787;** www.mastercard.

com) and **PLUS** (𝄇 **800/847-2911;** www.visa.com) networks span the country; you can find them even in remote regions. Go to your bank card's website to find ATM locations at your destination. Be sure you know your daily withdrawal limit before you depart.

Note: Many banks impose a fee every time you use a card at another bank's ATM, and that fee is often higher for international transactions (up to $5 or more) than for domestic ones (where they're rarely more than $3). In addition, the bank from which you withdraw cash may charge its own fee. To compare banks' ATM fees within the U.S., use www.bankrate.com. Visitors from outside the U.S. should also find out whether their bank assesses a 1% to 3% fee on charges incurred abroad.

Tip: One way around these fees is to ask for cash

back at grocery, drug, and convenience stores that accept ATM cards and don't charge usage fees (be sure to ask). Of course, you'll have to purchase something first.

Business Hours   Most banks are open Monday through Friday from 9am to 5pm as well as Saturday mornings. Many banks also have ATMs for 24-hour banking. (See "ATMs," above.) Most stores are open Monday through Saturday from 10 or 11am to at least 6pm, with shorter hours on Sunday. But there are exceptions: Stores in Chinatown, Ghirardelli Square, and Pier 39 stay open much later during the tourist season, and large department stores, including Macy's and Nordstrom, keep late hours. Most restaurants serve lunch from about 11:30am to 2:30pm and dinner from about 5:30 to 10pm. They sometimes serve later on weekends. Nightclubs and bars are usually open daily until 2am, when they are legally bound to stop serving alcohol.

Car Rental   See "By Car," under "Getting Around," above.

Cellphones   See "Mobile Phones," later in this section.

Crime   See "Safety," later in this section.

Disabled Travelers   Most disabilities shouldn't stop anyone from traveling. There are more options and resources out there than ever before.

Most of San Francisco's major museums and tourist attractions have wheelchair ramps. Many hotels offer special accommodations and services for wheelchair users and other visitors with disabilities. As well as the ramps, they include extra-large bathrooms and telecommunication devices for hearing-impaired travelers. The Visitor Information Center (p. 245) should have the most up-to-date information.

Travelers in wheelchairs can request special ramped taxis by calling **Yellow Cab** (✆ **415/626-2345**), which charges regular rates for the service. Travelers with disabilities can also get a free copy of the "**Muni Access Guide,**" published by the San Francisco Municipal Transportation Agency, Accessible Services Program, One South Van Ness, 3rd floor (✆ **415/701-4485**), which is staffed

weekdays from 8am to 5pm. Many of the major car-rental companies offer hand-controlled cars for drivers with disabilities. **Alamo** (✆ **800/651-1223**), **Avis** (✆ **800/331-1212**, ext. 7305), and **Budget** (✆ **800/314-3932**) have special hotlines that help provide such a vehicle at any of their U.S. locations with 48 hours' advance notice; **Hertz** (✆ **800/654-3131**) requires between 24 and 72 hours' advance notice at most locations.

Organizations that offer a vast range of resources and assistance to travelers with disabilities include **Moss-Rehab** (✆ **800/CALL-MOSS** [2255-6677]; www.mossrehab.com), the **American Foundation for the Blind** (**AFB;** ✆ **800/232-5463;** www.afb.org), and **SATH** (Society for Accessible Travel & Hospitality; ✆ **212/447-7284;** www.sath.org). **AirAmbulanceCard.com** is now partnered with SATH and allows you to preselect top-notch hospitals in case of an emergency.

Access-Able Travel Source (✆ **303/232-2979;** www.access-able.com) offers a comprehensive database on travel agents from around the world with experience in accessible travel, destination-specific access information, and links to such resources as service animals, equipment rentals, and access guides.

Many travel agencies offer customized tours and itineraries for travelers with disabilities. Among them

are **Flying Wheels Travel** (✆ **507/451-5005;** www.flyingwheelstravel.com) and **Accessible Journeys** (**610/521-0339;** www.disabilitytravel.com).

Flying with Disability (**www.flying-with-disability.org**) is a comprehensive information source on airplane travel. **Avis Rent A Car** (✆ **800/962-1434**) has an "Avis Access" program that offers services for customers with special travel needs. These include specially outfitted vehicles with swivel seats, spinner knobs, and hand controls; mobility scooter rentals; and accessible bus service. Be sure to reserve well in advance.

Also check out the quarterly magazine "**Emerging Horizons**" (**www.emerginghorizons.com**), available by subscription ($17 a year U.S.; $22 outside U.S.).

The "Accessible Travel" link at **Mobility-Advisor.com** (**www.mobility-advisor.com**) offers a variety of travel resources to persons with disabilities.

Discounts   For local discounts on attractions and restaurants, sign up for regular emails from **www.groupon.com** and **www.dailydeals.sfgate.com.** To be a "deal" on these websites, a merchant has to give a huge discount. I have received offers for Aquarium of the Bay tickets for $11 (regular price is $22), $70 worth of drinks and appetizers for $29 at restaurants listed in Chapter 5, $28 for a Blue and Gold Bay Cruise for Two (a $56 value), and many more great offers. You purchase the deal for future use; make sure to read the fine print. It is free to sign up for these deals; go online and make San Francisco your "home."

Doctors See "Hospitals" below.

Drinking Laws The legal age for purchase and consumption of alcoholic beverages is 21; proof of age is required and often requested at bars, nightclubs, and restaurants, so it's always a good idea to bring ID when you go out. Supermarkets and convenience stores in California sell beer, wine, and liquor. Most restaurants serve alcohol, but some serve only beer and wine. By law, all bars, clubs, restaurants, and stores cannot sell or serve alcohol after 2am, and "last call" tends to start at 1:30am. Do not carry open containers of alcohol in your car or any public area that isn't zoned for alcohol consumption. The police can fine you on the spot. And nothing will ruin your trip faster than getting a citation for DUI (driving under the influence).

Driving Rules See "Getting Around," earlier in this chapter.

Earthquakes In the rare event of an earthquake, *don't panic*. If you're in a tall building, don't run outside; instead, move away from windows and toward the building's center. Crouch under a desk or table, or stand against a wall or under a doorway. If you're in bed, get under the bed, stand in a doorway, or crouch under a sturdy piece of furniture. When exiting the building, use stairwells, *not* elevators. If you're in your car, pull over to the side of the road and stop, but wait until you're away from bridges or overpasses, as well as telephone or power poles and lines. Stay in your car. If you're outside, stay away from trees, power lines, and the sides of buildings.

Electricity Like Canada, the United States uses 110 to 120 volts AC (60 cycles), compared to 220 to 240 volts AC (50 cycles) in most of Europe, Australia, and New Zealand. Downward converters that change 220–240 volts to 110–120 volts are difficult to find in the United States, so bring one with you.

Embassies & Consulates All embassies are in the nation's capital, Washington, D.C. Some consulates are in major U.S. cities, and most nations have a mission to the United Nations in New York City. If your country isn't listed below, call for directory information in Washington, D.C. (☎ **202/555-1212**), or check www.embassy.org/embassies.

The embassy of **Australia** is at 1601 Massachusetts Ave. NW, Washington, DC 20036 (☎ **202/797-3000;** www.usa.embassy.gov.au).

Consulates are in New York, Honolulu, Houston, Los Angeles, and San Francisco.

The embassy of **Canada** is at 501 Pennsylvania Ave. NW, Washington, DC 20001 (☎ **202/682-1740;** www.canadianembassy.org). Canadian consulates are in Buffalo (New York), Detroit, Los Angeles, New York City, and Seattle.

The embassy of **Ireland** is at 2234 Massachusetts Ave. NW, Washington, DC 20008 (☎ **202/462-3939;** www.embassyofireland.org). Irish consulates are in Boston, Chicago, New York, San Francisco, and other cities. See the website for a complete listing.

The embassy of **New Zealand** is at 37 Observatory Circle NW, Washington, DC 20008 (☎ **202/328-4800;** www.nzembassy.com/usa). New Zealand consulates are in Los Angeles, Salt Lake City, San Francisco, and Seattle.

The embassy of the **United Kingdom** is at 3100 Massachusetts Ave. NW, Washington, DC 20008 (☎ **202/588-6500;** http://ukinusa.fco.gov.uk/en). British consulates are in Atlanta, Boston, Chicago, Cleveland, Houston, Los Angeles, New York, San Francisco, and Seattle.

Emergencies Call ☎ **911** to report a fire, call the police, or get an ambulance anywhere in the United States. This is a toll-free call. (No coins are required at public telephones.)

Family Travel If you have enough trouble getting your kids out of the house in the morning, dragging them thousands of miles away may seem like an insurmountable challenge. But family travel can be immensely rewarding, giving you new ways of seeing the world through smaller pairs of eyes.

To make things easier for families vacationing in San Francisco, we include two family-friendly lists that highlight the best hotels (p. 64) and attractions (p. 126) for parents and kids.

Recommended family travel websites include **Family Travel Forum** (http://myfamilytravels.com), a comprehensive site that offers customized trip planning; **Family Travel Network** (www.familytravel network.com), an online magazine providing travel tips; and **TravelWith-YourKids** (www.travelwith yourkids.com), a comprehensive site written by parents for parents, offering sound advice for long-distance and international travel with children.

Health If you worry about getting sick away from home, you may want to consider **medical travel insurance.** (See www.from-mers.com "tips and tools," then "insurance" for detailed information.) In most cases, however, your existing health plan will provide all the coverage you need, but be sure to carry

your identification card in your wallet.

If you suffer from a chronic illness, consult your doctor before your departure. Pack **prescription medications** in your carry-on luggage, and carry them in their original containers, with pharmacy labels—otherwise they won't make it through airport security. Visitors from outside the U.S. should carry generic names of prescription drugs. For U.S. travelers, most reliable healthcare plans provide coverage if you get sick away from home. Foreign visitors may have to pay all medical costs upfront and be reimbursed later.

Hospitals **Saint Francis Memorial Hospital,** 900 Hyde St., between Bush and Pine streets on Nob Hill (℃ **866/240-2087** or 415/353-6000; www.saint-francismemorial.org), provides emergency service 24 hours a day; no appointment is necessary. The hospital also operates a **physician-referral service** (℃ **800/333-1355** or 415/353-6566).

Insurance For information on traveler's insurance, trip cancellation insurance, and medical insurance while traveling, please visit www.frommers.com "tips and tools," then "insurance" for detailed information.

Internet & Wi-Fi You'll find that many cafes have wireless access, as do most hotels. Check www.wififree spot.com for a huge list of

free Wi-Fi hotspots—including every Starbucks and Peet's coffee shop, Barnes and Noble, Fed Ex office, and McDonald's. You can also log onto www.cybercafe.com. The Metreon Entertainment Center (p. 26) in SoMa is completely wired, as are City Hall (p. 117) and San Francisco International Airport. In July 2013, Google gave the city a $600,000 gift to cover the cost of free Wi-Fi in 31 parks for at least 2 years. San Francisco has a goal to have citywide Internet access as soon as possible.

When all else fails, ask a friendly local where you can get Wi-Fi nearby. Most will know a good spot.

Legal Aid While driving, if you are pulled over for a minor infraction (such as speeding), never attempt to pay the fine directly to a police officer; this could be construed as attempted bribery, a much more serious crime. Pay fines by mail, or directly into the hands of the clerk of the court. If accused of a more serious offense, say and do nothing before consulting a lawyer. In the U.S., the burden is on the state to prove a person's guilt beyond a reasonable doubt, and everyone has the right to remain silent, whether he or she is suspected of a crime or actually arrested. Once arrested, a person can make one telephone call to a party of his or her choice. The international visitor should call his or her embassy or consulate.

LGBT Travelers Since the 1970s, the Castro has acted as the city's center of gay life and nightlife in the city—though with society's changing norms, gay life has become less centralized (some might say less ghettoized) over the years. For some gay travelers, this is still The Place to Be, especially on a festival weekend, when the streets are filled with out-and-proud revelry; for others, the neighborhood is a quaint relic of the past to be visited occasionally (while shielding their children's eyes from the sex toys in the shop windows). For other San Franciscans and many travelers, it's a fun area with some wonderful shops.

Gays and lesbians make up a good portion of San Francisco's population, so it's no surprise that clubs and bars all over town cater to them. Although lesbian interests are concentrated primarily in the East Bay (especially Oakland), a significant community resides in the Mission District, around 16th and Valencia streets, in Hayes Valley, and Bernal Heights.

Several local publications concentrate on in-depth coverage of news, information, and listings of goings-on around town for gays and lesbians. The "Bay Area Reporter" (www.ebar.com) has the most comprehensive listings, including a weekly calendar of events. Distributed free on Thursday, it can be found stacked at the corner of 18th and Castro streets and at Ninth and Harrison streets, as well as in bars, bookshops, and stores around town. It may also be available in gay and lesbian bookstores elsewhere in the country.

The **International Gay and Lesbian Travel Association (IGLTA;** ✆ **954/630-1637;** www.iglta.org) is the trade association for the gay and lesbian travel industry, and offers an online directory of gay- and lesbian-friendly businesses and tour operators. **Purple Roofs** (www.purpleroofs.com) lists gay-friendly hotels, B&B's, travel agents, and tour operators. **San Francisco Travel** (www.sanfrancisco.travel/lgbt) has put together LGBT itineraries, and can help you plan your wedding in the city. **Gay.com Travel** (www.gay.com) owns **Out Traveler** (www.outtraveler.com). Both provide regularly updated information about gay-owned, gay-oriented, and gay-friendly lodging, dining, sightseeing, nightlife, and shopping establishments in every popular destination worldwide, including, of course, San Francisco. Many agencies offer tours and travel itineraries specifically for gay and lesbian travelers. San Francisco–based **Now. Voyager** (www.nowvoyager.com) has been making travel arrangements for the LGBT community for nearly 30 years. **Olivia** (✆ **800/631-6277;** www.olivia.com) offers lesbian cruises and resort vacations, as well as airline discounts. The Canadian website **GayTraveler** (www.gaytraveler.com) offers ideas and advice for gay travel all over the world. For travel guides, try **"Spartacus International Gay Guide"** (Bruno Gmünder Verlag; www.spartacusworld.com/gayguide), or the **Damron** guides (www.damron.com), both with separate, annual books for gay men and lesbians. **San Francisco Pride** (www.sfpride.org/travel) is another good resource for LGBT friendly travel in the city. For more gay and lesbian travel resources, visit Frommers.com.

Mail At press time, domestic postage rates were 34¢ for a regular postcard, 49¢ for a large postcard or a regular letter. Always include zip codes when mailing items in the U.S. If you don't know your zip code, visit www.usps.com/zip4. For international mail, a postcard costs $1.10. Look at www.usps.com to determine the price to send a letter.

If you aren't sure what your address will be in the United States, mail can be sent to you, in your name, c/o General Delivery at the main post office of the city or region where you expect to be. The addressee must pick up mail in person and must produce proof of identity (driver's license, passport). Most post offices will hold mail for up to 1 month, and are open Monday to Friday from 8am to 6pm, and Saturday from 9am to 3pm.

Medical Requirements
Unless you're arriving from an area known to be suffering from an epidemic (particularly cholera or yellow fever), inoculations or vaccinations are not required for entry into the United States.

Mobile Phones Just because your cellphone works at home doesn't mean it'll work everywhere in the U.S. (thanks to our nation's fragmented cellphone system). It's a good bet that your phone will work in major cities, but take a look at your wireless company's coverage map on its website before heading out; T-Mobile, Sprint, and Nextel are particularly weak in rural areas. If you need to stay in touch at a destination where you know your phone won't work, **rent** a phone that does from **InTouch USA** (☎ **800/872-7626;** www.intouchglobal.com), but be aware that airtime is pricey.

If you're not from the U.S., you'll be appalled at the poor reach of our **GSM** (Global System for Mobile Communications) **wireless network,** which is used by much of the rest of the world. Your phone will probably work in most major U.S. cities; it definitely won't work in many rural areas. To see where GSM phones work in the U.S., check out www.t-mobile.com/coverage/national_popup.asp. And you may or may not be able to send SMS (text messaging) home.

Money & Costs Frommer's lists exact prices in the local currency. The currency conversions quoted were correct at press time. Since rates fluctuate, before departing it is a good idea to consult a currency exchange website such as www.xe.com to check up-to-the-minute rates.

It's always advisable to bring money in a variety of forms on a vacation: a mix of cash, credit cards, and ATM cards. You should also have enough petty cash upon arrival to cover airport incidentals, tipping, and transportation to your hotel before you leave home. You can always withdraw money upon arrival at an airport ATM, but you'll still need to make smaller change for tipping.

THE VALUE OF THE U.S. DOLLAR VS. OTHER POPULAR CURRENCIES

US$	Can$	UK£	Euro (€)	Aus$	NZ$
1	1.10	0.60	0.72	1.07	1.16

WHAT THINGS COST IN SAN FRANCISCO

	US$
Taxi from SFO to downtown	$60
Inexpensive hotel room, double occupancy	$120–$150
Moderate hotel room, double occupancy	$150–$200
Cup of small coffee (Peet's or Starbucks)	$2
1 gallon of regular gas	$4
Admission to museums	$10–$35
Glass of Napa Valley red wine	$10–$15
Bus or streetcar fare for adults	$2
Cable car fare	$6

The most common bills in the U.S. are the $1 (a "buck"), $5, $10, and $20 denominations. There are also $2 bills (seldom encountered), $50 bills, and $100 bills. (The last two are usually not welcome as payment for small purchases.)

Coins come in seven denominations: 1¢ (1 cent, or a penny); 5¢ (5 cents, or a nickel); 10¢ (10 cents, or a dime); 25¢ (25 cents, or a quarter); 50¢ (50 cents, or a half dollar); the gold-colored Sacagawea coin, worth $1; and the rare silver dollar.

Credit cards are the most widely used form of payment in San Francisco: **Visa** (Barclaycard in Britain), **MasterCard** (Eurocard in Europe, Access in Britain, Chargex in Canada), **American Express, Diners Club,** and **Discover.** They also provide a convenient record of all your expenses and offer relatively good exchange rates. You can withdraw cash advances from your credit cards at banks or ATMs, but high fees make credit card cash advances a pricey way to get cash.

It's highly recommended that you travel with at least one major credit card. You must have a credit card to rent a car, and hotels and airlines usually require a credit card imprint as a deposit against expenses.

ATM cards with major credit card backing, known as **"debit cards,"** are now a commonly acceptable form of payment in most stores and restaurants. Debit cards draw money directly from your checking account. Some stores enable you to receive cash back on your debit-card purchases as well. The same is true at most U.S. post offices. Make sure your rental car company accepts debit cards; some require you to have a very large dollar amount available for them to "hold" until you return the vehicle in perfect shape. Other rental car companies do not accept debit cards.

Beware of hidden credit card fees while traveling. Check with your credit or debit card issuer to see what fees, if any, will be charged for overseas transactions. Recent reform legislation in the U.S., for example, has curbed some exploitative lending practices. But many banks have responded by increasing fees in other areas, including fees for customers who use credit and debit cards while out of the country—even if those charges were made in U.S. dollars. Fees can amount to 3% or more of the purchase price. Check with your bank before departing to avoid any surprise charges on your statement.

The important advice is to check with your bank before you travel, to find out about any fees and let them know you're going (so you don't find yourself turned away as a fraud at the ATM).

Newspapers & Magazines

The city's main daily is the "San Francisco Chronicle" (www.sfgate.com), which is distributed throughout the city. Check out the Chronicle's Sunday edition, which includes a pink "Datebook" section—a preview of the week's upcoming events. The free "San Francisco Examiner" (www.sfexaminer.com) is published Monday through Friday with a weekend edition. The free weekly "San Francisco Bay Guardian" (www.sfbg.com) and "San Francisco Weekly" (www.sfweekly.com), tabloids of news and listings, are indispensable for nightlife information; they're widely distributed through street-corner kiosks and at city cafes and restaurants.

Of the many free tourist-oriented publications, the most widely read are "San Francisco Guide" (www.sfguide.com), a handbook-size weekly containing maps and information on current events, and "Where San Francisco" (www.where magazine.com), a glossy regular format monthly magazine. You can find them in most hotels, shops, and restaurants in the major tourist areas.

Packing Dress warm, even in the summer. As the saying goes in San Francisco, if you don't like the weather, wait 5 minutes. Because of offshore breezes, microclimates, and the prevalence of fog in the summer, the temperature changes constantly in San Francisco, particularly if you're on the move. Even if it's sunny and warm at noon, bring a sweater or light jacket just in case—when the fog rolls in, it gets chilly fast. For more helpful information on packing for your trip, head to Frommers.com and click on the Tools section, which contains packing tips and information.

Passports Virtually every air traveler entering the U.S. is required to show a passport. All persons, including U.S. citizens, traveling by air between the United States and Canada, Mexico, Central and South America, the Caribbean, and Bermuda are required to present a valid passport. *Note:* U.S. and Canadian citizens entering the U. S. at land and sea ports of entry from within the western hemisphere must now also present a passport or other documents compliant with the Western Hemisphere Travel Initiative (WHTI; see www.getyouhome.gov for details).

Australia Australian Passport Information Service (℃ **131-232;** www.passports.gov.au).

Canada Passport Office, Department of Foreign Affairs and International Trade, Ottawa, ON K1A 0G3 (℃ **800/567-6868;** www.ppt.gc.ca).

Ireland Passport Office, Frederick Buildings, Molesworth Street, Dublin 2 (℃ **+353 1 671 1633;** www.foreignaffairs.gov.ie.

New Zealand Passports Office, Department of Internal Affairs, Level 3, 109 Featherston St., Wellington, 6040 (℃ **0800 22**

50 50 in New Zealand or +64 (4) 463 9360; www.passports.govt.nz).

United Kingdom Visit your nearest passport office, major post office, or travel agency or contact the **HM Passport Office,** 4th Floor, Peel Building, 2 Marsham St., London, SW1P 4DF (℃ **0300/222-0000;** www.ips.gov.uk).

United States To find your regional passport office, check the U.S. State Department website (http://travel.state.gov/content/passports/english.html) or call the **National Passport Information Center** (℃ **877/487-2778**) for automated information.

Police In an emergency, dial ℃ **911.** For nonemergency police matters, call ℃ **415/553-0123.**

Safety For a big city, San Francisco is relatively safe and requires only that you use common sense (for example, don't leave your new video camera on the seat of your parked car). However, in neighborhoods such as Lower Haight, the Mission, the Tenderloin (a few blocks west of Union Square), and Fisherman's Wharf (at night especially), it's a good idea to pay attention to yourself and your surroundings.

Avoid carrying valuables with you on the street, and don't display expensive cameras or electronic equipment. Hold on to your pocketbook, and place your billfold in an inside pocket. In theaters, restaurants, and

other public places, keep your possessions in sight.

Remember also that hotels are open to the public, and in a large hotel, security may not be able to screen everyone entering. Always lock your room door—don't assume that inside your hotel you are automatically safe.

Driving safety is important, too. Ask your rental agency about personal safety, and ask for a traveler-safety brochure when you pick up your car. Ask for written directions to your destination or a map with the route clearly marked. (Many agencies offer the option of renting a cell-phone for the duration of your car rental; check with the rental agent when you pick up the car.) Try to arrive and depart during daylight hours.

Recently, more crime has involved cars and drivers. If you drive off a highway into a doubtful neighborhood, leave the area as quickly as possible. If you have an accident, even on the highway, stay in your car with the doors locked until you assess the situation or until the police arrive. If you're bumped from behind on the street or are involved in a minor accident with no injuries, and the situation appears to be suspicious, motion to the other driver to follow you. Never get out of your car in such situations. Go directly to the nearest police precinct, well-lit service station, or 24-hour store.

Always try to park in well-lit and well-traveled areas. Never leave any packages or valuables in sight. If someone attempts to rob you or steal your car, don't try to resist the thief or carjacker. Report the incident to the police department immediately by calling ☎ **911.** This is a free call, even from pay phones.

Senior Travel   Nearly every attraction in San Francisco offers a senior discount; age requirements vary, and specific prices are listed in Chapter 4. Public transportation and movie theaters also have reduced rates. Don't be shy about asking for discounts, but always carry some kind of identification, such as a driver's license, that shows your date of birth.

Members of **AARP,** 601 E St. NW, Washington, DC 20049 (☎ **888/687-2277;** www.aarp.org), get discounts on hotels, airfares, and car rentals. AARP offers members a wide range of benefits, including "AARP The Magazine" and a monthly newsletter. Anyone 50 and over can join.

Recommended publications offering travel resources and discounts for seniors include the quarterly magazine "**Travel 50 & Beyond"** (www.travel50and beyond.com) and the best-selling paperback "**Unbelievably Good Deals and Great Adventures That You Absolutely Can't Get Unless You're Over 50 2009–2010 Edition"**

(McGraw-Hill), by Joann Rattner Heilman.

Smoking   If San Francisco is California's most European city in looks and style, the comparison stops when it comes to smoking in public. Each year, smoking laws in the city become stricter. Ergo, heavy smokers are in for a tough time in San Francisco. Smoking is illegal inside most buildings, at entryways, bus stops, public parks, beaches, and at any outdoor public events. Hotels are also increasingly going nonsmoking, though some still offer smoking rooms. You can't even smoke in California bars unless drinks are served solely by the owner (though you will find that a few neighborhood bars turn a blind eye and pass you an ashtray). San Francisco International Airport no longer has hazy, indoor smoking rooms; there are a few designated areas outside, pre-security.

Student Travel   A valid student ID will often qualify students for discounts on airfare, accommodations, entry to museums, cultural events, movies, and more in San Francisco. Check out the **International Student Travel Confederation** (**ISTC;** www.isic.org) website for comprehensive travel services information and details on how to get an **International Student Identity Card (ISIC),** which qualifies students for substantial savings on rail passes, plane tickets,

entrance fees, and more. It also provides students with basic health and life insurance and a 24-hour help line. The card is valid for a maximum of 18 months. You can apply for the card online or in person at **STA Travel** (☎ **800/781-4040** in North America, 134 782 in Australia, or 0333/321-0099 in the U.K.; www.statravel. com), the biggest student travel agency in the world; check out the website to locate STA Travel offices worldwide. If you're no longer a student but are still under 26, you can get an **International Youth Travel Card (IYTC)** from the same people; the card entitles you to some discounts. **Travel CUTS** (☎ **800/667-2887;** www.travelcuts.com) offers similar services for both Canadians and U.S. residents. Irish students may prefer to turn to **USIT** (☎ **01/602-1906;** www.usit. ie), an Ireland-based specialist in student, youth, and independent travel.

Taxes   The United States has no value-added tax (VAT) or other indirect tax at the national level. Every state, county, and city may levy its own local tax on all purchases, including hotel and restaurant checks and airline tickets. These taxes will not appear on price tags. Sales tax in San Francisco is 8.75%. Hotel tax is charged on the room tariff only (which is not subject to sales tax) and is set by the city, ranging from 12% to 17% around Northern California.

Telephones Many convenience groceries and packaging services sell **prepaid calling cards** in denominations up to $50. Many public pay phones at airports now accept American Express, MasterCard, and Visa. **Local calls** made from a pay phones cost 50¢—that is, if you can find one. They are a dying breed; only about 200 remain in the city. Most long-distance and international calls can be dialed directly from any phone. **To make calls within the United States and to Canada,** dial 1 followed by the area code and the seven-digit number. **For other international calls,** dial 011 followed by the country code, city code, and the number you are calling.

Calls to area codes **800, 888, 877,** and **866** are toll-free. However, calls to area codes **700** and **900** (chat lines, bulletin boards, "dating" services, and so on) can be expensive—charges of 95¢ to $3 or more per minute. Some numbers have minimum charges that can run $15 or more.

For **reversed-charge or collect calls,** and for person-to-person calls, dial the number 0 then the area code and number; an operator will come on the line, and you should specify whether you are calling collect, person-to-person, or both. If your operator-assisted call is international, ask for the overseas operator.

For **directory assistance** ("Information"), dial 🕜 411 for local numbers and national numbers in the U.S. and Canada. For dedicated long-distance information, dial 1, then the appropriate area code plus 555-1212.

Time The continental United States is divided into **four time zones:** Eastern Standard Time (EST), Central Standard Time (CST), Mountain Standard Time (MST), and Pacific Standard Time (PST). Alaska and Hawaii have their own zones. For example, when it's 9am in San Francisco (PST), it's 10am in Denver (MST), 11am in Chicago (CST), noon in New York City (EST), 5pm in London (GMT), and 2am the next day in Sydney.

Daylight saving time is in effect from 1am on the second Sunday in March to 1am on the first Sunday in November, except in Arizona, Hawaii, the U.S. Virgin Islands, and Puerto Rico. Daylight saving time moves the clock 1 hour ahead of standard time.

For help with time translations, and more, download our convenient Travel Tools app for your mobile device. Go to www.frommers.com/go/mobile and tap on the Travel Tools icon.

Tipping In hotels, tip **bellhops** at least $1 per bag ($2–$3 if you have a lot of luggage) and tip the **chamber staff** $1 to $2 per day (more if you've left a big mess for him or her to clean up). Tip the **doorman** or **concierge** only if he or she has provided you with some specific service (for example, calling a cab for you or obtaining difficult-to-get theater tickets). Tip the **valet-parking attendant** $1 every time you get your car.

In restaurants, bars, and nightclubs, tip **service staff** and **bartenders** 15% to 20% of the check, tip **checkroom attendants** $1 per garment, and tip **valet-parking attendants** $1 per vehicle.

As for other service personnel, tip **cabdrivers** 15% of the fare, tip **skycaps** at airports at least $1 per bag ($2–$3 if you have a lot of luggage), and tip **hairdressers** and **barbers** 15% to 20%.

The important thing is not to stiff those who depend on tips. Waiters are taxed based on the assumption you've given a tip, whether or not you actually have.

Toilets Those weird, oval-shaped, olive-green kiosks on the sidewalks throughout San Francisco are high-tech self-cleaning public toilets. They've been placed on high-volume streets to provide relief for pedestrians. French potty-maker JCDecaux gave them to the city for free—advertising covers the cost. It costs 25¢ to enter, with no time limit, but we don't recommend using the ones in the sketchier neighborhoods such as the Mission because they're mostly used by crackheads and prostitutes. Toilets can also be found in hotel lobbies, bars, restaurants, museums, department stores, railway and bus stations, and service stations. Large hotels and fast-food restaurants are often the best bet for clean facilities. Restaurants and bars in resorts or heavily visited areas may reserve their restrooms for patrons. For a list of "bathrooms for everyone," check out www.safe 2pee.org.

VAT   See "Taxes," above.

Visas   The U.S. State Department has a **Visa Waiver Program (VWP)** allowing citizens of the following countries to enter the United States without a visa for stays of up to 90 days: Andorra, Australia, Austria, Belgium, Brunei, Czech Republic, Denmark, Estonia, Finland, France, Germany, Greece, Hungary, Iceland, Ireland, Italy, Japan, Republic of Korea, Latvia, Liechtenstein, Lithuania, Luxembourg, Malta, Monaco, the Netherlands, New Zealand, Norway, Portugal, San Marino, Singapore, Slovakia, Slovenia, Spain, Sweden, Switzerland, and the United Kingdom. (**Note:** This list was accurate at press time; for the most up-to-date list of countries in the VWP, consult http:// travel.state.gov/content/ visas/english.html.) Even though a visa isn't necessary, in an effort to help U.S. officials check travelers against terror watch lists before they arrive at U.S. borders, visitors from VWP countries must register online through the Electronic System for Travel Authorization (ESTA) before

boarding a plane or a boat to the U.S. Travelers must complete an electronic application providing basic personal and travel eligibility information. The Department of Homeland Security recommends filling out the form at least 3 days before traveling. Authorizations will be valid for up to 2 years or until the traveler's passport expires, whichever comes first. Currently, there is one US$14 fee for the online application. Existing ESTA registrations remain valid through their expiration dates. **Note:** Any passport issued on or after October 26, 2006, by a VWP country must be an **e-Passport** for VWP travelers to be eligible to enter the U.S. without a visa. Citizens of these nations also need to present a round-trip air or cruise ticket upon arrival. E-Passports contain computer chips capable of storing biometric information, such as the required digital photograph of the holder. If your passport doesn't have this feature, you can still travel without a visa if the valid passport was issued before October 26, 2005, and includes a machine-readable zone; or if the valid passport was issued between October 26, 2005, and October 25, 2006, and includes a digital photograph. For more information, go to http://travel. state.gov/content/visas/ english.html. Canadian citizens may enter the United States without visas, but will need to show passports and proof of residence.

Citizens of all other countries must have (1) a valid passport that expires at least 6 months later than the scheduled end of their visit to the U.S.; and (2) a tourist visa.

For information about **U.S. visas,** go to http:// travel.state.gov and click on "Visas." Or go to one of the following websites:

Australian citizens can obtain up-to-date visa information from the **U.S. Embassy Canberra,** Moonah Place, Yarralumla, ACT 2600 (𝄞 **02/6214-5600**), or by checking the U.S. Diplomatic Mission's website at http://canberra.usembassy. gov/visas.html.

British subjects can obtain visa information by calling the **U.S. Embassy Visa Information Line** (𝄞 **020 3608 6998** from within the U.K. or 𝄞 **703/ 439-2367** from within the U.S. or by visiting the "Visas" section of the American Embassy London's website at http://london. usembassy.gov/visas.html.

Irish citizens can obtain up-to-date visa information through the **U.S. Embassy Dublin,** 42 Elgin Rd., Ballsbridge, Dublin 4 (𝄞 **353 1 668 8777** from within the Republic of Ireland; http:// dublin.usembassy.gov).

Citizens of **New Zealand** can obtain up-to-date visa information by contacting the **U.S. Embassy New Zealand,** 29 Fitzherbert Terrace, Thorndon, Wellington (𝄞 **644/462-6000;** http:// newzealand.usembassy.gov).

Visitor Information

The **San Francisco Visitor Information Center,** on the lower level of Hallidie Plaza, 900 Market St., at Powell Street (☎ **415/391-2000;** www.sanfranciscotravel. com), is the best source of specialized information about the city. Even if you don't have a specific question, you might want to request the free "Visitors Planning Guide" and the "San Francisco Visitors" kit, which includes a 6-month calendar of events; a city history; shopping and dining information; several good, clear maps; plus lodging information.

To view or download a free state guide and travel planner, log onto the **California Tourism** website at www.visitcalifornia.com. U.S. and Canadian residents can receive free travel planning information by mail by calling ☎ **800/CALIFORNIA** (225-4367). Most cities and towns also have a tourist bureau or chamber of commerce that distributes information on the area.

Wi-Fi See "Internet & Wi-Fi," earlier in this section.

Index

See also Accommodations and Restaurant indexes, below.

General Index

A

AA Bakery & Café, 145
Accommodations. *See also*
  Accommodations Index
  best, 2
  discounts, 50
  family-friendly, 64
  with free parking, 68
  historic, 58
  name brand, 54–55
  Napa Valley, 211–214
  northern Sonoma, 222–224
  San Francisco, 47–72
  Sonoma Valley, 218–220
Addresses, finding, 22
Air tours, 136
Air travel, 226–228
Alamo Square, 116–117
Alcatraz Island, 1, 9, 16, 102–104
Alice Marble & George Sterling Park, 154
"American" California, original street of, 143
American Conservatory Theater (A.C.T.), 177
Angel Island, 197–198
Antiques, 164
Aquarium of the Bay, 7, 16, 104
Aquatic Park Bathhouse Building, 106, 129
Architecture, best, 6
Area codes, 234
Armida (Healdsburg), 220–221
Armstrong Redwoods State Reserve (near Guerneville), 222
Art galleries, 164
Art Murmur (Oakland), 195
Asian Art Museum, 6, 7, 117
AT&T Park, 188
ATMs, 234
Ayala Cove (Angel Island), 197

B

Baker Beach, 129, 136
Balmy Alley Murals, 157
B&B accommodations, 49
Bank of America, 143
Bar Bocce (Sausalito), 201
Bars, 181–188
  gay and lesbian, 187–188
BART (Bay Area Rapid Transit), 230
Baseball, 188
BATS Improv, 178
Bay Area Discovery Museum (Sausalito), 200

The Bay Lights, 108
Bay Model Visitors Center (Sausalito), 200
Bay to Breakers Foot Race, 43, 139
Beach Blanket Babylon, 1, 10, 152, 178
Beaches, 136–137
The Beat Museum, 150
The beats (beatniks), 34
Belden Place, 78
Bella Vineyards & Wine Caves (Healdsburg), 221
Benziger Family Winery (Glen Ellen), 217
Berkeley, 190–192
Berkeley Repertory Theater, 177
Big Brother & The Holding Company, 40–41
Bike tours, 135
Biking, 4–5, 14–15, 137
Bimbo's 365 Club, 179
Biordi Art Imports, 152
Bi-Rite Creamery, 160
Bi-Rite Market, 160
Bliss Spa, 121
Blue & Gold Fleet, 135
Boating (boat rentals), 20, 137–138
Boat tours, 135
Books, recommended, 38–39
Bookstores, 165–166
The Boom Boom Room, 179
Bottom of the Hill, 179
Boudin at the Wharf, 104
Broadway, 150
Buddhist Church of San Francisco, 120
Buena Vista Park, 139
Business hours, 234–235
Bus tours, 135–136
Bus travel, 229–230

C

Cable Car Museum, 7, 20, 113
Cable cars, 8, 98–99, 229
Caffè Greco, 10
Caffe Trieste, 152
Calendar of events, 43–46
California Academy of Sciences, 7, 20, 123
California Coastal Trail, 129
California Historical Society, 6, 108
California Palace of the Legion of Honor, 131–132
California sea lions, 1–2, 7, 16, 99, 107
Cameron House, 145
The Candy Store on Main Street (Tiburon), 198
Canton Bazaar, 143
Cartoon Art Museum, 108–109
Car travel and rentals, 228, 231–233
Castello di Amorosa Winery (Calistoga), 208

The Castro, 5, 26, 121–122
  accommodations, 70–71
  restaurants, 95–96
Castro Theatre, 121
Cellphones, 239
Chandon (Yountville), 209
The Chapel, 180
Charles M. Schulz Museum and Research Center (Santa Rosa), 223
Chateau Montelena (Calistoga), 209
Chestnut Street, 163
Children's Creativity Museum, 109
Children's Zoo, 132
China Beach, 129
Chinatown, 1, 9–10, 20, 23, 114
  restaurants, 86
  shopping, 162
  walking tour, 140–147
Chinatown Gate, 114
Chinatown Gateway Arch, 142
Chinatown Kite Shop, 143
Chinese Culture Center, 146–147
Chinese Historical Society of America Museum, 145
Chinese New Year, 43
Chinese temples, 114
Cigars, 166
City Hall, 3, 117–119
City Lights Booksellers & Publishers, 151
CityPass, 105
City stair climbing, 138
Civic Center, 23, 26
  accommodations, 69–70
  exploring the neighborhood, 117–119
  restaurants, 91
Clarion Alley, 161
Cliff House, 20, 129–130, 137
Club and music scene, 179–181
Club Fugazi, 152–153
  Beach Blanket Babylon at, 1, 10, 152, 178
Coastal Trail, 4
Cobb's Comedy Club, 178
Coit Tower, 112
Columbus Tower, 150
Comedy and cabaret, 178–179
Community Garden, 156
Condor Club, former site of the, 151
Conservatory of Flowers, 123
Consulates, 236
Contemporary Jewish Museum, 6, 109
Cow Hollow, 23
  bars, 184
Credit cards, 240
Crissy Field, 129
Crocker Galleria, 174
Cruisin' the Castro, 133

D

Dance, 177
Debit cards, 240

Advance Praise

Hyun Chul Paul Kim presents a compelling commentary on the book of Isaiah, a book that would be considered politically incorrect in our contemporary world. He deftly combines the details of a diachronic or historical analysis of the various elements of the book with an overarching synchronic or literary perspective that unites the book as a whole. His work is fundamentally intertextual in that it explores the relationships between Isaiah and ancient and contemporary worlds. This accessible commentary will both prompt and enable students to engage this endlessly fascinating book.

—*Marvin A. Sweeney*
Professor of Hebrew Bible
Claremont School of Theology, Claremont, California
Professor of Tanak
Academy for Jewish Religion California, Los Angeles, California

Informed by the best scholarship in the field, Paul Kim's *Reading Isaiah* is as much a social commentary of our times as it is a penetrating interpretation of Isaiah. Students will find this book accessible, theologically rich, and exquisitely written. Teachers will find it indispensable for the classroom.

—*Louis Stulman*
Professor of Religious Studies
University of Findlay, Findlay, Ohio

Despite Isaiah's enduring appeal for both Jewish and Christian readers, it is arguably the Bible's most complex book. Paul Kim deals judiciously and fairly with numerous questions concerning Isaiah's structure and interpretation. His breadth of knowledge of the issues Isaiah raises for modern readers is impressive and is offered in an inviting, personable voice.

—*Patricia K. Tull*
A. B. Rhodes Professor Emerita of Old Testament
Louisville Presbyterian Seminary

READING ISAIAH

Smyth & Helwys Publishing, Inc.
6316 Peake Road
Macon, Georgia 31210-3960
1-800-747-3016
© 2016 by Hyun Chul Paul Kim

Library of Congress Cataloging-in-Publication Data

Names: Kim, Hyun Chul Paul, 1965- author.
Title: Reading the Old Testament : Isaiah / by Hyun Chul Paul Kim.
Other titles: Isaiah
Description: Macon : Smyth & Helwys, 2016. | Includes bibliographical
   references.
Identifiers: LCCN 2016046710 | ISBN 9781573129251 (pbk. : alk. paper)
Subjects: LCSH: Bible. Isaiah--Commentaries.
Classification: LCC BS1515.53 .K56 2016 | DDC 224/.107--dc23
LC record available at https://lccn.loc.gov/2016046710

Reading Isaiah

A Literary and Theological Commentary

Hyun Chul Paul Kim

SMYTH&HELWYS
PUBLISHING, INCORPORATED · MACON, GEORGIA

Also by Hyun Chul Paul Kim

You Are My People: An Introduction to Prophetic Literature

Ambiguity, Tension, and Multiplicity in Deutero-Isaiah

The Desert Will Bloom: Poetic Visions in Isaiah

Formation and Intertextuality in Isaiah 24–27

Concerning the Nations:
Essays on the Oracles against the Nations in Isaiah, Jeremiah, and Ezekiel

For my wife, Yijeong,
with
love, gratitude, and respect

Acknowledgments

"I don't know how to read Isaiah," said the acclaimed Isaiah scholar Chris Franke during an Isaiah panel session at a Society of Biblical Literature (SBL) annual meeting. This comment was not disturbing but rather encouraging to me. When I read and write on the book of Isaiah, I often feel clueless or even lost, as though plodding through a huge book of sixty-six chapters. Its words are so high and its ideas so deep that I easily feel as though I'm trying to find my way through a maze with high walls. Having completed this commentary, I am humbled at the recollection of so many mentors and colleagues, fellow servants of God, who have graciously provided incalculable GPS guidance and encouragement. I owe my genuine thanks to all of them, though I recognize there is not space enough to name everyone.

I thank all the Bible professors at Princeton Theological Seminary who have instilled my love for the prophet Isaiah, especially J. J. M. Roberts. Professors at Claremont have bestowed in me lasting scholarship and mentorship; particularly my *doktorvater* Rolf Knierim, who coached me to further develop my passion for this "beloved" prophet. In the larger SBL guild, I have been blessed to have met and been inspired by so many important Isaiah scholars, such as Ulrich Berges, Carol Dempsey, Joe Everson, Francis Landy, Margaret Odell, Gary Stansell, Archibald van Wieringen, Roy Wells, H. G. M. Williamson, John Willis, and many more; above all, I will forever cherish Roy Melugin's nurturing of my scholarly growth.

Special thanks to the scholars who have graciously read this manuscript. I am deeply grateful to W. A. M. Beuken for his tireless, meticulous, and accurate comments; Chris Franke for her keen, constructive critiques; Todd Hibbard for his cutting-edge feedback; Marvin Sweeney for his unmatched insights and for continuously mentoring me with his impeccable scholarship and extraordinary care; and Patricia Tull for her trenchant notes and suggestions. All shortcomings in this book remain solely my own.

Reinhard Kratz introduced to me the best of German scholarship during my research stay at Goettingen. For the rigor and advice of Louis Stulman, I am immensely indebted. Both the staff and many collaborative colleagues I have gotten to encounter at the Wabash workshops continue to share their sustaining wisdom and friendship. Colleagues from the Eastern Great Lakes region continue to be good academic dialogue partners. Nancy Bowen, Linda Day, and Carolyn Pressler (three musketeers) constantly model for me what camaraderie looks like in this highly individualistic culture. Fellow sojourners—including the African-American, Asian-American, and Latino/a scholars at SBL—and their resilient visions continue to inspire me. The pioneering joys and struggles of Korean-American mentors strengthen me beyond description, including Jin Hee Han, Chan-Hie Kim, Eunjoo Mary Kim, Seyoon Kim, Wonil Kim, Sang Hyun Lee, Seung-Ai Yang, and Victor Yoon. My special Korean-American 1.5 and second-generation colleagues continue to share the gifts of friendship, as well as scholarship (including Korean Biblical Colloquium), such as John Ahn, Paul Cho, Paul Huh, Johann Kim, Uriah Kim, Bo Karen Lee, Max Lee, Michelle Lee-Barnewall, Bo Lim, Paul Lim, Kang Na, Roger Nam, and Aaron Son.

My opportunity to conduct research as a Fulbright U.S. Scholar to Korea in 2015 has provided transformative perspectives on the importance of comparative studies on history, culture, and colonization. I am deeply grateful for the abundant hospitality and support of the hosting institution, Methodist Theological University. Heartfelt thanks to my institution, Methodist Theological School in Ohio (MTSO), for granting me the Faculty Fellowship research leave, which has been instrumental for the completion of this book; much thanks also to my wonderful colleagues (every faculty and staff) for the joy of collegiality and teamwork. Equally important, my completion of this book is possible, thanks to much laughter and challenge shared with my students at MTSO in the invigorating classroom discussions (esp. the Isaiah class). Students at the Course of Study School of Ohio have also enriched my interpretive effort to be relevant to diverse ministry contexts.

I would like to add my deep appreciation to Mark Biddle for inviting and nudging me to bring this enjoyable mission to completion, as well as for reading and commenting through the manuscript numerous times. My enthusiastic thanks to the editorial team at Smyth & Helwys, including Leslie Andres and Olivia Lovelady, for their superb editorial work and support.

Words cannot express my wholehearted gratitude to Rev. Hyung-Choon Yang and his family for their prayers and love all the way from Osaka, Japan. My mother's fervent prayer is the backbone and fertilizer of this product, just as the memory of my father's pastoral passion continues to sustain my vocational path. The boundless love of my wife and children, Anne and Ethan, constantly remind me that living out the lives of our *hesed* and hope together with communities, both near and far, matters just as much as (if not more than) putting black ink to white paper. *Kamsa hamnida!*

—*Paul Kim*
November 2016

Contents

Introduction

The book of Isaiah is politically incorrect. For that matter, so is the entire Hebrew Bible. Despite the many similarities of human traits in every place and time, the ancient setting of our biblical materials presents a great challenge due to immense temporal, cultural, and historical gaps. Isaiah lived when kings ruled, patriarchal authority was hardly questioned, and extreme starvation with limited goods each year was the norm for most of the populace.

Imagine a world in which a gifted athlete or musician would never get a chance to try out for the national team because he or she does not come from noble lineage or cannot bribe a powerful official to obtain an endorsement. Imagine a world in which affluent owners and employers earn ten or a hundred times more annually than do equally hard-working peasants or employees. Imagine a world, as in Suzanne Collins's novel *The Hunger Games*, in which different classes are virtually segregated from one another with impassible boundaries, except for the elites in the gluttonous capital who have incomparable freedom and privilege. In such a world, with no proper legal protections, the powers that be could take away one's property, rights, and even life at their will. Such was the ancient world, with all its charm and glory as well as ugliness and violence.

Ironically, many issues in today's world seem eerily similar to those in such an ancient world, hence the importance and pertinence of this ancient sacred book. When it comes to the scars of deep ruptures of society, rampant injustice against the vulnerable, and ongoing effects of trauma and bitterness deeply ingrained in the heartaches and tears of the victimized, the biblical world must have had no shortage of such examples. This awareness forms the foundation of the reading strategy for Isaiah. Prophets cried out amid and against undeniable corruption and haunting violence. Our humbling task is to get at the aspects of the ancient world through the study of the ancient text. In analogy, we are attempting to make the one-dimensional scroll come alive by retelling and re-presenting it in a 3-D or 4-D world. Before reading and interpreting the scroll, it is worthwhile to review select issues and scholarly observations regarding the following three areas: literary formation and features (text); historical, cultural, and sociopolitical data (context); and thematic and theological ideas (concept).

Literary Formation and Features (Text)

Breaks and Divisions

The book of Isaiah has sixty-six chapters. Considering that scholars debate whether Psalm 23 is a combination of two originally independent psalms (vv. 1-4 and vv. 5-6) or one developed unit, it is no wonder that interpreters have puzzled over the questions of how this bulky scroll of sixty-six chapters should have been put together. Where was it composed, over how many years, by how many scribes and/or editors, and so on?

Numerous commentaries review these questions in great detail in their introductions. Suffice it to say here that the possibility of multiple authorship was proposed as early as the time of a Jewish medieval commentator, Abraham Ibn Ezra (1089–1167 CE), who observed that the section including Isaiah 40–66 displays a scribal hand other than that of the prophet, a scribe who was active presumably after the exile: "The second part of the book of Isaiah, which contains allusions to events that took place long after the death of Isaiah, as to historical facts, is . . . not written by the same prophet" (Ibn Ezra 1873, 170). In the modern era, Bernhard Duhm championed isolating the sections of Deutero-Isaiah (chs. 40–55) and Trito-Isaiah (chs. 56–66), and the so-called four servant songs within Isaiah 40–55. While this perspective still stands as a theory with enormous consensus, recent scholars debate the specifics of the formation process, the location(s) of the author/redactor(s), and the resultant implications for reading the scroll in the present form as a whole.

Where is the major break, and how are we to make sense (synchronically) of—or redactionally reconstruct (diachronically)—the diverse editorial patches in these sixty-six chapters? On the one hand, scholars disagree on identifying a major break within the entire scroll. As has been perceived most commonly, many scholars identify a major thematic break between chapters 39 and 40, i.e., from the warning of the exile to the promise of homecoming. Yet others identify a major text-critical break between chapters 33 and 34. J. T. Milik has noted a distinct scribal break in a Qumran scroll of Isaiah, 1QIsaᵃ: "One detail is of some significance: chapter 33 finishes towards the foot of column XXVII, and the three ruled lines which follow are left blank. . . . Chapter 34 begins on a new sheet of leather, and the text thereafter continues without further interruption until the end of the book" (Milik 1959, 26–27). Emmauel Tov's observation is equally noteworthy: "Characteristic features of this scroll [1QIsaᵃ] are . . . the division of the scroll into two segments (Isaiah 1–34 and 35–66), written by two different scribes. . . . Although also in other Qumran scrolls two or more hands are visible (1QHᵃ, 1QpHab, 11QTᵃ), in no source is the text so neatly divided as in the Isaiah scroll" (Tov 1997, 501).

On the other hand, equally significantly, a major break within Isaiah 40–66 is not as apparent as has often been held. Admittedly, Duhm's influential argument for dividing this scroll into three sections deserves the attention of any interpreter interested in disjoints as well as joints within the scroll. Nonetheless, many scholars nowadays are not convinced that Isaiah 56–66 represent an originally independent composition: "It appears, therefore, that there is no conclusive reason to attribute chaps. 56-66 to a distinct and later prophet living in the mid-fifth century (or later). . . . One should not speak of two different personalities, but of a change in locus following the prophet's return to Israel" (Paul 2012, 11; cf. Berges 2012a, 388–93). Thus, more scholars recognize Trito-Isaiah "as the work of multiple writers" as opposed to that of a single writer (Sweeney 2014, 674). Furthermore, a recent Israeli research team led by Moshe Koppel developed computer software to analyze word style and frequencies in order to identify any major shift of authorship in the text, with the following intriguing result: "Instead of seeing the break between First and Second Isaiah as occurring between chapters 39 and 40, however, it situated it somewhat earlier in chapter 33. Also of interest is the fact that the program reported no change in authorship between chapters 55 and 56" (Niskanen 2014, xii–xiii).

Consequently, scholars are revisiting this question: Is there a distinct break between chapters 55 and 56? Notable key words from Isaiah 1–39, "righteousness" in particular, seem to resume most frequently from chapter 56 and on. However, this term connects to the immediately preceding chapters (Paul 2012, 450). Also, the evident shift from the singular "servant" to the plural "servants" leads many scholars to identify a break between chapter 53 and 54 instead (Seitz 2001; Berges 2014). Yet, as Shalom Paul has astutely discovered, there are many linguistic connections even within Isaiah 54–57 (Paul 2012, 415, 435, 450, 461). In terms of an earlier redactional layer, as Reinhard Kratz argues, the marker "a herald of good news" brackets the kernel from chapter 40 to chapter 52 together (Kratz 1993, 1994). Similarly, chapters 60–62, which many commentators take as a composite, separate entity, demonstrate linguistic correlations with the preceding and following chapters. In short, as Chris Franke asserts, "the strongest defense of single authorship [within Isa 40–66] is the consistent literary style throughout. A geographical change does not in itself warrant asserting a new author" (Franke 2014, 699). Joseph Blenkinsopp similarly cautions against reading too much literary separation rather than connection: "In subject matter, tone, and emphasis, chs. 56–66 are distinct enough to warrant separate treatment, yet they belong on the same textual and exegetical continuum as chs. 40–55" (Blenkinsopp 2003, 30). Perhaps it is time to bid farewell to the so-called Trito-Isaiah and expound literary and thematic continuity as much as discontinuity in Isaiah 40–66 (Steck 1989; Kim 2015a).

Structure
Hence, while respecting conspicuous literary discontinuity, the present study intends to explore another lens that looks at the book of Isaiah as a whole with particular attention to seams, brackets, and joints in continuity. As an interpretive premise, no matter how we subdivide it into various chapters or different "Isaiahs," the scroll invites us to read it as a unified whole in its final form. In fact, even chapters are at times misleading divisions, causing us to think there are many books in this scroll. Unlike the Twelve Prophets that do represent twelve individual, independent headings (although their interconnections as a composite whole deserves our interpretive awareness), the book of Isaiah lacks such isolating headings for the alleged three "Isaiahs" of the entire scroll (with exceptions such as 1:1; 2:1; 13:1). The scribes seem to have intended for readers not to forget to read the scroll in a holistic, sequential, and even cyclical continuum: "in a word, I do not believe that every structural division stems from an editorial decision. Rather, I would argue that what one can determine is the manner in which these chapters, however originally collected, have been shaped into a larger didactic composition" (Childs 2001, 200). With this premise in mind, we should highlight several literary features and related themes.

First, in terms of stylistic form and literary markers, Isaiah 40–66 seem more consistent and continuous than Isaiah 1–39. One visible marker occurs at the end of three sections in Isaiah 40–66, i.e., 48:22; 57:21; 66:24, evenly dividing the second half of Isaiah into chapters 40–48, 49–57, and 58–66— interestingly each in nine chapters (although the chapter system came later in the rabbinic era; cf. Muilenburg 1956, 11–21; Blenkinsopp 2003, 172–73). These markers closing each section in Isaiah 40–66 are somewhat akin to those in the five books of the Psalter, which function as unique doxological markers at the end of each book (Pss 41:13 [MT 41:14]; 72:20; 89:52 [MT 89:53]; 106:48; 150:6)—resembling the five books of the Pentateuch. Accordingly, although the most convincing approach continues to be to divide Isaiah into five parts (chs. 1–12; 13–27; 28–39; 40–55; and 56–66; cf. Seitz 1993; Tull 2010), this study intends to follow those distinctive closing markers in the second half of Isaiah, while taking chapters 36–39 as a crucial center of the whole, a circumstance that will be addressed below.

Second, once we subdivide Isaiah 40–66 into three parts (chs. 40–48, 49–57, and 58–66), it seems more plausible to divide Isaiah 1–35 into three parts as well. As most commentators recognize, Isaiah 1–12 and 13–23 appear to be quite distinct. This does not imply that these sections must have been originally independent compositions. The unique superscription that begins chapters 1–12 (1:1; cf. 2:1), however, likewise initiates chapters 13–23 (13:1), the latter congealed together as the "burden" (*massaʾ*) oracles against/about the nations. Within Isaiah 24–35—a section more loose and disjointed than the previous sections, but considered a third section by Bernhard Duhm (1892, 13–14)—chapters 28–33 neatly cohere as the "woe" (*hoy*) oracles. Although 24–27 can be linked to 13–23 as extended oracles, it is not necessary to glue 24–27 to these internally tight burden oracles. Hence, with 28–33 as a center, we can take 24–27 and 34–35 as brackets.

Third, of all the portions in the entire book of Isaiah, chapters 36–39 seem most out of place, instead of the so-called Trito-Isaiah section (Isa 56–66) or the so-called Isaiah apocalypse (24–27). Concerning the debatable issue whether the Kings account (2 Kgs 18–20) or the Isaiah account (chs. 36–39) is original, it is plausible to posit that both accounts may have come from a common source that has then influenced each editorial adaptation into Kings, Chronicles, and Isaiah. Be that as it may, whereas most scholars consider this middle section as a mere bridge that thematically closes the preceding chapters with the message of judgment and smoothly paves a way into the subsequent chapters with the message of consolation (in addition to the parallel narratives between the Ahaz account of Isa 7 and the Hezekiah account of Isa 36–39), the present study claims that this core section—"the only sustained section of the book in prose" (Davidson 2007, 96)—stands as the compositional and thematic center of the whole (Berges 2012c, 24, 42). In sum, the structure of Isaiah is, then, as follows:

Chs. 1–12: Isaiah's Vision about Judah and Jerusalem
    Chs. 13–23: Ten Oracles about the Nations
        Chs. 24–35: Tales of Two Cities and Parties
            Chs. 36–39: Hopeful Stories of Trust and Deliverance amid
                Imperial Threats
            Chs. 40–48: New Things to Anticipate for Servant Jacob-Israel via
                Cyrus
    Chs. 49–57: Good News of New Generations for Daughter Zion
Chs. 58–66: Glorious Future of Zion for the Righteous Remnants contra
    the Wicked Perpetrators

Reading the structure of Isaiah with this attention to stylistic form and literary markers, we can retrieve select underlying, major themes. First of all, the motif of *light* becomes a key thematic thread that holds this scroll together (Clements 1996 and 1997). In fact, the overall structure recalls the shape of the seven lampstands (menorah) in Exodus 25:31-40, which contains three branches on the left and three branches on the right, with the cap at the center. The word and motif of light are closely associated with YHWH as the true deity over the ancient Near Eastern sun gods. The term "light" occurs in numerous texts throughout the book of Isaiah, depicting the ideals of salvation and redemption over against darkness and captivity.

Second, related to the dichotomy between light and darkness, the symmetrical structure further underscores the dichotomy between *the obedient and the disobedient.* In a simplistic way, the fall of Jerusalem and the ensuing exile portray the fate of the guilty in the first half of Isaiah, while the return and restoration in Jerusalem anticipate the fate of the penitent in the second half. Instead of this twofold arrangement (which seems more evident in Ezekiel), however, the book of Isaiah casts the tension and struggle between the righteous and the wicked, in the way these two entities or groups are dispersed throughout the entire book, as though signifying that conflicts have continued and as though painting the subtlety or even interchange-ability between them, much the same way true prophets and false prophets are not so easily distinguishable.

Third, at the center of this great scroll, in Isaiah 36–39, implied readers encounter two ideal models of faith and hope, *Hezekiah and Isaiah* respec-tively, while learning of the bygone stories of the nation's crisis and miraculous deliverance. Regardless of historical accuracy, especially in comparison with the Sennacherib inscription, we learn two key names, among others, that play significant roles and symbolic functions. The first, Hezekiah, denotes the prophetic assurance or plea, "may YHWH strengthen." This king's defiant faith (with *strengthened* trust) and humble repentance demonstrate a model for all subsequent audiences to emulate. The second, Isaiah, denotes the divine promise: "YHWH saves." God's people, whether dejected in exile or despondent in Yehud (we will use the term "Yehud" to refer to the province of "Judah" after the exile during the restoration period under the Persian hegemony, prior to the designation "Jews" from the Hellenistic times onward; cf. Ezra 7:14; Dan 2:25; 5:13; 6:14; Becking 2011, 157), can rekindle their hope that this great prophet has demonstrated in his proclamation and confrontation in the face of daunting powers that be. Those who trust in the Lord, the creator and redeemer, shall be *saved*.

Historical, Cultural, and Sociopolitical Data (Context)

Theology without the guts and blood of social and political struggles can become merely sanitized, neutralized contemplation. Ancient texts thus testify to the multifaceted stories of the cries, laughter, sorrows, joys, hurts, and hopes of the real lives of real people. Therefore, although our primary aim is to analyze and interpret the texts, it would be an enriching endeavor to consider the historical, cultural, and political contexts of the surrounding ancient Near Eastern world. Thus, we will address some of the key events associated with the turbulent final years of the Judean monarchy vis-à-vis the surrounding international empires as well as the subsequent exilic and postexilic settings concerning the controversy over "the myth of the empty land" versus "the myth of the empty exile."

End of the Davidic monarchy vis-à-vis the Surrounding International Empires

The superscription (1:1) of the book of Isaiah introduces four kings of Judah: Uzziah (792–740 BCE), Jotham (750–732 BCE), Ahaz (743–715 BCE), and Hezekiah (728–686 BCE). While the prophet Isaiah's ministry ostensibly began during the year of king Uzziah's death (740 BCE) in Judah (6:1), this was the time when, after the long reign of Jeroboam II (793–753 BCE), the northern kingdom of Israel was on the verge of taking an escalating downward spiral. In less than the next three decades, various kings usurped and were deposed from the throne—Zechariah (6 months), Shallum (1 month), Menahem (752–742 BCE), Pekahiah (742–740 BCE), and Pekah (752?–732 BCE), ultimately leading to the last king Hoshea (732–722 BCE) during whose reign in 722 BCE Samaria fell to the Assyrian king Shalmaneser V (726–722 BCE). Concerning the major international events, we will rehash the following three issues.

First, one important political event, the Syro-Ephraimite War (735–732 BCE), characterized this turbulent era. During the Omri dynasty, northern Israel was under frequent attack by Aram. The Jehu dynasty subsequently formed an alliance with Assyria. King Pekah joined Aram's invitation to rebel against Assyria, however, trying to avoid paying heavy tribute to Assyria. Thus, in a joint campaign, Syria (Aram) and Ephraim (northern Israel) waged a war against Judah, pressuring king Ahaz to join their coalition against Assyria (Sweeney 2014, 681). King Ahaz could not make a leap of faith relying on the prophecy of a little child but instead resorted to submitting to the grown-up Assyrian king Tiglath-pileser III (744–727 BCE). The inscription of Tiglath-pileser III records the resultant devastation of Aram and northern Israel, the outcome of which will eventually considerably weaken Judah:

> I carried off [to] Assyria the land of Bīt-Ḫumria (Israel), [. . . its] 'auxiliary [army,'] [. . .] all of its people, [. . .] [I/they killed] Pekah, their king, and I installed Hoshea [as king] over them. I received from them 10 talents of gold, x talents of silver, [with] their [possessions] and [I car]ried them [to Assyria]. (COS II: 288; cf. 2 Kgs 15:30)

This rapidly changing international crisis provides the background for the Ahaz account (Isa 7–8), especially with regard to the political questions concerning which party to join and which superpower to serve as well as the theological issues of whether to seek and trust divine power or military might.

Second, another crucial international event, Sennacherib's invasion and siege of Jerusalem (701 BCE), occurred in the time of King Hezekiah of Judah. Among pertinent historical events, scholars suggest this incident as the backdrop of the key Hezekiah narratives (chs. 1; 30–31; 36–38). According to 2 Kings 18:13-16 (which has no parallel in Isa 36–39), upon King Sennacherib's threat, King Hezekiah succumbed and paid a huge sum of tribute. Interestingly, the ancient Near Eastern document resembles the biblical records at points. For example, the biblical text records that King Sennacherib of Assyria (704–681 BCE) "came up against all the fortified cities of Judah and conquered them . . . imposed upon king Hezekiah of Judah 300 talents of silver and 30 talents of gold" (2 Kgs 18:13-14). This correlates with the comparable details of Sennacherib's claim:

> As for Hezekiah, the Judean, I besieged forty-six of his fortified walled cities and surrounding smaller towns, which were without number. . . . He, Hezekiah, was overwhelmed by the awesome splendor of my lordship, and he sent me after my departure to Nineveh, my royal city, his elite

troops (and) his best soldiers, which he had brought in as reinforcements to strengthen Jerusalem, with 30 talents of gold, 800 talents of silver . . . . (*COS* II: 303; cf. 2 Kgs 18:13-14)

Likewise, Sennacherib's siege of Jerusalem, the definitive background for chapters 36–38, echoes the Assyrian king's avowal, although with an outcome that contrasts with the biblical account: "He himself, I locked up within Jerusalem, his royal city, like a bird in a cage. I surrounded him with earthworks, and made it unthinkable for him to exit by the city gate" (*COS* II: 303; cf. Isa 36:12; 37:33-38).

Third, after the Babylonian destruction of Jerusalem in 587 BCE, we learn from the Cyrus Cylinder of yet another significant event concerning the fall of Judah's hated enemy Babylon to the Persian king Cyrus II (559–530 BCE) in 539 BCE. On the one hand, the Isaianic texts embrace, if not appreciate, Cyrus as the liberator for the impending new exodus—analogous to Moses the liberator for the old exodus. That the menacing Babylonian empire would fall must have made a monumental impact in ancient Israel's historical, political, and theological paradigm shift. Whoever played a pivotally instrumental role in dethroning Babylon would be Israel's hero: hence the titles YHWH's "shepherd" (44:28) and YHWH's "anointed" (45:1).

Yet, on the other hand, just like the troubles that come with the monarchical system after the exodus and entrance into the land of milk and honey, the poets and prophets in the Isaianic community would acknowledge that they would still remain as "colonized" communities under another imperial power. The boss has changed, but we remain the same slaves, so to speak. One may ponder the following questions: What happened to those who served in the Babylonian court after the Persian takeover? Were they executed as the crooks, pawns, or puppets of Babylon, hence Persia's enemy? Did they retain their privileges even after the new empire took over, and, if so, how (cf. Dan 1:1-6; 5:31–6:3 [MT 6:1-4])? It is thus quite understandable that some of the Judean exiles remained doubtful or disappointed, while others refused to acknowledge any divine plan in the course of these historical events. Thus, there are subtle historical and thematic clues—also called "hidden transcripts" (Scott 1990)—that remind readers of the ruthlessness of the superpower empire as well as of the ever-present dangers of living as colonized people, not even a nation. In this sense, that the Isaianic text labels this Persian king as YHWH's "anointed" (45:1) may even be analogous to the self-propagandistic account:

When I entered Babylon in a peaceful manner, I took up my lordly reign
in the royal palace amidst rejoicing and happiness. Marduk, the great lord,
caused the magnanimous people of Babylon [to . . .] me, (and) I daily
attended to his worship. My vast army moved about Babylon in peace;
I did not permit anyone to frighten (the people of) [Sumer] and Akkad.
I sought the welfare of the city of Babylon and all its sacred centers. . .
. I gathered all their inhabitants and returned (to them) their dwellings.
In addition, at the command of Marduk, the great lord, I settled in their
habitations, in pleasing abodes, the gods of Sumer and Akkad, whom
Nabonidus, to the anger of the lord of the gods, had brought into Babylon.
(*COS* II: 315-16; cf. Isa 45:1; Ezra 1:1-4; 2 Chr 36:22-23)

At the outset, many historians considered the Persian conquest and
treatment of their subjects as a benign and benevolent policy. Some recent
interpreters, however, have questioned the reliability or accuracy of such a
claim by the king of an empire. In light of other related chronicles of the
Persian kings, it is legitimate to reexamine whether their claims bear historical accuracy or represent ideological propaganda.

Three cuneiform texts (the Nabonidus Chronicle, the Verse Account
of Nabonidus, and the Cyrus Cylinder) attest to divergent records of the
Persian occupation or conquest of Babylon. While the debate concerning
the historical and political pictures in these records continues (Kim 2012,
1043), it should be noted that these inscriptions more often than not may
betray the "ideological viewpoints" of the historiographers (Kratz 2003, 145)
and the pro-Persian propaganda intended "to insulate Cyrus from activities
associated with conquest" as can be detected in the graphic depiction of the
destruction of Babylon by the invading Persian army in Jeremiah 51:30-32
(Vanderhooft 2006, 362). A further debate concerns whether the Cyrus of
Deutero-Isaiah in fact may have been Cyrus II or Darius I (Albertz 2003a,
371–83). The main administrative systems of the Judeans remained under
the control of the Persian empire: "Far from being 'a network of "autono-
mous cities,"' the political economy of Palestine was tightly controlled by
the combination of a highly organized imperial infrastructure and locally
administered temple economies, which had the effect of enabling the limited
development of regionally individuated cultural identities" (Hobson 2013,
219). Joel Kaminsky and Joel Lohr's analogy is equally illuminating: "We
know from accounts outside the Bible that new emperors often did such
things to gain the favor of their citizens, perhaps like politicians today who
give large tax breaks upon being elected" (Kaminsky and Lohr 2015, 181).

What would these ambiguities in benign Persian policy versus imperial
propaganda imply in reading Isaiah? In understanding the struggles and hopes

of the people of Judah affected by the exile, we should, on the one hand, keep in mind the devastating impact of the Babylonian invasion and demolition of Judah and its capital Jerusalem. It would make sense for those victims and captives to welcome their new liberator Persia, expected to deliver them from bondage. At the same time, on the other hand, we should also picture this vulnerable people sandwiched among the towering superpowers. Now, the lot of the colonized nation Israel/Judah (or later, province Yehud) under the shadow of empire has merely shifted from one empire (Babylon) to another (Persia): "See, today we are slaves; in the land you gave to our ancestors to eat its fruit and its good; see, we are slaves today" (Neh 9:36; cf. Smith-Christopher 2002, 65). Just as they had to struggle to decide whether to ally with Egypt or Assyria in the first half of the book of Isaiah, soon they would also confront similar challenges to negotiate and survive as small colonies of Persia. We may hear from the texts the agonies of the lingering impact of the forced migration, deportation, and dispersion of this vulnerable minority group. We will also see examples of internal strife and schism amid their ongoing threats and daunting tasks to form a unified community—amid the tension between the righteous and the wicked—including the animosity between those who remained in the land of Judah and those who returned from Babylonian exile.

Exile and Diaspora vis-à-vis the Remainees and the Returnees between Judah and Babylon

What of the exile? How devastating was the exile? How many people were actually affected by the demise of the Judean kingdom? We would need to gather all the data from archaeology, history, sociology, anthropology, political science, literature, refugee studies, trauma studies, and many more. Admitting that this topic requires a vast amount of information from all disciplines and is constantly in need of updating, we will review some of the current debates, issues, and theories that can illuminate the interpretation of the book of Isaiah.

In light of the internal evidence, the biblical texts provide discrepant data as to how many people were exiled. According to 2 Kings 24:14, 16, during the first deportation in 597 BCE, as many as 10,000 elites—and possibly 7,000 soldiers and 1,000 artisans—were taken into Babylonian captivity except the poorest of "the people of the land" ('am ha'arets). Then Babylon further took those who defected to the king of Babylon in 587, again except some of the poor in the land (2 Kgs 25:11-12). According to Jeremiah 52:28-30, only about 3,023 elites were exiled during the first deportation, and then 832 inhabitants and then 745 Judeans, for a total of 4,600 captives.

This discrepancy has led some scholars to conclude that only a handful of people of Judah were exiled, whereas others argue for a substantial, if not massive, deportation and devastation.

In a comparable analysis, scholars similarly debate the archaeological data in the aftermath of the fall of Samaria in 722 BCE, from which some scholars observe no evidence for mass migration of northern Israelite refugees into Judah, while others find strong evidence for a drastic deportation from Israel into Judah, thereby suggesting parallel cases in our construction of the fall of Jerusalem in 587 BCE: compare thus the statements of Nadav Na'aman with those of Israel Finkelstein. Na'aman claims that

> the analysis of all the available textual and archaeological data from the Shephelah and Jerusalem demonstrates that the hypothesis whereby a flood of thousands of [northern Israelite] refugees arrived to the Kingdom of Judah in the late 8th century lacks concrete foundation. . . . Hence, unless supported by strong evidence, such theories should best be avoided. (2014, 13–14)

Finkelstein proposes that

> there is no escape from the unmistakable archaeological evidence of a dramatic demographic transformation in Judah in the Iron IIB, in the second half of the 8th century and the early 7th century BCE. And this transformation can in no way be explained as the result of natural population growth, economic prosperity or intra-Judahite movement of people. I maintain that many of the new settlers in Jerusalem, the highlands of Judah and the Shephelah emigrated from the territory of Israel, mainly from the southern Samaria highlands, where surveys seem to demonstrate deterioration of settlement activity after 720 BCE. (2015, 204)

Comparing the case that about 20 to 30 percent were deported in the fall of Samaria in 722 BCE and considering the number of war casualties and refugees, Rainer Albertz estimates that about 25 percent were deported from Judah around 587. This would amount to approximately 20,000 deportees out of a population of 80,000. We should also add another 20,000 casualties, including those killed, executed, and escaped during the battles. This would total 40,000—half the total population of Judah who were physically affected by the Babylonian invasion and exile. This number does not even include psychological effects on the surviving family members of those affected. John Ahn assesses the ongoing, repetitive transportation of the deportees as Babylon's carefully devised "socio-economic planning": "In contrast to a single punctuated mass deportation system of the Neo-Assyrians . . . the Neo-Babylonians imposed forced migration on conquered persons for work on their extensive and numerous primary, secondary, and tertiary canals" (2011, 32–33). Thus, considering these various factors around and behind the number recorded, Albertz asserts that "the Babylonian exile represents so massive a rupture in the history of Israel, even though life in Judah continued to go on" (2003b, 90).

As the discrepancy in the data demonstrates, scholars disagree regarding what it was like for the remainees to survive in the land of Judah post-587 BCE, in addition to how many people really were exiled and how many of them indeed returned. In the study of Isaiah, these questions lead to further pivotal questions: Where was the author of Isaiah 40–66 located, in Judah or in Babylon? Was Isaiah 40–66 compiled by the same author(s)/editor(s), whether in Judah, in Babylon, or returning from Babylon to Judah, or collected by the different schools or groups? Although it is not certain whether "a change in theology in the text implies a different author," as she asserts, Lena-Sofia Tiemeyer's questions touch on key interpretive options possible from various angles: "These different authors may either be *different persons*, i.e. various members of a 'Deutero-Isaiah group' who lived at different time and/or in different places and thus saw the world differently, or they may be *one person* who changed his mind throughout his life owing to changed historical and/or geographical circumstances" (2007, 369).

On one side, some scholars in the "myth of the empty land" school (Barstad 1996) argue that the author never left the land but wrote Isaiah 40–66, the exilic and postexilic collection, located in the land of Judah. This theory goes back to Charles C. Torrey in his 1910 proposal: "According to Torrey, the exile affected only a very small part of the population, . . . Judah was not devastated following the Babylonian campaign, and life for most Judeans continued pretty much as before 586 B.C.E. The land supposedly could not have been *completely empty* because the Babylonians would not have deported the *entire* population" (Faust 2011, 91–92). From archaeological data, especially of different sites and areas, Oded Lipschits cautiously notes that "by studying archaeological material in this way, even the most enthusiastic supporters of the 'empty land' and the 'Babylonian gap' theses could not assume that Judah was a truly vacant area" (2011, 84). Picking up the groundbreaking work of Hans Barstad and others, Tiemeyer presents a bold claim that "there is little in terms of specific knowledge of Babylon in Isa 40–55 and nothing that warrants the claim that Isa 40–55 was written in Babylon . . . the Babylonian provenance of Isa 40–55, with regard either to its entirety or to specific parts, is a house built on sand without a firm textual foundation" (2011, 130, 363; cf. 2014, 25). Recently, Fredrik Hägglund similarly proposes to identify the "servant" in Isaiah 53:4-6 as "the people exiled in Babylon" and the "we" as "the people remained in Judah" (2008, 22–32). While various intertextual correlations with psalm texts make this case quite strong, Hägglund's study does not take a closer look at equally valuable intertextual echoes of the prophet Jeremiah and his legacy of suffering.

Some of the key claims of this "myth of the empty land" (or the "myth of a mass return") school include the following reconstructions, summarized by Bob Becking:

> (1) The land of Judah did not lie desolate during the Babylonian period. (2) Mizpah and Bethel most probably functioned as administrative and religious centers for the people that remained. (3) Many exiled Judeans were settled in agricultural areas in order to supply the urbanized areas of Babylon with food. (4) These Judeans reached an acceptable standard of living and apparently were free to continue their religion. (5) The return from exile should not be construed as a massive event; the descendants of the exiled Judeans returned in waves and many remained in Babylonia. (6) The temple for YHWH was only rebuilt in the middle of the fifth century B.C.E. (2011, 166)

On the other side, scholars in what I would call the "myth of the empty exile" school admit that the number of the exiled people may have been embellished and that a great majority of Judeans may have remained in the land. Nonetheless, they do question whether the pained writings of the exiled elites (which were derived from their existential traumatic experiences of forced migration) exerted any literary and theological influence on the people in Judah, let alone on the composition of the Isaiah scroll. They further challenge the tendency to discount or dismiss the enormous impact that the war, demise, and exile of a country can make. In fact, both the survivors in the land and the exiles in the foreign land must have been severely affected by the aftermath of the brutality of war, such as death in battle, famine, epidemics, executions, and long-range factors. Likewise, a demographic decline in the aftermath of the war may have left catastrophic damages involving refugees, insecurity, and deportation.

Avraham Faust astutely avers,

> None of the scholars [John Bright and William F. Albright] who view the sixth century as a period of great demographic decline attribute this decline solely, or even primarily, to *forced migration* or *deportation.* . . . Clearly, the entire population was not exiled. But does this mean that most

of the population was left behind and prospered? Of course not. Because
there are other mechanisms of population contraction, deportation is not
the only factor that one must consider with when assessing the demographic reality in Judah during the sixth century. (2011, 95)

In a similar way, Dalit Rom-Shiloni emphasizes the intricate influence of the
community's locations in Babylon and then back in Jerusalem:

> Confronting what may seem quite a chaotic literary mix, I find that the
> concept of geographical discontinuity that, however, retains a thematic
> continuity serves as a valuable tool for sorting the materials in Isa 40–66,
> for accepting its division to Babylonian chs. 40–48, and to Jerusalem
> ones in chs. 49–66. . . . Group identity perspectives that surface in these
> prophecies . . . show that Isa 49–66 (in its miscellaneous character) follow
> Isa 40–48, and treat only the community of the Repatriated Exiles as the
> in-group of God's people. (2013, 102–103)

Interestingly, John Van Seters even argues that the Yahwist (J) of the Pentateuch was contemporary with Deutero-Isaiah in addressing many similar
issues amid the Babylonian *golah* (1999, 72).

Can we really neatly isolate and set apart those who remained and
those who returned, then? Are we looking, alternatively, at the issue from
two opposing but mutual angles, i.e., "Is the cup half full or half empty"
(Lipschits 2011, 85)? Could there have been pro-Persian and pro-Babylonian
groups both within the remainees and among the returnees? Are we making
an oversimplification when we identify and label all the remainees as one
group and all the returnees as another group? What if some of them changed
their ideology or allegiance over a period of time and/or via geographical
transition? Sure, any set rules would have functioned to implement many
societal principles (e.g., Ezra 10:16-19; Neh 9:1-3; 10:28-29). Nonetheless, as numerous biblical accounts testify, it is not simple, but complex and
complicated to make a clear-cut identification or "labeling" of key groups.
While the reconstruction of the remainees and the returnees is helpful, we
should be cautious about understanding various factions and groups in the
ancient society—and today's too—in a strict dichotomy.

What seems most convincing, whether the disputed scribes were in
Judah or in Babylon, must be the devastating impact of trauma both on the
remainees/survivors and on the exiles/returnees: "The murder and mayhem,
destruction of property, loss of the public institutions which sustained
communal living, the monarchy in the first place, created a situation of
extreme deprivation, disorientation, numbness, and anomie" (Blenkinsopp

2013, 54). While location of authorship may be less evident or significant, the hardship, shock, and trauma of the Babylonian captivity should not be discounted: "Irrespective of where [Isa 40–55] were composed, they envision a future restoration dependent on the return of the deported from other lands, in the first place from the Babylonian Diaspora" (Blenkinsopp 2014, 88). At the same time, we ought not to discount the complexity since most likely there were some faithful ones both among the remainees/Judah and among the exiles/Babylon (and Egypt and elsewhere). Likewise, opportunists would frequently have arisen in both locales as well. Inasmuch as we should categorize the people in Judah (those who were never exiled to Babylon) and the people in Babylon, we should also keep in mind the likely fluctuation and shifts (like chameleons) between the righteous and the wicked. To discount such shifting loyalties and flipping powers would be tantamount to grouping true prophets and false prophets by one lineage, class, or location.

In the aftermath of the September 11, 2001, national tragedy in America, many have witnessed, felt, and learned of its traumatic impact in the United States and beyond. Suppose, in the year 3000 or later, historians are studying this tragic event. What interpretation will they come up with? How will they compare and analyze this incident and from what numeric, demographic, and statistical data and records? Can we really say that such an event has impact only in one region (devoid of the other)? Can we thoroughly distinguish one community from another community? How about one class versus another class across the regions or communities in which we constantly find resurging tensions, injustices, and struggles?

Janet Rumfelt's assessment of trauma's rupturing effects on all those affected by war presents "triple displacement": physical, psychical, and relational displacement, with both short-term and long-term effects (2011, 324–25). Rumfelt calls attention to the pain-stricken words of a 1994 Rwandan genocide survivor with HIV/AIDS resulting from a gang rape: "I only half survived. I am still carrying death in me; not only the death that AIDS will bring. Others say they escaped from the sword, but the sword is still in my heart. Even in death, I do not believe I will find rest" (2011, 334). Consequently, despite the difficulty scientifically to reconstruct the exilic and colonized experiences in the aftermath of 587 BCE, recent interdisciplinary approaches to the exile "not as a singular event but as a broader phenomenon with sociological, anthropological, and psychological dimensions" provide stronger cases that the so-called "benign experience" of the Babylonian exile (as well as experience in the Yehud region) can no longer be the widely accepted view (Kelle 2011, 21).

Consequently, while we will address some of the economic, social, political, religious, and theological issues associated with the life of Judeans as the colonized or exiled people under the empires, the equally (if not more) pressing issue for the prophet and community in the book of Isaiah, whether in Babylon or in Judah, would have been the following theological challenges, insightfully summarized by Marjo Korpel:

- The apathy of those who asked themselves whether God had rejected [God's] people for ever.
- The apostasy of those who chose to worship the deities of their mighty opponents.
- The seemingly definitive end of the Davidic dynasty. (Korpel 1999, 91)

Thematic and Theological Ideas (Concept)

Reading the book of Isaiah in a holistic way can be enriching. This by no means indicates reading the book ahistorically or anachronically, disregarding the long historical and compositional development process. Yet, in this great scroll of poetic beauty and complex layers, scholars have discovered the validity and importance of reading it as a composite whole. One significant way to undertake this is to find key thematic threads that occur throughout the book as major connecting motifs. Just like the tapestry of various fabrics, there can be many leading threads that intersperse and intersect. Some threads disclose changing motifs via shifted settings or locales. Other threads show thematic tensions among contending groups or perspectives, in which "opposing voices compete for the reader's attention . . . to interact with the opinions of the various groups of people that formed their target audience" (Tiemeyer 2011, 51). Still others may be somewhat consistent throughout the whole book. Therefore, we ask, without intending to be exhaustive, what are some of the key thematic threads that hold the book of Isaiah together as a unified whole? We will survey five interspersed but interrelated threads that constitute a dialogical interaction or tension throughout the whole book.

The first is the dialogical tension of *the righteous versus the wicked*. At certain sections, this dichotomy exists between the poor and the powerful or, more foundationally, between good and evil. The righteous remnant identifies itself as the "we"-group, which seems to fluctuate in various sections while still occurring rather steadily and continuously. Who were these "we"-group people? Does the reference intend the same group consistently or different groups across changing locations and eras?

In the book of Isaiah, at times, the righteous "we"-group refers to the "remnant" (not to be confused or identified with the "remainees" during the exilic period) that escaped and survived the onslaughts of the Assyrian or Babylonian army—including the remnant of northern Israel that fled to Judah. At other times, they allude to the poor and the needy, the socially disenfranchised class that must endure the ongoing insults and injustices of the corrupt leadership.

Concerning the schisms, factions, or tensions of various groups during the exilic and postexilic era in the province of Yehud, scholars have developed a plethora of theories, including the notions that

(1) the so-called Trito-Isaiah adheres to the same ethos and ideology as those of the Ezra-Nehemiah group (e.g., Duhm 1892, 18–19 and 418–49; Rofé 1985, 213–17; Eidevall 2009, 195–200);

(2) the prophet (or party) can be identified as the marginalized Levites group (e.g., Hanson 1975, 173–79), lay leaders (e.g., Fishbane 1985, 128), or Levitical temple singers (e.g., Albertz 2003b, 111;), in their struggle for the control of Jerusalem temple authority over against the Zadokite/Ezekiel priests group (cf. 1 Sam 2:27-36; 1 Kgs 2:35);

(3) the prophet (or party) aspires the beliefs of the YHWH-only group over against those of the syncretistic religio-political group (e.g., Schramm 1995, 168–81);

(4) the prophet's (or party's) ethos aligns with that of the Ezekiel school of the Babylonian *golah* returnees versus the compromising group of Yehud remainees (e.g., Rom-Shiloni 2013, 133–36); and

(5) the perspective against the tendency to draw a clear line between two distinct groups (e.g., Japhet 1983, 103–25; Williamson 1989, 152; Smith 1995, 190–203).

Whichever reconstruction theory holds true, during and after the exile, the "we"-group evidently signified the penitent followers of the righteous prophet as the servant's disciples and Zion's offspring—whether the remainees or the returnees. Some scholars propose to identify this "we"-group as the Levites, or the levitical priests from the Diaspora remnant of the postexilic community, as opposed to the Jerusalem priests (Berges 2012c, 23–87). Rainer Albertz thus surmises that against the select few exilic leaders (descendants of David and Hilkiah) who pledged loyalty to Nabonidus and Belshazzar of Babylon, a prophetic circle from the former "temple singers" rooted in (Josianic) religious nationalism were inspired to mount an anti-Babylonian movement, and thus to choose a pro-Persian option (Albertz 2003b, 111). This hypothesis is in tune with the similar emphasis of

Chronicles concerning the leadership of the Levites: "The Chronicler gives surprising little attention to the high priests, who are often thought to have displaced the king in importance in the postexilic period" (Klein 2006, 45). Others, such as recently Stephen Cook, further divide leadership traditions into three (instead of two) groups in hierarchical order during the time of Isaiah 40–66, hence the final redactional stage: Zadokites (= Holiness School = Ezekiel); Aaronites (= Priestly Torah group = Deutero-Isaiah of chs. 40–66); and Levites (= Deuteronomy = Jeremiah). Parting company not only with the Zadokites but also with the Levites, this Aaronide Deutero-Isaiah group cherished the Priestly tradition and reconceptualized it for people in the exilic context. Rather than the conditional ("bilateral") covenant tradition upheld by the Levites, notable in Deuteronomy and Jeremiah, this Aaronide Deutero-Isaiah group took the perpetual, unconditional ("unilateral") covenant tradition of the "Priestly" Torah and reapplied its theology of YHWH's enduring commitment to the disheartened exiles (Cook 2015). This innovative study still needs to reconcile with the theory that identifies Deutero-Isaiah with the "Yahwistic" (J) strand of the Pentateuch (Van Seters 1992). Evidently, debate on these contending groups in schism will continue, as another complicating question is not only whether the Isaianic "we"-group refers to the Levites as opposed to the Zadokite priests but also whether the foreigners can be included as well (Paul 2012, 18–19, 448–49, 629–30).

Be that as it may, just like the anonymity of the servant's identity, it is fascinating to learn of this "we"-group. In Asian cultures, "we" can connote an entity that can blur societal boundaries. Whereas "I" tends to make its firm stance ("I think therefore I am") in the Western worldview, this non-individualistic or anti-individualistic tendency may offer an anthropological clue as to how to fathom this "we"-group. In other words, this "we"-group may not denote a fixed faction but instead a flexible, bending, and fleeing component with entry qualifications that may ever get narrower or wider: "We are now almost face to face with culture's double bind—a certain *slippage* or *splitting* between human artifice and culture's discursive agency" (Bhabha 1994, 196, emphasis added). Put another way, there should have been distinct entities or groups during the exilic and postexilic era—the righteous group and the wicked group. However, we should also keep in mind that, by being unspecified and anonymized, such ambiguity may caution readers that one can be a loyal member of the righteous group but can easily desert to the other, and vice versa, especially when it comes to the issue of power, greed, and survival.

Theologically and hermeneutically speaking, on the one hand, we should acknowledge our naiveté in claiming that we can distinguish the righteous from the wicked so easily and distinctively: "The outside is already inside."

'Over there' is right here. The enemy is us" (Miller 2007, 38). It is no wonder that Jesus' parable describes the need to wait until harvest time to be able to identify the wheat and the weeds (cf. Matt 13:24-30), let alone the fact that Jesus' traitor came out of his own twelve disciples (Matt 26:14-16). On the other hand, from the existential (and historical) locations of the marginalized and oppressed, especially those victimized in their aspiration to be righteous, their defiant condemnation against the wicked's overwhelming injustice would be as vivid as the shining stars at night. True prophets were so convinced that the outcry of the righteous, though dismantled and ridiculed, would ring loudly and clearly before God.

The second dichotomy is *light versus darkness*. Throughout the book of Isaiah, we find numerous occurrences of the recurring theme of light. Ronald E. Clements has presented significant studies on the theme of light as a main thread in Isaiah (1996 and 1997; see Dempsey 2012). It is indeed one of the main threads that connect many pieces of the book. A quick concordance check of the word "light" can evidence its numerous occurrences in crucial places throughout the book of Isaiah (e.g., 2:5; 5:20; 9:2 [MT 9:1]; 13:10; 30:26; 42:6; 45:7; 49:6; 50:10; 53:11; 58:10; 59:9; 60:1, 20). The opening call, "O house of Jacob, let us walk in the light of YHWH" (2:5), therefore provides an essential thematic thread that connects to the servant's task to be the "light to the nations" (42:6; 49:6) and then ultimately culminates in the divine everlasting Light that will arise and shine on both the exilic, colonized Judeans and all the nations and peoples (60:1, 3, 20).

Furthermore, notably, the language and imagery of light often occur with those of darkness. Among various motifs, in view of ancient Near Eastern texts and traditions, light connotes sun, salvation, justice, righteousness, and glory. Light in association with the theme of salvation then contrasts with darkness signifying the themes of bondage, sin, injustice, exile, and imprisonment (Hulster 2009, 213–28). Moreover, this dichotomous contrast between light and darkness also correlates with the capacities of seeing versus not seeing (blindness), hearing versus not hearing (deafness), and understanding versus hard-heartedness (obduracy). When criticizing recalcitrant leaders, the prophet describes them as being blind or as turning blind eyes to the truth. Contrarily, to the downtrodden people in the exilic setting, the message involves not only calling them blind and mute in sin and disappointment but especially also offering the hope of their seeing the light and even becoming the light to other nations and peoples.

Additionally, light is thematically linked to justice and righteousness. Thus, this motif functions to describe one of the key roles of the king. The king is supposed to reign with justice and righteousness, equity and fairness, in order to provide stability and peace. Ultimately, light, especially as a synonym for glory, depicts God: "Indeed, the final form of the book of Isaiah appears designed to persuade later generations of Jews that YHWH is indeed the true G-d of creation and that they should return to Jerusalem to acknowledge YHWH as the true sovereign of a restored Israel and Judah and the world at large" (Sweeney 2014, 674). Just as "glory" takes the representation of God into the post-biblical rabbinic era, so even within the postexilic time of Chronicles, scholars detect a tendency for "a marked preference for [God] over [YHWH] that must reflect something of the increasing reverence for the divine name itself" (Schniedewind 2003, 237). The light of God, as awe-inspiring and transcendent as the glory of God, can vanquish the unruly "kindlers of fire" (50:11), and at the same time immanently shine upon Zion and her devout pilgrims (60:19-20; cf. 2:2-4), with the result that all her people shall become righteous (60:21).

The third dichotomy is *human kingship versus divine kingship*. Within the realm of human kingship, there is a thematic contrast between good kings and bad kings. Since the people's request for a human king "like all the nations" (1 Sam 8:5), biblical texts have been ambiguous about the legitimacy and virtue of human kingship. In one place, YHWH has endorsed an unconditional, eternal promise for the Davidic dynasty (2 Sam 7:8-16). Yet, in another place, the divine promise is conditional, or conditionalized, upon the king's devout obedience (1 Kgs 3:14; 9:3-5; cf. Albertz 2003b, 294). Within this conundrum of virtues and vices of kings, the oracles of the prophets have vehemently chastised any abuse of power. Just as historians would evaluate good kings (Hezekiah) versus bad kings (Ahaz), so communities would reflect on true prophets versus false prophets. It is no wonder that most prophets' relationship with the ruling monarchs often went sour: "According to Jewish tradition, Isaiah was put to death by Hezekiah's evil son Manasseh, who sawed Isaiah in half after accusing him of being a false prophet (*b. Yev.* 49b; see also the pseudepigraphical work *The Martyrdom of Isaiah*)" (Sweeney 2014, 675).

In the study of Isaiah, besides the issues pertaining to good kings versus bad kings, one issue concerns the destiny of the Davidic monarchy. In Isaiah's firm belief in YHWH's grand and sure salvation of the people of Israel centered in Zion, how will the fallen dynasty fare? Questions in the post-monarchial (exilic and postexilic) era deal with the undeniable reality of the disappearing hope in the Davidic dynasty's final destiny. On the one hand, some scholars observe the tendency toward democratization, especially notable in Isaiah 55. As is widely accepted, the divine promise of eternal reign for David and his heirs (2 Sam 7) became democratized in the aftermath of the collapse of this dynasty so that the new covenant people would assume that role. This theological reconceptualization may have come in part due to a radical shift in embracing a foreign King Cyrus as a divinely anointed monarch, or due to the resolute perspective to return to Israel's old tradition before the times of monarchy, e.g., the times of patriarchy or of the judges (Albertz 2003b, 246–90). From this perspective, Judah's monarchy was a thing of the past, long gone with the fall of Jerusalem, and the collective community, with the leadership of the priests, would have to carry the legacy while charting a new path.

On the other hand, other scholars are not quite certain whether the book of Isaiah, as well as other exilic/postexilic literature, severed its hope in the Davidic monarchy (cf. Isa 11). Comparably, in his Chronicles study, Ralph Klein asks, "Did the Chronicler expect a restoration of the Davidic monarchy?" Citing H. G. M. Williamson, Klein posits that Chronicles "does see an abiding validity for the Davidic line, and that the building of the temple has confirmed, but not absorbed, this hope" (Klein 2006, 48). With similar reservations, J. Todd Hibbard ponders the end of hope for the Davidic dynasty: "Isa 55:3-5 is often described as 'democratizing' the Davidic kingship (which I doubt)" (2006, 91). Considering the scribes' location in a colonized environment, we may posit that perhaps such democratizing tendency may have arisen due to the necessity of secrecy (otherwise, any talk of another dynasty would be culpable to treason against Babylon or Persia). In this case, the book of Isaiah may have preserved "hidden transcripts" that would have furtively preserved the future of the Davidic lineage (cf. 2 Kgs 24:27-31; Jer 52:31-34). By "hidden transcripts," James C. Scott's groundbreaking definition is informative: "The hidden transcript is thus derivative in the sense that it consists of those offstage speeches, gestures, and practices that confirm, contradict, or inflect what appears in the public transcript" (1990, 4–5). At the least, we should note that there is a sense of open-endedness to this issue (Goldingay and Payne 2006b, 371–73), as even the Qumran literature preserves a tradition of two messiahs.

Eventually, however, the book of Isaiah is unequivocal concerning the issue of the identity of the true king of the universe. It is none other than YHWH God whose rule supplants any powers or threats of human kings (cf. 2:9-22). All human kings are mortal (2:22), including not only Israelite and Judean kings but also Assyrian, Egyptian, Babylonian, and Persian kings (Isa 13–14; 19–20; 45:1-5), who are like grass that withers and flower that fades (40:7). Yet the word of YHWH the King shall stand forever (40:8; cf. 33:22; 52:7).

The fourth tension concerns *universalism versus particularism.* One question with regard to this open-ended debate is, "How multicultural was ancient Israel in the ancient Near East?" Without doubt, there was no Internet and Wi-Fi for blazing fast communications across the globe. Villages, cities, and countries must have been more insulated from one another. Ironically, however, because of frequent wars, refugees, and forced migrations, and especially the location of the tiny Levant as a bridge connecting surrounding empires and continents, we read numerous words and ideas about people outside Israel. Terms include "nations," "peoples," "coastlands," "islands," "foreigners," and so on. Israel's international contacts seemed to have been constant and mutual.

Admittedly, oftentimes these nations were the thorny rivals that would easily stand in the way of Israel's stability. Yet, at other times, Isaiah labels them as the divine instrument to chastise Israel's misbehaviors. Still, in most cases, Israel strives to survive despite the incessant bullying of the daunting empires—Egypt, Assyria, Babylon, and Persia. From the perspective of the underdog Israel, events in this global arena would have had virtually everything to do with Israel's surviving and thriving. They would have had no choice but to cope with neighboring countries. In other words, whenever we encounter biblical records concerning Israel's or Judah's king making an alliance with some empire, we ought to keep in mind the irrefutable power imbalance between the (weak) vassal and the (dominant) suzerain. Likewise, they would have had to deal with foreigners both within and outside the land of Israel. Whether foes or friends, enemies or allies, Israel had to wrestle in interactions with many of them.

Thus, we should ask another pertinent question: "Does the book of Isaiah uphold and promote universalism or particularism?" Put differently, "Did the religious perspectives of the prophet and his disciples already have in mind the proselytization of people of other ethnicities or nationalities — a norm in later emerging Judaism?" In addition to numerous scholarly works on this issue, the following quotes may provide indication of where scholars stand at present:

> As Kaminsky and Stewart rightly observe, there is "a greater receptivity to the inclusion of some Gentiles within the elect group [as] appears even within the late texts of Third Isaiah in chapters 56 and 66" . . . . We should not assume, however, that the history of the book's development maps in any simple way on to a spectrum between particularism and universalism, as though the book moves from a narrow particularism to an all-embracing universalism. The history of the book's composition, and the development

of Israelite religion in general, is far more complex. To speak of particularism making way to universalism is to offer an algebraic solution when
only calculus will do. (MacDonald 2011, 55, 61)

Goldingay may be correct, however, in claiming that this tension [between
nationalism and universalism] represents "a false antithesis" and that these
two emphases are better understood as complementary. (Schultz 2009,
143; cf. Goldingay 2001, 143, 264)

Accordingly, at stake in this issue of "false antithesis" may be not so much
universalism versus particularism per se, but rather the social, ethnic,
economic, political, and ultimately theological aspects of "inclusivity" when
it comes to a group's self-identity and definition with other groups. In other
words, as would later become a full-blown issue in the debates of Second
Temple Judaism, the redactors and immediate audiences of the book of
Isaiah may already have had to wrestle with this issue of identity: "What are
the true Jews?"

A prime example of this in-group versus out-group tension appears in
the books of Ezra and Nehemiah. Contemporary scholars, especially Christians, tend to perceive Ezra-Nehemiah's reform attitude as exclusive in a
quite negative way. Although such a notion of xenophobic exclusivity may
be extant in this tradition, we must keep in mind that the people of Ezra-
Nehemiah, whether the Yehud remainees or (more likely) the *golah* returnees,
were a powerless, vulnerable minority under the colonial dominance of giant
empires.

With these disclaimers about our way-too-quick or way-too-one-sided
value judgment, we note that scholars have compared Ezra-Nehemiah with
Chronicles regarding this issue. Here the theology of Chronicles, in distinction from that of Ezra-Nehemiah (cf. Ezra 4:1-5; Neh 2:19; 4:1-9; 6:1-14),
may offer concepts similar to those in the book of Isaiah. Notably, even in
the genealogy section (1 Chr 1–9), Chronicles consistently adheres to a more
inclusive attitude, emphasizing that "all Israel"—both north and south—
descends from the patriarch Jacob (Klein 2006, 46; cf. Williamson 1977).
In fact, Sara Japhet further asserts, "According to the Chronicler's portrayal,
there are no Gentiles in the land of Israel; all its dwellers are 'Israel,' either
through their affiliation with the tribes or as the attached 'sojourners'" (1989,
46).

Turning back to read Isaiah, we evidently find a tension and an ambiguity. At one point, Isaiah is as exclusive as other books, not only against
tyrannical empires and oppressors but also toward foreigners in general.

Some scholars thus read Isaiah 60–62 as expressing a theme of exclusivity that is countered by 56 and 66, which express themes of inclusivity (Smith 1995, 198–99). These scholars interpret even the foreign nations of Isaiah 56 as the Israelite Diaspora among foreign nations. Likewise, those from all nations who are to serve as priests and Levites in Isaiah 66 (66:20-21) are in fact only the Judean families and clans returning from many nations. At another point, however, Isaiah is radically inclusive, no matter how idealistic it may seem (e.g., 2:2-4; 11:6-9; 44:28–45:1)—hence the (in)famous universalism of the book of Isaiah (Albertz 2003b, 138; Paul 2012).

Caught in this impasse, it seems that many, if not all, portions of the book of Isaiah do suggest "inclusive" attitudes, perspectives, and theologies toward the other. Nevertheless, other pertinent questions may be equally important, although difficult to definitively answer as well: To what extent, for what purpose, and from whose sociopolitical location does the Isaianic group or school promote inclusivism? Are they presenting one monolithic perspective? Did they compile contending traditions and beliefs into one composite collection? Were they inspired by the inclusive ideal, as they themselves had to endure hardship as a disenfranchised minority under their imperial overlords (cf. Exod 22:21 [MT 22:20]; Lev 19:33-34; Deut 23:7)? Were they pressured to sell this ideal in order to appease their imperial superiors, as the latter were only interested in levying taxes on the colonized inferiors in whatever communal identity or boundary these subjects would form?

For this open-ended debate, recurring anonymity may provide a clue, though not an answer by any means. Throughout the book of Isaiah, the Assyrian king, the Babylonian king, or the pharaoh tend to be anonymous, especially in the oracles about/against the nations section. There are exceptions to this as well. More important, Judean kings and heroes tend to be anonymous: "the stump of Jesse," the servant of YHWH, and so on. Whomever the prophet-poet may have intended in these figures, they became hidden in the name of anonymity: suppose a news report that reads, "Yesterday person 'A' went into the downtown center of the well-known city 'B,' where this person along with other followers proclaimed that their hero 'C,' inspired by God, will be coming to rescue them and many others over against the powerful yet abusive and cruel 'D'-leaders." As the text has its own life, such anonymous signifiers can not only prevent readers from finding out the detailed meanings but can also provide clues, like hidden transcripts, that can become applicable to new identities, inspire new insights, and thereby redefine their in-groups versus out-groups in ever-changing needs, situations, and even purposes.

The fifth dichotomy deals with the reciprocal correlations of *Zion-Jerusalem versus Jacob-Israel*. From the opening chapters (Isa 1–2) to the concluding ones (Isa 65–66), these identities tend to be mutually comparative and interdependent. In some texts, however, they seem to refer to two isolated or different entities. In fact, scholars do not agree as to whom or what "Jacob" refers and "Israel" signifies, especially in the book of Isaiah. It is not clear whether they—Jacob and Israel—refer to the same or different referents. Does "Jacob" refer to northern Israel (much the same way Ephraim or Samaria has functioned), especially in Isaiah 1–39, in contrast with southern Judah (one of the twelve sons of *Jacob*), to Zion-Jerusalem? Does Jacob symbolize one group (e.g., minority underclass) of the exilic community in distinction with Israel as another group in Babylon (e.g., the assimilated upper class; cf. Ahn 2011, 195–205)? Does Jacob function, in contrast, as in Chronicles, to allude to the patriarch from whom all the twelve tribes came, thereby signifying the unified pan-Israel of both north and south? Similarly, does "Israel" denote northern Israel over against southern Judah? Alternatively, does Israel eventually signify the twelve tribes, as the symbolic name change from Jacob may imply (Gen 32:13-32; cf. Kratz 2006; 2012)?

In some texts, we find similar distinctions, such as the "house of Jacob," the "remnant of Israel," the "house of David," and the like. It seems plausible that at an earlier compositional stage, these terms may have meant northern Israel and southern Judah. In the process of transmission amid the two nations' historical upheaval all the way down to their fall, exile, and beyond, however, many of these designations have become archaized code-names or symbols. On the one hand, these terms contain ancient history, tradition, and legacy. On the other hand, in the context of the final form of the text and beyond, they may mean something else.

For example, Jerusalem-Zion too may originally have had different names (cf. 2 Sam 5:6-9; 1 Kgs 8:1). This textual tradition seems to portray Zion as the city of David, as a district or province of the larger city Jerusalem. Likewise, if Jerusalem would mean an administrative district, Zion would then denote a cultic center. Then, at some point in Israel's history, the two names became synonyms, Zion-Jerusalem. Similarly, there are two covenant traditions in the Hebrew Bible: (conditional, Mosaic) Sinai covenant versus (unconditional, Davidic) Zion theology. Likewise, in the book of Isaiah, whereas this city could have depicted a place of power and gluttony of the elite leaders over against the poor peasants, ultimately it assumed the role of a symbol of divine protection, enduring covenant, and pilgrimage for both exilic/postexilic Israelites and all nations. By the same token, although more ambivalently, Jacob-Israel may have gone through semantic and symbolic changes. In the first half of the book of Isaiah, the terms "Jacob" and "Israel" often refer to northern Israel (9:8-9 [MT 9:7-8]; 10:20; 14:1; 27:6). Within Isaiah 40–66, this word pair occurs only in chapters 40–48, with the exception of 49:5-6.

In light of these observations concerning the interrelationship between the names Jacob-Israel and the names Zion-Jerusalem as two main threads, at least two interpretive options are possible. On the one hand, Jacob-Israel and Zion-Jerusalem may signify an exclusive redefinition of "true Israel" as especially those from the Babylonian *golah* community:

> It seems that Williamson perceived what I also recognize as Deutero-Isaiah's reidentification of the (entire) community of Babylonian Exiles as the exclusive new Israel. Thus, indeed, the concept of Israel has gone through a transition in Deutero-Isaiah, a transition that has reconceived the (entire) community of Babylonian Exiles (and Repatriates) as the "true Israel." (Rom-Shiloni 2013, 106)

Insofar as Zion-Jerusalem represents the capital of southern Judah (as opposed to Samaria, the capital of northern Israel), it may connote those who were exiled, especially the nobles, the royal and priestly upper class of the Jerusalemite hegemony during the monarchy.

On the other hand, however, Jacob-Israel and Zion-Jerusalem may inclusively symbolize complementary unity in the impending new era. Ironically, this ideal of a harmonious unity in a glorious future may be rooted in the divergent traditions and connotations of the terms, Jacob-Israel versus Zion-Jerusalem. Also, in the second half of the book of Isaiah, "within Isaiah 40–55 the use appears to be most quite stereotypical but its distribution shows that there is also a conscious shift at 49:1-6 from Jacob to Zion" (Williamson 2014, 228). Against this likely difference and even tension, we find an interesting pattern: sequential exchange between (servant) Jacob-Israel and (daughter) Zion, in an alternating format. As much as distinctions are noticeable, therefore, the scribal intention to put these two names as threads side by side is significant.

In the aftermath of the fall of Jerusalem and Judah, the prophet presents two laments—that of the (servant) Jacob-Israel in 49:1-13 and that of the (daughter) Zion in 49:14-26. These two complaints depict the distances and gaps between these two entities. Yet, at the same time, that these two are put together and occur in alternating fashion may signal the authorial hope for a cooperative, mutual solidarity of the two divergent groups—both male and female, both north and south, or both the disciples of the servant and the offspring of Zion. Not to be qualified by genealogy, ethnicity, or local origin (remainees or returnees), but rather by their ethical and religious adherence to YHWH's Torah (2:2-4) as well as justice and righteousness with true penitence (56:1; 57:15; 66:2), these common descendants of Abraham and Sarah (51:2) may together construct the interpretive thread for the ideals of unity, solidarity, and peace, in the midst of the ever-present schisms, tensions, and enmities among the sisters and brothers.

Isaiah's Vision about Judah and Jerusalem (First Branch of the Lampstand)

Isaiah 1–12

This initial section has two introductions (chs. 1–2) to the entire book of Isaiah, much the same way Genesis 1–2 and Psalms 1–2 present dual introductions to the Torah and the Psalter respectively (Mays 1994, 42–44). The double overture (Isa 1–2) extends to the illustrations of this overture in the divine accusation against Jerusalem's male and female leaders (Isa 3–4).

Next, the song of a vineyard (5:1-7) and the song of thanksgiving (12:1-6) bracket the subsequent segment. It contains, first of all, an enclosure of two series of woe-oracles against the wicked leaders, domestically (5:8-30), and the woe-oracle against Assyria, internationally (10:5-34). The unique phrase, "For all this his anger has not turned away, and his hand is stretched out still" (5:25; 9:11, 16, 20 [MT 9:10, 17, 21]; 10:4), further brackets this internal segment.

Inside these woe-oracles (chs. 5 and 10) and the unique catchphrases (chs. 5 and 9) lies the core that contains narrative reports about the prophet Isaiah, King Ahaz, and three children (chs. 6–8). Tradition-historically, this unit, called the "Isaiah Memoir" (*Denkschrift*), is considered to contain precise historical reports. In the literary form, this unit comprises the accounts in the first-person speech (chs. 6 and 8), which together sandwich the account in the third-person speech (ch. 7). Following the call of the prophet in the temple (ch. 6), readers hear the story of the conflict between Ahaz, king of Judah, and formidable kings in Judah's neighborhood (chs. 7–8). Yet there is another contention, i.e., between King Ahaz and the three little children (Shear-jashub, Immanuel, and Maher-shalal-hash-baz), as the latter function as signs for messages of warning and hope. Ultimately, the tension stands between the human king, who is a mere mortal, and the divine King, who is the creator and ruler of the world.

Resolutions of this tension culminate in the manifold oracles that echo and recapitulate key catchphrases of the earlier framing markers. First, the prophet proclaims the divine plan of yet another "child" (like the three little children), a righteous prince of peace in the line of David's dynasty (9:1-7). Next, this plan also accompanies divine punishment for the sins of Yʜᴡʜ's people, including Ephraim and Manasseh (9:8–10:4)—marked by key catchphrases that form a bracket with 5:25. Furthermore, the woe-oracle that focuses on and condemns the king of Assyria (10:5-34; cf. 10:1) connects a larger inclusio with the six woe-oracles in 5:8-24. Finally, this section concludes with the announcement of the ideal future world (ch. 11) and the song of thanksgiving (ch. 12), demarcated by the oracles about/against the nations (Isa 13–23) as another section.

Structure of Isaiah 1–12
The Twofold Overture to the Scroll of Isaiah, 1:1–2:22
Purging and Transformation of Jerusalem, 3:1–4:6
Signs and Warnings for the King and People of Judah, 5:1–10:34
An Ideal Future Kingdom, Starting from the Stump of Jesse, 11:1-16
A Song of Thanksgiving, 11:1-16

The Twofold Overture to the Scroll of Isaiah, 1:1–2:22

The primary addressees of this section are the people of Judah and Jerusalem, as the recurring superscriptions (1:1 and 2:1) indicate. Yet a bulk of this section also addresses the people of Israel, the "house of Jacob," whose fate is intricately intertwined with that of Judah and Jerusalem. The preposition ('al) in both superscriptions denotes "about" or "against" Judah and Jerusalem (cf. 13:1). In other words, even though the superscriptions hint that these oracles are proclaimed for the sake of ("about") Judah and Jerusalem first and foremost, the contents involve vehement sociopolitical and religious criticisms directed toward ("against") Judah and Jerusalem. The four kings of Judah likewise imply that all these oracles are set against the very tangible, concrete political arenas of Judah's turbulent history.

The two visions (1:1; 2:1) further present thematic introductions to the entire book of Isaiah. Just as Genesis 1–2 introduces not only the Pentateuch (Torah) but also the entire Bible with the dual theme of Yʜᴡʜ's majestic transcendence (Gen 1) and meek immanence (Gen 2), so recent scholars observe that Psalms 1–2 function as a two-part introduction to the whole Psalter, offering key themes of the Torah instruction for righteous happiness (Ps 1) and Yʜᴡʜ's reign over the human world (Ps 2; deClaissé-Walford, Jacobson, and Tanner 2014, 56–57). Similarly, the two chapters introduce two key themes for the entire book of Isaiah: (a) the divine pathos in judgment and mercy toward Yʜᴡʜ's people (Isa 1) and (b) the humiliation of humankind versus the exaltation of Yʜᴡʜ, the true King (Isa 2).

Thesis One: Admonitions for Justice via Divine Mercy, 1:1-31

Chapter 1 contains three main subunits, as indicated by the clues of literary genres and persons addressed. Verses 1-9 address Israel, "*my* people," although they also portray the vulnerable plight of daughter Zion. The call to heavens and earth to "hear" (*shimeʻu*) in v. 2 envisions a courtroom setting. Verses 10-20 target the powerful rulers of Zion, addressed in the second-person masculine plural ("you"), whom the prophet as the plaintiff accuses and admonishes (interestingly, the oracles in Isa 65 similarly accuse the wicked as "you" [pl.] versus the righteous as "*my* servants"). The call to "hear" (*shimeʻu*) in v. 10 denounces the unceasing hypocrisy and recalcitrance of Jerusalem's religious and political leaders. Verses 21-31 finally turn to Zion, addressed in the second-person feminine singular ("you"), whose wonton sinfulness YHWH the judge exposes, along with the divine promise of her eventual restoration. Commonly considered a postexilic expansion, at the end of this oracle (vv. 27-31), YHWH assures redemption for the penitent in Zion, as opposed to reprobate sinners ("you") whom God will ultimately punish.

Isaiah 1:2-9 starts an opening indictment. The divine call to heavens and earth as witnesses in v. 2 is a unique feature that occurs elsewhere only in Deuteronomy 32:1 (Kim 2004). The Psalter starts with the declaration of the happiness of the righteous (Ps 1:1, "Happy are those"), as if echoing the ending part of the Torah (Deut 33:29, "Happy are you, O Israel"). Similarly, Isaiah 1:2 addresses both heavens and earth as if echoing both the beginning (Gen 1:1) and the concluding part (Deut 32:1) of the Torah. This creator reared the children of Israel, but they have transgressed against YHWH.

Verse 3 identifies YHWH's children as Israel, "my people." Later on, the prophet contrasts Judah's stubborn grown-up kings and leaders with obedient children—infants and youths—who learn and obey "good" faster (cf. 7:3, 15-16; 8:3-4; 9:6-7 [MT 9:5-6]; 11:6, 8). But here, the prophet likens the people of Israel to egotistical children (cf. v. 4; 3:4; 40:30). They are contrasted with the basic domestic animals (ox and donkey), who like Balaam's donkey (Num 22:21-35) know their owner. Contrarily, Israel neither knows nor understands its owner. Whereas, in Psalm 32:9, animals like horse and mule that lack understanding need to be secured, now, ironically, human beings so ignorantly—or rather, stubbornly—behave in uncontrolled and unruly ways. It is as though the prophet shames such stubborn human beings: when it comes to ethical integrity and socio-religious conscience, you people are worse than animals! Israel's obduracy lays a thematic foundation for the entire book of Isaiah, especially with the catchwords, "knowing" and "understanding" (e.g., 6:9; cf. Gen 2:17; 3:22). As Patricia Tull observes, "Isaiah's vision points toward one of the book's prevailing themes: the human inability to see what God wants seen" (2010, 50).

Verses 4-6 then present shocking metaphors. The invocation of "woe" ("woe to a sinful nation") initiates this subunit. It lists numerous sins of Israel, and then express name-calling follows: "sinful nation, people laden with iniquity, offspring who do evil, children who deal corruptly (lit., 'sons of corruption')" (v. 4). That the people of Israel who forsake YHWH have become "strangers" is significant because of the issues of insider-outsider tensions that will surface toward the end of the book of Isaiah. Yet, whereas those who have "rejected the Torah of YHWH of the army and spurned the word of the Holy One of Israel" (5:24; one of the woe-oracles in Isa 5) target the privileged segments of the population, here those who have "abandoned YHWH and spurned the Holy One of Israel" refers to the entire people (Williamson 1997, 270–71).

The sins of Israel result in sickness and disease in the "whole head" and the "whole heart" in v. 5. Verse 6 graphically describes the metaphors of sin's contaminating effects as "bruises," "sores" (cf. 53:5), and "raw wounds." Modern psychologists tend to consider addiction as a form of disease: "[Dependence] is a more scientific and clinically accurate term for addiction. It describes the brain disease associated with impaired control over drug use" (Erickson 2007, 244). This ancient oracle perceptively diagnoses Israel's propensity to sin as a sickness with mortal wounds that are extremely difficult to cure.

Verses 7-9 pick up the metaphors of disease but shift into the settings of military invasion. While sinful Israel has become strangers (v. 4), land and cities throughout Israel are burned and devoured (lit., "eaten"; cf. 1:20) by the strangers (v. 7). Key phrases closely reverberate with those of the Assyrian royal inscriptions:

> Tiglath-pileser I/Sargon II: The city devastated, destroyed, burned with fire, consumed it; Isa 1:7: Your country is a desolation; Your cities burned with fire; Your land, in your very presence, Aliens consume it. (Machinist 1983, 724)

The unique consecutive expressions—"desolation . . . burned with fire . . . consume it"—evidence the Isaianic text's explicit adoption of the well-known Neo-Assyrian idiom, thereby heightening the historical reality and military urgency of the prophetic warning. Now only Jerusalem, daughter Zion, is left like "a hut in a cucumber field" (v. 8). The expressions "booth" and "hut" may mirror the imagery of Zion's destruction like a "garden" in Lamentations

2:6—common expressions in the Mesopotamian laments of a deity's turning a magnificent temple into a dilapidated hut (Dobbs-Allsopp 1993, 68–70). Likewise, in the records of the Assyrian king Sennacherib's siege warfare, one of the battle tactics was the destruction of crops. Roy Melugin offers the observation that "the food and eating imagery holds this composition together" (2009, 9); the devouring of food and drink both concretizes the devastating effects of warfare and magnifies the threats of the giant empire (Abernethy 2014, 31–33). Although scholars have proposed various historical backgrounds for this text, Sennacherib's assault on Judah in 701 BCE provides a momentous setting for Zion's vulnerable fate, on the verge of annihilation, besieged "like a bird in a cage" by these strangers, i.e., the Assyrians (Sweeney 1996, 77; Blenkinsopp 2000a, 193).

Regardless of the various contexts, this subunit provides notable literary and thematic cues in light of the speakers and addressees. Verses 2-4 describe Israel in the third-person plural form ("they"). Next, vv. 5-8 address these corrupt addressees in the second-person masculine plural ("you"). Then, in v. 9, the speaker announces the divine rescue of a few survivors in the first-person plural ("we"). This "we"-group—the righteous and penitent remnants, whom Ulrich Berges calls a "model [postexilic] remnant community" (2012a, 40, 52; cf. Hobson 2013, 202—"Yehud group")—will play significant roles in the theological development throughout the book of Isaiah (e.g., 7:14; 8:10; 53:1-6; cf. 65:21-25; 66:2). In its immediate context, the correlation of vv. 8-9 portrays panoramic views of the destruction of the land that reaches toward Zion. As W. A. M. Beuken elucidates, "v. 8 depicts the daughter of Zion *ad extra* as a besieged city in a devastated land, v. 9 portrays her *ad intra* as a town in which only a few survivors are found" (2004a, 462). Zion stands as a defenseless survivor, if not by divine mercy (cf. Lam 4:6).

Isaiah 1:10-20 then specifies the divine litigation against the leaders of Judah—addressed in the second-person masculine plural—concerning the topics of ritual (vv. 11-15), righteousness (vv. 16-17), and repentance (vv. 18-20). The same imperative verbs ("hear" and "give ear") in both v. 2 and v. 10 open their subsequent subunits, while "Sodom" and "Gomorrah" in v. 10 link to the same words in v. 9 (Williamson 1997, 266). Whereas the prophet calls heavens and earth to "hear" and "give ear" in v. 2, now the call to "hear" and "give ear" targets the "rulers of Sodom" and the "people of Gomorrah" in v. 10. The divine accusation against these evildoers in direct address (the second-person masculine plural "you") will recur later in the book of Isaiah in the accusation against "you" (pl.) versus "my servants" (cf. 65:13-15). Analogous to the name-calling in v. 4, we hear comparable expressions of insult against the whole population but against the powers that be of Jerusalem in particular. Who of aristocratic privilege in the ancient Israelite society would like to have been called the "rulers of Sodom" and the "people of Gomorrah"? Even in today' world, no sane leaders would want to be likened to cruel dictators or tyrants of the past. It thus speaks volumes to hear them labeled with no other place than Sodom and Gomorrah: "God takes a particular interest in the leadership" (Seitz 1993, 33; cf. v. 23).

Verses 11-15 concern a ritual that the people outright abused. YHWH's abject denial and negative reactions are startling. Against the ancient Near Eastern viewpoint of sacrifices as human beings' "feeding gods," concerning the multitude of sacrifices, YHWH expresses utter distaste, "I am fed up" (v. 11): "If these meals were meant to signify fellowship with YHWH, YHWH is excusing himself from the table" (Abernethy 2014, 34–36; cf. Williamson 2006, 74). Offerings that are supposed to produce a pleasing aroma to YHWH (Lev 2:9) are called "worthlessness" and an "abomination" (v. 13). Echoing the divine pathos against empty ritual without justice in Amos 5:21-23, our text declares that YHWH's "soul hates" new moon and festival practices (v. 14). Contrary to the prophet's call to listen to YHWH's "instruction" (*torah*) in v. 10, YHWH considers these sinners' rituals a "burden" (*torakh*, v. 14). Indeed, YHWH has become sick and tired of them. Israel's prayers are callous, and the people's lifted hands only expose the bloodstains of cruelty. According to the Mesopotamian ritual-prayers of šuilla (lifting of the hand[s]), through the hand-lifting gesture "the superior status of deities over humans was expressed in relative spatial terms [and] . . . the hand-lifting of the human was imagined to be reciprocated by the deity" (Frechette 2012, 15, 88; cf. Esth 5:2). In contrast, YHWH reacts to these prayers by becoming obdurate toward Israel: "I will hide my eyes . . . I will not listen" (v. 15).

Verses 16-17 concern righteousness and justice, a central issue regarding the laws and instructions of YHWH. If YHWH will not accept wrongful rituals, what can the people do to receive God's acceptance? Almost like the Decalogue, this subunit provides nine verbal imperatives that center on two phrases in the middle: "stop evil" and "learn good" (vv. 16-17; cf. Amos 5:14-15; Prov 8:13). Stopping evil is the prerequisite for cleansing (v. 16), and defending the orphan and fighting for the widow exemplify learning good (v. 17).

Verses 18-20 concern repentance and divine mercy. Despite the anticipated verdict of doom, YHWH casts a hint of divine mercy. Divine pathos with warnings of judgment (vv. 14-15) paradoxically accompanies a solemn offer of divine mercy, as though God like a parent repeats the ultimatum: okay, this is really the final chance for you! Sins that are irreparable and irrevocable can be forgiven, but only on conditional terms, quite like the blessing and curse covenants in Deuteronomy (v. 18). If the people do good (v. 17), they are promised to eat the good of the land (v. 19). But if they refuse to obey, they will be eaten by the sword (v 20; cf. 1 Kgs 22:38; 2 Kgs 10:36; Ps 53:4 [MT 53:5]). This association of food and land mirrors the Assyrian ideology that the king owns these resources. This oracle thus underscores the polemic that YHWH, not the imperial king, is in fact the supreme owner of land and crops (Abernethy 2014, 44–45). Put differently, the prophet appeals to the people's repentance not through abstract doctrines but through the daily sustenance of eating. In a nutshell, according to Andrew Abernethy's study on the thematic function of food in Isaiah, vv. 19-20 project a key introductory theme for "the larger schema of envisioning Zion's judgment and restoration": the divine provision of food for the obedient (v. 19) and the divine deprivation of food for the disobedient (v. 20; Abernethy 2014, 91). These accusations against the sin-laden people (also called "rulers of Sodom" in the second-person masculine plural, "you")—bracketed by the framing catchphrase, "for the [mouth of] YHWH has spoken" in v. 2 and v. 20—now transition to the accusations against Zion (addressed in the second-person feminine singular, "you"; cf. 1:1, 8).

Isaiah 1:21-31 focuses its final attention on Zion. Similar to the litigation against Israel (1:10-20), it is a form of prophetic judgment speech: "an indictment [vv. 21-23] followed by 'therefore' with an extended messenger formula [v. 24a], and then the announcement of judgment [vv. 24b-25]" (Williamson 2003, 425). Thus, this subunit uncovers Zion's socio-ethical fornication (vv. 21-23). Just as Israel is admonished to turn away from evil and learn good, Zion's cleansing will require painful smelting and refurbishing (vv. 24-26). Afterwards, in the restored Zion, the righteous, penitent ones will receive redemption, but the wicked rebels will perish.

Verses 21-23 deliver the indictment in a lament form describing how Zion failed to obey YHWH's instructions. Reminiscent of Israel's wayward wife in Hosea (Hos 2:7; 3:3; 4:13-15; cf. Jer 13:27), the comely Lady Zion played the whore and her justice and righteousness have turned to murder (v 21; cf. Lam 1:1). Sharon Moughtin-Mumby observes a subtle word play on the verb "to lodge" (*lin*), which may be suggestive of spending the night (cf. Song 1:13). This sexual innuendo hints that Jerusalem outright changes her partner from "righteousness" (singular) to "murderers" (plural). At the same time, Zion's "prostitution" here has a far-reaching connotation, more than infidelity, that points to socioeconomic decline and political perversion of justice (Moughtin-Mumby 2008, 118–20; Williamson 2006, 136). Thus, essential export goods of Israel's economy (wine, grain, olive oil), as well as silver and gold, have become diluted and polluted (v 22). Royal officials, who neither "defend the orphan" nor "fight for the widow" (v 23; cf. v. 17), championed corruption. According to F. W. Dobbs-Allsopp, resonant with the Mesopotamian city laments, the prophet here "utilizes the reversal motif, except here the imagery appears to depict Israel's sin rather than the chaos which results from the city's destruction" (Dobbs-Allsopp 1993, 151).

Verses 24-26 pronounce the sentence of divine judgment, portraying the process of drastic cleansing. The society is so corrupt that YHWH's enemies are amid those oppressors; the enemies are within (v. 24). Against the hypocritical worshipers who merely extend their hands (v. 15), now YHWH will stretch the divine hand against Zion (v. 25). Silver that has become dross (v. 22) will now be smelted away (v. 25). Through YHWH's reformulation, Zion in the upcoming bright future will have judges who actually practice justice (v. 26; cf. v 21). Only afterwards will Zion, which once accommodated "righteousness" and was named the "faithful city" (v. 21), regain her reputation as the "city of righteousness, faithful city" (v. 26)—note the inclusio of vv. 21-26 by the bracketing catchwords.

Verses 27-31 wrap up the entire chapter by adding a thematic summary that echoes Psalm 1. The announcement of the dichotomy between the righteous (v. 27) and the wicked (vv. 28-31) now delineates the promise and process of Zion's renewal (vv. 24-26). The righteous will be found among the "repentant ones" in Zion (v. 27). In contrast, the wicked, identified as the rebellious ones (*pasha'*, cf. v. 2) alongside the sinners (*hata'*) and the forsakers (*'azab*) of YHWH (cf. v 4), shall all perish (v. 28).

Verses 29-31 address the wicked predominantly in the second-person masculine plural ("you" except "they" in v. 31). This makes a sharp contrast with vv. 21-26, which address Zion in the second-person feminine singular ("you" except "she" in v. 21). It is as though the prosecuting attorney turns from the witnesses now directly to the defendant, the wicked, as vv. 29-31 function as "an explication of the fate of the sinners" of v. 28 (Sweeney 1996, 65). Likewise, in vv. 29-31, these rebels and sinners anticipate the wicked who will later receive YHWH's condemnation in the second-person masculine plural ("you") over against YHWH's faithful "servants" in 65:13-15. Furthermore, the description of these wicked as "an oak whose leaf withers," "without water" (v. 30), echoes the opposite expression of the righteous in Psalm 1, which depicts the righteous as "a tree planted by streams of water" whose "leaf does not wither" (Ps 1:3). Overall, readers may wonder whether this prophetic book is hopeful or tragic (imagine a movie with a happy or sad ending). Isaiah 1 as an overture casts a note of hope, especially for the repentant and righteous, but the overall tone has explicit refrains of the undeniably impending exile.

Thesis Two: Visions for a Whole New World—Human Hubris versus Divine Exaltation, 2:1-22

Following the theme of divine pathos expressed in the accusatory litigations and call for repentance addressed to Israel and Zion (Isa 1), now Isaiah 2, as the flipside of a twofold overture, presents the theme of human lowliness versus divine loftiness. The scene expands from the specific locales of Israel to the universal horizons of nations and peoples to embrace all mortals and nature in general.

Yet, at the same time, the focal point remains consistently rooted in Zion, the mountain of the house of YHWH (e.g., 1:8, 21-31; 2:2-4). Thus, in a narrow sense, Isaiah 2 points out the contrast between Zion's glorious future (2:2-4) and Jacob's sinful debasement (2:5-8). Ultimately, however, Isaiah 2 highlights the contrast between all mortals, who should remain humble, and YHWH, who alone should be exalted (2:9-22). Read together, we find a roughly symmetrical match in terms of targeted addressees and their genders:

1:1-20—Israel and its leaders, addressed as "you" (2mp)
   1:21-31—Zion, addressed as "you" (2fs; except 1:27-31)
   2:1-4—Zion, purified and respected
2:5-22—Jacob and its house, humbled of haughtiness

Isaiah 2:2-4 (cf. Mic 4:1-5; Sweeney 2001; Joel 3:10 [MT 4:10]; Nogalski 2011, 247), introduced by the second superscription (2:1; cf. 1:1), pronounces a vision of a new world set out by the futuristic expression, "in later days" (v. 2). Just as Zion shall be the top mountain above other lower hills, "analogous to the temples and oracle loci of other gods throughout the world," so YHWH shall take over the highest place surpassing any other deities or powers (Groenewald 2012, 60). Following the divine purging of Zion's sinfulness (1:21-31), this renewed Zion shall inspire the pilgrimage of all the nations (2:1-4).

Key intertextual allusions construct this vision. First, the notion that all nations "stream" (*nahar*) to Zion (v. 2) may allude to Genesis 2:10, where "a river (*nahar*)" flows out of Eden. Just as four rivers flow out of Eden (Gen 2:11-14), now nations and peoples shall return to the Eden-like Zion. Likewise, the river "flowing forth" (*yatsaʾ*) further alludes to the constantly flowing living waters from the temple threshold in Ezekiel's vision of the new temple (v. 3; cf. Ezek 47:1, 8, 12; Groenewald 2012, 60–61). This new Jerusalem shall have ever-flowing waters (cf. 12:3), with the Torah firmly rooted as its foundation.

Second, the motif of nations and peoples marching toward Zion may allude to Psalm 2:1-3, which depicts the tumultuous commotion of nations and peoples against YHWH. Contrary to their vain plot to march against YHWH in Psalm 2 (cf. Isa 36:1), here their journey will constitute a pilgrimage up to Mount Zion (v. 3; cf. Ps 24:3; Ezra 1:3; 2 Chr 36:23) to learn YHWH's ways. Whereas the king in Zion is said to "break" and "dash" the conspiring nations in Psalm 2:9, now the nations "shall beat *their* swords into plow-shares, and their spears into pruning hooks" (v. 4). Similarly, Patricia Tull observes intertextual contrasts with select psalms of Zion: "Whereas in the psalmic tradition [e.g., Psalm 46] it is the tribes of Israel who make pilgrimage to Jerusalem, while the nations come only to attack, here it is the nations themselves coming to be instructed by God" (2010, 85). Thematically, in relation to the servant's task to "bring forth justice to the nation," Alphonso Groenewald comments, "The [servant] brings forth justice to the peoples [Isa 42:1], while Zion receives the nations who are coming to her" (2012, 61; cf. Williamson 1994, 152). Therefore, just as Isaiah 1 may echo Genesis 1 and Psalm 1, so Isaiah 2 mirrors the language and motifs of Genesis 2 and Psalm 2.

Scholars debate the theological meanings of this subunit (cf. Roberts 2007, 119–28; Fischer 2008, 151–65). On the one hand, an element of political polemic states that Zion shall be the highest, most influential mountain (v. 2) and that YHWH will disarm imperial forces (v. 4), just as YHWH God vanquished mythological chaos (Gen 1:1-5). This polemic sketches a powerful reversal of Babylon's *akītu* New Year's festival, when the emissaries of subject nations march in procession to succumb to the Babylonian throne at the ziggurat as the center of the earth. Through the triumphal procession from the outside steppe as a realm of chaos, the *akītu*-procession into the city was "to celebrate the re-establishment of order, to visualize the power and presence of the king and to inspire the people with confidence" (Nissinen 2001, 205; cf. Sweeney 1996, 99). Similarly, with the historical events of the Persian (Cyrus, Darius, and Xerxes) overthrow of Babylon, this Isaianic text may echo the Jeremianic oracle: "I will punish Bel in Babylon; I will cause to bring forth [*yatsa*] what he swallowed out of his mouth; and the nations shall not stream [*nahar*] to him; even the wall of Babylon has fallen" (Jer 51:44; Groenewald 2012, 66). Indeed, nations shall instead stream (*nahar*) to Zion. Whereas the Persian Empire conquered Babylon in ancient Near Eastern history, the prophet pronounces YHWH as the truly mighty God over all empires and the Jerusalem temple as the loftiest center of all nations.

On the other hand, this passage signifies a concept of radical peace, in which formidable nations make pilgrimage to Zion not to wage war but rather to learn YHWH's teaching (v. 3). Although its thematic multivalence may be intentional, the present form suggests that the final redactor adapted the theme of imperialistic ideology to the underdog Zion's superior future and reconceptualized it as the theme of radical peace, inclusive of many nations and peoples. Whereas the callous Israelites, labeled "rulers of Sodom" and "people of Gomorrah," are to hear the "word" and "teaching" of YHWH (1:10), here nations initiate their yearning to learn YHWH's "teaching" and "word" from Zion (v 3). As YHWH takes over to arbitrate all the affairs of the peoples, thereby assuming the place of the true King over all kingdoms, nations shall neither raise swords nor devour others (1:20) but shall learn war no more (v. 4). Accordingly, the dual themes of the purification of Zion (Isa 1) and the pilgrimage of the nations to Zion (2:2-4) may eventually represent a dissenting theological voice that counters Ezra-Nehemiah's policies on Zion's reform and identity, and on foreigners (Ezra 9–10; Neh 13:23-31). No longer a place of war and subjugation, but a place where "peace and harmony mingle within diversity" (Schökel 1987, 172), the redeemed Zion shall be a center of peace that embraces not only Jacob-Israel but also nations and peoples who shall all yearn for a world governed by Torah (Groenewald 2012, 66–67).

Isaiah 2:5-22 continues the theme of vv. 2-4 by presenting a profound theological rationale. Why should nations and peoples desire to make a pilgrimage to YHWH? It is because YHWH alone is the most exalted and trustworthy God.

Verse 5, which bridges vv. 2-4 and vv. 6-22, is pivotal in its thematic relations to both preceding and following subunits. Here the addressee, "house of Jacob," either refers to the whole people or, as in Isaiah 40–66, alludes to the exiled Israelites in the final form (cf. 46:3; 48:1; 58:1; Williamson 2006, 188). They are now called to join the "we"-group ("let us") to "walk in the light of God," just as nations and peoples aspire to "walk" in the paths of the God of Jacob (v. 3; Sweeney 1988, 135). The thematic irony, or radicality, is that, rather than leading, the house of Jacob is led to join the pilgrimage of nations and peoples. Previously, Isaiah 1 portrayed Israel as lower than animals (1:3). Now, the house of Jacob (2:5-6) is to follow (surprisingly not to lead) both nations and peoples, both empires and diasporas, in the worldwide stream toward YHWH's light in Zion.

Accompanying Zion, the house of Jacob is to walk in the "light" of YHWH. This association of light with YHWH may reveal the ancient biblical correlation between YHWH and the sun—as "light" is a common motif in "depictions of the divine in the ancient Semitic world" (Strawn 2007, 105). Against the backdrop of the sun-god Shamash, the prophet reaffirms that

YHWH is the true source of the sun, light, and righteousness (Groenewald 2012, 64; cf. Gen 1:3). What then would it mean to "walk" in the light of God (v. 5) and to "walk" in God's path (v. 3)? It means to walk in the humble obedience of the Torah—the teachings and commandments—of YHWH (1:10; 2:3). It means to walk in the righteous path, indeed a narrow and rugged road, as opposed to the wide and easy but wicked road of evil and destruction (cf. 65:2; Ps 1:1; Matt 7:13-14). It ultimately means, as the light essentially signifies, to live in utter trust and obedience toward God, the true source of light and salvation (cf. Ps 27:1).

Verses 6-11 start with the causal or asseverative preposition, "for, surely" (*ki*), and end with the phrase, "on that day." These bracketing markers hold together this subunit, and then similarly vv. 12-17, in the otherwise somewhat messy unit of vv. 5-22. Here, whereas international nations and peoples pursue YHWH's law and justice (vv. 3-4), the house of Jacob contrarily has forsaken YHWH by pursuing the political values and religious practices of other nations: diviners, soothsayers (v. 6), silver, gold, horses, chariots (v. 7), and idols (v. 8)—"Israel has become 'foreign'" (Seitz 1993, 41). Here the Hebrew word translated "full of" occurs four times, highlighting the key essences of a self-aggrandized, gluttonous society—money, weapons, and idolatry. Walter Brueggemann's remark aptly captures its theme: "The actual effect of such *fullness* is an inescapable *emptiness*, life emptied of well-being, security, and joy" (Brueggemann 1998a, 29). The result is the utter humiliation of human insolence.

Asserting that "the prophet Isaiah subverts the terms used in Neo-Assyrian claims of empire," Shawn Zelig Aster notes the comparable motif of arrogance and loyalty: "In Deuteronomy, arrogance leads the Israelites to forget the loyalty they owe YHWH, and in Neo-Assyrian royal inscriptions, the weaker power's failure to acknowledge a suzerain is often portrayed as a result of the vassal's arrogance" (2012, 206). Just as they "bow down" (*shakhah*) to the work of their hands (v. 8), they will be "humbled" (*shakhah*) and brought low (v. 9). This subunit then closes with a climactic thematic refrain (which will recur in vv. 17 and 22). In a broader horizon, the prophet warns not just the house of Jacob but all of humanity (*adam*) to find shelter in the rock, YHWH, who alone shall be exalted (vv. 10-11).

Verses 12-17, like vv. 6-11, start with the causal preposition, "for" (*ki*), and end with the phrase, "on that day." Further development of themes from vv. 6-11 is evident here. The "day of YHWH" is pronounced (v. 12; cf. v. 2). Contrary to the common ancient perception, this day of the Lord will be the day of divine punishment against all the pompous and haughty (v. 12; cf. Hos 5:9; Joel 1:15; 2:11; Amos 5:18-20; Zeph 1:14-16; Nogalski 2011, 89,

320). Subsequent descriptions with numerous occurrences of the preposition (*'al*, "upon, against") not only illustrate the meanings of YHWH's coming against the proud and lofty but also accentuate the ironic contrast between Zion versus Lebanon, Bashan, and Tarshish (vv. 13-16). In the ancient world, without today's towering skyscrapers, high mountains and lofty towers were symbols of pride and fear. Concerning such daunting forces, there is a famous ancient Korean poem with related expressions: "Although the Great Mountain is extremely high, / Seen from the heaven it is just another mountain . . ." (by Sa-eon Yang, 16th century CE; author's translation). The refrain reaffirms how all seemingly magnificent mountains shall collapse and crumble in the face of YHWH's majesty with the holy abode lifted up (v. 17).

Verses 18-22 are considered a *relecture* or *Fortschreibung* (inner-biblical expansions of previous phrases and motifs) of previous subunits, but they also function as a climactic finale with additional rhetorical and thematic emphases. Referring back to Israel's obsession with idols (cf. v. 8), the prophet announces that idols will pass away (v. 18) and admonishes idol-worshipers to hide in the caves of the rock (v. 19; cf. v. 10, v. 21). The "on that day" phrase opens vv. 20-21, which warns all of humanity (*adam*) again to throw away the idols of silver and gold (cf. v. 7). The syntactical ambiguity allows an alternative reading: unlike as in vv. 10 and 19, the disempowered and abandoned idols are to enter the clefts and crevices in v. 21 (Aster 2012, 209). This reading heightens not only the theme of the mortification of haughty leaders but also that of the incapacity of idols.

The final verse, v. 22, concludes the double overture of Isaiah 1–2. Echoing the climactic closures of previous subunits ("YHWH alone shall be exalted on that day," v. 11 and v. 17), this conclusive verse reiterates the climactic theme in a rhetorical question, "For what is a human worth?" As if reiterating the command in Isaiah 1, "Stop (*hadal*) doing evil" (1:16), here, at the end of Isaiah 2, the prophet adds another profound command, "Stop (*hadal*) relying on mortals," and thus trust and obey YHWH. Remember that mortals, whose life comes from "breath" in "nostrils" (2:22; cf. Gen 2:7), are, after all, creatures formed by God.

Purging and Transformation of Jerusalem, 3:1–4:6

Oracles against Male Upper Class and Female Elites in Jerusalem, 3:1–4:1

This unit (Isa 3–4) picks up the previous unit (Isa 1–2) with regard to common vocabulary and motifs. Accordingly, scholars consider Isaiah 1–4 a unit—e.g., with two parallel introductions in 1:2–2:5 and 2:6–4:6 (Beuken 2004a, 457). Chapters 3–4 can be read, however, as detailed evidence for the indictment from chapters 1–2. In addition, chapters 3–4 share key catchwords with the following unit, including chapter 5. Hence we will treat this unit (chs. 3–4) as a legitimate bridge between 1–2 and 5, with its own thematic importance. Isaiah 3 has two parts: condemnation of oppression addressed to the male leaders of Jerusalem and Judah (vv. 1-15) and to the female elites (vv. 16-26; Tull 2010, 99).

Isaiah 3:1-15 illustrates the haughtiness and humiliation of the male leaders of Jerusalem. The prophetic announcement of moral disarray in Jerusalem and Judah (vv. 1-7) includes the presentation of witnesses of social corruption (vv. 8-12) that culminates in the indictment of the criminals (vv. 13-15).

Verses 1-7 start with the same causal preposition, "for" (*ki*), as in 2:6 and 2:12. In response to the people's refusal to "remove" evil (1:16), and thus as a demonstration of how YHWH will "remove" all alloy (1:25), now YHWH intends to "remove" (v. 1) all the powerful administrative officers in Jerusalem and Judah (vv. 1-3). The entire society will fall apart, starting from the most essential economic resources such as bread and water (v. 1), extending to military, judiciary, and governmental officials (v. 2), and ending in the law enforcement, education, and civic arenas (v. 3). John D. W. Watts astutely considers this a description of a besieged city. With water and food resources blocked, military and civil personnel would be lost: "without its supporting area and population a city is helpless. . . . This is how a sustained siege over a considerable period of time could bring a city down without ever breaching its walls" (Watts 2001, 214).

The consequence would be a society in utter breakdown (vv. 4-5). The descriptions here obviously portray Jerusalem and Judah as a country in the upside-down havoc of anarchy. Yet key words may also connote a literary irony. In other words, on another level, this is in fact the society the prophet has been accusing in Isaiah 1, where "princes are rebels, pals with thieves" (1:23) and self-indulging oppression is the norm. Throughout the book of Isaiah, readers will encounter references to sons, daughters, and youths. While they are commonly looked down upon as naïve and immature beings, the prophet's ideal society in fact advocates the uncompromised courage and unselfish passion of the young ones (v. 4; cf. 11:6, 8), in stark contrast with the obdurate, calculating, and cowardly minds of the grown-ups and elders (v. 2; cf. vv. 12, 14). The society is so unfair and corrupt that reform is impossible and change is nonsensical.

Moreover, this declaration of a "world-turned-on-its-head" is a common motif in ancient Near Eastern prophetic oracles (e.g., Mesopotamian Marduk prophecy and the Syro-Palestinian Balaam inscription), as the result of divine absence or intervention and as the result of human wickedness. In the Isaianic texts, likewise, as a result of YHWH's hiding on the people's wickedness (1:15; cf. 8:17; 54:8; 64:7), the social, political, and economic systems of Jerusalem and Judah will crumble down to utter chaos (vv. 4-5; Kruger 2012, 58–76).

Unlike the dialogues of nations on their pilgrimage to Zion (2:3), the dialogues of the citizens of Jerusalem only disclose a community in shambles (vv. 6-7). In fact, key words here may allude to the time of Judges in regards to internal tension and distrust. For example, the "wanton ones" who "shall rule over them" (v. 4) may allude to Abimelech, a son of Gideon through a concubine (Judg 8:31), who dared to "rule" over his people (Judg 9:2). Likewise, the clan members' intention to appoint their own "leader" (vv. 6-7) may echo similar episodes of Gideon (Judg 8:22-23) and Jephthah (Judg 11:6, 11). Similarly, the "cloak" used as a qualifier to be a ruler (vv. 6-7) may remind one of Gideon, who self-servingly collected golden earrings in his cloak (Judg 8:24-27).

Verses 8-12 start with the same causal conjunction, "for" (*ki*), as in 3:1 (cf. 2:6, 12), presenting the witnesses of the guilty party. They are none other than Jerusalem and Judah, shamefully placed on the witness stands (vv. 8-9). They are humiliated because their tongue and actions defy the "eyes" of YHWH's glory (v. 8). They do not hide their guilt (v. 9) as YHWH "hides" YHWH's eyes (1:15) or as YHWH commands humans to "hide" in the dust (2:10). Indeed, by publicly exhibiting their sin, they have become like Sodom and Gomorrah (v. 9; cf. 1:10). Therefore, inasmuch as YHWH expressed "my soul hates" in 1:14, the divine pathos now turns its head against them: "Woe to their soul" (v. 9).

Then readers hear the opposite fates of the righteous versus the wicked (vv. 10-11), which reprises 1:27-31. The righteous (*tsaddiq*), pronounced "good," shall "eat" the fruit of their works (v. 10; cf. 1:19). YHWH denounces the wicked (*rasha'*) by saying "woe to the wicked" who are evil (v. 11; cf. 6:5).

Afterwards, YHWH identifies the true culprits (v. 12). Yet, even in this accusation, readers can sense a tone of divine compassion and anguish. For the first time since 1:3, now readers hear the expression "my people," in fact two times! The accusation contains emotional offense by calling their oppressors little kids and comparing their rulers to women. According to Herbert Huffmon's elucidation, akin to the ancient Near Eastern curse expression that "warriors become women" in the letter from Samsi-Addu, king of Assyria, to his son Yasmah-Addu, king of Mari, the father chides his overindulgent son for being a "baby" (Huffmon 2006, 278–79). The feminization of male leaders (cf. 19:16; Judg 4:21-22; 9:53-54) is also congruent with the comparable rhetorical devices in Hosea and Ezekiel (Yee

2003, 81–109; Launderville 2013, 193–214). Who are the criminals? They are the oppressive but ignominious and incompetent rulers.

Verses 13-15 culminate the whole process of litigation by directly accusing the criminals. The previous subunit (vv. 8-12) addressed these corrupt rulers in the third-person masculine plural. Now, they are addressed in the second-person masculine plural. In a covenant lawsuit formula, YHWH now takes the stand of the righteous judge to plead the case and adjudicate the peoples (v. 13; cf. 1:17, 23; 2:4). The unveiled defendants are the oppressive elders and princes who are devoid of a speck of conscience (v. 14; cf. 1:23). In the explicit address, "you," YHWH accuses them of devouring the vineyard (v. 14; cf. 5:1, 5; 1 Kgs 21:1-29). Their crime is the oppression of YHWH's people, now explicitly identified as the poor (v. 15). Readers can hear YHWH's impassioned fury against the rich, powerful rulers, who, with their hypocritical and haughty "faces" (v. 9), crush and grind the tearful "faces" of the poor (v. 15).

Isaiah 3:16–4:1 exemplifies the haughtiness and humiliation of the female leaders of Jerusalem. Whether or not there were influential female political leaders in Judah during this time, the addressees seem analogous to the kind of first ladies of Jerusalem's urban monopoly, whose flaunting of overpriced accessories exposes the elites' excessive consumption of items purchased "with the skin off the back of an oppressed peasantry" (Blenkinsopp 2000a, 201). YHWH mocks the proud walks of the daughters of Zion (vv. 16-17) and vows to remove all luxurious ornaments that adorn the wealthy female elites (vv. 18-23). The result will be their utter shame and sorrow (3:24–4:1).

Verses 16-17 start with the similar causal conjunction, "for" (*ki*), as in 3:1, 8 (cf. 2:6, 12). In Isaiah 2, we read how all human arrogance and pride shall be humbled (2:11, 17). Here, in the second-half of Isaiah 3, not only the male leaders but also the female leaders of Judah learn of YHWH's humbling of their haughtiness (v. 16). Daughters of Zion, who parade around with pomp and gluttony (v. 16), will be afflicted with scabs on their heads and with shamefully exposed private parts (v. 17).

Verses 18-23 recall the expectation of the day of YHWH proclaimed in 2:12. What will happen "on that day" (v. 18; cf. 2:11, 17, 20; 3:7) resembles the expression and content of the reversal of fortune in 3:1-3. Just as YHWH warned that YHWH was about to "remove" from Jerusalem and Judah all bread, water, warrior, prophet, elder, and so on (vv. 1-3), now YHWH declares the intention to "remove" all the ornaments of beauty—which most commoners could not afford—that cover every body part of these female elites (vv. 18-23).

Verses 24-26 reiterate the calamity that will befall these haughty female rulers with the vivid descriptions of a war. Although readers will later hear the promise of restoration for Zion in 61:3 ("to give them a garland instead of [*takhat*] ashes, the oil of gladness instead of mourning, the cloak of praise instead of a faint spirit"), here the rich are condemned to be covered with stench, rope, baldness, sackcloth, and shame "instead of" (*takhat*) perfume, sash, silky hair, robe, and beauty (v. 24). Their men shall fall in the battle (v. 25), Zion's gates shall be ravaged, and her women shall sit on the ground (v. 26; cf. 47:1; Job 2:13; Lam 1:9-10; 2:10).

Isaiah 4:1 resembles the aftermath of the social debacle illustrated in 3:6-7. The catchwords, "bread" (*lekhem*) and "cloak" (*simelah*), here echo the same words, "bread" (*lekhem*) and "cloak" (*simelah*) in 3:7 (note also the catchphrase "on that day" in 3:7 and 4:1). The setting is more specifically related to exile and military destruction, however. Because of the enormous casualty of male warriors (3:25), "on that day" (cf. 3:7), seven women will contend for one man and desperately yearn to "take away" their disgrace.

Recently, biblical scholars from Africa have presented diverse interpretive possibilities and challenges in reading this passage with regard to both ancient culture and the contemporary world. On the one hand, Edouard Kitoko Nsiku (DR Congo) observes the relevant criticism concerning the ideal women in that today's African women too tend to prefer external displays, adorning with excess jewelry and decoration, over highlighting their internal qualities. Women too, especially those obsessed with power and greed, need to hear these voices of prophetic criticism. On the other hand, finding parallels between Judah's struggle under the Babylonian empire and black people's hardship in post-apartheid South Africa, Makhosazana Nzimande (South Africa) observes a condescending attitude toward women, the bias of which may entwine the prophet's voice with the colonizer's voice, thereby "depicting black women as oversexed" (Holter 2014, 84–87). Hence, while it is important to hear the resounding criticism against women abusing power and privilege, in both ancient and today's societies, we also ought to be mindful of any unintended interpretive nod to the ongoing bias vis-à-vis gender and class.

Renewal of Mount Zion and Its Survivors, 4:2-6

This unit (4:2-6) wraps up the theme of divine purging and renewing of Jerusalem by giving a promise to the remnants in Jerusalem. The initial declaration of Zion's attraction among the nations (2:1-5) bookends with the announcement of Zion's resurgence as Israel's holy abode (4:2-6; cf. Beuken 2004a, 458). After the purging of the corrupt rulers, both male and female

(Isa 3), the next generation of survivors will bring the hope of restoration in Zion (Isa 4). Adding to the similar futuristic expression, "on that day" (v. 2), readers now hear a positive message regarding the survivors in Zion (vv. 2-3). The survivors of Israel (v. 2) shall become the "branch" of YHWH and regain their lost "beauty" (3:18). Key words in v. 2 may echo Genesis 19:25 where God's annihilation of Sodom and Gomorrah included the "branch" (*tsemakh*) of the ground. Now the remnants of Zion will receive the name of the "branch" (*tsemakh*) of YHWH. Thus, echoing the confession of the "we"-group in 1:9, who were miraculously "left" (*yatar*) as survivors, those "left" (*yatar*) in Jerusalem (v. 3) shall become holy.

The conclusion of this unit (vv. 4-6) delineates the theme of the purging of Jerusalem in further climactic details. The filth and bloodstains of the daughters of Zion (cf. 1:15) are to dissolve not only by smelting (cf. 1:25) but also by the spirit of judging and burning (v. 4). Notably, fire and water function as "a merism for extreme danger" as in Psalm 66:12 (Hossfeld and Zenger 2005, 146). The purified Mount Zion will then be as glorious as Mount Sinai, re-created by a cloud by day and a flaming fire by night (v. 5). Zion will no longer be the unprotected "shelter" in a vineyard (cf. 1:8). Unlike Sodom and Gomorrah on which sulfur and fire "rained" (Gen 19:24), this renewed Zion will become a refuge from storms and "rain" (v. 6).

Signs and Warnings for the King and People of Judah, 5:1–10:34

This extensive and complex segment shows a rough chiastic format. It is bracketed by the parallel song or woe-oracles (a-a') that hold the whole pieces together, especially with the solemn condemnation against the wicked (b-b'). The death of King Uzziah connects to its counterpart by the birth of a royal child (c-c'). In the core portion of this envelope, there are announcements of three little children (d). Of these three children, Immanuel accentuates the key theme of this entire segment, i.e., God is with us.

a. A Parable-Song of the Vineyard (5:1-7)
   b. Six Woe-Oracles against the Many Wicked (5:8-30)
      c. Death of Uzziah, King of Judah, and the Call of the Prophet
         Isaiah (6:1-13) (*first person speech*)
         d. Three Children as Signs of Warning and Hope (7:1–9:21)
            (i) King Ahaz's Test and the Child Immanuel as a Sign
               (7:1-25) (*third person speech*): center (3 children, esp.
               "With Us God")
            (ii) Child Maher-shalal-hash-baz as a Warning against "this
               people" (8:1-22) (*first person speech*)
      c'. Birth of a Child of Light, a Prince of Peace (9:1-7)
   b'. Resumed Woe-oracles against the Wicked (9:8–10:4)
a'. A Woe-oracle against Assyria, Yʜᴡʜ's Weapon (10:5-34)

Within the internal sections, in terms of the genres, Isaiah 6 is a vision report issuing a call of the prophet; Isaiah 7 is a salvation oracle; Isaiah 8 contains a symbolic prophetic action; 9:1-6 again a salvation oracle; and 9:8–10:4 contains woe-oracles (linked with 5:8-30 of six woe-oracles).

A Parable-Song of the Vineyard, 5:1-7

Isaiah 5:1-7 starts a new section, but it also functions to bridge the preceding and following sections (as will be discussed). In terms of its genre, this unit may be a love song, a juridical parable, or an oracle. All these elements seem to be extant so that even though the speaker sings a song, the entire song is in fact a parable, which unveils decisive messages.

This song starts with the repeated usage of the word "beloved." "Beloved" occurs three times in v. 1 and denotes a deep affection between lovers. This parable of stern judgment actually starts with the unmistakable emphasis on divine love. Similar phrases and nuances with the Song of Songs—"My vineyard, my very own, is for myself. . . . Make haste my beloved . . ." (Song 8:12, 14)—heighten the imagery of intimacy between "my beloved" (God) and the "vineyard" (Israel) in this Isaianic love song. At the outset, accordingly, this love song chimes not the "icy indifference of a judge, but . . . the mixed sorrow and anger of a lover who has been deeply wounded" (Fretheim 2014, 59).

Words for "love" may also have implicit puns. The word "love" (consonants, "*dwd*") in the phrase "love song" sounds similar to the name "David" (consonants, "*dwd*"). Likewise, the word "my beloved" (*yedidi*) resonates the name "Solomon" (*yedideyah*; cf. 2 Sam 12:25). Together these words may then allude to the kings of the golden era of Judah, the beloved of Yhwh (cf. 1 Sam 13:14; 2 Sam 12:24).

With regard to puns, read intertextually, this song may also adduce a parody-like allusion to King Uzziah, a Davidic descendant whose name appears in the superscription in 1:1. According to 2 Chronicles 26, there are both positive and negative reports about this king. During his fifty-two years of reign, in addition to building (*banah*) cities and towers (*migdal*) especially in Jerusalem, Uzziah is said to have "hewed out" (*hatsab*) many cisterns with farmers and vinedressers in the hills, for "he loved the soil" (2 Chr 26:10). Some of the linguistic expressions are strikingly similar: "He built (*banah*) a watchtower (*migdal*) in the midst of it, and hewed out (*hatsab*) a wine vat in it" (Isa 5:2). It is Uzziah's positive achievement that Yhwh the real builder, farmer, and vinedresser would trump. Likewise, Uzziah's consequent pride and empty offerings (2 Chr 26:16; cf. Isa 2:15; 5:15-16) may mirror the criticism against the hubris in Isaiah 2. Isaiah's oracles thus may allude to the rise and fall of King Uzziah as well (2 Chr 26:22; cf. Seitz 1993, 48).

All these lexical puns involving Judah's kings accentuate not only the nostalgic memory of their high regimes but also the scathing criticism of social decay that usually started with these monarchs (cf. 3:12-15; 5:8-10). At the same time, in the present form, this vineyard song or allegory insinuates that the prophet's "beloved" is none other than Yhwh, the owner and creator of the vineyard. No less than five verbs, "dug, cleared of stones, planted, built, and hewed," describe the divine care for the vineyard (v. 2). God's deep affection accompanies tangible sweat and toil via divine action for the precious vineyard (cf. 1:8). Nevertheless, this choice vineyard would only produce worthless, rotten grapes (cf. 3:14).

Accordingly, a court is in order. The first "now"-speech summons the people of Jerusalem and Judah (vv. 3-4; cf. 1:1; 2:1; 3:1, 8). Yhwh the prosecutor presents the case, and neither defendants nor witnesses can rebut. Terence Fretheim trenchantly observes that God raises two questions here: "what?" and "why?" (2014, 63). Readers may then posit a thematic connection to the Garden of Eden episode with the relationship between God and the first human couple in Genesis 3. There God asks three ontological questions: "where?" (omnipresence), "did you eat?" (omniscience), and "what?" (omnipotence; cf. Gen 3:9, 11, 13). In our love song, the "what?" question entails every best effort this beloved God—indeed not human—could possibly have done, presumably underscoring God's unmatched power. Yet, ironically here, we also sense the God who still vulnerably had to wait and hope for the outcome. The dice, or power, was cast by God's people, endowed with choices and blessings. Furthermore, the "why?" question can be directed against the people of God, whose failure to produce good grapes provides an unequivocal answer. Yet, paradoxically here, this question may also be directed toward God. Rather than the question as to who is to blame, this text further highlights divine dependence on human agents, whether obedient or disobedient. At the same time, moreover, this question emphatically hints at the divine pathos of God, who is not only deeply disappointed but also deeply hurt because of the affection and love this "beloved" God cannot discard: "God's sorrow rather than the people's tragedy is the theme of this song" (Heschel 1962, 85; cf. Fretheim 2014, 64–65).

In the second "now"-speech, YHWH the judge declares the verdict (vv. 5-6). The consequence, announced with the concentrated series of verbs, "remove, ravage, make waste, and command the clouds to withhold rain," reverses divine acts of care. Instead of the oppressive rulers who devoured the vineyard (3:14), now YHWH will let the vineyard be devoured (v. 5). Instead of the canopy or tabernacle that should serve as a shelter from rain (4:5-6), now dark clouds block any rain (v. 6; cf. Deut 11:13-17).

This parable ends with explications (v. 7). The vineyard is the house of Israel and the planting is Judah. Rather, to be more precise, "those trapped into self-condemnation by the parable" are the "ruling elites of Judah and Israel, led by the two dynastic houses and their sitting dynasts" (Chaney 1999, 117). In a surprising irony, the audience becomes "the judges of their own conduct (like David listening to Nathan's parable, 2 Sam. 12)" (Schökel 1987, 166). Readers recall that Israel the vineyard is YHWH's beloved and the planted Judah is YHWH's delight. Alas, instead of good grapes defined by justice and righteousness (cf. 1:17, 21, 23), they can only taste bitter grapes defined by the stench of bloodshed and outcry (cf. 1:11, 15; 4:4). The well-known word plays on "justice" (*mishpat*) and "righteousness" (*tsedaqah*) replaced by "bloodshed" (*mispakh*) and "outcry" (*tse'aqah*) in Hebrew respectively heighten the somber irony, because the previous outcry Israel howled over their hardship under the Egyptian taskmasters has now turned to Israel's excruciating outcry against its own kindred (Goldingay 2014, 22).

Six Woe-Oracles against the Many Wicked, 5:8-30
Isaiah 5:8-10, the first woe-oracle, picks up the motif of the "vineyard" (v. 10) from the previous unit (vv. 1-7). The lavish houses and fields ostensibly castigate the corrupt rulers (v. 8). Soon these rulers who illegally and abusively hoard all the wealth will diminish, like the defenseless booth in a vineyard (cf. 1:8). With the impending debacle those hoarded houses will become empty (v. 9) and their fields will yield little (v. 10).

Isaiah 5:11-17, the second woe-oracle, also picks up the motif of the vineyard (vv. 8-10) through the mention of hard liquor and wine, products of the vineyard. These leaders pursue intoxication from dawn till twilight, incapable of recognizing either YHWH's works or the plight of the destitute (vv. 11-12; cf. 1:23). Two "therefore"-speeches declare their downfall (vv. 13-14): first, Israel, "my people," shall go into exile where hunger and thirst will strike the nobles (v. 13); and second, all the privileged, jubilant ones in Jerusalem shall go down into the gulf of Sheol (v. 14).

The insert-like refrain (vv. 15-16) plays a significant role because this refrain reminds readers that these woe-oracles decisively connect to the thesis passage of Isaiah 2. The motif of bringing low mortals, and especially haughty subjugators (v. 15), cites 2:9, 11, 17 almost verbatim. The addition to these citations highlights not only that YHWH alone is the most exalted but also that this holy God will bring about justice and righteousness (v. 16). In a dramatic reversal, strangers shall devour the ruins of the filthy rich (v. 17; cf. 1:11).

Isaiah 5:18-19, the third woe-oracle, illustrates the leaders' sin and iniquity. In an indirect allusion to 1:3-4, as if they carry the oxen in the cart (cf. Num 7:3-8), these profane oppressors drag down people with sin and iniquity (v. 18). These arrogant leaders even dare to "hurry" (*mahar*) and "hasten" (*hush*) the divine plan and presence, as if they can "see" and "know" them (v. 19). Yet all they learn will be their obdurate seeing but not knowing (cf. 6:9), because YHWH will "hurry" and "hasten" the sign, Maher (*maher*)-shalal-hash(*hash*)-baz, and weapons of judgment (cf. 8:1-8; 10:6).

Isaiah 5:20, the fourth woe-oracle, is brief and concise just like the next oracle (5:21). Nonetheless, this verse contains one of the most foundational themes of this entire chapter. Also, if we include the seventh woe-oracle (10:1-4) in a larger corpus, 5:20 may be another center of a rough chiastic structure within 5:8-25 and 10:1-4, as will be elucidated below (Berges 2012a, 75). This central oracle depicts the crookedness of this society that distorts good and evil as well as perverts bitter and sweet (cf. Jer 4:22; Mic 3:2). Sandwiched between these two similar phrases, the middle phrase reclaims the thesis statement of 2:5—light should overcome darkness (cf. Gen 1:2-3).

Isaiah 5:21, the fifth woe-oracle, continues the denouncement of the leaders. Its expression coincides with 5:18-19, repeating the words "seeing" and "knowing" (v. 19), and "eyes" and "understanding" (v. 21). Together, 5:18-19 and 5:21 as chiastic counterparts frame 5:20 at the center. Moreover, the self-proclaimed "wise" (*hakam*) and "discerning" (*bin*) ones who are actually only such in their "faces" (*paneh*), may echo those "nobles" (*paneh*), "expert" (*hakam*), and "skillful" (*bin*) powers that be whom YHWH mocks in 3:3.

Isaiah 5:22-25, the sixth woe-oracle, constructs an outer chiastic counterpart with 5:11-17. The expressions of "wine" and "hard liquor" in v. 22 form an inverted chiasm with "hard liquor" and "wine" in v. 11. Similarly, the two "therefore"-speeches (*laken* and *'al-ken*) in v. 24 and v. 25 match the two "therefore"-speeches in v. 13 and v. 14.

Here again, just as 5:21 echoes 3:3, the terms "warriors" (*gibor*) and "valiant ones" (*'ish milkhamah*) in 3:2 recur as "heroes" (*gibor*) and "valiant ones" (*'aneshe-khail*) in 5:22. The thematic irony is consistent with the feminization of these would-be macho abusers (cf. 3:12): contrary to the job descriptions of these warriors of valor, these high officials have become war heroes in drinking affairs (v. 22). They are so intoxicatedly corrupt that they declare the wicked to be righteous and hamper the rights of the truly righteous ones (v. 23).

The first "therefore"-speech (v. 24) identifies these unrighteous leaders as "chaff" (cf. Ps 1) whose root will rot (cf. 3:24). Notably, the word "rot" (*maq*) occurs only in Isaiah 3:24 and 5:24 in the entire HB. Where did this corruption start? From their "despising" the Torah and word of YHWH (cf. 1:4, 10; 2:3).

The second "therefore"-speech (v. 25) announces the verdict: the doom of this arrogant and stubborn people. Just as the empty worshipers "spread out their palms" (1:15), so now YHWH will stretch out a divine hand against them. Just as the people's corruption lingers on, so YHWH's anger has not turned away (this refrain-like phrase will form a further literary envelope with 9:8–10:4; Sweeney 1996, 114).

Thus far, in the overall placement, we should note the literary and thematic links between vv. 1-7 and vv. 8-25. At the outset, the vineyard parable-song (vv. 1-7) and the woe-oracles (vv. 8-25) seem as unrelated as water and oil. Yet the vineyard imagery and key words such as wine and drunkenness (vv. 10-12, 14, 22) intricately connect these two subunits. Accordingly, the general accusation against Israel and Judah in the vineyard parable-song is specifically illustrated in the detailed accusations of the woe-oracles: Whose fault is it? Who is to blame? Who is the culprit for producing evil grapes? It is the ruling class, those privileged affluent leaders who are seasoned experts at perverting justice and devising evil (Sweeney 1996, 128). The vineyard and wine as economic commodities in viticulture make explicit the contrast between the agonizing toils of the rural peasants as abused victims and the luxurious debauchery of the urban elites as vicious perpetrators. In the ancient setting, these upper-class elites would yell at the farmers for their failure to produce satisfactory amounts of wine. Like a slap on their face, YHWH now rebukes those abusive owners. Woe to the ruling elites of the dynastic houses of Israel and Judah for their economic and political oppression of the poor peasants (Chaney 1999)!

Isaiah 5:26-30 is not a woe-oracle, and thus seems to be an odd subunit in Isaiah 5. Nevertheless, this subunit makes a nice bracket with 5:1-7, enveloping the six woe-oracles. Furthermore, key words and notions link this unit with its preceding units. Just as YHWH stretches out a divine hand (v. 25), so YHWH raises a signal for nations far away (v. 26). The expression that these distant forces—presumably Assyria—hurry (*meherah*; v. 26) may allude to similar phrases in v. 19 that anticipate the name of Isaiah's son Maher-shalal-hash-baz (8:1-8). The repetitive phrases in vv. 27-28 likewise match nicely the repeated occurrence of verbs for YHWH's judgments in vv. 2, 5-6. The repeated use of the negation "not" (*lo'*) similarly occurs in v. 6 ("it shall not be pruned or hoed") as well as in v. 27 ("none slumbers, none sleeps, not a loincloth is loose, no sandal-thong broken"). Moreover, in relation to those described in the immediately preceding subunit (vv. 22-25), this army from a nation far away never tires (v. 27). It is fully equipped with virulent weapons (v. 28). This army contrasts sharply with the totally intoxicated heroes of Judah (v. 22).

The final metaphors (vv. 29-30) describe this army's roaring (*sha'ag*) like a lion (v. 29)—quite opposite from the love-song (*shir*) of YHWH's beloved (v. 1). Marvin Chaney elucidates the rhetorical effect of the figurative speech against the abusive elites on poor peasants: "The rapacious elite may 'overtake' the persons and fields of their peasant prey . . . they may even 'fence about' the land they have taken, but they will not be able to 'drag off into security' the prey upon which they have pounced. Fields cannot be carried into exile" (Chaney 2006, 158). Accordingly, now it will soon be the elite wealthy leaders' turn to experience what it is like to become prey and get bullied by the more powerful, i.e., the Assyrian empire (cf. Ps 109:6). In fact, "on that day," Assyria's roaring will be like that of the unruly mythological sea (v. 30). In the end, therefore, because of these shrewd oppressors who distorted darkness and light (v. 20), darkness and clouds shall cover the whole land (cf. v. 6; 8:22).

Death of Uzziah, King of Judah, and the Call of the Prophet Isaiah, 6:1-13

Isaiah 6:1-7 presents the initial report—in the first-person singular—of the call and commissioning of the prophet Isaiah who "saw" (v. 1) and later "heard" YHWH (v. 8): "the first half of the chapter [vv. 1-7] will be dominated by the description of what Isaiah saw, and the second half [vv. 8-13] by what he heard in his dialogue with God" (Williamson 2007, 127). Scholars have debated whether Isaiah 6, which oddly does not open this prophetic book, is indeed a call narrative, a throne council vision (Wildberger 1991, 236), or a commission in the heavenly assembly (Steck 1972, 191). Ellen White analyzes five of the six features of a call narrative, originally presented by Norman Habel's form-critical study:

• divine confrontation (vv. 1-2);
• the introductory word (vv. 3-7);
• the commission (vv. 8-10);
• the objection (v. 11a);
• the assurance (vv. 11b-13);
• [a sign of confirmation (cf. Isa 7)].

Also, this chapter contains a series of threes, further building a literary unity: the three sets of wings (v. 2); the trishagion—"holy, holy, holy" (v. 3); "Adonay" (*adonay*; vv. 1, 8, 11); "Yhwh" (vv. 3, 5, 12); "people" (*am*; vv. 5, 9, 10); "full" (*ml'*; vv. 1, 3, 4); "sit, dwell" (*yashab*; vv. 1, 5, 11); and three clauses in v. 7, v. 5, and v. 11 (White 2014, 83).

King Uzziah does not appear in the preceding chapters, except the opening superscription (1:1). Although the scroll of Isaiah likely went through numerous redactions in a complicated transmission process, sequential readers may posit that the time of Uzziah, the first of the four kings in the superscription (1:1), has ended. According to 2 Kings 15:1-7 (cf. 2 Kgs 15:32-38; 2 Chr 26:19-21), Uzziah (also called Azariah) reigned over Judah for fifty-two years. But due to his leprosy, his son Jotham became his co-regent. During the unstable time following the death of Uzziah, who reigned over Judah for such a long era with Jotham, "Isaiah was confronted with the real King [Yhwh]" (Achtemeier 1988, 27). Whereas Uzziah, the proud but unconsecrated human king, entered the temple only to be struck by leprosy (2 Chr 26:16-21), Isaiah the obedient and penitent prophet enters the Jerusalem sanctuary to witness the glory of Yhwh, the true King, and to receive the divine commission (vv. 1-4; Williamson 2007, 124–26). Yhwh alone is truly "high" (*rum*) and "lofty" (*nasa'*), rightfully taking the throne (cf. 66:1). In light of West Semitic iconography, Yhwh would be seated on the wings of the cherubim above the ark, while the skirts of Yhwh's robe filled the whole temple (cf. 66:1-2), where the "platform, forming the seat of [Yhwh's] throne, stood one and a half times as high as a modern NBA basketball goal" (Roberts 2002, 200–204). This atmosphere itself would easily nullify, if not terrify, any mortals who pretend to be "proud" (*rum*) and "lofty" (*nasaʾ*; cf. 2:12-14, 17). This true King with glory has the ability to command the army ("the Lord of hosts")—an essential prerequisite of a king's authority in ancient times—not only to fight for Israel but now also even to "deploy against Israel" (Williamson 2007, 135).

In this scene, readers first learn of the seraphim who, like the cherubim, guard the ark (Exod 25:18-22), attend to YHWH (v. 2), and proclaim YHWH's holiness and glory (v. 3). This holy theophany then accompanies earthquake and smoke, depicting YHWH's descent upon Mount Sinai (Exod 19:18). These seraphim, the terrifying two-winged cobras in ancient Near Eastern iconography, especially in the Egyptian sources, would spread their wings to protect the deity from any harm. On the contrary, in Isaiah's temple vision, they are covering and protecting their own faces and feet, i.e., private parts, at the presence of holy God. The seraphs have lost their original duty: "The only function left to them is to point to the sole majesty of [YHWH]" the exalted King in their loud chants with "effects of a modern rock concert" (Roberts 2002, 204–208).

Although this text contains elements of a call narrative, according to Rolf Knierim's analysis, it also exhibits key signs of a judicial process or lawsuit: e.g., YHWH as the chief judge, the call of the seraphim proclaiming the royal judge, and the prophet's confession of guilt (Knierim 1968). Victor Hurowitz further observes the intertextual allusion in v. 3 ("the whole earth is full of his glory") to Numbers 14:21 ("YHWH's glory will fill the entire earth"), which describes YHWH's intention to pass judgment on the disobedient generation in the wilderness (Hurowitz 1989, 82).

Thus, the prophet utters his confession amid implied legal procedures over against the glorious chants of the seraphim (vv. 5-7). Isaiah's humility makes yet another contrast with the haughtiness of human kings. Amid the lament of this prophet of unclean lips, readers nonetheless learn that this contrite prophet has witnessed the true "King, YHWH of the army" (v. 5). That the prophet, an unclean human being, stands before God should have been a shock to the audiences—it is no wonder the prophet cries, "Woe to me!" Whereas the ritualist initiates the purification process in Mesopotamian cultic activities, here YHWH initiates and controls the device. The prophet unexpectedly learns of the assumed judgment (Hurowitz 1989, 82–83). Nonetheless, readers learn of an unforeseen theme. Despite the expected punishment upon this impure human, God grants gracious forgiveness (White 2014, 86).

Furthermore, comparable to the Mesopotamian *mīs pî* mouth-purification rituals (vv. 6-7), cleansing and atoning of the prophet's mouth is "symbolic of total purity" (Hurowitz 1989, 41). In addition, seraphim evoke the tradition of the touch of the prophet's lips (cf. v. 6) by the "fiery serpent-rod" in the Egyptian mouth-opening rites (Glazov 2001, 121). Not unlike Moses whom God called unexpectedly in the wilderness, this prophet Isaiah receives the divine call while ritually impure. Thus, just as YHWH declared the divine intention to "remove" their filthy alloy (1:25), this holy God, merciful to the confession of the prophet, readily cleanses and calls him (v. 7; cf. 1:4, 18; 5:18). In the literary depiction, Isaiah's cleansing may not have been pain-free. Considering that the seraphim were holding the live coal in the tongs, "imagine, then, how it must have felt on Isaiah's lips" (Roberts 2002, 211). This purging of sins by fire recurs in Ezekiel's vision, when the cherub gives burning coals to the man clothed in linen to spray them over Jerusalem (Ezek 10:1-7). Whereas this refining in Ezekiel implies an outright burning of the city, the Isaianic vision emphasizes not only the danger of judgment by fire but also the possibility of purifying the prophet's lips and so also the remnants' (Roberts 2002, 211–12). Now the purified prophet is ready to speak the divine oracles. In short, contrary to the mouth-purification ritual associated with incapacitated idols in the ancient Near East, the Isaianic narrative pronounces not only that the prophet is forgiven but also that YHWH empowers this human being to transmit divine words (Glazov 2001, 148–49).

Isaiah 6:8-13 reports the divine commissioning in dialogues between the prophet (first-person singular) and YHWH. In both dialogues (vv. 8-10 and 11-13), Isaiah makes proactive responses, but YHWH offers the closing statements. In the first dialogue (vv. 8-10), Isaiah obeys the divine commissioning. Yet here Isaiah's willful and obedient response (v. 8), after his seeing (v. 1) and hearing (v. 8), makes an ironic contrast with "this people" who keep hearing and seeing but do not know at all (v. 9). The subsequent task for the prophet is to make this callous people's heart more stubborn (v. 10).

This contrast between the prophet and the people signifies the theme of the reversal of the exodus tradition. Instead of the hardened heart of Pharaoh and the Egyptians (Exod 7:3), it is Isaiah's audience, the people of YHWH, whose heart is obdurate. On this difficult concept of the hardening of the heart, there are divergent interpretive thrusts that are equally valid and significant. First, the obduracy text functions like the hardening of Pharaoh insofar as the motif functions to highlight the dynamics between Isaiah, like Moses, and the people (esp. King Ahaz), like the Pharaoh/Egyptians. The more they hear, the more arrogant and rebellious they will become. Second, connected to the first interpretive thrust, in light of the "theme of hardening" as a key thread, the prophet's task to harden this people may be taken as a part of divine judgment already pronounced in the preceding chapters. As an essential component of divine punishment, the moral and theological shipwreck is unavoidable, and this hardening is in fact a "strategy of prolongation" in the divine verdict (Uhlig 2009a, 141–42). Third, there is a theme of divine mystery. On a comparable text of divine deception in the encounter between the prophet Micaiah and the king Ahab in 1 Kings 22:1-28, C. L. Seow's remark is noteworthy: "[This depiction of God who deceives] forces us to deal with a God who is a sovereign, a God who is absolutely free to use any means—even those contrary to human reason or standards of morality—in order to bring divine purpose to fulfillment" (Seow 1998, 166–67).

Finally, in the present literary form, it may serve a rhetorical effect. On the narrative of divine deception in 1 Kings 22, quoting the insight by J. M. Hamilton, Terence Fretheim shares the following interpretation: "Deception exposed is no longer deception but something more complicated. It hands over to the person whom one intends to deceive the capacity of choosing whether to be deceived or not" (1999, 125). Likewise, we should note the discrepancy of the popularity contest between 127,400 prophets as false prophets, "yes men" for the king, and Isaiah (like Micaiah and like Jeremiah) as a true prophet; receptivity toward the latter would have been marginal at best (Fretheim 1999, 127). It would be analogous to the modern-day freedom of speech (i.e., the prophet has revealed the top-secret plan to harden this perverse people) as well as its abject denial by the press, media, and populace (i.e., the powers that be silence this information and the brainwashed people join in outright derision of true prophets).

Nevertheless, even in this harsh statement, readers can overhear a tiny hint of divine pathos, as the leaked-out code may "soften" instead of "harden" this people: if the unholy people truly repent and return, they can still be healed (cf. 1:19). According to the study of Gregory Glazov, several key words in this narrative resonate with the Exodus and wilderness traditions of Exodus 15–17 and Numbers 11–21: e.g., the seraphim (Num 21:5-7), the antiphon to the trishagion (Num 14:21), the fiery coals (Num 17:11), and so on. In terms of the prophet's repentance and healing by the seraph, therefore, the prophet epitomizes the recalcitrant people in that Isaiah symbolizes uncleanness, obduracy, and eventual healing through piercing repentance and divine cleansing (Glazov 2001, 143, 156–62; cf. Oswalt 1986, 174–75). Whereas this people "really hear" and "see" but do "not know" at all (v. 9), YHWH is the caring God who has "really heard," "seen," and "known" the affliction, cry, and suffering of the people in Egypt (Exod 3:7). Nonetheless, the indisputable outcome here will be that this people's "heart" is about to become more stubborn, quite the opposite of what God desires in the Sinai covenant: "Love YHWH your God with all your heart, all your soul, and all your everything" (Deut 6:5).

Terrified by the outlook of hardening their hearts, in the second dialogue (vv. 11-13), Isaiah cries out, "How long, my Lord?" (v. 11a). Although this question evidently concerns the temporal extent as indicated in the divine answer in v. 11b, Isaiah's cry is somewhat similar to the psalmist's complaint in the lament psalms (cf. Pss 6:3 [MT 6:4]; 80:5; 90:13). Citing Harold Kushner's profound criticism of Job's friends, Denise Hopkins emphasizes that the question of "How long?" in lament is not a question for information regarding the duration of the pain and agony but rather a reaction to the urgency of the hard-pressed situation. It does not require a question mark but instead an exclamation mark. Through this question, the speaker expresses, "This has gone on long enough! I can't take it anymore!" (Hopkins 2002, 83). Or, to rephrase in the prophet's complaint, "This is way too heavy and harsh! I can't endure its devastating effect!" This vision report first and foremost underscores the heaviness of the stubbornness of this people. YHWH's response contains an ultimatum of desolation, albeit with a slight glimpse of hope. The verdict is grim at the outset. Yet, as when the deity assured Jeremiah of his presence by touching Jeremiah's mouth (Jer 1:9, 17-19; cf. Exod 3:12), Isaiah is to carry out this task with the divine purpose (cf. Isa 7:14; 8:8).

Cities and land will become ruins (the Hebrew word is *shoah*), and houses will be uninhabited (v. 11). Such a misfortune, which was pronounced earlier (5:6, 8-9; cf. 1:7), is now about to take place. This will result in the exile of many people (v. 12). Just as ten acres of vineyard will produce a mere bath (5:10), now even the tenth part will be burned (v. 13). Whereas the coal did not burn the prophet's lips but purified him, Judah with its recalcitrant people will be burned down (Beuken 2004b, 77).

Moreover, amid this terrifying calamity, there will be remnants: "Its stump shall be a holy seed" (v. 13; cf. Ezra 9:2). This phrase "holy seed" occurs elsewhere only in Ezra in the entire HB (Neh 9:2). Regardless of the compositional influence of these books, if there were any phraseological correlation, it is worthwhile to ponder the pertinent meaning and theology. On the one hand, "the holy seed" in all these texts may denote the same socio-ethnic identity, i.e., the in-group of true Israel, commonly defined as the *golah* (exile)-returnees from the Babylonian captivity of Ezra and Nehemiah. The holy seed of Isaiah, then, would likewise refer to the Judean survivors from the exile. On the other hand, however, the holy seed of Isaiah may allude to a group counter to that of Ezra-Nehemiah. In this sense, the Isaianic holy seed may connote the out-group of Ezra-Nehemiah's true Israel. Mark Brett, for example, takes the "holy seed" here synonymously with the "holy people" of 62:12 (cf. Lev 19:2), thereby interpreting that "the Abrahamic seed reflected in 61:8-9 would necessarily include descent groups beyond the borders of Yehud, beyond the genealogical borders of Jacob-Israel, and thus beyond the narrowed circle of holiness in Ezra-Nehemiah" (Brett 2013a, 201; cf. Brett 2013b). Whether the remainees as a remnant or even those of mixed marriage, as can be found from other parts of the book, Isaianic holy seed signifies a radically inclusive theology.

Isaiah 6 is enveloped by the catchwords "death" (v. 1) and "seed" (v. 13). This polar correlation depicts an underlying concept that whereas the earthly king and his followers are to topple, the heavenly King intends to redeem the holy seed. Like a stump, the country will meet its demise. Admittedly, the stump can look so unappealing and as dead as it can be. Yet the stump is resilient and tough to kill, and oftentimes or over a long time it can regrow. It even regrows with many sprouts and numerous new trunks. Ultimately and miraculously, therefore, out of the stump a seed will grow (cf. 11:1). Who can ever make such a miracle occur? It is YHWH, proclaimed "holy, holy, holy" by the seraphim, who is capable of preserving and restoring the "holy" seed (Beuken 2004b, 75–78).

Three Children as Signs of Warning and Hope, 7:1–8:22
King Ahaz's Test and the Child Shear-jashub as a Warning, 7:1-13
Isaiah 7 shifts the prophetic speech from the first-person singular (Isa 6) to the third-person singular. This shift, which will revert back to the first-person singular in Isaiah 8, may mark Isaiah 7 as loosely fitted in the larger corpus. In contrast, as illustrated above, Isaiah 7 stands out and can be seen as a focal center of Isaiah 5–10.

Isaiah 7:1-9 displays a certain linguistic and thematic continuity as well. Here we learn of a new king (vv. 1-2) and have the first report of YHWH's speech (vv. 3-9). In a sequential reading, the chronological mention of the names Uzziah and Jotham fits wells with the Deuteronomistic history's account of the co-regency of these two kings (2 Kgs 15:5; 2 Chr 26:21). Following their co-reign, now Ahaz is the king. The historical setting is the Syro-Ephraimite War (735–732 BCE).

Here the invasion by the military alliance of Syria and Ephraim (northern Israel) against Jerusalem mirrors the expression of 2:3, where nations propose, "Let us go up" to Jerusalem (cf. 7:6). The neighboring nations plotted and "went up" to attack Jerusalem (v 1; cf. 36:1; Ps 2:1). Ironically, even though the intention of their going up toward Jerusalem is different, the results seem the same: just as the nations will not wield a sword and will learn war no more (2:4), so these ally nations "could not attack" Jerusalem (v 1; cf. 2 Kgs 16:5). Likewise, equally ironically, paralleling the "house of Jacob" (2:5-6; 5:7), now the reaction of the "house of David" (v. 2) contrasts with the atmosphere of the temple in Isaiah 6. Whereas the foundation of the thresholds "shook" (*nua'*) in 6:4, now it is the panic-stricken heart of King Ahaz that "shook" (*nua'*).

Verses 3-9, reporting the first speech of YHWH, further demonstrate the obstinate heart of King Ahaz as an object lesson of the task of the prophet's commissioning (6:9-10): "chapter 7 offers the first illustration of the hardening process at work in King Ahaz's rejection of the challenge of faith" (Childs 2001, 62). Near the Gihon spring, where the king is inspecting the defense system against the siege and infiltration attack through the relatively spacious underground tunnel, God provides the prophet's first child, Shear-jashub ("a remnant shall return"), as a sign of warning and hope (v. 3). Concerning the political context of King Ahaz and his intention to seek Assyria's aid, not YHWH's, there may be a literary pun with the name of this child. The Hebrew word for the "remnant" (*she'ar*) in the name Shear-jashub sounds quite similar to the word for Assyria (*ashur*). To the fearful, desperate King Ahaz and his policymakers, the news that "Assyria will return" to them would have been the most anticipated good news. Through the name of Isaiah's son, YHWH overturns their cunning international policy and forebodes the haunting news that "A remnant shall return"; i.e., Ahaz's kingdom will eventually fall, be exiled, and only "leftovers" will survive (Goldingay 2014, 25).

Thus, the divine message to the king in this national crisis is, "Do not fear" (v. 4; cf. 10:24; 37:6; 41:10, 13; 43:1, 5; 44:2). The divine assurance against the alliance's attack (vv. 5-6) recalls the theme of human lowliness versus YHWH's exaltation (Isa 2). Hence, the alliance's evil scheme will fail and not stand (v. 7). Each "head" of Aram and Ephraim—the word "head" occurs four times in vv. 8-9—cannot be a match for Jerusalem, already promised to be the "head" of all mountains (2:2). Ultimately, therefore, this divine promise comes with an admonition to "trust" (*amen*), echoing the divine covenant with the house of David in the Nathan oracle (2 Sam 7:16). Yet the conditional statement with "if" in v. 9 connotes a "qualification"—though not a "repudiation"—of the Davidic covenant, not unlike the conditional promise to Solomon (1 Kgs 8:25) in contrast with the unconditional promise to David (2 Sam 7:15-16; cf. Collins 2010, 229).

Isaiah 7:10-17 reports the second speech of YHWH that begins with the word "additionally" (v. 10; cf. Jonah 3:1). This time God gives Ahaz an offer to ask for a sign, which Ahaz declines (vv. 11-12). Margaret Odell posits that signs, even as symbolic acts, are not inherently decipherable but oftentimes "require faith in order to be perceived" (Odell 2005, 62; cf. Sweeney 2013, 38). Analogous to the "down payment" (or the inquiry to "mirror, mirror" in the fairy tale "Snow White"), according to Hans Wildberger, the divine offer of a sign "as deep as Sheol or as high as heaven" denotes "two opposites" for every possibility, thereby underscoring "the generosity of Isaiah/[YHWH]" (Wildberger 1991, 304). With regard to the sign YHWH offers, Ahaz parallels Hezekiah (37:30; 38:7, 22; cf. 37:7), together posing a question: "How will the sign be received—gratefully or with caution? Ahaz responds one way, Hezekiah another" (Seitz 1993, 78). The "house of David" hears divine chastisement due to the king's "wearying" of YHWH and the king's refusal to trust (v. 13). This is much like the way Israel's false sacrifices made YHWH become "weary" (1:14). Readers may wonder what huge difference it would imply for the king not to ask a sign from YHWH. In light of the pertinent content in 2 Kings 16:5-18, however, we can infer that the king's policy of rejecting YHWH's sign equals his outright submission to the Assyrian king, Tiglath-pileser III.

Throughout the history of the ancient Near East, puppet kings, exemplified by Ahaz, would succumb to become servants of Assyria in order to retain their power, courtesy of the Assyrian king's protection, support, and rewards for subservient subjects via the *Pax Assyriaca*. Who would object to the idea of buttering up the most powerful top dog of the era? Notably, whereas most Assyrian diplomatic expressions use "your servant" in the king's self-address, King Ahaz describes himself as Tiglath-pileser's "servant *and son*" (2 Kgs 16:7). Paul-Eugène Dion conjectures that this additional expression "son" may betray the disgruntled biblical narrator's intention to "emphasize Ahaz's servility" (Dion 2006, 137). In an intertextual reversal of Psalm 2, where YHWH declares to the Davidic king, "you are my son" (Ps 2:7), Ahaz now renounces this sonship and becomes Assyria's slave and son (Seitz 1993, 77). King Ahaz, through the overwhelming superpower of Assyria, could succeed in circumventing the stronger forces of the Syro-Ephraimite coalition. But the author of 2 Kings denounces this policy "not as an expression of political strength or genius but rather as the inception of a dangerous dependency" (Wright 2011, 117).

In addition to paying tribute to Assyria (2 Kgs 16:7-8), Ahaz further built an altar as a replica of one in Damascus and pillaged sacred adornments from the Jerusalem temple (2 Kgs 16:10-18). In fact, Ahaz is the first king of Judah who "made his son pass through fire"—"a rite of Molech in the Valley of Hinnom" (2 Kgs 16:3). Such syncretistic practices were to please their Assyrian masters in order to maintain their royal security. We should wonder how Manasseh, another syncretistic vassal who paid heavy tribute, managed to reign for so long, almost fifty-five years. Ahaz would thus easily resort to demoting YHWH "into a minor deity (2 Kings 22) due to [YHWH's] inability to protect Judah from the powerful Assyrians and Tiglath-pileser's defeat of Israel in 732 BCE" (Perdue and Carter 2015, 65).

We should further note that this policy meant more than a symbolic reliance or idolatry per se, for forming an alliance also had massive ramifications on the economic, social, and political dimensions of the country's life (Fretheim 2013, 10–11). Jacob Wright posits that, when paying tribute to the imperial superpower, the kings of Israel and Judah often taxed substantial portions of money, not from the temple or palace but from "all the wealthy landowners" and people of the land (Wright 2011, 117–18; cf. 2 Kgs 15:17-20; 23:31-35). This would in turn have produced a domino effect in the economic ladder of the society, mostly affecting the poor peasants who would often have had to match the increasing amounts of agricultural export goods their landowners would demand, regardless of famine, war, or any other conditions. Ahaz managed to keep his throne by way of the cowardly bribe for Tiglath-pileser, but eventually at the expense of his country's wealth and sovereignty. While saving himself and his political clout, there would be worsening economic hardships for the rest of the population, especially the lower class. More significantly, by offering himself as a slave to Assyria, Ahaz is turning his back toward YHWH.

Immanuel as a Sign of Divine Admonition to Trust YHWH's Protection, 7:14-25

Verses 14-17 (as part of the second YHWH speech, vv. 10-17) narrate YHWH giving a sign to Ahaz (cf. Judg 6:17; Isa 20:3; 38:22). This sign involves another child, Immanuel, from a young maiden ripe for marriage (*'almah*) through a birth announcement formula (v. 14; cf. Gen 16:11; Judg 13:3; Childs 2001, 65–66). The child's name implies YHWH's abiding presence and thus the continuity of the Davidic dynasty. The name refers to the "we"-group ("God is with us"). Accordingly, contrary to a monarch in charge of the Israelite or Judahite state and population, the prophet for the "we"-group frequently took up the role of a "freely recruited and enlisted emissary for the CEO of the universe—direct spokesperson for the Sovereign of all the world" (Boling 1999, 173). At the same time, it connotes a positive note of salvation that God is able to provide for this frightened king and his people. Here this child's ability to refuse evil and choose good makes a hyperbolic contrast with the grown-ups, the monarchs, who love evil and hate good (v 15; cf. 1:16-17; 3:4; 5:20).

Why a child metaphor? Faith in God requires our resolute belief, like a quantum leap, in every dimension and affair of life, both in theory and praxis: "Faith is a refusal to give in to the threats of undoing posed by these small northern neighbors, and to proceed in confidence in the face of such self-evident danger" (Brueggemann 1998a, 67). The prophet Isaiah constantly reminds his audience of this mystery of the simple yet utter trust of children as opposed to the complicated yet hollow assurance of adults, as John Oswalt lucidly explicates: "The book of Isaiah indicates frequently that God is powerful enough to destroy his enemies in an instant, yet when the prophet comes to the heart of the meaning of deliverance, a childlike face peers at us" (Oswalt 1986, 245; cf. Matt 18:3). Jacqueline Lapsley further elucidates the metaphorical functions of children in the book of Isaiah that, on the one hand, how the society treats children, especially the orphans (1:17, 23; 10:1-2), is "a barometer that indicates how far Israel is from keeping the Torah" and, on the other hand, not just the three children addressed as signs and portents of divine judgment (8:18) but also Israel itself is a child (alongside daughter Zion) in relationship with God as their compassionate parent (Lapsley 2008, 86–87).

That Hezekiah is Ahaz's son accentuates the dynamic contrast between the recalcitrance of Ahaz the grown-up father and the receptiveness of Hezekiah the young son—in fact, some scholars propose to identify Immanuel as Hezekiah rather than one of Isaiah's sons or another Davidic heir (Seitz 1993: 65). Assuredly, in such a short time, YHWH pronounces the impending fall of Syria and Ephraim to the king of Assyria who will act as YHWH's mere instrument (v. 16; cf. 10:5).

Isaiah 7:18-25 continues and expands the warnings concerning the king of Assyria in the four "on that day" passages (cf. v. 17). Concerning the first subunit (vv. 18-19), YHWH whistling for the fly forms a literary bracket with YHWH whistling for a nation from the north (5:26-30). The "fly" from Egypt (v. 18) may echo the "swarms of flies," one of the ten plagues that afflicted the Egyptians (Exod 8:20-32). Even though the Hebrew words for the "fly" are not the same, it is noteworthy that YHWH also offers a "sign" ('ot) using this plague (Exod 8:23), just as Ahaz was given a "sign" ('ot) here (v. 14). Both flies and bees, referring to Egypt and Assyria, are attracted to curds and honey (v. 15 and v. 22), implying not only that Ahaz should not rely on these superpowers but also that they can easily turn against such vulnerable vassals at whim (Sweeney 1996, 155–56).

The second subunit (v. 20) elaborates the same motif in light of shaving hairs, which was equivalent to shaming by unmanning and castrating since beards were symbols of male power in the ancient Near East—an image of utter defeat and humiliation (2 Sam 10:1-5). Moreover, along with the word "bee" (v. 18; cf. Judg 14:8), the notion of shaving with a "razor" may allude to the Philistines' disarming of Samson (Judg 13:5; 16:17-19). Now the king and people of Judah will be violated by the king of Assyria.

The third subunit (vv. 21-22) depicts the effects of this Assyrian invasion. Referring to the "curds and honey" of v. 15, this passage predicts that the remnants of the land will have to rely on a young cow and a couple of flocks (v. 21) to produce curds and honey (v. 22). In an ironic twist, the curds and honey, which could indicate abundant food (cf. v. 15), now connote "the produce of the uncultivated land," implying the impending hardship until God's deliverance (Collins 2010, 233–34).

The last subunit (vv. 23-25) echoes the "briers and thorns" of 5:6 and, with the threefold use of these words in each verse, recapitulates the devastating overthrow of the vineyard (5:1-7). Just as the vineyard on a fertile hill would not be "hoed" (5:6), so all the hills that used to be "hoed" (v. 25) shall be full of briers and thorns (the verb "to hoe" [*'adar*] occurs only in 5:6 and 7:25 in the entire HB). That these choice vines will become thorns and briers fulfills the judgment announcement of the song of the vineyard in Isaiah 5 (Seitz 1993, 80). Forming a bracket with v. 21 by the catchwords (young cow and flocks), this subunit concludes that where the powerful rulers used to "trample" like beasts (1:12), only oxen and sheep will loosely "trample" on that day (v. 25; cf. 5:5).

Child Maher-shalal-hash-baz as a Warning against "this people," 8:1–22

Isaiah 8 shifts the speaker back to the first-person singular, thereby together with Isaiah 6 (also the first-person singular speech) enveloping the Immanuel passage of Isaiah 7 as the literary and thematic center. In that center, the primary theme was the divine invitation for the king and people to have faith in YHWH in their policy and practices. Now Isaiah 8 resumes the theme of the preceding chapters with regard to the warning concerning the impending doom of Syria and Ephraim through the king of Assyria, doom that now affects Judah as well. Yet, in the present form, Isaiah 8 shares many thematic affiliations with Isaiah 7 (Collins 2010, 226).

Isaiah 8:1-4 introduces another child, Maher-shalal-hash-baz (8:1, 3), as a sign of YHWH's message. Together with Shear-jashub (7:3) and Immanuel (7:14), this child makes a triad in this core section. Just as the motif of the name Shear-jashub ("a remnant shall return") continues the preceding occurrences of the similar motif (cf. 1:9; 4:2-3), so the name Maher-shalal-hash-baz ("the spoil speeds, the prey hastens") picks up the pertinent tunes sounded previously (cf. 5:19, 26).

Similar to the episode concerning the common language of Judah instead of Aramaic in the Rabshakeh's siege (36:11-13), here in the initial speech YHWH commands Isaiah to record in plain characters, comprehensible to all (v. 1), and with "faithful" (*amen*) witnesses (v 2; cf. 7:9). That Isaiah's wife, as some scholars posit, may have been a female prophet, hence a public figure, seems to bolster the theme of influential witnesses (v. 3). Being a public figure, possibly the predecessor of the prophetesses' office held by Huldah, her child with Isaiah could have attracted broader attention, thereby reinforcing the reliability of Isaiah's prediction against the northern coalition (Williamson 2010, 73–75). Following the same expression in 7:16 ("before the child knows . . ."), this child too functions as a sign for the demise of Damascus and Samaria (v 4): there (7:16) the timeline was the child's weaning in a couple of years or three years (hence 735–732 BCE), when the child becomes a toddler; but now (v. 4) we hear a sense of more urgency, barely a year away, when the child can say its first words, "mama and papa."

Isaiah 8:5-8 presents the second speech of YHWH, initiated by the word "additionally" (v. 5), much like the two speeches of YHWH in Isaiah 7 (7:3, 11). The causal sentence elucidates how "this people" has rejected YHWH (cf. 5:24), who is likened to the gentle, reassuring Shiloah (v. 6; cf. Neh 3:15). The consequential sentences then reverse this imagery into the inundating waters of the river, Assyria, that will fiercely "go up" and flood Judah (vv. 7-8). Similar to the shift from the judgment against Judah (Amos 2:4-5) to that against northern Israel (Amos 2:6-16), when Ahaz and his conclave delight in hearing the downfall of their enemy nations up north (vv. 1-4), Isaiah hurls another sign of warning directed to none other than Judah (vv. 5-8). Here, the name Immanuel recurs (v. 8; cf. 7:14), but this time this sign highlights trouble on the way to Ahaz.

Isaiah 8:9-15 follows the message of dual threat (against Judah's northern enemies in vv. 1-4 and against Judah in vv. 5-8) with an imperative command, which then will correlate to a second imperative command subunit in 8:16-22.

Verses 9-10 extend the addressees to "peoples" and "all remote places of the earth" (v. 9). This hymn mocks all daunting nations in their forming alliances together, announcing that they will be "shattered"—the word "shattered" occurs three times in v. 9. It is as though the prophet is taunting the allied forces of Aram and Ephraim, who will be "shattered" (*hatat*) according to 7:8, just as all military pacts will be "shattered" (*hatat*) according to v. 9. YHWH declares that any political scheme shall not "stand" (7:7, 9), therefore, such military and political plots will not "stand" (v. 10). In contrast, the hymn resoundingly avers who is in charge: Immanuel, or "God is with us" (v 10; cf. v. 8).

Verses 11-15 reveal the religio-political tension in Judah by reiterating the contrast between "this people" who fear the allied forces and the smaller "we"-group that fears YHWH. The phrase "this people" (vv. 11, 12) picks up the same group in v. 6, which then indicates Ahaz and his circle. Countering the previous aspiration to "walk in YHWH's paths" (2:3), now the prophet is not to walk in the way of "this people" (v. 11). It should be noted that the phrase "this people" occurs only in select passages throughout the book of Isaiah (6:9-10; 8:6, 11-12; 9:16; 28:11, 14; 29:13-14; cf. Haran 2010: 95–103). Whoever "this people" may represent, they may have had a close association with the king. They were influential in charging Isaiah and his disciples with conspiracy (v. 12). Contrary to what these thugs fear and dread, however, Isaiah and his faithful disciples and community are to fear YHWH alone (v. 13).

Over and against the powers that be in Jerusalem, YHWH declares the divine intention to become the very sanctuary. This divine attack targets the two "houses of Israel" and the citizens of Jerusalem (v. 14). Csaba Balogh delineates the various terms of v. 14 as follows: YHWH "will become a sanctuary (for the disciples [cf. vv. 16-18]); but a stone one strikes against and a rock one stumbles over [YHWH] will be for both houses of Israel (Ephraim and Manasseh; cf. Isa 9:20), a trap and a snare for the inhabitants of Jerusalem" (Balogh 2013, 13). Reinhard Kratz offers another insightful analysis: considering the political meaning of "house" and the social meaning of "Israel," and also in light of 7:17, the expression "the two houses of Israel" highlights "both the two kingdoms and the ideal of a unified 'Israel'" (Kratz 2012, 168, 179). YHWH as the "sanctuary" (*miqdash*) constitutes a thematic pun with a "snare" (*moqesh*) for the hard-hearted leaders of the two kingdoms (Ephraim and Judah) as well as Jerusalem, who will stumble, fall, and be broken (v. 15; cf. 3:8).

Isaiah 8:16-22 starts another subunit with imperatives. This time, though, the prophet's command does not concern the citizens of Jerusalem and other peoples in distant lands (vv. 9, 14) but instead his disciples who adhere to God (v. 16; cf. 1:10; 2:3; 5:24).

Verses 16-18, with their "restricted audience," present a central message in the larger section (Balogh 2013, 4). Despite the fact that YHWH threatened to hide the divine face from the "house of Jacob" (2:5-6; cf. 1:15), Isaiah vows to wait for the Lord, even if the Lord seems absent to many people (v. 17). In fact, YHWH is neither hidden nor absent but dwells in Mount Zion and has already provided Isaiah and his children as "signs" (v. 18; cf. 7:3; 8:3;

20:3). Nevertheless, that the divine messages are sealed is consistent with the motif of hardening this recalcitrant people and the motif of the hiding of YHWH (Uhlig 2009b, 81). "This people," who love to utter self-serving "counsel" and "word" (cf. v. 10) and devise wrongful "conspiracy" (cf. v. 12), will meet the fate of false prophets and perverse leaders. In contrast to "this people" with callous hearts, YHWH will later make another signal out of the branch of Jesse (11:1, 10).

Verses 19-20 expand the theme of divine absence in vv. 16-18. Comparable to the murmuring of the Israelites (cf. Exod 32:1-4), this people seek ghosts, local gods, and the dead for instruction and testimony (cf. 1 Sam 28:5-25). The words "instructions" (*torah*) and "testimony" (*te'udah*) in v. 20 bracket an inverted chiasm with the words "testimony" (*te'udah*) and "instructions" (*torah*) in v. 16. It is no wonder that, because these divine messages are rolled up and sealed, people cannot access them (cf. 29:11). Indeed, those who resort to such ungodly routes will have no light (v. 20; cf. 2:5; 5:30).

Verses 21-22 elaborate the situation by describing how recalcitrant people will walk in the dark. Reminiscent of the wilderness wandering recorded in the Pentateuch, this people, in their hunger, will curse their king and their own gods (v. 21; cf. v. 19). In fact, everywhere they look, there will only be distress and darkness (v. 22) much in the same way that they have perverted light into darkness (cf. 5:20). According to Ulrich Berges, this catchword "darkness" in 8:22 builds an inner ring structure with the same word in 5:30. The outer ring structure of the woe-oracles of 5:8-24 and 10:1-4 also surround this darkness theme. The theme centers chiastically on the Immanuel theme, God's abiding presence with the devout remnant. The theme of darkness further anticipates the dawn of the light that the following chapters depict (Berges 2012a, 73–80).

Birth of a Child of Light, a Prince of Peace, 9:1-7 (MT 8:23–9:6)

Like an oasis in the desert terrain, this unit is refreshing. It rings a melody of hope amid oracles of judgment. This unit shifts its main addressees from Ahaz and his circle, also referred to as "this people," to Isaiah and his devotees who represent the "we"-group. In turn, its overall mood also shifts from gloomy doom to hope for an era of light with a righteous ruler. The dawn of the generation of light will embrace the colonized regions of Israel (v. 1). This time will also usher in the birth of a child of hope, a prince of peace, proclaimed by a chorus of thanksgiving (vv. 2-7).

Isaiah 9:1, though closely connected to the preceding subunit, reverses the motif of gloom. Contrary to those who consult pagan gods and who will be thrust into "gloom of anguish" (8:19-22), those who were in "anguish" will be free from "gloom" (v. 1). Both Zebulun and Naphtali, the northern-most regions of Israel ravaged by Tiglath-pileser III in 732 BCE, will experience glorious restoration (cf. 2 Kgs 15:29).

Isaiah 9:2-7, a royal hymn, recounts the exodus deliverance and the settlement in Canaan (vv. 2-5), followed by the annunciation of the birth of a royal child (vv. 6-7). Verses 2-3, recalling the miraculous exodus deliverance, proclaim YHWH's ongoing salvific guidance. In one of the plagues the Egyptians experienced "thick darkness" (cf. Isa 8:22) and could not see at all, contrary to the Israelites who enjoyed light (Exod 10:21-23). Likewise, YHWH will lead the people into light with joy and exultation, just as the Hebrews plundered the Egyptians in their redemption (Exod 12:35-36).

Verses 4-5 follow up with two causal *ki*-clauses, and a third instance of the clause recurs in vv. 6-7. This subunit further recalls the divine victory over the enemy oppressors during the time of Judges (Judg 6:1-6). God enabled Gideon and his meager three hundred soldiers miraculously to defeat the Midianites (Judg 7:2, 12-25). Similarly, it will be only YHWH who will defeat the oppressors.

Verses 6-7 climactically proclaim YHWH's anointing of a royal king in the Davidic kingdom, as anticipated by the "we"-group ("unto us")—this first-person plural voice may have originally echoed the responses of the divine council, not unlike those of the seraphim of 6:3, in the Egyptian coronation ritual (Roberts 2002, 143–56; cf. Ps 2:7). Reverting back to the account of the death of King Uzziah (6:1), now the prophet announces the birth of a new king. The "Mighty God" together with "unto us" in v. 6 makes a fitting reference to "God with us," Immanuel, of 7:14. The preceding promise of a son finds its first fulfillment here in a royal birth (Seitz 1993, 87).

Although Hezekiah makes a good candidate for this king, the king's identity is anonymous, leaving open expectations for future heirs to the Davidic dynasty. Rather, the name of this child includes "prince of peace" (*sar-shalom*), which hearkens back to Solomon (*shelomoh*) of the past golden era. Certainly, this divinely appointed king will be granted "peace without end" (cf. 2 Sam 7:12-16; 1 Chr 17:11-14) so that he can build the kingdom with justice and righteousness. We learn the foundational purpose behind God's providing this child, i.e., to establish and protect the kingdom with "justice" and "righteousness"—key concepts of Isaiah's wholesome society (Williamson 1998, 255). This final clause affirms that it is not human strength but divine zeal that will accomplish this (cf. 37:32).

Resumed Woe-Oracles against the Wicked, 9:8–10:4

This unit has four subunits, consistently ending with the phrase, "For all this his anger has not turned back; his hand is still stretched out" (9:12, 17, 21; 10:4). This catchphrase connects the unit back to 5:8-25, which also ends with the same phrase (5:25). Similarly, the six woe-oracles in 5:8-25 resume in the seventh woe-oracle in 10:1-4. All together, these two units, 5:1-25 and 9:8–10:4, envelop the internal core section of 6:1–9:7. A thematic shift from Isaiah 5 to Isaiah 9 may thus coincide with the transition of the locale of accusation from Judah back to northern Israel. Nevertheless, these two units share the same thematic thread, i.e., vehement criticism against the abusive leaders of northern Israel.

The first subunit, 9:8-12, clearly identifies the target of its accusation as Jacob-Israel. Reading sequentially, in the aftermath of the demolition of many towns in northern Israel, YHWH's word "fell" on Israel and Israel's bricks "fell" as well (vv. 8, 10). Yet the privileged leaders in the capital Samaria display no penance but still have arrogant hearts (v. 9), foreshadowing the haughty hearts of the king of Assyria (10:7) and the king of Babylon (14:13). As a result, YHWH "exalts" (cf. 2:11, 17) their enemies—Aram from the east and Philistia from the west—to "devour" Israel (vv. 11-12; cf. 1:7, 20).

The second subunit, 9:13-17, continues the theme of human hubris as sin, portrayed by how the people neither returned to nor sought YHWH (v. 13). Who are the primary culprits? High ranks of various offices in leadership: first the "heads," such as elders and dignitaries with haughty faces, and then the "tail," such as false prophets (vv. 14-15; cf. 3:2, 5, 14). The masterminds of "this people" as well as their subjects are corrupt, resulting in a total crumbling of the society: everyone is godless and evil (vv. 16-17; cf. 1:4; 10:6).

According to the third subunit, 9:18-21, matters will become even worse. The consequence of the prideful sins of Israel's leaders led first to the uprooting of towns by military invasion (vv. 8-12) and then to the disintegration of the social system (vv. 13-17). Now, hubris has led to a horrendous, harrowing civil war. Whereas the desolate land became "briers and thorns" (5:6; 7:23-25), now wickedness will consume those places (v. 18). Just as the boots of Israel's attackers burned as "fuel for fire" (9:5), now Israel is to become "fuel for fire" (v. 19). Even more dreadfully, these depictions are not mere metaphors but instead agonizing portrayals of the reality of the nation in domestic warfare (vv. 20-21). Once they knew each other as brothers, Manasseh and Ephraim, two sons of the same father Joseph (Gen 41:51-52). Now they are only busy devouring each other, the flesh of their own kindred, while simultaneously attacking Judah. Can a society get any worse than this? Where did all this inhumane brutality start?

The last subunit, 10:1-4, which also resumes the woe-oracles of 5:8-25, discloses the diagnosis of all this violence. Once again, and unequivocally, the main blame goes to the most powerful and privileged leaders. Woe to the movers and shakers, both in Israel and in Judah, who obliterate fair dealings, bend the rules against the needy, and rob justice from the poor of "my people" (vv. 1-2; cf. 3:15). The prophet cries a scathing lament in rhetorical questions on behalf of the widows and orphans to the thickened ears of these stubborn leaders: In the days of your punishment, who will protect you and where will all your hoarded wealth go?

A Woe-Oracle against Assyria, YHWH's Weapon, 10:5-34

The previous collection of woe-oracles (5:8–10:4) detailed the divine condemnation of the upper-class rulers (5:8-25), the hardening of the heart of "this people" (6:1-13), the demise of Syria and northern Israel (7:1-17; 8:1-4), the warning of punishment on Judah (8:5-22), and again the judgment against the stubborn leaders of Jacob/Israel (9:8-21), including those in Judah (10:1-4). Just as in the song of the vineyard (5:1-7), readers also hear the chorus of a royal hymn (9:1-7).

In this composite collection, which mainly covers the domestic realm, the prophet also hinted at the influence of Assyria in the international arena (5:26-30; 7:18-25). Indeed, Assyria is a menacing empire. Nevertheless, its people are merely a weapon for the divine plan, summoned by YHWH who gently hints "psst" to them (5:26; 7:18). Now the prophet declares another woe-oracle, but this time it aims at Assyria (Sweeney 1996, 198–99). This woe-oracle projects at least two key themes: first, YHWH will humble any human hubris, not just that of the abusive upper-class of Israel and Judah but also that of the impregnable and arrogant Assyria; second, the humiliation of the Assyrian empire will thus guarantee and usher in the redemption of the penitent remnants of Israel and Judah. There is a rough temporal movement from the present to the future, mirroring the demise of Assyria and the return of Israel's remnants (Beuken 2002, 19–22).

Isaiah 10:5-11 thus shifts the condemnation of woe onto Assyria. This subunit reveals the plans of both YHWH and the Assyrian king. Like the Pharaoh in the exodus, this Assyrian king is unnamed, though scholars consider Sargon II (721–705 BCE) during his westward military campaign against Egypt and Philistia in 720 BCE, prior to Sennacherib's campaign in 701, a likely candidate (Sweeney 1996, 204–209).

Verses 5-6 describe YHWH's plan. Just as God provided Moses the "staff" as a tool for the deliverance of Israel (Exod 4:2-5; 7:1–10:20; 14:16), Assyria is the "rod" and "staff," a mere instrument, for divine anger against the godless nation, Israel (cf. 9:17). In light of numerous parallel expressions describing the Assyrian kings as the "weapons" of the patron gods in the Neo-Assyrian royal inscriptions (e.g., Sargon II: "By means of the power of Ashur, Nabu [and Marduk], the great gods, my lords, who have raised my weapons, I slew my enemies"), Michael Chan claims that this subversive Isaianic oracle dethrones not just the imperial king but also the imperial gods, thereby concocting a "theological and rhetorical coup d'état" (Chan 2009, 724–26). In an echo of the name, Maher-shalal-hash-baz (8:1-4; cf. 5:26), this Assyrian king is summoned "to take spoil and to seize plunder" (*lishelol shalal welaboz baz*). This weapon will accomplish YHWH's intention to "trample" the rotten vineyard (5:5).

Verses 7-11 unveil Assyria's plan. As if echoing the dismissal of the wicked in Psalm 1—"Not so (*lo'-ken*) the wicked" (Ps 1:4)—they expose the gruesome but foolish "heart" of the Assyrian king —"This is not (*lo'-ken*) what he devises" (v. 7; cf. 14:13; Pss 14:1; 53:1). The speech of this king exhibits nothing short of arrogance expressed in rhetorical questions (vv. 8-11). From the annals of Sargon, we find similar records that the Aramean cities (with Ilu-bi'di as their leader) fell under his campaign:

> In my second regnal year, . . . Il[ubi'di] of Hamath, not the rightful holder of the throne, not fit(?) for the palace, who in the shepherdship of his people, did [not attend to their] fate, [but] with regard to the god Aššur, his land (and) his people he sought evil, not good, and he treated contemptuously. He gathered Arpad and Samerina, and he turned (them) to his side [. . .] h[e] kill[ed] [a]nd he did not leave anyone alive [. . .] I raised [my hand to Aššur]; and in order to conquer H[a]math. . . . (*COS* II: 295)

Against this background, this king boastfully but ignorantly claims that Jerusalem's God, misunderstood as "idols" (*'elil*), is no more powerful than the images of Samaria or other sizable kingdoms.

Isaiah 10:12-19 states the divine rebuttal against the taunt of this Assyrian king. Following the divine chastisement of Jerusalem, YHWH will crush the haughty eyes of this king (v. 12; cf. v. 3). As in the previous taunt speech (vv. 8-11), this Assyrian king boasts that his "hand" has no match or limit in power (vv. 13-14; cf. v. 10).

Against this insolent claim, YHWH mocks the Assyrian king who is neither a human nor a hand to YHWH but is a mere inanimate ax, saw, rod, or staff (v. 15). This striking metaphor criticizes the cutting down of trees by the Assyrian army (cf. 37:24; Deut 20:19-20). The metaphor further underscores that this ax will soon become mere material for burning (vv. 16-17). Whereas Israel met the fate of "briers and thorns" to be consumed by wickedness (9:18), now Israel's light, its Holy One, shall devour Assyria's "thorns and briers" (v. 17). In this destruction, just as remnants of Judah will be minimal (6:13), now the remnants of Assyria will also be few (vv. 18-19). Mirroring the Neo-Assyrian siege warfare, the descriptions of vv. 16-19 shift the judging overlord from the Assyrian king to YHWH: "Ironically, the agent of judgment (the Assyrian king), has now become the object of judgment" (Chan 2009, 730).

Isaiah 10:20-26—the first "on that day" subunit—turns to the real audiences, the people of Jacob/Israel (vv. 20-23) and of Zion/Judah (vv. 24-26), with the message of their survival and rescue. It is as though this passage resumes the oracles against northern Israel (9:8-21). Amid the process and aftermath of the Assyrian invasion, northern Israel will fall completely (vv. 20-23). Its remnant will survive, however. Israel's fate will be an object lesson for Judah's renewal and hope for divine mercy (vv. 24-27a).

Verses 20-23 focus on the remnant of Jacob-Israel. This subunit reveals a thematic tension, especially with the double meaning of the name Shearjashub ("a remnant shall return") in 7:3. Negatively, countering the positive tone of promise of Hosea 1:10 ("the number of the children of Israel shall be like the sand of the sea"), only the remnant shall escape in the nation's complete end (vv. 22-23). Yet, positively, there is a sure tone of hope for them. Previously, it was YHWH, to whom the people did not return, who struck them (9:13). Now the striker is not YHWH but presumably Assyria, on whom the remnant should not lean as did the murmuring Israelites who yearned to go back to serve the Egyptians (v. 20; cf. Exod 14:11-12). This theme of the faithful remnant relates to the stories of the four leprous men in the outskirts of Samaria who not only saved themselves but also the whole people against the Aramean camp in 2 Kings 6–7 (cf. Naaman in 2 Kings 5):

> In the little traditions, in the folktales from the scroll of Kings, common people and roving bands of their prophetic champions move among farming villages and rural holy sites (Mount Carmel, Mount Horeb, the Gilgal monuments from Joshua's day), sustaining the Mosaic faith and supporting one another in spite of evil governments. They constitute the faithful remnant that the writing prophets always promised would make it

through any disaster (Isa 10:20-21 . . .), the righteous who survive because of their faithfulness (Hab 2:4). (Mobley 2009, 133)

The emphatic statements that the remnant will "never again" lean on a pharaoh or any tyrannous king but instead will "truly" lean on YHWH (v. 20) assert this hopeful news. As a result, this "remnant of Jacob" is assured of its return to "Mighty God" (v. 21), echoing one of the names of the royal child (9:6).

Verses 24-26 focus on the Jerusalemites, with vv. 24-25 as "an oracle of encouragement for the people in Jerusalem" (De Jong 2010, 86). As a consequence ("therefore") of Jacob's demise and the remnant that escapes to Judah, YHWH admonishes Zion, "my people," not to fear (v. 24). Here the message alludes to the exodus tradition. Like the Egyptians, the Assyrians beat them with the "rod" and the "staff" (v. 24; cf. v. 5). But soon YHWH's "fury" and "anger" (v. 25) will turn against the very tool of divine "anger" and "fury" (cf. v. 5). The catchphrase "the way of the Egyptians"—or "the road to Egypt" (De Jong 2010, 91)—at the end of both v. 24 and v. 26 envelops this subunit. Indeed, just as the "staff" of Moses with his outstretched hand divided the sea (Exod 14:16, 21), now YHWH will lift the "staff" over the sea and strike Assyria (v. 26).

Isaiah 10:27-34—the second "on that day" passage—recapitulates the Assyrian invasion, depicted in graphic reports of the military march and assault on Judah. Verse 27 connects to v. 26 with key catchwords: staff, shoulder, and yoke. Once YHWH broke the yoke and staff on their shoulders in the time of the judges (9:4), now YHWH, who will extend the staff over Egypt (v. 26), promises to break Assyria's yoke on "your [Israel's]" back and shoulder (v. 27). Read together, Matthijs J. De Jong considers vv. 26-27 as presenting the reciprocal themes as two sides of the same coin: "[YHWH's] punishment of Assyria" in v. 26 and "the liberation of Judah" in v. 27 (De Jong 2010, 95). At the same time, however, the shift to the second-person masculine singular ("your") as well as the "on that day" phrase marks v. 27 as a start for a new subunit. The rhetorical effect of this shift signifies that now YHWH will tell Jerusalem how the yoke and staff on "your" shoulder (v. 27) will crumble (vv. 28-32).

Verses 28-32 report the towns where the Assyrian troops raided. Text-critically, v. 27b may refer to the Assyrian king's initial attack on Rimmon. The next towns subjugated are Aiath, Migron, and Michmash (v. 28). Then fall Geba, Ramah, and Gibeah, which are closer to Jerusalem (v. 29). Outcries of carnage arise from Gallim, Laishah, and Anathoth (v. 30). Madmenah and Gebim are taken (v. 31), and "today" his troops are stationed at Nob, with his "hand" directed at Mount Zion (v. 32). The effect is as though the sentinels send the terrible news that towns and fortresses surrounding Jerusalem have succumbed to the Assyrian army, one by one, from the farther outskirts of the northeast of Jerusalem to all the way near Nob, overlooking Jerusalem.

Verses 33-34 dramatically counter the clear and present threat against the vulnerable city Jerusalem. Miraculously, YHWH of the army will appear and marvelously dismantle them. This conclusion climactically culminates with the matchless power of divine deliverance, depicted with echoes of the tree metaphors: "The highest trees will be cut down and the lofty ones brought low" (v. 33; cf. 2:11-12, 17; 5:15).

An Ideal Future Kingdom, Starting from the Stump of Jesse, 11:1-16

Somewhat abruptly, but as if restating the vision for a whole new world from Isaiah 2, the prophet offers the blueprint of an ideal future kingdom in vv. 1-9. In this world, the good ruler empowered by YHWH's spirit will uphold justice and integrity (vv. 1-5), and all classes of people will live in mutual trust and harmony (vv. 6-9). The stump of Jesse will bring about this utopia (vv. 1, 10), elucidated further in vv. 10-16, by vanquishing all threatening forces and consolidating a peaceful unity of Israel and Judah.

Isaiah 11:1-9—emphatically initiated by the first "stump of Jesse" statement—envisions the coming of a restored era. A great leader from Jesse's lineage will receive anointing of YHWH's spirit (vv. 1-5), and the trustworthy reign will establish a community of hope and trust (vv. 6-9).

Verses 1-5 ingeniously pick up the tree motif of the preceding passage. Whereas YHWH will uproot the tall trees of the Assyrian empire (10:33-34), now a true leader will come out of a lowly stump of Jesse (v. 1). W. A. M. Beuken remarks that this insight is "far from recent," since C. Vitringa's 1715 commentary had already observed the antithetical link between "the tall and lofty trees of Lebanon" (10:33-34) and "the shoot from the stump of Jesse" (11:1)." In a larger scope, accordingly, the two preceding collections (10:5-34 and 11:1-16) coalesce with contrasting themes that culminate in the closing psalm (Isa 12): "The prophet's song of thanksgiving (ch. 12) is preceded by a diptych: the woe-oracle concerning Assyria that is to be hewn down 'like mighty trees' (10:5-34), and the promise of salvation for the shoot of Jesse, upon whom the spirit of YHWH shall rest and who will be raised as an ensign for the nations (11:1-16)" (Beuken 2002, 17).

The reference to the hacked stump may hint at the fall of the Davidic monarchy. On the contrary, the phrase "stump of Jesse"—instead of "stump of David" (cf. an additional phrase: the "bud of David" in 4Q285 Frag.

5)—does not imply negative judgment but rather points to the positive future involving the new, righteous Davidic ruler (Williamson 1998a, 263). Comparable to Ezekiel 17, 31, and Daniel 4, here the tree represents a king, firmly rooted and growing in supernatural marvel (Mazor 2004, 82). This Davidic king will be endowed with the spirit of YHWH and equipped for perfect governance.

Reminiscent of the world of creation in Genesis 1–3, vv. 2-5 advocate key prescriptions of good leadership. Possibly, echoing the six days of complete creation in Genesis 1, the sixfold attributes of YHWH's spirit (cf. Gen 1:2) imply perfect qualifications of "good" dominion (v. 2; cf. Gen 1:31). No longer is there a dangerous tree with the knowledge of good and evil (Gen 2:17) because YHWH's spirit alone will provide good knowledge. The sixth attribute, "fear of YHWH," depicts the ability to judge beyond outward seeing or hearing (v. 3; cf. 6:9), motivated neither by matters desirable to the eyes (Gen 3:6) nor by the "fear" of nakedness (Gen 3:10).

In another intertextual correlation, these virtues of a good king allude to their origin in Lady Wisdom, who grants prudence, knowledge, discretion, fear of YHWH, counsel, efficiency, understanding, and valor (Prov 8:12-14). Indeed, a good king must delight in the fear of God (Isa 11:2-3). The ancients thought of a king as divinely elected and endowed, almost with divine qualities, as the son of God (cf. Ps 2:7). Yet such a divine approval of the kings did not reside in their special status but rather in their acknowledging the deity. Hence, the human king ought to fear the divine King. Human kings must wield authority and power in abject humility and total trust toward the power and stipulations of God (Prov 8:15-16).

Furthermore, these descriptions allude to the Davidic dynasty. Thus, YHWH's spirit, which "rushed upon [David]" (1 Sam 16:13), will rest upon this shoot from Jesse (v 2). References to this Davidic heir, endowed with the spirit of "counsel and might," echo the theophoric names of the divinely elected child, "Wonderful" Counselor and "Mighty" God (9:6; cf. Williamson 1998a, 259). In the selection of David, the youngest among the siblings, YHWH chides the prophet Nathan that "humans see according to the sight of their eyes, but YHWH sees into the heart" (1 Sam 16:7). Thus, this spirit-filled branch "shall not judge according to the appearance in his eyes" (v. 3; cf. Mazor 2004, 87). The statement that this anointed ruler will not govern according to what his eyes see or his ears hear makes a deliberate contrast with the recalcitrant people (6:9-10).

Should readers perceive these ideals to be too abstract, good leadership is exemplified in concrete, socioeconomic domains (v. 4). Fair reign means providing justice and righteousness for the poor and the weak, first and foremost (cf. 1:17; 3:14-15; 5:7; 10:2). Unlike the "rod" and "staff" the Assyrian king assumed as a tool in 10:5, the righteous shoot (as though a little child) will wield the "rod" of his mouth and the "spirit" of his lips in slaying the wicked. Instead of the arrows and bows for Assyria's "belt of loins" (*'ezor halatsayw*, 5:27-28), righteousness and faithfulness will be the "belt of loins" (*'ezor halatsayw*, v. 5). Read sequentially from Isaiah 10 to Isaiah 11, therefore, the prophecy of the Davidic shoot may function as a prophecy against Assyrian imperialism. It is no longer an Assyrian king but a Davidic king who will establish governance with the ideal attributes of wisdom, strength, and fear of Yhwh (Weinfeld 1986, 169–82). Put another way, the arrival of an ideal peaceable kingdom (vv. 6-9) "presupposes a rupture . . . with this world" (Beuken 2002, 23).

Verses 6-9 further expand the portrayal of an ideal society. Under the system of righteous leadership (vv. 1-5), all natural enemies in food chains will not attack but will cohabit with one another; they are peaceful enough to escort a little child (v. 6; cf. 7:16; 8:4). While a literal reference to the Garden of Eden is plausible, some tones of symbolism may be possible as well. Thus, the "young lion" (*kepir*) may connote not only the specific species of the animal kingdom but also the "impious" as opposed to the "pious" seekers of Yhwh (Roberts, 262–65; cf. Ps 34:10 [MT 34:11]). Assyria, whose "roaring is like a lion" (5:29), will no longer behave like a predator but rather like the ox—that "knows its owner" (1:3)—peacefully led by a little child. In this ideal society, no threatening carnivores like lions will attack oxen (v. 7; cf. Gen 1:29-30). In this new world, enmity between the snake and human beings will cease (cf. Gen 3:14-15) and an infant baby will play safely with the cobra and viper (v. 8). That this oracle focuses on the "lad," "suckling child," and "toddler" emphasizes both the innocent yet sheer faith of young children and the vulnerability of the powerless, as they will become the primary beneficiaries of the peaceful cosmic era (cf. Mazor 2004, 78). On Zion, where "the Assyrian lion was finally halted and caged" (Seitz 1993, 107), hostile superpowers will cause no evil or catastrophe (like fratricide or flood in Genesis), and Yhwh's knowledge will fill the earth as powerfully as the mighty acts at the Red Sea (v. 9; cf. 2:2-4).

This oracular vision is more, however, than a mere return to or repetition of the glory of David and the Garden of Eden. As Walter Brueggemann puts it, "this poem is about the impossible possibility of the new creation!" (1998a, 103). In the midst of the incessant denial and failure of such a just world, Isaiah's vision finds its root in the spirit and knowledge of Yhwh, who is the sole source to usher in a whole new world. Lea Mazor judiciously expounds on this concept in the following comment:

The myth of the Garden of Eden places perfect existence at the beginning
of days, while the vision of the Shoot envisions it for the future. Thus,
the Garden of Eden is a utopian past, while the vision of the Shoot is a
utopian future. . . . If the Garden of Eden is a myth about a Nowhere
Land, then the vision of the Shoot is a prophecy about Everywhere Land,
for the entire land, according to Isaiah, will be filled with knowledge of the
Lord like water flooding the seas. (Mazor 2004, 89)

Isaiah 11:10-16—juxtaposed by the second "root of Jesse" statement—
further explicates the processes of building this ideal world. Verse 10, the first
"on that day" passage, asserts that this Davidic king will become a glorious
signal to nations and peoples (cf. 2:2-3; 5:26).

Verses 11-16, the second "on that day" passage, describe YHWH's intention
to gather the remnants of Israel and Judah to rebuild a unified, harmonious
kingdom. Previously YHWH stretched out a hand to chastise YHWH's own
people (5:25; cf. 10:10), but now this same hand extended for the second
time will be to acquire the remnants from far regions such as Assyria, Egypt,
and coastlands of the sea (v. 11). Also, instead of the "signal" entrusted to
Assyria (5:26), now the stump of Jesse will take the role of YHWH's "signal"
to peoples and nations to assemble the scattered remnants of both Israel and
Judah (vv. 10, 12).

Significantly, the gathering of the remnants of both Israel and Judah
depicts the end of their mutual hatred (v. 13). On the one hand, looking
back on Israel's history, the rivalry may allude to the enmity and hostility
between north and south during the divided monarchical period (Beuken
2002, 24–25). Throwing off the former oppressors' yoke on Israel's shoulder
(9:3-4), now the united forces of Israel and Judah will together counter the
Philistine yoke on its shoulder and plunder Edom, Moab, and Ammon,
following the exodus from Assyria (v. 14). On the other hand, the harmonious relationship between Ephraim and Judah may betray the conflict and
harassment between Samaria and Yehud, as well as between the remainees (in
Yehud) and the returnees (from the exile) during and after the Babylonian
exile.

Additionally, the extended hand of YHWH will "completely destroy"
(*haram*; cf. Deut 7:2; Josh 6:21) both Egypt and Assyria, the two most
intimidating superpowers, thereby replacing Baal by crushing Yamm (sea =
Egypt) and Nahar (river = Assyria), both figures from the ancient Canaanite
mythology, the Baal Epic. It is not Anat, the consort of Baal, who slayed
Leviathan into seven pieces, or the twisted serpent with seven heads: "I
[Anat] have smitten 'Ilu's beloved, Yammu, / have finished off the great god

Naharu. / I have bound the dragon's jaws, have destroyed it, / have smitten the twisted serpent, / the close-coiled one with seven heads" (*COS* I: 252). Rather, YHWH will split the river, Assyria, into "seven streams" for people to cross on foot like the old Exodus (v. 15). Like the glorious deliverance from Egypt, the remnant will return on the king's highway from Assyria (v. 16). Amid the concrete yet complex recollections and projections of Israel's topsy-turvy history, this prophetic text ultimately affirms YHWH's sovereignty: "For YHWH, the acting persons in world history are mere instruments: the king of Assyria a rod, the shoot a bearer of his spirit. They do not establish epochs. Past, present and future stand before YHWH, who is present on the mountain of Zion" (Beuken 2002, 33).

A Song of Thanksgiving, 12:1-6

Isaiah 12 wraps up the first section (Isa 1–12) with a song that reflects and sums up the whole section. Subdivided by "you will say on that day" phrases (v. 1 ["you" sg.] and v. 4 ["you" pl.]), the two subunits construct a hymn of chorus, or antiphony, echoing between the second-personal singular and plural forms and reaffirming YHWH as the savior from Zion for all nations.

Verses 1-3 start with the "on that day" phrase, as if extending the preceding "on that day" passages of 11:10, 11. In an I-thou utterance, the singer, individually and personally, gives thanks to YHWH by summarizing a key theology of Isaiah 1–12: "Though you were angry with me, your wrath is revoked and you comfort me" (v. 1; cf. 40:1). Thesis-like theological confessions, "God is my salvation (*yeshu'ah*)," chiastically envelop v. 2, echoing the very name Isaiah (*yesha'yahu*)—the whole book of Isaiah is about the historical testimony that "God saves!"—which further forms an inclusio with the name "Isaiah" in 1:1 (Blenkinsopp 2000a, 270). Between the inclusio in v. 2, two pairs of phrases complement each other: "I will trust, I will not be in dread"; "YHWH is my strength and my praise."

The hymnic expressions of v. 2, moreover, intertextually echo those of Exodus 15:2. The recalcitrant corruptions of Ahaz and his corrupt "this people" caused the devastation of the entire country by the Assyrian army. Yet, promised by Isaiah's own two sons and a royal child Immanuel, remnants are to return in an era of light over darkness. The meager shoot from the stump of Jesse will then triumph over the tall trees of Assyria, ushering in a new era of peace and harmony both domestically and internationally. This festive hymn, therefore, fittingly alludes to the victory song in Exodus 15. Just as Moses and Miriam, together with their communities, sang the songs of thanksgiving for the defeat of Egypt in the old exodus, so the devout remnants and witnesses gathered in Zion are to sing praises at the defeat of Assyria, and eventually Babylon, in the new exodus (Blenkinsopp 2000a, 270).

Verses 4-6, with another "on that day" phrase, expand the call of v. 1 to the whole audience by using the plural "you" (cf. v. 3). Now communally, "you" are to "give thanks to YHWH" (v. 4). The worshiper's individual praise of God therefore challenges the addressees to join the praise of God among the peoples and nations, in fact throughout all the earth (v. 5). The invocation includes making known YHWH's salvific works to peoples, validating the preceding oracles that YHWH's name is exalted (cf. 2:11, 17)—note that v. 4 is almost verbatim as Psalms 9:11 (MT 9:12); 105:1; 1 Chronicles 16:8. Who are the addressees of this glorious task of praising and witnessing God's majesty? The final clause specifies "the inhabitants of Zion"—or the pilgrims to Zion in later contexts—as the addressees to carry out such a task (v. 6), similar to the previous vision that Torah and word of YHWH shall go forth from Zion to many peoples and nations (2:2-3).

In closing this first section, the prophet commands wholehearted praise to God, not only by himself but also by the inhabitants of Zion and indeed all those who aspire to follow and trust in God. What does it mean to praise God? Walter Brueggemann profoundly elaborates that "doxology is the exuberant abandonment of self over to God" (2014, 47). In a theological nutshell, to praise God therefore means not to praise one's own self or any other powers and principalities. To praise God is to deny self—like the prophet's genuine confession "Woe is me" (6:5)—in utter trust in the creator. To praise God is to de-absolutize any other candidates for "gods," including those towering superpower empires and menacing nations that the prophet will dismantle in resolute theological assault in the following section (Brueggemann 2014, 42).

Ten Oracles about the Nations (Second Branch of the Lampstand)

Isaiah 13–23

This second section, commonly called the "Oracles about/against the Nations" (hereafter, OAN) transitions the setting from Judah into the international arena. This change seems abrupt with regard to language and content. There is, however, a thematic continuity from the preceding section (Isa 1–12), as will be discussed below. Even the language of the superscription in 13:1 neatly correlates to 1:1 and 2:1:

• The vision (*hazon*) of Isaiah son of Amoz which he saw (*hazah*) about Judah and Jerusalem in the days of Uzziah, Jotham, Ahaz, and Hezekiah, kings of Judah (1:1);
• The word which Isaiah son of Amoz saw (*hazah*) about Judah and Jerusalem (2:1);
• An oracle against Babylon which Isaiah son of Amoz saw (*hazah*; 13:1).

Furthermore, this section coheres around the tenfold occurrences of the word "oracle" (*massa*; lit., "burden"), which mainly targets various foreign nations as though echoing the ten plagues in the exodus tradition. Admittedly, the loose organization of this section makes it difficult to analyze any systematic pattern. Scholars have observed an internal bracket, framed by oracles against Babylon (Isa 13 and Isa 21), which may have been a prototypical pattern. The place and function of the oracle against Jerusalem (Isa 22) may replicate those of the oracles against the nations in Amos 1–2, where the climactic targets are not only foreign nations but also Judah and, indeed, Ephraim.

For our study, considering the significance of both form and content, we will trace the internal pattern in light of the ten appearances of the word "burden" (*massa'*). Moreover, two sets of five oracles surround the symbolic action of Isaiah 20. Each set of five begins with an oracle against Babylon and ends with oracles against sea-related nations, Egypt (Yamm) and Tyre (on the

Phoenician coastline). Isaiah 22 puts Jerusalem on the line with the nations, as one of those nations, if not a climactic one! Even though proportionately not so evenly balanced, this reading can provide further interpretive insights (Kim 2015b; cf. Beuken 2007, 18–26; Kaiser 1974, 1–2):

massa' (Concrete/Named Nations)	massa' (Cryptic/Symbolic Nations)
13:1 = *Babylon* (w/ Assyria)	21:1 = "wilderness of the sea"
14:28 = Philistia	[*Babylon*]
15:1 = Moab	21:11 = Dumah
17:1 = Damascus/N. Israel/Cush	21:13 = "desert plain" [Arabia]
19:1 = *Egypt*	22:1 = "valley of vision" [Zion] (cf. 22:25)
	23:1 = *Tyre* (sea coastland)

The first half addresses mainly specific, concretely named nations. They mirror the nations listed in the preceding passage, e.g., 11:14-15 (Philistia, People of the East [or, Syria?], Edom, Moab, Ammon, Egypt, and Assyria). Accordingly, this list smoothly picks up the preceding section (Isa 1–12; cf. Seitz 1993, 115–19). Likewise, the second half addresses mainly symbolic or cryptic, if not unnamed, nations. Such a tendency nicely paves the way into the following section with more abstract, mythological targets (Isa 24–27).

Why do we have this OAN section here in the book of Isaiah? How did it come about? What functions do the oracles purport to serve? Several aspects concerning the original setting(s), functions, and implications may be worthwhile to explore. First, as to the origin and development of the OAN, scholars have proposed either a cultic setting (e.g., the New Year's festival in Israel) or war oracles (before and during military battles). Linked to the latter background, OAN as war oracles would convey the prophet's efficacious magical spells of judgment against the enemy (e.g., Isa 7:4-9). In this case, always accompanying the announcement of the enemy's defeat, the OAN also project a promise of victory for Israel. Rainer Albertz surmises that this uniquely biblical feature of the dual functions of the OAN—curse on the enemy and salvation for Israel—exhibits the theological development of the exilic period, "a radical shift from their preexilic function" to "a medium of retaliation against a superior opponent, invulnerable in the political arena" (Albertz 2003b, 185, 188).

Second, the OAN deal with many of Israel's surrounding nations. We should keep in mind that Israel was a country surrounded by many powerful, often stronger nations. After the exile, Israel met the fate of a "colonized" nation under the colonial, hegemonic empires. In that historical upheaval, the fates of neighboring nations had a major impact on the Israelites and their morale. On the one hand, these ten oracles concerning various neighboring countries function to depict nations in havoc, as if portraying the world wars of the ancient time. Israel was like a tiny boat in the ocean; worldly affairs of these nations would surge powerful winds and waves that would significantly affect the little boat. Admittedly, as other nations' misfortune may have meant Israel's fortune, the downfall of these nations denoted Israel's salvation. The constant threat of the military forces of the empire "from the north" (cf. 14:31; Jer 1:13-15; Ezek 38:6, 15)—the news of wars, killings, and refugees in the surrounding countries—however, stirred up psychological panic and fear in the Levant. In some oracles, Israel and Judah learned that they were not so superior to other nations (Amos 1–2; Isa 19:16-25; 22:1-14).

On the other hand, the ups and mostly downs of these nations implicitly signaled their demise under the superpower empires; in fact, most of them were under the vassal servitude to these imperial suzerains. It is no coincidence that Babylon takes a major place in this OAN section (cf. Jer 50–51). Interestingly, in Isaiah 13–14, Babylon eclipses Assyria. To the less powerful nations, including Israel and Judah, it would have been a world-shattering shock to learn not only that Assyria would fall (612 BCE) but also that Babylon—the new and improved terminator—would wield an even stronger threat over them. Precisely against this background, the OAN declare that just as Assyria falls to Babylon, then Babylon too shall soon collapse (cf. Isa 47).

Third, whereas world history would record that Assyria fell to Babylon and that Babylon succumbed to Persia, the OAN present a different historical interpretation: neither Babylon nor Persia but YHWH is sovereign over all nations. We have noted that the two parallel columns start with Babylon, the superpower force symbolized as a "river," and conclude with Egypt and Tyre, the daunting forces closely attributed to the "sea." According to Csaba Balogh, the perimeters of the river and the sea form the larger structure of Isaiah 13–23 as the royal "stele of YHWH" (cf. 19:19), in parallel with the Mesopotamian royal stele, which portrays the Assyrian king and his patron deity in control over the Mediterranean Sea (upper sea) and the Persian Gulf (lower sea). The Isaianic OAN expand the territory even to the farthest corner, as far as Egypt, implying that YHWH is the true ruler of the greater world. Its thematic polemic asserts that various nations are subject to the world ruler—not the Mesopotamian king or deity but only YHWH (Balogh 2011, 348–49).

Similarly, according to Marvin Sweeney, the list of all these foreign nations in the given form signifies "the hegemony of the Persian empire over these nations," underscoring the implied polemic that YHWH from Zion, not the Persian deity or king, is in control of this world (Sweeney 1996, 216–17). Whereas the OAN of Isaiah start with Babylon and end with sea-powers, especially Egypt in the middle, the OAN of Jeremiah (MT) start with Egypt (Jer 46) and end with Babylon (Jer 50–51). Steed Vernyl Davidson interprets these two poles of empires—Egypt and Babylon—as "flip sides of a vinyl record" between exodus and exile, with geographical, historical, and theological tensions between survival through "escape and withdrawal" (exodus) and survival through "adjustment and adaptation" (exile). These tensions betray the "consequences of empire, with all that empire entails," amid the theopolitical contexts of the Diaspora world (Davidson 2011, 172–76). Within this dialectical trajectory of empires, the OAN indomitably affirm the theological statement that YHWH is in control not only of Israel and Judah but also of all the nations, including these apparently insurmountable empires.

Structure of Isaiah 13–23
First Oracle—Against Babylon and Assyria, 13:1–14:27
Second Oracle—Against Philistia, 14:28-32
Third Oracle—Against Moab, 15:1–16:14 (cf. Jer 48)
Fourth Oracle—Against Damascus and Ephraim vis-à-vis Cush, 17:1–18:7
Fifth Oracle—Against Egypt, 19:1–20:6
Sixth Oracle—Against "the Desert of the Sea" [Babylon], 21:1-10
Seventh Oracle—Against Dumah, 21:11-12
Eighth Oracle—Against "The Desert Plain" [Arabia], 21:13-17
Ninth Oracle—Against "The Valley of Vision" [Jerusalem], 22:1-25
Tenth Oracle—Against Tyre, 23:1-18

First Oracle—Against Babylon and Assyria, 13:1–14:27

An Oracle against Babylon, 13:1-22
Strange it seems that Babylon appears here in 13:1 (cf. Hab 1:1). Reading sequentially, the prophetic literature appears to have a rough pattern from Isaiah 1–39 to 40–66, e.g., from judgment to consolation, or from preexilic to exilic and postexilic settings. The order of prophetic books does not align chronologically, however, as is also the case in the Twelve prophetic literature (Stulman and Kim 2010, 202–204).

In other words, this shift from Assyria to Babylon may not be so strange. The larger thematic flow of Isaiah may hint that, after the oracles accusing

Judah of its sins (Isa 1–12), the oracles will now condemn the evil wrought by Babylon, followed by other nations (Isa 13–23). Alternatively, placed at the start of this section, Babylon may function rhetorically as a symbol for any "enemy par excellence." Historically, Babylon was indeed the empire that consummated the fall of Jerusalem in 587 BCE. Throughout, the book of Isaiah mentions superpowers such as Assyria as YHWH's instrument or Persia as YHWH's anointed shepherd. In fact, even Egypt and Assyria are to join the nations in their pilgrimage and allegiance to YHWH (cf. 19:18-25). But not Babylon (except cf. Jer 25:9; 27:6)! Judah's trauma caused by this enemy kingdom may have been too painful to say anything favorable about it at all. The sole destiny of this most hateful, despised enemy is to crumble.

Isaiah 13:2-5 opens the oracle with an urgent military call; YHWH summons the army for battle. This summon harkens back to the "signal" YHWH raised previously—for the Assyrian army (5:26) and the remnants of Israel and Judah (11:10, 12). Now, YHWH commands messengers to raise their "signal" and "voice" at the gates so that the nobles can hear the news that YHWH is summoning "my" warriors (vv. 2-3). The "voice" of tumult and the "voice" of uproar from kingdoms and nations, from the end of the "heavens" to all the "earth," highlight the potency of YHWH's army (vv. 4-5).

Isaiah 13:6-16 is the main body of this unit, composed of three subunits initiated by the "day of YHWH" phrases (vv. 6-8; 9-12; 13-16; cf. 2:12) and each escalating into shocking imagery. Equally striking, the word Babylon does not occur until v. 19 in this oracle. Hearing the oracle in vv. 2-18, the audience may wonder, "Who is this enemy YHWH so ferociously threatens to demolish?" Readers will have to hear the tumultuous sounds (vv. 2-5) and the threefold announcements of the fearful day of YHWH before they find out who the doomed nation is—none other than Babylon.

Verses 6-8 proclaim the initial "day of YHWH" (cf. 2:12; 10:3). In another rhetorical irony, the initial call to wail (*helilu*; v. 6) sounds eerily similar to the call to praise (*halelu*; cf. Isa 38:18; 62:9; 64:10; Ps 150:1). Just as YHWH will quell the "hand" of power and the pompous "heart" of which the Assyrian king boasts (10:10, 12-14), now all human "hands" and every human "heart" will melt (v. 7) with pangs like a woman in labor (v. 8; cf. 7:14, 16; 8:4).

Verses 9-12 declare, for a second time, the "day of YHWH." Here the motif of the day of YHWH adumbrates the creation tradition for a message of chilling decimation of sinners. Not unlike the upside-down reversal of "earth" to "heaven" (cf. Jer 4:23), the earth will become desolate (v. 9) and the sun, moon, and stars in heaven will grow dark (v. 10). Who are the targets of this un-creation? The sinners (v. 9)—the evil, the wicked, the insolent, and the haughty tyrants (v. 11). Creation is so overturned that humankind will be scarcer than fine gold (v. 12).

Verses 13-16 intensify, for a third time, the "day of YHWH's burning anger." This unique phrase "burning/fierce anger" (Isa 13:9, 13) occurs more frequently in Jeremiah (Jer 4:8, 26; 12:13; 25:37-38; 30:24; 49:37; 51:45; cf. Zeph 2:2). YHWH's army will shatter heaven and earth (v. 13). All the people—presumably of Babylon—will disperse as gazelle and sheep run away (v. 14). Even in their escape, they will be captured and massacred (v. 15), including infants and wives (v. 16). This is reminiscent of the most gruesome Babylonian assault the psalmist decried in the Psalter (cf. Ps 137:8-9). Admittedly, this is a seriously troubling idea and expression to modern culture. Yet, like the imprecatory or curse psalms, as Erich Zenger profoundly interprets, these verses are not

> a "blessing" on child-murderers; they are a passionate outcry of the powerless demanding justice! . . . [This outcry] is an attempt, in the face of the most profound humiliation and helplessness, to suppress the primitive human lust for violence in one's own heart, by surrendering everything to God—a God whose word of judgment is presumed to be so universally just that even those who pray the psalm submit themselves to it. (Zenger 1996, 48)

Isaiah 13:17-22 finally names the one who will meet this catastrophic fate: Babylon. YHWH will stir up the Medes (v. 17; cf. 41:2, 25; 45:13) who are too fierce to care for gold, let alone human beings, and so can easily slaughter children (v. 18; cf. v. 12; Jer 51:11, 28). In the history of the rise of the Neo-Babylonian empire, it is noteworthy that the Medes were instrumental in the Babylonian king Nabopolassar's overthrow of the Assyrian empire: "The conquest of the Assyrian capital of Nineveh in 612 was a shared victory of the Median-Babylonian coalition" (Albertz 2003b, 50). It is thus telling that the oracle now warns that the would-be ally Medes will become the weapon aimed at Babylon (cf. Dan 8:20). The final subunit (vv. 19-22) reveals that Babylon is the object of this horrific onslaught. Once foreigners "overthrew" Judah like Sodom and Gomorrah (1:7, 9), but now readers learn that Babylon will soon suffer the worse blow (v. 19): "This prophecy threatens the inhabitants of Babylon with the same kind of atrocities that the Jerusalemite population suffered in 587 BCE" (Eidevall 2009, 112). Utterly destroyed, this once glorious city shall become a wasteland with its houses and palaces where only ostriches and jackals will run around wildly

(vv. 20-22; cf. 34:13). Contrary to the fate of Jerusalem to be the paradise renewed (11:6-9), Babylon awaits the fate of paradise extinguished.

Israel's Taunt Song against Babylon, 14:1-23

This oracle actually continues Isaiah 13. Yet here Israel joins the divine denouncement of Babylon with a taunt song jabbed at this accursed city. Babylon is not only the arch-oppressor of Judah and Jerusalem but also the arch-arrogant rebel against YHWH (cf. Isa 10). As such, the Babylonian king now gets the treatment of abject humiliation that has been announced in 2:6-22 (Beuken 2004c, 99–100).

Like Isaiah 13, this unit also has the introductory (or transitional) subunit (vv. 1-2), which leads to the main song, the climactic curse (vv. 3-21), and ends with reasserting the condemnation of 13:17-22 (vv. 22-23). The dual themes of YHWH's compassion for Jacob-Israel (vv. 1-2) and YHWH's destruction of Babylon (vv. 22-23) thus envelope the central song (vv. 3-21).

Isaiah 14:1-2 turns its attention to Jacob and Israel, to whom YHWH will show compassion. It predicts that this exiled northern Israel will return safely to Israel proper, even with aliens who will join the "house of Jacob" (v. 1). As many of the OAN and anti-imperial taunt songs imply, the themes of God's resettling Jacob-Israel in their homecoming and the subjugation of the captors may be reminiscent of Israel's—and later Zion's—own destruction and captivity. The portrayal of their yearning to return home is relevant to the victims of war and captivity during World War II. We can see the haunting images of sorrowful tears of the people captured in trains that took them to the dreadful concentration camp. Many Korean grandparents tell the stories of how, as young kids, they had literally thrown rocks at the running train that snatched away their older sisters and brothers to an unknown place and forced labor by Imperial Japan (1910–1945). To them, and to their loved ones, homecoming and reunion would be nothing short of a miracle. The prophet declares that such a miraculous homecoming is to occur soon.

How will such a homecoming of Jacob's exiles occur? The depiction here differs significantly from the one in 2:2-4. Nonetheless, the text signifies Israel's captivity by Assyria in 722 BCE, after which in the imminent future, nations will assume the role of the attendants, indeed as male and female slaves. Although the description seems different, the underlying theology of subversion is continuous in that the fate of the "house of Israel" and that of their oppressors will finally switch (v. 2).

Isaiah 14:3-21 presents the powerful taunt song, which Israel, delivered from exile, will sing. In time of rest (*nuah*) from oppression and slavery (v. 3; cf. vv. 1-2; Deut 12:10; 25:19), this redeemed Israel will lift up a satirical taunt against the king of Babylon (v. 4a). The taunt parable or song itself comprises the two "how" (*'ek*) clauses (vv. 4b-11 and 12-21).

Verses 4b-11 start with the first "how"-clause: "How the oppressor has rested (lit., 'sabbathed')!" (v. 4). Whereas the redeemed Israel will enjoy "rest" from war and torment (cf. 30:15; Ps 116:7), the imperial oppressor will "rest," i.e., cease to be. The credit for the tyrant's downfall goes to YHWH. YHWH has broken the "staff" and "rod" of the wicked, not those of Assyria who acted as YHWH's instrument (cf. 10:5, 15) but of Babylon, who struck "peoples" and "nations" (cf. 2:2-3) with unlimited brutality (vv. 5-6).

First, the earth, being at rest (*nuah*), rejoices over the demise of Babylon (vv. 7-8). The stout cypresses and cedars of Lebanon, vulnerable for hacking down (cf. 2:13; 10:34), now rebuke Babylon's king addressed in second-person speech: "You are laid low and cannot rise up."

Second, in Sheol, far beneath the earth, a commotion begins to welcome the king of Babylon. It is as though one wonders how low this pompous tyrant can go. Other dead kings and ghosts jeer at him: "You too have become weak like us. . . . Your pomp is brought down to Sheol. . . . Maggots are your bed and worms your blanket" (v. 11).

Verses 12-21 follow with the second "how"-clause: "How you have fallen from heaven!" (v. 12; cf. 2 Sam 1:19, 25, 27). Babylon's asinine boast, "I will ascend to heaven" (v. 13), is not unlike the fools who say in their hearts, "There is no God" (Pss 14:1; 53:1; cf. 10:13). This contemptuous scheme to go up to heaven betrays the ancient Near Eastern theogony in which the lower gods revolt against the superior gods. Babylon's assertion that it will climb all the way to the highest Mount Zaphon and to Elyon (vv. 13-14) alludes to the comparable Canaanite mythology (cf. Ps 48:2 [MT 48:3]): "Thereupon terrible 'Attaru / climbs the heights of Ṣapānu, / sits on Mighty Ba'lu's seat" (*COS* I: 269).

There are several responses to such a vain claim. First, this king of Babylon has booked the bottom of the Pit instead of the highest rank in the pantheon. The chorus scoffs at this king: "You are dragged down to Sheol" (v. 15). We find an express contrast between Babylon's claim to reach "the furthest reaches of the north" with his transport into Sheol, "the furthest reaches of the pit" (Sweeney 1996, 225). Again, stunned, those in Sheol will welcome this pitiful newcomer—he who once so fearfully moved the earth, shook up the kingdoms, and toppled the world into desert (vv. 16-17).

Next, this song powerfully concludes with a scornful dirge over the dismantled king (vv. 18-21). All the kings of the "nations" vanquished by this king of Babylon (v. 12) at least lie in their tombs (lit., "home"; v. 18). Contrary to the "branch" (*netser*) that will grow out of Jesse's stump (11:1),

Babylon's king will drift like a disfigured "branch" pierced and trampled (v. 19)—much the same way YHWH declared the intention to cut down the lofty boughs and branches of Assyria (10:33-34). W. A. M. Beuken posits a possible literary pun with the word "branch" (*netser*) here (14:19) and the Akkadian word "Nebuchadnezzar" (Akk.: *nabû-kudurri-uṣur*), which further heightens the dramatic contrast between the fate of the branch of Jesse and that of the branch of Babylon (Beuken 2004c, 103): the former, the upcoming ruler of justice and faithfulness, will arise, while the latter, the pompous and malicious oppressor, will fall down and disappear.

Oaths of curse follow this tormenting funeral dirge (vv. 20-21). This Babylonian king will receive no proper burial. The seed of this evildoer will be no more (v. 20). Here again, a literary interconnection contrasts YHWH's protective deliverance, "they shall not hurt or destroy (*shakhat*) on all my holy mountain" (11:9), with the condemnation of the Babylonian king for his atrocious crimes, "you have destroyed (*shakhat*) your land, you have slain your people" (v. 20; Beuken 2004c, 104). For his iniquity, his sons will vanish never to rise again (v. 21; cf. 13:16, 18).

Isaiah 14:22-23 wraps up the oracle against Babylon, with YHWH's sure plan to rise to punish the king of Babylon. YHWH will cut off this king's name and descendants for eternity (v. 22). The broom of extermination will sweep away Babylon, the invincible empire, forever (v. 23). Contrary to Zion's future of peace and equity in a cosmic realm (11:6-9), Babylon's future will see her regress into an uninhabitable marshland. Whereas Zion, also stained with iniquity, shall survive and revive with the remnants (11:11, 16), Babylon, devoid of any remnant, will be completely annihilated (Beuken 2004c, 105, 108–10).

Here, although this taunt song condemns the anonymous Babylonian king, scholars conjecture Sargon the Assyrian king as the template of his hubris and mortification. Sargon II (721–705 BCE), when killed in battle, was not buried properly; his corpse was abandoned in the battlefield (vv. 18-20). Assuming this conjecture, it is significant to consider the impact of northern Israel's devastating fall and deportation by this Assyrian king— along with Shalmaneser V before him, who captured the capital Samaria (2 Kgs 17:1-6; 18:9-12), and Sennacherib after him, who devastated many Judean cities except Jerusalem (Isa 36:1–37:38). Just as the Babylonian king's invasion traumatized southern Judah later, so the Assyrian king's gory attacks would have left lasting damage on the northern Israelites, their refugees to the south, and even the prophet, as the subsequent oracle against Assyria demonstrates (Sweeney 1996, 232–38).

An Oracle against Assyria, 14:24-27

Even though this subunit concerns Assyria, it thematically connects to its preceding unit on Babylon, while also paving a smooth transition to subsequent oracles against other nations. At the outset, this unit reads more like the woe-oracles of 5:8-30 and 10:1-34. In fact, its vocabulary echoes those passages. If we delete the word "Babylon" in 13:1, 19; 14:4, 22, however, the preceding oracle against Babylon can flow smoothly with the following unit. In the present form, therefore, the taunt against Babylon sets the initial frame of this entire section (Isa 13–23), with this oracle against Assyria as a follow-up accusation against another ferocious empire, as if the two empires—Babylon and Assyria—coalesce to be punished and shattered together.

Rather than the apparent chronological gap, we find a thematic juxtaposition between the upcoming Babylonian attack in 587 BCE (14:1-23, esp. vv. 22-23) and the antecedent Assyrian threat in 701 BCE (vv. 24-27). Read together, 14:24-27 provides a flashback message: just as YHWH breaks down Assyria, illustrated in Sargon's mortifying demise (Sweeney 1996) or exemplified in Sennacherib's siege in retrospect (Clements 1989), so surely YHWH's oracles and plans against Babylon will come true: "The passage serves redactionally to unite the destruction of Assyria with its latter counterpart Babylon, and to join in the one plan of God the destruction of the arrogant oppressor from both the eighth and sixth centuries" (Childs 2001, 124).

The key phrase "YHWH of the army," in v. 24 and v. 27, brackets this unit (cf. v. 23). At the outset, YHWH affirms in first-person speech that the divine intention will stand securely (v. 24). Just as YHWH has broken (*shabar*) the "staff" and "rod" of the wicked rulers of Babylon (14:5), YHWH is about to "break" (*shabar*) Assyria (v. 25), formerly the "rod" and "staff" of YHWH's anger (10:5). Just as YHWH removed the "yoke" and "burden" from the "shoulders" of the oppressed (9:4; 10:27), now YHWH will remove ferocious empires in YHWH's mountains (v. 25). YHWH's mighty, outstretched hand overpowers all nations (vv. 26-27; cf. 5:25; 9: 12, 17, 21; 10:4).

Second Oracle—Against Philistia, 14:28-32

This oracle is unusual, not only due to its relative brevity but also due to its chronological and narrative-type statement. Further, the phrase "In the year of the death of King Ahaz . . ." (v. 28) is exactly the same as the phrase "In the year of the death of King Uzziah . . ." (6:1). In Isaiah 6, we read the call narrative of the prophet. Here, no such significant information is available, except the report that the oracle ("burden") came.

Concerning its significance, on the one hand, a sequential reading implies that the rest of the accounts may be taken to consider King Hezekiah as a background. Just as with the sophisticated placement and composite aspects of Isaiah 13 with the oracle against Babylon, however, the scribes of Isaiah may not have intended to arrange all in rigid chronology. One should consider it more of a thematic sequence. Thus, on the other hand, its thematic significance may be that it elicits a historical or literary reference to King Ahaz in association with the Philistines. Accordingly, we should note that the report of Ahaz's death (14:28) follows the announcement of the demise of Assyria (14:24-27). Ahaz was an acquiescent vassal to Tiglath-pileser (2 Kgs 16:5-9; cf. Isa 7). Recalling that the Assyrian king Tiglath-pileser's campaign not only pillaged Syria and northern Israel but also the Philistine region during the Syro-Ephraimite war, one may posit Sargon's subsequent invasion on Philistia. Archaeological excavations on a Philistine site, Ashdod, provide further information concerning mass burials during Sargon's conquest of the city, signifying a massacre and even decapitation during and after the battle (Faust 2011, 97–98). Regardless of the exact (original) setting of this oracle, therefore, it is conceivable that this oracle thematically follows the oracle against Assyria, with the correlated message of warning that Judah's regime (Hezekiah?) should not attempt a coalition with the Philistines (Sweeney 1996, 233–34).

Verses 29-30 contain the first imperative: "Do not rejoice, Philistia" (v. 29). Here their joy came as a result of YHWH's "breaking" (*shabar*) the rod of Assyria—whether Tiglath-pileser's death in 727 or Sargon's in 705 (cf. v. 25; 10:5), hence making a smooth connection to the preceding passage. The subsequent statement alludes to the peaceful kingdom passage (cf. 11:6-9), except with an opposite outcome. Whereas the child plays peacefully with the adder in an ideal Davidic kingdom (11:8), there will be a threatening serpent amid Philistia (v 29). This "snake" and "flying serpent" allude to the mythological chaos monsters in Baal Epic, symbolizing a menacing empire that will consume Philistia (cf. 27:1). Whereas cows and bears "graze" (*ra'ah*) and their young "lie down" (*rabats*) together (11:7), now only the poor will "graze" (*ra'ah*) and the needy "lie down" (*rabats*) together (v. 30). Similarly, whereas the "root" (*shoresh*) of Jesse will be a glorious signal for the "remnant" (*she'ar*) of YHWH's people (11:10-12), as for the Philistines, YHWH will slay their "root" (*shoresh*) and "remnant" (*she'erit*) altogether (v. 30).

Verses 31-32 pronounce the second pair of imperatives: "Wail, O gate, and cry, O city!" (v. 31). The command to "wail" harks back to the same call toward Babylon (13:6). The smoke signal is to come from the "north" (in Hebrew "Zaphon"), alluding to the summit of YHWH's abode (cf. 14:13). Its messenger will reassert the fundamental theological statement, reinforcing v. 30 and many previous texts—that YHWH has founded Zion (cf. 2:3; 4:5;

8:18) and that the community of the poor, the destitute, and the afflicted shall find refuge here (v. 32; cf. 3:14-15; 10:2; 11:4).

Third Oracle—Against Moab, 15:1–16:14 (cf. Jer 48)

Moab Is Ruined, 15:1-9

From Babylon, Assyria, and Philistia, we now move to Moab, whose judgment oracle consists of the genre of a dirge: the lament proper (15:1-9); the appeal on behalf of the refugees for Judah's shelter (16:1-5); the resumed, final lament over Moab (16:6-12); and a summary (16:13-14). Readers may hear satirical mockery from the Israelites whose refugees the Moabites betrayed in their fickle treatment of their adjacent neighbors (cf. Isa 47; Obad 10-14). Alternatively, there may be a genuine sense of sadness over the devastated country that the tribes of Reuben and Gad once shared (cf. Num 32; Childs 2001, 131).

Isaiah 15 has a chiastic framework, indicated by key markers:

a—"for" (*ki*) . . . "for" (*ki*) . . . (v. 1)
  b—"therefore" ('*al-ken*) . . . (v. 4)
    c—"My heart goes out" . . . "for" . . . (vv. 5-6)
  b'—"therefore" ('*al-ken*) . . . (v. 7)
a'—"for" (*ki*) . . . "for" (*ki*) . . . (vv. 8-9)

Read this way, it can be divided into three subunits: the vivid messenger reports on the invasion of the towns of Moab (vv. 1-4); the statement of the prophet's pathos over Moab's misfortune (vv. 5-6); and the description of the Moabite refugees (vv. 7-9).

Isaiah 15:1-4 sketches the devastation of major cities in Moab. The destructions of Ar and Kir by night imply a sudden military attack (v. 1). Dibon, Nebo, and Medeba—major cities of Moab—wail with head and beard shamefully shaved (v. 2; cf. 13:6; 14:31; Num 21:21-30). The whole country is in havoc as everyone wails not only in temples and high places (v. 2) but also in streets, on rooftops, and in squares (v. 3). Further major towns (such as Heshbon, Elealeh, and Jahaz) add to the calamity, while numerous occurrences of verbs of mourning (e.g., weep, wail, cry, shout, quiver, and tremble) intensify the picture of Moab's sorrow (v. 4).

Isaiah 15:5-6 expresses the prophet's emotional reaction. Just as Moab's soul trembles (v. 4), now the prophet's heart aches for Moab as he learns of Moab's fugitives frantically fleeing to hills and roads (v. 5). The refugees are similar to stray sheep and can find no water or grass (v. 6). Amid this lament from "my heart," readers can imagine the vivid pictures of havoc wreaked by the war. Jacob Wright has presented some of the key Neo-Assyrian military tactics, which include not only siege warfare but also its accompanying stoppage of water resources, destruction of fruit trees, flooding (hydraulic warfare), burning down temples, and taking away massive resources (Wright 2008; 2011). These warfare techniques of mass-scale destruction frequently resulted in famine, disease, and more casualties.

Isaiah 15:7-9 further describes the pitiful caravans of Moab's refugees in turmoil. All their possessions once secured in treasure stores futilely drift down to the Wadi of Willows (v. 7). Wailing reaches more towns like Eglaim and Beer-Elim (v. 8). The picture of the humiliated, wailing caravans is similar to many portrayals of defeated captives in the ancient Near East. For example, the Lachish Frieze displays the Judeans from the town of Lachish in captivity to Assyria, from the siege attack by Sennacherib in 701 BCE: "Men, women, and children with scant belongings and emaciated animals are driven from the city. Two men are flayed alive, and another is stabbed" (Tull 2010, 353). In this subversive vision, the prophet now depicts such a fate of exile to be placed upon the Moabites. Likewise, as if the Egyptian plague returns, the waters of Dimon will turn to blood while lions await those refugees and remnants (v. 9; cf. 2 Kgs 17:25-26). The imagery of lions further correlates with Amos 3:12, which portrays "two legs and an ear" in the lion's mouth: "As it is for Israel in Amos, so it will be for Moab here" (Brueggemann 1998a, 140).

A Righteous Ruler in the Land, 16:1-5

In light of the reports on Moab's debacle, the people of the city of refuge, presumably Zion, are to support these helpless fugitives in the era of a merciful judge from the tent of David. Walter Brueggemann contrasts two contending scholarly views: Otto Kaiser, on the one hand, considers this hope for the fugitives as a promise of future salvation "only to Jews" (Kaiser 1974, 73); Hans Wildberger, on the other hand, interprets this promise to be applicable even to "the peoples" (Wildberger 1997, 140–45). Admittedly, the text's meaning is ambiguous (Brueggemann 1998a, 142). However, in light of the comparable theme in another portion of the OAN (cf. 19:16-25), it is possible to retrieve a theme of mercy, not violence, in an international scope. From the unequivocal contrast between the defenseless daughters of Moab and the defended daughters of Zion, the poet derives potential for an era when Zion welcomes the needy and the weak even from the nations, with the righteous ruler from the throne of David (cf. 2:2-4; 11:1-9; Ruth 4:16-22).

Contrary to the lion (15:9), a lamb as an offering from Sela shall reach the ruler of the mountain, daughter Zion (v. 1). Desperately seeking a helping hand from daughter Zion, daughters of Moab linger defenselessly around the Arnon River, which is Moab's border (vv. 2-3). But, when the oppressor disappears, and destruction and gang violence in the aftermath of war-led anarchy are gone, Zion can provide asylum and shades for these fugitives and even let them "sojourn" in the land: "let the outcasts of Moab sojourn among you" (v. 4; cf. 11:6; Ruth 1:1). In Zion's land, a hiding place for the remnants of Moab, all oppressors will disappear and instead a throne shall arise in the tent of David, executing all aspects of virtue—mercy (*hesed*), honesty (*'emet*), justice (*mishpat*), and righteousness (*tsedeq*; v. 5).

The Pride of Moab Is Utterly Toppled, 16:6-12

While daughter Zion is to show compassion toward the routed daughters of Moab (vv. 1-5), Moab will ultimately expire. The "we"-group recalls, "We have heard of the pride of Moab, an extreme, unmeasurable pride" (v. 6). Three "therefore" reactions follow (vv. 7-12).

The first "therefore" (*laken*) response is to invite everyone in Moab to wail over the once abundant raisin-cakes of Kir-hareseth, the lush fields of Heshbon, and the fertile vines of Sibmah (vv. 7-8). The second "therefore" (*'al-ken*) response contains the prophet's ("I will weep") crying over the calamity in Jazer, Sibmah, Heshbon, and Elealeh, where joy and gladness of fruitful harvests have ceased (vv. 9-10; cf. 9:2). The third "therefore" (*'al-ken*) response intensifies the prophet's ("my intestines" and "my inward part") somber lament over Kir-hareseth. Moab's prayers upon the "high places" and "sanctuary"—the catchwords that form a larger inclusio with 15:2—will no longer have any effect at all (vv. 11-12).

The Judgment on Moab Updated and Confirmed, 16:13-14

This short subunit concludes the whole segment of oracles concerning Moab. The unique phrase "this is the word" (*zeh hadabar*) in 16:13 may further pick up the similar phrase "this oracle" (*hamasa' hazeh*) in 14:28. Accordingly, this subunit not only wraps up the oracle against Moab (Isa 15–16) but also forms a bracket with the oracle against Philistia (14:28-32). Likewise, it transitions to new oracles in this section.

As if reiterating the "on that day" passages, the prophet recaps the oracle of YHWH announced to Moab thus far (v. 13). Now, this oracle will not be about the past but instead a revitalized decree so that, in three years—thus in a short while (cf. 7:16; 8:4)—Moab's glory will shrink, leaving only a small remnant (v. 14).

Fourth Oracle—Against Damascus and Ephraim vis-à-vis Cush, 17:1–18:7

This oracle is rather a loosely combined unit, seemingly lacking coherence. Unlike the oracle against Moab (Isa 15–16), it does not name many towns specifically. In fact, other than referring to locales such as Damascus (17:1, 3) and Jacob (17:4), this section does not denote any concrete targets, somewhat resembling the main oracles against Babylon (13:2-16; 14:4b-21).

Nevertheless, scholars have noted several clues for the backdrop of this fourth oracle. First, the combination of Damascus and Ephraim recalls the Syro-Ephraimite coalition and their threat to Judah in Isaiah 7–8 (Wildberger 1997, 164; Blenkinsopp 2000a, 303). Second, 18:2 points to northern Israel's attempt to form a political alliance with Egypt, at the time ruled by the Nubian dynasty. Third, 17:8 brings up the issue of idolatry, which the prophets often associate with alliances with foreign nations (cf. Isa 30–31). Moreover, Isaiah 18 appears to target Cush (also called Nubia or Ethiopia) in the region of Ethiopia, which anticipates and links with Isaiah 19–20 that target Egypt and Cush. Therefore, certain geographical, historical, and thematic connections of these locales—Damascus, Ephraim, and Cush—seem to cohere. Whereas the subsequent oracle in Isaiah 19–20 targets Egypt, however, the present unit (Isa 17–18) does not target Cush per se, but rather the nations' attempt to send envoys in reliance upon Cush: "In this context, Cush is representative of the nations at large" (Sweeney 1996, 260). Thus, the oracle warns Judah not to trust in Cush.

Furthermore, certain key linguistic markers correlate these disjointed subunits. Most distinctly, agricultural imagery (harvesting and gleaning) functions as a key component that ties this unit thematically (Sweeney 1996, 254). Beyond the fact that the "oracle"/"burden" (*massaʾ*) unites Isaiah 17–18 as a unit, the oracle against Damascus (17:1-3) neatly links to the three "on that day" subunits, primarily against northern Israel (17:4-6, 7-8, 9-11). Then, two "woe"-oracles expand this unit (17:12-14; 18:1-7), of which the one concerning Cush functions as a hinge between the preceding (Isa 17) and the following segments (Isa 19–20). We will therefore discuss these oracles together as a composite whole. W. A. M. Beuken summarizes the thematic coherence of Isaiah 17–18, which "opens with the fall of Damascus, the capital of Aram (Isa. 17:1-3), and closes with Mount Zion," where gifts will come to YHWH from as far as Cush (Beuken 2011, 63–64).

An Oracle against Damascus, 17:1-3

Here, Damascus, the capital of Aram, falls into abject misery: it will no longer be a city but a mere heap of ruins (v. 1). This place will be devoid of inhabitants with only flocks grazing (v. 2). In fact, YHWH taunts the robust coalition of Aram and northern Israel: Ephraim's fortresses and Damascus's dynasty will desist (cf. 13:11; 14:4; 16:10) and Aram's remnant will eclipse the forgone glory of Israel (v 3; cf. 16:14).

Oracles against Northern Israel, 17:4-11

Isaiah 17:4-6—the first "on that day" subunit—rushes on to northern Israel. What will the "glory" of Israel be like (v. 3)? Jacob's "glory" will sink (v. 4). Israel's demise will be so swift and effortless that it will be like harvesting standing grain and dense ears in the Valley of Rephaim near Jerusalem. Consequently, only a few berries and branches will remain (vv. 5-6).

Isaiah 17:7-8—the second (and concentrically central) "on that day" subunit—predicts the eventual effects of Jacob's downfall: everyone (*'adam*) to look to their Maker, the Holy One of Israel (v. 7). They will not look to any altars, Asherah poles, or incense that their own hands or fingers made (v. 8).

Isaiah 17:9-11—the third "on that day" subunit—expands the preceding subunits in terms of the idol worship practices that were rampant in northern Israel. Israel's fortified cities shall become like the abandoned forests of the Hivites and Amorites once defeated by the entering Israelites (v. 9). The oracle of Israel's breakdown connects to the causal ("for") and consequential ("therefore") utterances (vv. 10-11). Expounding vv. 7-8, but in the direct accusation of second-person feminine singular address, v. 10 rebukes Israel for having forgotten the God of "your" salvation and the Rock of "your" refuge. An echo of the Song of the Vineyard (5:1-7) describes the consequences of Israel's sin: even though "you" plant, sow, and build a fence for it, the harvest will yield only incurable illness (vv. 10-11).

Two Woe-Oracles against Many Peoples-Nations vis-à-vis Cush, 17:12–18:7

Isaiah 17:12-14—the first woe-oracle—expands the target to many "peoples" and "nations" (cf. 2:3) that echo the unruly forces of the ancient Near Eastern mythology which will crumble at YHWH's rebuke. The thundering uproar of the nations resembles to the tumult of the sea and waters (v. 12; cf. Ps 2:1). Yet, at YHWH's rebuke, they will turn to mere chaff blown by the wind (v. 13; cf. Ps 1:4). Here, the contention between the righteous and the wicked resurfaces as the "we"-group contends that all those who plunder "us" shall evaporate by night (v. 14).

Isaiah 18:1-7—the second woe-oracle—introduces a new target: Cush. Although its geographical location connects this chapter closely with Isaiah 19–20, which deal with Egypt, this subunit forms an equally close tie to the preceding woe-oracle. Scholars also posit the context of the Syro-Ephraimite War (735–732 BCE) during which the Syria-Ephraim coalition attempted to ask Cush to join them in their fight against Assyria (2 Kgs 17:4).

Verses 1-3 target Cush described as the land of the Nile with menacing people, tall and smooth (vv. 1-2). The depiction of "tall and smooth-skinned" (v. 2) underscores "the ability of this foreign people in warfare," implying that "the people of Cush would be a fear-inspiring military opponent" (Eidevall 2009, 81). The Hebrew word for the envoys (*tsir*) resembles the Akkadian word (*tsiru*) for "foreign high-ranking emissaries," alluding to the Assyrian imperial regime. Likewise, tributes from the envoys "far and away" (cf. v. 7) recall the common practice of paying homage to the empire (Balogh 2011, 350–51). As in the preceding subunits, the addressees embody the inhabitants of the world, who are to "see" the signal and "hear" the horn, witnessing YHWH's patronage of all subject nations (v. 3). The implied message becomes evident that the warning actually targets the Judeans in their propensity to rely on the lands of Nile rather than on YHWH.

Verses 4-6 present two causal ("for") statements that recapitulate the agricultural imagery of 17:9-11. Like the invisible heat and dew at the "harvest," YHWH will stealthily watch from the holy abode (v. 4). Just before the "harvest," YHWH will use the "pruning hooks," formerly used as spears, to cut off shoots and branches (v. 5; 2:4; cf. Mic 4:3; Joel 4:10). These leftovers will feed wild birds and beasts (v. 6).

Verse 7 then drastically projects the preceding situation into the future ("at that time"). Echoing the expressions of v. 2 verbatim as brackets, and possibly recalling the visit of the queen of Sheba to Solomon's kingdom (cf. 1 Kgs 10:1-13), it predicts that these Ethiopians will bring gifts of homage to YHWH in Mount Zion as a fulfillment of the nations' pilgrimage (cf. 2:2-4). The expression of "the people tall and smooth" in this verse has been the most well-known and inspiring phrase to many Sudanese Christians in our time. Having learned from the community of Dinka refugees from South Sudan in the aftermath of the atrocious civil war and genocide during the two decades prior to 2005, M. Jan Holton presents how the prophetic records of the exile and restoration of ancient Israel have provided powerful interpretive connections for the Sudanese Christians' resilient hope for God's redemption amid the painful memories and impact of war and displacement (Holton 2011).

This closing verse (18:7) provides key clues pertaining to the overall thematic unity of the fourth oracle (Isa 17–18). First, it sounds the theme of the confrontation of YHWH with arrogant nations, such as Aram, Ephraim, and Cush. One by one, the oracle addresses these daunting forces as though painting a map of daring and formidable nations. Yet the prophet assuredly pronounces their downfall: in particular, Damascus and even Samaria, the nations threatening Zion, are to collapse (cf. 7:8-9). At the same time, readers should anticipate that just as Samaria is not immune to divine judgment on their arrogant wrongdoings (Isa 17), so Jerusalem should be ready to heed the same warning (Isa 22).

Second, the language and idea of "harvest," functioning as a strong unifying theme, tie this oracle together (17:5-6, 10-11, 13; 18:5-6). This imagery of the desolation of the fields and shortage of crops occurs in crucial places in this oracle, together signifying the theme of impending catastrophe. Here, however, readers also find a depiction of YHWH who quietly awaits the harvest (18:4). This imagery of a veiled God implies that this oracle, which concerns the nations, also addresses the inhabitants of Jerusalem. The audience would then hear another surprising message in that whereas those haughty nations will be punished at the harvest time, the Ethiopian nation, Nubia, shall bring tribute to God—the very "harvest" that YHWH intends to gather in (Beuken 2011, 75, 78).

Finally, the geographical shifts betray not only the historical backgrounds of the Syro-Ephraimite crisis but also the literary progress that extends from Damascus and Ephraim, via Cush, to Zion, thereby contributing to the thematic contrast between Damascus-Samaria and Mount Zion. This oracle thus attests the foundational theology of the nations' acknowledgment of the Torah in 2:2-5, of which W. A. M. Beuken trenchantly states, "If at the beginning of the fourth *massa'* oracle, 'Damascus / the fortress of Ephraim' represent powerful city-states that adore alien gods but neglect the God of Israel, at the end of this composition Mount Zion comes to the fore as the place where a dreaded nation, Nubia, will pay homage to Yhwh" (Beuken 2011, 78). Ultimately, both the devastation of the arrogant nations, Syria-Ephraim, and the embrace of the humble nation, Nubia, highlight the theme that the one who governs all the events of world history is YHWH alone, whom all these nations, without exempting Israel and Judah, should faithfully acknowledge.

Fifth Oracle—Against Egypt, 19:1–20:6

The Nile Will Dry Up, 19:1-15

This oracle against Egypt, prior to the "on that day" passages (vv. 16-25), has a rough chiastic format:

Verses 1-4 = "spirit" (*ruakh*) (v. 3)
    Verses 1-4 = "a mighty king" + declares YHWH of the army (v. 4)
        Verses 5-7 = Nile will dry up
        Verses 8-10 = fishers + workers + weavers
    Verses 11-12 = princes/counselors/sages + YHWH of the army (v. 12)
Verses 13-15 = "spirit" (*ruakh*) of confusion (v. 14)

In light of the linguistic bracketing by vv. 1-4 and vv. 11-15, the central part (vv. 5-10) essentially focuses on the river Nile, its devastation, and its impacts on Egypt. The Nile is the pivotal symbol of the Egyptian civilization and the heartbeat of its economy. The news of the Nile's depletion accentuates the monumental collapse of Egypt. This core part divides into two subunits: descriptions of the Nile drying up (vv. 5-7) and of its effects (vv. 8-10). The result of this division vividly portrays how the very land, which "the rivers divide" (18:2, 7), has been divided in havoc and disarray.

Verses 1-4 declare YHWH's intent to punish Egypt. Echoing the Canaanite myth of Baal riding the clouds, YHWH comes to Egypt, whose heart will melt (v. 1; Blenkinsopp 2000a, 314). Also, the impending infliction of trembling and panic alludes to the Assyrian royal inscriptions, implying YHWH not Assur as the sovereign Lord whose arrival in Egypt overwhelms enemy forces (Balogh 2011, 350). As a result, there will be incessant civil wars (v. 2; cf. the turbulent Intermediate periods of Egyptian history). Just like the "heart" (v. 1), now the "spirit" of the Egyptians will deteriorate (v. 3) and the Egyptians will serve as slaves under the hard masters, a reversal of fortune from the Exodus (v. 4; cf. Exod 1:14).

Verses 5-10, as a literary center, graphically describe the Nile being parched. Symbolically, the Nile represents Egypt's pride and foundation (vv. 5-7). Yet, literally, the drought devastates its entire economic and social system (vv. 8-10). Various verbs meaning "to be dry" occur repeatedly throughout vv. 5-7. Echoing the Canaanite myth, the Nile will meet the fate of the "sea" (*yam*) and the "river" (*nahar*), and will thoroughly dry up (v. 5). Consequently, vv. 8-10 forecast the collapse of Egypt's economy, which heavily relies on the stability of the Nile that provides vital resources for fishers, garment weavers, and hired workers.

Verses 11-15 culminate with the political incapacity of Egypt's ruling class. Princes of Zoan (or Tanis or Ramses as a city) are foolish, the wise counselors of Pharaoh are ignorant, and the princes of Memphis (the capital in Lower Egypt) are delusional (vv. 11-13; Oswalt 1986, 371). All this is because YHWH has poured out a "spirit" of corruption and, in turn, all of Egypt's upper class ("head and tail, palm branch and reed"; cf. 9:3-4) will become ineffectual (vv. 14-15).

Egypt's Transformations—Six "on that day" Passages, 19:16-25
These six "on that day" passages expand the preceding unit with more dramatic, futuristic projections of Egypt's transformation (as if signaling a thorough six-day makeover of Egypt). This transformation will impose the unmanning of Egypt's armies and will usher in a revolutionized Egypt that fears and honors YHWH. In a sense, these passages predict the future glorious restoration of the exiled Diasporas who will turn to YHWH whether in Susa or in Elephantine (cf. Amos 9:7-10).

Verses 16-17—comprising the first "on that day" passage—emasculate the formidable Egyptian power, causing Egypt's complete demoralization (cf. 3:12; 5:22). The reversal of its fate signals the empowerment of the land of Judah, which will become a formidable threat to Egypt (v. 16). The simile that compares the Egyptian male warriors to women mirrors common ancient Near Eastern texts intending to negate and ridicule the warriors' capabilities. A similar expression in an Akkadian treaty, found at Nineveh, between Ashurnirar and Mati'ilu of Arpad appears in the Assyrian king's curse upon his vassal subject: "If Mati'ilu sins against this treaty of Ashurnirari, king of Assyria, may Mati'ilu become a prostitute and may his warriors become women" (Bergmann 2008, 135). Hence, words describing "trembling," "dread," and "terror" abound, highlighting the incomparable power of YHWH's hand (vv. 16-17).

Verse 18—the second "on that day" passage—depicts the consequences of Egypt's utter disbandment. Here again, allusions to the Mesopotamian royal inscriptions depict the implicit theme highlighting YHWH as the true sovereign Lord. Israel's influence will be so immense that Hebrew will be *lingua franca* in the five metropolises of Egypt as they pledge an oath to YHWH. This idea of an oath in a foreign language is pertinent to the Assyrian vassals who were obliged to swear allegiance to their overlord. The city Heliopolis ("sun") in Lower Egypt will obtain a new name with a thematic pun in Hebrew meaning "the city of destruction" (Wildberger 1997, 262–63). This renaming further echoes the Assyrian expressions for a destroyed city, "ruin hill" (*til abube*; Balogh 2011, 350).

Verses 19-20—comprising the third "on that day" passage—express further impacts of the reversal of the fate. Transformation will impact not only the five major cities (v. 18) but also religious centers in Egypt, where there will be an altar of YHWH as well as a monument ("stele" or "inscription") to YHWH on the borders (v. 19). Here we find features strikingly similar to the Assyrian royal inscriptions. Often in the context of the conquest of vassal nations, the erection of the stele represented a sign of their subordination to Assyria. The stele also entailed a cultic reminder of their treaty obedience to the suzerain. In fact, the Mesopotamian stele may even have functioned "as a substitute" for the ruler. The underlying theme of "the stele of YHWH," contrary to the ancient Near Eastern tradition, avers that it is YHWH —not Assur, Marduk, or Ahuramazda—who is the ultimate, unmatched Lord of all the seemingly daunting but actually fleeting empires and their gods (Balogh 2011, 350–52). Subsequently, when Egypt will soon fall in harm's way, YHWH will raise a savior to deliver them, as in the time of the judges (v. 20).

Verses 21-22—comprising the fourth "on that day" passage—indicate the religious transformation of the Egyptians who will not only "know" YHWH (v. 21; cf. 1:3; 6:9; 11:2, 9; 19:12) but will also worship and sacrifice to YHWH, no longer revering Egypt's popular gods. YHWH will then respond, both striking them for their wrongs and healing them for their prayers (v. 22).

Verse 23—the fifth "on that day" passage—projects a pilgrimage all the way from Egypt to Assyria, where there will be a "highway" (cf. 11:16; 35:8; 36:2; 40:3; 49:11; 62:10) and both Egyptians and Assyrians will come to worship YHWH. Whereas according to 11:16 the highway will mainly enable the Israelite remnants and exiles to return, in this passage the highway guides Assyria and Egypt—Israel's two imperial oppressors—to come and worship the God of Israel (Childs 2001, 144–45; cf. 2:2-4).

Verses 24-25—comprising the sixth "on that day" passage—conclude this unit with yet another reversal motif in that Israel becomes third, next to Egypt and Assyria, for the channels of blessing on earth (v. 24; cf. 2:5; Gen 12:2-3). The transformative divine blessing will embrace all these peoples: "Blessed be Egypt my people (cf. Isa 1:3; Exod 5:1), Assyria the work of my hands (cf. Isa 29:23; 60:21), and Israel my inheritance" (v. 25; cf. Exod 34:9; Deut 32:9; 1 Kgs 8:51; Pss 28:9; 74:2; 78:71; 94:5, 14; 106:40).

This gradual yet dramatic transformation moves beyond a mere reversal of fortune against Egypt. It further envisions a future era when Egypt, Assyria, and Israel may live in mutual peace together. We have read and will encounter key passages throughout the book of Isaiah, here and there, that resonate, like the chorus refrains, the ideals of peace and unity. For example, "in later days," many nations and peoples shall go up to Zion, not waging war but rather learning peace (2:2-4; cf. 36:1; Ps 87:4-7). Likewise, the peaceable kingdom will come when there will be no harm or destruction between predators and prey, between the powerful and the weak (11:6-9; cf. 65:25). Thus, "on that day," the enmity between Ephraim (northern Israel) and Judah will cease and turn to unity (11:13; cf. 9:21 [MT 9:20]). Such a vision of radical peace and harmony seems out of place, quite nonsensical and unrealistic, especially considering the oppressive abuses Egypt and Assyria wielded in the history of Israel. Nonetheless, if the prophet could dream such dreams, we too may envision a world where nations (especially those nations of recent animosity or current hostility) in Far East Asia, Middle East, Africa, Europe, Americas, and elsewhere can live in mutual reconciliation and peace. Dreams and visions indeed. But we remember the dreams Martin Luther King, Jr., dreamed for such a possible future, "on that day." Desmond Tutu's prayer directs toward a similar hope: "Lord, we praise you in Europe's cathedrals, in America's offerings, / And in our African songs of praise. / Lord, we thank you that we have brothers and sisters in all the world. / Be with them that make peace. / Amen" (Tutu 1995, 65–66).

The Prophet's Street Performance about Egypt's and Ethiopia's Exile, 20:1-6

Isaiah 20:1 introduces a new chronological heading, somewhat akin to 6:1 and 14:28. Its historical context refers to the military campaign of Sargon II of Assyria against the revolt of satellite countries with Egypt as its instigator. The Assyrian king sent Tartan, the commander-in-chief, whose conquered regions cover the Philistine city Ashdod. Now the threat lurks in the land of Judah (2 Kgs 18:17).

Verses 2-5, initiated by the temporal phrase "at that time," provide the divine oracle to Egypt and Ethiopia. First, the prophet's symbolic action of walking without sackcloth or sandals, naked and barefoot, for three years would unequivocally convey the message of the impending captivity of Egypt (v. 2). Depicting the Assyrian practice of "depriving war prisoners of their clothes," this barefooted nakedness implies humiliation and disgrace "at the national level" (Eidevall 2009, 93–94). Next, the explanation of this symbolic action as "a sign and a portent" (cf. 8:18) indicates the Assyrian defeat of Egypt and Ethiopia in their subsequent exile and captivity (vv. 3-4). Previous predictions of the Nile becoming "bare places" (*'arot*, 19:7) are soon to become the sure reality of the shame of nakedness (*'arom*).

In light of the ancient Egyptian history, Cush reached the apex of its political power with the Cushite (twenty-fifth) dynasty on the Egyptian throne during the mid-eighth and mid-seventh centuries BCE. Together with the previous oracle in Isaiah 18, Cush and Egypt thus compare as politically, economically, and militarily strong nations (Holter 2014, 76). Similar to the effect of hearing the news of the fall of Assyria or of Babylon, the announcement of the defeat of these African empires should have shocked the audiences, not to mention those Israelite leaders betting on these empires for saving their own skin.

Verse 6, initiated by the "on that day" phrase, recapitulates the dire context of these captives expressed in the speech of the coastlands. The "hope" (*mabat*) that many had in Cush and Egypt (v. 5) will be dashed and realized as a false "hope" (*mabat*). Not just Judah but also the coastlands that have leaned on Assyria for deliverance now regretfully wail their own "we"-lament: "How shall we escape?"

Sixth Oracle—Against "the Desert of the Sea" [Babylon], 21:1-10

A Harsh Vision, 21:1-5

Unlike the previous "burden" oracles (Isa 13–20), which address nations with specific names, here we find a more cryptic, abstract target. As analyzed above, we can subdivide the overall arrangement of the OAN section in two ways: (1) the Babylon oracles frame the core parts within Isaiah 13 and 21; or (2) the Babylon oracles initiate each of the two parts in Isaiah 13–20 and 21–23. Either way, this unit concerning Babylon plays a pivotal role, whether as a bracketing conclusion of the core segment or as the bridging initiation of another segment, if not both.

Even more startling is the not-so-specific description of the target, which the heading designates "the wilderness of the sea." Except in v. 9, nowhere does this oracle mention Babylon. We can infer that "the wilderness of the sea" may refer to the geographic region near Babylon, possibly the "marshy delta of the Tigris and Euphrates in southern Mesopotamia" (Blenkinsopp 2000a, 324). In addition to its abstractness, however, both desert and sea as antonyms may signify both ironic and symbolic implications, as "desert" and "sea" occur frequently throughout the book of Isaiah (cf. 16:8; 50:2), not to mention ancient Near Eastern mythologies. Furthermore, this "desert" may complement "coastlands" (20:6; cf. 21:13; 23:2, 4, 6, 11), together signifying the vast territory of a superpower empire that YHWH will obliterate: "The designation 'Desert of the Sea' would be quite apposite as a symbol for the whole of Babylonia" (Uffenheimer 1995, 678).

Verses 1-2 forecast the surge of militant forces from the desert, far away. Heavy tornadoes, a metaphor for invincible forces (cf. 5:28; 17:13; 66:15), will pass through from the desert region of Negev (v. 1). The harsh vision given to the prophet informs listeners that the violent oppressors—betrayers and treacherous ones—are unleashing their wickedness, and this wickedness has caused much "sighing" in petty kingdoms like Israel (cf. Lam 1:22). To challenge these violent forces, YHWH is mustering Elam and Media, the neighboring countries that often fought against Assyria or Babylon (v. 2). In fact, the Median-Babylonian coalition affected the fall of Nineveh and the Assyrian empire (Albertz 2003b, 50; cf. 13:17-18). Yet Elam and especially Media may have been crucial allies in the Assyrian king Sennacherib's revolt against Babylon (around 700 BCE; cf. Sweeney 1996, 279–83).

Eventually, this previous history was adapted to depict the fall of Babylon by Cyrus of Persia, whose supremacy embraced and far surpassed the regions of Elam and Media (539 BCE; Liverani 2014, 561–62). In light of this broad historical background, however, we should remember Babylon as Judah's arch-oppressor. The oracle's allusions to Elam and Media may have been a powerful rhetorical reminder of Babylon's volatile past history, leaving a deep scar. In analogy, Elam and Media were to Babylon just as Edom—the traitor and bystander—was to Judah (cf. Obad 10-14; Ps 137:7). In another respect, to the powerless Judeans, Babylon's weak past may be a reminder that this menacing empire too is liable and shall collapse someday.

Verses 3-5 display the resultant horror and emotional anguish continuously in first-person speech. Using imagery of a birthing woman, the prophet describes himself as too distraught from the stern news to "hear" or "see" anything (v. 3; cf. 6:9). Even his "heart" pounds with panic and fear (v. 4; cf. 6:9). The prophet's instant reaction combines both "acute physical pain" and "spiritual confusion" (Uffenheimer 1995, 684). Then the scene portrays the contrast between the lackadaisical leaders of Babylon, boasting of their security, and the bellicose warriors of Elam and Media, eager to go to the battle (v. 5). Here, through remarkable intertextual twists, Babylon's false sense of safety meets abject denial. Just as the psalmist affirms that "you prepare a table (ta'arok . . . shulkhan) before me" (Ps 23:5), so "they prepare a table ('arok hashulkhan)." Yet, contrary to Babylon's volatile wish that in front of the enemies "you anoint my head with oil" (Ps 23:5), the prophet relays the roars of the soldiers ready to assault Babylon, "Rise up, captains, oil the shields!" (cf. Sweeney 1996, 279–83; Tull 2010, 337).

A Message from the Watchtower: "Fallen, Fallen, Babylon," 21:6-10

The divine vision allowed the prophet to see and hear the rousing of the invaders against Babylon, albeit dimly (vv. 1-5). Now the divine word directs the prophet to hear the long-awaited news from the battle sentinel, not unlike a marathon reporter.

Verses 6-7 extend the emotional tension that escalated in the prophet's vision in the preceding passage. As Benjamin Uffenheimer observes, "the prophet's intense agitation is betrayed mainly by repeated sounds, words, and indeed entire phrases": e.g., "spreading the rug [or, 'let the watchman watch']" (*tsapoh hatsapit*) in v. 5 and "lookout" (*hametsapeh* and *mitseppeh*) in vv. 6, 8; "horsemen in pairs" (*tsemed parasim*) in v. 7 and v. 9; and, climactically, "fallen, fallen" in v. 9 (Uffenheimer 1995, 685). The divine instruction this time is thus for the prophet to appoint a lookout who is about to witness the very onslaught upon the city of Babylon (v. 6). The watcher is to see warriors riding chariots, donkeys, and camels, with the effect being as though readers too are witnessing countless bands of troops marching fiercely (v. 7).

Verses 8-10 present the watcher's report of Babylon's termination. The sentinel, who looks out vigilantly day and night (v. 8), finally sees the troop of riders (v. 9). The prophet and readers have to wait out a moment of suspense. What will the report of the sentinel be? How did the battle turn out? The message is simple and precisely delivered by the signals of flags and torches: "Fallen, fallen, Babylon" (v. 9; cf. 2 Sam 1:19, 25; Amos 5:2). In terms of possible historical settings, A. A. Macintosh (1980) calls it a "palimpsest"; "two major events, one in the eighth century and one in the sixth, are reflected" (Childs 2001, 154). On the one hand, in light of the preexilic context of Judah's alliance with Merodach-baladan against Assyria, Babylon's defeat would have dashed the last resort the Judean leaders had bet on for their selfish survival, virtually careless of the rest of the population.

On the other hand, alternatively, the two messages may be the two sides of the same coin: "fallen, fallen, Babylon" equals "comfort, comfort, my people" (Isa 40:1)! Who among those in days, years, and decades of exilic torment and agony would ever have imagined that the empire Babylon—the most powerful superpower of the time—would fall? Walter Brueggemann puts it this way: "[the fall of Babylon] is a cosmic happening that signifies a revolutionary redefinition of the world" (1998a, 171). The report repeatedly declares the fall of the tyrannical kingdom of Babylon along with its gods. Thus, in this announcement of the most incredible event, the prophet wraps up the report of his vision (v. 10; cf. v. 2).

Together with Isaiah 13–14, this oracle announcing the fall of Babylon in Isaiah 21 forms a ring structure and accentuates the demise of the superpower. In one respect, the OAN section presents anachronistic content by introducing Babylon, which does not fit properly in chronological sequence. In another respect, however, the present arrangement can display a fundamental theme: (1) the oracles about the fall of Jerusalem (587 BCE) and (2) those about the fall of Babylon (539 BCE). If, as scholars have rightly noted, the fall of Jerusalem in 587 BCE was one of the most devastating and impactful events in Israel's biblical history, then now we should add that the fall of Babylon in 539 BCE could have been a second most revolutionary event. That Jerusalem and its Davidic dynasty ended must have shattered many foundations of Israel's theological traditions and beliefs. Equally significant, that the most powerful and oppressive superpower Babylon could collapse may have engendered radically new and shifted perspectives to the faithful YHWH-devotees, pro-Babylonian defectors, numerous opportunists, and so on (Stulman and Kim 2010, 246–67).

Thus, even though it may seem anachronistic, the pronouncement of the downfall of Babylon in the present form of the OAN section presents a valuable message. Perhaps the later audiences could not fathom or endure the hardship this menacing empire inflicted on them. Or perhaps the scribes could not wait any longer for the good news of liberation. What seems like a "spoiler alert" in the case of a novel or movie, the present arrangement exhibits a powerful theme that God had already pronounced the fall of Babylon. Together with the fall of Jerusalem, sequential readers thus encounter the tales of two cities—the fall of Jerusalem (Isa 1–12) and the fall of Babylon (Isa 13–23). In a broader perspective, these tales of two cities, two deities, and two symbols will continue later in Isaiah 24–27 and beyond (Isa 40–48).

Seventh Oracle—Against Dumah, 21:11-12

This short oracle is replete with cryptic and mysterious meanings. The location "Dumah" may refer to the northern oasis in Arabia, yet its cognate form may allude to "the land of the silent dead" (Pss 94:17; 115:17), reinforcing the demise of Babylon in the preceding unit. Literarily placed in the middle of Isaiah 21, this unit of two verses may function not only as a hinge but also as the core of the surrounding units. Accordingly, it extends the roles of the sentinels from vv. 6-9 and at the same time suspends the impact of the fall of the Babylonian empire.

One sentinel shouts from Seir, located in Edom (cf. Gen 36:8-9), inquiring of another sentinel as to what has transpired in the night (v. 11; cf. v. 8). Another sentinel's response assures that, with the verb "to come" framing the speech, morning will come, as will night (v. 12). Yet the emphasis highlights the night. Just as Moab was undone, "by night, by night" (15:1), Dumah or the land of the silent dead shall suffer the fate "of night . . . of night" (v. 11).

Eighth Oracle—Against "The Desert Plain" [Arabia], 21:13-17

With regard to the literary arrangement, this oracle parallels the oracle of vv. 1-10. In Isaiah 21, these two oracles (vv. 1-10 and vv. 13-17) bracket the internal one (vv. 11-12). Likewise, thematically, the oracle against "the *desert* of the *sea* [Babylon]" (vv. 1) corresponds nicely with the oracle against "the *desert* [Arabia]" (v. 13)—we will also cover another "*sea*" oracle in Isaiah 23.

Verses 13-14 warn of the impact of Babylon's demise on the region of Arabia. As in v. 1, correlating to the coastlands (20:6), this desert area consists of two cities, Dedan and Tema, which will be prevented from escaping the devastating war (cf. Jer 25:22-24). Dedan's caravans will have to lodge in the thickets of the desert (v. 13). Tema will be a town busy hosting war-torn refugees amid shortage of water and bread (v. 14).

Verses 15-17 provide the rationales for Arabia's doom, with the further announcement of another city, Kedar, another likely ally of Judean regime. The first "for"-clause passage (v. 15) describes the refugees fleeing from swords and bows. The second "for"-clause passage (vv. 16-17) conveys the divine message against Kedar. Kedar's glory will fade within a year, with only a few remnants of warriors and bows.

Ninth Oracle—Against "The Valley of Vision" [Jerusalem], 22:1-25

The Valley of Vision, 22:1-14

This oracle continues and extends the cryptic targets within the second part of the OAN section. The oracle against the valley of vision (vv. 1-14) picks up the oracles against the wilderness of the sea, Dumah, and the desert (21:1-17). The oracle against Tyre, a coastland territory, will then follow (23:1-18). This oracle situates Jerusalem on the same line with the nations and just before Tyre (sea nation), similar to the way Ephraim (northern Israel) stands among the nations followed by Egypt (sea nation). The way the OAN section culminates therefore does not stop with Babylon but ends with the verdicts on two proud capitals—Jerusalem and Tyre—under God's judgment! The harsh "vision" (*hazut*) the prophet saw (21:2) connects now to the "valley of vision (*hizayon*)" (22:1). As a narrative insert or doublet, the valley of vision unit (vv. 1-14) coincides with the messages concerning Shebna and Eliakim (vv. 15-25).

Verses 1-8a recall the symbolic places of earlier oracles, such as wilderness or sea (21:1), and desert (21:13). Now this subunit introduces the valley. In close linguistic affinity with 40:3-4, "wilderness," "desert," and "valley" may symbolize the harsh terrains of hopeless exile where the prophet later hears the admonition to prepare a highway for YHWH's triumphal return.

Just as "wilderness" and "sea" seem paradoxical (21:1), so it is oxymoronic to expect a "vision" in a steep "valley" that naturally obstructs one's vision (22:2; cf. Ps 23:4). Read together, however, just as "the wilderness of the sea" signifies Babylon (Isa 21), here "the valley of vision" denotes Jerusalem; the tales of two cities stand put side by side.

The opening part of the oracle (vv. 1-4) shifts the focus from the third-person plural, "they" (21:1-9, 15-17), to the second-person feminine singular, "you." This direct address echoes more closely the taunt song against the king of Babylon (14:4b-20a; cf. 21:10-14). Read together, just as the oracle of the mocking song accuses Babylon in the second-person masculine singular (Isa 14), now this oracle accuses Jerusalem in the second-person feminine singular (cf. 1:22-26). As it resembles the rhetorical punch line of the OAN in Amos 1–2, which targets Judah and climactically northern Israel, the Jerusalem readers would now learn of the powerful message against themselves, as the famous saying goes: "We have met the enemy and the enemy is us."

Ironically, the vision from the low valley is vivid. The women of Jerusalem have fled, going up to the rooftops (v. 1). Denoting this people's desperate attempt to hide away (cf. 2:10), their going up to the rooftops signifies the lack of faith, making an ironic contrast with the nations' going up to Zion (cf. 2:3) or even the positive Hezekiah (cf. 37:14; 38:22; Beuken 2005, 53).

Akin to the "roaring" of Jacob (17:12), the prophet chides the "roaring city" as well as the "jubilant town" (*qiryah 'alizah*) in v. 2. The "jubilant town" (*qiryah 'alizah*) will later recur in the similar denouncement of the complacent women in the fortified Jerusalem in 32:13. Equally notably, the feminine personification of Jerusalem alludes to the similar denunciation of the noble women in 3:16-26. Whereas Isaiah 3:25 reports that Jerusalem's male warriors have fallen valiantly, or even honorably, by the "sword" (*hereb*) in the "battle" (*milkhamah*), now (v. 2) they will not even have such an honorable death, neither slain by the "sword" (*hereb*) nor killed in the "battle" (*milkhamah*). Instead, these commanders have fled only to be captured, tied up, and taken away (v. 3). The prophet describes the bitter laments of Jerusalem's women, vulnerable and deprived of being "comforted" (v. 4). Jerusalem, called "the daughter of my people," is a city in ruins.

The subsequent segment (vv. 5-8a) extends the depiction of the gruesome battle scene described as the upcoming day of YHWH. We further hear an inner-biblical allusion with regard to the expression of the day of YHWH:

• "For YHWH of the army has a day against . . ." (2:12);
• "For Adonay YHWH of the army has a day of tumult, trampling, and turmoil in the valley of vision . . ." (22:5; cf. 13:6-13).

This unique phrase occurs elsewhere only in 34:8 in the book of Isaiah. The literary expansion here illustrates YHWH's day by the alliteration of three repetitious words (*mehumah wumebbsah wumebukah*) so that the readers may hear the very tumult, trampling, and turmoil in the valley of vision (v. 5).

Literary puns continue, heightening the sounds of havoc in the deep valley, "a wrecking of walls" (*meqarqar qir*) and "an outcry to the mountain" (*shoaʾ ʾel-hahar*, v. 5). Interestingly, one of the three alliterations, "trampling," has the connotation of "treading down" (*mebusah*), which occurs elsewhere only in 18:2, 7 in the OT. Together, the vocabulary of "treading down" (*mebusah*) and "wrecking down" (*meqarqar*) in v. 5 sounds similar to the phrase in "a conquering and trampling (*qaw-qaw wumebusah*) nation," which depicts Ethiopia (18:2, 7).

Both Elam, the city stirred up to invade Babylon (21:2), and Kir, the town to which the king of Assyria transported the captives of Damascus (2 Kgs 16:9), now aim their quivers and shields against Jerusalem (v. 6). Pointing to Sennacherib's invasion of Judah, as construed by many scholars, chariots and cavalry encamp at the major valleys and gates (vv. 6-7). As a result, accompanying the wrecking down of the walls (cf. v. 5), the defensive barricades of Judah are now removed, literally "denuding Judah of its cover" (v. 8a; Blenkinsopp 2000a, 333). It is unclear who the agent of this removing action is—whether the Assyrian king Sennacherib (Isa 36–37) or YHWH (v. 5). Yet, in the present form, because of the likely inclusio of the alliteration with the word "covering" (*masak*), it points to YHWH of the army who musters a formidable empire against Judah.

Verses 8b-11 extend the preceding subunit about the day of YHWH with another "on that day" passage. Whereas the oracle in vv. 1-8a addressed Jerusalem's complacent women ("you") in the singular, this subunit now addresses Jerusalem's male counterparts ("you") in the plural form (cf. 3:1-26). The detailed report recounts the building project of the Siloam Tunnel in Jerusalem in preparation for the siege of Sennacherib during the time of King Hezekiah (2 Kgs 20:20; 2 Chr 32:3-5, 30), although the cryptic, subtle clues to the historical aspects of the whole unit (Isa 22:1-14) exhibit "an amalgam of various calamitous events which befell the city: the siege of 701, the downfall of 586, and other comparable dangers to its survival" (Beuken 2005, 60–61).

The initial masculine singular "you" refers to Hezekiah (v. 8b). Many of the words and motifs are strikingly similar to those of 2 Chronicles 32:3-5. Just as Hezekiah made many weapons and shields (2 Chr 3:5), so "he" prepared the weapons (v. 8b). Now, the fact that the masculine plural addressee, "you," saw the breaches in "the city of David" (v. 9) coincides with Hezekiah's fortification of the citadel, or Millo, in "the city of David" (2 Chr 3:5). The fortification of the inner and outer walls (v. 10) likewise reflects Hezekiah's renovation of the walls (2 Chr 3:5). Finally, the construction of the reservoir between the two walls (v. 11) reflects Hezekiah's tunnel documented in the Siloam Tunnel Inscription (2 Kgs 20:20; 2 Chr 32:30): "This is the record of how the tunnel was breached. While [the excavators were wielding] their pick-axes, each man towards his co-worker, . . . Then the water flowed from the spring to the pool" (*COS* II: 145–46). Recent archaeological studies estimate that this massive labor project, which employed many refugees from southern territories of northern Israel (after their fall in 722 BCE), took at least four years (Burke 2011, 50–51).

Despite these courageous efforts (vv. 8b-11a; cf. 2 Chr 32:7-8), this oracle accuses Jerusalem of lacking utmost trust in God (v. 11b). Two key words form a bracket around the subunit. While Hezekiah "gazed" (*nabat*) at the weapons (v. 8b) and all his officials "saw" (*ra'ah*) many breaches in Jerusalem (v. 9), this ruling class (plural "you") hears divine denunciation that they neither "gaze" (*nabat*) at the Maker nor "see" (*ra'ah*) the Planner (v. 11b; Tull 2010, 346). This verdict underscores how human efforts to strengthen military resources (vv. 8b-11a) can be useless without genuine prayer and trust in God (v. 11b; cf. 2 Chr 32:25). Ultimately, the oracle does not specify these addressees but conveys a theme paramount in the whole oracle—that it is not Hezekiah alone but rather all the ruling class who should rely on YHWH, the Maker and Planner of all things.

Verses 12-14 add another "on that day" passage, with its climactic episode involving the people's perverse debauchery, scorning YHWH's admonition to communal repentance. The prophetic call in such a time of national crisis is to mourn in communal penitential acts such as putting on sackcloth (v. 12). Alas, the people in Jerusalem are taking the opposite actions, in disregard of the divine warning, in their self-indulgent, sumptuous feasts of oxen, sheep, meat, and wine (v. 13). Jerusalem's guilt is due not only to Epicurean indulging in festivities but especially to their utter disregard of the divine expectation of justice and righteousness (cf. 1:21-26; 28:16-17; Beuken 2005: 57). Therefore, in light of the foregoing accusation (vv. 1-13), the prophet communicates the verdict (v. 14) that YHWH will not forgive their iniquity (cf. 1:18; 2:9): "Inappropriate rejoicing and self-indulgences such as 'eating, drinking, and making merry' lead to a voice in the night that addresses, 'Fool' (Luke 12:19-20)" (Brueggemann 1998a, 178).

Shebna the Steward of Hubris and Eliakim the Servant of YHWH, 22:15-25

Just as the narrative account of the prophet's symbolic actions concerning Egypt and Cush in Isaiah 20 interrupts the preceding burden-oracles, so the narrative account of two high officials of Jerusalem in 22:15-25—Shebna (vv. 15-19) and Eliakim (vv. 20-25)—interrupts the preceding burden-oracles. The exact historical identifications of Shebna and Eliakim remain disputed. The recurrences of the same but contradictory figures in 36:3, 11, 22; 37:2 further complicates this matter. Regardless of the issue of specific historical accounts of these two officials, the place of this narrative account evidently functions as an illustrative object lesson for the preceding oracle against Jerusalem (22:1-14) while at the same time presenting two contrasting individuals as symbols of two contending religio-political groups, e.g., the wicked versus the righteous, the insolent versus the penitent.

Verses 15-19 narrate the case of Shebna, opening with the messenger formula ("Thus says YHWH"), which functions in most prophetic texts as an announcement of judgment, or what Brueggemann calls "the firing of a top employee" (1998a, 179). The title, "this Shebna . . . in charge of the house [of David]" (v. 15), may rank him just beneath the king (cf. 2 Kgs 15:5; 2 Chr 26:21: "Jotham was in charge of the king's house"). The divine exhortation for the prophet to "go" (*lek*) to Shebna nicely parallels the command to "go" (*lek*) to perform signs and portents (20:2; cf. 21:6). Initially, the divine word accuses Shebna of hubris related to his privileged but self-serving high rank, symbolized by his tomb built on the height (v. 16).

Readers may still wonder why this kind of act would deserve such severe punishment. Tova Ganzel suggests that Shebna's paramount sin is not just hewing his tomb on high but especially also its prohibited location in proximity to the temple. From the ancient Egyptian traditions of kings' burial near sacred precincts, this incident may point to Hezekiah's reform, whose religious purification would have included removing any defilement, such as graves and idolatry, from the temple (cf. Ezek 43:6-9). Shebna's act may thus both represent defiance of God and contrast with Hezekiah's ultimate piety (Ganzel 2015, 473–81).

Readers can hear the irony in the threefold usage of the word "here," as if YHWH is rebuking Shebna that he does not belong here, on high. Where does he really belong then? The subsequent denunciation depicts Shebna's downfall (vv. 17-19). As though YHWH assumes the role of a javelin thrower or of a blazing baseball pitcher, Shebna will be rolled up like a ball and hurled away to the lowest burial place or the farthest exile. Numerous repeated words ("hurl," "grasp," and "wind up") emphasize the emotional condemnation.

Whereas "here," at the peak of Jerusalem, Shebna desires to claim his lofty power (v. 15), "there," as the prophet asserts, he will die and his glorious chariots will crash (v. 18; cf. v. 14). Shebna will thus bring "shame" to the house of his master, presumably the house of David, and lose his office (vv. 18-19).

Verses 20-25, led by the "on that day" phrase, narrate the case of Eliakim. That YHWH calls Eliakim "my servant" (v. 20) intensifies the deliberate contrast between Shebna and Eliakim. The subversive elevation of this lowly servant suggests the transfer of power, expressed by the repeated uses of possessive pronouns, from "your" (Shebna's) tunic, belt, and authority to "him" (Eliakim) in v. 21. Eliakim is endowed with the title of "a father ('ab) to the inhabitants of Jerusalem and to the house of Judah" (v. 21), a possible allusion to the high status of Joseph as "a father ('ab) to Pharaoh, lord of all his house, and ruler over all the land of Egypt" (Gen 45:8). In fact, the key to the "house of David" shall rest on his shoulder (v. 22; cf. Isa 9:6 [MT 9:5]). Thus, in contrast to Shebna, who is to bring "shame to the house of his lord" (v. 18), Eliakim will become a "throne of honor to the house of his ancestors" (vv. 23-24).

The additional "on that day" passage (v. 25) stands as an anomaly. Strangely, it reverses the honor conferred upon Eliakim. According to it, YHWH will take away "the peg that was fastened in a secure place" (cf. v. 23) and cut off the load or "burden" (massa') on it. Two interpretive options may be possible. On the one hand, taking the references to the "tent peg" or "pin" as another parallel to vv. 15-19, some scholars propose to identify the first "pin" as Shebna (v. 23), whose grim dismissal will lead to the second, stronger "pin" as Eliakim (v. 25; Ganzel 2015, 485–86). On the other hand, identifying the "pin" consistently as Eliakim (which seems a plausible reading), this seemingly anticlimactic passage—which ironically coincides with the questionable depiction of King Hezekiah in Isaiah 39—may be an additional warning that no human office is immune to the wrongful lure of power and the resultant disempowerment by YHWH: "even after the removal of Shebna and the appointment of the faithful Eliakim, the city will not stand forever" (Ganzel 2015, 486).

Tenth Oracle—Against Tyre, 23:1-18

The OAN section may conclude properly with the oracles against Babylon (Isa 21) and Jerusalem (Isa 22). Yet that is not the case in its present form. This section ends with an oracle targeted against Tyre, a somewhat unexpected and strange city. Despite the oracle's awkward appearance, however, certain literary elements may offer some clues to its placement.

First, following the oracles against Egypt and Cush at the end of part one (Isa 13–20), the heading of part two (Isa 21–23) includes an interesting phrase: "An oracle against the *desert* of the *sea*" (21:1). In this second part, even though Babylon may not be a desert or wilderness, the subsequent oracles point to Dumah (21:11) and the "desert plain" of Arabia (21:13). Now Tyre is evidently a seaport in the coastlands. Accordingly, Isaiah 21 (*desert*) and Isaiah 23 (*sea*) form a bracket, enveloping the central oracle concerning Jerusalem, the *valley* of vision (Isa 22). Thus Tyre coincides with Babylon, Dumah, and Arabia, together sandwiching Jerusalem in the middle.

Second, key catchwords construct this unit as a bridge between the preceding and following passages. For example, the Hebrew word for "Tyre" (*tsor*) sounds similar to the word "rock" (*tsur*). Although the exact word does not occur in the preceding chapter, we read about the "rock" (*sela'*) upon which Shebna the high official boasted to have built his tomb (22:16). Tyre thus denotes a symbol of pride as a city of luxurious commerce that is still not a match for YHWH the true Rock (*tsur*) of refuge (17:10). Likewise, the "jubilant (*'alizah*)" city (23:7) picks up on the same term in 22:2, anticipating another usage in 24:8.

Third, as one of the crucial coastlands, Tyre was a major trade port and defense fortress. Josephus's record that Nebuchadnezzar besieged Tyre for thirteen years hints at the importance of Tyre as a highly defensible harbor city, an island adjacent to the Phoenician coast, and explains the Babylonian interest in setting up a blockade against Egypt's sea trade through this seaport (Albertz 2003b, 57). In the introductory discussion of this section, we mentioned the importance of the maritime imperial forces, especially Egypt (19:1) and Tyre (23:1), each concluding one of the two major segments of this OAN section. We should further note that in the OAN of Ezekiel (Isa 25–32), both Tyre (Isa 26–28) and Egypt (Isa 29–32) take up the largest portion as two last, climactic nations. It seems likely that there may have been compositional paralleling between Isaiah and Ezekiel, especially with regard to the importance of Tyre, as well as Egypt (Kim 2015b, 13–16).

Notably, likewise, the word "coastlands" occurs frequently in the second half of the book of Isaiah (41:1, 5; 42:4, 10, 12; 49:1; 51:5; 59:18; 60:9; 66:19). In certain texts, "coastlands" replaces "nations," hence the phrase "coastlands . . . peoples" (49:1) instead of "nations" and "peoples." In other texts, "coastlands" accompanies "ends of the earth." Tyre may function for both literary effect and thematic meaning. Accordingly, it seems plausible to argue that Tyre now represents one of those "coastlands" (cf. 24:15) in addition to the list of preceding targets, objects, and addressees in the OAN as "nations" and "peoples."

Fortresses of Tyre and Sidon Destroyed, 23:1-14

This unit seems disjointed, with many repeated phrases. In the final form, however, this unit manifests a rough chiastic format, framed by the same phrase in v. 1 and v. 14:

a—"Wail, O ships of Tarshish, for your [royal] house is destroyed" (v. 1)
 b—"the fortress (*ma'oz*) of the sea" (v. 4)
  c—"Pass over (*'abar*) to Tarshish" (v. 6)
   d—"Who has planned this against Tarshish . . . ? YHWH of the army has planned it" (vv. 8-9)
  c'—"Pass over (*'abar*) to your land" (v. 10)
 b'—"to destroy its fortresses (*ma'oz*)" (v. 11)
a'—"Wail, O ships of Tarshish, for your fortress is destroyed" (v. 14)

Verses 1-3 start with the initial imperatives. The first command to "wail" (vv. 1, 6, 14) forms a larger bracket with Isaiah 13 involving the same imperative to "wail" against Babylon (13:6; cf. 14:31) within the OAN section. As the ships of Tarshish (cf. 2:16) return from the island of Cyprus, the news reports that Tyre's fortress has toppled (v. 1). The second command addresses the inhabitants of the coast and Sidon, whose merchants are to be silent, even as they cross over many waters trading the harvest of the Nile (vv. 2-3).

Verses 4-5 proceed with the third imperative, addressed to Sidon, who will experience the shame of her commercial and military barrenness (v. 4). Patricia Tull comments, "But the watery harbor is an empty womb, a sorrowing woman disclaiming having given birth to children (probably colony ports) after all" (2010, 358). In fact, at the port of Nile in Egypt, Sidon will hear the news of Tyre's fall in dismay (v. 5).

Verses 6-7 continue with the fourth imperative, addressed to the inhabitants of the coast (cf. v. 2) to cross over to Tarshish and wail (v. 6). Not unlike the once-jubilant town of Jerusalem (22:2), Tyre and Sidon are now condemned to sojourn, being carried far away (v. 7).

Verses 8-9, as the chiastic center of this unit, do not contain an imperative but a pivotal question and an answer. In the question concerning the identity of this planner against Tyre, readers recall the pride of Tyre, whose merchants were princes and traders, the honored of the earth (v. 8). The answer unequivocally identifies this planner as YHWH, who will assuredly humiliate the "pride of all beauty" of Tyre (v. 9; cf. 13:19).

Verses 10-12 continue with the fifth imperative addressed to daughter Tarshish. As in v. 6, she ought to "cross over your land like the Nile," the imagery of which may insinuate the Passover traditions of the Exodus

(v. 10). Y<small>HWH</small>'s mighty acts, exemplified by the outstretched hand over the sea (cf. Exod 14:26-27; 15:12), command the Canaanite cities to destroy Tyre's fortresses (v. 11). The violated virgin daughter Sidon, even in her flight to Cyprus, will find no rest (*nuakh*, v. 12).

Verses 13-14, seemingly a gloss, momentously culminate this unit concerning Tyre and Sidon. The abrupt introduction of the Chaldeans that have ceased may originally have referred to the Assyrian invasion of Babylon in 703 BCE, prior to the subsequent demolition of Tyre in 701 BCE. It will lie uninhabited for the next seventy years.

Tyre's Exile and Restoration after Seventy Years, 23:15-18

This unit—led by the "on that day" phrase—adds a prophetic treatment of Tyre in chronologically and thematically extended material. First, the prophet announces Tyre's captivity of seventy years (vv. 15-16). Tyre will be forgotten for seventy years, the period denoting not only one's average lifetime (Ps 90:10) but also Judah's own captivity in Babylon (Jer 25:11-12; 29:10; Zech 1:12; 2 Chr 36:21). It is Tyre's turn to taste the bitter hardships of exile. Just as the tormentors teased Zion's captives to sing a song of Zion by the rivers of Babylon (Ps 137:1-3), during this shameful seventy-year exile, Tyre, taunted and tormented, would resort to singing a song of the prostitute (v. 15). The song may have been a popular folk song about an aging harlot searching for customers (Childs 2001, 169). Now, analogous to Zion's song to the captured Judeans not to forget but to "remember" Zion (cf. Ps 137:1, 5-7), the personified Tyre as a "forgotten prostitute" would struggle to rediscover her identity and dignity: "Pluck the strings, multiply songs, so that you may be remembered" (v. 16).

The second reference to "the end of the seventy year exile" (v. 17; cf. v. 15) envisages a dramatic reversal in that Tyre shall return and be restored, albeit with her harlotry in base wages. Eventually, however, Tyre will regain her honor, though minuscule, in that the wages of her harlotry will contribute toward supplying those who dwell in the presence of Y<small>HWH</small> (v. 18).

One can discern several themes, vis-à-vis intertextual correlations, concerning these descriptions of the radical reversal of Tyre's fortune. First, that the wages of Tyre's "harlotry" shall be "holy" to Y<small>HWH</small> (v. 18) coincides with other similar passages in the OAN, where nations and "all the kingdoms of the earth" (v. 17), transformed in the future "on that day," shall honor God and reconcile with Israel—in the cases of Moab (16:5), Cush (18:7), and Egypt (19:16-25; cf. Childs 2001, 169).

Second, Tyre's commercial goods will provide "satisfying food and fine clothes" through trade to those who remain faithful to Y<small>HWH</small> (v. 18). This theme correlates with the plentiful food and drink that will be freely provided to those who are thirsty and poor (Isa 55). On a global scale, all the righteous ones who yearn for YHWH shall be able to eat and not starve, especially those disenfranchised (cf. 2:2-4).

Third, the opening chapter called Zion the pernicious "prostitute" (1:21), while YHWH's own people heard the admonition to obey and "eat" good, rather than to disobey and be "eaten" by the sword (1:19-20). Here, the text labels Tyre no less than three times with the word "prostitute." If God can turn Tyre into a servant of the temple (cf. Isa 56), however, through divine judgment and her repentance, will God do the same and more for Jerusalem, if only she will repent and return to justice (1:21-31)? The prospect of the personified Tyre should bring the personified Jerusalem—the real audience—both the warning of shame and the possibility of restoration.

Tales of Two Cities and Parties (Third Branch of the Lampstand)

Isaiah 24–35

This section is the least cohesive in the first half of the book of Isaiah. The main reasons for grouping Isaiah 24–35 as one of the seven overall sections are threefold: (1) its preceding section (Isa 13–23), held together by the key word *massa'* ("burden, oracle"), clearly demarcates itself as independent; (2) the tripartite division of Isaiah 40–66 (Isa 40–48; 49–57; 58–66) makes it legitimate to divide Isaiah 1–35 equally into three parts (Isa 1–12; 13–23; 24–35), both formally and thematically, enveloping Isaiah 36–39 as the center of the whole; and, (3) as will be discussed below, Isaiah 24–27 and 34–35 share similar motifs, especially in terms of the thematic contrasts of two cities or nations—between Babylon and Jerusalem (Isa 24–27) as well as between Edom and Zion (Isa 34–35)—together bracketing the internally cohesive woe-oracles (Isa 28–33) that exhibit a neat format alternating between judgment and salvation. Accordingly, while key phrases and patterns may help this section to cohere, it is the theme closely associated with "the tale of two cities/nations/groups" that profoundly integrates Isaiah 24–35.

Within Isaiah 24–27, readers learn of the tension between the two cities—between the "chaos city" and the "strong city." Admittedly, the divine chastisement of the mythological chaotic forces in a cosmic dimension here connects smoothly with the previous oracles of judgment against many nations in Isaiah 13–23. Yet Jerusalem is included as one of the targets of punishment in the OAN section of Isaiah 13–23. On the contrary, here we have two main entities whose tension and ultimate fates take center stage. The "chaos city" is also called the "fortified city" or "lofty town" (24:10; 25:2; 26:5; 27:10), depicting the locus of the tyrants. The "strong city" (26:1-2; cf. 24:23; 25:6-9) represents the locus of the powerless and the poor, the hallmark of the devout "we"-group. Thus, together they represent the chaotic forces versus the faithful ones. Symbolically, the two cities denote Babylon, soon to be destroyed, versus Jerusalem, assured to be protected (Seitz 1993, 118). Ultimately, the wicked will fall (Isa 24 and 26:4-6; 27:10-11) while the righteous will experience their vindication (Isa 25; 26:1-3; 27:7-9; cf. Polaski 2001; Sweeney 1996, 312–13; Hibbard 2006, 107).

Just like the mythological chaotic forces, this chaotic city is too powerful for Jerusalem, a colonial city. Divine intervention will be necessary to fight against such chaotic forces, which will then guarantee the resurgence of the "strong city" of Jerusalem. The three songs (25:1-5, 9-12; 26:1-6), bracketed by the prophetic-eschatological discourse at the beginning (24:1-23) and at the end (27:6-13), function to "express confidence that Israel will survive the terrors of the *eschaton* so vividly described in the surrounding discourse" (Blenkinsopp 2000a, 363).

Within Isaiah 28–33, which cohere tightly around the key word *hoy* ("woe, ah, alas") and hence are called woe-oracles, the targets of divine chastisement are the leaders both of Israel and especially of Jerusalem and Judah. We may wonder how this section relates to the preceding section (Isa 24–27). It should be noted that the word "earth" (*erets*) in Isaiah 24–27 has a double meaning, denoting either "earth" or "land." The former meaning refers to the wider nations and peoples in the international arena and cosmic realm (cf. Isa 13–23). The latter meaning anticipates the domestic rulers and their wrongdoings in the land of Ephraim and Judah. Isaiah 28–33 illustrate this latter meaning in the six variant but connected oracles.

Similarly, the term "city," occurring so frequently and significantly in Isaiah 24–27, plays a key function in Isaiah 28–33 as well. In fact, it is the city as the citadel of the urban court system and urban elite upper class over against the rural farmers and poor peasants that the prophet vehemently chastises in Isaiah 28–33 (Chaney 2006; cf. Mic 6:9). The nonspecific identification of the city throughout 24–27, therefore, may highlight the prophetic condemnation of the city life in general, with all its vain glory and cruel abuse (Seitz 1993, 174). Isaiah 28–33 exemplify and expose the ugliness of the policymakers, the rulers, and the king of the city—the metropolis of the privileged and the castle of the powerful.

In Isaiah 34–35, the theme of the judgment on the wicked and restoration for the righteous culminates. Just as in the tale of two cities—chaos city and strong city, or Babylon and Jerusalem—so now we have the tale of two nations, Edom (ch. 34) and Israel-Judah (ch. 35). Obviously, as will be discussed below, with regard to the redactional/compositional perspective, one of the key functions of chapters. 34–35 is to bridge the preceding (Isa 1–33) and the following (Isa 40–66) portions. Yet, at the same time, in the overall arrangement of the final form and in light of the overarching thematic progress, Isaiah 34–35 also function to reemphasize the fate of the oppressive forces versus that of the faithful penitent people, as illustrated in Isaiah 24–27.

Structure of Isaiah 24–35

Chaotic Forces of the Earth, 24:1–27:13

Six Woe-Oracles—Five against the Leaders of Israel and Judah plus One against the Superpower Destroyers of Zion, 28:1–33:24

Doom to the Enemies and Restoration for the Faithful, 34:1–35:10

Chaotic Forces of the Earth, 24:1–27:13

An Oracle about the Earth, 24:1-23

It seems strange that the earth (*erets*)—occurring sixteen times in this chapter—is the target of divine judgment, not a nation, a city, or a ruler. In fact, this word has a double meaning—"earth" or "land"—that can complicate our reading but can also enrich our interpretive imagination (Kim 2013).

For example, on the one hand, the text flows more smoothly if the term is read as the "land." The frequent use of this term with no accompanying description, however, makes it difficult to come up with a specific identity. Nonetheless, readers may hear an elliptical nuance in the repeated term, such as "the people of the land" (*am-ha'arets*; 24:4; cf. Gen 23:7; Lev 20:2; Jer 1:18; Ezek 7:27; Hag 2:4; Zech 7:5; Ezra 4:4; Neh 10:30 [MT 10:31]), "the good of the land" (Isa 1:19; Ezra 9:12), and so on. In particular, the phrase "people of the land/earth" in Isaiah 24:4 deserves close attention. It will be discussed below.

On the other hand, the flow of the text makes reading the term as "earth" smoother. In ancient society, the earth was a vital source of essential products, especially for economic survival and blessings (cf. Lev 26:4, 20; Deut 1:25; 7:13; Isa 1:19; 4:2). Ironically, even in today's technologically advanced world, the importance of the earth has become a major issue, be it related to ecology, environmental sustainability, or sheer survival. In fact, God's creation started with the heavens and the "earth" (Gen 1:1; 2:4). Although employing a different word, the ground (*'adamah*) was cursed (Gen 3:17). As Erhard Gerstenberger attests, "Humanity as a whole is sitting in a single boat. Epidemics and pollution of the environment recognize no national boundaries. Many catastrophes have consequences entering immediately or in the longer term for many or for all the countries on earth" (2011, 535). Thus, the desolation of the earth can have broad impact and drastic ramifications on many parts of the whole world. Overall, Isaiah 24–25 projects a future era when, following the divine vanquishing of enemy forces, YHWH will construct the divine kingdom built on Zion (Hibbard 2006, 119).

Isaiah 24:1-13 projects the devastation of the earth and its aftermath. Against an ancient Near Eastern background, especially various treaty curses, the earth as the target of punishment is significant (cf. Lev 26; Deut 28–29). Relatively consistent portions of three verses (vv. 1-3, 4-6, 7-9, 10-13) consecutively and sequentially progress from one incident to another.

Verses 1-3 pronounce the opening statements of the divine plan to over-turn the earth. The initial word, "look" (*hinneh*), plays a significant role here much like the similar initial word (*hen*) in 32:1 (cf. 17:1; 19:1). This vocative word "look" in v. 1 frames this segment with the oracular formula "for YHWH has spoken this speech" in v. 3. Likewise, key wordplays—"devastate" (*bqq*) and "demolish" (*blq*) in v. 1 as well as "devastate" (*bqq bqq*) and "destroy" (*bzz bzz*) in v. 3—bracket this segment. Additionally, the key word "YHWH" in vv. 1a and 3b bounds this segment as well: this description of the disman-tling of the cosmic creation is "a thoroughly [YHWH]-centered statement" (Brueggemann 1998a, 190).

This earth-quaking devastation will affect the inhabitants who will scatter away (v. 1). Sandwiched between similar words and motifs, the core verse of this subunit (v. 2) delineates a socioeconomic and religious upheaval or revolution. A phrase akin to "like father like son" identifies opposing classes to be shuffled and reversed: "Like people like priest, like male servant like his master, like female servant like her mistress, like buyer like seller, like lender like borrower, like creditor like debtor." Joseph Blenkinsopp cites similar expressions in the "Egyptian Teaching of Ipu-Wer," through which the text portrays a society turned upside down in terms of social class and economic power groups: "Poor men have become the possessors of treasures . . . all maid servants make free with their tongues . . . noble ladies are now gleaners and nobles are in the workhouse" (*ANET*, 441–42, cited in Blen-kinsopp 2000a, 351).

Verses 4-6 elaborate the outcomes of the earth's devastation. The initial word of this subunit, "dry up" (*'bl*)—eliciting the crisis of drought—will recur as the initial word of the next segment (vv. 7-9). The alliteration of the letters in v. 4 is striking, as though presenting a panoramic view of the earth-quake spreading out (*'bl nbl . . . 'ml nbl . . . 'ml . . .*). Here the initial word can denote to "mourn" (BDB) or to "dry up" (HALOT) so that the double meaning of v. 4 may be deliberate: (a) "The earth *dries up* and withers, the world dwindles and withers, the heaven dwindles with the earth" (cf. NRSV; CEB); (b) "The earth *mourns* and withers, the world languishes and withers, the exalted of the people of the earth languish" (cf. NASB, TNK).

Whether the earth is personified or whether the "height" (*merom*) denotes the heavens (paralleling the earth) or the high rulers, the subsequent content in v. 5 elucidates how the earth's pollution intimately correlates with its inhabitants, who have unashamedly violated the laws (plural of *torah*), the statutes, and the eternal covenant (*berit 'olam*). The two "therefore" clauses in v. 6 intensely expose the crime of human beings. In this depiction of the return of the curse upon the earth (cf. Gen 3:17; 8:21), the guilty party is the earth's inhabitants, whose transgression sadly reverses the Noachic covenant (cf. Gen 9:16).

Verses 7-9 further report the earth's loss of crops and joy. Just as the earth "dries up" or "mourns" in v. 4, now the wine "dries up" or "mourns" (v. 7). In consequence, the joyful sounds of tambourine or harp will cease (lit., they are "sabbathed," implying an effect of judgment, v. 8; cf. 14:4). Indeed, as if echoing Jerusalemite high society's banquet with "hard liquor," "wine," "harp," and "tambourine" in one of the previous woe-oracles (5:11-12), now all those components of merriness will turn to bitterness (v. 9).

Verses 10-13 explicate the preceding segments with the introduction of the "chaos town (*qiryat tohu*)" (v. 10). It is the town in utter chaos, not unlike pre-creation chaos (Gen 1:2; cf. Jer 4:23). Here the word "chaos" (*tohu*)—alongside "deep" (*tehom*)—is cognate to the Akkadian word for "Tiamat" (*ti'amatu*) the sea-monster goddess, whom Marduk the Babylonian city god vanquishes in the Babylonian creation epic, Enuma Elish. Against this background, the "chaos town" may connote a polemic against Babylon the tyrannical empire, "designed as a deliberate pun to call to mind Tiamat and to question the self-proclaimed role of Babylon as the center of world order" (Sweeney 1996, 318).

As "all those joyous of heart" groan (v. 7) and "wine" lacks melody (v. 9), so they cry for "wine" and "all joy" grows dark (v. 11). As the "merriment" (*masos*) of tambourine and harp has ceased (v. 8), now the "merriment" (*masos*) of the earth goes into exile (v. 11). Only desolation and wrecked gates are surviving remnants of the town (v. 12). This segment culminates with a commentary-like exposition that just as YHWH purposed to obliterate the "earth" and its "inhabitants" (v. 1), such will be the fate of the "earth" and "peoples" (v. 13). Here, the expression "beating the olive tree" (*noqep zayit*) and "gleaning" (*olelot*) echoes 17:6, in inverted chiasm. Whereas it had denoted the destruction of northern Israel (17:6), here the same phrase signifies the destruction of the nations (Sweeney 1988).

Isaiah 24:14-23 extends the impact of the divine judgment upon the earth, especially the "chaos city," again through the progressing crescendo of themes and expressions (vv. 14-16, 17-20, 21-23). Verses 14-16 portray the worldwide exaltation of YHWH in response to divine punishment of the chaos city. People from the western seacoast and from the east sing praises to the majesty, glory, and name of YHWH (vv. 14-15). From the ends of the earth, they shout songs of honor to the "Righteous One" (v. 16). But the prophet's reaction is puzzling: "Woe to me!" (v. 16). Perhaps, as J. Todd Hibbard proposes, this subunit as the core of this section depicts the "improper joyous display" of the peoples that leads to the prophetic response (2006, 68). The prophet's response brings to mind the human propensity to praise and pledge reverence to YHWH while actually having no clue as to whom they believe and what this true God expects.

Here both the backdrop of the choral exaltation of YHWH and the utterance of the prophet seem to mirror the call narrative in Isaiah 6 (Tull 2010, 373). If this intertextual echo is intentional, then this segment may depict how the prophet is appalled at now witnessing the large-scale debacle that involves the unruly invasion of an empire, such as Babylon, Persia, or even a later kingdom: "until cities lie waste without inhabitant, and houses without people, and the land is utterly desolate . . . vast is the emptiness in the midst of the land" (6:11-12; cf. Seitz 1993, 184). Just as the expression of Israel's destruction (17:6) recurs, referring to the earth and nations (24:13), similarly, unique terms depicting Babylon (*haboged boged wehashoded shoded*) in 21:2 now allude to the unruly conquering forces (*bogedim bagadu wubeged bogedim bagadu*) in v. 16 (cf. 33:1; 48:8). The rhetorical effect may thus insinuate that despite the message of the divine plan to destroy the "chaos city" along with its inhabitants, the prophet aches over the ensuing devastation, except that here the prophet does not voice a complaint, "How long, O Lord?" (cf. 6:11).

Verses 17-20 culminate this whole unit with the recurring descriptions of the shattering of the earth, thus bracketing with vv. 1-3 or even vv. 4-6. Yet here we find further developed motifs and expressions. First of all, key phrases from vv. 17-18 are verbatim citations of Jeremiah 48:43-44. Strikingly, just as Jeremiah 48:28-38 picks up numerous statements in Isaiah 15:1–16:12, so now vv. 17-18 reapply Jeremiah 48:43-44, although with a thematic shift: whereas in Jeremiah 48:43-44 the target is the "inhabitant of Moab" (*yosheb mo'ab*), here the target broadly denotes the "inhabitant of the earth" (*yosheb ha'arets*). There is also a thematic shift from one particular country, Moab, to an abstract, universal entity, "earth" or "land."

Second, the text makes another intertextual allusion, in this case to the flood tradition, through another inverted chiasm. Just as "all the springs of the great deep burst forth and the windows of the heavens were opened (*arubot hashamayim niptahu*)" (Gen 7:11), now "the windows on high are opened (*arubot mimmarom niptahu*) and the foundations of the earth shake" (v. 18). Further echoes include Isaiah 24:1 and Genesis 11:1-9 as well as Isaiah 24:5

and Genesis 9. These allusions depict the judgment on the earth in a larger scale, implying the thematic analogy that the eschatological punishment will be as devastating as the debacle in the primeval era. Such an analogy implies yet another thematic reminder that human corruption and divine punishment originated back in the beginning of human history, as "the device of human heart is evil from youth" (Gen 8:21; cf. 6:5; Hibbard 2006, 69).

Third, the alliterations in v. 17 and v. 19 suggest the very sounds of the earthquake and collapse. Thus, "terror" (*pakhad*), "trench" (*pakhat*), and "trap" (*pakh*) in v. 17 anticipate the flood-like upheaval of the cosmic realm in v. 18, which results in the "breaking, breaking" (*ra'a' ra'a'*) "crumbling, crumbling" (*parar parar*), and "tottering, tottering" (*mot mot*) of the earth in v. 19 (TNK).

The closing verse (v. 20) of this segment personifies the earth with echoes of various other texts. For example, the earth is likened to a "drunkard," a comparison that anticipates the sin-intoxicated "drunkards" of Ephraim (28:1, 3). Also, the earth embodies a "booth" (*melunah*), a term occurring elsewhere only in Isaiah 1:8 in the entire OT and denoting the besieged, vulnerable daughter Zion. Why is the earth so deeply in trouble? It is because of the "transgressions" of the earth, which make it so heavy it can never rise again.

Verses 21-23, with an initial "on that day" phrase, may appear to be a mere appendix. This segment is an essential part of this unit, however, because the "on that day" phrases, occurring seven times in Isaiah 24–27, present essential themes of the polemic against ancient Near Eastern mythological ideology. Several issues highlight the key theme of universalism in this subunit—YHWH's reign in "non-covenantal and universalistic" ways centered on Mount Zion as the new center of the devastated earth (Hibbard 2006, 92, 117).

YHWH's punishment of the host of heaven and kings of the earth echoes ancient Near Eastern mythological themes (v. 21). Chaotic forces, as well as moon and sun, will succumb to divine control—not to Ashur, Marduk, or Baal, but to YHWH (vv. 22-23a). Echoing the mythological plot of the seventy gods feasting under the deity, Moses together with seventy "elders" went up to the mountain as the "glory of YHWH" dwelled on Mount Sinai (Exod 24:1, 9, 16). The "elders," alluding to the exodus tradition, underscore communal leadership without the priestly qualification, highlighting the divine reign not only over Israel but over many nations, and in fact over all humankind (Hibbard 2006, 77–83; 92–93). Now, YHWH is about to reign on Mount Zion, in Jerusalem, and the divine "glory" will dwell with the "elders" (v. 23b; cf. Mic 4:7). This community of a faithful remnant in

Zion will be "the new Noah" (Brueggemann 1998a, 196). The divine reign of YHWH from Zion (cf. 52:7) will cover the entire host of heaven and kings of the earth with a more universal outlook than that of human kingship (Hibbard 2006, 91).

A Feast at Mount Zion, 25:1-12

Isaiah 25:1-5, a hymn of thanksgiving, picks up key themes of the preceding chapter and provides additional cues of the tension between the two cities—the "chaos, fortified, lofty town" of the tyrants (24:10; 25:2; 26:5) versus the "strong city" of the poor and needy "we"-group (26:1; cf. 25:3). In the overall flow, Isaiah 24–25 (esp. 24:14-23 and 25:1-10) do not stand as detached pieces but rather fit "within a dramatic course of events" (Beuken 2000b, 144). Here the beginning verses of the two subunits (25:1-5 and 25:6-12) describe God's past "works" (*'asah*, v. 1) and future "works" (*'asah*, v. 6). Accordingly, 25:1-5 praises God for what God has done, while 25:6-12 prophesies what God will do (Beuken 2000b, 141).

Verse 1 introduces the prophet's first-person thanksgiving addressed directly to YHWH ("you"). Although apparently abrupt, this hymn responds to YHWH's wondrous works that subdue unruly earthly forces and resume the divine reign on Mount Zion described in Isaiah 24. Within Isaiah 25, the prophet's "exalting" (*rum*) YHWH (v. 1) forms a nice inclusio with its thematic counterpart, YHWH's "laying low" (*shapel*) and "bringing down" (*shakhakh*) of Moab's pride (vv. 11-12). These verses echo the foundational theme of humbling human pride and exalting YHWH in Isaiah 2 (2:9, 11, 17).

Verses 2-3 present the first causal ("for") rationale for the psalmist's thanksgiving. Here we should note, however, that in hymns, the asseverative *ki* ("truly") often introduces the subject matter of the praise. In this syntactical nuance, the psalmist does not praise God "because" but proclaims the divine deeds, i.e., "surely" or "indeed" or "wow!" (Nowell 2013, 81). The fortified town and the foreign citadel will become a heap of ruins (v. 2). Consequently, "strong people" (*'am 'az*)—compare "a strong city" (*'ir 'az*) in 26:1—and cities of tyrant nations will honor and fear YHWH (v. 3).

Verses 4-5 present the second causal ("for") rationale that highlights the divine protection of the poor and needy over against the stormy roar of foreigners and tyrants. Now the prophet expresses his solidarity with the group for whom YHWH will be a shelter, i.e., the poor and the needy. In contrast, YHWH vows to vanquish the "foreign" (v. 5; cf. v. 2) and "tyrant" (vv. 4-5; cf. v. 3) nations. Notably, the "tyrant" (*'arits*) nation, a phrase that occurs three times in vv. 3-5, refers to Babylon in 13:11 (cf. 49:25; Hibbard

2006, 100–102). At the same time, in Isaiah 25, the target of divine subjugation is Moab. Thus, these tyrants function to denote not only Babylon or Moab but also other oppressive forces, the latter of which thematically paves the way for Isaiah 29 (cf. 29:4-5). For the linguistic and thematic similarities between 25:11-12 and 29:4-5, see the discussion of Isaiah 29 below; similarly, note that the motif of refuge, shelter, and shade in vv. 4-5 will recur in 28:15, 17; 30:2-3; 32:2.

Isaiah 25:6-8 shifts the tone and nuance, no longer addressing (second person) but speaking of YHWH (third person), yet it stands as the core of this unit, marking the thematic high point, bracketed by vv. 1-5 and 9-12. This powerful subunit, which reflects well-known ancient Near Eastern mythological traditions, integrates the masterfully concatenated double usages of the phrases "on this mountain" (vv. 6-7) and "he will swallow up" (vv. 7-8). Here without the thematic flow from the preceding chapter (24:23), it may not be clear as to what locale "on this mountain" designates, because nowhere in Isaiah 25 does the word "Zion" occur. In fact, the phrase "on this mountain" (*bahar hazeh*) occurs only in 25:6, 7, 10 throughout the book of Isaiah.

On this mountain, YHWH promises to provide a bounteous banquet for "all peoples" (v. 6a). Alliteration and repetition of the words for wine sketch a panoptic view of sumptuous meals (v. 6b). In the previous chapter, wine dried up on an earth without music, only an outcry (24:7, 9, 11). Now, the extravagant wine YHWH gives will overflow to all. Read together, 25:6-8 presents a climactic message: in contrast with the depletion of wine as judgment over the tyrants' sin (Isa 24), YHWH promises to offer choice wines to the obedient (Isa 25; Abernethy 2014, 90).

Here, as Paul Cho and Janling Fu surmise, in comparison with the feast of Ashurnasirpal II, who claims to offer a banquet to seventy thousand people for the founding of the capital Nimrud, this celebratory banquet signifies YHWH as the King who rules over all peoples, including those in Zion (Cho and Fu 2013, 133–36). John Day similarly elucidates the interpretive shift from the ancient Near Eastern mythology (especially Enuma Elish and the Baal Epic) to this biblical tradition, from the celestial to the terrestrial domain: "It has hitherto remained unnoted that 'the seventy sons of Asherah' invited to the feast, corresponding to the totality of the divine pantheon, account for the universality of the banquet in Is. 25:6, where '*all* peoples' come" (Day 1985, 149; cf. Kim 2013, 30).

Furthermore, the vocabulary of "mountain," "peoples," and "nations" in vv. 6-7 makes an inner-biblical allusion to 2:2-4. A thematic development occurs here, from merely "many nations" and "many peoples" (2:3-4) to "all peoples" and "all nations." In fact, the word "all" (*kol*) occurs five times in this subunit (cf. 2:2), just as there are five actions of YHWH in the subunit, vv. 6-8 (Tull 2010, 384). In this intertextual correlation, in addition to the development from "many" to "all," we further note that whereas nations and peoples would make a pilgrimage to Zion for divine teaching (2:2-4), now the teaching will incorporate divine food for all (cf. 55:1).

Verse 7 states that YHWH "swallows up" the shroud over all peoples and all nations. In a thematic development according to v. 8, YHWH will "swallow up" death forever. This motif manifests deep associations with the ancient Canaanite Baal Epic, where Mot, the god of death with insatiable appetite, swallows up Baal. According to Cho and Fu's judicious argument, the grammatical vagueness in the MT may leave room for misreading Mot as the subject of the verb "to swallow up." The ingenious effect is that, to the audience who would be familiar with the Baal Epic, our text claims that YHWH will swallow Mot, the swallower (Cho and Fu 2013, 120–25). This surprising polemic coheres well with the overall syntax in vv. 6-8, where YHWH is the sole agent of all five actions, including wiping away tears from all faces.

Isaiah 25:9-12, introduced by the "on that day" phrase, wraps up chapter 25 by resuming words and motifs that correspond to and overturn those of vv. 1-5. In v. 1, the prophet exalted YHWH ("you") with thanksgiving. Now, in v. 9, the collective "we"-group cherishes YHWH's salvific answer: "Look, *this is our God* for whom we have waited that he may save us; *this is YHWH* for whom we have waited, let us rejoice and be glad in his salvation." Put differently, the prophet's song, "You are my God" (v. 1) has been extended to the community's song, "This is our God" (v. 9). Like those who endured the long years of colonial regimes or those who fought as underground resistance during World War II in modern history, this devout group utters, perhaps with tears of joy, that their faithful waiting was not in vain: "Those who have believed have waited a long time, seemingly without justification" (Brueggemann 1998a, 200).

Verses 10-12 follow the "we"-group's thanksgiving with causal ("for") statements (cf. vv. 2, 4). YHWH's hand will rest (*nuakh*) "on this mountain." In contrast, Moab, and all arrogant forces, will march into a dung-pile (v. 10; cf. Zeph 2:8). While the history of Moab's hostility remains (Isa 15–16), Moab here symbolizes all the nations that arrogantly and recalcitrantly deride God's intention, and thereby, on that day, will meet the fate of divine punishment (Hibbard 2006, 117). While the fate of the poor and needy marks a sharp contrast with that of the foreign tyrants (vv. 4-5), now Moab's fate will be the opposite of Zion's (vv. 10-11). Ultimately, whereas YHWH alone will be exalted, while the fortified town turns into rubble (vv. 1-2), the fortifications of Moab's ("your") walls will tumble to the ground, to the dust (vv. 11-12).

The Fates of the Righteous and the Wicked, 26:1-21

As a result of YHWH's vanquishing the god of death, Mot, and providing a sumptuous feast, a so-called "victory song"—in the "we"-group speech—will fill the land of Judah (26:1-6; cf. 25:1-5). The central portion of this unit (26:7-19) depicts the strenuous reality of the tension between the righteous (whose blessing was exemplified in Isa 25) and the wicked (whose destruction was illustrated in Isa 24; cf. Polaski 2001, 207–12, 219). Hence, the devout people—speaking in the first-person singular—lament their sufferings under the staggering forces of the wicked (the "they"-group) and petition God to bring peace. This middle portion may have been a combination of two divergent subunits (vv. 7-13 and vv. 14-19), but in the final form they combine to constitute a core part of this chapter, highlighting another dimension of the tension between YHWH and mythological deities. The final admonition (26:20-21)—in the first-person singular—calling for the "we"-group, "my people," to wait for YHWH's vindication wraps up this unit (Beuken 2014, 253).

Isaiah 26:1-6, beginning with the "on that day" phrase, contains a song of praise in the "land" (the same word for "earth") of Judah. Verses 1b-3, introduced by a thesis statement (v. 1b), stress positive aspects of the righteous people. Opposite the collapsing "chaos town" (24:10), the "we"-group exclaims that "we" have a "strong city" with walls erected by YHWH's salvation (v. 1b).

The first imperative ("open the gates") introduces the assured endorsement of the fate of the righteous (vv. 2-3). The expression—"Open the gates so that X may enter"—may echo similar psalmic phrases: "Lift up your heads, O gates . . . so that the King of glory may enter" (Ps 24:7, 9); "Open the gates of righteousness for me, so that I may enter through them and give thanks to YHWH" (Ps 118:19). In the Isaianic passage, only the nation that is righteous and honest will enter the gates (v. 2; cf. Ps 24:3-4). Because they trust in YHWH, they will obtain "peace, peace" (v. 3; cf. 39:8; 57:19; Jer 6:14; 8:11).

The second imperative ("trust in YHWH") announces the downfall of the wicked (vv. 4-6). The righteous who "trust" in YHWH now exhort their audiences to "trust" in YHWH the everlasting rock (cf. Isa 2:10; 17:20)—notably, the last word in v. 3 and the first word in v. 4 are the same. Verses 5-6, introduced by the causal conjunction ("for"), reiterate another thesis statement underscoring the reversal of fortune (cf. 2:6-22). Joseph Blenkinsopp observes that key words and themes of Isaiah 26 echo those from the "Great

Arraignment" passages of Isaiah 2:6-22, as well as Psalm 1 (Blenkinsopp 2000a, 369–71). This drastic reversal contrasts the "lofty town" on high and its pompous inhabitants that will fall all the way down to the earth, in fact to the dust, while the feet of the poor and needy will trample them (cf. 1:12; 2:10). Ancient audiences would recall the popular Baal Epic: "The powerful one will fall to the earth, / the mighty one to the dust" (*COS* I: 248). Readers today can think of the scenes depicting how the oppressed mass finally gets to see the inside of the hypocritical dictator's luxury summer and winter mansions or how the great populace would tear down the colonizer's prison buildings where they ruthlessly tortured innocent demonstrators (Brueggemann 1998a, 203). Yes, pride (cf. Isa 2) is the essential reason for this town's ultimate downfall (Hibbard 2006, 134).

At the same time, there is another subtle message. Inasmuch as it is difficult to accurately identify the "strong city" (of the "we"-group) in v. 1 versus the "lofty town" (of the wicked) in v. 5, there may be another layer of ambiguity in the dialect and addressees. Scott Neogel thus discovers numerous examples of northern Israelite dialect in Isaiah 26 that display a case of the author's "style-switching." Taken this way, this victory song in 26:1-6, which is presumed to be a song for Judah, may have been intended as a song for Israel. Its rhetorical effect, with northern Israel in this "addressee-switching" device, may offer several interpretive implications. First, the consistent occurrences of the northern dialect support the literary integrity of Isaiah 26. Second, by introducing northern dialect addressing Ephraim (much like the opening subunits of Isa 28 that address the drunkards of Ephraim), the prophet makes an "appeal to northern sensitivities" through a "sense of solidarity." Third, the Judean addressees would then hear the impact of the switch, prompting their own humble penitence and devout trust in YHWH: "upon hearing in the song a scathing indictment, the people of Jerusalem would be forced into a defensive posture and roused to action" (Noegel 1994, 192).

Isaiah 26:7-19, a lengthy, complex subunit, may be divided into two segments: (a) vv. 7-13, bracketed by key words in v. 8 ("YHWH," "your name [*shem*]," "your memory [*zeker*]") and in v. 13 ("YHWH," "we remember [*zeker*]," "your name [*shem*]") and (b) vv. 14-19, bracketed by key phrases in v. 14 ("the dead [*mut*] will not live," "ghosts [*repa'im*] will not rise") and in v. 19 ("your dead [*mut*] will live," "my corpses will rise," "the earth will cause the ghosts [*repa'im*] to be reborn"). Yet the consistent use of the first-person plural ("we") connects these segments, contrasting the fates of the righteous versus the wicked, on the one hand. At the same time, on the other hand, this whole portion centers on the contrast between the trustworthy YHWH and all other null deities (note the first word "YHWH" in each of vv. 11-13, hence a total of three times, in contrast to the one word "the dead" in v. 14).

Verses 7-13 explicate the preceding song of praise with elaborated descriptions of the righteous and the wicked. First, as in the previous song (vv. 1-6), the righteous (*tsaddiq*) receive primary attention (vv. 7-9; cf. Ps 1:1-3). The path of the righteous is straight (v. 7). The righteous "we"-group professes that their hope lies in the justice, name, and memory of YHWH (v. 8). The prophet's personal longing for YHWH by night asserts how YHWH's "justice" on earth will influence the whole world to learning "righteousness" (v. 9). Next come the wicked (*rasha‘*) in strongly contrasting but very brief portrayals (v. 10), much like the quick dismissal of the wicked in Psalm 1:4 ("Not so the wicked"). Although the inhabitants of the world may learn righteousness (v. 9), the wicked, even when they seem to be in divine favor, do not learn righteousness and cannot see YHWH's majesty (v. 10; cf. 2:10).

Then, the lament proper, with threefold petitions to YHWH, both summarizes and highlights the core theme of this entire chapter (vv. 11-13). Because the wicked cannot see YHWH's majesty (v. 10), they cannot see YHWH's hand lifted high (v. 11a). As if resonating the concluding verses of Psalm 1:5-6, the fire of divine anger will consume the wicked (v. 11b), while the righteous will obtain peace (v. 12). These confessions culminate with the declarations of the righteous who pledge their allegiance to YHWH over other false deities (v. 13). Literary puns heighten the exclamation marks, as the devout "we"-group vows to keep their faith amid the perilous battle between YHWH ("YHWH our God . . . only you") and chaotic mythological forces ("other lords [*’adonim*] besides you have ruled [*ba’al*] us").

Verses 14-19 reiterate the trying situation when the righteous struggle to keep faith. The description of this dire situation appears in the framework between "the dead" who cannot live (v. 14) and "your dead" who will live (v. 19). As though the distressed community were walking through the dark valley of death (cf. Ps 23:4), these verses encircle it with phrases regarding the dead. First, the speaker declares the contrasting fates in that YHWH will destroy the wicked chaotic forces and increase the righteous nation (vv. 14-15). Here "the dead" (*mut*) may allude to the Canaanite mythological god, Mot, already swallowed by YHWH (v. 14; cf. 25:8). At the same time, this term together with "ghosts" may signify the dead kings (6:1; 14:9, 28). Accordingly, the wicked are like the dead, which can neither live nor rise, but rather will "perish" (*’abad*; cf. Ps 1:6). In stark contrast, the presumably "righteous" nation (cf. 26:2) will increase and give glory to YHWH (v. 15).

Next, the following segment records a series of dialogues that involve various speakers and addressees (vv. 16-19). The lamenter recounts how "they" earnestly poured out "whispers of prayer" in times of distress (v. 16). Their prayers comprise the "we" speeches in the feminine imagery of giving birth (vv. 17-18). This "we"-group expresses their anguish from their feminized point of view (v. 17), reminiscent of human (rather, Babylon's) agony in 13:8. Claudia Bergmann, who cites pertinent ancient Near Eastern texts, distinguishes the texts that compare warriors in crisis with women giving birth from the texts that depict defeated warriors as women. Unlike the latter metaphor that only describes warriors of foreign nations in negative notions, the former metaphor—"like a woman giving birth"—holds women in high honor, invoking the readers' "feelings of sympathy," uplifting esteem for those under a crisis, and even regarding them (warriors) as "heroes of their people" (Bergmann 2008, 141–42). Against this background, rather than a child as a prophetic sign (cf. 7:14; 9:6 [MT 9:5]) and despite the intention to give birth to salvation for the earth and the inhabitants of the world, they now only give birth to wind (v. 18). Contrary to the divine promise of successful delivery of Zion's heirs (66:7-9), her prospective progeny seems distant (Hibbard 2006, 159). Despite the previous promise of YHWH's conquest of death (25:8), now the community laments their present reality that seems as dead (cf. v. 14).

Ultimately, however, the prophetic rebuttal (cf. Mic 6:8) pronounces not only a successful birth but also a miraculous rebirth in high honor (v. 19). This promise in the form of the salvation oracle deliberately rebuts the complaints of the lamenting community: whereas the wicked heard that "the dead will not live" and "ghosts will not rise" in v. 14, the righteous will hear the promise that "your dead will live" and "my corpses will rise" in v. 19. Joseph Blenkinsopp notes the deliberate contrast between these two groups: "*your* dead will live (19) but . . . *their* dead will not (14)" (2000a, 371). Text-critically, the MT reads "*their* corpses" as "*my* corpses." In this case, readers may hear not only the priest's words of assurance but also YHWH's own care to resuscitate "my [YHWH's]" people. As a result, even "those lying down in the dust" (cf. 25:12; 26:5) are to wake up and rejoice, as the earth will cause the rebirth of "ghosts" (cf. 26:14). This birthing imagery, symbolic of Judah's exile and return, culminates in the national resurrection, more than individual resurrection, with YHWH's loud vow once more to protect and provide for the barren, widowed—exiled—Jerusalem (Doyle, 87).

Isaiah 26:20-21 concludes with the prophet's admonition to "my people" to hide in resolute hope during the imminent time of divine judgment. The call to "enter into your rooms" (v. 20) echoes the similar call to "enter into the rock" (2:10). From other texts, this expression also alludes to the divine protection of the righteous remnant (cf. Gen 7:7; Exod 12:12). All these passages direct the righteous, humble, "my people" to hide from the large-scale disaster. The divine punishment (lit. "visitation") of the host on high and the kings of the earth (24:21-22) now subsumes the inhabitants of the earth for their iniquity and bloodshed (v. 21; cf. Mic 1:3).

A New Song of the Vineyard, 27:1-13

If many of the recurring phrases and patterns within the book of Isaiah are deliberate scribal products in the form of inner-biblical exegesis, then the placement of the new song of the vineyard in Isaiah 27 is not coincidental. In Isaiah 5, we have the (original) song of the vineyard (5:1-7), followed by a series of six woe-oracles (5:8-25). Likewise, this (new) song of the vineyard (27:2-56) initiates an expanded series of six woe-oracles (Isa 28–33). Accordingly, in the present arrangement, resembling the first vineyard song that bridges the preceding oracles (Isa 1–4) with the subsequent woe-oracles (5:8-25), the second vineyard song bridges the preceding section (Isa 24–27) with the following woe-oracles (Isa 28–33).

Within this unit, we further find a symmetrical pattern. A conventional view regards v. 1 as a part of 26:20-21. Aside from the abrupt thematic flow, however, the "on that day" phrase in 27:1 does not link smoothly to 26:20-21. In the final form, 27:1 can maintain its literary and thematic integrity with the subsequent passages as well, thereby forming a pattern of five "on that day" passages that center on v. 6 in terms of its core theme and literary function as a hinge for the two parts of Isaiah 27 (interestingly, also in Isa 22, we find one "day of YHWH" passage plus four "on that day" passages; 22:5, 8, 12, 20, 25):

v. 1—"*on that day*"
   v. 2—"*on that day*"
      vv. 2-5—a new song of the vineyard
         v. 6—"*in coming days*" Jacob-Israel will blossom
      vv. 7-11—purging of Jacob versus the fortified city
   v. 12—"*on that day*"
v. 13—"*on that day*"

Isaiah 27:1-6 proclaims YHWH's upcoming victory over chaotic forces (v. 1; cf. 11:15; 25:8), which will lead to a new song of the vineyard (vv. 2-5), followed by a parable-like elucidation (v. 6). Verse 1, with the initial "on that day" phrase, announces the impending future when YHWH will vanquish unruly enemy forces. Following the announcement that YHWH will return to punish (*paqad*) the inhabitants of the earth (26:21), YHWH will wield divine power to punish (*paqad*) the primordial chaotic forces. Scholars wonder whether these forces denote three different or one identical seven-headed monster(s): Leviathan the slippery serpent, Leviathan the twisting serpent, and the sea dragon. Scholars also speculate whether these creatures symbolize an empire, e.g., Egypt (Isa 30:6-7; cf. Pss 74:13-14; 87:4), Assyria, Babylon, Persia, Greece, or the like. What is certain remains the scribal intention to mirror the Baal Epic, so as to assert that YHWH will assuredly use the "fierce, great, and strong sword" to win victory over those overwhelming forces:

> I [= Anat, or Baal?] have smitten 'Ilu's [= El] beloved, Yammu [= sea], have finished off the great god Naharu [= river]. I have bound the dragon's [cf. *tannin*] jaws, have destroyed it, have smitten the twisting serpent [cf. *nahash 'aqallaton*], the close-coiled one with seven heads. (*COS* I: 252)

Verses 2-5 restate expressions from v. 1—"on that day" (v. 2) and "to punish (*paqad*)" (v. 3)—and introduce a new song of the vineyard according to which YHWH will no longer be the punisher but the pledged protector. In fact, YHWH calls it again "a vineyard of delight" (v. 2), echoing the words "a plant of delight" (5:7; cf. Amos 5:11).

Naturally, inner-biblical allusions to the first song of the vineyard (5:1-7) are evident. Despite the divine care for the vineyard, it only yielded spoiled grapes, which resulted in the removal of the fence (5:2, 4-5). Now, however, YHWH promises to protect it so thoroughly that, following the emphatic subject "I YHWH," v. 3 starts and ends with the verb "to guard" (*natsar*), as if portraying the vineyard securely shielded by YHWH the keeper. Contrary to the divine command not to rain (5:6), YHWH promises to water it every moment (v. 3). Whereas YHWH vowed to bring "briers and thorns" upon the recalcitrant vineyard (5:6), now no longer angry (cf. 5:25), YHWH vows to march against any "briers and thorns" that threaten the vineyard (v. 4). Thus, the vineyard and its surroundings are invited to trust in and make peace with YHWH (v. 5). Whereas the divine denouncement in the first vineyard song in Isaiah 5 is an irrevocable decision, here in the second vineyard song it undergoes a thematic transformation with the divine invitation for the people to make peace and join in the restored relationship with YHWH.

Verse 6 is a hinge that wraps up the song of the vineyard (vv. 2-5) while at the same time connecting to the following subunit (vv. 7-11). Here the resemblance with the first song of the vineyard (5:1-7) makes it legitimate to read this verse as a summary explication. Located at the core of the whole unit, however, this verse unveils a central theme: whereas the vineyard previously symbolized the "house of Israel" and the "people of Judah" devoid of justice and righteousness (5:7), soon "in days to come" Jacob and Israel will be restored. The statement that Jacob will take "root" (*sharash*) and Israel will "sprout" (*parakh*) may further echo and reverse the sixth woe-oracle in Isaiah 5: "their root (*shoresh*) will become rotten and their sprout (*perakh*) go up like dust" (5:24; cf. 11:10). The vineyard as the symbol of agricultural sustenance and poetic affection was once uprooted and destroyed (Isa 5) but, in days to come, will assuredly regain its place for hope of nourishment and renewal (Isa 26).

Isaiah 27:7-13 restates the divine plan to purge Jacob's iniquity and sin in counterpoint to the demise of the fortified city (vv. 7-11), culminating in the glorious return of the exiles into Jerusalem on that day (vv. 12-13).

Verses 7-11 appear to transition abruptly with ambiguous contents. Nonetheless, we may detect certain intertextual clues that suggest subtle meanings, highlighting a contrast between the penitent "Jacob" soon to be forgiven and the wicked "fortified city" soon to be destroyed.

First, Jacob's restoration presents an image antithetical to the fate of Philistia (vv. 7-9; cf. 14:29-30). The alliteration of the same root words (v. 7) parallels similar features elsewhere (21:2; 33:1). Yet here, together with v. 6, several key words resemble those in 14:29-30. Vocabulary such as the "blow" (*makkah*) one strikes (*nakah*) and "to kill" (*harag*) in v. 7 appears near the beginning and the end of 14:29-30, just as the key words "root" and "fruit" occur in both texts (although the words for "fruit" are different in Hebrew; cf. 5:24). In light of this intertextual comparison, the message becomes apparent: in contrast to the case of Philistia, whose doom remains irrecoverable (14:29-30), "Israel's punishment . . . is not comparable to the punishment inflicted on other nations; it is severe but not terminal" (Blenkinsopp 2000a, 377).

Similarly, YHWH's "fierce (*qasheh*) spirit/blast" that led Jerusalem into exile with the "east wind" (v. 8) echoes YHWH's "fierce (*qasheh*), great, and strong sword" that will slay the chaotic forces (v. 1). The exiled Jacob will gain divine forgiveness of its "iniquity" and "sin," following the demolition of the altar stones and Asherahs (v. 9; cf. 1:4; 5:18).

Next, in contrast to the exiled and penitent Jacob, the obstinate and haughty "fortified city" learns of its doom (vv. 10-11). The identity of the "fortified city" ('*ir betsurah*) is unclear—Samaria, Jerusalem, or a foreign city, each with boundless pride. The literary flow suggests that this "fortified city" is a menacing city in a foreign empire, e.g., the "fortified town" (*qiryah betsurah*) of 25:2 (cf. 26:5). Yet its ambivalence may connote a double meaning, thus also referring to a sinful city in Israel or Judah (cf. 2:15; Ezek 21:25). Either way, the theme is clear that contrary to the ideal, peaceful city where "the leopard will graze with the young goat" (11:6), now in the deserted city, "there . . . there" (cf. Ps 137:1, 3), the calves will graze (v. 10). Hence, reading the "fortified city" as a foreign imperial city can make a thematic connection to the OAN section of Isaiah 13–23.

Furthermore, the "people without understanding" (v. 11) may allude to YHWH's opening oracle, "my people do not understand" (1:3). This recalcitrant people will not experience divine comfort (cf. 9:17 [MT 9:16]; 14:1) or favor (cf. 26:10). Therefore, reading the "fortified city" as a symbol of the wicked separate from the righteous (cf. 26:10) makes a thematic connection to the subsequent woe-oracles section of Isaiah 28–33.

Verse 12, with another "on that day" phrase, predicts the impending event when YHWH will gather the offspring of Israel from the Euphrates to the Nile, one by one, like threshing the grain. The streams and torrents in Assyria and Egypt parallel the irrigation channels of Babylon where the captives had to endure the hard labors of slavery (Ps 137:1; cf. Ahn 2008, 277–80).

Verse 13, with the final "on that day" phrase, climactically concludes the image of the glorious future when the exiles will enter into Jerusalem and worship YHWH. Instead of the "great" sword YHWH will wield to slay Leviathan (v. 1), now the "great" horn will ring. Instead of the wicked who will "perish" (Ps 1:6; cf. Isa 26:14), those who are "perishing" in the "land" of Assyria and banished in the "land" of Egypt will return. This ingathering of the "outcasts" from all corners of the world, especially from the wadi of Egypt and the Euphrates river, echoes the comparable oracle in Isaiah 11:10-16. Though comparable, whereas the oracle in 11:10-16 envisages the restored monarchy and political unity, the culminating oracle in 27:12-13 presents the reconceptualized theme of YHWH as the true King under whose reign the restored community will be reunited not through political qualifications but rather through cultic requirements, opening an ideological path to a more universal worldview (Hibbard 2006, 204–208).

This concludes the collection of oracles (Isa 24–27) that have proclaimed divine judgment of mythological forces and divine transformation of the faithful of the earth/land as encrypted symbols. The chastisement and cleansing of the "earth" ('erets) have gradually progressed toward those of the "land" ('erets; cf. 27:13): the former portion that highlights "earth" connects to the preceding collection (Isa 13–23) whereas the latter portion that underscores "land" leads to the following collection (Isa 28–35). Likewise, the references to Egypt and Assyria in 27:12-13 may pave the way into the subsequent collections (Egypt—30:2, 3, 7; 31:1, 3; cf. 36:6, 9 and Assyria—30:31; 31:8; and frequently in Isa 36–38), to which we now turn.

Six Woe-Oracles—Five against the Leaders of Israel and Judah plus One against the Superpower Destroyers of Zion, 28:1–33:24

This section seems out of place within the larger corpus, both thematically and chronologically. Yet several features may help make sense of the pattern in the present arrangement. First, following the OAN (chs. 13–23) and the oracles against the earth/land, chaos/empire, and the wicked of the world (chs. 24–27), this section shifts its focus back to the political arena in the domestic and international affairs of the Levant. Inasmuch as Isaiah 24–27 addresses the "earth" and mythological forces in its broader spectrum, the double meaning also builds a link to the issues related to the "land" and the rulers dealing with the "empire," which are the primary concerns of Isaiah 28–33. In fact, as will be addressed below, there are numerous linguistic and thematic connections between Isaiah 24–27 and 28–33.

Second, the six woe-oracles (Isa 28–33) preceded by the new song of the vineyard (27:1-6) represent inner-biblical *relecture* of the six woe-oracles (5:8-25) preceded by the song of the vineyard (5:1-7): "Chapters 1–5 and 28–35 are stylistically linked: each section contains six oracles beginning with 'woe' (*hwy*). These twelve woes (with the exception of 33:1) are directed against the misguided leadership within the community" (Conrad 1991, 125–26). The prophetic criticism voiced concisely earlier in Isaiah 5 now recurs in detailed elaborations here. Accordingly, there are linguistic and thematic correlations between these two independent woe-oracles sections that we will examine below. We have observed that a rigid chronology does not account for the final shape of the book of Isaiah, as Babylon already appears in Isaiah 13–14 and 21. Nonetheless, historical settings appear to point roughly to the times of Uzziah and Ahaz for Isaiah 5–12 and the times of Hezekiah and beyond for Isaiah 28–33. (We may speculate that, in his early regime, Hezekiah [728–687 BCE] may have been a co-regent under his father Ahaz [735–715 BCE]; cf. Goldingay 2014, 52.) Concerning the compositional process, Reinhard Kratz provides the analysis that "chs. 28–31 as a whole are to be regarded as a successive rewriting of earlier states of the text in chs. 1–12 (and 13–23) [chs. 5–10 in particular], that is, as an ongoing rewriting of Isaiah in the book of Isaiah" (2010, 263–64).

Third, despite the lack of clear literary or thematic cohesion, this section exhibits a distinct marker, i.e., "woe" (*hoy*) phrases, just as Isaiah 13–23 uniquely cohere around the "burden" (*massa'*) phrases. Chapters 28–33, accordingly, function as the kernel of Isaiah 24–35 (Fohrer 1996, 4). In the OAN section, contrary to the oracles targeted against foreign nations, Isaiah 22 concerns Jerusalem and Judah. Interestingly, this kind of oddity resurfaces in 28–33 where, amid predominantly scathing oracles of judgment against the rulers, chapter 32 pronounces a righteous king and government. Redactionally, scholars consider Isaiah 28–31 messages of judgment upon Jerusalem's leaders (five woe-oracles), followed by 32–33 with messages of salvation through a righteous spirit-anointed leader (Isa 32, which I propose to call a "weal-oracle" or "wow-oracle") and divine punishment of super-power destroyers, Israel's enemies (Isa 33; sixth woe-oracle). Synchronically, taking the present form, Gary Stansell lays out the following diagram that displays a consistent pattern of "doom-salvation," thereby connecting various sections of the six woe-oracles as "their own kind of structural unity" (Stansell 1996, 71; cf. Blenkinsopp 2000a, 426; Berges 2012a, 184):

	Woe		*Woe*		*Woe*
Judgment	28:1-4	28:7-22	29:1-4	29:9-14	29:15-16
Salvation	5-6	23-29	5-8		17-24

	Woe	*Woe*		*Woe*
Judgment	30:1-17	31:1-4	32:9-14	33:1
Salvation	18-26	5-8; 32:1-8	15-20	2-24

First Woe-Oracle—Against Drunkards of Ephraim and Scoffers of Jerusalem, 28:1-29

The first woe-oracle targets the elite leaders of Ephraim and ultimately of Jerusalem, indicting their recalcitrance and predicting their consequent demise. The oracle depicts northern Israel's leaders as drunkards, heavily intoxicated with confusion and ignorance (vv. 1-13). Judah's leaders do not fare any better. Worse yet, by making a covenant with death, they will become miserable, even though YHWH will cancel their covenant (vv. 14-22). This unit concludes with an allegory of a farmer, emphasizing that the ultimate purpose of plowing and threshing is not to destroy but to build (vv. 23-29).

Isaiah 28:1-13 introduces the first target of indictment, the self-indulgent and self-intoxicated leaders of Ephraim. The glistening crowns of the drunken rulers will crumble, replaced by the true crown of honor for the remnant of YHWH's people (vv. 1-6). Priests and prophets in the intoxication of obstinacy will only lead "this people" (cf. Isa 8) with power and privilege to collapse and captivity (vv. 7-13).

Verses 1-6 target the royal rulers of Ephraim, whose political ineptness equates to drunkenness (vv. 1-4) and whom YHWH will dethrone (vv. 5-6). Regarding compositional development, J. J. M. Roberts claims that vv. 1-4 were originally addressed to northern Israel during the Syro-Ephraimite

War, which the prophet then reapplied against southern Judah during the later Assyrian era. Its hermeneutical implication would be illuminating: the Judean leaders were "just as irresponsible as the northerners had been" (vv. 7-13; Roberts 2002, 302).

In verses 1-4, following the direct "woe to . . ." accusation, readers hear numerous repetitions, puns, and intertextual echoes. Kings, queens, and princes (cf. Jer 13:18) hear divine condemnation of their wonton gluttony, the drunkenness of their corruption (v. 1). Intertextually, where the earth quaked terribly like a "drunkard" (*shikkor*, 24:20), now the powerful rulers are mere "drunkards" (*shikkor*). Similarly, the crown of "majesty" (*ge'ut*) implies a sharp thematic contrast with YHWH's "majesty" (*ge'ut*), which the wicked cannot see (26:10). Not the wine but the arrogance and pride of these leaders in their "majestic crowns" are what lead them to utter humiliation and ruin (Eidevall 2009, 149). Thus, whereas Jacob and Israel will blossom (*yatsis*), the majestic crowns dangling on their heads will turn to fading flowers (*tsits*). The "fading flower" (*tsits nobel*) anticipates the similar expression, "the flower fades" (*nabel tsits*), in 40:7, just as the "valley" may presage 40:4. Indeed, in light of the Neo-Assyrian iconography depicting the rosette emblem as a symbol of royalty, Rolf Jacobson posits the double meaning of the "fading flower" both as a symbol of royalty and as a symbol of transitoriness, implying that "as quickly as the flowers of the field fade, so too the King of Ephraim would disappear" (Jacobson 2009, 136). The "fertile" valley also echoes the "fertile" hill in the song of the vineyard (5:1), just as the language of "strong drink" (*shekar*) and "wine" (*yayin*) closely correlates to the previous woe-oracles in 5:11, 22.

Their doom accompanies the dawn of their devastator, YHWH's instrument (v. 2; cf. 10:5). This agent is "strong" (*hazaq*) and "mighty" (*'ammits*). The sounds of the Hebrew terms recall the names "Hezekiah" (*hizqiyahu*) and Isaiah son of "Amoz" (*'amots*). These key words describing the foreign invader may reflect "Hezekiah's speech to the people to 'be strong and of good courage' (*hizqu we'imtsu*) in the face of the projected Assyrian attack (2 Chr 32:7)" (Sweeney 1996, 368). We should keep in mind that nowhere in Isaiah 28–33 do we find the name Hezekiah. Nevertheless, the originally intended setting seems to betray the time of Hezekiah and his negative political policies, which may have motivated the concealment of the king's name here, in contrast to the explicit specification of the name Hezekiah with positive portrayals in Isaiah 36–39. In this case, the root word echoing the name Hezekiah ironically depicts the upcoming divine agency. The intended audience would hear hidden criticism of Hezekiah (or Hezekiah's co-regency with his father Ahaz), who neglected the policy of a righteous king (cf. 2 Sam 12:7; 2 Kgs 18:13-16).

Verbatim wordplays, with shifted motifs, describe the resultant upheaval of the royal dynasty (vv. 3-4). Thus, "the shining crown of Ephraim's drunkards" (v. 1) will soon be trampled under foot (v. 3; cf. 1:12; 26:6). Also, "the fading flower of its glorious beauty at the head of the fertile valley" (v. 1) compares to an early fig that the attacker will soon "swallow" (v. 4; cf. 25:7-8): "Assyria will gulp down Israel!" (Brueggemann 1998a, 221).

Opposite the majestic drunkards of Ephraim's rulers (vv. 1-4), in vv. 5-6, which begin with the "on that day" phrase, the oracle declares a society transformed by divine renewal, consisting of devout remnants—the twelve-tribe "descendants of both kingdoms" (Blenkinsopp 2000a, 390). In fact, YHWH will become the "glorious crown" and "beautiful diadem" for the remnant (v. 5; cf. vv. 1, 3). While YHWH's "spirit of wisdom and understanding" was to rest on Jesse's descendant (11:2), now YHWH promises to be the "spirit of justice" for the new righteous ruler (v. 6). Like the "spirit of strength (*geburah*)" (11:2), YHWH promises to be "strength" (*geburah*) for the warriors at the gate (v. 6).

Verses 7-13 continue the portrayals of the intoxicated leaders, this time targeting the priests and prophets of northern Israel, with the same repetitive and rhetorical expressions. Now, the oracle exposes the identity of this corrupt class—the priest and the prophet (v. 7). Yet readers wonder whether these accused audiences would pay heed; after all, they are heavily drunk. The Hebrew expressions are so repetitive, as Patricia Tull remarks, that "like the reeling of the drunkards, their descriptions circle round and round the same terms: they reel with wine, stagger with liquor, reel with liquor, are confused (or, ironically, swallowed) by wine, they stagger from liquor, reel in their visions, and stumble even when engaged in court decisions" (2010, 422). In the preceding section (Isa 24–27), we have learned that YHWH will swallow up death forever (25:8). Here, sadly, wine has swallowed these leaders. The portrayal of the tables at a banquet scene in v. 8 is reminiscent of the ancient Canaanite *marzēaḥ* ritual, when the leaders would orgy all night long, leaving vomit, spew, urine, excrement, and odor everywhere (Asen 1996; Blenkinsopp 2010b).

The rhetorical question in v. 9 ("To whom [*'et-mi*] will he teach knowledge and to whom [*'et-mi*] will he expound the report?") echoes the questions of commissioning in the divine council: "Whom (*'et-mi*) will I send and who (*mi*) will go for us?" (6:8). If the question in Isaiah 6 was the divine search for a willing agent, now we hear the prophet's lament over the absence of any sane agent. Not only insanely intoxicated, these religious and social leaders are also compared to infants and babes (v. 9). Their ethical and juridical fluency would be at the level of childish "blah, blah, blah" gibberish (v. 10).

Whereas Isaiah's unclean "lips" received cleansing (6:5-7), now this people will hear only a stammering "lip" (v. 11). Not unlike "this people" that kept seeing and hearing but did not understand (6:9), YHWH vows to speak to "this people" in a foreign tongue—which may refer to the Akkadian language (v. 11; cf. 36:11; Perdue and Carter 2015, 80). The message delivered to them treats the theme of "rest (*nuakh*)" (v. 12). Enveloped by phrases conveying the assurance of a resting place, the chiastic center of the three phrases in v. 12 admonishes them to "give rest to the weary." Whereas the obdurate people in Isaiah's call at least really heard although they could not understand (6:9), now these folks abjectly refuse to listen. In the end, the word of YHWH will only sound like rote repetition to them, as the message in v. 13a is a verbatim recitation of v. 10. Here the divine purpose of such a hidden or incomprehensible message coincides with that of Isaiah's call. Earlier, the prophet received the divine commission to engender the people's heart to become more obstinate, "lest" they may repent and be healed (6:10). Now, they will only hear the covert message "in order that" these intoxicated leaders will totter backward, be broken, and captured (v. 13b; cf. 8:15).

Isaiah 28:14-22 is the central piece of the three subunits in chapter 28, where the audience hears the most intensified negative accusation as well as the positive foundational message. The divine word now addresses the rulers of Jerusalem, the ultimate target (vv. 14-15). Despite the seemingly irrecoverable downward spiral of Judah, courtesy of the rulers' covenant with death, YHWH asserts the intention to cancel that covenant by overthrowing the wrongful leaders and restoring justice and righteousness (vv. 16-20). Indeed, the announcement of YHWH's rise to accomplish this plan wraps up this unit (vv. 21-22).

Verses 14-15 switch the attention from Ephraim to Jerusalem. More precisely, we learn that the climactic target has been not northern Israel but actually southern Judah (cf. Amos 1–2; Ezek 23). In the preceding unit, the "word of YHWH" was unrecognizable to the leaders of Ephraim; after all, they were drunk (v. 13). What about the scoffers, who rule "this people" in Jerusalem (v. 14; cf. v. 11)? The report is grisly: the royals at Jerusalem made a covenant with death and received a divination from Sheol (v. 15), as if daring to revoke YHWH's defeat of death (25:8). Mot, the Canaanite god of death, was the lord of Sheol. The rhetorical mockery is vivid: who in their right mind would enter into a deal with such lethal forces? Who could sever their own covenant relationship with YHWH (cf. 24:5)? None other than Jerusalem's ruling elites in their alcohol-free, sober, and thus all the more cold-blooded decisions. At least Ephraim's leaders were too intoxicated to do anything proper. But now Jerusalem's leaders are sober, making lies and falsehood their shelter in their rational minds.

In light of the larger section (Isa 28–33), scholars conjecture that this covenant with death may allude to Jerusalem's political alliance with Egypt's Pharaoh in their survival struggle with Assyria (cf. 30:1-5; 31:1-3). Though different words, the catchwords for "refuge" in Pharaoh and "shelter" in Egypt (30:2) thematically connect to our text. Here, concerning the correlation of death with Egypt beyond the Canaanite background of Mot, Christopher Hays proposes to read Isaiah 28 over against the ancient Egypt's major mother goddess Mut. This Egyptian goddess, Mut (meaning "mother"), is portrayed as a vulture with protecting wings, thereby symbolizing both a protector with terrifying power and a destroyer of rebels. In fact, the notions of "flower garlands and heavy drinking" in 28:1-4 may also allude to key components of Egyptian religious practices (lotus flowers and inebriation), thereby implying not only Egyptian goddess Mut's mythology but also her cult (Hays 2010, 225–26). Against this Egyptian backdrop, the Isaianic oracle condemns Judah's elites for seeking "protection from Egypt by means of a covenant with . . . the mother goddess Mut" (Hays 2010, 239). The rhetorical and thematic criticism becomes all the more vehement: Jerusalem's policymakers are foolish and stubborn, driving the whole nation toward a cliff at full speed.

Verses 16-20 present YHWH's stern rebuttal and retort. Zion, contaminated by the distorted cohort of Sheol, has to comply with its foundation, a precious cornerstone, so that those who trust will not perish (v. 16; cf. 7:9). In this verse, the Hebrew text has a grammatical paradox in that the particle "Behold [I am about to]" (*hineni*) leads to a third-person Piel perfect verb "I have laid" (*yissad*). Most English translations render as "Behold I am going to lay . . . ," implying the futuristic notion of YHWH's salvific act. Faithful to the text-critical difficulty, however, its alternative reading emphasizes the past tense, asserting YHWH's already-assured foundation of Zion that may be hidden away but will never be shattered amid the resounding announcement of judgment in this core subunit (Dekker 2007, 124–30). Judah's political and religious submission to (Canaanite) Mot or (Egyptian) Mut may seem a dismal central theme of this text. But such a negative accusation is not the final word. Proposing the judgment oracle of 28:14-22 as a thesis-like guide for Isaiah 28–33, Jaap Dekker expounds this oracle's theological axiom that "Zion serves as the point of conjunction between Isaiah's preaching of judgement [*sic*] and his preaching of salvation. . . . The conviction that YHWH would uphold the salvific institutions [YHWH] had once established

(Zion being the most important)—even in and through judgement—must
be understood as characteristic of the preaching of Isaiah" (Dekker 2007,
264 and 352–53).

The prophet affirms a foundational theme with the imagery of YHWH
the carpenter, not unlike the beloved vinedresser or a farmer (vv. 16-17;
cf. 5:1-2; 28:23-29). YHWH affirms not only laying in Zion a sure foundation
(v. 16; cf. 14:32) but also reestablishing justice and righteousness (v. 17).
Here, J. J. M. Roberts proposes to translate "a tested stone" (*'eben bokhan*)
as "a massive stone of refuge," in light of the Egyptian loanword *bakhan*
("fortress, tower, watch tower") and Qumran texts. This rendition unveils a
literary framework, highlighting the centrality of v. 16, which is bracketed
by the expressions of the leaders' "refuge of falsehood" (v. 15) and the subsequent punishment upon the "refuge of lies" (v. 17). Therefore, this building
imagery in vv. 16-17 signifies a thematic contrast between two rival structures—between the flimsy shelter built by Jerusalem's rulers and the refuge
city Zion of unwavering bulwark built by YHWH (Roberts 2002, 294–99 and
303–304).

Additionally, a couple of intertextual allusions are noteworthy. First,
YHWH's intention to set up "justice" (*mishpat*) as the measuring "line" (*qaw*)
may allude to the gibberish sentences in vv. 10, 13. The paranomasia of the
word "line" here thus may function to overwrite the "line upon line" (*qaw
laqaw*) that the drunkards from Ephraim were babbling in denial. The "line"
in vv. 10, 13 is therefore "justice" that they disregarded, just as the word
"precept" (*tsaw*) is a partial form of the root word "to command" (*tsawah*;
cf. Deut 4:5; 6:1; Hos 5:11). Like Ephraim's drunkards, Jerusalem's leaders
are guilty of disdaining justice, statutes, and commandment. Hence, "line"
and "plummet" do not refer to the foundation of the physical temple, where
God is not boxed in, but rather to the divine "blueprint . . . for a city built
by justice and righteousness" (Roberts 2002, 309).

Second, the word "plummet" (*mishqelet*) occurs elsewhere only in
2 Kings 21:13 in the OT: "I will stretch out against Jerusalem the line of
Samaria and the plummet of Ahab's house." Together with the word "line"
and its similar motif, the close intertextual affinity is significant. In 2 Kings
21, the culprit is Manasseh, King Hezekiah's son. Manasseh built altars for
Baal and Asherah (2 Kgs 21:3, 7; cf. Isa 27:9). Although our text reveals
no historical references, we can deduce that the "scoffers in Jerusalem"
(v. 14) may allude to the cabinet members of either Hezekiah or Manasseh.
Read intertextually, whereas Manasseh worshiped Baal and Asherah in
2 Kings 21, the ruler in the Isaiah text made a covenant with Mot (an equally
villainous god of Ugaritic mythology who once swallowed Baal) or with Mut

(a formidable goddess of Egyptian mythology with dual aspects of protection and destruction). Accordingly, these gibberish words evoke "strange" words of foreigners, making Jerusalem's leaders guilty of idolatry in their denial of YHWH (Hays 2010, 234).

Therefore, YHWH's revocation of the Jerusalemites' pact with Mot or Mut requires the trampling down of those corrupt leaders, just like the trampling of Ephraim's drunkards (v. 18; cf. v. 3). The failure of Jerusalem's leaders to construct the city with justice and righteousness necessitates YHWH's "urban renewal project," the divine demolition work (Roberts 2002, 310). While waters suggest that the Assyrian flood will "overpower" (*shatap*) the shelter of falsehood (v. 17; cf. v. 15), now the "overpowering" (*shatap*) whip will pass over them (v. 18), day and night (v. 19). Here, proposing to read "vision" instead of "pact, agreement" in the phrase "a pact (*hazut*) with Sheol" (v. 18), Christopher Hays expounds another interpretive option: "the prospective of a covenant with Mut certainly could have looked like 'a vision of hell' to a prophet of YHWH" (2010, 237).

We note a linguistic and thematic correlation between v. 9 and v. 19. The previous question added suspense and fear concerning the fate of Ephraim's rulers: "To whom will he expound (*bin*) the report (*shemu'ah*)?" (v. 9). Now readers should ponder the ghastly fate of Jerusalem's rulers: "It will be a sheer terror to expound (*bin*) the report (*shemu'ah*)" (v. 19). The outcome recalls the ill fate of the king of Babylon, whose pomp went down to Sheol, with the "bed" (*yutsa'*) of maggots and "blanket" (*mekasseh*) of grubs (cf. 14:11, 15). Now the "bed" (*matsa'*) will be too short and the "blanket" (*massekah*) too narrow to shelter Jerusalem's royals (v. 20; cf. 25:7).

There is another significant linguistic and thematic marker between v. 15 and vv. 18-19—the catchword "to pass over" (*'abar*). This word is closely tied to the exodus tradition, in which, through the Passover ritual on the tenth plague, YHWH "passed over" (*'abar*) to strike the Egyptians, excepting the Israelites who placed the blood of the lamb on the doorpost (Exod 12:23). Thus in v. 15, the scoffers of Jerusalem, who made a covenant (lit., "cut a deal") with death (Mot or Mut), claim that "when the overwhelming scourge passes over (*'abar*) it will not enter us." YHWH's rebuttal dramatically annuls their miscalculation: "When the overwhelming scourge passes over (*'abar*), then you will become its trampling place. Each time it passes over (*'abar*), it will take you; for morning by morning it will pass over (*'abar*)" (vv. 18-19; cf. 1:12; 28:3). Like Faust who sold his soul to the devil, these rulers of Jerusalem cut a deal with death, as though thinking that they would escape death because they bowed to it and hoping that death will only hit the powerless poor and helpless needy as has been throughout human history. Alas, God has read every inclination of their deadly schemes. Those immovable rulers of Jerusalem are to meet the fate of Pharaoh and his submissive adherents.

Verses 21-22 wrap up this central subunit (vv. 14-22) with recurring motifs and bracketing words. Contrary to Jerusalem's leaders who will be trampled (v. 18) and put down on a mini-bed (v. 20), YHWH will rise to accomplish divine plan (v. 21a). Strikingly, divine work will be "strange" and "foreign," just as the divine word was like "another" language to all those incapable would-be experts in politics (v. 21b; cf. v. 11). If Mount Perazim, geographically proximate to Jerusalem and Gibeon Valley, alludes to David's victory over the Philistines (2 Sam 5:17-25; 1 Chr 14:8-17), then such allusions imply that the divine intervention would shock the audience: instead of YHWH intervening on their behalf, according to this oracle "YHWH's imminent intervention is to be directed against [YHWH's] people"—indeed strange and alien (Dekker 2007, 162). Having made a covenant deal with foreign gods and their alien rituals, these callous leaders are to experience the foreign and strange wrath of YHWH (Hays 2010, 239). The command not to "scoff" in v. 22 brackets this subunit with the term "scoffers" in v. 14. Earlier the prophet warned Ephraim's drunkards of their intoxicated recalcitrance (vv. 1-13), and now Jerusalem's scoffers are to witness the annihilation of the entire "land" (v 22).

Isaiah 28:23-29, picking up the preceding oracles of punishment against the rulers of Ephraim and Jerusalem, contains an interlude with a para-ble-like metaphor of plucking up and replanting. Not unlike the smelting of contaminated Zion (1:21-31) and the song of the vineyard (5:1-7), this parable of the farmer employs its unique agricultural vocabulary of plowing and threshing to convey the messages of both solemn warning against the sinners and anticipatory restoration for the survivors. The farmer metaphor here plays a significant rhetorical and thematic function. If we consider the divine accusation against the "city" in Isaiah 24–27 as a vehement socioeco-nomic criticism against the ruling class, then here we may hear a comparably deep-seated socioeconomic allegory of divine judgment, excerpted from the cries of the vulnerable, agrarian, and rural peasant farmers.

Verses 23-26 pose rhetorical questions. The call to "listen" to YHWH's voice and "hear" the word (v. 23) echoes, in inverted chiasm, the equivalent calls in the introductory oracle (1:2, 10; cf. 32:9). The rhetorical questions probe whether or not plowing and harrowing, presumably the process of uprooting, will stop. The pertinent message is that once the ground is replenished, the farmer will plant and sow dill, cumin, wheat, barley, and rye (vv. 24-25). Another implied message, reading socioeconomically, hints that the farmer puts everything in order; why, then, do the elite rulers confound and corrupt the fair system? The crucial conclusion, which brackets this subunit with v. 23, asserts that the farmer can surely do everything properly because YHWH, not the perverted elite, guides and instructs "justice" (v. 26).

Verses 27-29 provide answers and clarifications implied in the questions of vv. 23-26. After plowing and harrowing, the dill and fennel will be planted and not be threshed or rolled over by a cart wheel. Dill and cumin are tiny seeds vulnerable to damage by farming implements. How ironic that the elite rulers so brutally crush and roll over the disenfranchised peasants! That the rod and the staff will thresh those cruel leaders buoys a hope for the divine guidance of the true King and Shepherd (v. 27; cf. 9:4 [MT 9:3]; 10:5, 24; 27:12; Ps 23:4). Whereas the oppressive elite class schemes to destroy the people, the good farmer guided by YHWH will let the remnant breathe and regrow (v. 28). This hope is real because YHWH is indeed the wondrously trustworthy farmer and the wonderfully wise planner (v. 29).

Second Woe-Oracle—Against the Rulers of Ariel-Jerusalem, 29:1-14

This second woe-oracle extends the negative assessment toward Jerusalem from the preceding text (28:14-29), which then will lead to the positive promise of restoration for the house of Jacob in the third woe-oracle (29:15-24). This woe-oracle has two thematically distinct parts: "the attack and subsequent deliverance of Ariel" (29:1-8) and "the withholding of understanding" (29:9-14; Exum 1981, 340).

Isaiah 29:1-8 rhetorically portrays the siege of Jerusalem, surrounded and attacked by none other than YHWH. Jerusalem will then be saved miraculously. Some of the historical clues in this subunit suggest the event of the Assyrian siege of Jerusalem and its subsequent dramatic rescue during the time of Hezekiah. Although no Assyrian king appears in the text, readers may picture Jerusalem under Sennacherib's siege (701 BCE).

Verses 1-4 convey the divine judgment to besiege Jerusalem. In the dual occurrence of the name, "Ariel, Ariel," readers hear a note of divine pathos (v. 1; cf. Gen 22:11; Exod 3:4). This city (*qiryah*) recalls the "chaos city (*qiryah*)" in the preceding references (cf. 1:21, 26; 22:2; 24:10; 25:2-3; 26:5). This town is about to experience oppression, to be filled with "lamenting and mourning" (v. 2). Notably, the phrase, "lamenting and mourning" (*ta'aniyyah wa'aniyyah*), occurs elsewhere only in Lamentations 2:5. The descriptions of YHWH's siege of Jerusalem likewise echo the detailed expressions in Lamentations (vv. 3-4; cf. Lam 2:4-5). In connection with Lamentations, where the siege and capture of Jerusalem evidently denote the fall of Jerusalem to the Babylonian king Nebuchadnezzar (587 BCE), the emphasis in the Isaianic text underscores that it is not a foreign king but rather YHWH who intends to pillage the fortifications of Jerusalem and bring them low, down to the dust (cf. 25:12; 26:5, 19). Repetition of the assonance—*wetsarti* ("to siege"), *mutsab* ("intrenchment"), *metsurot* ("siegeworks"), all from the same root *tswr* ("to besiege")—accentuates that "the city is under siege" (Exum 1981, 363).

Furthermore, the twofold naming of Jerusalem, "Ariel, Ariel," may allude to the Assyrian "Hymn to the City of Arbela," dating to the seventh century BCE (SAA III 8:1-18):

> Arbela, O Arbela [*Arbail Arbail*]!
> Heaven without equal, Arbela! City of merry-making, Arbela!
> City of festivals, Arbela! City of the temple jubilation, Arbela! . . .
> Arbela is as lofty as heaven. Its foundations are as firm as the heavens . . . .
> (Nissinen 2001, 177)

Ancient Near Eastern cities, including Arbela, symbolized the convergence of the divine and human worlds, hailed as "heaven without equal." The city Zion, called "Ariel, Ariel" in our oracle, would experience, like Arbela, the reversal of all the lofty glory and honor. Instead of "festivities" (v. 1), similar to the merry-making and jubilation of Arbela, Jerusalem will soon be making "lamenting and mourning" (v. 2). Instead of the exultation Arbela enjoys "as lofty as *heaven*," Jerusalem will be "brought low" and will only speak "from the *earth*" (v. 4; cf. 2:9-12, 17).

Verses 5-8 describe a reversal of fate, divine deliverance, so that the enemies will soon become like the dust, indeed will suddenly disappear. All the multitude of foreigners and tyrants will become like fine dust and chaff at the time of the divine theophany with thunder, earthquake, whirlwind, and fire (vv. 5-6). This depiction of an instant retreat of the enemy army resembles the miraculous defeat of the 185,000-strong Assyrian army during Sennacherib's siege of Jerusalem (37:36-37; cf. 2 Kgs 19:35-36; 2 Chr 32:21). Here, however, the text adds a didactic lesson framed by the phrase that emphasizes "all the nations" (vv. 7-8). These verses contain bookend phrases: "the multitude of all the nations that wage war against Ariel" (v. 7) and "the multitude of all the nations that wage war against Mount Zion" (v. 8). Accordingly, not only Assyria but also "all the nations" that threaten Jerusalem will vanish like a dream, a night vision (cf. Job 20:8). This dream and night vision is a nightmare: "[The attackers] think they have Jerusalem in their grasp, but discover their anticipated victory to be an illusion" (Exum 1981, 346). Put another way, the recurrent alternations between dream and reality point to the prophetic criticism of the "unreality" of military and political power over against the abiding "reality" of YHWH (Blenkinsopp 2000a, 402).

Echoing the call narrative (6:9-10), Isaiah 29:9-14 then expounds the drunkenness of the obstinate leaders, who are blinded (cf. 6:10) by the spirit of deep sleep. Alternatively, to note the thematic transition, "from the dream of the preceding poem, we move to the deep sleep of this one" (Exum 1981, 347). The command to be dumbfounded and blinded is fraught with cynicism. Why cynical? It is because their drunken state is worse than before. In the previous woe-oracles, the recalcitrant leaders wielded their socioeconomic abuse against vulnerable peasants, luxuriously consuming wine and liquor (5:11, 22). Now, worse than the leaders and drunkards of Ephraim (28:1, 7), these policymakers of Jerusalem are condemned not for their intoxication with wine and liquor (v. 9) but rather for their spiritual incapacity. Who are these blind and deaf leaders? They are the so-called spiritual leaders, the prophets and diviners, whose spiritual alertness has fallen into a deep hiatus (v. 10)—and can only be reawakened by divine intervention (cf. 32:15).

These somnambulating false prophets cannot read or proclaim the vision (vv. 11-12). The verb "to seal" (*hatam*) occurs only in two places in the book of Isaiah (8:16 and 29:11). It would be embarrassing or rather useless if these diviners could not decipher the "vision" (v. 11; cf. Gen 41:8; Dan 2:1-11; 4:1-7). In light of 8:16, readers recall the instruction as the good news sealed by Isaiah's faithful disciples. Contrary to those devout disciples, these diviners with titles and prestige are incapable of either proclaiming or reading the vision.

Now we hear the punch line of the divine dismissal of these dull leaders (vv. 13-14). Again, echoing the call narrative (6:9-10), the text charges "this people" of unclean lips (6:5) with honoring YHWH only with their filthy mouths and lips, while their obdurate "hearts" are remote from divine commandments (v. 13). Therefore YHWH announces the intention to chastise "this people" with the result that wisdom of the would-be sages will "perish" and the understanding of those reputed to have "understanding" (cf. 6:9) will depart (v. 14). The preceding woe-oracle ended by announcing YHWH's wondrous (*pala'*) counsel and wisdom (28:29). Similarly, this woe-oracle now ends by proclaiming YHWH's wondrous (*pala'*) works against "this people" (29:14; Exum 1981, 350).

Third Woe-Oracle—Against the Tyrants and Scoffers of Jerusalem, 29:15-24

This woe-oracle continues the chastisement of the religious and political leaders who continue to lead their people astray, while pronouncing YHWH's trustworthy plan to redeem the house of Jacob.

Verses 15-17 accuse the royal counselors whose shrewd policies will be exposed and revoked. These leaders are master planners in the dark (v. 15; cf. 5:20). Readers can hear a double message. On the one hand, they are so skilled in covert schemes that they confidently ask, "Who can see us and know us?" (cf. 6:9), believing that they can keep their secrets not only from Isaiah, their trouble-maker, but even from YHWH (Roberts 2002, 289)! Yet, on the other hand, they are indeed in the dark, lost in cluelessness and ignorance of the light. Direct address, "you [pl.]," tumbles their worldview upside down (v. 16; cf. 5:20). Earlier the prophet warned that the ax or the saw cannot boast over the one who handles it (cf. 10:15). Likewise, the clay should not dare try to control the potter (cf. Jer 18:1-6). Three key words in v. 16—"Maker" ('asah), "Shaper" (yatsar), and "understand" (bin)—recall the vocabulary of 27:11—"understanding" (binah), "Maker" ('asah), and "Shaper" (yatsar). Read together, the stupidity of this people becomes more apparent in that these leaders, themselves lacking understanding and miscalculating that God is absent, dare to charge their creator with a lack of understanding.

YHWH's rebuttal contains familiar figurative language conveying the theme of the reversal of fortune: Lebanon will become a garden-land, whereas a fruitful field will become a lush forest (v. 17; cf. 2:13; 10:34). Csaba Balogh observes chiastic parallelism in this verse with regard to semantic and thematic correlations:

"return" (shab)   "Lebanon" (lebanon)   "garden-land" (karmel)
// "garden-land"(karmel)   "as a forest" (layya'ar)   "considered" (yekhasheb)

Taking this chiastic pattern as a literary clue, some interpreters posit that Lebanon and its forest do not allude to the region north of Israel but symbolize Jerusalem. Read this way, the reversal of Lebanon into a fruitful land signifies the glorious restoration of the presently desolate Jerusalem (Balogh 2009, 51–52).

Verses 18-21 begin with the "on that day" phrase and function as the central subunit of this woe-oracle (sandwiched by vv. 15-17 and vv. 22-24). Whereas many "on that day" passages tend to appear at the end of units, often as appendix-like subunits, this subunit takes center stage not only in its literary arrangement but also with its thematic climax: the themes of the differentiation between the righteous and the wicked and of the reversal of their fortunes.

In this dichotomy, the righteous group includes the deaf, the blind, the poor, and the needy (vv. 18-19). Contrary to the power-blinded prophets and diviners who cannot read the "words of the book" (dibre hasseper,

vv. 10-11), the deaf will hear the "words of a book" (*dibre seper*, v. 18).
Contrary to the blinded leaders (v. 9) and the counselors who operate in the
"dark" (v. 15), the blind will see amid darkness (v. 18). Who are these people
who can hear and see? They are the poor and the needy who tend to be easy
prey to the socioeconomic and political abuse of the drunkards, but whose
joy and gladness YHWH will increase assuredly (v. 19).

On the opposite side, the wicked group includes the tyrants and the
scoffers (vv. 20-21). Their fate is horrible: both tyrants and scoffers will
be destroyed and those who plot evil will be cut off (v. 20; cf. v. 5). Why
should they receive such a sentence? It is because of their devious and brutal
perversions of justice, prevalently conducted at the city gates: concealing
wrongdoings while blaming the innocent, entrapping just witnesses in legal
proceedings, and overturning the legal system against the righteous (v. 21).

Verses 22-24 enclose this woe-oracle with the introduction of new main
characters and implied messages. The first character, Abraham, appears only
here (v. 22) other than in 41:8; 51:2; 63:16. Abraham, who left Chaldea
(Babylon) to enter Canaan, can set a precedent for the exiles' return from
Babylon to Yehud. The second character, Jacob, another representative of
the exilic community, will be neither ashamed nor will his face turn pale.
The word "to be pale" (*hawar*) has the connotation "to be white," which
implies a pun with the name Laban (meaning "white"), Jacob's uncle whose
seasoned tricks supplant those of Jacob. Like genetic transmission, the shame
of mischief and disloyalty can transfer to children and descendants. This
shameful cycle of tricking and being tricked will cease. Instead, Jacob's
descendants ("the house of Jacob"), set free of the tyrants' oppression and
their own shame, will sanctify the Holy One of Jacob, the God of Israel
(v. 23). Finally, no longer overshadowed by the "spirit of deep sleep" (v. 10),
those who err in "spirit" will surely understand and learn (v. 24).

Fourth Woe-Oracle—Against Judah's Plan to Make Alliance with Egypt, 30:1-33

This woe-oracle extends a similar denouncement of obstinate leaders, drunkards of Ephraim (28:1), and scoffers of Jerusalem (28:14), but now in the
context of their religio-political reliance on Egypt. The two initial subunits
(vv. 1-7 and vv. 8-17) that comprise the first half of this unit offer detailed
descriptions of the international policy of these opportunistic fearful souls.
The two subsequent subunits (vv. 18-26 and vv. 27-33) turn the table and
proclaim that YHWH, not Egypt or Assyria, is the truly reliable source of
their deliverance. These four subunits together center on the thematic apex
in v. 18.

Verses 1-7 target the international policymakers, the top officials, who are choosing to place their trust in Pharaoh, not YHWH. The setting of the plot mirrors Hezekiah's sending of envoys to Egypt in his rebellion against Assyria (2 Kgs 18:7-8). Here Judah's movers and shakers are called "rebellious kids" (v. 1; cf. Deut 21:18, 20). Their political scheme does not come from "my spirit," says YHWH, because it comes from false prophets and diviners, intoxicated in "a spirit of deep sleep" (29:10). Instead of trustworthy refuge and shelter from YHWH (4:6; 25:4; cf. 32:2), these rulers seek refuge and shelter from Pharaoh (v. 2). Robin Routledge finds an intertextual allusion of catchwords from Psalm 46:1 to v. 2 here: Psalm 46:1—"God is our refuge (*makhaseh*) and strength (*'oz*), a help very near in trouble-times"; and Isa 30:2—"[who] look for help to Pharaoh's protection (*ma'oz*) to Egypt's shade for refuge (*hasah*)." The linkage intensifies the theological message that sure refuge and strength in times of trouble should not be sought from Pharaoh or any human mechanism but first and foremost from YHWH (Routledge 1992, 185). The shelter of Egypt will turn to Jerusalem's shame and misery (v. 3; cf. 29:22). Even though Jerusalem's princes and envoys march through Zoan and Hanes, northern and southern regions of Egypt (v. 4), they will receive no help but will experience only shame and disgrace (v. 5).

An oracle on the beasts in the Negev desert further elaborates this chastisement (vv. 6-7). These caravans make the arduous trip on the humps of camels through the desert full of lions and flying serpents (v. 6; cf. 14:29). To these policymakers, such a perilous trip to the mighty nation Egypt would seem worth the risk. Yet the prophet dismisses the policy because Egypt's help is unreliable and fleeting (v. 7). Indeed, echoing the mythological tradition, Egypt is compared to "Rabab" that has ceased to be (cf. 51:9; Pss 87:4; 89:10 [MT 89:11]; Job 26:12).

Verses 8-17 specifically expose the society whose system is corrupt. This subunit consists of two parts dealing with the unimaginable arrogance of the sociopolitical leaders (vv. 8-11) and YHWH's stern reaction to them (vv. 12-17).

Previously Isaiah wrote on a tablet as an impending sign (8:1). Now another tablet will be inscribed as a witness (v. 8). The tablet starts, not unlike the discussion of corrupt children in 1:4, with enraged name calling: rebellious, deceptive children who refuse to listen to YHWH's law (v. 9). Indeed, they are neither novices when it comes to shrewd falsehood nor amateurs in their bold refusal of divine teaching. How corrupt have they become? The previous oracle informed that YHWH had obstructed "prophets" and "diviners" (29:10). Now, these perverse leaders dare to demand—or, more likely, threaten—"seers" and "diviners" to deviate from truth and only spread false reports (v. 10). Imagine a system in which public reports conceal the real story and only convey manipulated, false messages! Or imagine a ruling body, fearful of the leakage of the government top secrets (concerning making a treaty with Egypt and thereby breaching the vassal contract to Assyria) and the subsequent commotion out of the damaged public morale, that thus plots to do whatever necessary to threaten the dissenting prophet (Roberts 2002, 285–90; cf. Amos 7:10-12; Jer 36:20-26; 37:11-21)!

Likewise, the leaders' secret request or deal to the seers and prophets to "speak to us smooth things" (v. 10) exposes the leadership quality gone awry. In every system, whether political or religious, it is natural for leaders to favor those who flatter and praise them. Who, of ancient or today's world, would have enough guts to speak directly to the king, e.g., "Your majesty, you are wrong" (cf. 2 Sam 12:7; 1 Kgs 22:8; Jer 28:6-9), as opposed to the sweet swan songs, e.g., "Your majesty got it right again" (cf. 1 Kgs 22:6)? Yet, oftentimes, true leaders should not only be cautious of those "yes"-men and "yes"-women but also be willing to listen to those who criticize and speak the truth with genuine care and respect. Even in our time, both in government and in ecclesia, the society can steer more securely, metaphorically speaking, when our captains remain vigilant to those who warn of the storm or iceberg on the way. When the foolhardy and delusional captains ignore those warnings, the ship—be it a company, a community, or a nation—is destined to be shipwrecked. Brett Younger's scathing criticism of today's ethically anesthetized church, and society too, connects to our prophetic message:

> The early church believed for a time that affluence is a sin against those who are starving. They soon discovered that preaching that message tended to keep wealthy people from joining, so the church does not consider wealth a sin any more. The economic preferences of a materialistic society, rather than Jesus, have shaped our theology. (Younger 2013, 297)

Alas, they are so daring as to derail the right way, the proper path, ultimately forbidding people to call upon "the Holy One of Israel" (v. 11).

Nonetheless, "the Holy One of Israel" (v. 12), just censored by the governing system, retorts with righteous indignation against those hard-hearted leaders. God addresses them (pl.) directly, accusing them of rejecting the divine word (v. 8) and relying on a ludicrous protocol, i.e., "extortion and fraudulence." Alas, they do not know that "this iniquity"—the norm their regime values most—is the very cause for their society's sudden fall (v. 13). In fact, the regime's collapse will be like an entire wall so thoroughly shattered that not a single piece of a sherd can be found to scoop water from a puddle

(v. 14; cf. 29:16). J. Cheryl Exum elucidates the poetic technique involving similes that use many words like "crack, running down, bulging, breaking, shattering, smashed, fragments, and sherd," all painting both a slow-motion panoramic view and the thoroughness of the collapse of the wall. Its effect assures that "there is a certain aesthetic pleasure that comes from having our anticipation delayed and then confirmed" (Exum 1981, 334–35). Put another way, the poet is so emotionally enraged by the societal corruption, which seems like an insurmountable wall, that readers can sense the emotion put into the very utterances of poetic outcry—as though the poetic words and pictures are shattering the iron wall of the crooked regime.

Once again, "the Holy One of Israel" (v. 15) counters with the reminder as to what their secure route and value system should be: salvation through quiet repentance and strength through calm trust. To this reminder, their unambiguous response is, "No thanks!" (cf. v. 9). Therefore, soon they will flee (v. 16; cf. Lev 26:36-37). Their rapid flight will leave only a few of them remaining like a lonely flag on a hill (v. 17; cf. Deut 32:30).

Verses 18-26, as the counterpart or second half of this chapter, present divine assurance of deliverance if the inhabitants of Jerusalem will respond and act properly. Placed roughly at the center in the framework of chapter 30, v. 18 presents a core theme of this whole unit. Indeed, this verse too is itself chiastic, signifying a concept of what this unit is all about:

a—YHWH *waits* (*hakah*) to be gracious to you
   b—YHWH rises to have *compassion* on you
   b'—YHWH is a God of *justice*
a'—Happy are all who *wait* (*hakah*) for him

It is YHWH who "waits" to extend divine grace to the people. We should note that the HB does not refer to YHWH as the subject of the verb "to wait for" except in this verse: "A common term used to describe the human act of waiting in anticipation for God's benevolent intervention is transferred to YHWH in order to create a theological point of departure for the proclamation of renewed salvation after judgement [*sic*]" (Beuken 2000a, 171). As a counterpart, the motif of human waiting resumes in a wisdom admonition, "Happy are all who wait for him." Between these statements of assured hope, readers find two attributes of YHWH—the imagery of God's compassion (*rakham*), which shares the root of the word for "womb" (*rekhem*), and the imagery of God's stern justice.

Following this thematic refrain or chorus (v. 18), two subsequent illustrations elaborate on the thesis. In both cases, YHWH is the initial agent whose acts of grace result in the renewal of the people and nature (vv. 19-21 and vv. 22-26).

The first case (vv. 19-21) expounds the motif of hearing and seeing (cf. 6:9-10). As a counterpart to the self-serving royals who are busy crying out to Egypt, YHWH, who promised to be "gracious" (v. 18), now asserts the intention to be "gracious" to the outcry of the inhabitants of Zion (v. 19). With the emphatically repeated expressions, "in Zion . . . in Jerusalem," the prophet asserts the theme fundamental to the whole woe-cry, i.e., the divine promise of the renewal and repopulation of Zion. Because of this divine initiative of grace, the people will be able to "see" their Teacher with their eyes (v. 20) and "hear" divine direction on the path with their ears (v. 21).

The second case (vv. 22-26) demonstrates the ongoing impact of divine mercy, which extends not only to the people of Jerusalem (vv. 19-21) but also to the areas of ritual, agriculture, commerce, and even the cosmos. First, these repentant people will throw away the idols of gold and silver (v. 22; cf. Exod 32:4). Then, YHWH will provide rain and bread (v. 23a). In consequence, "on that day," cattle will graze (v. 23b) and be well fed (v. 24).

Moreover, streams will flow forth from "all high mountains" and "all lofty hills," on "the day" of the great massacre when "towers" fall (v. 25). Here the "towers" that fall recall the introductory thesis statement announcing YHWH's "day" against "all high mountains," "all lofty hills," and "every high tower" (cf. 2:12, 14-15). Ultimately, like the creation of the universe (Gen 1), even the moon will be bright and the sun seven times brighter (v. 26). This will be "the day" when YHWH binds up and heals the wounds of YHWH's people.

Verses 27-33 build upon the preceding subunit (vv. 18-26) and thereby wrap up this entire chapter with the culminating depiction of YHWH's irresistible power over Assyria. In order to parallel a formidable mythological character, towering over far inferior forces of Egypt or Assyria, this subunit illustrates various bodily and sensory parts of YHWH (vv. 27-30). Accordingly, not unlike mythological heroic figures, YHWH's anger produces smoke, and YHWH's "lips" and "tongue" consume fire (v. 27). YHWH's "breath" likewise compares with a gushing torrent thwarting nations and peoples (v. 28). Then, YHWH's people are to march with glad songs toward the holy mountain (v. 29). Theophany will not only introduce the divine "voice" but also reveal the divine "arm" (v. 30).

As a result of YHWH's glorious return, Assyria, which once boasted of its proud status as the "rod" of YHWH's anger and the "staff" of YHWH's indignation (10:5), will meet its demise (vv. 31-33). In an intertextual intensification, all key words in the earlier Assyrian woe-oracle—"rod, anger, staff, indignation" (10:5)—recur here in a dramatic fashion (30:27, 31-32) with the notion that, just like a boomerang that returns, Assyria, the rod and staff, will be shattered by YHWH's rod (v. 31) and staff (v. 32). A massive fire-pit is established, ready to be ignited by YHWH's "breath" (v. 33). Several key words—dense cloud (v. 27), night/darkness (v. 29), and rod/staff (v. 31)—in this prophetic denunciation are reminiscent of those in the Balaam Inscription, uttered by Balaam, son of Beor (*COS* II: 143).

Fifth Woe-Oracle—Against Judah's Reliance on Egypt, 31:1-9

This fifth woe-oracle continues the fourth woe-oracle in terms of the thematic focus on Judah's reliance on Egypt. Yet, while alluding to and commenting on the key linguistic and thematic notes of Isaiah 30, Isaiah 31 also has its own literary integrity, presenting decorated, heightened messages. This unit comprises three subunits. First, the condemnation targets the stubborn top officials who have become numb to any criticism (vv. 1-3). Next, in the central segment, the prophet reveals a secretive report of divine rescue hinted by YHWH (vv. 4-5). Finally, the call to return embraces the children of Israel, with the resumed reminder of Assyria's downfall (vv. 6-9).

Verses 1-3 unashamedly chastise Judah's policymakers. This woe-phrase, though reminiscent of 30:1-2, underscores a sharp contrast between the horses-chariots of Egypt and YHWH, the Holy One of Israel (v. 1). A key word in this subunit, the "helper" ('*ezrah*), appears in each verse. Notably, the word "helper" often refers to YHWH as the reliable source of rescue and protection (Pss 22:19 [MT 22:20]; 27:9; 63:7 [MT 63:8]; cf. Gen 2:18). Alas, these movers and shakers in the palace are going down to Egypt for help (v. 1). YHWH intends to bring evil upon these mischievous calculators, who are called the "house of" evildoers and the "helpers" in doing iniquity (v. 2). Because the Egyptians are mere mortals (cf. Pss 60:11 [MT 60:13]; 108:12 [MT 108:13]), against the outstretched hand of YHWH, such a volatile "helper" will stumble, fall, and come to an end (v. 3).

Verses 4-5, as the center of this chapter, shift attention to the prophet's own report of YHWH's impending glorious return. Here readers hear two images of YHWH's power. First, like a youthful menacing lion, YHWH will come down to Mount Zion to fight the threatening animals who are no match (v. 4). Second, like a swift flying bird, YHWH will hover and protect Jerusalem (v. 5). Here there is a sense of irony. Normally, a lion growling over its prey or a bird hovering in the sky denotes an image of attack. Yet these similes function to portray a reversed motif, connoting images of YHWH's protection as the One who will "defend, deliver, spare, and rescue" the faithful (Exum 1981, 338). Moreover, this imagery of YHWH as a protecting bird is significant if we read it against the backdrop of Sennacherib's siege of Jerusalem during the time of Hezekiah, when this Assyrian king described Jerusalem "like a bird in a cage." Here, the prophet counters such a pompous claim, affirming that YHWH indeed is coming as the most formidable and victorious bird.

Verses 6-9 reaffirm YHWH's salvific triumph over Assyria. In contrast to the prophet's denunciation of the "house of evildoers" (v. 2), he now exhorts the "children of Israel" to repent (v. 6). Following the "on that day" phrase, this penitent people are to throw away the idols of silver and gold (v. 7; cf. 30:22). This time there will be a role reversal in which the Assyrian king will fall by the sword (v. 8), consumed by YHWH's fire in Zion, in Jerusalem (v. 9).

Weal/Wow-Oracle—A Righteous Royal Savior under the Divine Spirit, 32:1-20

This unit does not start as one of the "woe" (*hoy*) oracles in Isaiah 28–33, but instead starts with a word somewhat akin to "wow"—"behold" or "look" (*hen*). Yet, in Hebrew, these words sound similar, both starting with the letter "h." Its rhetorical emphasis highlights the surprise factor when readers hear the word that virtually means the opposite of "woe." Nonetheless, Isaiah 32 continues key themes in connection with both the preceding and following chapters. In one respect, much as Isaiah 22 with the oracles against Jerusalem may function as a climax of the OAN section in Isaiah 13–23, Isaiah 32 may constitute the culmination of this woe-oracles section (Sweeney 2014, 692). Accordingly, in the final form, Isaiah 32 (weal-oracle or wow-oracle) provides the twofold closure of the five preceding woe-oracles in terms of the following overarching themes: the righteous leaders versus the male fools (Nabals) and the female royal oppressors, who will meet their just desserts when the spirit from on high comes in order to implement the prophetic words.

The oracle announces the dawn of a righteous king and justice-driven princes (vv. 1-2). This era will usher in an ideal world in which nobles and poor will be acknowledged but asinine male villains will stumble by their foolishness (vv. 3-8). As counterparts of the oppressive yet foolish male leaders of Jerusalem, the contemptuous female leaders of Jerusalem will meet the same ruinous fate (vv. 9-14). This vision of a better world will become available when the spirit from above comes, establishing a kingdom of justice, righteousness, peace, quietness, and security forever (vv. 15-20).

Verses 1-2 introduce the first of various groups—king and princes—this chapter will address (e.g., villains, knaves, poor, needy, complacent women, and "my people"). Over against the fragile sources of help in Egypt and the self-serving rulers of Judah (Isa 30–31), a righteous king will arise (v. 1).

Unlike the "princes" of Assyria who will run away in panic (31:9), the "princes" of this new era will rule with justice (cf. Prov 8:15-16). In this time of justice, the righteous ruler will be like a hiding place, like a cleft of the rock, and like the "streams of water" (v. 2; cf. Ps 1:3; Prov 21:1).

Verses 3-8 portray this era in a topsy-turvy reversal of fortunes so that villains will fall by their treacherous acts and nobles will receive their honor. This subunit contains two subparts, each starting with the negative particle "not" (*lo'*)—vv. 3-4 and vv. 5-8. In the first subpart (vv. 3-4), we find intertextual allusions. Whereas the obstinate people kept hearing but did "not" (*'al*) understand and kept seeing but did "not" (*'al*) know with the result of their eyes being further "blinded" (6:9-10), now their eyes will "not" (*lo'*) be "blinded" and those with ears will listen (v. 3). Whereas earlier they neither "understood" nor "knew" due to their stubborn "heart" (6:9-10), now the governing "heart" will "understand" and "know (v. 4a). Whereas the prophet announced divine message with stammering lips and foreign "tongue" (28:11), now the "tongue" of the stammerers will speak eloquently (v. 4b).

In the second subpart (vv. 5-8), readers find scathing mockery of elite male leaders, now identified as fools, as if echoing the episode of Nabal whose name means "folly" (1 Sam 25:25). The second negative particle indicates that this era will set right a corrupted society in which nobles and scoundrels will "not" (*lo'*) be confused (v. 5). The prophet exposes villainous rulers as fools who utter nonsense, act foolishly against YHWH, abandon the hungry empty, deprive the thirsty of drink (v. 6), devise evil deeds against the poor, and withhold justice from the needy (v. 7). Contrary to the wicked who will not "stand" but perish (cf. Ps 1:5-6), however, those who preserve and practice honorable deeds will "stand" (v. 8).

Verses 9-14 accuse and denounce elite female leaders, just like their male counterparts—all the Nabals (vv. 5-8). Alas, unlike Abigail who prudently escaped her foolish husband's ill fate (cf. 1 Sam 25), these pretentious women will meet the same fate as the corrupt male thugs. The first address to these arrogant women (vv. 9-10) calls them to "stand" (cf. v. 8). It is now their turn to hear the solemn judgment. By next year around this time, these confident women will learn of the failure of the harvest. The second address then unveils the impending doom of these arrogant women (vv. 11-14). No longer standing, they are to be terrified and troubled, ordered to undress and put on sackcloth (v. 11). They are to cry loudly concerning their delightful fields, which they have been hoarding and abusing over against the poor (v. 12). "Thorns and thistles" (cf. 5:6) will come upon the land, which was meant for YHWH's people and not just for the rich and the powerful few, and also against the "exultant city" (v. 13; cf. 22:2; 23:7). Their secure palace and crowded city will be deserted (v. 14).

Verses 15-20, however, present YHWH's proclamation of the dawn of a new era for the glorious restoration of "my people" after divine judgment upon corrupt leaders. This time will arrive through the outpouring of the spirit (vv. 15-17). In contrast to the arrogant women who are chastised to "lay bare" ('*arah*, v. 11), the time of hope will come when the spirit on high is made manifest ('*arah*, v. 15). Justice and righteousness will blossom, whether in the desert or in the garden-land (v. 16). Now there will be genuine peace, tranquility, and security (v. 17).

The theme of highs versus lows accentuates the reversal of fortunes. The anointing of the spirit "*from the height*," from the exalted God, makes a sharp contrast with the downfall of the military and political powers of the haughty human beings. Earlier, the prophet announced a doom to those who "go down" to Egypt for help (31:1), as YHWH is said to "rise up" against those evildoers (31:2) and "come down" to fight them on Mount Zion (31:4). How is it so? It is because Egyptians are human and their horses are "flesh," not "spirit" (31:3), while Assyrians too will "fall" (31:8). The forest will "come down" and the city be "laid low" (32:19). Thus, when God "rises up" to be "exalted" and dwell "on high" (33:3, 5, 10), God promises to lift up not the sinners and godless but those humble and upright to dwell "*on the heights*" (33:14-16; cf. 32:15; Kim 2014, 151–52).

Like the flock led in green pastures (cf. Ps 23:2), "my people" will dwell in a peaceful resting place (v. 18). Contrary to the "complacent" (*sha'anan*) elite women (vv. 9, 11), this people will live in the truly "secure" (*sha'anan*) places. This will be the time when the proud city will crumble down, bad news to the high officials (v. 19). In contrast, YHWH calls the downtrodden, righteous people to be happy, since they will sow beside the waters (cf. Ps 1:3) and safely shepherd the ox and the donkey that appreciate their trustworthy owners (v. 20; cf. 1:3).

Sixth Woe-Oracle—Against the Superpower Empires, Zion's Enemies, 33:1-24

This sixth woe-oracle functions both as the conclusion of the section of six woe-oracles (Isa 28–33) and also as a transition to the subsequent sections (Isa 34–35 and Isa 36–39). At the same time, Isaiah 33 is an additional closure, as though an adaptation (*Fortschreibung*) of the preceding five woe-cries. While the first five woe-oracles pronounced condemnation against the leaders of Jerusalem (Isa 28–31), the sixth woe-oracle rebukes the superpower destroyers, in defense of Zion (Isa 33). In the broader scope, Isaiah 33 also functions both as a concluding summary of Isaiah 1–32 and as "an editorial bridge" between the two halves of the book of Isaiah (Balogh 2008, 477).

By reiterating key words and motifs from Isaiah 28–32, chapter 33 wraps up this woe-oracle section and reprises several themes in culmination. First, unlike the preceding woe-oracles that condemn the haughty rulers of Israel and Judah (Isa 28–29) and their reliance on Egypt (Isa 30–31), YHWH now condemns the unruly superpowers, Assyria and Babylon, that will soon encounter their own doom. Second, whereas the preceding oracle announced the rise of a righteous human king over the foolish, corrupt male and female leaders of Jerusalem (Isa 32), now the announcement is that YHWH will come to rule and protect as the exalted, divine King. Third, amid the "we"-group's laments over the reality of ongoing hardships and incessant oppression (Isa 28–32), now the prophet announces the indispensable restoration and renewal of Zion, where the penitent and the upright will find refuge. Furthermore, Isaiah 33 also shares many key terms with Isaiah 34–35, thereby forming close compositional and thematic ties, which we will delineate below.

This unit contains three subunits. First, the prophet sounds the liturgy of communal lament on behalf of the "we"-group amid rampant oppression while at the same time denouncing the oppressor and declaring YHWH's exaltation in Zion (vv. 1-9). Next, the prophet conveys the divine answer to the preceding petition that YHWH will rise to purge the wicked enemies but to provide a shelter to the upright (vv. 10-16). Finally, the prophet exhorts the faithful "we"-group that it will experience miraculous deliverance and flourish under divine guidance in Zion (vv. 17-24).

Verses 1-9 report the communal lament of the "we"-group to whom the prophet promises that the deity will vanquish its oppressors. The "king" in 32:1 is anonymous. Similarly, here the "smasher" and the "betrayer" are not identified (v. 1; cf. 21:2). Yet one thing is certain: the impending doom of these undefeated oppressors. Here the prophecy, that after they are done destroying they will be destroyed, echoes the similar expression concerning Assyria as the tool of divine purpose and subsequent punishment in 10:5-19. Likewise, the Hebrew word for the "smasher" (shoded . . . shadud) with its strong "sh" sound may imply a pun with the word "Assyria" (ashur). The intended setting of Sennacherib's siege of Jerusalem around 701 BCE further heightens the likelihood that this smasher or shatterer is Assyria (Balogh 2008, 494–95). We may wonder, however, whether, by the same token, the word "betrayer" (boged . . . bagedu) alludes to the word "Babylon" (babel). Since Joseph Blenkinsopp posits that both the serpent and Rahab function as "code names" for Egypt (cf. 27:1; 30:7), at one point, these terms may have functioned similarly as "code names" (Blenkinsopp 2000a, 372 and 383). In this case, on the one hand, the prophet may be using code words to take a more audaciously derogatory shot at these daunting empires. On the other hand, the anonymity may open the possibility that subsequent readers can identify the oppressor with any contemporary enemy power. Be that as it may, YHWH denounces the smasher and betrayer in direct address, "you."

Next we hear the communal lament of the "we"-group (vv. 2-4). As if responding to the divine mercy promised in the central statement of the fourth woe-oracle, "YHWH waits to be gracious to you . . . Happy are all who wait for him" (30:18), now the people ask God, "Be gracious to us, we wait for you" (v. 2). At the divine roar, "peoples" and "nations" will flee away (v. 3; cf. 17:12-13), running about like the swarm of locusts (v. 4; cf. Joel 1:4; 2:25).

Now the prophet offers words of assurance (vv. 5-6). Here the prophet reaffirms who the truly exalted one is, who will govern Zion with justice and righteousness (v. 5; cf. 2:11, 17), and who is the source of salvation (v. 6; cf. v. 2). We note that the "ox" and "donkey" in the previous oracle (32:20) forms a nice bracket with the "ox" and "donkey" of the opening oracle of the book of Isaiah (1:3). By the same token, here the notion of YHWH's exaltation (33:5) builds another inclusio with the initial thesis oracle (2:11, 17). Likewise, Zion, once "full of justice and righteousness" (1:21), will regain her lofty place when YHWH will "fill Zion with justice and righteousness" (33:5; Williamson 1994, 233–34). Chapter 33, accordingly, not only wraps up the woe-oracles of Isaiah 28–32 but also together with chapter 32 forms a bracket with Isaiah 1–2.

Yet this subunit continues to the description of the grim reality of desolation (vv. 7-9). Here the valiant warriors are crying out in the street (v. 7; cf. 19:16). The valiant ones (or, "the people of Ariel"; 'er'ellam) recall the city Ariel ('ari'el) in 29:1, just as the phrase "the Arielites cry out in the street" ('er'ellam tsa'aqu hutsah) in 33:7 shares similar phonetic tones with the phrase "I will bring distress to Ariel" (hatsiqoti la'ari'el) in 29:2. Together we find a common theme: just as the proud city where the great warrior king David once encamped is to become a city of mourning and lamentation (29:1-2), the valiant warriors of Ariel will be subdued and humiliated (33:7; cf. Balogh 2008, 497). Whereas the exilic prophet will call for the "herald of peace" (mebaser . . . shalom, 52:7; cf. 40:9), at present the "messengers of shalom" (mal'aki shalom) weep bitterly. Highways are deserted and the covenant is broken (v. 8; cf. 24:5; 35:8; 40:3). As a result, the earth mourns, just as shame and decay will cover Lebanon, Sharon, Bashan, and Carmel (v. 9; cf. 2:13; 35:2; Nah 1:4).

Verses 10-16 pronounce YHWH's answer to the "we"-group's collective petition. This subunit highlights the contrast between the wicked and the upright in the international (vv. 10-12) and domestic realms (vv. 13-16). Now, in the worldwide realm, YHWH declares the intention to arise and be exalted (*rum . . . nasa'*, v. 10; cf. 6:1). This exalted Lord addresses the wicked as "you" (pl.), as the begetters of "chaff" and "stubble" (v. 11; cf. 5:24). Recalling the "wind" (*ruakh*; cf. Ps 1:4) that blows away the chaff, the prophet rebukes them, "your breath (*ruakh*) will devour you like a fire." Peoples too will be like thorns burned by fire (v. 12; cf. v. 3).

Next, divine admonition covers the addressees in both far (international) and now near (domestic) settings (v. 13; cf. 57:19). Here readers learn of another group, the "sinners" and the godless within Zion, who also lament in the first-person plural. The text depicts the wicked, also present in Zion, as "sojourning" (*gur*) in the midst of everlasting flames. On the other hand, again echoing the righteous who do not walk in the path of sinners (cf. Ps 1:1), the prophet illustrates six qualifications for the righteous: (a) walking righteously, (b) speaking uprightness, (c) rejecting gain from extortion, (d) waving away bribery, (e) blocking ears from tempting lures of bloodshed, and (f) shutting eyes from evil. As a reward, unlike the wicked, the righteous will cherish security and nourishment, "dwelling" in the heights, the fortresses of rocks (v. 16).

Verses 17-24—"the climax of the entire chapter" (Sweeney 1996, 425)—culminate this unit with the promise of a righteous reign and protection for the "we"-group in Zion. It is not clear whether the king in v. 17 is a human king or the divine King YHWH. If the former, this king corresponds to the good Davidic king promised in 32:1, who will accomplish a righteous reign with charisma, no longer with extortion or stammering words (Beuken 2000a, 246–47). The description of this virtuous human king would then form a neat inclusio surrounding Isaiah 32–33, at the beginning (32:1-8) and at the end (33:17-24; Blenkinsopp 2000a, 445). If the latter, this subunit complements the implementation of the new era: overthrowing the oppressive ruler prepares for the appearance of YHWH as the divine King (Sweeney 1996, 422–25). Turning the audience from the wicked ("you") in v. 11 now to the upright ("you"), the prophet passionately consoles the lamenters (vv. 2-4) with the vision and hope for the restoration of Zion where the upright will dwell under perfect governance.

What would the faithful people's secure future look like? The prophet previews a foretaste of this glorious future in the emotional dialogues with "you" (vv. 17-19). This era indeed will be marvelous, bringing a miraculous reversal of the previous time of rebellion and obstinacy (6:1-12). No longer blinded by bloodshed or evil (cf. v. 15), and no longer reserved only for the prophet (cf. 6:1, 5), the whole people's "eyes" will behold the divine King in beauty and majesty (v. 17). No longer sent "far away" (*rakhaq*, 6:12), they will see the territory of the new king that reaches "far away" (*merekhoq*). Moreover, no longer made dull (6:10), their "heart" will meditate in awe concerning the disappearance of the harsh taskmasters, tax collectors, and overseers (v. 18). Likewise, the menacing foreign attackers will disappear—those folks with speech too strange to "hear" and too stammering to "understand" (v. 19; cf. 6:9-10; 28:11).

What then will they see? They are called to behold Zion, Jerusalem (v. 20), where the penitent and upright will no longer sing a song of lament (vv. 2-4) but of salvation (vv. 21-22). They will not only see the trustworthy King (v. 17) but also behold Zion, Jerusalem, the city of YHWH and the center of their homeland (v. 20). Here, bracketed by the passages addressing "you" (vv. 17-20 and vv. 23-24), the song of salvation (vv. 21-22) marks the structural and thematic center of this subunit. Surely, in Zion, the seasonal festivals will resume (cf. Lev 23; Deut 16) and the sacred temple of "secure abode" will never be destroyed or uprooted (cf. 32:18). All the exiled people—the repentant and the devout alike—will shout the song of salvation that "there" (*sham*; cf. Ps 137:1), back in Zion, "YHWH will be for us" (v. 21; cf. 7:14; 8:8, 10). There, in Jerusalem with rivers and streams wider than Nile or Euphrates, no ships threatening attack will ever enter (cf. Num 24:24; Ezek 30:9). As though a recurring refrain of a popular song, this "we"-group then sings of YHWH, "our judge . . . our commander . . . our king," their savior (v. 22; cf. vv. 2, 6). Readers can picture the *akītu* festival when the new Assyrian king would be installed and the Sangu priest would proclaim, "Ashur is King! Ashur is King!" (Perdue and Carter 2015, 37). Against this backdrop, the song subversively counters, "YHWH is our King!" (cf. Pss 93:1; 95:3; 96:10; 97:1; 98:6; 99:1).

How can the people regain their status? Whereas the Assyrians seized spoil and took plunder (10:6), in this coming era even the lame will seize the spoil of their former oppressors (v. 23; cf. Exod 12:35-36). Whereas the entire population of Judah, from top to bottom, were "sick" (1:5-6), now no inhabitant will become "sick" anymore (v. 24). Residents of this restored Zion will be forgiven their iniquity (cf. 1:4; 5:18; 22:14; 40:2). This promise of forgiveness entails significant thematic implications. On one level, just as one individual's—the prophet Isaiah's—iniquity was forgiven (1:6), now the whole people of Zion will receive forgiveness. On another level, consequently, the people who will receive deliverance and the protection of the divine King may not be limited to the upright ones per se but may include all those who humbly return and repent (cf. 30:15).

Doom to the Enemies and Restoration for the Faithful, 34:1–35:10

Many books of the HB have more than one conclusion. Whether due to redactional additions or for the sake of emphasis, somewhat similar to the "Pomp and Circumstance" orchestral music, readers can find repeated wrap-ups. Thus, in the present form, we can consider chapters 32, 33, and 34–35 as closures of the first half of the book of Isaiah.

First, Isaiah 32 forms an inclusio with Isaiah 1. The beatitude-like closure in 32:20, with the catchwords "ox" and "donkey," forms a legitimate bracket with the same catchwords in 1:3 (Beuken 1998, 23–24). The people condemned as more asinine and rebellious than ox and donkey in Isaiah 1, thus, are now admonished to gain blessing in a new era of a righteous king in Isaiah 32.

Second, W. A. M. Beuken calls Isaiah 33 a "mirror text" (*Spiegel-text*) for the book of Isaiah (Beuken 1991, 27–28): Isaiah 1–2 and Isaiah 33 together are a pair of bookends that holds what is between them. In particular, it announces the cure of sickness and forgiveness of sins (33:24) that will reverse Israel's status of sickness (1:5). Also, the qualifications of the righteous, especially those with power and authority (33:14-16), correspond to the expectations detailed previously (1:16-17, 21-26; Sweeney 1996, 430). Similarly, the description of YHWH's exaltation (33:5, 10) builds a nice inclusio with the thematic expressions of humbling all that are high and proud (2:11, 17). Likewise, the lofty trees of "Lebanon" and "Bashan" (2:13) recur in the comparable motif of their shameful withering (33:9). Put together, therefore, we may surmise that Isaiah 32–33 is the closing bracket to Isaiah 1–2, thereby enclosing the first part of the book of Isaiah (Blenkinsopp 2000a, 445).

Finally, Isaiah 34–35 conclude the first half of the final form of the book of Isaiah. Although Isaiah 32 and 33 may have been compiled to be conclusions at certain redactional stages, the final form continues with Isaiah 34–35. Marvin Sweeney addresses key echoes of Isaiah 1 in Isaiah 34: "the call to attention (Isa. 1:2; 34:1); YHWH's vengeance (Isa. 1:24; 34:8); unquenchable burning (Isa. 1:24; 34:10); YHWH's mouth has spoken (Isa. 1:20; 34:16); the sword of punishment (Isa. 1:20; 34:5-6); sacrificial blood and fat (Isa. 1:11-15; 34:6-7); Sodom and Gomorrah (Isa. 1:7-10; 34:9-10); and wilting leaves (Isa. 1:30; 34:4)" (2014, 695). These parallels between the two chapters evince that "the portrayal of YHWH's judgment against Edom and the nations in ch. 34 is designed to provide a complement and counterpoint to the portrayal of judgment against Israel and Zion in ch. 1" (Sweeney 1996, 442).

Accordingly, scholars have insightfully identified Isaiah 34–35 as the bridge that connects the preceding and following sections, especially through the themes of punishment (ch. 34 wrapping up Isa 1–33) and of restoration (ch. 35 anticipating Isa 40–66): "The two major themes of the chapters, namely, the divine judgment of the nations [Isa 34] and the return of the redeemed to Zion [Isa 35], point both backward to the earlier Isaianic prophecies as well as forward to the ensuing chapters" (Childs 2001, 253; cf. Steck 1985, 39–79; Mathews 1995, 157–79). Furthermore, the present study proposes that Isaiah 36–39 is the center of the entire book of Isaiah—as will be discussed in the next section. From this perspective, it is possible to consider Isaiah 34–35 as another conclusion to the first half of the final form of the Isaiah scroll, which also paves the way thematically not only for Isaiah 40–66 but especially for Isaiah 36–39, the apex of the whole book of Isaiah.

Doom of Edom/Enemies—YHWH Has a Day of Retribution, 34:1-17

This oracle (Isa 34) is one side of a single coin: the message of Edom's doom paired with its opposite counterpart, the message of Judah's bloom (Isa 35). Reading consecutively thus far, it seems out of place that Edom occurs here as a target of divine punishment, because it would fit more appropriately within the OAN section (Isa 13–23). When compared with the Twelve Prophets, however, it is noteworthy that Obadiah concerns Edom while the subsequent Jonah and Nahum both concern Assyria. In Isaiah, we have the oracle concerning Edom (Isa 34) and then narratives concerning Assyria (Isa 36–39). It is plausible to posit that the final redactor(s)—of Isaiah and of the Twelve Prophets—intended to preserve the comparable pattern. Alternatively, some textual references depict Phoenicia (Isa 23) and Edom (Isa 34) as the "two nations that oppressed the Judeans most severely during the exilic period" (Albertz 2003b, 228; cf. Ezek 25:12; 35:5, 10, 12, 15; Amos 1:9-12; Obad 10-14; Ps 137:7). Be that as it may, Isaiah 34 singles out Edom (vv. 5-6), entwined with the "nations" (vv. 1-2), as a symbol for "all nations, both now and in the future, who would dare to rise up against YHWH" (Beuken 2000a, 286; cf. Dicou 1991, 30, 34–35; Seitz 1993, 237–38). The prophet announces their doom to the whole world, demonstrating the surety of YHWH's vindication and instilling hope in the downtrodden.

Verses 1-15 contain the main oracle of this chapter, as vv. 16-17 are more like a summary appendix. This main oracle reveals a chiasm that centers on Edom's doom (vv. 5-11) and ultimately on the day of YHWH (v. 8):

vv. 1-4—Ban (*haram*) on all the nations
   vv. 5-7—Sword will "go down" on Edom
      v. 8— *The day of YHWH*
   vv. 9-11—Smoke will "go up" forever
vv. 12-15—No kingdom and princes

The ban on all the nations (vv. 1-4) echoes and inverts the call to heaven and earth in Isaiah 1 as well as the worldwide pilgrimage of nations and peoples in Isaiah 2. Whereas YHWH calls "heavens" and "earth" to hear the divine message (1:2), now the call starts from the earth (v. 1) and moves toward the "heavens" (v. 4; cf. Gen 2:4b). Likewise, the call to "nations" and "peoples" here alludes to the pilgrimage of "nations" and "peoples" in Isaiah 2 (2:2-4). Countering the claim of worldwide peace when nations will learn war no more or reinterpreting the claim as disarming of superpowers (2:4), now the prophet proclaims divine war against nations with utter destruction and slaughter (v. 2). Instead of the nations' pilgrimage to "go up" (*'alah*) to YHWH's mountain (2:3), now the corpses of the nations will "go up" (*'alah*) and mountains will melt with blood (v. 3). Reverting back to the primordial time of chaos, all heavenly forces will wither away (v. 4).

The middle segment (vv. 5-11) portrays slaughter (vv. 5-7) and burning (vv. 9-11) in the most horrific ways imaginable, as if graphically reporting the utter destruction (ban) of Edom. Sandwiching the central statement of the "day" of YHWH's vengeance and the "year" of YHWH's vindication (v. 8), these two surrounding subunits employ directional expressions of going down and going up to depict the cities in war and debacle.

As though the announcement of the cosmic and global upheaval (vv. 1-4) were only an overture, the brutal slaughter hits Edom hard (vv. 5-7). Thus, the divine sword from the heavenly battle will "come down" upon Edom with the ban of complete annihilation (v. 5). Whereas the hands of the rebellious generation were "filled with blood" (1:15), now YHWH's sword will be "filled with blood" (v. 6). Echoing Israel's futile burnt offerings (1:11), this passage now declares that the whole land of Edom is to become burnt offerings (v. 7; cf. v. 10).

At the center of this whole unit, the prophet declares the day of YHWH—the day of vengeance and the year of retribution (v. 8), reminiscent of the day of YHWH in Isaiah 2 (2:12; cf. 61:2; 63:4).

Corresponding to the depiction of slaughter (vv. 5-7), the description of the day of YHWH further details the drastic burning of Edom (vv. 9-11). Again, as though the entire land of Edom becomes the burnt offering, burning consumes its streams and territories into "brimstone" like Sodom and Gomorrah (v. 9; cf. Gen 19:24). Unlike on Mount Sinai where "the smoke went up" accompanying divine theophany (Exod 19:18), now on Mount Bozrah "the smoke will go up" in a devastating conflagration (v. 10). Edom will ultimately revert back to a "formless void" (*tohu . . . bohu*; v. 11), the state of chaos prior to creation (Gen 1:2). The "line of chaos" (*qav-tohu*) and the "stones of turmoil" (*'abne-bohu*) further echo the "line" and "cornerstone of the world" in Job 38:5-6, the creation language of which hints that YHWH "is engaged in a work of uncreation" (Blenkinsopp 2001, 42).

The announcement of Edom's demise is not over yet. If readers consider the preceding subunit to be a legitimate climax on Edom's doom, they are mistaken. We now hear the louder climactic tones of curse upon Edom (vv. 12-15). Adding to the expression of the "formless void" of primordial chaos in Genesis (v. 11), the prophet now nullifies Edom as "no (*'eyin*) kingdom there" and its princes as "nothing (*'epes*)" (v. 12), echoing the expression that occurs uniquely in Isaiah 40–48 (cf. Isa 40:17; 41:12; 45:6, 14, 22; 46:9; 47:10). Further expressions of Edom's desolation consist of "thorns" and "briers" (v. 13), albeit with different Hebrew words than those in previous texts (5:6; 7:23-25). There, the fact that Edom will turn into the habitat for "jackals" (*tan*), "ostriches" (*ya'anah*), "hyenas" (*'i*), and "goat-demons" (*sa'ir*) also equates Edom's fate with that of Babylon (vv. 13-15; cf. 13:20-22).

Verses 16-17, despite their appendix-like content, marvelously echo key phrases and motifs from Isaiah 1, much the same way vv. 1-15 share expressions with Isaiah 1. At the same time, by echoing Isaiah 1, these sentences wrap up the entire previous collection (Isa 1–34). Hence, the catchphrase, "for the mouth of YHWH has commanded" (v. 16), brackets with that of 1:20, "for the mouth of YHWH has spoken." Thus, YHWH not only assures the trustworthiness of this scroll (v. 16) but also guarantees the lot securely provided for the faithful people (v. 17), for whom the subsequent song of restoration resonates (Isa 35).

Bloom of Judah—A Transformative Future, 35:1-10

This oracle, with hope for the joyful restoration of Judah and Zion, is the literary and thematic counterpart to Isaiah 34. When read together, the dichotomy between Edom and Judah stands out through key linguistic and thematic contrasts. The wicked will perish and the righteous will stand; Edom will meet its doom and gloom but Judah will bloom and blossom.

Numerous intertextual citations of and allusions to other texts in the book of Isaiah aside (e.g., with chs. 1–2; 33; 40–41; cf. Kim 2009, 166–73), this unit exhibits intriguing rhetorical formats that, by way of the first words of each verse, form a chiastic whole:

v. 1—"rejoice" (*sus*)
v. 2—"blossom" (*parakh*)
   v. 3—"strengthen" (*hazaq*) [imperative]
   v. 4—"say" (*'amar*) [imperative]
      v. 5—"then" (*'az*)
      v. 6—"then" (*'az*)
   v. 7—"and it will be" (*hayah*)
   v. 8—"and it will be there" (*hayah-sham*)
   v. 9—"it will not be there" (*lo'* + *hayah-sham*)
v. 10a—"the ransomed" (*padah*)
v. 10b—"rejoicing" (*sason*)

The initial statements (vv. 1-2) instantly contrast the desolated Edom (Isa 34) with the rejuvenated desert and wilderness. Thus, the "desert" and "wilderness" will rejoice (v. 1; cf. v. 6). Countering the previous shame (33:9), Judah will attain the majesty of Lebanon, Carmel, and Sharon and "see" the glory of YHWH (v. 2; cf. v. 5; 40:5). A triad of fertility—Lebanon-Carmel-Sharon—will now replace what Walter Brueggemann calls the triad of deathliness—wilderness-dry land-desert (1998a, 275). Desert and wilderness symbolize drought and death. Nonetheless, the Israelites of the first exodus generation persevered on the long journeys through the wilderness, which led them into the land of milk and honey. For this miraculous vision, the poet anticipates that the desert is "the ultimate starting point of the journey" in joyful return to Zion and to life (Beuken 2000a, 311).

The two imperatives (vv. 3-4) accentuate the addressees for whom God shows utmost concern—those with "weak hands," "shaking knees" (v. 3; cf. Job 4:3-4), and "anxious heart" (v. 4; cf. 6:9-10). Whereas YHWH's day of "recompense" (*naqam*) in 34:8 accompanies Edom's doom, God's coming with "recompense" (*naqam*) in 35:4 entails Zion's salvation. This catchword underscores the intricate thematic linkage of chapter 34 and 35 in that "Edom and Israel are each other's counterparts" (Dicou 1991, 42). Furthermore, whereas the earlier salvation oracle admonished only King Ahaz "to fear not" (7:4), now this message addresses many who are discouraged and disheartened. Interestingly, these verses start with the word "to strengthen" (*hazaq*; a root word in the name Hezekiah) and end with the word "to save" (*yasha'*; a root word in the name Isaiah). On one level, as the subsequent core section (Isa 36–39) will highlight, both Hezekiah and Isaiah will play crucial roles in setting examples of faith and deliverance. Yet, on a deeper level, both names, Hezekiah and Isaiah, emphasize the source of such strength and salvation, YHWH, who "will save you" (v. 4).

The central piece of this oracle underscores the most socially ostracized group, announcing their renewal (vv. 5-6). Echoing and reversing the hardening of the hearts of recalcitrant people (6:9-10), this oracle proclaims the intensified transformation of the blind, deaf, lame, and mute.

Even animals and nature will experience dramatic reversal and restoration (vv. 7-9). Thus, through the surging streams of water (v. 6), there will be a dramatic transformation of not only the dry soil into well-watered fertile fields but also of the habitat of jackals into rushes for choice produce (v. 7; cf. 34:13; Beuken 2000a, 322). There will be a highway in the wilderness for the second exodus (v. 8). This highway undergoes a metamorphosis into a holy way. The motif of the "way" is a key thread that binds the entire book of Isaiah together (Mathews 1995, 131–35): "The most explicit link is the theme of the highway or processional route with which ch. 35 ends and ch. 40 begins" (Blenkinsopp 2000a, 457). Moreover, this way is "holy" in that no "unclean," no "fools," no "lions," and no "ferocious beasts" can enter it (vv. 8b-9a; cf. Hos 5:14). W. A. M. Beuken connects the word "fool" here with the same word in 19:11 for the "foolish" princes of Egypt who led the land astray. Also related to the foolish elites ("Nabals") of Jerusalem (32:5-8), we can deduce that those leaders who shrewdly put their reliance in superpowers or elsewhere than God are indeed fools who cannot join this glorious journey (Beuken 2000a, 324). Who then can walk in the way? Like the weak and feeble (v. 3), and the blind, deaf, lame, and mute (vv. 5-6), the disenfranchised yet redeemed will walk on it (v. 9b; cf. Lim 2010, 157).

The closure of this glorious song of return (cf. 51:11) reasserts the glorious future of these transformed people: the ransomed of YHWH, all those downtrodden yet repentant and faithful, will return to Zion (v. 10). Whereas Isaiah 51 primarily focuses on the return of those in exile, here Isaiah 35 projects the transformed world in more inclusive and universalistic ways (Harrelson 1994, 254).

Hopeful Stories of Trust and Deliverance amid Imperial Threats (Central Branch of the Lampstand)

Isaiah 36–39

Most interpreters nowadays no longer consider Isaiah 36–39 an oddity, appendix, or insertion that has virtually nothing to do with the rest of the book of Isaiah. Rather, many scholars find valuable redactional and thematic functions of this section, especially as a bridge between the two halves of the book of Isaiah. In light of recent approaches to reading the book as a unified whole, the present study proposes that this section is not just a hinge or bridge but rather the core of the entire book of Isaiah. Reading the book of Isaiah as a literary cathedral comprising seven acts, Ulrich Berges similarly proposes this section as the center: "Contrary to the widespread opinion that these chapters are only an 'historical appendix', . . . [these chapters] are the centrepiece [sic] of the dramatic unfolding of the book as a whole" (Berges 2012c, 42). We should further note that Isaiah 34–35 and 40–41 share many linguistic parallels, thereby together sandwiching and bracketing 36–39 as the apex of the entire scroll (Kim 2009; Childs 2001, 301–302).

Compositionally, this section has its parallel account in 2 Kings 18–20. Scholars have debated as to whether the Isaiah text borrowed from the Kings text or the Kings text borrowed from the Isaiah text. Despite the plausibility of both theories—whether Isaiah 36–39 is dependent on 2 Kings 18–20 (Williamson 1996) or 2 Kings 18–20 is dependent on Isaiah 36–39 (Seitz 1991)—it seems evident that the diachronic development went through much more complex venues and routes. More probably, therefore, an original document found its way into both 2 Kings and Isaiah, and even 2 Chronicles, and underwent different adaptations in each text and context (Beuken 2010, 379–80). Although there are many parallels in both accounts, differences are notable and deserve careful attention for some valuable interpretive insights. We should thus note not only the overall arrangement of various units and subunits in both accounts but also the function of the passages that are unique in each account, e.g., 2 Kings 18:14-16 (only in 2 Kings) and

Isaiah 38:9-20 (only in Isaiah). We will compare the Hezekiah account in 2 Chronicles 32 as well, which can shed further light.

Historically, the primary setting connects this account with Sennacherib's siege of Jerusalem in 701 BCE, especially Isaiah 36–37, if not Isaiah 38 as well. The Assyrian royal inscription claims that he has successfully invaded and pillaged the city of Jerusalem: "The Assyrian Annals report 46 cities of Judah conquered, 205,105 prisoners led away, and Hezekiah locked up like a bird in a cage" (Berges 2012a, 259). To the contrary, the biblical accounts assert that YHWH's miraculous intervention defeated the Assyrians and Sennacherib was assassinated back in Nineveh.

These chapters display numerous intertextual allusions, including linguistic and thematic ties with the rest of the book of Isaiah (Williamson 1998a, 249). Besides the most obvious ones (2 Kgs 18–20 and 2 Chr 32), this section should be read in dialogue with Isaiah 7 (Ahaz), as well as the book of Jonah (two similar episodes concerning Assyria). Because Jonah stands beyond the scope of this study, we will compare the narratives of Ahaz and Hezekiah, which Peter Ackroyd has already astutely expounded (Ackroyd 1987, 105–20).

Overall, an initial comparison with 2 Kings 18–20 and Isaiah 7 yields the following observations and insights. Whereas 2 Kings presents a more sober historical report on Hezekiah as a king with fragile faith who grows through dramatic events, and so repents and matures in faith, Isaiah portrays Hezekiah from the outset as an ideal role model, a symbol of devout faith. Whereas King Ahaz pays tribute, makes a vassal alliance with Assyria, and so fails to trust in YHWH, King Hezekiah does not succumb to Assyria but rather appears as a human leader of courage and piety.

Thematically at the center stage, and literally and rhetorically as the central piece within the book of Isaiah, it is not Ahaz but Hezekiah who receives the spot light. This is significant because the root of the name Hezekiah (*hazaq*) denotes "trust" (lit., "to strengthen [faith]"). The theme of "trust" plays a significant role in the theology of the book of Isaiah (Isa 7:9; 28:16; 30:15; cf. Isa 39:1; 2 Chr 32:5, 7). In this respect, there is another key character in the spotlight. The root of the name Isaiah (*yasha'*) denotes "save." The word "to deliver, save" likewise presents a major theme: "Does their use of a different term for deliverance contain some acknowledgement of the name Isaiah ('YHWH saves')?" (Beuken 2000a, 340).

In a way, we may say that, from the viewpoint of the central section of Isaiah, this book is really about the model prophet *Isaiah* and the model king *Hezekiah*. Historically or redactionally speaking, it is not certain how reliable the variant biblical sources are in reconstructing Hezekiah's political record vis-à-vis his alleged model faith. Theologically speaking, however, the pivotal event and collective cultural memory of 701 BCE must have constituted a lasting legacy for the Isaianic community. Some contemporary analogies of the impact of such historic legacy might be the invasion of Normandy for the allied forces, the liberation of the nation of Korea on August 15, 1945, after forty-five years of occupation by Imperial Japan, or the end of apartheid in South Africa in 1993, two years after Nelson Mandela's release from imprisonment. This one punctual event of YHWH's miraculous delivery of the disempowered, besieged Israelites in Jerusalem would have formed lasting memories of hope for all those who would remember, reread, and retell the mighty acts of this saving and trustworthy God.

Last but not least, therefore, the ultimate character in this section is YHWH, the only true God. Against the overwhelming threat of the Assyrian empire (Isa 36–37), the crisis of personal illness (Isa 38), and controversial piety and security facing the Babylonian empire (Isa 39), YHWH's saving power on behalf of those who trust sustains the besieged people, heals the ailing king, and gives hope to each generation, especially the people colonized in Yehud and exiled in the Diaspora.

Structure of Isaiah 36–39
The Model King—Hezekiah amid the Assyrian Siege, 36:1–37:38
The Healed King—Hezekiah amid His Illness and Babylonian Threat, 38:1–39:8

The Model King—Hezekiah amid the Assyrian Siege, 36:1–37:38

The First Assyrian Threat and King Hezekiah's Plea to Prophet Isaiah, 36:1–37:8
This unit (36:1–37:8) introduces the first Assyrian threat against Jerusalem, which will recur in a second version (37:9-38). It portrays the Assyrian invaders encamped against the Gihon Spring outside the wall of Jerusalem, whereas the second episode highlights the scene inside the Jerusalem city, with Hezekiah's prayer and Isaiah's report of the divine oracle of assurance.

Set on the battlefield outside the Jerusalem wall, this unit contains two instances of the Assyrian official Rabshakeh's taunt: first, directed against Hezekiah followed by the response of Judah's top three officials (36:1-12); second, directed against the Judeans followed by the response of the Judeans, Judean officials, and King Hezekiah (36:13–37:8).

Isaiah 36:1-12 narrates the threat against the besieged, defenseless city of Jerusalem from the opening taunt by the Rabshakeh encamped outside the Jerusalem wall. This narrative starts with the description of the intense crisis at the battlefield (vv. 1-3). The event is set in the fourteenth year of King Hezekiah, 701 BCE, when the Assyrian royal annals record that King Sennacherib undertook a military campaign against the southwestern region of the Levant and conquered forty-six fortified cities in Judah (v. 1).

Ironically, whereas one day the nations will aspire to "go up" (*'alah*) to learn the way of YHWH (2:3; cf. 40:3), here the foreign nation Assyria "went up" (*'alah*) to capture the cities of Judah. Whereas many (*rab*) nations will come to Zion to follow YHWH's teaching "in later times" (2:2), now Jerusalem is in dire crisis, besieged by the mighty Assyrian army and taunted by the Rabshakeh, which may literally mean the "chief (*rab*) of the officers" (v. 2). Will Jerusalem surrender like the rest of Judean cities? Will Jerusalem, Judah's capital, succumb to become a vassal to Assyria? Or will it experience an impossible, miraculous deliverance?

The literary expression, "at the water channel of the upper pool on the highway of the laundry-washer's field" (v. 2), repeats almost verbatim the similar account of Syria-Ephraim's threat against King Ahaz (7:3; Williamson 1998a, 247–48). The book of Isaiah has two major historical narratives (Isa 7 and Isa 36–37), portraying "two sieges of the city" (Watts 2001, 214). Contrary to prophet Isaiah's advice, King Ahaz did not trust in YHWH but succumbed to the Assyrian king. Now readers wonder whether King Hezekiah would do the same, which would then exhibit the same disheartening example of faithlessness and thereby signal the powerlessness of YHWH.

Scholars have insightfully compared and contrasted the two kings, Ahaz and Hezekiah, and their parties and policies (Ackroyd 1987, 181–92). In addition to the records in the book of Isaiah, there are other detailed records available in 2 Kings and 2 Chronicles. These variant historical accounts provide additional glimpses of these kings. While we will discuss these variant accounts of Hezekiah below (esp. in the discussions on Isa 38–39), we will also find helpful information concerning Ahaz. In particular, although 2 Kings 16 depicts Ahaz as a rebellious king, 2 Chronicles 28 gives him far worse evaluations. In fact, the Chronicler views Ahaz even worse than Manasseh: "'Faithlessness' is characteristic of the reign of Ahaz, the worst king of Judah according to Chronicles (2 Chr 28:19, 22; 29:6)" (McKenzie 2004, 56). In the book of Kings, Manasseh is the worst king of Judah. Yet, in Chronicles, Ahaz is the worst king of Judah, because in Chronicles even Manasseh repents (2 Chr 33), but not Ahaz.

Hezekiah, the son of Ahaz, encounters comparable challenges and tasks for himself and his people. We should keep in mind that children play significant rhetorical and thematic roles in the preceding texts (esp. Isa 1–12). Accordingly, readers will discover, through the comparison between Ahaz and

Hezekiah, not only a theological comparison between one king (disobedient) and another king (trusting) but also a symbolic sapiential contrast between a grown-up (arrogant) and a youth (repentant). Against this backdrop, Judah's chief officials—Eliakim, Shebna, and Joah—go out to the battlefield to meet with the chief commander of Assyria (v. 3).

In the summit, Assyria's chief commander taunts boisterously (vv. 4-10). This taunting message recalls key oracles from the preceding chapters (esp. Isa 28–33), as if this foreign commander is well informed about Israel's prophetic messages. Admittedly, the implied audiences can hear select rhetorical themes for their own theological debate.

The first and supreme theme addresses the issue of trust: "What is the source of your confidence?" (Blenkinsopp 2000a, 470). Significantly, the word "to trust" (*batakh*) occurs seven times in this subunit. Here the Assyrian commander denounces Judah's military "counsel" and strength as "empty" words (v. 5; cf. 29:15, 13; 30:1). The second theme concerns King Hezekiah's alliance with Egypt (v. 6; cf. 30:1-3; 31:1). Readers hear arrogant sarcasm from the Assyrian commander in that he is willing to provide his enemy Judah some weapons, two thousand horses, which would count more than the trained chariot riders of Jerusalem (vv. 7-9; cf. 30:16; 31:1-3). The third theme more subtly echoes King Hezekiah's reform, which involved removing the high places. The Rabshakeh may remind his audience of this reform in order to degrade Judah's unity and morale, and thereby stir potential commotion from those parties who did not appreciate Hezekiah's reform (v. 7; cf. 2 Kgs 18:3-7). The last theme plays on the true versus false prophets, tricking that YHWH endorsed this Assyrian attack as the divine tool to chastise YHWH's own people (v. 10; cf. 10:5-11).

The rhetorical taunt sounds rather persuasive and heavily demoralizing. Recent archaeological excavations and cuneiform tablets studies for the reigns of Sargon and Sennacherib have demonstrated the widespread Assyrian efforts to establish administrative centers at key locations bordering Judah. It seems most likely that Judah's elite bureaucrats were well informed about or even educated in the Neo-Assyrian imperial language, culture, and ideology, including the theological challenge of "the invincible power [*melammu*] of Assur and his king" (Aster 2007, 251–53). Likewise, diplomatic exchanges of Judah's envoys would have enabled "the oral transmission of Assyrian royal propaganda to Judah's intellectuals" (Morrow 2011, 192). It is no wonder that Judah's multilingual officials plead with the Assyrian commander to speak in Aramaic and not in Hebrew (v. 11; cf. 28:11; 33:19). Put another way, "the officials respond: *Let's not speak our own language; let's speak the language of the empire*" (Hays 2013, 67). Nevertheless, the Rabshakeh's retort reveals that he means for all the people of Judah amid the siege to hear his taunt and become swayed to follow the Assyrian imperial ideology (v. 12; cf. 2 Kgs 6:24-33).

Isaiah 36:13–37:8 portrays the threat now directed against all Judeans, both citizens and refugees desperately surviving in Jerusalem. The more thundering and explicit taunt of the Assyrian commander, in Hebrew (v. 13), now entices Judean soldiers to surrender by belittling King Hezekiah and even YHWH (vv. 14-20). Just as the word "to trust" occurs seven times in the preceding subunit (vv. 1-12), here the word "to deliver" (*natsal*) occurs eight times, emphasizing the question of the identity of the true deliverer.

The first half of the Rabshakeh's speech is full of prohibitive commands ("Do not," vv. 14-18a). The first command is, "Do not let Hezekiah deceive you," disclaiming the authority of King Hezekiah (v. 14). The second command is, "Do not let Hezekiah make you trust in YHWH," denying the power of YHWH (v. 15). The third command is, "Do not listen to Hezekiah," enticing the besieged and starving people to exit the city walls and alluring them with words about eating, drinking, and "a land of grain and new wine, a land of bread and vineyards" (vv. 16-17; cf. 2 Kgs 9:30-33). The fourth command recaps the focal theme of the first two commands, "Do not let Hezekiah trick you, saying, 'YHWH will deliver us'" (v. 18a).

The second half of the Rabshakeh's speech contains approximately six rhetorical questions (vv. 18b-20). The initial questions cover major Aramean cities, such as Hamath, Arpad, and Sepharvaim (vv. 18b-19; cf. 10:9; 2 Kgs 17:24). To the questions whether any of the gods of Syria has delivered them, the implied answers are no. These questions culminate in the case of Samaria, the capital of northern Israel, which did not survive the Assyrian attack (v. 19b). In the same rhetorical formula, the ultimate question centers on the case of Jerusalem, the capital of southern Judah, "Surely will YHWH deliver Jerusalem from my hand?" (v. 20b).

Here the Assyrian superpower emperor's arrogance reveals his unmatched arrogance and blinded *naïveté*. The Assyrian king's pompous question, "Who among the gods of these countries have delivered their land from my hand?" (v. 20a), recurs in the Babylonian king Nebuchadnezzar's hubris in Daniel 3, "Who is the god who can save you from my hand?" (3:15). These tyrants boast of their invincibility, as though they have become gods themselves. Indeed they are too powerful for any underdogs to challenge them. However, human history has taught us that just as absolute power absolutely corrupts, so any human power is bound to be supplanted by another. Likewise, any individual, no matter how strong and powerful, is like the grass that withers and fades away. This haughty Assyrian king will meet his fate of being killed by his own sons (Isa 37:38). The prophet aptly reminds of the frailty of all human oppressors. The prophet also asserts that the creator God, rather than any nonexistent gods, has dealings with all cruel tyrants.

How then will the people inside Jerusalem respond (vv. 21-22)? Many of them would be on the verge of surrendering to Assyria. Yet, against those boisterous prohibitive commands, King Hezekiah rebuts with his own, "Do not answer him" (v. 21). At that moment of agony, Judean officials tear their garments and convey the words of the Rabshakeh to King Hezekiah (v. 22; cf. Jonah 3:5-6).

Now King Hezekiah responds and dispatches delegates with his request to the prophet Isaiah (37:1-8). King Hezekiah's reaction reveals a panic-stricken, albeit penitent ruler, asking the prophet Isaiah to pray on behalf of the people (vv. 1-4). That the king tore his clothes and covered himself with sackcloth is not in and of itself a sign of penance, as other kings reacted similarly in a time of terror (v. 1; cf. 1 Kgs 21:27; 2 Kgs 5:7; Ezra 9:3; Esth 4:1). Yet Hezekiah's entry into the house of YHWH suggests that he is a devout king. The king dispatches two of the three officials along with the elders of the priests to Isaiah (v. 2).

The request contains the metaphor of birth pangs with the possibility of dramatic rescue (vv. 3-4). The metaphor of birth pangs signifies the day of distress with a dual connotation of death and life (v. 3). If the baby does not come out, both the baby and the mother are in mortal danger. But if the baby comes out, both will be alive (cf. 7:14-17). Hezekiah's earnest request for prayer implores Isaiah in direct address: "YHWH your God . . . if you will lift up prayer" (v. 4). In the second episode (37:9-38), however, King Hezekiah will offer his prayer directly to YHWH. The king's request with the word "perhaps" (cf. Joel 2:14; Amos 5:15; Jonah 1:6; 3:9; Zeph 2:3) seems to exhibit a sign of humble faith. Here in 37:3-4, it is "not about Jerusalem or the temple, but about the living God . . . [who] will silence the blasphemer" (Berges 2012a, 275).

YHWH's response to Hezekiah here is brief but significant (vv. 5-7). Opposite the Assyrian king's babbling prohibitions (36:14-16, 18), YHWH assures Hezekiah, "Do not fear" in the form of a priestly oracle of salvation (v. 6; cf. 7:4; Beuken 2000a, 358). Whereas King Hezekiah and his officials are in utter dismay before the Assyrian army, not unlike Ahaz whose heart shook with fear (7:3), divine assurance ridicules the envoys of the Assyrian king as mere "lads" or "babies" without strength (cf. v. 3; 7:16; 8:4). YHWH's spirit will allure the Assyrian king to return to his land and fall miserably in a coup (cf. 2 Kgs 7:6-7). Indeed, the Rabshakeh retreats because of the

news that the Assyrian king had left the city of Lachish (v. 8). Thus ends the
episode of the first crisis—round one of the battle—in Jerusalem.

The Second Assyrian Threat and King Hezekiah's Prayer to YHWH, 37:9-38

The unit is similar in content and format to the preceding unit. But there are
different patterns involving new thematic emphases, in terms of the shorter
version of the Assyrian threat speech (vv. 9-13), Hezekiah's prayer (vv. 14-35),
the lengthier oracle of divine rescue (vv. 21-35), and the concluding report of
Sennacherib's demise (vv. 36-38).

Verses 9-13 introduce another episode of Assyrian taunting—round two
of the battle—against Jerusalem. Tirhakah, the king of Cush, comes to fight
against Assyria, possibly as a result of Judah's alliance (v. 9; cf. 18:1-2; 20:1-4;
36:3). The Assyrian king then sends another taunting speech through his
messengers (vv. 10-13). The tone and content of this taunt are more flamboyant. Whereas the previous taunt attacked the status of King Hezekiah
("Do not let Hezekiah deceive [*nasha*] you"; 36:14), this taunt dares to mock
YHWH ("Do not let your God deceive [*nasha*] you"; v. 10). Admittedly, this
empire's military conquest is impressively daunting, fomenting the survivors'
potential revolt, "Can we really be delivered?" (v. 11; cf. 20:6). Thus, subsequent rhetorical questions unveil the full-blown arrogance of the Assyrian
king, denying any gods or kings of their power (vv. 12-13; cf. 10:8-11,
13-14; 36:18-20).

Verses 14-20 record King Hezekiah's earnest prayer to YHWH. Instead of
melting with fear like King Ahaz (7:12), King Hezekiah goes up to the house
of YHWH (v. 14; cf. Ps 27:4-6). Whereas Hezekiah previously asked prophet
Isaiah to pray on his behalf (v. 4), now the king himself prays (v. 15).

Hezekiah's prayer exhibits a roughly chiastic structure (vv. 16-20):

v. 16—"*You alone are God over all the kingdoms of the earth*"
> v. 17—"Hear . . . see . . ."
>> v. 18—"The kings of Assyria have dried up all the lands"
>>> v. 19a-b[1]—"**They are not gods**"
>> v. 19b[2]—"[The kings of Assyria] destroyed them"
> v. 20a—"Save us"
v. 20b—"*All the kingdoms of the earth* shall know that *You alone are God*"

Although not all corresponding words neatly match in this chiasm, we can
detect a rhetorical design that conjoins three related themes. The prayer starts
and ends with recognizing and pointing to God. Within these bookends,

the prophet pleads for Y<small>HWH</small> to hear, see, and save the Jerusalemites. Ironically, the central portion directly addresses the formidable campaigns of the Assyrian kings. Here then is the first theme concerning the tortuous reality of Sennacherib's assault. The cruelty of Sennacherib's onslaught in a way parallels that of Pharaoh, as if plotting a connection between the memories of threat and deliverance "from Assyrian and Egyptian domination" (Hobson 2013, 205). Without doubt, this Isaianic text acknowledges the all-powerful reality of the Assyrian dominance.

Nevertheless, at the core is the firm confession that those gods Assyria subdued are no gods. In Isaiah's subversion of the Assyrian ideology, "while accepting and even affirming the reality of Assyrian power, it denies the enduring nature of Assyrian sovereignty" (Aster 2007, 257; cf. Isa 2:5-22). Inasmuch as this structure highlights the reality of Assyria's military accomplishment, the second theme underscores the sheer fact that there are no other gods and that imperial kings are only transient. By implication, thus, Y<small>HWH</small> will prove to be the only living and sovereign God, which is the third theme.

Interestingly, this symmetry paints and reverses the very situation of Jerusalem's siege. Whereas the mighty Assyrian army encircles Jerusalem, like a bird in a cage, this prayer encircles the king of Assyria, as if God besieges Sennacherib and his army. Bracketing these is Hezekiah's humble plea for Y<small>HWH</small> to hear, see, and save the people of Jerusalem. The outer frames that envelope this prayer thus signify the third theme: All the kingdoms of the earth shall know that Y<small>HWH</small> alone is God.

Verses 21-35 follow Hezekiah's moving prayer with the empowering speech of Y<small>HWH</small>. Y<small>HWH</small> directly addresses and retorts the Assyrian force ("you" singular), as if projecting a valiant battle hymn while protecting daughter Zion under the wings. Against the derisive message the king of Assyria "sent" (*shalakh*) to Hezekiah (v. 9; cf. v. 14), the prophet Isaiah "sent" (*shalakh*) the divine word to Hezekiah (v. 21). In the answer to King Hezekiah's prayer directed to none other than God, here comes not only the divine speech that assures Hezekiah but also the divine fury that outright denounces Sennacherib.

The first of the two-part format of the divine speech (vv. 22-29) starts with the word "this" (*zeh*) in v. 22 and ends with the phrase "I will expel (*shub*) you by the way you came" in v. 29. That the divine word comes "against him [Sennacherib]" asserts Y<small>HWH</small>'s unmitigated scorn for the Assyrian king (addressed as "you" throughout this subunit), thereby assuring divine support for the Judean king and his beleaguered people. It is now daughter Zion's turn to mock the invader. The rhetorical question affirms that arrogant Sennacherib blasphemed the Holy One of Israel—yes, it is a big mistake to challenge the living God (v. 23).

The content of Sennacherib's self-exaltation concerning his subjugation of Syria (v. 24) and defeat of Egypt (v. 25) resembles the previous pompous claims of Tiglath-pileser III (10:13-14; cf. Machinist 1983, 725). Peter Machinist has identified common motifs concerning the military campaigns to the western mountains and cutting down the trees in the Neo-Assyrian inscriptions, "demonstrating the heroism of the king and the long reach of his might":

> Shalmaneser III: I went up to the mountains of the Amanus and cut down logs of cedar and juniper. My royal image I set up before the Amanus.

> Isa 37:24: With my numerous chariotry, I am the one who ascended the heights of the mountains, the inner recesses of the Lebanon. I cut down its tallest cedars, its choicest junipers, I came to its uttermost height, its garden-like forest. (Machinist 1983, 723)

The subsequent rhetorical questions state that YHWH is the one who planned the Assyrian king's conquest of the fortified cities in the region surrounding Israel (vv. 26-27). Here one finds another Neo-Assyrian royal idiom:

> Sennacherib: (The place x) I conquered and turned into a ruin;

> Isa 37:26b: And it was (that you) would make fortified cities crash (?) into ruined heaps. (Machinist 1983, 725–26)

This common idiom may reflect Israel's familiarity with these Neo-Assyrian literary expressions and imperial ideologies. Thus, the Isaianic text may have adapted the Assyrian king's pompous claims and turned them against him, to his ignominy. Accordingly, in addition to the depicted "visual and oral propaganda," these Assyrian literary influences represent the "official written propaganda" in which, in the Isaianic text, the Assyrian becomes "what the 'enemy' was in his own inscriptions" (Machinist 1983, 729, 733). Like a modern spy camera, YHWH knows Sennacherib's moves and intentions inside and out (v. 28; cf. Ps 139:2). No matter how high this Assyrian king may claim to have risen, his loftiness is still way too low to catch any notice from on high in the heavens; consider that despite the Babylonian effort to build a tower to reach the heavens, they are so low that YHWH had to "scoop down" to see what they were building (cf. Gen 11:4-5). YHWH retorts that "because your arrogance has [barely] come up to my ears," YHWH will put a hook in Sennacherib's nose like a chained captive and a bridle on his lips like a tamed donkey, so as to drag him back to Assyria (v. 29; cf. Ps 104:25-26; Job 40:15–41:2 [MT 40:15-26]).

The second part of this divine speech also starts with the word "this" (*zeh*) in v. 30 and ends with the phrase "by the way he came, he shall return (*shub*)" in v. 34, with an additional culminating statement in v. 35. Now YHWH directly yet gently addresses Hezekiah ("you"), along with his frightened Jerusalemites (vv. 30-32). The divine "sign" conferred here recalls the "sign" given to Ahaz (7:14-16; cf. 8:18; 19:20; 20:3). The previous sign with Immanuel ("God with us") implied the retreat of Syria and Ephraim within several (most likely "three") years of the child's weaning, a sign that Ahaz rejected (Isa 7). Now this sign deals with three years when crops will grow gradually but steadily (v. 30). Moreover, the survivors of the land of Judah, many of whom escaped to Jerusalem, will rebuild and disperse from Jerusalem throughout all Judah (vv. 31-32). Paralleling the vision that YHWH's teaching is said to go forth from Zion (2:3), Judah's remnants shall surely go forth from Zion (v. 32).

YHWH's speech shifts the divine rebuke back to the Assyrian king, but now in the third-person address with a clear focus on Jerusalem, "this city"—this phrase occurs three times (vv. 33-35). Jerusalem is no longer the vulnerable, besieged city. Rather, YHWH will so protect Jerusalem that Assyria's arrow, shield, and attack will not reach "this city" (v. 33). Without any further military success, Assyria shall retreat away from "this city" (v. 34). An additional but essential assurance concludes the entire divine speech as YHWH vows to save (*yasha'*) "this city" for YHWH's sake and for the sake of David, YHWH's servant (v. 35).

Verses 36-38 bring the whole episode of Sennacherib's siege to a closure (cf. v. 8). Here what may have been a relevant ancient Near Eastern history is reported from a theological perspective (Blenkinsopp 2000a, 478). The "angel of YHWH"—this phrase occurs only here in Isaiah—overpoweringly strikes 185,000 Assyrian soldiers in their camp overnight (v. 36; cf. 2 Kgs 19:35). This motif of YHWH's nocturnal defeat of Assyria echoes that of Egypt in the Exodus account (Exod 12:23, 29; Hobson 2013, 207; cf. Num 22:23, 31; 2 Sam 24:16-17; 1 Chr 21:15-16). With the drastic defeat of the massive army, Sennacherib's dismal escape seems similar to Sisera's flight from the battlefield on foot (Judg 4:17), except that Sennacherib made his way back to Nineveh (v. 37). Alas, as a stark contrast to Hezekiah who prays at "the house of YHWH" (vv. 1, 15) and receives the promise of divine deliverance, Sennacherib gets killed by two of his own sons during the time of his worship at "the house of Nisroch" his god (v. 38; cf. Judg 16:30): "The obvious irony is that he who assumed incorrectly that [YHWH] could not protect Israel was not protected by his gods from his own family" (McKenzie 2004, 350). Kings and rulers honoring (e.g., Hezekiah's faithfulness) divine authority receive divine protection, whereas those disregarding (e.g., Sennacherib's hubris) divine sovereignty will fall (Hobson 2013, 214; cf. 2 Macc 8:19; 15:22; 3 Macc 6:5; Sir 48:18; *2 Bar.* 63).

The Healed King—Hezekiah amid His Illness and Babylonian Threat, 38:1–39:8

Like the preceding section (36:1–37:38), this section has two units with different portrayals of Hezekiah—Isaiah 38 (positive) and Isaiah 39 (positive, albeit with ambiguous open-endedness). Diachronically, scholars posit that Isaiah 38–39, with the event of Merodach-baladan's revolt against Assyria, precede the accounts of the Assyrian siege of Jerusalem of Isaiah 36–37. Synchronically, however, chapters 38–39 in the current placement fulfill various literary functions and thematic purposes.

The present form, synchronically, arranges the sequence of a model king in national crisis (Isa 36–37), followed by a model king in personal threat (Isa 38), who becomes a beneficiary of peace (Isa 39). The Hezekiah account in 2 Kings 18–20 starts with the flawed king (2 Kgs 18:14-16, which is not in Isa 36–39) followed by the model king Hezekiah—painting a king whose "faith . . . grew over a lifetime" (Hens-Piazza 2006, 358; cf. Isa 30–31). In contrast, the Isaiah account emphasizes the model hero of faith in Hezekiah from the outset. The anticipation of the captivity of Hezekiah's descendants (Isa 39) forebodes and functions to pave the way for a literary transition to the time of exile and beyond (Isa 40–66). However, most distinctly, the prayer of thanksgiving (Isa 38:9-20, which is not in 2 Kings 18–20) dramatically highlights the theme of Hezekiah's personal piety, despite the ambiguous, open-ended conclusion in Isaiah 39.

Hezekiah's Miraculous Healing and Thanksgiving Prayer, 38:1-22

The parallel account in 2 Kings 18–20 does not have the poetic segment, i.e., Hezekiah's thanksgiving prayer (Isa 38:9-20). It seems possible that the Isaiah account splits the common source of the 2 Kings account and inserts the core prayer of Hezekiah. Thus, Isaiah 38:1-8 and 38:21-22 (unified in 2 Kgs 20:1-11) as two split-up parts envelop Isaiah 38:9-20, Hezekiah's psalm, "as its centerpiece" (Blenkinsopp 2000a, 484). Then Isaiah 39 (which resembles 2 Kgs 20:12-19) follows the episode:

(cf. 2 Kgs 18:13-16 only in Kgs)

2 Kgs 20:1-6	= Isa 38:1-6
2 Kgs 20:9-11	= Isa 38:7-8
	Isa 38:9-20 (only in Isaiah)
2 Kgs 20:7-8	= Isa 38:21-22
2 Kgs 20:12-19	= Isa 39:1-8

Isaiah 38 manifests a roughly chiastic pattern, enveloped by narrative accounts, that emphasizes the lengthy central poetry of Hezekiah's prayer (vv. 9-20):

vv. 1-8—narrative
   vv. 9-20—poetry
vv. 21-22—narrative

Verses 1-8 narrate King Hezekiah's personal crisis of illness (vv. 1-3) and divine healing in response to his prayer (vv. 4-8). Intricately related to the preceding episodes of Judah's national crisis (chs. 36–37), this account may depict King Hezekiah as a symbol for the entire nation—especially the exiled Diasporas of later generations. As Peter Ackroyd notes, "the illness of Hezekiah and the death sentence upon him thus become a type of judgment and exile" (1987, 165). The opening chapter of the book of Isaiah describes the whole people of Israel and Judah as sick (1:5-6). Just as the prophet Isaiah, whose cleansing from the unclean lips, symbolizes the cleansing of the penitent people (Isa 6), so here the king Hezekiah functions as a type for all who yearn for the divine healing and rescue.

When the royal narrative reports that a king becomes mortally ill, readers would anticipate the death of that king and a transition to the next king in typical regnal formulae (v. 1; cf. 1:5). We find such reports of the deaths of King Uzziah (6:1; cf. 2 Chr 26:16-21) and King Ahaz (14:14). But that is not the case for King Hezekiah. In fact, whereas 2 Kings 20:21 records Hezekiah's death and his son Manasseh's succession, there is no description of Hezekiah's death in the Isaiah account. Contrary to the initial warning that Hezekiah "shall die and not live" (v. 1), somewhat like Enoch or Elijah, Hezekiah never dies, at least not in the scroll of Isaiah. This pious, upright, and symbolically immortal king prays fervently, weeping loudly (vv. 2-3).

Isaiah receives the divine answer to Hezekiah's prayer (vv. 4-5; cf. 37:17, 21). If Hezekiah here symbolizes the people of Judah, 15 years of restored life may signify 150 years of Judah's time of peace prior to the exile (Blenkinsopp 2000a, 482). Indeed, YHWH promises to rescue both Hezekiah and "this city" from Assyria (v. 6; cf. 37:35). Recalling the sign of deliverance given previously (37:30), YHWH provides Hezekiah another sign that depicts God in control of the sun (vv. 7-8).

Verses 9-20 highlight the moving psalm of the healed Hezekiah. This subunit contains corresponding key words that form a loose chiasm, though not perfectly matching in each counterpart:

vv. 10-11—"I said . . . I said"
  v. 10—"Sheol"
    v. 11—"YHWH, YHWH" (*yah yah*)
      vv. 12-13—"put an end" (*shalam*, 2x)
        v. 14—"Adonay"
          v. 15—"It is he who has done it"
        v. 16—"Adonay"
      v. 17—"wholeness" (*shalom*)
    v. 18—"Sheol"
  v. 19—"the living, the living" (*hay hay*)
vv. 18-19—"Sheol will not thank you . . . the living will thank you"

Following the heading, "the writing belonging to Hezekiah" (v. 9), Hezekiah the psalmist recounts his complaint amid dire illness (vv. 10-14). Sheol approaches and encircles the stricken psalmist (v. 10), making it difficult for him to see YHWH in the land of the living (v. 11). Hezekiah describes his vulnerability in sickness with various metaphors (vv. 12-14):

v. 12—"like a shepherd's tent" (psalmist)
  v. 12—"like a web" (psalmist)
    v. 13—"like a lion" (YHWH)
  v. 14—"like a swallow" (psalmist)
v. 14—"like a dove" (psalmist)

Like a shepherd's tent and like a web, Hezekiah is about to be removed (v. 12). Like a lion, YHWH crushes the psalmist (v. 13; cf. Hos 5:14; 11:10; 13:7-8; Amos 1:2), making the psalmist as helpless as a dove (v. 14; cf. Jonah 2—note that the name Jonah means "dove"). Whereas Jonah was in the belly of the fish three days and three nights (cf. Jonah 1:17 [MT 2:1]), Hezekiah is about to be finished off from day to night. This helpless dove cries out, "my Lord has oppressed me," petitioning God to "pledge security to me" (Sweeney 1996, 493).

The psalmist then proceeds to another petition, leading to thanksgiving and a vow of praise (vv. 15-20). In the chiastic central verse, the psalmist reports that YHWH answered (v. 15). Then in phrases that are extremely difficult to translate, Hezekiah petitions or testifies that YHWH is the true source of life and spirit (v. 16). Hezekiah even acknowledges that the purpose of bitterness was for his wholeness, as YHWH cast his sins away (v. 17). No more does Hezekiah need to depict himself as a dove against a lion. Rather, he eagerly joins the living as opposed to the dead: Sheol, death, and the pit cannot "thank" YHWH for the divine "faithfulness" (v. 18), but the living will "thank" YHWH and make known to future generations the divine "faithfulness" (v. 19).

The concluding statement expands the liturgist of this psalm from the individual speaker Hezekiah to a community of "the living," with whom Hezekiah expresses solidarity: "YHWH will save *me*, and *we* will play the stringed instruments all the days of *our* lives in the house of YHWH" (v. 20; cf. Ps 23:6). Therefore, while vv. 10-11 and vv. 19-20 correspond chiastically, there is thematic development. At the beginning of the psalm, Hezekiah sang and prayed alone. But in the climactic end, Hezekiah and later generations, together as "we," sing praises to YHWH in the temple.

This psalm of Hezekiah, missing in the Kings narrative, thus suggests a pivotal theological theme: "Whereas in the Kings account the focus of attention is entirely on the individual Hezekiah, in Isaiah his restoration is seen typologically as adumbrating the restoration of the community, and of the royal line in particular, characterized by worship in the house of the Lord" (Williamson 1996, 52; cf. van Wieringen 2015, 488–89). Accordingly, this "house of YHWH" also signifies the theme of hope for the later servant community, as eunuchs, foreigners, and, in fact, all faithful can be admitted (56:7; Berges 2012a, 297). Placed at a chiastic centerpiece within chapter 38, Hezekiah's prayer in vv. 9-20 ultimately points to the faithfulness and mercy of God (cf. 37:16-20). A renowned biblical scholar once shared that it took her more than twenty years of teaching experience to learn that the preeminent step in exegesis, as in anything else in our work and life, is "to pray." Putting aside his own power and privilege, the human king Hezekiah thus both exemplifies a humble psalmist who resolutely trusted in the seemingly invisible God and models a praying creature who, in the childlike fear of God, refused to fear other mortals, including the daunting imperial king—still a mere creature.

Verses 21-22 resume the account of the prophet's treatment to heal Hezekiah. Intertextually, we find a significant thematic shift from its parallel account in 2 Kings 20. In 2 Kings 20, Hezekiah's request for the "sign"

(2 Kgs 20:8) refers to the prophet Isaiah's preceding remark that "on the third day" Hezekiah will go up to the house of YHWH (2 Kgs 20:5—note that the phrase "on the third day" is missing in Isa 38). Indeed, the prophet immediately responds to Hezekiah's question by announcing the "sign" of the change in the shadow of the sun (2 Kgs 20:9-11). In contrast, in Isaiah 38, the prophet already confers the "sign" of the sun's shadow (Isa 38:7-8) as part of a divine answer to Hezekiah's prayer. The lengthy psalm of Hezekiah follows (Isa 38:9-20). Then, we encounter the seemingly anticlimactic question of Hezekiah with no pertinent answer: "What is the sign that I shall go up to the house of YHWH?" (Isa 38:22; cf. 2 Kgs 20:8).

The implication of this intertextual shift is noteworthy. In the Isaiah account, by placing Hezekiah's quest for the sign at the end of the episode, its thematic function does not refer to the sign of the sun's shadow. Instead, by placing it after the divine assurance and the subsequent psalm, the text conveys Hezekiah's question as a climactic conclusion of this episode. Greg Goswell observes the shift from "the house of David" (38:1) to the climactic yearning for "the house of YHWH" (38:22): "The initial concern of prophet and king in Isaiah 38 appears to be the continuation of the house of David, but by the close of the chapter that has been subsumed under the higher priority of the house of YHWH and its worship. The final focus on divine kingship is made all the more pointed by the fact that it is King Hezekiah who voices it" (Goswell 2014, 186). Following the thanksgiving vow collectively to offer praise in "the house of YHWH" (38:20), Hezekiah's culminating question coherently portrays him as a pious king eager to go up to "the house of YHWH" (38:22). To the later exilic and postexilic audiences, this inquiry further underscores King Hezekiah's exemplary desire to "go up" to the house of YHWH, just as the exiled Diasporas would be exhorted to "go up" (cf. Isa 2:3; 2 Chr 36:23; Ezra 1:3).

Open-ended Prayer of Hezekiah amid Babylon's Infiltration and Judah's Exile, 39:1-8

As has been widely perceived, this unit, which resembles the similar culminating episode in 2 Kings 18:12-19, seems anticlimactic in the overall flow of Isaiah 36–39. Yet there are key phraseological and theological differences through which the Isaiah account presents certain significant literary implications and thematic messages.

Verses 1-4 report a new episode of the empire's visit to Hezekiah. This time King Merodach-baladan (Marduk-apla-iddina) of Babylon attempted a revolt against Assyria around 705–701 BCE. In light of the historical and political milieu, the reason for the Babylonians' visit to Hezekiah was not the news of Hezekiah's physical recovery per se. Rather, the Babylonian imperial palace had "an interest in Hezekiah's wealth and his attractiveness as an alliance partner after his deliverance from Sennacherib" (Wright 2011, 118).

Whereas the Assyrian king sent a taunt letter (*separim*, 37:14), now the Babylonian king sends a letter (*separim*) as a present to Hezekiah for his regaining strength (*hazaq*) from sickness (v. 1). Whereas Isaiah 36–38 depicts a close relationship of trust and prayer between Hezekiah and YHWH, Isaiah 39 illustrates a close communication between Hezekiah and Babylon. Whereas in Isaiah 36–37 the Assyrian army could not penetrate the besieged Jerusalem, in Isaiah 39 "Babel comes to Jerusalem and, in contrast to Assur, even enters into Jerusalem" (van Wieringen 2015, 496). Hezekiah, being "pleased" (compare "good" in v. 8), shows them every treasure in his house (v. 2; cf. 1 Kgs 10:1-13; 2 Kgs 18:14-16; 2 Chr 32:25-26).

Then, the prophet Isaiah comes and asks Hezekiah about this incident (vv. 3-4). Hezekiah's replies are somewhat ominous in that he describes these emissaries as being from "a land far away" (cf. 13:5) and reports that there is nothing in his "house" not shown to them. The repeated occurrences of the "house" of Hezekiah (vv. 2, 4) may make a sharp thematic contrast with the "house" of YHWH in the preceding section (37:14; 38:20, 22). At the same time, the king's "house" often connotes his dynasty (cf. 2 Sam 7:11-13; 1 Chr 17:10-14). Readers will learn of its upcoming downfall in the future.

Verses 5-8 convey the prophet Isaiah's pronouncement of a divine oracle, followed by Hezekiah's reaction. The divine oracle announces future days when all in Hezekiah's house will go to Babylon (vv. 5-6; cf. 2 Kgs 24:8-17; 25:1-21; 2 Chr 36:5-21). Because there was nothing in his house Hezekiah did not show to Babylon (cf. vv. 2, 4), there will be nothing left in the event of exile. Even some of the kings of Judah will be taken into captivity and become eunuchs (v. 7; cf. 56:3-5). Hezekiah's response to this oracle contains an enigmatic statement: "The word of YHWH that you have spoken is good . . . for there will be peace and security in my days" (v. 8). Its thematic flow seems abrupt and the whole conclusion quite anticlimactic. Nevertheless, in comparison with its parallel account in 2 Kings 20:12-19 and in light of the larger literary plot, Hezekiah's statement can provide important clues for reading the core of this section, if not the entire section, of the book of Isaiah.

First, as many scholars have interpreted, Hezekiah's statement together with this unit helps build a literary bridge between Isaiah 1–39 and 40–66. Like the appearance of Babylon in Isaiah 13–14 (albeit anachronistic), Babylon (vv. 6-7) may function literarily in Isaiah 39 by foreshadowing the ensuing Babylonian exile and thereby paving the way for the oracles with exilic and postexilic settings in Isaiah 40–66. On the one hand, Hezekiah's illness and healing foreshadow the ensuing experiences of the Judean people in the aftermath of the Babylonian exile. On the other hand, the death of the imperial king and the rescue of the Judean king foreshadow "the respective destinies of their peoples in a proximate future" (Blenkinsopp 2000a, 483).

Second, this ending with Hezekiah's comment on "peace/wholeness" and "security/faithfulness" in his era (v. 8) functions to sustain Zion theology as a major concept in the book of Isaiah. Notably, as discussed above, this passage does not report Hezekiah's death, contrary to other pertinent accounts (cf. 2 Kgs 20:20-21; 2 Chr 32:32-33; Isa 6:1; 14:28). Furthermore, amid the abrupt transition from Isaiah 39 to 40, there is no explicit record of the destruction of Jerusalem. This thematic lacuna seems deliberate and significant in that, in the final form of the Isaiah scroll, just as Hezekiah the ideal king never dies, so Jerusalem's violation is missing, as if Zion's inviolability remains intact at least in the textual world (cf. 2 Kgs 24:10-16; 25:1-11; Lamentations).

Third, compared to 2 Kings 20, Isaiah 39 depicts Hezekiah in a more pious way. In 2 Kings 20:19, Hezekiah's rationale for taking the divine oracle positively appears in the form of a question: "Is it not so, if there will be peace and security in my days?" The expression may be somewhat analogous to the popular attitudes toward contemporary issues on the global environment, as though the current generation may claim, "It won't affect our generation, so why should we care?" The expression tends to highlight Hezekiah's self-concern. In contrast, Isaiah 39:8 describes Hezekiah's reaction in a more humble way: "Surely there will be peace and faithfulness in my days." Taking this as similar in expression and content to Josiah's statement, "I will gather you to your ancestors, and you shall be gathered to your grave in peace" (2 Kgs 22:20), Christopher Seitz interprets this statement not as "selfish *après moi le déluge* but a realistic appraisal of God's mercy directed to him . . . without a hint of gloating or selfish disregard" (1993, 263, 266). It is further noteworthy that Luther translates this verse close to the LXX, Vulgate, and Targum, as a sober prayer: "Let there be peace and faithfulness in my days" (Beuken 2003, 52).

Equally important, the catchwords "peace" and "faithfulness" in 39:8 point to the divine covenantal promise to the house of David (2 Sam 7:16, 28-29; cf. Isa 9:6-7 [MT 5-6]; 16:4-5; 42:3; 48:18-19; 52:7; 54:14; 55:3). King Hezekiah's "faithfulness" (38:3, 18-19) underscores his "exemplary role at the point of transition"—or at the core—between Isaiah 1–39 and Isaiah 40–66 (Beuken 2003, 54). We should note that, linguistically and rhetorically, the terms "peace" (*shalom*) and "faithfulness" (*'emet*) of 39:8 form brackets with Hezekiah's ardent "faithfulness" (*'emet*) and "whole heart" (*leb shalem*) of 38:3. These catchwords also occur toward the end of Hezekiah's psalm: "wholeness" (*shalom*) in 38:17 and YHWH's "faithfulness" (*'emet*) in 38:19. Additionally, just as Hezekiah's psalm starts with the two repeated words—"I said (*'mr*) . . . I said (*'mr*)" (38:10-11), so Hezekiah's final episode ends with the two repeated words of Hezekiah's speech—"he said (*'mr*) . . . he said (*'mr*)" (39:8). Read together, Isaiah 38–39 further frame and highlight the "wholehearted faithfulness" of Hezekiah, enveloped by key catchwords at the start, middle, and end of Hezekiah's crucial life and words (Beuken 2010, 389). Contrary to the "wicked," as well as wicked kings, who will be precluded from peace (48:22; 57:21; 66:24), this king epitomizes faithfulness and peace.

Fourth, this solemn reaction in Isaiah 39:8 emphasizes the importance of prayer, repentance, and trust in each generation. From one angle, the passages that occur only in 2 Kings 18:13-16 (Hezekiah's tribute to King Sennacherib) and 2 Chronicles 32:24-26 (Hezekiah's pride; cf. 2 Chr 26:16) accentuate Hezekiah's shortcomings, although they are truncated in comparison with more extensive descriptions of his positive accomplishments. Even in 2 Chronicles 29–32, which depicts Hezekiah as the most pious king next to David and Solomon, "the account is not entirely positive, since the Chronicler revealed the stories of Hezekiah's sickness, which he linked to Hezekiah's arrogance" (Boda 2010, 382). That these accounts are missing in Isaiah 36–38 elevates Hezekiah as the most impeccable king among the books of Kings, Chronicles, and Isaiah (Sweeney 1996, 510–11). From another angle, the prayer of Hezekiah occurs uniquely in Isaiah 38:9-20. Considering that "The Prayer of Manasseh" in the Apocrypha testifies to the Chronicler's emphasis on Manasseh's penitent prayer (2 Chr 33:18-19), it is remarkable that the book of Isaiah also emphasizes Hezekiah's penitent prayer. Hezekiah's prayer is unique and pivotal to the overall theme in Isaiah, underscoring this king's and his community's exemplary faith that shines more brightly than in Kings, and even Chronicles.

That Hezekiah's generation ("in my days") will have peace and security may thus imply that the king leaves it to YHWH with humble trust. Although his son Manasseh's generation and then subsequent generations, minus Josiah, will eventually fail in devout faith, Hezekiah's generation stands out as a model for the later audiences to look back on. In the Deuteronomistic historiography, Manasseh's sin trumps over other generations' virtues (2 Kgs 23:26-27). In the book of Isaiah, however, Hezekiah's faith sets him apart as a symbol of light amid darkness, deliverance amid calamity: "Hezekiah is remembered as a role model. . . . This figure from the past, who lived before the bad times of Manasseh, was a role model for the *bene golah* ('children of the exile') and all those who supported their measures" (Becking 2013, 188). Read sequentially, it is as though the compiler censored any records of brutality against Jerusalem. Rather, the abrupt jump from Isaiah 39 to 40 seems to underscore this theme: the prayer of Hezekiah for "peace" and "faithfulness" (39:8) is immediately and assuredly answered by YHWH's utterance of "comfort, comfort" (40:1).

Finally, nonetheless, this sudden closure of the episode evidently leaves this section (Isa 36–39) in an open-ended debate. Not unlike the end of the book of Jonah that concludes with a question (Jonah 4:11; cf. Nah 3:19; Kim 2007), this episode ends with a thematic ellipsis—in fact, Isaiah 38 too concludes with a question (cf. 2 Kgs 20:19; 2 Chr 32:31). Despite the predominant signals of Hezekiah's growth, repentance, and prayer, this open-ended episode may leave room for the interpretation that Hezekiah too, like all the other virtuous kings of Judah, is a frail mortal, especially before the divine King YHWH (Cohn 2000: 144). Hezekiah was a great devout, model king indeed, yet not without blemish as a finite human being. This open-endedness both at the end of Isaiah 38 and Isaiah 39 seems to exhibit the deliberate thematic imprints of the redactor(s). Its effect is as though the text raises its theological question to its audiences: Will each generation respond piously or unfaithfully? Which model of the Judean king shall we pursue, Uzziah, Ahaz, or Hezekiah? Whose letter or word shall we heed, Babylon's (or Assyria's) or YHWH's? On whose side shall we stand? Ultimately, whom shall we trust, Marduk or YHWH? W. A. M. Beuken profoundly ponders: "Maybe [readers] are inquisitive enough to continue on and look for an answer in the second half of the book of Isaiah" (2010, 390). In the meantime, careful readers may have detected key hints, e.g., from the name Isaiah ("YHWH is Savior"), as this lengthy scroll is ultimately about God and as the following sections will "report on the saving acts of the LORD" (Widyapranawa 1990, 264).

New Things to Anticipate for Servant Jacob-Israel via Cyrus (Fifth Branch of the Lampstand)

Isaiah 40–48

There is an advantage to analyzing distinct aspects distinguishable in Isaiah 40 and on, as many notable interpreters have contributed in the past, such as Abraham Ibn Ezra (1089–1167 CE), Ludwig von Döderlein (1775), Johann Gottfried Eichhorn (1783), and Bernhard Duhm (1892; cf. Sweeney 2006, 243–48). Yet, at the same time, we can equally find significant insights from reading the entire book of Isaiah as a unified whole, as recent Isaiah scholars have proposed and demonstrated. This study will thus explore reading in light of holistic, sequential, and intertextual interconnections, while also being mindful of some likely historical transitions vis-à-vis sociopolitical settings.

The first section (Isa 40–48) centers on Jacob-Israel as the focus, while the next section (Isa 49–57) highlights the restoration of Zion (Berges 2012a, 301). Many scholars conjecture that the first section points to a setting in the Babylonian exile. Recently, some scholars have proposed that the actual setting may have been in Yehud; in this case, we should call it the Babylonian "colonization" rather than "exile" per se. Whether in the colonizer's territory through forced migration (exile) or in the colonized locale back in the homeland (Yehud), Isaiah 40–48 contain various anti-imperial polemics, notably in the passages against idol-fabrication and climactically against Bel (= Marduk), Nebo, and daughter Babylon.

Trying not to forget but rather alluding to the exodus tradition of the past, the prophet encourages the downtrodden people to anticipate the new exodus with a new agent of liberation: "Second Isaiah urges his fellow exiles to regard Babylon as the Egypt of old that their ancestors had known" (Perdue and Carter 2015, 101). Babylon will meet the fate of Egypt of the old exodus. The new exodus will happen. How is it so? Here we find an essential theology of monotheism: YHWH is the only living God and this God is about to set off for the return to Zion on the royal highway. To many dejected exilic or colonized people, this may have sounded nonsensical. During the colonized era of Japanese occupation in Korea (1910–1945), many leaders who once fought for Korea's independence and liberation abandoned their fidelity and became key conspirators for imperial Japan's secret police. In a recent blockbuster movie titled *Assassination*, after Korea is liberated in August 15, 1945, a resistance leader in Korea who has turned into a Japanese police informant is reproved by former resistance comrades as to why he betrayed them. This traitor replies, "I had never thought that my country would be liberated . . . I had thought it was all over." Amid the darkness of exilic and colonial life, YHWH commissions a servant to be the light and covenant. To many doubters and deserters, the messenger shouts that this God returns, raising an agent of deliverance, guiding them through the wilderness journey back home, and vanquishing the seemingly impregnable empire Babylon. In the ebb and flow of political upheavals, just as Babylon took over Assyria less than a century ago, Babylon will fall as the new superpower Persia under King Cyrus rises on the horizon.

Isaiah 40–48 also shares many linguistic and thematic interrelationships with 49–57 as well as with 1–39. We will address some of the cases in the discussion below, especially those interconnections that can help shed some light on our interpretation. Concerning the structure of this section, scholars agree that it is unclear as to where the divisions should stand. Indeed, the seams marking divisions within Isaiah 40–66 are not clear at all (e.g., Isa 1–12 are demarcated by the new superscription in 13:1, or Isa 13–23 hold together by the "burden"-oracles). Acknowledging that numerous catchwords and motifs connect most parts of Isaiah 40–48 in a concatenated way, we will subdivide this section as follows.

Structure of Isaiah 40–48
Oracles of Salvation for Doubting Jacob-Israel amid the Babylonian Exile, 40:1–42:17
YHWH Claims Jacob-Israel as the Servant, 42:18–45:8
From Anti-idols Satires to Anti-Babylon Polemics, 45:9–48:22

Oracles of Salvation for Doubting Jacob-Israel amid the Babylonian Exile, 40:1–42:17

Albeit loosely, certain elements of Isaiah 40–42 may mirror the opening overture, Isaiah 1–2. This does not mean that Isaiah 40–42 are a new introduction to the second half of the book of Isaiah—we have one whole scroll of sixty-six chapters. Nevertheless, some words and patterns seem noteworthy. Isaiah 1 concerns the fates of Israel and Zion (with regard to their sins and warnings); Isaiah 40 concerns the fates of Jerusalem and Jacob-Israel (with regard to their laments and salvation oracles as divine responses). Isaiah 2 discusses the nations and peoples; Isaiah 41–42 deal with the coastlands, nations, and peoples. While nations and peoples desire to stream to Zion for YHWH's teaching with justice and Torah (2:1-4), now YHWH will commission the servant to bring forth justice to nations as the nations wait for the Torah (42:1-4). In fact, the servant is to execute the role of a covenant to the people(s) and a light to the nations (42:1-10). Read together, there are literary links and parallels between Isaiah 1–2 and Isaiah 40–42. Yet there are also thematic developments in the latter, especially with the new role divinely bestowed upon the servant, Jacob-Israel.

Even though this study will not adhere rigidly to the following structural pattern, John Goldingay and David Payne's analysis on the internally repetitive "parallel" sequences and patterns within 41:1–42:17 can be illuminating regarding these loosely but fascinatingly juxtaposed oracles. This chart is condensed (Goldingay and Payne 2006a, 136):

41:1-7	**41:21-29**
Who lies behind political events?—the nations are asked	Who can explain political events?—the nations' gods are asked;
Only YHWH;	Only YHWH;
They are helpless	They are helpless
41:8-16	**42:1-9**
The commitment YHWH makes to servant Israel— it will see the defeat of its oppressors	The commitment YHWH expects from a servant— bringing deliverance to the oppressed
41:17-20	**42:10-17**
YHWH turns desert to garden	YHWH turns garden to desert

Comfort to Zion and Confidence for Jacob-Israel, 40:1-31

The double command, "comfort, comfort" starts this unit—in fact the entire second half of the book of Isaiah—with divine pathos. The command to comfort "*my people*" (v. 1) forms loose bookends with the rhetorical questions, "Do you not *know*? Have you not heard" (vv. 21, 28), thereby together correlating with the opening remark in Isaiah 1, "Israel does not *know, my*

people do not understand" (1:3). There is also a shift of concern from Jerusalem and Zion (vv. 2, 9) to Jacob and Israel (v. 27). In light of the stylistic
shift, we divide this unit into two parts: the divine commissioning of Zion
to proclaim the good news (vv. 1-11) and a series of rhetorical questions
suggesting who YHWH is, the creator of the ends of the earth (vv. 12-31).

Verses 1-11 introduce the opening scene of divine commissioning in
the heavenly council. Throughout the subunit, it is not clear as to who the
speakers are. Scholars consider the possibility that such a lack of clarity may
be intentional and instructive, thereby highlighting "what is said" rather
than "who speaks" (Goldingay and Payne 2006a, 80). As will be elaborated
below, this subunit displays substantial linguistic and thematic links to the
prophet's call in the heavenly council in Isaiah 6 (concerning the intertextual
echoes of Isa 28, see Goldingay and Payne 2006a, 59). Leading imperative
verbs subdivide and yet join this subunit together in sequence—vv. 1-8 and
vv. 9-11: "Comfort, comfort . . . speak. . . ." (vv. 1-2) and "Go up . . . Raise
up your voice . . . raise it up . . ." (v. 9).

The initial imperatives address the members of the divine council
(vv. 1-8). Certain key words neatly hold this segment together. The word "all"
(*kol*) occurs six times in vv. 2, 4 (two times), 5, 6 (two times). Likewise, five
phrases involving YHWH in the construct form connect with one another:

v. 2—"hand of YHWH"
    v. 3—"way of YHWH"
        v. 5—"glory of YHWH"
    v. 5—"mouth of YHWH"
v. 7—"breath ['spirit'] of YHWH"

The double occurrences of the word "comfort, comfort" (v. 1) relate to the
"double" punishment placed upon Jerusalem for her sins (v. 2). Besides the
coincidental fact that the word "double" (*kiplaim*) occurs elsewhere only in
Job 11:5 and 41:5, the epilogue in the book of Job contains God's double
restitution of Job's fortunes (Job 42:10). Connected to the legal principle of
repaying double for any robbery (cf. Exod 22:4, 7, 9), in both Job 42:10 and
Isaiah 40:2, YHWH hints at divine pathos toward these wounded protagonists
as though YHWH feels guilty for inflicting excessive pain upon them.

Furthermore, the divine concern for "my" people (v. 1) may correlate
with "this" people in 6:9-10. If so, readers can sense a dramatic reversal. The
phrase "this people" has occurred in numerous places thus far denoting the
corrupt, sinful people of Israel and Judah. Now, divine pathos with compassion calls them again passionately, "my people," reverting all the way back

to 1:3, "Israel does not know, *my people* do not understand." Likewise, the threefold particle "for" (*ki*) in v. 2 contrasts with the threefold occurrences of "for" (*ki*) in 6:5 (Goldingay and Payne 2006a, 58). Moreover, whereas the prophet's "iniquity" (*'awon*) and "sin" (*hatta't*) were forgiven through the cleansing of his lips (6:7) in the call narrative of Isaiah 6, YHWH now directly accepts and pardons (cf. Jer 5:1, 7) the payment of Jerusalem's "iniquity" (*'awon*) and "sins" (*hatta'tot*). Reading Isaiah 40 intertextually in relation to Isaiah 6, therefore, there is a thematic reversal and development: "As 6:1-13 authorizes the *theme of judgment* in chapters 1–39, so 40:1-11 now authorizes the *theme of deliverance* for the remainder of the book" (Brueggemann 1998b, 17).

Just as the prophet heard the "voice" (*qol*) of YHWH's commissioning (6:8), now the prophet—conventionally called Deutero-Isaiah—hears the "voice" (*qol*) with divine commands (v. 3). We hear collective voices, especially in the first-person plural ("a highway for *our* God"), similar to the inquiry in the divine council ("who will go for *us*?") in 6:8.

The initial command in the divine commissioning is to restore a highway for God (cf. 33:8; 35:8). This highway will pave the way for God's royal return to Zion through the wilderness (cf. 52:7-10). As the "wilderness" may denote YHWH's regular home, outside the holy abode in Jerusalem, the highway for the king's march then connotes that, no longer departing and abandoning Jerusalem (cf. Ezek 10:18-22; 11:22-23), YHWH is returning to comfort her (Goldingay and Payne 2006a, 73–75). Here YHWH's "way" conflicts and coalesces with the people's "way." Clearly YHWH's way is superior to the people's way (cf. 55:8-9). At the same time, however, it is important to note that YHWH has already given the divine order to build a road through the wilderness, *before* the people would make an allegation against YHWH that their "way" is hidden (cf. 40:27). For the subsequent passages and unfolding events, ultimately, "the way of YHWH also becomes the way of the people," in that the divine engineer's plans to construct a highway through the desert will make it "passable" even for the lost, exiled Judeans (Lund 2007, 101).

Metaphorically speaking, as various scholars have proposed, the "desert" can denote not only the literal terrain distant from Jerusalem but also the figurative symbol for the people's "punishment and trial" in the aftermath of the fall of Jerusalem. By the same token, the "way" of YHWH can connote YHWH's "saving power" in Psalm 67:2 (MT 67:3), "saving acts" in Psalm 103:7, and indeed "comfort, comfort" in v. 1 (Lund 2007, 85, 90–91, 101). This way of YHWH will accompany dramatic reversals of fortune, echoing the similar thesis oracle of Isaiah 2: "All valleys shall be lifted up (*nasa'*) and all mountains be brought low (*shapel*)" (v. 4a; cf. 2:9, 12-17; Ps 97:5).

Here readers may hear a pun: the expression that "uneven ground (note in Hebrew: 'aqob) becomes straight (*mishor*)" can signify that "Jacob [*ya'aqob*] shall become upright" (v. 4b). For this literary pun and thematic link to the Genesis story, Iskandar Abou-Chaar observes that "the problem posed in Isaiah 40–49, for which answer is given in Isaiah 50–55, is precisely how to make of Jacob an upright person!" (Abou-Chaar 2013, 121).

Then, the "glory of YHWH"—the central one of the five descriptions for YHWH here—shall appear through the highway, which "all flesh" shall see (v. 5; cf. Ps 97:6). The divine glory echoes the call narrative in Isaiah 6, which also emphasizes "the revelation of the glory of God to the whole world" (Korpel 1999, 93; cf. 6:3; 35:2). The announcement confirms this initial command: "for the mouth of YHWH has spoken" (cf. 1:20; 34:16).

The voice continues, this time, with the command to "proclaim" (v. 6). Then, another voice, perhaps that of the prophet, questions, "What shall I proclaim?"—instead of "Whom shall I send?" (cf. 6:8). Not unlike the prophet's confession to be among "the people of unclean lips" (cf. 6:5), this voice appeals to the reality that "all flesh" is grass that withers away (vv. 6-7; cf. Ps 90:5-6; 103:15-16). Readers can picture the trying situations of the dejected exilic community: "When the 150 years have passed the reader finds [herself or himself] in a nightmare. The city, Jerusalem, is fallen" (Lund 2007, 99). Against this dismal reality of human fickleness and ephemerality, the divine commission concludes with a passionate rebuttal: "Grass withers, flower fades, but the word of our God shall stand forever" (v. 8; cf. 1:10; Eccl 1:4).

Commissioned and charged by the heavenly council, the prophet now calls Zion to proclaim the good news of YHWH's glorious return to deliver and heal the people (vv. 9-11). The call to Zion to "go up" (*'alah*) to a high mountain is reminiscent of the intention of nations and peoples to "go up" (*'alah*) to the mountain of YHWH (v. 9; cf. 2:3). Whereas an unknown group hears the command (in the second-person plural) to comfort the people of YHWH, suggested by the phrase "says your [pl.] God" (v. 1), now the prophet calls Zion to "fear not" and to declare to the cities of Judah, "Here (*hinneh*) is your [pl.] God" (cf. 35:4). In a defiant counterargument, the prophet rebuts the theological challenges of Lamentations. Deutero-Isaiah urges Daughter Zion, sitting lonely (Lam 1:1; 2:9-10) and dejected on the ground (Lam 2:2), to get up and climb the elevation to regain her lofty place (Korpel 1999, 95).

The prophet pronounces the arrival of the deity first as a victorious warrior (v. 10). Twice more the word "here" (*hinneh*) occurs to affirm YHWH's arrival with "strength" (*hazaq*; cf. 35:3-4 and the name "Hezekiah" throughout Isa 36–39). Second, at the same time, as a gentle shepherd, YHWH will rescue

this people, presumably out of Babylon, and lead them into YHWH's bosom—
"an image of love and tender individualized care" (Paul 2012, 137; v. 11;
cf. 49:10; 53:6; Ps 23).

Verses 12-31 contain a series of rhetorical questions asserting who the
true God is, i.e., none other than YHWH. A total of seven interrogative questions (six times with "who" and one time with "what") may echo the events
of creation in Genesis 1. The repeated rhetorical "who" questions contrast
with the "nothingness" of the nations in the first segment (vv. 12-17). Then
the rhetorical questions, "to whom" (v. 18 and v. 25) and "Do you not know?
Have you not understood?" (v. 21 and v. 28), multiply sequentially in the
second (vv. 18-24) and third segments (vv. 25-31):

v. 12—"Who . . . ?"
v. 13—"Who . . . ?"
v. 14—"Whom . . . ?"
  v. 18—"*To whom . . . ?*"
  v. 18—"To what likeness . . . ?"
  v. 21—"*Do you not know? Have you not understood?*"
    v. 25—"*To whom . . . ?*"
    v. 26—"Who . . . ?"
    v. 28—"*Do you not know? Have you not understood?*"

The first segment contrasts the incomparable YHWH with the nations that are
"nothing," in fact, "empty nothingness" (vv. 12-17). Alluding to the ancient
Near Eastern mythological motifs of the powerful gods, the prophet portrays
the heavens, earth, mountains, and hills as so tiny to the creator that they can
fit in the palm of YHWH (v. 12). Whereas, in the Enuma Elish, another god,
Ea, instructed and guided Marduk, the Babylonian god, no gods in fact exist
to guide the "spirit of YHWH" (vv. 13-14; cf. v. 7; Paul 2012, 140).

The sequential statements concerning the nations, with illustrative analogies, have key similar-sounding words that not only cohere together but
especially progress toward the culminating theme of the utter chaos ("empty
nothingness"; cf. Gen 1:2) of the nations:

v. 15a—"look" (*hen*)
  v. 15b—"look" (*hen*)
    v. 16a—"not" (*'en*)
      v. 16b—"not" (*'en*)
        v. 17a—"not" (*'en*)
          v. 17b—"empty nothingness" (*'epes watohu*)

Not unlike the lengthy oracles about/against the nations (Isa 13–23), the prophet dismisses what most Judeans in Yehud or Babylon would fear—the menacing forces of surrounding nations. It seems likely that the poet writes in Babylon, the fearful empire of the time. Whether in Babylon or in Yehud, however, the poet counters the mighty military campaigns of these superpowers: "nations are like a drop in a bucket. . . . All the nations are like nothing before [God]": "Deutero-Isaiah is the prophet who made 'all' and 'nothing' into determinative concepts" (Westermann 1969, 53).

Next, the second segment crescendos with rhetorical questions that contrast the living God with vain idols and rulers (vv. 18-24). What entities may dare claim to resemble God (v. 18)? The prophet considers an idol (v. 19). Yet, just like nations, idols are mere collections of gold, silver, and trees that are crafted and assembled together by human metalworkers and woodcutters (v. 20; cf. Ps 115:4-8). Here, the divine work takes the audience back to the time of origin, "in the beginning" (v. 21; cf. Gen 1:1). From the creator's standpoint, human beings are like minuscule locusts and the earth like a tent spread out (v. 22; cf. Ps 19:4 [MT 19:5]). In subsequent statements, as in the previous segment (cf. vv. 15-17), readers hear repetitive negatives:

v. 23a—"not" (*'en*)
   v. 23b—"nothingness" (*tohu*)
      v. 24a—"not . . . not . . . not . . ." (*bal*)

Not only is the whole world in God's hand (cf. v. 12), but the rulers of the earth also are nothing before God (vv. 23-24). Indeed, as the grass withers (cf. vv. 7-8), and also like the fate of the wicked (cf. Ps 1:4-6), those menacing rulers will wither away like stubble (v. 24).

Finally, the third segment reaches its climax, repeating the pattern of interrogative and rhetorical questions [v. 18=v. 21 // v. 25=v. 28] and yet presenting more intensified messages (vv. 25-31). Reiterating the questions concerning who may substitute for God (v. 25), the prophet exhorts the audience to lift up their eyes to see the wonders of creation and acknowledge the creator God who counts every creature (v. 26). Shalom Paul observes an intertextual connection involving the key words "the Holy One" and "high" between 40:25-26 and 57:15—we should note that Isaiah 40 starts the initial section (Isa 40–48) and Isaiah 57 concludes the second section (Isa 49–57) within Isaiah 40–66. At any rate, here lies the prophet's polemic against the Babylonian religious tradition that Marduk "established (in) constellations the stars, their likenesses" (*COS* 1:399; cf. Paul 2012, 152). Carol Newsom interprets this counterclaim against the imperial domination by way of the "command and execution" sequence in Daniel 3: e.g., Nebuchadnezzar orders the officials and subjects to gather and bow, and they immediately comply and prostrate themselves. According to Israel's prophet, it is not the imperial king but YHWH "Who calls them each by name . . . Not one fails to appear" (v. 26, TNK; cf. Pss 33:9; 148:5; Newsom 2014, 106).

In this climactic segment, just as YHWH commissions to comfort Jerusalem/Zion (v. 2), now the prophet chides the complaint of Jacob-Israel. As will be true frequently throughout Isaiah 40–48, scholars disagree as to the identification of "Jacob-Israel." On the one hand, the name may denote Judean exiles in Babylon. On the other hand, it may connote the twelve tribes, thereby signifying the unified people of northern Israel and southern Judah, now from various corners of the Diaspora (Goldingay and Payne 2006a, 125–26). Be that as it may, in the exilic reality, not knowing the divine plan to restore the "way" of YHWH (v. 3), Jacob-Israel laments, "My way is hidden from YHWH" (v. 27). Not knowing their own blindness and deafness in their ancestors' paths and amid their predicament (cf. 42:16, 18), they ignorantly protest that their God is "blind, deaf and ignorant" toward them (Lund 2007, 166).

In the culmination, the prophet reaffirms that YHWH is the eternal God, creator of the ends of the earth (v. 28): "Isaiah is not concerned so much with how many gods there are . . . as with the question of who is God" (Goldingay 2014, 63). This powerful God shows utmost care for the weary and the powerless (v. 29), not for the empires (vv. 12-17) or the rulers (vv. 18-24). The contrast instead targets the youths, who can indeed grow weary and stumble on their ways (v. 30). Who then cannot become weary or disempowered? Here is the punch line of the message: "those who wait for YHWH" shall renew their strength (v. 31; cf. Ps 27:14). As Marjo Korpel observes, the hiphil form of the verbs ("renew" and "mount up") implies that this waiting for YHWH is not passive but rather active. It is the resolute waiting of the downtrodden, fighting to keep faith and practice hope together, like marathon runners who persevere to their exhaustion—from accelerating to running and eventually to walking (Korpel 1999, 98). On the wilderness journey of the old exodus, YHWH carried Israel "on eagle's wings" (Exod 19:4). In the impending new exodus, YHWH will go further to strengthen even the elderly and the feeble to make their journey successfully with never-ending energy, without fatigue or detour. Moreover, as the winged sun disk in ancient Egypt, Mesopotamia, and Syro-Palestine frequently symbolized divine protection and authorization primarily of the king, we may even conjecture that not merely the king (cf. Ezek 17:3, 7) or the cherubim (Isa 6:2) but now the common people who trust in YHWH will mount up with "wings" in truly royal and divinely provided strength (Deut 32:11-12; cf. LeMon 2015, 269–73).

Furthermore, climactically, the question "to whom will you liken God . . . ?" (v. 18) hints that its answer is to be found in Genesis 1:26—no idols but rather the one God has created: *adam* in the image of God (Schaper 2014, 158). Here, however, this theme is qualified through a contrast between the youth and the weary. Whereas the youth—and those with power and privilege—shall falter (v. 30), the weary—and those vulnerable and abused by the sociopolitical injustice and suffering from theological doubt—shall be able to press on in their march, as they indomitably and defiantly wait upon the Lord (v. 31; cf. Ps 103:5).

YHWH's Court Procedure with the Nations as the Defendant and Servant Jacob-Israel as the Witness, 41:1-29

Although this unit reiterates many key words and themes from Isaiah 40 and also anticipates recurring motifs in Isaiah 42, it has its own inherent chiastic format as well. In the larger scope, two correlated divine trial debates with the nations frame this unit (vv. 1-7 and vv. 21-29). These two surrounding subunits—as if the surrounding empires threaten the fate of Israel—envelop the central subunit that resoundingly proclaims YHWH's salvific deliverance of "Jacob-Israel" as well as "the poor and the needy" (vv. 8-20):

vv. 1-5—"Who has . . . ?" (2x) + "from the east" + "from the beginning"
    vv. 6-7—idol-makers mocked
        vv. 8-13—"*Israel . . . Jacob*" + "Fear not, I will help you"
        vv. 14-20—"Fear not . . . I will help" + "*Jacob . . . Israel*"
    vv. 21-24—idols or other gods mocked
vv. 25-29—"I have" / "Who has . . . ?" + "from the north" + "from the beginning"

Verses 1-7 present a courtroom setting in which YHWH challenges coast-lands and peoples to answer the trial interrogations. Whereas those who hope in God learned the promise to "renew strength" (40:31), now nations and coastlands who are like a drop and a fine dust (cf. 40:15) hear the chiding taunt to "renew strength" (v. 1).

The initial question concerns who is in charge of current international affairs (vv. 2-4). The rhetorical, interrogative questions (vv. 2, 4, 26) build stylistic continuity with the previous chapter (cf. 40:12-14, 18, 25-26). Earlier YHWH appointed an Assyrian king to chastise Israel (10:5-6). Now who is the planner, the one who subdues nations and kings like dust (cf. 40:12, 15), and who is the "righteous one" summoned to serve at the feet of the planner (v. 2)? YHWH is the divine planner, and the "righteous one"—YHWH's instrument—is Cyrus the Persian king (v. 4). The Hebrew term "generation" (*dor*) is "cyclical," connoting the idea of cycles in progress (Dijkstra 2002, 61). This concept of periods, dynasties, or eras is consistent with ancient Near Eastern historiography, evoking continuity between the past and the future. The Isaianic text here mirrors this pattern, asserting the "coherent sequence and alternation of periods guided through a kind of divine plan" (Dijkstra 2002, 69). The distinctive polemic in this prophecy is the concept that the source of "the former and coming/new things" (41:22-23, 27; 42:9) is founded here in none other than YHWH, "the first and the last." Chris Franke's observation adds to this theme: "A distinctive feature in this section is God speaking in the first person, . . . An English translation of 41:1–44:8 reveals over 130 occurrences of first-person pronouns" (2014, 702).

As a result, coastlands fearfully tremble at the court (v. 5). From another angle, amid the "then" current affairs of the upheaval that witnessed the collapse of Babylon and the rise of Persia in the 540s, we can imagine that not only the Babylonians but also many puppets of the Babylonian empire, including many nations and coastlands that praised Babylon, would have panicked (Goldingay 2014, 64). Even in the aftermath of World War II, we often picture the scenes of people joyfully dancing and celebrating their liberation. In contrast, not only the Nazi and their allies but also many traitors and renegades within the liberated countries must have panicked in fear of their acts of betrayal. Against these backdrops, the oracle mocks their panic-driven idol-fabrication and the impotence of their gods (vv. 6-7). Opposite YHWH who comes with true "strength" (*hazaq*, cf. 40:10), the nations attempt to "strengthen" (*hazaq*, occurring three times in vv. 6-7) their idols. Looking at the welding of their idols, they even dare to claim, "It is good" (cf. Gen 1:4, 10, 12, 18, 21, 25, 31), to no avail.

Verses 8-20, the central portion, shift the attention from coastlands and nations to Israel-Jacob with divine "oracles of salvation" addressed directly to Israel-Jacob and assuring them not to fear (Westermann 1969, 67–73). This central portion underscores whom YHWH loves most. It is not the coastlands, and not even Cyrus ("the righteous one" from the east). Rather, it is Jacob-Israel, the poor and needy, whom YHWH upholds most preciously.

The first part of this subunit names Israel-Jacob—in inverted chiasm with Jacob-Israel (cf. 40:28; 41:14)—as "my servant" and "my chosen," singled out with the emphatic pronoun "you" (vv. 8-13). Contrary to the ineptness of the idols for nonexistent gods (vv. 5-7), now, recalling the great commissioning of Abraham and Sarah (Gen 12:1-3), God elects and claims Israel-Jacob as YHWH's own royal servant (vv. 8-10). According to Shalom Paul's extensive comparison of numerous seventh century BCE Mesopotamian royal inscriptions and Neo-Assyrian prophecies, expressions of the deity concerning an individual king whom the deity chooses and admonishes not to fear have now been transferred to the whole collective people—Jacob-Israel, all the seed of Abraham (v. 8; Paul 2012, 163–67).

Describing the five "fear not" oracles (41:8-13, 14-16; 43:1-4, 5-7; 44:2-5; cf. 55:3-5) as "war oracles," instead of "salvation oracles," Edgar Conrad likewise argues that not just the king, as was common in ancient tradition, but also the whole community will benefit from YHWH's victory in a new era (Conrad 1985, 99–111). From "the ends of the earth" that shake in fear over witnessing the vain "strengthening" of the idol-makers (vv. 5-7), YHWH "strengthens" and chooses Jacob-Israel, declaring, "You are my servant" (v. 9). As if reasserting the Immanuel theme (cf. 7:14; 8:8), YHWH assures Israel, "Fear not, for I am with you," promising to uphold by the divine righteous right hand (v. 10). Reviewing Joachim Begrich's earlier study, Rainer Albertz elucidates that the expression "Do not fear"—a key phrase in the oracles of salvation—functions as a positive response to individual laments. Thus, this phrase "must not be interpreted as an exhortation to be brave but as a word of comfort in the sense of, 'There is nothing to be afraid of'" (Albertz 2003b, 169).

YHWH's choosing Israel further accompanies the divine vanquishing of all that oppress and attack Israel (vv. 11-13). Just as the prophet derides the powerlessness of the idols (vv. 5-7), so the prophet conveys the divine annulment of the formidable military forces of the empire. All that furiously threaten Israel shall be ashamed, become nothing, and perish (vv. 11-12; cf. 40:17). The divine assurance to strengthen Israel's right hand culminates this first segment (v. 13; cf. v. 10).

The second part of the subunit—a salvation oracle—extends the theme of Israel's reversal of fortune (vv. 14-20). The inverted chiasm of Israel-Jacob (v. 8) into Jacob-Israel (v. 14) ties the two parts (vv. 8-13 and vv. 14-16) neatly together. Yet, unlike the lofty title "my servant," now Jacob bears the designation "worm" (v. 14). The term "worm" (*tole'ah*) elsewhere suggests lowest status, worthlessness (cf. 14:11; Ps 22:6 [MT 22:7]; Job 25:6). From a *corrido* (a narrative song of an individual's cultural memory as a model for a community), Gregory Cuéllar observes a comparable expression of "worm" as a trope for the "unseen and unnoticed" plight of many Mexican immigrants on the margins of US society: "When they touched the river's edge / The guards fired at them / And they pitted their lives / Against the Americans

/ and there they ended up / Like worms" (Cuéllar 2008, 68 and 85–86). The divine promise to uplift such a worm, exiled and viewed as minority, amplifies how great YHWH's might and compassion truly can be (cf. Jonah 4:7).

Thus, YHWH promises to make this "worm" into a sharp "threshing-sledge" (*morag*) that will crush mountains and hills (v. 15; cf. 2:14; 40:12). Israel will become YHWH's valiant weapon to smash those daunting nations "like chaff" that the "wind" will carry away (vv. 15-16; cf. 41:2; Ps 1:4). The worm, now wondrously transformed, will "rejoice" and "glorify" the Holy One of Israel (v. 16).

This oracle further elucidates the theme of reversal of fortunes in light of the poor and the needy (vv. 17-20). Once called "worm," Jacob-Israel now denotes the destitute and the afflicted in exile. Yet, contrary to the daunting empires that will become "nothing" (vv. 11-12), for the exiles who find "nothing" in their search for water, YHWH now promises to answer them and not abandon them (v. 17; cf. v. 9).

Such transformative reversal of fortune will not only involve Israel (worm, slave) or nations (nothing) but also the natural habitat of the desert, which will become springs of water surrounded by productive trees for the sake of the vulnerable in exile (vv. 18-19; cf. 35:1-7). Through such a transformation, they will all "see" and "know" that YHWH has done all this (v. 20; cf. 6:9).

Verses 21-29 resume the courtroom scene. YHWH directly charges the idols of the nations to prove that they are gods, only resulting in the unequivocal evidence that they do not even exist to answer at all. Shifting the address from Israel to the would-be gods in the second-personal plural, YHWH directly disputes them (vv. 21-24). The "King of Jacob" thus challenges the gods that claim to guide the kings of empires (v. 21). Can these gods declare what has happened and what is to occur in human history (vv. 22)? Can they predict the future or even do any good or evil (v. 23)? With the emphatic pronoun "you," YHWH has pronounced that "you are my servant" (v. 9). In a dynamic contrast, YHWH now derides the idols, questioning whether "you are gods" (v. 23). The verdict is undeniable: these gods are "nothing" (v. 24; cf. vv. 11-12; 40:17, 23).

Concerning the importance and impact of the "gods" in the exilic and postexilic settings, we should read this prophetic polemic over against the rampant culture when the discouraged people easily fell into paying homage to the gods of other nations and peoples (Newsom 2014, 108–109). Some may have embraced a syncretistic practice for the sake of survival under the imperial culture and religion. Others may have welcomed the foreign gods for political compromise and socioeconomic advancement. In another aspect of metaphorical signification, analogous to today's world, "the other gods might be the idols of state, race, gender, economic theory, or any preference or practice that is turned into an absolute" (Brueggemann 2014, 42). To them who believe that turning to other gods, cultures, or superpowers was the best way to achieve fortune and fame, the prophet counters that those "gods" will bring no genuine restoration, hope, and meaning.

YHWH's definitive answers conclude this whole unit (vv. 25-29). To the initial question as to who has roused a righteous one from the east to "subdue" kings (v. 2), neither coastlands nor idols could provide an answer. Now the audience can hear, loudly and convincingly, that it is YHWH who roused this one from the north, from the rising of the sun, to "trample" rulers (v. 25). Likewise, to the question as to who has planned and announced this "from the beginning" (v. 4), YHWH reaffirms that "surely there was no one"—note that this expression occurs three times—who did such "from the beginning" (v. 26). The culminating answer reasserts that YHWH is the "first" who exists and who gives the good news to Zion (v. 27; cf. v. 4). In contrast, no idols can utter a word because they are "nothingness" (*'epes*), nonexistent "formless" (*tohu*) spirit (v. 28; cf. 40:17).

YHWH's Servant as a Covenant to the People(s) and a Light to the Nations, 42:1-17

As iterated above, this unit appears to start a new section with the introduction of the "servant." However, in light of the servant's role in close connection to the nations, peoples, and coastlands, we take this unit as a follow-up expansion of Isaiah 40–41, with some introductory themes for the second half of the book of Isaiah. The divine commissioning of the servant (vv. 1-9) leads to the call to the earth to sing praises (vv. 10-12), which is followed by the assurance of the divine warrior's return along the royal way (vv. 13-17).

This unit introduces one of the four so-called "servant songs" (cf. 49:1-6; 50:4-11; 52:13–53:12). For centuries, interpreters have wrestled with the perennially ambiguous question of the identity of the servant with so many candidates, both individual and collective figures. What remains evident in the present form, however, is the complexity between explicit and implicit clues. Explicitly, the text identifies the servant as none other than Jacob-Israel. At the same time, implicitly, the servant is often anonymous, thereby suggesting other individual figures, such as Cyrus, a Davidide, a prophet, and the like. At the outset, the final editor put together a radical perspective that a collective group called "Jacob-Israel"—not unlike the "we"-group of the first half of the book of Isaiah—takes the role of YHWH's servant. Whether the people back in Yehud or those in Diasporas scattered outside Israel, this servant group now hears the rejuvenating messages of divine election and endowment for greater missions.

Verses 1-9 introduce divine commissioning of the servant, Jacob-Israel, to the noble tasks of functioning as a covenant to the people(s) and a light to the nations. This servant, anonymous, is introduced in a radically royal yet modest way (vv. 1-4; cf. Zech 9:9). Through the divine election and the divine spirit upon him, the servant is to establish justice among the nations (v. 1). How this servant fulfills justice is unconventional, thus marvelous. The servant does not need to make a boisterous noise (v. 2). Whereas the previous empires, Assyria or Babylon, have crushed the reed of Egypt (cf. 36:6; Kim 1999, 116–19), this servant will bring about justice virtually nonviolently (v. 3; cf. 2:4). Indeed, coastlands eagerly await justice and Torah through the servant (v. 4; cf. 2:3).

Now, the prophet ascertains how the servant's task will be successful—because YHWH the creator is behind all this (vv. 5-9). The description of God (v. 5) is reminiscent of the dual creation accounts in Genesis, i.e., the one who created heavens, earth, and all the earthlings (Gen 1:8, 10-12, 24-25) and who gave breath and spirit to animals and human beings (Gen 2:7). Moreover, according to Christine Mitchell's comparison of the creation formula and Old Persian inscriptions (on many Persian kings from Darius I to Artaxerxes III), this Isaianic oracle with the creation sequence of heaven–earth–humanity–ruler strongly resonates with the Achaemenid royal inscriptions:

> A great god is Ahuramazda
> Who established this earth
> Who established that sky
> Who established humanity
> Who established peace for humanity
> Who made Darius king
> One king of many
> One commander of many. (Mitchell 2014, 305)

Various polemics are evident. Instead of Ahuramazda, the Persian deity, it is YHWH who is the true creator of heavens, earth, and humankind. It is not Ahuramazda but YHWH who appoints human rulers, be they Darius, Cyrus, or another anonymous servant. Whereas the Achaemenid order too will come to an end (cf. Zech 12:1-8), the new order of YHWH will shine in the world forever (Mitchell 2014, 306–308). Thus, the first "I am YHWH" speech (vv. 6-7) echoes ancient Near Eastern royal election language, yet with additional elaborations that YHWH appoints the servant as "a covenant to the people(s)" and "a light to the nations" (v. 6; cf. 2:2-5; 9:2 [MT 9:1]).

Mark Smith finds in the phrase "covenant of the people(s)" (*berit 'am*) a phonetic resemblance with "eternal covenant" (*berit 'olam*), through which, "playing on the memory of the Davidic covenant theology" (2 Sam 23:1-7), the former phrase hearkens back to the dynastic tradition but now with the new role given to Jacob-Israel toward the nations. Whereas the old covenant tradition depicts the enemies as being crushed (2 Sam 22:32-50), now, in the new era for the exilic community, "the nations no longer represent the archetypal enemies" (Smith 1981, 242). Instead, Jacob-Israel will assume the role as a new covenant and "mediate the blessings to the peoples" (cf. Gen 12:1-3).

Accordingly, just as the servant is called to "bring forth" justice (vv. 1, 3), so the servant as a covenant is to "bring forth" prisoners from the dungeon (v. 7). Whereas the obstinate people looked blindly on the prophetic message (6:11), now the servant as a light will open blind eyes (v. 7). Likewise, the second "I am YHWH" speech (vv. 8-9) echoes the exodus tradition where Israel learns of the divine name and the divine glory unlike any futile images (Exod 24:16; 40:34-35; Isa 6:3). With the theophany approaching, the exiles will soon hear of new things, a new exodus (v. 9).

Verses 10-12 contain the anticipatory praise of the earth. Reminiscent of the songs of the sea (Exod 15:1, 21)—especially that of Miriam and women ("Sing to YHWH"), this new song invites even "those who go down to the sea," along with the wilderness and the mountains, to praise YHWH (vv. 10-11; cf. Exod 15:21, "horse and rider he has hurled into the sea"). As "glory" and "praise" do not belong to any idols (cf. v. 8), all creatures ought to give "glory" and "praise" to YHWH (v. 12).

Verses 13-17 advance with a dramatic proclamation of the new exodus, the return of the exiles across the wilderness. Here as a new divine dispute directed toward Israel, the prophet provides reasons to praise YHWH (vv. 13-17). The divine warrior will shout a war cry (v. 13; cf. v. 2) in the first-person singular (vv. 14-16). Similar to the combination of warrior and nursing mother imagery earlier (cf. 40:10-11), the divine warrior's battle cry (v. 13) coalesces with that of a woman in labor, groaning and gasping (v. 14).

Moreover, due to the shifts of genre and imagery, commentators often divide v. 13 and v. 14 into two separate subunits. Nonetheless, as some scholars have insightfully argued, the intentional correlation of these two images can provide a powerful effect, in that YHWH as both a warrior (v. 13) and a woman in labor (v. 14) "is both destructive and creative, both masculine and feminine. Yet the warrior is not only destructive; the warrior saves. Birth is not only creative, it is life-threatening" (Dille 2004, 72; cf. Løland 2008, 100–28). God has the power to turn the world order upside down (vv. 15-16). Thus, YHWH will dry up mountains and pools (v. 15). YHWH will also turn darkness into light and rough places into level ground (v. 16). This realignment of the world has the purpose of sociopolitical upheaval: to guide the blind through the dark wilderness (v. 16; cf. v. 7; 40:27) and to shame the idol-worshipers (v. 17).

From one perspective, this subunit (42:13-17) wraps up this section by forming a rough inclusio with 40:1-11. The images of YHWH as a warrior and a woman in labor (vv. 13-14) recap the comparable masculine and feminine images in the opening announcement (40:10-11). Likewise, YHWH will directly level the "mountains" and "hills" and turn crooked places into "flat ground (*mishor*)" (vv. 15-16), echoing the divine command to make low all the "mountains" and "hills" and turn the rough ground into "flat ground (*mishor*)" (40:4). On the very "way" the divine council was requested to prepare (40:3), YHWH will now not only gloriously return but also guide the blind on the "way" of the new exodus (v. 16). Who are the blind people here? The following section will elaborate on this question: in terms of the intertextual and thematic relations with the blind and deaf, the callous people in 6:9-10. In the meantime, this section ends with the divine accusation of the reprobate idol-worshipers, the wicked puppet-leaders of the Babylonian hegemony (v. 17; cf. 48:22; 57:21). Together with 40:1, v. 17 forms a contrasting inclusio: divine comfort for "my people" (40:1) as opposed to divine condemnation for those who vow to idols, saying "you are our gods" (42:17). This expression contrasts starkly with the I-thou relationship YHWH desires and approves: "you shall be my people and I shall be your God" (Jer 7:23; 11:4; 30:22; Ezek 36:28; cf. Hos 2:23 [MT 2:25]; Isa 51:16).

YHWH Claims Jacob-Israel as the Servant, 42:18–45:8

It is difficult to demarcate larger units within this section because there are so many concatenated semantic lines through repeated literary genres. If we take 42:18–45:8 as a section, we find a long discussion on the theme of divine election of Jacob-Israel as the servant for the commissioned task. Although hints of Cyrus occur in many key texts, none name Cyrus "the servant." The key role Cyrus will play as YHWH's agent against Babylon will thus receive fuller description in the next section (Isa 45–48). In this section, the fate, status, and role of Jacob-Israel as YHWH's servant takes center stage.

Here again, John Goldingay and David Payne's analysis of the internally mirroring "parallel" sequences and patterns within 42:18–45:8 can be informative (Goldingay and Payne 2006a, 304):

42:18-25
Israel has been too blind to be YHWH's servant, in its failures; Israel's deafness simply asserted

43:22-28
Israel has made YHWH its servant, with its failures; Israel's actual shortcomings emphasized

43:1-7
YHWH delivers those who bear YHWH's name; Promise of salvation from . . . (protection, rescue)

44:1-5
YHWH recreates a people to bear YHWH's name; Promise of positive blessing (fruitfulness, increase)

43:8-13
Israel's God is the only one, others are futile; Israel still to be witnesses

44:6-23
Israel's God is the only one, others are futile (developed in vv. 9-20); Israel's sins swept away

43:14-21
YHWH will defeat Babylon (named for the first time); New journey through desert

44:24–45:8
YHWH will rebuild Jerusalem by means of Cyrus (named for the first time); New land, city, and temple

Accordingly, we will divide this section into two parts: (1) 42:18–43:21 and (2) 43:22–45:8. Part one starts with the divine rebuke concerning the blindness of the servant, now in exilic darkness (42:18-25), which shows a fundamental change in the direction of speech in preparation for the subsequent subunits. This subunit then connects to the reminder of the divine commitment to Jacob-Israel (43:1-7). This part continues to the divine speeches concerning the new exodus and new things (43:8-21), linked by the imperative of v. 8 (to the blind and the deaf; cf. 42:18), which is directed to the nations of vv. 9-10. Part two resumes the accusation of Jacob-Israel, expressing the divine weariness over their apathy to YHWH's law and mercy (43:22-28), followed by a statement of what God is going to do about that (44:1-5). Even though the description of idolatry (44:6-23) has a kind of autonomy, it puts an end to the sham of the so-called gods that have been refuted in the preceding subunits. Part two concludes with a sort of summary (44:24–45:8), which still deals with YHWH's election on the servant. At the end, a topic implied in the preceding section (Isa 40–42), Cyrus, is resumed in anticipation of the next section (Isa 45–48). What YHWH has achieved through Cyrus ("the things which have come," Isa 41) demonstrates that the divine plans through the servant Jacob-Israel are now about to unfold ("the new things"):

Part One = 42:18–43:21 = 42:18-25 + 43:1-7 + 43:8-21
Part Two = 43:22–45:8 = 43:22-28 + 44:1-5 + 44:6-23 + 44:24–45:8

Part One: New Exodus and Wilderness Guidance for Jacob-Israel, 42:18–43:21

Isaiah 42:18-25 transition from what YHWH has started doing (vv. 10-17) to the interpretation of the past: the past does not testify against YHWH. Picking up the imperatives of the previous texts, "Comfort, comfort" (40:1) and "Be quiet toward me, coastlands" (41:1), the prophet now admonishes the exilic audience, "Hear . . . and look" (v. 18). Interestingly, the first word here in 42:18—"Deaf ones (*hakhereshim*), hear"—is almost identical to the first word in 41:1—"be quiet (*hakharishu*) toward me, coastlands." Read together, whereas the previous oracle challenged the coastlands, nations, and peoples to be quiet (and quietly listen) to YHWH, now the present oracle admonishes YHWH's own obdurate but exiled people to hear.

The first interrogative question—"Who?"—identifies this people (vv. 19-22). They are none other than the servant of YHWH—Jacob-Israel—who has been unable to really see, hear, and keep the divine words (vv. 19-20; cf. 6:9-10). Against the expectations of divine righteousness and Torah (v. 21), this people have been trapped in caves or viper's hole (cf. 2:10, 19, 21; 11:8) and imprisoned in exile (v. 22).

The second interrogative question—"Who?"—reflects back on the history of Israel and Judah's demise (vv. 23-25). Now the prophet, addressing them in the second-person plural ("you"), passionately asks whether any of "you" will pay heed (v. 23). In acknowledging their sinful past, the prophet embraces this "we"-group in solidarity of repentance: "Was it not YHWH against whom *we* have sinned?" (v. 24). Contrary to their complaint that their "way" is hidden from YHWH (40:27), it was this people who were not willing to "walk" in the ways of YHWH. As a result, divine anger consumed with war and fire, yet the ancestors of the penitent, righteous remnant did not put their "heart" aright (v. 25; cf. 6:10).

Isaiah 43:1-7 starts with the "thus says YHWH" phrase (cf. vv. 14, 16). This subunit continues the unified theme of divine plan and assurance toward Jacob-Israel, whom YHWH created, loves, and is willing to forgive. The chiastically enveloping verses reassert that YHWH has "created" and "formed" Jacob-Israel (v. 1 and v. 7; note also the inclusio of the catchwords "Jacob" and "Israel" between v. 1 and v. 28, as well as between v. 22 and v. 28). As foundational themes, the theme of creation here intricately accompanies that of election and redemption (Van Seters 1999, 82–84).

In this bracket, Jacob-Israel, "whom YHWH *called by* your *name*" (v. 1), encompasses inclusive groups of Israel's exilic descendants, "*all* who are *called by* my *name*" (v. 7). This climactic statement for "all" extends and embraces the divine invitation to Jacob-Israel, the scattered Diaspora, and even beyond (cf. Childs 2001, 335). Likewise, the salvation oracle ("fear not . . . I am with you," vv. 1-2) recurs to assure Jacob-Israel ("fear not [for] I am with you," v. 5). Similarly, the promise of divine protection for Jacob-Israel amid four aspects of danger ("waters," "rivers," "fire," and "flame") in v. 2 is recapitulated in the promise of divine gathering of the children of Jacob-Israel from the four diasporic corners ("east," "west," "north," and "south") in vv. 5-6.

Here the imagery of "fire" and "flame" may allude to exilic hardship, just as "waters" and "rivers" recall the old exodus memories. In this reading, the metaphorical linkage between the exile and the "refining fire" (48:10) may point to the immense threat and agony the exilic experiences would bring. Daniel Smith-Christopher discusses an intertextual echo of this fire imagery in the dreadful decree of the Babylonian king Nebuchadnezzar and the fiery furnace to which Daniel's three friends as disloyal subjects were thrown: "If this Isaiah passage was in the mind of the storyteller [of Daniel 3 generations later], the implication that the exile (which is compared by Isaiah to the exodus) was like a fiery threat ought once again to give pause to those who argue that the exile was 'not that bad'" (1996, 65).

In the new exodus, this salvation oracle reaffirms the Immanuel theme ("I am with you," vv. 2, 5; cf. 7:14; 8:8) of God's mysterious yet abiding presence and guidance through waters, rivers, and flames, mirroring the same theme of the old exodus, as Thomas Long elucidates on a comparable psalm text:

> In other words, when all hell broke loose on Israel as it faced extinction by the Egyptian army, God intervened. But God did not take them out of the troubled sea, but *through* it. . . . In this psalm [77:19 (MT 77:20)], the turning point comes not when the absent God finally hears the lament and acts, but when the grieving sufferer recognizes, through an act of willful

memory, that God has been redemptively present in his suffering all along. (2014, 26)

Similarly, we also note several striking intertextual correlations, especially with Psalms 22–23. First of all, the psalmist's lament ("My God, my God, *why* have you forsaken [*'azab*] me?") in Psalm 22:1 (MT 22:2) echoes the lament of Israel ("*Why* do you say, O Jacob, and speak, O Israel, 'My way is hidden from YHWH?'") in Isaiah 40:27 (cf. 49:4) and that of Zion ("Zion said, 'YHWH has forsaken [*'azab*] me . . . forgotten me'") in Isaiah 49:14 (cf. 54:7; Lam 5:20). In the canonical arrangement, the psalmist's complaint in Psalm 22 conjoins with the psalmist's confidence in Psalm 23. Walter Brueggemann addresses a similar kind of transition that displays three patterns of psalm speech (Brueggemann 1984, 155):

lament	*salvation oracle*	*song of confidence*
I am afraid	Do not fear	I will not fear
(cf. Ps. 56:3)	[Isa 41:10, 13-14; 43:1, 5]	[Ps 23:4]
Why have you forsaken?	I am with you (Isa 41:10; [cf. 7:14; 43:2, 5])	You are with me (Ps 23:4)
[Isa 49:14; Ps 22:1]		

In this closely intertwined pattern, the salvation oracle of the Isaianic passages stands as a significant bridge between the lament and the song of confidence. As though mirroring each other in the "I-Thou" relationship between God and the petitioner, the lament of "I am afraid" transitions to "I will not fear" by way of the Isaianic exhortation of "Do not fear." Likewise, the complaint "Why have you forsaken me?" becomes a resolute testimony of "You are with me" through the prophet's transmission of the divine promise, "I will be with you." Read together, our Isaianic oracle of salvation plays a pivotal role between the dramatic leap from lament to song of trust in the psalm traditions, concocting a rhetorical admonition to the exilic community to give their own answer—like the answer King David or the psalmist uttered: "Even though I *walk through* the darkest valley, I fear no evil, for you are with me; your rod and your staff, they *comfort* me" (Ps 23:4). How shall the hard-pressed, exilic community—elected as Servant Jacob-Israel and Daughter Zion—answer (cf. Ps 73:23)?

Readers will have to listen to more of their laments in the subsequent oracles. However, readers already know what God has said and promised: "When you pass through the waters, I will be with you . . . when you *walk through* the fire, you will not be burned" (Isa 43:2). Indeed the second half of the book of Isaiah started with the announcement of the divine readiness to "*comfort, comfort* my people" (Isa 40:1). Now will they put their hope in the good news of the new exodus amid the realities of dark valley? "Psalm 23 knows that evil is present in the world," Brueggemann writes, "but it is not feared. Confidence in God is the source of new orientation" (1984, 156).

Sandwiched by these framing catchwords in vv. 1-2 and vv. 5-7, the central piece highlights the impact of the old exodus and the new exodus on superpowers. In the old exodus, YHWH had given "Egypt, Cush, and Seba" as a ransom for the deliverance of Israel (v. 3; cf. 45:14). Now, in the new exodus, YHWH will give "humans and peoples" in exchange for Israel's life (v. 4b). Why is YHWH willing to do so? Readers hear the answer in YHWH's threefold confession of love from this unit's central apex, i.e., v. 4a—"because you are precious in my eyes, you are honored, and I love you." Whereas the Mesopotamian royal inscriptions record gods' love for their king, here YHWH expresses divine love for the whole people, for whom YHWH is willing to pay nations and peoples in exchange (Paul 2012, 207). Equally significant, no longer called a worthless "worm" (41:14), this people devoid of self-esteem or self-worth will now regain their long-lost identity and long-denied dignity through the prophetic assurance of God's approval: "You are my worthy and honored children."

Isaiah 43:8-21, as a trial speech, expands the salvation oracle of the preceding subunit (vv. 1-7) with the theme of court witnesses. YHWH the plaintiff summons Jacob-Israel and the nations (vv. 8-9). Previously called "heavily iniquitous people" (1:4), "this people" (6:9), or "plundered, despoiled people" (42:22), the exiled Jacob-Israel, now called "blind people" (v. 8; cf. 42:18-19), are to see and hear how marvelous God is. The blindness and deafness of this exiled people trace back to the recalcitrant generation, whose hardened heart made them turn blind and deaf to the prophetic shouts (cf. 6:9-10). In this sense, they are not unlike the nations. Nevertheless, despite their present plight, with the agency of the servant of YHWH, they will overcome hardening in the future (Uhlig 2009a, 187–88). Hence the divine command to release them from the exilic imprisonment (Goldingay and Payne 2006a, 282; cf. Ps 142:7 [MT 142:8]). Conversely, YHWH challenges nations and peoples to reply as to who has been in charge of the course of human history (v. 9). Understandably, the nations, the coastlands, and even idol-worshipers cannot answer (cf. 40:15-17; 41:1-5).

Against these mute, speechless nations and coastlands, YHWH calls Jacob-Israel YHWH's servant: "You (pl.) are my witnesses" (vv. 10-13). Whereas nations and peoples cannot bring their "witnesses" (cf. v. 9), YHWH elects the deaf and blind Jacob-Israel as "my witnesses" with astonishing influence that will reach the nations (v. 10a; cf. v. 12). In a larger scope, the election of Israel—both exiled and colonized—functions to serve a theological purpose: to bear witness to the uniqueness and universality of YHWH. Hence, "chosenness serves a larger purpose. . . . [The chosen people] are the particular witnesses—and beneficiaries—of universalism" (Levenson 1996, 155). In the past, this people acted like the blind and the deaf who kept hearing but did not understand and kept seeing but did not know (6:9). Now, they will "know" and "understand" that "I, I am YHWH and there is no savior besides me" (vv. 10b-11). Recurring expressions emphasize that it is "I," YHWH the only God, who elects the witnesses (vv. 12-13).

The next segment (vv. 14-21), starting with another "thus says YHWH" phrase (cf. v. 1 and v. 16), presents a powerful announcement of the new exodus that mirrors yet surpasses the old exodus. The initial premise, in the messenger formula, asserts YHWH's unparalleled authority (vv. 14-15). YHWH's plan to send a divine instrument, presumably Cyrus, to thwart the Babylonian oppressors is in fact for the sake of Jacob-Israel, again addressed in the second-person plural (v. 14). What does this divine intention mean? It heightens that YHWH the creator of all Israel, not Marduk or any Babylonian or Persian king or would-be deity, is the true King (v. 15).

This true King naturally has the surest authority to promise the new exodus for the exiles in Babylon. This oracle, opened by another messenger formula ("thus says YHWH"), recalls YHWH's mighty acts of the old exodus (vv. 16-17). It is YHWH who made "a way in the sea" and "a path in the mighty waters" (v. 16; cf. Exod 14:21-22), who also drowned the Egyptian horses, chariots, and army (v. 17; cf. Exod 14:26-28; 15:1, 4-5, 19). YHWH exhorts them, however, not to remember and linger over the "former things" of such past glory (v. 18). This exhortation to the heavily Babylonized generation is an apodictic command, "mimicking the language of the Decalogue": "Do not remember the former" (Ahn 2011, 159). To many exiles who became accustomed to the Babylonian colonial lifestyle (recalling their forebears in the wilderness who yearned for their slave lifestyle back in Egypt), the words of the old exodus, such as the chariot, horse, and army, may have been mere cliché from ancient history that had nothing to do with them in Babylon. Moreover, to these groups who had become comfortable and prosperous in the Marduk civilization, the challenging journey through the wilderness would not be appealing or inspiring at all (Hanson 1995, 72–73).

To such dejected or complacent communities, the prophetic admonition is to have a dream about new things—even the freedom journey from Babylon to Jerusalem. Just as YHWH did in the former exodus, now YHWH is about to make "a way in the desert" and "rivers [or, paths] in the wilderness" (v. 19; cf. v. 16; Exod 15:22-27; Num 20:1-13). John Oswalt lucidly posits, "Clearly, God hates doing the same thing twice. One has only to look at the myriads of flower species in the spring to know that" (2004, 387). Just as new things will marvelously sprout up, wild animals of the desert, such as jackals and ostriches (cf. 13:21; 34:13), will honor YHWH because of Jacob-Israel, YHWH's chosen people (vv. 20-21; cf. Exod 15:16). Indeed, no longer labeling them as "this people" of recalcitrance (6:9-10; 8:12; 28:11), now YHWH identifies "this people" (v. 21) as "my chosen people" (v. 20), those who shall glorify and praise YHWH. Once chastised as callous, sinful people in the first half of the book, now the exilic community obtains a clean slate to start a new beginning, to launch a new identity and mission. It is easy to bog down in past troubles and present travails, saying "we've never done it that way before" (Oswalt 2004, 388). God admonishes those deprived of any hope to look toward new challenges, new possibilities, and new things.

Part Two: Empty Idol-Makers versus YHWH the Creator and Redeemer, 43:22–45:8

Isaiah 43:22-28 resumes the direct address to Jacob-Israel, once blind and mute (cf. v. 8; 6:9; 42:18-20), who now receives the divine promise of forgiveness of sins. First, though, this oracle revisits the past sins of Jacob-Israel, via a transition from promise to indictment, paralleling the divine indictment in 42:18-25 (vv. 22-24; Goldingay and Payne 2006a, 305). Contrary to the divine promise to bring all who are "called by my name" (vv. 1, 7), this people have "not called on me" (v. 22a). Like the immature youths who grow "weary" (40:30), Jacob-Israel grew "weary" of YHWH (v. 22b). Echoing the earlier accusations of the empty rituals and corrupt social ethos (1:11-17), YHWH accuses the people of improper worship in various ways (v. 23). Rather, in the opposite extreme of v. 22, instead of YHWH's making them "serve" with offerings (v. 23), their sins made YHWH a "servant of Israel" and their iniquities "wearied" YHWH, reversing 40:28—"YHWH does not grow weary" (v. 24; Goldingay and Payne 2006a, 311).

Nonetheless, YHWH now utters the promise to forgive their sins (vv. 25-28). Just as YHWH enjoined this people not to "remember" the former things (v. 18), so now YHWH promises not to "remember" their sins (v. 25). Now they turn to the dismal sinful past (vv. 26-28). As in the previous legal trial, "Let us reason it out" (1:18), now YHWH requests, "Let us judge it together" (v. 26). As YHWH has earlier given them choices (1:19-20), YHWH reminds them of the sins of the former ancestor, like Abraham (cf. 41:8) or Jacob, and interpreters like priests and prophets (v. 27). The figure Jacob and his sin may mirror the story of the patriarch "Jacob, the cheat" in Genesis 27–32, with numerous literary links in vv. 22-28 (Baltzer 2001, 180–83). That is why YHWH polluted the officials of the sanctuary, handing over Jacob and Israel to the dreadful threat of "the ban," as though Jacob-Israel were YHWH's enemy (v. 28; cf. 11:15; 34:2, 5; Deut 7:2, 26).

Parallel to 43:1-7, Isaiah 44 transitions into the salvation oracle ("fear not"), assuring the promise of restoration and denouncing the colonizer's idols and powers. While key themes and expressions from preceding units continue, although with a shift of focus, now readers will hear an extended polemic against idols and idol-makers, symbolizing not only idol worship but also imperial powers and culminating in the introduction of another imperial ruler by the name of Cyrus. Although various catchwords can factor into dividing this unit form-critically, we will follow the three "thus says YHWH" phrases as markers of subunits (vv. 1-5, 6-23, 24-28).

Isaiah 44:1-5 contains the first "thus says YHWH" phrase—"Thus says YHWH, your Maker and Shaper from the womb" (v. 2). The catchwords, "Jacob" and "Israel," bracket this subunit (v. 1 and v. 5), as they frame the preceding subunit (43:22 and 43:28; note also 43:1 and 43:7, as well as 43:1 and 43:28). Here in this subunit we find numerous examples of *relecture* (literary expansion). Thus, key expressions echo previous occurrences: e.g., "Jacob my servant, Israel whom I have chosen" (v. 1; cf. 41:8; 42:1; 43:1, 10); "your creator/maker . . . your shaper from the womb" (v. 2; cf. 43:1), "fear not . . . I/who will help you" (v. 2; cf. 41:10, 13-14; 43:1, 5).

Roy Melugin astutely observes the intentional juxtaposition of 43:22-28 and 44:1-5, which betrays a larger thematic flow from past into future. This thematic development throughout these sections signifies not only literary continuity but also an implied message: "the past is a model for the future. . . . The memory of [YHWH's] past acts proves [YHWH's] deity, yet memory . . . must go beyond being mere memory. Memory must be transcended by hope" (Melugin 1976, 104). Likewise, John Goldingay and David Payne elucidate a thematic movement among the "fear not" oracles in chapters 41, 43, and 44: "the first (pair) [41:8-20] promised deliverance from opposition and obstacle, the second (pair) [43:1-7] the reconstitution of the community, the third [44:1-5] the community's increase and new commitment" (2006a, 320).

In these concatenated and intensifying expressions of assurance, YHWH reminds the addressee of the divine election of Jacob "from the womb" (v. 2a). Readers may recall the enmity and struggle between Jacob and Esau even "from the womb" and through various courses of the patriarch Jacob's life (Gen 25:23-26). But now YHWH promises to "help" Jacob-Israel throughout the restoration process. Here our subunit introduces a new term, "Jeshurun," in parallel with Israel (v. 2b). This word occurs elsewhere only in Deuteronomy 32:15; 33:5, 26, with the connotation of the ancient Israel's election, while denoting "upright, straight" with the allusion to the name "Israel" (Kim 2004; Goldingay and Payne 2006a, 323). Likewise, the recurring phrase, "I will pour out my spirit upon your offspring" (v. 3), echoes the similar phrase, "I have put my spirit upon him" (42:1). In our text, YHWH's spirit espouses a collective people, especially the exilic descendants of Jacob-Israel who shall spring forth (vv. 3-4). No longer like captives by the rivers of Babylon who hung up their harps upon the "willows" (Ps 137:1-2), the exilic offspring shall receive divine spirit and blessing and thus sprout like "willows" by flowing streams (Goldingay and Payne 2006a, 326). Through the renewal of the divine spirit, they shall regain unity as belonging to YHWH, known collectively by the names of their common ancestors, Jacob and Israel (v. 5).

Isaiah 44:6-23 presents the second catch phrase—"Thus says YHWH, the King of Israel and its Redeemer" (v. 6). This bulky subunit, parallel to 43:8-21, first declares the incomparability of YHWH (vv. 6-8). Expressions describing YHWH, the prosecutor, as the insurmountable God frame this segment: "besides me there are no gods" (v. 6) and "is there any God besides me? There is no other rock" (v. 8; cf. Deut 32:4, 37). Here coastlands or idols cannot answer the rhetorical question "who is like me?" (v. 7; cf. 40:18, 25; Mic 7:18). As a result, YHWH appoints the servant Jacob-Israel, "you are my witnesses" (v. 8).

How is it that idols and idol-makers are powerless? A lengthy mocking illustration demonstrates their ineffectiveness (vv. 9-20). First, idol-makers are nothing and utterly shamed (vv. 9-11). Contrary to YHWH the true "shaper" (*yatsar*) of Jacob-Israel and all creation (v. 2), the "shapers" (*yatsar*) of idols are nothing, naught (*tohu*) (v. 9; cf. 41:29). Unlike YHWH's newly designated "witnesses" (*'ed*), Jacob-Israel (v. 8), these empty "witnesses" (*'ed*) will neither see nor know but only find shame (v. 10; cf. 6:9). Since the artisans are mere humans, idol-makers and idol-worshipers will be put to shame (v. 11). Chris Franke trenchantly observes that "critique of the gods [esp. Marduk] is critique of Babylonian politics. [Deutero-Isaiah's] exilic audience would relish the disarray of Babylonian's inept and divided leadership" (2014, 704).

Accordingly, the detailed descriptions of idol fabrication ridicule not only the incapacity of idol-makers but also the powerlessness of the formidable empires (vv. 12-17): "Biblical humour [sic] is . . . dark subversive disparagement releasing social aggression and undermining convention and authority"

(Goldingay and Payne 2006a, 333). Whereas God created the world with divine command, shaping human beings in God's own image (Gen 1–2; cf. Exod 20:4), the fabricator of iron shapes an image and works with his "strong arm," except he gets hungry and tired (v. 12; cf. 40:28-31). The fabricator of wood similarly fashions an impressive idol in human form (v. 13). Ironically, however, human beings created in the image of God are planting and nurturing the trees to use some of them for heat, others for cooking, and then others for images to bow down to (vv. 14-15). The humorous satire against the images of imperial deities mocks that it is not mortals who are burned or whose flesh is eaten (cf. 9:18-20 [MT 9:17-19]) but rather mere trees that burn and provide roasted meat (v. 16). It is not the "remnants" of Israel and Judah whom YHWH promised to rescue (10:20, 22; 11:16; 37:31-32) but instead the "remnants" of the piece of wood that human beings make into a god, worship, and pray to (v. 17).

Here again we find an anti-imperial polemic. In the ancient Near East, the invading army would not only deport the wealth of the subjugated country but also demolish and desecrate sacred objects, dismembering the images of the enemy gods or rulers and burning down the sanctuary. The Hebrew Bible also attests to this ancient tradition (cf. Deut 7:5, 25; 12:2-3; 2 Sam 5:21; 2 Kgs 23:4; 1 Chr 14:12; 2 Chr 25:14-15). Borrowing from Hanspeter Schaudig's study, Jacob Wright correlates dismembering the trees of divine images with the ideology of the Assyrian imperial desecration of enemy gods "back to raw wood": "At his [Marduk's] command, the hostile gods are bound, and dressed in soiled garments; they are cut to pieces like *mēsu*-trees" (Esaĝil Chronicle line 36; Wright 2011, 122). The table is turned now. It is at YHWH's command that the images of Marduk will return back to raw wood.

Finally, this polemic exposes the nothingness of the idols (vv. 18-20). No longer a metaphorical expression of YHWH's people not knowing or understanding (6:9), now the idols do not "know or understand" because "their eyes cannot see or comprehend with their mind" (v. 18). Equally ridiculously, idol-makers and idol-worshipers are all ignorant of such an "abomination" (v. 19), with their hearts too deceived to recognize, "Is not this thing in my hand a fake?" (v. 20).

Yet this mocking illustration turns to the real audience, Jacob-Israel, reminding them to remember that they have not been forgotten (v. 21). YHWH promises to forget their transgressions and sins, with a moving call of divine pathos: "Return to me, for I have redeemed you" (v. 22; cf. Joel 2:12; Amos 4:6, 8-11; Hag 2:17; Zech 1:3; Mal 3:7). The closing hymn calls for all creatures—heaven, earth, mountains, and especially "all trees" (no longer idols)—to acknowledge and praise YHWH, the true redeemer of Jacob and Israel (v. 23). Therefore, remembering (vv. 21-22) and praising (v. 23) go side by side as essential theological components. Claus Westermann makes an astute interpretation of the reciprocal theme of "praising" and "not forgetting" in Psalm 103:1-2 ("Bless/praise the Lord, O my soul . . . forget not all his benefits"), as a foundational theological premise for the entire Psalter: "The coordination of 'bless' and 'forget not' expresses a profound truth: only those who praise do not forget. One may indeed speak about God, and still have forgotten [God] long ago. One may reflect upon the nature of God, and still have long since forgotten [God]. Forgetting God and turning away from God always begins when praise has been silenced" (1980, 6).

Isaiah 44:24–45:8 starts with the third catchphrase—"Thus says YHWH, your Redeemer and Shaper from the womb" (v. 24). This subunit introduces a key character, Cyrus the king of Persia. Nevertheless, the underlying concept remains the same: God is in charge of all forces and human courses, including heavens, earth, the deep, and Cyrus.

This subunit exhibits a rough chiastic structure (Kim 2003, 115):

a—"I am YHWH who made all" (44:24b)
  b—heavens and earth (44:24b)
    c—nullifies their knowledge (44:25)
      d—his servant and messengers (44:26a)
        e—Jerusalem/Judah (44:26b)
          f—deep/rivers (44:27)
            g—Cyrus (44:28a)
        e'—Jerusalem/temple (44:28b)
            g'—Cyrus (45:1)
          f'—darkness/bronze (45:2-3)
      d'—Jacob-Israel as servant (45:4a)
    c'—not knowing YHWH (45:4b-6)
  b'—forms, makes, and creates (45:7a)
a'—"I am YHWH who made all these" (45:7b)

Although 45:1 may originally have started a new unit (as some scholars think), in this chiastic format, YHWH, the creator who is in charge of all, envelops the whole text. At the center, or joining the two segments (44:24-28 and 45:1-8), lie the dual references to the name Cyrus. Indeed, this new founder of a new empire is the would-be savior of the captive and colonized Israelites. This text accordingly culminates in the explicit introduction of the hero of Israel, i.e., Cyrus. In a way, how YHWH is to bring about the plan to comfort Jacob-Israel and Zion, announced in the preceding texts, now becomes clearer by the name of Cyrus. However, as will be discussed below, this oracle equally underscores both the ignorance of Cyrus and the more significant emphasis on the rebuilding of the Jerusalem temple. Thus, Cyrus is a mere instrument in the divine plan, much like the Assyrian king (Isa 10), appointed by YHWH to restore Jerusalem and its temple.

That YHWH alone controls all things is evident in the emphatic recurrences of the active participial verbs of which YHWH is the subject. Thus, God is the "maker" of all, including heaven and earth (v. 24). YHWH nullifies diviners and turns the wise into fools (v. 25). YHWH confirms the words of YHWH's servant and messengers (v. 26a).

Furthermore, as though highlighting the prowess of God's creation through divine speech (cf. Gen 1:3), the remaining participial verbs use the word "to say/tell/call" (*'amar*) accompanied by the sure promises of fulfillment. God "tells" Jerusalem and the cities of Judah to be inhabited and rebuilt (v. 26b). God "tells" the deep to dry up (v. 27). God "calls" Cyrus, "my shepherd," who will fulfill the divine desire. God "tells" Jerusalem's temple to be reestablished (v. 28).

Scholars have addressed the historic campaign of Cyrus who permitted the rebuilding of the city and temple of Jerusalem (cf. Ezra 1:1-4; 2 Chr 36:22-23). Apparently, there must have been strategic economic gain in the Persian policy of allowing reconstruction and semi-autonomy in Yehud. Yet, at the same time, we should also note the ideology of *Pax Persica* over its subject nations. We can find similar ideology in the Assyrian royal inscriptions as well: e.g., the reason for Esarhaddon's rebuilding of Akkad was "doubtless its symbolic and religious significance as the ancient capital. . . . By means of this event Esarhaddon [the Assyrian king] not only paid homage to time-honored Babylonian traditions but also demonstrated and enacted his kingship over Babylonia" (Nissinen 2001, 203). Accordingly, "the return of gods (the cult statues) to various sanctuaries throughout Greater Mesopotamia was also good policy, one that followed age-old Mesopotamian patterns" (Waters 2014, 47).

By the same token, the oft-cited benign policy involving Cyrus's permission for the reconstruction of Jerusalem reveals Persian imperial ideology. Such a colonial ideology—that Cyrus fulfills both YHWH's and Marduk's desires—was "carefully tailored by the Persian conquerors to justify their takeover": the new conqueror would do well to vilify the rival regime that causes divine anger, such as Nabonidus in the case of Cyrus's takeover of Babylon (Waters 2014, 47, 64). The ideology of Cyrus's claim that Marduk, the Babylonian deity, blessed him to rebuild the city Babylon reverberates in our text: i.e., YHWH, Israel's deity, has anointed him to rebuild Jerusalem. How will this unfold? What ramifications does this signify? Who is really in charge of this world-shattering event? We will find out in the subsequent texts.

In the context of changing world affairs and anticipating the demise of Babylon, the next segment (45:1-8) asserts who anoints and authorizes Cyrus the Persian king to take over Babylon. It is not Marduk (Bel), as was widely recognized in the Babylonian *akītu* or New Year festival in 539 BCE. Rather, it is YHWH who created heaven and earth and reigns over the people of Israel and the entire world. Cyrus, the founder of a new empire and the vanquisher of Babylon, Israel's evil oppressor, is YHWH's appointed instrument (cf. 10:15). That YHWH calls Cyrus "my anointed (*mashiakh*=messiah)" (v. 1a) can connote a double meaning (much the same way YHWH's departure from Jerusalem temple in Ezekiel 8–11 implies both the threat of divine abandonment of the rulers in Jerusalem and the assurance of divine presence with the exiled people in Babylon): on the one hand, considering Cyrus a "foreign" king as the anointed widens the theological horizon especially in recognition of the exiles in Babylon who should no longer be deemed unworthy but as divinely loved and elected; on the other hand, this widened horizon intensifies claims concerning YHWH's utter control over the imperial rulers and kingdoms, including Cyrus. While the two prestigious titles of Judean kings— YHWH's "shepherd" and "anointed"—were conferred upon the most powerful foreign ruler of the time, "Cyrus's power is, to be sure, only temporary" (Boling 1999, 176–77).

The expressions of the divine actions, mostly described with YHWH as the subject "I," resemble the descriptions of the Cyrus Cylinder (Paul 2012, 251). Thus, YHWH, who grasps the right hand of Cyrus (cf. 41:10, 13), subdues nations and opens the doors so that gates will remain open (v. 1b). YHWH shatters bronze doors and iron bars (v. 2). YHWH provides secret treasures to Cyrus (v. 3). These expressions compare with elements of the Cyrus Cylinder:

> He [Marduk] surveyed and looked throughout all the lands, searching for a righteous king whom he would support. He called out his name: Cyrus, king of Anshan; he pronounced his name to be king over (all the world). . . . He ordered him to march to his city Babylon. He set him on the road to Babylon and like a companion and friend, he went at his side. . . . I am Cyrus, king of the world. . . . (*COS* II: 315)

In light of the echoes of the Cyrus Cylinder, readers can hear the emphatic polemic of the Isaianic oracles that it is not Marduk but YHWH who made all this possible (Clifford 2010, 272–73). Interestingly, the Cyrus Cylinder records Cyrus's own claim—in first-person speech—that Marduk appointed him to conquer Babylon. In stark contrast, the Isaianic oracle relegates Cyrus to the third person in that YHWH not only appoints Cyrus but also corrects Cyrus's ignorance. One notes the repeated reminders to Cyrus, "though you have not known me" (vv. 4-5; cf. 44:25). Considering that one's not knowing God in Psalms connotes one's being foolish (e.g., Pss 14:1, 4; 53:1, 5; 73:11; 79:6; 82:5; cf. Isa 6:9; 44:19; 45:20), this expression achieves the double purpose of both subjugating the foreign deity and rulers and at the same time elevating YHWH alone (Kim 2014, 158). Moreover, the recurring phrase, "I am YHWH," occurs five times (vv. 3, 5, 6, 7, 8) as if alluding to the exodus tradition of the Pentateuch (e.g., Exod 6:2, 6-8) and thereby reaffirming YHWH's imminent deliverance in the new exodus.

Last but not least, YHWH's incomparable power further reinterprets the creation account of Genesis 1. Whereas the Genesis account reports God's creation (*bara'*) of heavens and earth out of, or over against, "darkness," amid the chaotic forces of the deep (Gen 1:2; cf. Enuma Elish), this oracle proclaims that God not only makes light and peace but also creates (*bara'*) "darkness" and evil (v. 7; cf. v. 3). Whether or not intended to subvert the dualistic traditions of Zoroastrianism in Persia, our Isaianic oracle asserts a monotheism that nullifies the existence of any other deities. The Behistun (or "Besitun") Inscription dating to the time of Darius I, after Cyrus, not only contains many gory descriptions of the Persian emperor's brutal execution of the rebellious subjects but also depicts the Ahuramazdaean worldview. One of the king's duties as the agent of Truth and Good was to fight against the Lie and overcome the forces of chaos, Evil, so as to return the empire "to its proper order" (Waters 2014, 63). Underlying Darius's dualistic imperial ideology, however, "the Mazdaist dualism between Good and Evil, Truth and Lie, Order and Chaos, was a reflection of the dynamic and punitive aspects of the empire, its ambition towards further conquests and its repression of revolts and oppositions" (Liverani 2014, 570). Against this religious and ideological backdrop, the hymn aptly acknowledges that YHWH has "created" it all, including righteousness and salvation on heaven above and earth below (v. 8). The doxology here avers that YHWH is indeed the true God in total control of all daunting forces, such as the Babylonian gods or Cyrus, willing to restore salvific righteousness to mistrustful Jacob-Israel (Brueggemann 1998b, 77).

From Anti-Idols Satires to Anti-Babylon Polemics, 45:9–48:22

Who Brings about the Fall of Babylon? Not Bel-Nebo but YHWH! 45:9-25

Following vv. 1-8 which announce YHWH's claim and control over Cyrus, vv. 9-13 proclaim the divine rebuke over people's objections. Subsequently, vv. 14-17 reassert the incomparability of Israel's God, backed up by the court trial, validating YHWH as the one true God to the ends of the earth in vv. 18-25.

Isaiah 45:9-13 illustrates divine rebuttal of a theological challenge concerning the divine plan to employ Cyrus as an agent. Reminiscent of one of the six woe-oracles in Isaiah 28–33 (cf. 29:15-16), YHWH condemns those theological objectors in rhetorical questions with the analogy of the clay to the potter as well as an infant to the parents (vv. 9-10; cf. Jer 18:1-6).

The divine rebuttal, led by the "thus says YHWH" phrase, ascertains YHWH as Israel's potter and begetter, while responding with comparable rhetorical questions (v. 11). The subsequent answer is irrefutably clear: this same God who created earth and heaven (v. 12) is the one who righteously—that is, with every right—stirred up Cyrus (v. 13). It becomes evident that as R. Norman Whybray asserts, "[Cyrus] is merely [YHWH's] instrument in carrying out a task whose real purpose is the liberation of Israel and the universal honouring [*sic*] of God's name" (1975, 106). This God will "make straight" the paths (cf. 40:3) so that Cyrus may rebuild YHWH's city and redeem the exiles.

Verses 14-17, initiated by the "thus says YHWH" phrase, continue to describe the effect of divine plan on Cyrus as YHWH's instrument. Here its impact will reach the regions of Egypt, Cush, and Seba (v. 14; cf. 43:3). Something remains unclear here though. Whereas in vv. 1-5 YHWH's direct address to Cyrus was in the masculine singular ("you"), here in v. 14 it is in the feminine singular ("you"). Is the addressee Cyrus or Zion-Jerusalem? If the former, the statement portrays a menacing conqueror Cyrus to whom the captives come in chains and bow down—if so, this record starkly contrasts with the self-claim of Cyrus on his peaceful entry and occupation of Babylon in the Cyrus Cylinder (Kuhrt 2007, 49, 70–74). If the latter, the nations' acknowledgment makes sense for the people of Israel, "Surely God is with you, and there is no other god" (cf. 7:14; 8:8, 10) and "you are a God invisible (or who protects)" (v. 15; Paul 2012, 266). In either case, in front of this living God, all idol-makers will be humiliated (v. 16), while Israel will inherit "everlasting salvation," never to be humiliated (v. 17).

Verses 18-25 resume the court trial in which YHWH makes climactic remarks and declares final verdicts. Unlike other gods of chaotic forces,

YHWH is the true God who created heaven and earth, not as a chaos but rather to be inhabited (v. 18). Unlike the idols confined to the land of darkness and chaos, YHWH speaks righteousness and uprightness to the offspring of Jacob (v. 19). Amid the rampant hardship and despair of exilic life as life in the land of darkness, the prophet asserts that their life is governed not by "chaos" but instead by the faithful God.

The divine imperatives to appear in court reach out to the "survivors of the nations" with paradigmatic contrary choices to follow, i.e., between the idols that cannot save (v. 20) and YHWH the righteous God, the savior (v. 21). Another divine imperative follows, but this time with an invitation to "all the ends of the earth" to turn to YHWH and be saved (v. 22). Through YHWH's decree and invitation, every knee shall bow and every tongue confess that "only in YHWH are righteousness and strength" (vv. 23-24a). In the final verdict, just like the unequivocal distinction between vain idols and reliable God, "*all* who rebel against YHWH shall be put to shame" (v. 24b) while "*all* the offspring of Israel shall find vindication and glory" (v. 25).

Marduk versus YHWH, 46:1-13

This oracle continues the depictions of Babylon's downfall via YHWH's agent Cyrus. Yet it also expands the anti-idol satires into dramatic anti-Babylon polemics, nullifying the formidable images of Bel (Marduk) and his son Nebo. With a loosely chiastic arrangement, this unit exhibits two main subunits: YHWH's subjugation of Bel and Nebo (vv. 1-7) and YHWH's employment of Cyrus (vv. 8-13). At the same time, three key verses starting with imperative verbs form a chiastic linkage:

v. 3—"Listen to me" (*shim'u 'elay*)
    v. 8—"Remember" (*zikru*)
    v. 9—"Remember" (*zikru*)
v. 12—"Listen to me" (*shim'u 'elay*)

Here the central portion highlights the divine admonition for Jacob-Israel to remember the former things, i.e., the only living God.

Verses 1-7 derisively depict the powerlessness of Babylonian gods—mere heavy "things" that are carried by animals (vv. 1-2) and by people (vv. 5-7). These statements bracket the core theme of the maternal image of YHWH's undying love toward Jacob-Israel (vv. 3-4).

The opening phrases present a vivid pun with alliterations (vv. 1-2). The seemingly fearful Babylonian gods are bowing down and cowering (cf. 1 Sam 5:1-4). Bel, another name for Marduk, and his son Nebo were the primary

deities paraded through the city streets of Babylon during the New Year's
festival followed by the boisterous crowd (Albertz 2003, 105). Now, instead
of their pompous march, they are merely "carried, loaded burdens" that
animals carry (v. 1). Here the verb "to cower" (*qores*) sounds similar to the
name "Cyrus" (*koresh*). If the pun is intended, it would imply that Marduk
is bowing down and Nebo is "Cyrus-ing," i.e., Cyrus is subordinating and
replacing Babylon. In fact, these burdensome deities seemingly parading
through the city's main street will process all the way into captivity, just as
Babylon will succumb to Persia (v. 2). Colonized Israelites would have used
the mechanism of "mimicry" as "camouflage" in reaction to the influence of
the colonizing empire, as Homi Bhabha theorizes: "What they all share is a
discursive process by which the excess or slippage produced by the *ambivalence* of mimicry (almost the same, *but not quite*) does not merely 'rupture'
the discourse, but becomes transformed into an uncertainty which fixes the
colonial subject as a 'partial' presence" (1984, 127).

Scholars have discovered striking similarities between this Isaianic polem-
ical oracle and the Babylonian "processional omens." According to Hanspeter
Schaudig, the passage indicates that the Judean deportees witnessed this
Babylonian procession in their exile. During the *akītu*-festival in the month
of Nissan at the beginning of a year (i.e., in spring), the statue of Marduk
accompanied by his son Nabu would make a procession "from his temple
Esaĝil at Babylon to the *akītu*-house outside of the city" (Schaudig 2008,
558). In the Babylonian "processional omens," the statues' bowing down to
the right or left could mean good omens, while their being twisted or turned
bad omens. Each processional occasion would thus increase the Babylonians'
fear of auspicious misfortune. The prophet here points to such an anxiety
involved in every swaying and staggering move of the statues but ultimately
portrays the statues and idols as impotent spoils. Whereas customarily people
(e.g., soldiers) would carry the statues, the prophet here reinterprets and
depicts these idols as fastened to animals about to be abducted (Schaudig
2008, 566–69).

Contrary to the Babylonian gods that will be "carried" away, YHWH vows
in a powerful maternal image the divine promise not only to "carry," "bear,"
and "rescue" Jacob-Israel from birth but also to protect them all the way
into their old age of gray hair (vv. 3-4). Hanne Løland, in her meticulous
linguistic and literary analyses of 46:3-4, identifies the female imagery for
God as a mother (cf. 42:13-14) in that "YHWH is also said to have a womb
. . . and is depicted as a pregnant woman. The image shifts as YHWH acts
as the midwife who lifts up the child at birth" (2008, 160). Indeed YHWH
has carried the "house of Jacob" and "all the remnant of the house of Israel"

from the womb (cf. 44:2, 24). All the key verbs in v. 1—"carry," "bear," and "rescue"—which Bel and Nebo could not execute now recur in v. 4, accentuating that YHWH is capable of doing all these.

The metaphor makes a striking contrast between vv. 1-2 and vv. 3-4. Whereas the Babylonian idols had to be "carried away" by the beasts (vv. 1-2), God will affectionately and faithfully "carry" the people of Israel (vv. 3-4). This divine parental care will nurture God's people from their time in the womb all the way into their old age, yes, until they turn into gray hairs! Thus, as Walter Brueggemann expounds, the exiles are not a "one-generation community." They need the unchanging and unfailing nurture throughout intergenerational ebbs and flows by the steadfast love of God, "the endlessly reliable guardian and advocate of Israel" (Brueggemann 1998b, 88).

A question echoes the previous ones (40:18, 25) but now implies indirect contention with Marduk: "To whom will you compare me . . . that *we* are alike?" (v. 5). Undeniably, Marduk, the feared deity of Babylon (and Persia), is a mere idol that people assemble out of gold and silver (v. 6), which however cannot move, answer, or save them (v. 7). With regard to the issue of money associated with idols (cf. 40:19; 43:24; 55:1), whereas these idols depend on the money (gold and silver) from their makers, YHWH requires no money from worshipers but instead provides for them free of charge (Abernethy 2014, 132). The illustration makes another thematic contrast between vv. 3-4 and vv. 5-7. Whereas God faithfully promises to "carry" and protect Israel, God's children, from the womb to the old age (vv. 3-4), this despondent exilic people "carry" the idols of gold and silver on their shoulders (vv. 5-7; Brueggemann 1998b, 89).

Verses 8-13 shift the attention from Bel or Nebo toward Cyrus, the attacking bird summoned by YHWH's whistle. Against the exiles who are acculturated into the magnificent marches of Bel and Nebo, as some of them may have been carrying them, YHWH casts the twofold imperatives to "remember" (vv. 8-9; cf. Ps 25:6-7). Who are to remember? They are the "transgressors" of heart, like Jacob-Israel's preexilic ancestors (v. 8; cf. 43:27). What are they to remember? YHWH exhorts them to remember "the former things of old" that "I am God and there is no other" (v. 9).

What of this God, unlike any other false gods? The three participial verbs illustrate the divine acts in the course of human history (vv. 10-11; Franke 1994, 59). First, this God declares what will come after the former times (v. 10a). Second, God states the plan that will assuredly stand (v. 10b). Third, YHWH is the one who calls the bird of prey—Cyrus—from the east (v. 11; cf. 41:2). Accordingly, in the course of history during the exilic time, many may have wondered as to how the mighty Babylon would fall. The prophet conveys not only that this empire's demise is sure to come but also that YHWH has already engineered this ebb and flow, including the rise of Cyrus.

The culminating call to listen reconnects the addressees with "the house of Jacob" and "all the remnant of the house of Israel" (v. 3) but now described as "those stubborn of heart" and "those far from righteousness" (v. 12). The LXX similarly renders it "the faint of heart," a rebuke or wake-up call not unlike the preceding passage against those who are prone to doubt and give up (e.g., 42:18-19; 43:27-28). Yet the MT actually contains "those mighty [lit., bull-like stubborn] of heart" (cf. v. 8; 6:10) which then may imply a contrast between the true "Mighty One of Jacob" (cf. 49:26; 60:16), YHWH, and Jacob-Israel's inability to be truly mighty. Finally, this all-encompassing and all-powerful God personally yet climactically addresses Zion and Israel, promising to give salvation to Zion and to restore the divine glory to Israel (v. 13). It is not Jacob-Israel, with hearts fossilized with iniquity, but rather YHWH who will bring about righteousness and salvation to them.

A Taunt Song against (Virgin Daughter) Babylon, 47:1-15

As though a counterpart to the immobile "Bel and Nebo (masculines)," this oracle now derides the haughty "daughter Babylon (feminine)." Defiant and accusatory commands to daughter Babylon open the taunt song (vv. 1-6). Then, in the central portion, YHWH or the prophet twice retorts Babylon's pompous claims with the irrevocable sentence of disaster and destruction upon her (vv. 7-11). Another command wraps up this unit with impassioned mockery and condemnation, pronouncing that daughter Babylon will be dethroned (vv. 12-15).

Verses 1-6 convey YHWH's taunting commands against daughter Babylon (vv. 1-4), backed up by the rationales of the divine intention to reverse Babylon's fortune (vv. 5-6). The opening imperatives coincide with the opening verse of Isaiah 46. Whereas Judah "went down" (*yarad*) from his brothers (Gen 38:1) and Joseph was "taken down" (*yarad*) to Egypt (Gen 39:1), in this exilic context, Bel and Nebo "cower" (46:1) and virgin daughter Babylon is going to "go down" (*yarad*; v. 1). The motif of going *down* heightens the theme of dramatic downfall of the Babylonian empire.

Moreover, the taunt to daughter Babylon to "sit in the dust" and "without a throne" mirrors the reversed fortune of daughter Zion's sitting on the ground (Lam 1:1; 2:10). Notably here, the word "sitting" (*yashab*) occurs six times in this chapter (vv. 1 [two times], 5, 8 [two times], 14). Readers may recall the lament song of the exilic Judeans who "sat down" by the rivers of Babylon amid the taunting oppression of daughter Babylon (Ps 137:1, 8). Now it is daughter Babylon's time to sit down, humiliated and accursed.

This mocking taunt does not stop there. No less than six imperative verbs follow (v. 2). These expressions quite likely reflect the memories of Judeans' exilic humiliation when Babylon took them captives. The phrase "grind meal" may echo the story of Samson who was blinded and bound in chains to grind mill in the prison (Judg 16:21; cf. 2 Kgs 25:7). Babylon's "nakedness" and "shame" may be reminiscent of Jerusalem's disgrace (v. 3; cf. 32:11; Lam 5:1). These expressions imply the exposure of the personified city's genitalia. Now reversed, virgin daughter Babylon shall meet her own doom for her brutality and abuse of Jerusalem (Franke 2014, 708). Hearing this incredible taunt against Babylon, the chorus joins the "we"-group to proclaim YHWH as "our redeemer" (v. 4).

The command to "sit silently" opens the subsequent segment (vv. 5-6). Now daughter Babylon will enter into darkness, thus into exile (v. 5; cf. 8:22; 42:7, 16). Israel's demise was not because of Babylon's might but rather because of YHWH's anger (v. 6). Readers hear a tone of divine pathos as YHWH affectionately calls Israel "my people" and "my inheritance."

Verses 7-11, the central subunit, provide the double speeches about Babylon's hubris (vv. 7-9 and vv. 10-11). Each time, the oracle reverses Babylon's boastful claim and throws it back at her. In the first instance, Babylon said (cf. 49:14), "I shall be a queen forever" (v. 7; cf. v. 5). The rebuttal accuses Babylon as the sensuous one, who "sits" in security (v. 8). Reminiscent of the haughty claim of the Babylonian king (14:13; cf. Ps 53:1), daughter Babylon claims, "I am, and there is no one besides me"—the claim only YHWH can deservedly make (cf. 43:11; 44:6; 45:5, 6, 18, 22; 46:9). On the contrary, the disaster of loss of children and widowhood—what many Judeans experienced—shall come upon Babylon (v. 9).

In the second instance, daughter Babylon again arrogantly yet ignorantly boasts two times: "No one sees me" and "I am, and there is no one besides me" (v. 10). Twice daughter Babylon uttered her oppressive hubris. Now, the divine rebuttal casts threefold curses—evil, disaster, and destruction (v. 11; cf. Jer 14:12; Ezek 5:17; 1 Chr 21:12).

Verses 12-15 start with an imperative, like v. 1 (cf. v. 4), and climactically present the mocking taunts and irreversible denunciation against daughter Babylon. The mocking taunts are akin to the humorous derisions aimed at idol-makers. Whereas YHWH earlier commanded daughter Babylon to "go down" and "sit" (v. 1), now the exhortation is for her to "stand up" (v. 12). The invitation is for her to use as many spells and sorceries as she can (cf. v. 9; Exod 8:18-19 [MT 8:14-15]). There is even an encouragement twice, "perhaps," not unlike the prophetic support or wish (e.g., Isa 37:4; Joel 2:14; Amos 5:15; Jonah 1:6; 3:9; Zeph 2:3). In actuality, however, it is a divine challenge for the Babylonian astrologers, magicians, diviners, and sorcerers to "stand up" and "save" Babylon (v. 13).

The final verdict is a solemn condemnation. Babylon's rulers, queens, and soothsayers are "like stubble," soon to be consumed by fire (v. 14). The wooden idols were at least useful to warm the idol-makers (44:16). Yet Babylon will not even have a fire to "sit" around. The polemic against the military might, religious hegemony, and commercial power of the Babylonian empire—including those exiles who may have followed the ethos, rituals, and systems of Babylon—thus culminates in one phrase: "There is no one to save you" (v. 15).

Significantly, whereas prophetic marital metaphors are typically negative (cf. Hosea 4–14, Jeremiah 2–4, and Ezekiel), those in the second half of Isaiah are uniquely optimistic, positive. Accordingly, the strikingly negative metaphor on Babylon in Isaiah 47 is a notable exception (Moughtin-Mumby 2008, 122, 137, 153).

Amid this metaphorical language, there is a sharp double edge—painfully paradoxical—for interpretive tension. On the one hand, despite their powerful anti-imperial and anti-hegemonic conceptuality, these metaphors have the potential to be misread or misused to justify violence in our time. We should keep in mind that metaphors, like parables or illustrations, should remain metaphors, first and foremost. We ought to distinguish the literary and rhetorical functions of metaphors, or even poetic imprecatory curses (e.g., Ps 109:6-19; 137:8-9), from the actual historical and military events. Considering the ill consequences of the vicious cycles of war, these metaphors disclose painful reminders that war and violence devastate so many innocent people. In light of the implicit but resolute idea that all human beings are God's children, the vulnerable populace, especially women and children, are hauntingly reminded that in war's brutality, no one wins: "The command for Babylon to 'sit in silence and go in darkness' is chilling for its echoes not only of the silence of the female elsewhere in the prophetic texts, but also with the responses of flesh-and-blood women to such violence" (Moughtin-Mumby 2008, 139). Hence, "reading all the metaphors critically in context" is indispensable in order to avoid "mistaking the metaphor for the message" (Clifford 2010, 278).

Yet, on the other hand, ironically and sadly, it is the silence of the victimized female that beckons the vivid, albeit painful, voicing and retelling of such violence and brutality. Walter Brueggemann has forcefully warned about the "costly loss of lament" in our interpretive discourses and theological guilds:

"what happens when appreciation of the lament as a form of speech and faith is lost, as I think it is largely lost in contemporary usage? . . . In the absence of lament, we may be engaged in uncritical history-stifling praise" (1986, 59, 67). History not correctly remembered is bound—and doomed—to be repeated: "Things I'm going to say, not shout. I've long given up shouting" (Fanon 2008, xi).

In a society where equilibrium is tilted, justice is twisted, and voices of the victims are silenced, someone needs to keep records, tell stories, and shout pains. During the Japanese occupation in 1910–1945, many Koreans, both male (7 million) and female, were forcefully taken away as forced service laborers, military sources, and so on. Among them, approximately, if not more than, 200,000 young girls of Korea were forcefully taken to serve as sex slaves (aka "comfort women"). Against the threats of brutal beating and inhumane butchering, they had no choice but to be sexual slaves for tens, hundreds, and thousands of raping soldiers. After decades, when historians are still trying to cover up, distort, or outright deny such a policy, many surviving victims cry out, demanding a genuine, truthful, and especially "official" apology by the representative of the Japanese government. Like the Holocaust Memorial *in Berlin*(!), history must be recorded and taught, lest some can easily deny any criminal acts, such as the German Nazis' mass murder of more than six million Jews during the same era.

During the discussion session after a thought-provoking seminar at my school on the topic of the mass incarceration and racial discrepancy still rampant in the United States, an African-American student gently expressed, "White people don't *need* to hear about this stuff, it's okay." Immediately afterwards, a Caucasian woman replied, "Actually, we white people do need to hear what you black people have to tell us, and hopefully learn and work together to heal and reconcile," followed by the main speaker's caring challenge, "Go talk to the 70 percent of white people who don't know that there is such a problem in the past and now in our country." The "comfort women" victims—some of them are indeed "alive" as genuine witnesses, albeit in the average age of ninety or older—shout out that what they want is not being pitied or paid but being heard, not being labeled but recognized as human beings in their truthful testimonies. To the question, "What would you wish if you can go back to your youth?" a survivor in an interview once answered, "I only wish that I could have a normal 'average' life, such as getting married, building a family, and having kids—that would be my wish."

Thus, to the war-torn and devastated victims, such metaphors of reversal, revenge, or even curse upon the malefactors would have been one of the few—if not only—venues to confront and defy their hardship and to have any chance of surviving and rebounding toward hope and meaning-making:

> In telling their stories, victims are no longer frozen in time; rather, they are advocates, ones who tell a story in the present about the past so as to create a better future. . . . They may not be able to return to their "homely," pre-trauma, just-world assumptions about the world . . . but they can construct a narrative with a conceptual basis in which they can feel at home, and where they can invite others to join with them in creating a society that is more just because it recognizes and mitigates fortune's injustices. (Rumfelt 2011, 339)

Revisiting, reminding, and retelling stories of human pain and atrocity would be excruciatingly painful and often dangerous. Nonetheless, it is precisely because such pains and dangers can recur due to our ignorance, indifference, or denial that such stories and histories must be voiced, heard, recorded, recognized, and retold. The testimony of Jan Ruff-O'Herne, a Dutch "comfort woman" victim for the Japanese army in Indonesia during World War II, rings such an outcry of truth:

> The world ignored these atrocities for almost fifty years. It has taken fifty years for these women's ruined lives to become a human rights issue. . . . It is by telling my story that I hope these atrocities against women in war will never be forgotten and will never happen again. (2005, 3 and 8)

If the victims' voices are silenced and mouths shut, how else and who else will tell them?

Get out of Babylon . . . Back to Zion! 48:1-22

The resolute polemic against the Babylonian empire, which followed YHWH's employing Cyrus, consisted of the divine taunt toward Marduk and the personified city of Babylon. This oracle rehashes divine control of world history in terms of "former things," Israel's past rebellion and exile (vv. 1-11), and "new things," the liberation of exiles via Cyrus (vv. 12-16). The prophetic proclamation culminates with the urgent call to get out of Babylon (vv. 17-22).

Verses 1-11 describe the former things and the new things, thereby reiterating who has been in control of world events. First of all, the addressees of this oracle cover a broad spectrum: the house of Jacob, those who call themselves by the name of Israel, those who came from the waters of Judah, those who swear by the name of YHWH (cf. 56:6), those who invoke the

God of Israel (v. 1), and those who call themselves residents of the holy city (v. 2). Notably, the imperative "listen" is plural. Admittedly, these are various expressions for comparable groups. Yet, despite differences, all these entities—both Jacob-Israel and Judah—attain equal opportunity or equal treatment (cf. 46:3, 12). At the same time, there is inherent ambiguity between negative assessment (their not seeking God in "true righteousness") and positive consideration (their leaning on God) (Franke 1994, 173–75).

Now, the oracle recalls the "former things" (v. 3; cf. 41:22; 42:9; 43:9, 18; 46:9). Israel's former description as the "stiff-necked" people in the wilderness tradition resurfaces (v. 4; cf. Exod 32:9; 33:3, 5; 34:9; Deut 9:6, 13; 31:27). In the midst of the divine guidance and provision of the manna, this grumbling people "treated the *abundance of the creation* as though it was the *scarcity of Pharaoh*" (Brueggemann 2014, 65). The reference to iron "sinew" may allude to the "sinew" of the hip, Jacob's thigh (Gen 32:32). As suggested by the phrases that echo the golden-calf rebellion, this stubborn people ought not to fall to the dominant Babylonian culture: "My idol did them" (v. 5).

Next, the oracle reintroduces the "new things" (v. 6; cf. 42:9). These new things indicate liberation and freedom from the long, agonizing exilic life, analogous to the famous expression of Martin Luther King, Jr.'s dream speech: "Free at last, Free at last, Thank God almighty we are free at last." God has recently "created" these new things so that they cannot say, "I knew them" (v. 7). However, echoing the call narrative, YHWH asserts what traitors and rebels this obdurate people have been from their birth (v. 8; cf. 6:9-10; Gen 8:21).

Then the theme of the merciful God resounds amid the deafening tones of Israel's stubborn sinfulness. Inasmuch as Israel's corruption resurfaced in the preceding subunits, the oracle asserts that YHWH is "slow to anger" (v. 9; cf. Exod 34:6). Accordingly, Israel's hardship and exile are processes of refining (v. 10; cf. 1:25). Here we find a double meaning: The Qumran scroll (1QIsa[1]) reads, "I *tested* you in the furnace of affliction"; MT reads "I *chose* you in the furnace of affliction." Bracketing this subunit, readers learn of the foundational theme of divine compassion, i.e., because of who God is, "for the sake of my name . . . my praise . . . my glory" (v. 9 and v. 11; cf. Ezek 20:9, 14, 22, 44; 36:21-22, 32).

Verses 12-16 delineate the divine plan to utilize Cyrus to deliver YHWH's people out of Babylon. A series of three imperatives (vv. 12, 14, 16) takes up a central place of this chapter. The first imperative resumes the opening imperative (vv. 12-13; cf. v. 1). Whereas the opening call to "listen" addresses diverse groups in the plural, however, now the call targets Jacob-Israel in the singular (v. 12). What are they to hear? Jacob-Israel, divinely elected, should note that YHWH is the one who created the earth and heaven (v. 13).

The second imperative charges "all of you" to gather (v. 14). Briefly, the prophet intervenes and discloses the divine love for a foreign, superpower king Cyrus: "YHWH loves him." Much like when YHWH calls Cyrus "my shepherd" (44:28) and "my anointed" (45:1), this description can be scandalous. This description of divine "love" occurs elsewhere only for Abraham (41:8) and Jacob-Israel (43:4). Yet, at the same time, in light of the ancient Near Eastern royal inscriptions, readers may learn that it is not Marduk but YHWH who loves and appoints Cyrus to fulfill YHWH's "delight," the plan against Babylon: "Cyrus . . . whose rule Bel (i.e., Marduk) and Nabu love" (COS II: 315). The emphatic repetition of "I, I have spoken and called him" supports this notion (v. 15).

The third imperative addresses all of them to hear that YHWH has been there from the beginning (v. 16). The prophet affirms the ongoing effect of divine plan and word through the claim that God, who is the first and the last (cf. v. 12), has "sent me with his spirit."

Verses 17-22 conclude this unit with the recollection of the covenants (vv. 17-19) and the climactic admonition to leave Babylon en route to Zion (vv. 20-22). In fact, this subunit wraps up the whole section of Isaiah 40–48 by way of the bracketing passages of 40:12-40 and 48:17-22—both sharing pertinent expressions and themes: YHWH's knowledge of the future as well as power over military-political events (Lund 2007, 227–29). With the "thus says YHWH" phrase, this subunit reasserts that "I am YHWH" who teaches and leads Israel on the right path (v. 17). Somewhat similar to the double meaning in vv. 1-2, the particle of wish ("O that you would . . .") can connote not only undeniable regret of the past but also promise embedded in the conditional covenant: if you keep my commandments, then you will have the blessings of shalom, triumph, and many descendants (vv. 18-19).

Finally, the urgent command is to "go out" and "flee" from the soon-to-be-collapsing Babylon (v. 20; cf. Gen 19:17; Exod 5:1). Just like the early exhortation to proclaim, "Here is your God" (40:9), now the prophet dispatches the message of the good news to the end of the earth: "YHWH has redeemed his servant Jacob!" In the new exodus out of Babylon, YHWH will assuredly provide gushing water through the desert (v. 21; cf. Exod 17:6; Num 20:11). It should be noted here, however, that when they flee from Babylon (which is the ultimate goal of the previous oracles on the transition between former things and new things), "they not only have to leave the geographical place but also their Babel-likeness" amid their current exilic predicament of sinfulness and idolatry—all things negative in their identity, self-worth, and ways of life (Uhlig 2009a, 217; cf. vv. 8, 12). This section then ends with a scribal marker in v. 22. Whereas those who keep divine commandments will have peace (v. 18), there is no peace for the wicked, Babylon included.

Good News of New Generations for Daughter Zion (Sixth Branch of the Lampstand)

Isaiah 49–57

Although many verbal links exist between Isaiah 40–48 and this section (hence the term Second Isaiah for chs. 40–55), some shifts in content and pattern are noticeable. From chapter 49 and on, readers encounter no "former things" and the related command whether or not to remember former things. There is no anti-idol polemic, and mentions of Babylon or Cyrus are no more. Also, except for 49:5-6, the pair of terms "Jacob" and "Israel" does not occur anymore (Paul 2012, 321). Rather, the primary emphasis lies on Zion-Jerusalem, where God will resume divine kingship (Blenkinsopp 2002, 114). Joseph Blenkinsopp even argues that, in distinction with the style and situation of chapters 40–48, already from chapter 49 and on, "the hand of a Trito-Isaianic editor is in evidence" (2002, 80).

On the one hand, we note literary and thematic discontinuity. Chapter 49, for example, functions like a prism or a hinge involving two laments reflecting the exilic context: (a) Jacob-Israel's lament (49:1-13) and (b) Zion's lament (49:14-26). Read this way, the first lament wraps up the preceding section centering on Jacob-Israel, while the second opens up the present section centering on Zion. On the other hand, at the same time, there is continuity, especially in pattern and sequence. In this section, the "male" Servant and "female" Zion pattern will recur in alternating sequences: Servant (49:1-13), Zion (49:14–50:3), Servant (speaking, 50:4-11), Zion (51:1–52:12), Servant (52:13–53:12), and, finally, Zion (ch. 54; cf. Tull 1997, 105). This pattern signifies various thematic implications, not only the gender balance and mutuality (comparable to the male and female imageries for God) but also the inherent diversity of the two symbolic entities or groups as well as their potential, ideal unity.

In the previous section, the grim predicament of the Babylonian exile discloses the exiles' hardened hearts (42:18-25) and sinfulness (43:16-28), indeed a familiar tendency from birth (48:8). We learn of divine solutions to those problems: YHWH elects the Servant to bring the people out of prison in preparation for their homecoming (49:8-12), to help their "de-hardening" (50:4-9; cf. 48:16), to atone for their sins and make them righteous (52:13–53:12), and ultimately to accomplish their dramatic transformation out of the Babylonian captivity and the hardships in colonized Yehud (55:12-13; Uhlig 2009a, 247–48).

The previous call to witness (41:1) highlighted YHWH's taunt against the idols of the empire, with the subsequent illustrations of the demise of daughter Babylon through Cyrus and the expectation of the new exodus and new things (Isa 40–48). Now the new call to witness (49:1) focuses on the Servant's vocation and daughter Zion's return and renewal out of exile (Isa 49–57). Toward the end of this section, we find a trend involving increasing tension between the lowly Servant/Zion and the corrupt oppressors. This opposition becomes more distinct in the contrasts between the marginalized and the dominant between the poor and the wealthy (Isa 55); between the outsiders and the insiders (Isa 56); and between the righteous and the wicked (Isa 57).

Structure of Isaiah 49–57
The Servant Consoled and Zion Comforted, 49:1–52:12
The Servant Will Prosper, Zion's Offspring Will Multiply, 53:13–54:17
The Marginalized Righteous versus the Dishonorable Wicked, 55:1–57:21

The Servant Consoled and Zion Comforted, 49:1–52:12

The Servant's Complaint and Zion's Lament, 49:1-26
Despite numerous recurring exchanges and seemingly disjointed dialogues between the Servant and YHWH, as well as between Zion and YHWH, this unit coheres around two main parts, both initiated by complaints—of the Servant (vv. 1-13) and of Zion (vv. 14-26).

Verses 1-13 begin a new section and present the Servant's complaint and divine response, recalling a court scenario. Scholars have incessantly debated issues related to the Servant, especially concerning his identity and the historical setting of this unit. The elusive ambiguity of the text militates against any firm theory. Yet, as far as the present form is concerned, the Servant is explicitly and consistently identified as Jacob-Israel.

The call to listen addressed to the coastlands and peoples afar (vv. 1-3) resumes the previous call (41:1), but now with a new message. Whereas YHWH previously addressed the Servant directly, "who formed you from the womb" (44:2, 24; 46:3; cf. Gen 25:23-26), now the Servant speaks, "YHWH has called me from the womb" (v. 1). This description of the divine election from the womb not only mirrors the special appointment of royal Assyrian monarchs, such as Ashurbanipal, but also echoes the prophetic call of Jeremiah (Jer 1:5; Paul 2012, 324). Just as Yᴴᴡᴴ put divine words in Jeremiah's mouth (Jer 1:9), now Yᴴᴡᴴ has made the Servant's mouth like a sharpened sword (v. 2; cf. 11:4). In the military nature of the Servant's equipment, Joseph Blenkinsopp detects political language, "a political manifesto . . . in the political sphere that Cyrus was unwilling to perform [Isa 40–48] will now be undertaken by Israel itself by means of its prophetic representative" (2002, 300). Thus, echoing the motif of the prophetic legacy and the ancient Near Eastern royal ideology, Jacob-Israel representing the exilic community hears again, "You are my servant" (v. 3).

The Servant's complaint states that, unlike those who wait for Yᴴᴡᴴ (40:30-31), the Servant has grown weary (v. 4; cf. 43:22-24). Key words, such as "chaos" (*tohu*) and "vapor" (*hebel*; cf. Eccl 1:2; 12:8), heighten the situation in which there is no theophany but only a hollow image (Goldingay and Payne 2006b, 160). Then we learn of the servant's mission: to bring back Jacob and Israel, presumably from the exile (v. 5). The logical lacuna is, how can the Servant (if Jacob-Israel) help itself (Jacob-Israel) return? We should note that the word pair, Jacob-Israel as the Servant, occurs only within Isaiah 40–48, and not in 49–66, except in 49:5-6. In a way, there seems to be a conceptual shift in 49:5-6, where the Servant's task expands beyond the horizons of Jacob and Israel. Whoever the prototype of the Servant may have been, therefore, the present text conveys a concept that this Servant has the task of helping bring back the people from the Diaspora and beyond.

Further delineation of, or midrashic commentaries on, the two catch-phrases expands this thesis statement of the Servant's commissioning. These expansions constitute an inverted chiasm with 42:6: "a light for the nations" (vv. 5-7) and "a covenant to the people(s)" (vv. 8-11). The first inner-biblical commentary (vv. 5-7)—on the phrase "a light for the nations"—describes Yᴴᴡᴴ's plan as more than raising up the tribes of Jacob and returning the survivors of Israel (v. 6a). Rather, the divine plan is to make the Servant "a light for the nations," implying that Yᴴᴡᴴ's salvation will cover "the end(s) of the earth" (v. 6b; cf. 40:28; 41:5, 9; 42:10; 43:6; 45:22; 48:20; Acts 13:47). Put differently, the servant is to bring salvation to the ends of the earth, as Abraham is to be a channel of blessing to all the families of the earth (Gen 12:2-3; Goldingay and Payne 2006b, 166; Knight 1984, 48).

At present, the nations despise and abhor the Servant; he is not their light (v. 7a). Shalom Paul discovers a double entendre in the word "nation" (*goy*), which can also be vocalized to mean "body, back" (*gewih*). Accordingly, the phrase read as "whose *body* is abhorred" can modify its preceding phrase, "the person despised," while the phrase read as "abhorred of *nations*" can complement its following phrase, "slave of rulers" (Paul 1996, 370). Thus, sandwiched between the two catchphrases for the identity of this "Servant of YHWH"—"a light to the nations" (vv. 5-6) and "a covenant to the peoples" (vv. 8-11)—we should note this possible third identity: "a slave of rulers" (v. 7a), a despised person, spurned by the nations.

We should then note a linguistic and thematic contrast between the "Servant" (*'ebed*) of YHWH and the "slave" (*'ebed*) of rulers. Jacob-Israel, or some individual as a divine agent, is both the "slave of imperial rulers" and "slave of YHWH." Through a double meaning, this term connotes both a royal "servant" and a subservient "slave." But "[*'ebed*] is mostly a slave, that is, an inferior, a non-autonomous social agent whose life is contractually controlled by a master" (Brenner 1997, 146). In this semantic nuance, the juxtaposition of these two phrases—slave of rulers and servant of YHWH —may reflect the physical, social, and emotional hardship experienced by slaves in the Babylonian empire on the one hand, and also the sense of the lofty transfer to the noble status as slaves of God on the other hand. This thematic contrast is intrinsic to the shift of the status of the Israelites from being "slaves" to the Egyptian Pharaoh and taskmasters (Exod 3:7) to becoming "worshipers" (*'abad*, lit. "slaves") of YHWH (Exod 3:12; cf. Lev 25:55): "Unlike Israel's harsh enslavement by Pharaoh, Israel's service to God is an affirmation of life's highest possibilities, often characterized by . . . God's blessing flowing outward and resulting in material and spiritual fulfillment for God's people and the larger world" (Kaminsky and Lohr 2015, 72–73). This juxtaposition leads smoothly to the theme of reversal, heightening the dramatic future when the imperial kings and princes will submit to the colonized, captive slaves (v. 7b).

The second inner-biblical commentary (vv. 8-11)—on the phrase "a covenant of the people(s)"—underscores the "day" of salvation, when YHWH will elect the Servant for this task (v. 8). This status entails rescuing the prisoners as a light, releasing those in darkness, and also guiding the sheep to safely graze in lush pastures under the protection of the good shepherd (v. 9; cf. 40:11). Darkness symbolizes the exile, from which these prisoners will depart without hunger or thirst (v. 10). On the highways that YHWH will help construct, not only YHWH but the exilic people will march on their homecoming journey (v. 11). Here one finds a thematic correlation between 44:9-20 and 49:8-11. Contrary to the idol-makers who will starve and pass out without water (44:12) and the idol-worshipers who will "graze" on ashes (44:20), God's redeemed will neither hunger nor thirst, safely led along springs of water (49:9-10; Abernethy 2014, 134–35).

Yet this is not empty utopianism. Rather, it is the call for the Servant to take a significant role in the divine plan "aimed at the restoration of the entire creation to justice and peace, to [*shalom*]" (Hanson 1988, 97). The call for the Servant to be the "light for the nations" and the "covenant of the people(s)," therefore, does not merely depict a passive rescue from the dark, exilic imprisonment. Rather, it envisions an active, grandiose role of the community of Israel "as the center of the world of nations" (Gerstenberger 2011, 491). Out of the depths (Ps 130:1), Israel is not only to survive barely but rather to thrive with the marvelous dreams and visions to encourage one another and bless the whole world as well. James Logan's profound call for the inspired people to rekindle hope and rebuild love in the midst of the Ferguson, Missouri, tragedy of a white officer killing an unarmed black man (and the resulting violene) prompts a similar kind of resilient and sublime vision:

> Even when God's love appears to be all but dead and buried, out of the ground and heavens of Christian hope we still find ways to celebrate life in the midst of struggle: we dance, make love, sing and shout, make art, we think and reason and imagine a human present and future bound by God's Love, even if by a tread. I would ask that fighters against the ravages of *Everywhere Ferguson* hold on tight to even a tread of hope. (Logan 2016)

Thus the returnees in the new exodus will come from north, west, and even Sinim (southern Egypt)—not only from Babylon but also from various regions of the Diaspora (v. 12; cf. 43:5-6). The closing hymn calls heaven, earth, and mountains to rejoice at the divine "comfort" for YHWH's people, the afflicted exiles, because "the command to comfort YHWH's people (40.1) is being fulfilled" (v. 13; Goldingay and Payne 2006b, 178).

Verses 14-26 present daughter Zion's lament and the divine response. This subunit is a counterpart to the preceding subunit, vv. 1-13. Just as the servant's complaint finds an answer in the divine promise of the new exodus, now female Zion's lament draws the divine assurance of the triumphant and royal return of countless children of mother Zion (Maier 2008, 164–67). Intertextually linked to the imagery and catchwords of Jeremiah 13, this Isaianic text reverses the oracle of doom into one of return and repatriation (Willey 1997, 203–204). In a larger scope, following E. Hessler's analysis, John Goldingay and David Payne discover another counterpart, in a reversal parallel, again with the complaints of Jacob-Israel in 40:12-31 (interestingly, ch. 40 starts Isa 40–48, while ch. 49 starts the Isa 49–57 section; Goldingay and Payne 2006b, 180):

49:14-17	40:27-31	Plaint and response
49:18-21	40:25-26	A challenge to lift eyes and look
49:22-23	40:21-24	YHWH's sovereignty over kings
49:24-26	40:18-20	YHWH's incomparable power
50:1-3	40:12-17	YHWH's lordship over the created world

Moreover, it is noteworthy that the pattern of gender combination of both *male* (Servant) and *female* (Zion) alternates not only in Isaiah 49 but also in its preceding and following chapters. The double complaints of male Servant and female Zion, placed right next to each other, together form a divergent yet harmonious theological duet.

Rather than conjecturing two groups (or locales) from the Servant oracle (49:1-13) and Zion lament (49:14-26), Uta Schmidt proposes that Isaiah 49 presents two interpretive options—two theological positions or "models"—toward envisioning the future amid desolate ruins. According to her, the Servant-model demonstrates the attitude of unshaken, optimistic trust in YHWH despite harsh realities. Contrarily, the Zion-model displays an alternative reaction to the exilic hardships, a more pessimistic confrontation of Judah's miserable environs, with no conciliatory tone. Together, therefore, these two models portray two different but equally legitimate ways for the exilic people to lament and find meaning for the future amid ongoing devastation and captivity: "the Servant-model assumes a positive and trusting attitude in spite of suffering" whereas "the Zion-model takes serious the experience of utter suffering, loneliness, and abandonment" (Schmidt 2011, 90).

Just like the complaint of the male Servant (v. 4), now the female personified Zion laments over the plight of the Babylonian exile, as though forsaken by her husband YHWH (vv. 14-21). Reading the complementary counterparts of vv. 1-13 and vv. 14-21, Patricia Tull identifies daughter Zion as the female Servant (Willey 1997, 175–81)! Echoing Zion's cry in Lamentations ("Why do you forget [*shakak*] us continually and abandon [*'azab*] us for many days?" Lam 5:20; cf. Ps 22:2) in an inverted chiasm, Zion laments, "YHWH has abandoned (*'azab*) me, my Lord has forgotten (*shakak*) me" (v. 14). The divine rebuttal to Zion's accusation comes in the personification of YHWH as a mother (v. 15). Here the bodily connection between mother and child through breastfeeding heightens the portrayal of YHWH's fidelity toward Zion (Løland 2008, 188–92; cf. 66:11-12). A mother cannot forget the child from her "womb" or "belly" (cf. 44:2, 24; 46:3; 48:8; 49:1, 5). Even if a human mother may do so (cf. Ps 27:10), the divine Begetter vows never to forget Zion.

YHWH has inscribed Zion as a permanent tattoo (v. 16; cf. 44:5). A series of alliterations marvelously describes the rapidly coming reconstruction of the city Zion, with the recurring sounds of the word "to hurry" (*mahar*): "Your sons [or "builders"] will hurry (*miharu*) to come; your destroyers (*meharsayik*) and your devastators (*makaribayik*) will go away from you" (v. 17). There is another double entendre here, which, with different vocalization, can denote either "your sons" (*banayik*)—supported by the MT, Symmachus, and Syriac (Peshitta)—or "your builders" (*bonayik*)—attested by the LXX, Aquila, Theodotian, Vulgate, and 1QIsaa. The literary pun with double vocalization signifies a double meaning: "Zion's returning 'children' are to be her future 'builders'" (Paul 1996, 372).

Here the location too may have shifted. YHWH addresses the personified female Zion from the location of city Jerusalem (Paul 2012, 321). From her locale, she is to see all her children come back to her from the scattered exilic regions (v. 18). Many ruins and desolate places around Jerusalem will become overpopulated (v. 19). In this verse, the decisive word "now" (*'attah*) insinuates a turning point amid the "tension between announced and experienced circumstances"—a tension between the "already" embraced hope in the divine intervention and the "not yet" happened time of its fulfillment (Schmidt 2011, 88). Also, this passage connects intertextually with 5:8-9 and 6:11-12: whereas earlier the prophet warned of the impending desolation of Israel and Judah "without inhabitants" (5:9; 6:11), now Jerusalem will become too crowded for the "inhabitants," her gathered offspring (Williamson 1994, 53–54).

Zion's long-lost children will flock over the entire metropolis of Jerusalem (v. 20). Despite a conjectured shift of locale from Babylon to Jerusalem, there is a thematic continuity and contrast, which Mark Biddle elucidates in light of the correlation between Babylon (Isa 47) and Jerusalem (49:14-26): "In Isaiah 47 Lady Babylon arrogantly reacts to [YHWH's] plan to unseat her; in Isaiah 49.14-26 Lady Zion humbly anticipates [YHWH's] plan to restore her" (1996, 131). Contrary to the conceited queen Babylon who spoke foolishly in her "heart" (47:8, 10), now the wife Zion, exiled and deserted, will speak in her "heart" with marveled delight as to who has reared so many of these children of hers (v. 21).

How will these children of Zion, exiled and scattered in Babylon and beyond, return to their deserted capital? In a reversal of fortune, their return will be far more glorious than the old exodus into the promised land through the powerful deeds of YHWH the warrior (vv. 22-26). Earlier YHWH's lifting up the hand was to wield divine judgment upon Israel (5:25; 9:12, 17, 21 [MT 9:11, 16, 20]; 10:4), just as raising a signal to Assyria was to chastise Israel (5:26). Now YHWH will lift up the divine hand and raise the signal to nations and peoples so that they will bring back Zion's sons and daughters (v. 22; cf. 11:10, 12). This role reversal embraces a dramatic polemic against the memory of Zion's past humiliation: now the imperial kings and queens will serve as guardians and nursing mothers, as if they would take the roles of the sister and mother of Moses in Egypt (v. 23; cf. Exod 2:7-10).

An additional question addresses the impossibility—and hopelessness—of any captives being rescued from the confinement of a tyrannical empire (v. 24). YHWH dismisses any threat posed by the menacing empire —presumably Babylonian—and instead pledges to save Zion's children (v. 25). The mighty works of the divine warrior will bring the imperial oppressors themselves to the point of cannibalism, eating their own "flesh," both literally and metaphorically (cf. 36:12; 2 Kgs 6:24-30). In the climactic outcome, a theme progresses from Zion's knowing YHWH (v. 23) to "all flesh" knowing that "I am YHWH" and that YHWH is Zion's savior, the Mighty One of Jacob (v. 26; cf. 40:5; 47:4; Melugin 1976, 152).

Mother Zion Reassured, the Servant Reaffirmed, 50:1-11

This unit expands on the previous chapter in many ways (Paul 2012, 345). Through the continued dialogues and monologues, the Servant conveys more reflections and themes. This unit exhibits a rough chiasm: the divine questions to Zion's children, "you (pl.)" (vv. 1-3); the Servant's confession (vv. 4-7); the Servant's questions to "all of you (pl.)" (vv. 8-11). From another angle, especially that of gender dynamics, Athalya Brenner's delineation is noteworthy: the prophet portrays the people "as a discarded wife-mother" whom YHWH will bring back (vv. 1-3); and then, among the redeemed "slaves"/servants, the representative Slave/Servant will sing a poem (vv. 4-11; 1997, 149).

Continuing the pattern of questions (49:21, 24), now YHWH poses copious questions to the Servant Jacob-Israel as Zion's offspring (vv. 1-3). The Servant Jacob-Israel, once obstinate, now confesses how YHWH opens the ear especially to sustain the weary and the powerless (vv. 4-7). Mirroring divine questions in vv. 1-3, now the Servant challenges the would-be powerful, those who walk in darkness (vv. 8-11), with multiple questions.

Verses 1-3 pose many questions to Zion's beleaguered children, "you" (pl.). Opened by the "thus says YHWH" phrase, YHWH asks, "Where is your mother's divorce document? Who is my lender to whom I sold you?" (v. 1; cf. Deut 24:1, 3, 10-11; Jer 3:1). The presumed answer is that despite the iniquity and transgression of Zion's children, YHWH has not expelled her. YHWH's "hand" is not too short to ransom; rather, alluding to the Ugaritic Baal Epic, YHWH replaces the position of Baal with the power to dry up the sea, Yamm (v. 2). God is "in control not only of the sea, but of the heavens as well" (Paul 2012, 349). God the creator can bundle up the heavens with darkness (v. 3; cf. 45:7; Exod 10:21-22).

Verses 4-7 present the Servant's defiant confessions of faith. The Servant points to key human body parts to illustrate a dramatic transformation. Earlier the Servant's mouth has become like a sharpened sword (49:2). Now YHWH has given the Servant the "tongue" of the learned elites (v. 4; cf. 8:16). The Servant may have once been robbed of elite status, but now the Servant has the capacity to awaken the weary (cf. 40:28-31), as YHWH awakens the Servant's "ear" to hear like those elites. This time when YHWH opens the "ear," the Servant will not be obstinate (v. 5; cf. 6:9-10). Like the afflicted man of Lamentations, the Servant confesses to have given his "back" to the strikers, his "cheeks" to the pluckers, and his "face" to insulting spits (v. 6; cf. 49:7; Lam 3:30): "the first two items on this list of travails—flogging and tearing of the hair—appear in the same order in the Assyrian Law Code (MAL A.44, 59) as punishments of debasement" (Paul 2012, 351). These descriptions of the bodily assault allude to the physical torture of a convicted criminal, suggestive of the imprisonment (cf. 42:7, 22; 49:9; 61:1), albeit here the Servant is wrongfully accused. Nonetheless, despite abject humiliation by the oppressors, the Servant can set his "face" like a rock (v. 7).

Verses 8-11 resume the questions, but this time not from YHWH but from the Servant. Confessing that the righteous God is near—as the "key witness . . . standing nearby in court" (Goldingay and Payne 2006b, 213)— and trusting the divine promise to "contend" with Zion's adversaries (49:25), the Servant spurns those who "contend" with him (v. 8). Such a devout faith comes from the Servant's confession that "YHWH will help me" (v. 9; cf. v. 7; 41:10-14; 44:2). Against the harsh reality of betrayal and injustice, the Servant defiantly condemns to decay like a mothy garment those who condemn him.

The dichotomous tension between the humble Servant and the contentious foes in vv. 8-9 recurs in the distinction between the God-fearers (v. 10) and the wonton "kindlers of fire" (v. 11; Paul 2012, 354-55). Turning to the audience directly in search of the faithful God-fearers (cf. 51:1, 7), the speaker (whether the prophet or YHWH) asks whether any of the community would vow to fear YHWH (cf. 11:3; Ps 22:23 [MT 22:24]; Prov 1:7) and obediently trust in God amid their walk in "darkness"—i.e., exilic hardship—without "light" (v. 10; cf. 2:5). An impassioned denunciation concludes this unit.

Because the wicked ("all of you") do not walk in the "light" of YHWH (2:5) but instead walk in the "light" of fire they perversely set ablaze (v. 11; cf. 7:4), their doom will come from "my hand," declares YHWH. They will lie down in torment.

This unit comprises two opposite metaphors: the water metaphor in v. 2 and the fire metaphor in v. 11 (Brenner 1997, 143). Read together, they suggest that just as YHWH has the power to subdue the sea and the rivers, so YHWH will castigate the "kindlers of fire." We also find an intertextual allusion. Earlier the prophet earnestly exhorted in the first-person plural cohortative: "House of Jacob, come, let us walk in the light of YHWH" (2:5). Contrarily, the prophet now accuses these inflamers in the second-person plural: "Walk in the light of your (pl.) fire" (50:11). This bunch of contenders against God is not any different than the impudent "smoking firebrands" (7:4)—Aram and Ephraim—that scorned YHWH. Like the wicked chaff that will be blown away (Ps 1), these haughty conspirators will walk into their own flame of condemnation.

YHWH Will Guide the "Justice-Seekers" into Zion, 51:1-16

A new group appears in 51:1: "those who pursue justice." Put another way, these "justice-seekers" and "God-fearers" are those who obey the call of 50:10, "Who among you (pl.) fears YHWH?" Like the call ("listen to me") to coastlands and peoples afar (49:1; cf. 46:3; 48:1), now YHWH calls this community of righteousness. All the imperatives in 51:1, 2, 4, 6, 7 address them, inspiring the new generation of those who pursue righteousness and seek YHWH, the descendants of Abraham and Sarah (vv. 1-8). Not only seeking righteousness and fearing God, they epitomize the overcoming of obduracy (Uhlig 2009a, 247). In the next subunit, in the I-thou interchanges, their prayer to awaken YHWH's arm (vv. 9-11) elicits a reply promising divine comfort (vv. 12-16). The language in this chapter is a performance act, somewhat analogous to dialogue "as *appeal* and *response*" (Brueggemann 1998b, 129). In a larger scope, therefore, this unit (51:1-16) addresses the justice-seekers, while the following unit (51:17–52:12) addresses the same group now called "Zion."

Verses 1-8 contain divine address to the heirs of Zion, subdivided by three calls to listen (vv. 1-3; 4-6; 7-8). Who are they? Which ethnic group? What social class? This may have been a hotly debated issue especially at the dawn of the return of the exiles to Jerusalem and Yehud (cf. Ezra; Nehemiah). Our subunit offers its own definition of this group, albeit a rather loose and thereby more inclusive definition.

In the opening call to listen, YHWH addresses those who pursue righteousness and seek YHWH (v. 1). The echo of Isaiah 1 helps define this community as those no longer obdurate (6:9-10) who aspire to obey the divine commands (1:17). Not only to "hear," they are also admonished to "see" (cf. 6:9) Abraham and Sarah—the rock and the quarry, respectively— their common ancestors (v. 2). We should note the rare occurrence of the two ancestral names together—Abraham and Sarah—whose stories of the promise of election, progeny, and blessing resonate in the thematic, and even compositional, juxtaposition between the exilic compiler of Genesis and Deutero-Isaiah (Van Seters 1999, 81–83). From the intertextual connections between Ezek 33:24-29 and Isa 51:1-3, David Carr delineates the common expression ("Abraham was one"; Ezek 33:24 and Isa 51:2) in both texts with contrasting themes: Ezekiel, just prior to the fall of Jerusalem, criticizes people's blind reliance on the tradition of Abraham, whereas Deutero-Isaiah, during and amid the exilic setting, proclaims for the exiles to find hope in Abraham: "In the time between the beginning and end of exile we have moved from Abraham as a false hope to Abraham as the rock on which hope should be based. Whereas current figures like 'Daughter Zion' and the anonymous servant of Second Isaiah symbolized the exiles' suffering, ancestral figures like Abraham become a way for exiles to envision hope" (Carr 2014, 95).

Furthermore, outside Genesis and here, Sarah occurs nowhere else in the OT. It poses a metaphorical connection between Sarah the barren woman and Jerusalem the barren city (Abou-Chaar 2013, 115). In addition to Abraham, why does the prophet mention Sarah here? George A. F. Knight delineates that God can "raise Israel up out of the womb of death, for new life can spring forth for Israel now in Babylon as truly as new life once came from Sarah's womb" (Knight 1984, 151).

Moreover, it is not priestly lineage or social ties, not even north versus south, but rather the common ancestral background that connects this people. Analogous to this intention, we should note that, according to Antonios Finitsis, Haggai and Zechariah 1–8 present a similar thematic appeal for the unity between remainees and returnees, by way of directing the attention to their common enemies (such as foreign empires or wealthy neighbors) or their common heritage (same exodus tradition, same ancestors, and so on). During the early postexilic period, neither Haggai nor (Proto-)Zechariah "paints such a polarized picture as the one found in the books of Ezra and Nehemiah . . . their stance stems from the prophets' desire to build a new cohesive group identity for the people in Yehud" (Finitsis 2011, 116–17; cf. Blenkinsopp 2002, 326). Abraham and Sarah were only one family, but through divine blessing they have become numerous (cf. Gen 12:1-3; Ezek 33:24). Yet that was ancient history. Can the same occur to Zion amid her ruins? It will be so because YHWH is about to "comfort" Zion and turn her wilderness of the new exodus into Eden, the garden of YHWH (v. 3; cf. 40:1; 49:13). Villainous schism and rivalry will come to the surface in later (con-) texts (cf. Isa 58–66). But, at least in its early restoration period, not only were the stakes high but also their hopes and aspirations for unity and reconciliation were high as well.

The second call to listen addresses "my people" (v. 4). Readers learn of an important inner-biblical commentary. That YHWH's Torah (law and teaching) goes forth with divine "justice" (2:3) is an explication of a "light to the peoples" (42:6; 49:6). All the peoples and coastlands (cf. 41:1; 42:4; 49:1) will wait and hope for YHWH's "arm" (v. 5; cf. 40:31). Just as Abraham and Sarah looked at the heaven for the promise of many heirs like the stars (Gen 15:5-6), now Zion's faithful heirs are to look at the heaven and earth (v. 6). This time they learn that heaven and earth may pass away, yet YHWH's "salvation" and "vindication" stand forever (cf. 40:8).

The third call unveils a situation of harsh oppression or tension, within which those who know righteousness and Torah, presumed to be the outnumbered minority group, are exhorted not to fear the majority group of revilers (v. 7). The corrupt will perish like moth and worm, contrary to YHWH's "vindication" and "salvation"—note the inverted chiasm with v. 6—which will remain forever (v. 8).

Verses 9-11 present the group's or community's urgent appeal for YHWH to act for them. This plea implores the arm of YHWH to awake, echoing key ancient Near Eastern mythological traditions. As though the great arm of YHWH has become dormant amid the rebellious monster gods (Yamm and Tiamat), the prophet voices the people's lament. This brief psalm, according to Rainer Albertz, betrays the communal lament possibly recited during the Babylonian exile (2003b, 147). It recalls YHWH's slaying of Rahab, the dragon (v. 9; cf. 27:1; Job 26:12), the sea (Yamm), and the deep (Tiamat; Heb. *tehom*) that echoes the old exodus victory (v. 10; cf. 50:2; Gen 1:2; Job 7:12). If the terms "Rahab" and "sea" symbolize the empire of Egypt that YHWH vanquished in the old exodus tradition (Isa 30:7; cf. Pss 87:4; 89:9-10 [MT 89:10-11]), then, as Shalom Paul notes, these expressions now in the new exodus theme contrast with 47:1-2, which depict Lady Babylon as crossing "rivers" in her decline into captivity (Paul 2012, 370). The earnest hope for the new exodus from Babylon echoes verbatim the expression for the return to Zion with "everlasting joy" (v. 11; cf. 35:10). Together, the slaughtering of Rahab and the redemption of the exiles constitute one divine victory over "cosmic" and "historical" chaotic forces (Berges 2011, 110–11).

Verses 12-16 contain the divine response to the plea of vv. 9-11, promising to comfort and deliver the captives against the oppressors (vv. 12-16). YHWH neither slumbers nor fails to answer their call (cf. Ps 121:4). Mirroring the double entreaty "awake, awake" (*'uri 'uri*) of v. 9, YHWH responds with emphasis, "I, I (*'anoki 'anoki*) am the one who comforts you (pl.)," chiding them for fearing mortals that are only grass (v. 12; cf. 40:6-8). Their fear of the human oppressor thus means their having forgotten the creator of heaven and earth (v. 13). Indeed the imprisoned—whether in Jerusalem or in Babylon—shall be set free, lacking no bread, possibly suggesting the settings of the return following 540 BCE (v. 14; cf. 55:2, 10; Goldingay and Payne 2006b, 243). This assurance of deliverance comes from YHWH who controls the sea (v. 15; cf. Jer 31:35). Echoing the call of the prophet Jeremiah, YHWH assures the devout ones in colonial captivity that "I have put my words in your mouth" (cf. Jer 1:9), while "planting" (cf. Jer 1:10) the heavens and saying to Zion, "You are my people" (v. 16; cf. Hos 2:23 [MT 2:25]). Strikingly, now Zion is equated with "my people" (cf. v. 4). In other words, the justice-seekers are identified as the (new) Zion: "Zion can be both the city that people left and the people who left it" (Goldingay and Payne 2006b, 247). Thus, this divine election of Zion is rooted in both YHWH's saving power over chaotic forces and creational power over all creatures: hence Jerusalem is not going to be "built" but "created" anew (cf. 65:17-18; Berges 2011, 111–12).

Zion, Awakened out of the Exilic Mortification, Hears the News of YHWH's Royal Return, 51:17–52:12

The justice-seekers and God-fearers in the preceding unit are now called by the name of their city, Jerusalem, divinely empowered to arise and behold a marvelous reversal of fortune (51:17-23). In this way, the new people of God, "my people," is created in Zion (52:1-6). They will witness the impending victorious entry of YHWH as the divine King in Jerusalem (52:7-12).

Isaiah 51:17-23 shifts the call to "awake," which was addressed to the arm of YHWH in the preceding text (51:9-11), to Jerusalem. Personified as a bereaved mother, she is exhorted to hear the news of divine renewal. Jerusalem, fallen by the cup of divine wrath and the cup of reeling, is to rise up (v. 17; cf. Jer 25:15; Amos 5:2). Because of devastation and sword—two things that befell her (cf. 40:2; 47:9; Jer 11:22; 25:16, 27, 29), "there is no one to guide her" and no one to comfort her (vv. 18-19; cf. Lam 1:17). Jerusalem's children lay vulnerably at the time of her destruction (v. 20).

Yet now the prophet communicates the divine message of Jerusalem's restoration. The addressees are the "afflicted" (or the "poor" or "humble") and those "drunk" but not with wine, hence not those of upper class (v. 21; cf. 28:1, 7). YHWH now pledges to remove the "cup of reeling" and the "cup of wrath"—note the inverted chiasm with v. 17—from Jerusalem (v. 22). Once again, depicting Jerusalem's humiliation, YHWH promises to give the cup to her tormentors who have walked on the back of the fallen city (v. 23). The tormentors' mockery, "Get down so that we cross over you," is hauntingly gruesome, as though such an expression only seems a metaphor. Unfortunately, many repeated incidents in the history of human war and brutality have shown otherwise. In the current century, we have seen the barbarous torture and abuse committed against the Iraqi prisoners in Abu Ghraib. In the twentieth century, during World War II, many Korean independence movement leaders, poets, and common participants were imprisoned. Some of them died in inhumane biological experiments, such as how humans freeze, how many bullets go through the human body, lethal chemical or vaccination injection tests (note the expression of "drinking" the "cup of wrath" of v. 10), and so on. Thus, the description of the mortifying attack on daughter Zion in the ancient world is not merely elegant poetic imagery but rather a grisly yet vivid testimony of those who suffered, those who told the stories of their suffering, and those who have heard those stories with excruciating tears.

Isaiah 52:1-6 presents an intensified and climactic call to daughter Zion to "awake, awake" (cf. 51:9), to regain her past glory and holiness (cf. 1:21). Whoever calls Zion to wake up no longer looks at her with pity and sorrow but rather with renewed strength. The prophet calls the personified Zion, raped by the uncircumcised and the unclean during the time of the city's fall in 587 BCE (cf. Lam 1:9-10) but now called the "holy city," to clothe herself anew with beautiful garments (v. 1). Since she is no longer cast to the dust with chains upon her neck (cf. Lam 1:14; 2:10)—which will soon become queen Babylon's ghastly fate (cf. 47:1-3)—it is time now for the captive Zion to rise up (v. 2).

Whereas the preceding segment addresses Zion with repeated feminine singular imperatives (vv. 1-2), now, led by "thus says YHWH" phrases (v. 3 and v. 4), the subsequent segment concerns "my people" (vv. 3-6; cf. 51:4). YHWH's people will be ransomed without money (v. 3; cf. 45:13; 50:1; 55:1). Echoing the old exodus from Egypt, YHWH also deems Assyria's atrocity against Israel undeserved (v. 4). Now, *seeing* that "my people" went to exile without cause and *hearing* the beastly taunting of the imperial rulers' howling (v. 5), YHWH envisions that "my people" will *know* the divine name on that day when YHWH appears to them, "Here I am" (v. 6; cf. Exod 3:7). Earlier the prophet saw and heard the divine call and obediently responded, "Here

I am" (6:8). Now, after seeing and hearing the empire's mockery of Zion and her God, YHWH passionately responds with the vengeful commitment, "Here I am."

Isaiah 52:7-12 introduces the announcer of the good news of YHWH's coming kingdom to Zion (vv. 7-10), thereby prompting the exiles to make a new exodus out of "there"—Babylonian captivity—en route back to Jerusalem (vv. 11-12). Whereas earlier the prophet called Zion the *female* messenger of good news to proclaim to the cities of Judah (40:9; cf. 41:27), now the prophet charges the *male* messenger who announces to Zion that "Our God is king" (v. 7; Tiemeyer 2012, 236–37). The prophet lauds the beautiful "feet" of the messenger, who would travel through the arduous routes of hills, valleys, streams, and desert terrains—an essential qualification of a model servant and minister, later, during the Reformation paintings and also equally validly in the present time: "There is nothing very beautiful about feet—except when they are wearing the running shoes of the [good news] and taking it to the world" (Wright 2016, 224).

Here the intertextual correlations with Nahum (cf. Nah 1:15 [MT 2:1]) and Psalms are noteworthy. Both Nahum and Isaiah 52 pronounce good news to Zion, in light of pivotal world events: the fall of Nineveh in 612 BCE and the ensuing fall of Babylon in 539. Just as the Assyrian empire fell, so too the Babylonian empire will crumble and lose its menacing power (Tull 1997, 119–20). As though a sportscaster jubilantly shouts that our heroine or hero has won the championship, the messenger proudly proclaims that YHWH has won the battle and is about to return victoriously as the true King (cf. Pss 93:1; 95:3; 96:10; 97:1; 98:6; 99:1).

The guards of the city walls lift up their voices for YHWH's triumphant return to Zion (v. 8; cf. Ezek 43:1-5; Zech 8:3). Finally, YHWH is returning (cf. Ezek 43)! This royal return and entrance of the divine warrior into Zion forms a thematic correlation with the preceding announcement of YHWH's departure as a valiant warrior (cf. 42:10-13; Oosting 2002, 159). The invitation to rejoice addresses both the "ruins of Jerusalem" and her people, because the divine command to "comfort" (40:1) is now being fulfilled (v. 9). Just as Jerusalem is now the "holy city" (cf. v. 1), so YHWH's "holy arm" (cf. 40:10; 48:14; 51:5, 9) will bring about the saving acts of the new exodus that all nations and ends of the earth will witness (v. 10). Zion's people, amid recurring disappointment and hardships, may still be reluctant to acknowledge YHWH. The heralds and the sentinels shout the good news, because their eyes have seen that YHWH—indeed "the salvation of *our* God" (in solidarity with the "we"-group)—is on the way to Zion. Notably, "they are the first who are mentioned to have eyes and who do see (cf. Isa 42:7; 43:8)" (Oosting 2002, 166).

The subsequent twofold imperatives—"depart, depart"—echo the previous command to leave Babylon (cf. 48:20). Calling Babylon ("there") a remote, unclean place (cf. Ps 137:1, 3), the prophet exhorts the exiles to purify themselves and proceed on the new exodus journey (v. 11). This call to "depart . . . do not touch unclean things" makes an intertextual reversal of the similar call to "depart, unclean . . . depart, depart, do not touch" in Lamentations 4:15: "In Lam 4:15 the priests and prophets, fleeing *from* Jerusalem, are so defiled by blood (i.e. crimes) that they are not even allowed to stay among the nations. In Isa 52:11 the dispersed Jews are reminded not to touch anything unclean because they are supposed to go *back* to Jerusalem" (Berges 2011, 116–17; cf. Tull 1997, 125–30). Consequently, unlike the hurried escape of the old exodus (cf. Exod 12:11), they will return in good time, as Yhwh the King (cf. v. 7)—the mighty warrior and gentle shepherd (cf. 40:10-11)—will safely guide them on the front and back of the returnees (v. 12; cf. Exod 13:21-22).

The Servant Will Prosper, Zion's Offspring Will Multiply, 52:13–54:17

The Servant's Humiliating Demise yet Glorious Vindication, 52:13–53:12

The chiastic arrangement and consistent theme hold together this unit, the so-called Suffering Servant passage. Yet, despite the abrupt transition, this unit apparently continues the pattern of the previous texts. From chapter 49 on, we have read the alternating descriptions of the Servant Jacob-Israel (49:1-13; 50:1–51:8) and Zion the personified daughter (49:14-26; 51:9–52:12). This pattern continues here with the depiction of the Servant and his offspring (Isa 53) and of Zion and her offspring (Isa 54).

Numerous studies throughout the last two millennia have addressed the issue of the identity of the Servant. The ambiguity and anonymity of its descriptions make it difficult to conclude whether the Servant is an individual (e.g., Moses [Baltzer 2001, 18–22, 42–44], Cyrus as the new Moses [Watts 2005, 650–58], the prophet Deutero-Isaiah in the legacy of Jeremiah, a Davidic king such as Hezekiah, Josiah, Jehoiachin, and Zerubbabel, etc.), or a collective entity (e.g., Jacob-Israel, a "steadfastly righteous minority" among Jacob-Israel [Paul 2012, 398], etc.). While respecting such debates, it seems plausible that the Servant may have indicated an individual figure that then was collectivized to represent a larger group of people, analogous to the "we"-group.

Key subunits of the symmetrical feature correspond as follows (compare also Goldingay and Payne 2006b, 277):

a—52:13-15, future tense [he-they-"many"] = "my servant" (v. 13)
   b—53:1-3, past tense [he-we] = "no form, no splendor, no appearance"
      (v. 2) = "he was despised and rejected" (v. 3)
      c—53:4, past tense [he-we-Elohim]
         x—53:5, central theme = transgressions + shalom
      c'—53:6, past tense [he-we-YHWH]
   b'—53:7-9, past tense [he-we] = "he was oppressed . . . and afflicted"
      (v. 7) = "no violence, no deceit" (v. 9)
a'—53:10-12, future tense [he-they-"many"] = "my servant" (v. 11)

Isaiah 52:13-15 present a sudden shift in content from the preceding passages. Yet, when read sequentially, they show that the theme of the Servant's exaltation despite abject mortification corresponds with that of Zion's renewal and comfort amid unforgettable humiliation (52:1-12). This Servant at present must be one in the lowest status, as YHWH declares the reversal that "my Servant" will be "exalted and lifted up (*rum . . . nasa'*)" (v 13; cf. 6:1; 57:15). Whereas YHWH has determined to lower all the proud forces that are "exalted and lifted up (*rum . . . nasa'*)" (2:12-14; cf. 37:7, 23-24; 46:1-2; 47:1), now this Servant will be truly uplifted.

As will be suggested below, scholars have noted a number of linguistic and thematic links between this text and Isaiah 6. In particular, the phrase "exalted and lifted up" of v. 13 is a verbatim replica of the phrase in 6:1. There it is YHWH who is exalted so high. Here, this lofty God declares the intention to exalt and uplift this presumed lowly, hard-pressed Servant. Read intertextually, there is a sense of descending and ascending—dramatic reversal of highs and lows (Kim 2014, 152–54). The divine promise to the exiles that "wait for" God depicted them as "fly[ing] on wings like eagles," then as "run[ning]," and then as "walking," as though their physical strength would decrease but nonetheless be divinely sustained (40:31). Now, we read three verbs that display ascending effects as the servant is to "arise," "exalt himself," and "be very high" (Goldingay and Payne 2006b, 289). By the same token, in the concluding chapter, we learn of another dramatic reversal: God, whose throne is in the exalted heaven, vows to look upon the lowly—"the humble and the crushed in spirit" (66:2).

Just like daughter Zion's utterly disempowered status (51:18-20; 52:1-2), so this Servant's disfigured appearance stuns many (v. 14; cf. 39:7). Indeed, the Servant will "startle"—or "sprinkle"—many nations and kings (v. 15;

cf. 2:3-4), and, contrary to the obdurate monarchical Israelites, these "many" peoples will see and understand things never seen or heard (cf. 6:9-10).

Isaiah 53:1-9 makes a swift turn from "many" (or "they") to "we." On the one hand, this "we" speaker may be the very many nations and kings (52:14-15) who are now talking about what they have witnessed. On the other hand, and more likely, it could be the penitent and devout "we"-group who, amid the exilic calamity, finally reflects and acknowledges the righteous words and works of the Servant—"the experience of conversion to discipleship," according to Joseph Blenkinsopp (2002, 351). Some scholars posit that this "we"-group, in vv. 4-6 in particular, should be identified with "the people who stayed at home," i.e., those who remained in the land of Judah (Hägglund 2008, 32), and the Servant as "the returning group of exiles" (Berges 2012b, 491). Although the overly generalized grouping of the remainees (who were never exiled) and the returnees (who were exiled to Babylon) seems much too simplistic, if not problematic, it is worthwhile to ponder the fact that various groups would now recognize, with their own awe and transformation, the legacy of the Servant whose words and life demonstrate righteousness.

The initial segment describes the Servant's undesirable appearance at present contrary to his honorable upbringing (vv. 1-3). Comparable to the earlier "Who?" questions (cf. 42:19, 23; 50:8), now the "we"-group asks (v. 1). Here the "arm" of YHWH echoes the preceding oracles where coastlands and nations are told to witness YHWH's "arm" (cf. 40:10; 51:5; 52:5, 9-10, 15). This Servant's undesirable shape sharply contrasts with his noble youth as a "young plant" and a "root" (v. 2). The phrase "young plant," "a sucker" (*yoneq*), denotes a baby boy and may signal that this servant's origin is of ordinary people, neither of upper-class nobles nor of royal majesty (Goldingay and Payne 2006b, 299–300). Furthermore, this root or plant growing out of the parched wasteland evokes the picture of the unattractive "desert weed" (Barré 2000, 12). Far from being a root as a signal to nations and peoples (cf. 11:1, 10), this Suffering Servant is now despised, stricken with sickness, and considered the "most frail of human beings" (v. 3; Goldingay and Payne 2006b, 302). As though not so distant from today's utilitarian world controlled by our self-centeredness and self-promotion, the people "despised" the servant as worthless and useless, regarding him "of no account," i.e., a dehumanized *thing* or *object* with zero value (Cook 2010, 117).

Then, in the central piece of this chiastic unit, the "we"-group reflects on their relationship with the Servant, confessing that his affliction bears their wrongdoings (vv. 4-6). Although undeserving of God's whole-scale punishment, the Servant carried their sickness (v. 4; cf. Jer 10:19). The adverb "surely" (*'aken*), which is morphologically quite similar to "certainly" (*'amen*), marks a new awakening—a transforming moment—of the "we"-group (Cook 2007, 116). As a scapegoat or a sacrificial lamb, it is the Servant's wound that turned their "transgressions" and "iniquities" into "shalom" and "healing" (v. 5). The Servant's chastisement now actualizes the possibility of "well-being" (*shalom*) posited but unresolved previously (48:18; cf. 52:7). Not just a few, but "all of us" have gone astray like sheep (v. 6; cf. Jer 10:21). Unlike the obedient ox and donkey (1:3) or rather than walking in the paths of YHWH (2:3), this group confesses that they have turned to their own "way" (cf. 8:11). Stephen Cook observes the close intertwining of the second-person plural ("we") and the third-person singular ("he"), which points to the salient theme of "intimacy" between the chorus and the Servant in this Servant Song: "By setting pronouns such as 'our' and 'we' together next to pronouns such as 'he' and 'him,' the poetry of vv. 4, 5, and 6 conveys the narrators' new experience of relationship to the Servant and each other" (Cook 2007, 116–17). Like the sheep that acknowledges its Shepherd (Ps 23:1), this wayward people finally came to realize who their true shepherd and leader should have been.

What then happened to this Servant (vv. 7-9)? Despite the torment, "like a lamb led to the slaughter," the Servant remained silent (v. 7; cf. Jer 11:19). By a corruption of justice and the transgression of "my people," the Servant died ("cut off from the land of the living," v. 8; cf. Jer 11:19). Equally trag-ically, although there was no falsehood in his "mouth" (cf. 49:2; 51:16), he was disgracefully buried with the company of the wicked and the nefarious rich (v. 9). Several interpretive options are possible with regard to the identity of the Servant and the implications of the Servant's mission and legacy.

On the first level, the key phrases that echo Jeremiah 11 beckon for consideration of the legacy of the prophet Deutero-Isaiah, in addition to Jeremiah, in understanding the impact this Servant must have had. Just as the descriptions of Jeremiah mirror those of Moses (cf. Jer 1:6-8; Exod 3:12; 4:10), so here the descriptions of this righteous Servant replicate those of Jeremiah (cf. Dell 2010, 133–34). If there were any true prophet, this "we"-group now acknowledges and ascertains that it ought to have been this Servant: "In Second Isaiah's poetic narrative of cultural resistance, it is apparent from the fourth Servant Song that the hidden transcript of the prophet of the exile becomes public and leads to his execution" (Perdue and Carter 2015, 100).

On the second level, there is a royal description. Besides the root or plant signifier (cf. 11:10), key phrases—"YHWH struck (*naga'*) him"

(cf. 53:4) and "he was cut off (*gazar*) from the house of YHWH" (cf. 53:8)—
hint at verbal and thematic links with King Uzziah (2 Chr 26:20-21). Some
scholars posit that the servant was not killed literally, but rather excluded
from the temple (Barré 2010, 19, 23). Revisiting E. Sellin's study in 1901,
M. Goulder recently proposed identifying King Jehoiachin as the Suffering
Servant. Taking the title "servant" as denoting "the highest position in the
land, normally to be king," Goulder considers Jehoiachin's likely torture
and affliction as a vassal (2 Kgs 24:11-16; cf. 2 Kgs 25:7) and his disfigured
appearance after thirty-seven years in a dungeon as allusions for a dignified
example of the rightful heir, reflected by the historian and people in Jerusalem, not in Babylon (2 Kgs 25:27-30; cf. Jer 52:31-34; Goulder 2002,
178, 181–89). Although many correlations between Jehoiachin and the
Suffering Servant seem much too loose and somewhat typological, nonetheless, whether historically or metaphorically, and also whether individually
or collectively, this Servant does take the place of royalty amid repugnant
affliction. Alternatively, this Servant may symbolize a positive counterpart
who contrasts the negative legacies of Jehoiachin (Jer 22:24-30) or Zedekiah
(Jer 23:5-6; Goldingay and Payne 2006b, 283, 322).

On the third level, though less linguistically evident, the key words "cut
off" in Isaiah 53:8 and "grave" in 53:12 may resonate with the same words
in Ezekiel 37:11 and 37:12, respectively. In this correlation, the Servant
could refer in a collective sense to "the people in exile," much like the bones
utterly dried up then will yet live (Hägglund 2008, 27; cf. Pixley 1999, 97).
Accordingly, in light of this Servant's function to represent and symbolize
countless heroes and heroines of devout faith and righteous courage, Jorge
Pixley highlights the social location of the Servant. In the context of the
exiles in Babylon, Pixley distinguishes two ideas or communities, which he
coins the "pro-Babylonian party" versus the "Servant-party" (or "pro-Persian
party" or *ipso facto* "anti-Babylonian party"). It would be natural to assume
that the pro-Babylonian party members would prosper, while the Servant-
party would often run into harsh oppression or death (Pixley 1999, 96–97).
The excruciatingly unjust persecution and death of the Servant-party leaders
and members, through the outright betrayal and report of pro-Babylonian
party culprits, would devastate the mission of the Servant-party. Worse yet, if
we read the "wicked" and "rich" in v. 9 as describing "Babylon" (Goldingay
and Payne 2006b, 316), then it would be an enormously mortifying insult
and dishonor for the Servant (possibly the leader of the Servant-party) to be
wrongfully labeled as one of the pro-Babylonian party members.

Nevertheless, the Servant-party's visions would not die out but resurge
and sprout. Their collective struggles for a glorious homecoming like the old

exodus, and even their ancestral mission to be a blessing to many nations (cf. Gen 12:1-3; Levenson 1996, 151–52), would not be in vain. Calling the Servant's death martyrdom, Pixley expounds in analogy to the Nicaraguan people's struggle for a nation that should embrace the poor: "Martyrdom, then, is not a value in itself, but a life-affirming value when it is assumed to be an element in the struggle for life in its fullness . . . the mission of realizing justice among a people denied life for centuries must pass through defeat on the way to becoming part of the national life" (Pixley 1999, 98).

Isaiah 53:10-12 resumes the divine speech, asserting that such a shameful demise of the Servant is not the end. Instead the Servant will see prolific offspring and learn of an honorable vindication. The Servant's legacy will continue on through disciples and the devout "we"-group (v. 10). Opting for the third interpretive level discussed above, Ulrich Berges interprets the implication of the "guilt offering" ('asham) as follows: "Analogous to the priestly sin-offering that atones for the sins of the sacrificers, [YHWH] has deployed and accepted the sufferings of the returnees as redemption of sin for the many, that is, for all the people of Israel!" (Berges 2012b, 493). Now vindicated, this righteous Servant—characterized by "other-centeredness" (Cook 2007, 123)—will make "many" righteous, assuming the role and task expected of royalty or sages in the ancient world (v. 11; cf. Dan 12:3). Although taking the shame of association with transgressors (cf. 1:5-6), yet having suffered for the sake of those transgressors, the Servant will ultimately inherit a glorious future as do the mighty and the strong (v. 12).

Childless Zion Will Be Comforted by YHWH with Numerous Children, the Servants of YHWH, 54:1-17

Just as the ill-treated Servant will be exalted with a prosperous legacy (Isa 53), so the ill-fated Zion will regain divine love, restored with the divine covenant and abundant offspring (Isa 54). Just as Zion is to awaken and arise out of the devastated dust of captivity (51:17; 52:1), now Zion the abandoned and barren wife is to sing for joy (54:1) for the everlasting love her husband YHWH will rekindle (vv. 1-10) and the righteous future of her plentiful children, the "servants" of YHWH (vv. 11-17).

Verses 1-10 resume the divine reminder that YHWH never divorced the personified Zion, the mother of Jacob-Israel (cf. 50:1-3). Personified as the wife of YHWH (cf. Hos 1), Zion, desolated and destroyed, will find her husband again and have prodigious progeny (cf. 49:17-21). Therefore, Zion must sing (v. 1). But can she? Claus Westermann observes poignantly that for the barren Zion to sing a song would sound "extremely paradoxical" (Westermann 1969, 272). Also, why and what should she sing? Intertextual echoes

relate to the song Hannah sang when YHWH delivered her from misery with
the gift of Samuel (1 Sam 2:1-10). Barren Zion also echoes the matriarchs,
such as Sarah, Rebekah, and Rachel in Genesis. Equally significantly, readers
may also muse on the connection between Sarah the migrating sojourner
from Ur of Chaldea and Zion the destination for the returnees from Babylonian captivity. Paralleling the divine miracle for the righteous Servant's
offspring (Isa 53), the undercurrent here is the "theme of transformation"
in which, like the numerous progeny of Sarah and many other matriarchs,
barren Zion will have many children. Indeed, the concept of "illogicality"
is central to this passage with the prophet's daring transformation of Zion's
pitiful reality (Moughtin-Mumby 2008, 132).

To achieve the rhetorical effect of the reversal of fortune, "in six verses
(54:1-6), the prophet lists all the previously used epithets of the defeated
people and then overturns them" (Franke 2014, 714). With the reversal of
fortune, Zion will enlarge her habitation for her bountiful children (v. 2;
cf. Jer 10:20). In light of intertextual connections to 33:20, which shares tent
imagery with regard to Zion, H. G. M. Williamson notes that 33:20 emphasizes Zion's security while v. 2 highlights Zion's expansive size (Williamson
1994, 228). Her seed will repopulate cities across and beyond Judah (v. 3).
Just as divine mercy sanctified the widowhood of Ruth, Zion's shame of
widowhood will disappear (v. 4).

How can this come true? Zion learns that her husband ("ba'al" in
Hebrew) is not Baal or any other imperial deity, but rather YHWH, the one
who created her (v. 5) and who is calling her back (v. 6). YHWH's anger, the
hiding of the divine face (cf. 8:17), was only temporary as YHWH intends
to comfort her with a "great compassion" (v. 7) and "everlasting faithfulness (hesed)" (v. 8). Notably, in this section (Isa 49–57), we find repeated
depictions of the reversal and contrast of the fates of Babylon and Zion.
Whereas YHWH's mercy and redemption will replace Zion's shame and
widowhood, Babylon will encounter divine anger, will fall, and will dissipate:
"The Babylon portrayed in Isaiah 47 is the polar opposite of the Jerusalem
depicted in Isaiah 49; 51–52; and 54" (Biddle 1996, 133).

The reference to the days of Noah gives further assurance that Zion
will never encounter such agonizing punishment (v. 9). Rather, reminiscent
of the theme and expression of Psalm 46, YHWH vows that, although mountains may move and hills may "shake" or "quake" (mot), the divine "faithfulness
(hesed)" and "covenant of shalom" will abide with Zion—God is with us
(v. 10; cf. Ps 46:2-3, 5-7 [MT 46:3-4, 6-8]).

Verses 11-17 reassert YHWH's resolute pledge to restore Zion and bless
her children. Zion, afflicted (cf. 51:21) and shaken (cf. v. 10), will soon

regain gemstones and foundations of sapphires (v. 11). Jerusalem's towers, gates, and walls will boast of precious jewels, recalling statements about the dazzling appearance of Mesopotamian temples and palaces (v. 12; cf. Ezek 28:13; Paul 2012, 427).

Furthermore, Zion's children will become erudite "disciples" of YHWH (v. 13; cf. 50:4; Jer 31:34). Firmly founded in righteousness, Zion will be far from oppression or terror (v. 14). Like the divine promise to curse those who curse Abraham (cf. Gen 12:3), YHWH vouches to frustrate any assault or weapon against Zion (vv. 15-17a). Such will be the astonishing lot and vindication for the "servants" of YHWH—the righteous offspring of Zion, by the identity of Jacob-Israel (v. 17b). Here the "servants" (pl.), as successors of the Servant (sg.), are introduced for the first time. They will play a major role in the subsequent section, especially Isaiah 63–66 (cf. 56:6).

The Marginalized Righteous versus the Dishonorable Wicked, 55:1–57:21

Despite notable catchwords and themes that connect to the preceding chapters, Isaiah 55–57 stand uniquely on their own. Isaiah scholarship has profoundly, and convincingly, isolated Isaiah 56–66 as a composite, yet self-standing section, the so-called Trito-Isaiah. Its chiastic format, as well as its apparent shifted historical setting (postexilic), has occasioned recent trends to read Isaiah 60–62 as a distinct section, enveloped by 56–59 and 63–66. Recently, however, scholars have also challenged the legitimacy of the originally independent authorship of Isaiah 56–66. In fact, as will be discussed below, Isaiah 54–57—the presumed heterogeneous chapters (between Isa 54–55 and 56–57)—share many linguistic and thematic similarities (Paul 2012, 415, 435, 450, 461; cf. Kim 2015a). To push the argument further, the literary continuity of Isaiah 40–66 seems as evident and legitimate as its literary discontinuity. Therefore, like the recent approach to read the book of Isaiah as a unified whole, thereby even reading Isaiah 39 and 40 with eyes for connection rather than disconnection, so we intend to read Isaiah 55, 56, and 57 with the ideas and implications of conjunction rather than disjunction.

A Banquet for All, Especially the Afflicted, the Poor, 55:1-13
This section does not mention Zion, Jerusalem, or the Servant (except 56:6, "servants") at all—in fact, there is no explicit reference to Zion even in Isaiah 54. What then holds Isaiah 55–57 together? What may have caused the final arrangement of these three chapters as the end of the second section (chs. 49–57) of Isaiah 40–66? Isaiah 55–57 not only share many similar phrases

and motifs—especially the concerns for the more inclusive addressees and the marginalized, excluded, righteous—but also contain distinct intertextual allusions to Isaiah 1–2, which will be referenced below. In the present form, thematically, the banquet invitation to "all" wraps up the consistently alternating concerns for the male "Servant of YHWH" (explicitly Jacob-Israel) and the female "daughter Zion," especially culminating the treatment of these two entities in Isaiah 53 and 54 respectively. Now the invitation encompasses "all," except with a clear modifier—i.e., "all who are *thirsty* . . . who have *no money*."

Verses 1-5 present an invitation to all, but especially the impoverished and powerless, to the everlasting covenant. Concerning the likely setting for this text, Andrew Abernethy surmises three proposed options: (a) a formal invitation to a sacral feast (cf. Prov 9:1-6, 11); (b) wisdom tradition (cf. Sir 24:19-22); and (c) marketplace—of which he considers the third option most likely: "Isa 55:1-3a presents a street merchant calling on the audience to eat and drink while incorporating wisdom elements into this form" (Abernethy 2014, 120–23).

If considered as a feast, not unlike the eschatological feast, it is all the more important that YHWH promises to provide for all peoples (25:6-8; cf. Prov 9:5): "God's purpose in the Servant. . . . is the redemption not only of Israel herself but of all [humankind]" (Knight 1984, 189). Moreover, in the ancient Near East, the king would provide meals to his subjects in a hierarchical arrangement (cf. Gen 43:33-34). Israel's prophet subverts the situation so that it is not the imperial king but YHWH who will provide meals.

At the same time, the recipients of the meals are, first and foremost, those who cannot afford. It is admittedly a communal banquet as implied by the collective exhortation: "Come" (v. 1; cf. 1:18; 2:3, 5). Yet the accompanying modifiers qualify this invitation to "all" in order to emphasize the divine care for those who are thirsty and who have no money. Those with "thirst" frequently pair with those with "hunger," together signifying the poor, the needy, and the exiled (cf. 5:13; 32:6; 41:17; 49:10; Ps 22:24, 26 [MT 22:25, 27]). Likewise, the expressions "without money" (cf. 46:6; 52:3) and "without cost" (cf. 45:13) reassert YHWH's unmerited deliverance of the marginalized and the powerless, thereby implicitly marginalizing the powerful and the affluent under the empire: "The everlasting covenant was now to be expanded beyond the privileged elite to embrace the entire community of those obedient to God's word" (Hanson 1995, 179).

John Ahn, in his sociological analysis, conjectures at least two socioeconomically stratified groups or communities in Deutero-Isaiah. Although it is difficult accurately to reconstruct and identify various contending groups during the post-monarchic era, some literary clues can offer helpful insights. On one side, there is a group who joined the mainstream Babylonian system (whether in Babylon or in Yehud) with their trades and skills: e.g., artisans, goldsmiths (41:7), idol-makers, and carpenters (44:9-20). On the other side, there is a group who were pushed to the margins in this colonial system: e.g., prisoners (49:9-10), the thirsty, and those without money (55:1). Comparatively, during the Japanese occupation of Korea, those Koreans who worked as delegates (or "puppets") for the imperial regime greatly prospered socio-economically and politically, whereas the family members and descendants of the incarcerated or persecuted resistance leaders became extremely impoverished, generation after generation. Against the backdrop of such a socially, economically, and morally distressed and contentious society, the prophet's call to the feast implies a vision of unity that encompasses not only aspirations for the return to and restoration of Yehud but especially advocacy for the poor, vulnerable underclass (Ahn 2011, 174–76).

The interrogative question "why" continues the previous rhetorical questions (v. 2; cf. 40:27; 50:2). The phrase "really hear me" (*shime'u shamoa'*) occurs elsewhere only in 6:9. The admonition to "eat the good" echoes the divine exhortation in the covenant lawsuit, "if you consent and obey, you will eat the good of the land" (1:19; cf. 1:16-17). YHWH will renew the "everlasting covenant" the preexilic ancestors had broken (cf. 24:5) as well as the "everlasting faithfulness (*hesed*)" promised in the Davidic covenant during the monarchy (v. 3; cf. 54:8, 10). Just as YHWH elected David as a witness, prince, and commander of the "peoples" (v. 4; cf. 1 Sam 13:14; 25:30), now the whole exilic community will embrace such a role for the "nations" (v. 5; cf. Isa 2:2-3).

It is not clear whether this passage implies severing of the Davidic line along with the age-old Davidic covenant. On the one hand, scholars aptly detect the democratization of David in this passage ("you" [pl.] in v. 3) and also throughout the second half of the book of Isaiah. However, on the other hand, in the larger scope, readers come across two human ruling figures in the second half—Cyrus (44:24; 45:1) and David (55:3). Read this way, while Cyrus takes a central role in Isaiah 40–48, albeit for the sake of Jacob-Israel, David returns to the stage in 49–57, closely linked with Zion theology (cf. Blenkinsopp 2002, 370).

In either reading, what seems clear is the expansion of this tradition into embracing the penitent, faithful exilic and postexilic communities of faith in a changing era: "it is thus a covenant that YHWH makes 'for you' not 'with you'" (Goldingay and Payne 2006b, 371). Under the governance of YHWH as commander-in-chief but with no Judean monarch, the covenant promise is "indeed unconditional, but it is not made, as formerly, to the power elite, centering in a royal family" (Boling 1999, 179). The invitation is to all, and the offer is free of charge—anticipating the inclusion of socio-ethnic outsiders (Isa 56) and the politico-economic disenfranchised (Isa 57).

Verses 6-13 elucidate the preceding call to the communal feast (vv. 1-5) with resounding assurances of divine mercy and restoration. Four causal or emphatic statements—led by "for, surely" (*ki*)—explicate the plans and purposes of merciful YHWH in this subunit. Goldingay and Payne summarize the analysis of Grimm and Dittert with regard to the fourfold *ki* themes in vv. 7b, 8, 10, and 12, as "Yes" answers concerning the Second Temple community's anxious question, "Where is YHWH's word? Let it come now" (Jer 17:15; Goldingay and Payne 2006b, 366).

The first rationale for "Yes" is that YHWH compassionately desires to forgive (vv. 6-7). The call is to "seek YHWH" (v. 6), just as the community was earlier called to "seek justice" in repentance and reform (1:17). Whereas nations and peoples march to Zion in order to walk in YHWH's "ways" (2:3), now the prophet exhorts the people to forsake their own "ways" and "thoughts" (v. 7). Here, however, the exhortation is not a condemnation per se but an invitation to the wicked for repentance. What shall we make of this compassionate call, "Let the wicked forsake their ways (*derek*)" (v. 7), which intertextually echoes the doomed "way" (*derek*) of the wicked in Psalm 1:6 (cf. Ps 37:1, 5)? Retrieving back to the core passage of Hezekiah as the model king of righteousness (as opposed to Ahaz the wicked), Peter Ackroyd's theological caution against too simplistic a distinction provides a profound caveat: "Ahaz bad, Hezekiah good, Manasseh bad, Josiah good, Jehoiakim bad . . . it is a pattern which makes for good preaching, but is it not just a little too good to be true?" (1987, 192). Lest we fall into the unrealistic fallacy that we human beings *never* change our own behavior or loyalty, the divine call to return provides not only a palpable caveat that we all can become wicked but also a hopeful promise that we the wicked can change our hearts and ways in genuine repentance (cf. 1 Kgs 8:46-50; Jonah 3:10; 2 Chr 7:14).

Amid the harsh reality of the world saturated with human depravity and dominated by the wicked (which will be the topic of Isa 57), this oracle underscores a significant theological premise: "To be righteous is *not* a matter of *being sinless but* a matter of *being forgiven*, In fact, as Psalm 32 [as a corrective against misunderstanding Psalm 1] suggests, sin and its effects are pervasive *in the life of the righteous*" (McCann 1996, 805, emphasis added). Put another way, the oracle here does not presuppose that "we" are inherently righteous and "they/others" are wicked. Rather, we "all" have the dangerous capacity and propensity to cross over and morph into the wicked. Accordingly, the divine call here does not target an exclusive group of the wicked yet. Rather, it is a call—like a last call as an ultimatum—with one more chance, one more plea to "all" those who are willing to humble themselves (57:15; 66:2) and return to God in penitence (30:15; 44:22; 45:22). The message is not condemnation of the wicked per se yet, but rather admonition for all God's people to return in their earnest prayer and repentance: "Prayer becomes a way of life for those who know that their own accomplishments, capabilities, and intentions are always inadequate" (McCann 1996, 806). The divine call to "comfort, comfort my people" (40:1) thus reverberates loudly in the promise of divine compassion for those who are willing to return to YHWH.

The second rationale for "Yes" is that YHWH has a plan to deliver the people (vv. 8-9). This theme contrasts the "way" of YHWH with that of the sinners (v. 8; cf. 40:3; Ps 1:1, 6). It also compares the gap between heaven and earth, both created by God, highlighting the chasm between YHWH's thoughts and human thoughts (v. 9). Together, vv. 8-9 refer back to Jacob-Israel's excruciating lament: "my way is hidden from YHWH" (40:27). The community now hears the divine answer, loudly, that YHWH's way far outreaches human ways. Concerning the incredible yet sure works of divine intention, Ehud Ben Zvi cites Alexander Rofé's judicious interpretation: "Rather than the Word being fulfilled, it fulfills. . . . The true purpose of the Word of God can never be known, as [God's] thoughts are beyond human comprehension, just as the heavens are beyond the earth" (Ben Zvi 2010, 99). Furthermore, there is an intertextual correlation between Isaiah 55:9 ("as the heavens are higher than the earth") and Psalm 103:11 ("as the heavens are high above the earth"). In both texts, the unfathomable and unreachable divine nature, like the heavens, highlights God's unmerited mercy and compassion, ready to relent the plan to punish and ready to forgive all, even the penitent wicked (Isa 55:7; Ps 103:8-13).

The third rationale for "Yes" is that God's reliable word will come true (vv. 10-11). This rationale uses metaphors of the rain, snow, heaven, earth, seed, and bread, underscoring the surety of YHWH's word (vv. 10-11; cf. 1:20; 34:16; 40:5; 58:14). Nili Samet observes two Sumerian texts that contain similar expressions and ideas:

> May that 'storm-day,' like rain pouring down from heaven, never return to its place! ("Lamentations over the Destruction of Ur," l. 409)

> [N]ow, like rain pouring down from heaven, [al]as, I cannot turn back to brick-built Urim. ("Death of Ur-Nammu," l. 164)

The idiom of falling rain in these parallel Sumerian texts conveys the theme of irreversibility, somewhat akin to the expression "spilled milk." The Isaianic expression here emphasizes different ideas: not only that the rain ultimately returns to heaven but also that it ought to fulfill its task of watering the earth. Evoking the common culture, the prophet underscores the theme of the "absolute dominion of God" even over precipitation (cf. Gen 1; 6–9; Exod 14–15): "Far from being the uncontrollable natural force depicted in the Sumerian phrase, the rain and the snow . . . are devoted messengers of God . . . carrying out their duty" (Samet 2010, 440).

Moreover, the rain, snow, seed, and plants collectively operate to provide food to the "eater." In a way, this oracle of the divine promise of the inclusive marketplace or eschatological feast initiates and concludes with food (vv. 1-2 and v. 10). Just as food and drink play significant roles in other texts, especially Isaiah 1, 25, and 58, so here the meal signifies key themes. First, food hits home to everyone's everyday necessity. Food is vital for any creature's survival. Thus, the free offer to those without money or privilege in this invitation sends a radical message. Divine consolation reaches out primarily, if not exclusively, to those disadvantaged economically, socially, and politically. Second, food is a communal commodity. It becomes available through many farmers' toils to feed many people. In the ancient world, contrary to the contemporary "fast food" culture, families and villagers would normally dine together. There was a strong sense of community—perhaps pointing to an egalitarian aspect or ideal (cf. 11:7)—as the phrase "sharing the meal together" means even today. Third, food is more than an ingredient for sustenance. It can nourish and revive one's body and soul. The admonition to "eat the *good*" (v. 2; cf. 1:19) thus has significant ramifications, metaphorically and theologically, more than feeding the empty belly—although this too was a major challenge to the poor and needy in ancient times, as it is even now. This food will "satisfy" (v. 2). This food is the word of YHWH that "goes forth from his *mouth*" and will not return empty but freely and richly sustain the penitent and obedient (vv. 10-11). Those who return and desire to taste this food (cf. Ps 34:8 [MT 34:9]) will experience "transformation in all realms of life" (Abernethy 2014, 138).

The fourth rationale for "Yes" projects a glorious return of the exiles, Jacob's children, in their new exodus from Babylon back to Zion (vv. 12-13; cf. 48:20-22; 52:11-12). This return will be full of joy and shalom (v. 12). The previous oracle called for leveling the mountains and hills for constructing the highway of YHWH's glorious return to Zion (40:4; cf. 2:2, 14). Now even those mountains and hills—those intimidating towering forces or even enemies—will not only become amicable companions on the journey but will also sing praises together, with trees clapping hands over the marvelous divine ways and plans for the new exodus (cf. Lund 2007, 289–91). Instead of thorn bush and nettle, there will be cypress and myrtle (v. 13a; cf. 5:6; 7:19, 23-25; 34:13). YHWH's "everlasting sign" (cf. 51:11; 54:8; 55:3) will not be "cut off" (v. 13b; cf. 48:19; 56:5).

A House of Prayer for All, Especially the Immigrants and the Eunuchs, 56:1-12

Notably echoing Isaiah 1–2, this unit sustains the subversive theme of the inclusion of all in God's house, especially the disenfranchised groups—much like the righteous, penitent "we"-group. In Isaiah 55, the reference to this group implies those who are thirsty, hungry, and penniless. Isaiah 56 expands the identification of this group to include the immigrants and the eunuchs exemplifying those most left out in their community (vv. 1-8), in stark contrast with the shepherds who are labeled as nothing short of "mute, greedy dogs" (vv. 9-12).

Verses 1-8 construe the happy group as those who are just and righteous, who keep the Sabbath, and who shun evil. The section identifies this group as immigrants and eunuchs. Starting with the "thus says YHWH" phrase, the opening command to "keep (*shamar*) justice and do righteousness" (v. 1) is a fitting expansion (*Fortschreibung*) of the previous command to "seek YHWH" (55:6; compare "seek justice" in 1:17). Echoing the expression for the righteous one in Psalm 1:1, the opening statement also depicts the "happy" one as a "human being" (lit., "son of Adam") who "keeps (*shamar*)" the Sabbath and "keeps (*shamar*)" his hands from doing all evil (v. 2).

Thematically and logically, reading vv. 1-2 together, keeping the Sabbath equals keeping justice and righteousness. How is it so? It is because the Sabbath observance, one of the key ceremonial practices for maintaining their identity in the Babylonian *golah* community (together with circumcision and dietary regulations; cf. Albertz 2003b, 106–108), is equivalent to being holy in the Holiness Code (Lev 19:2). Comparable to Rolf Knierim's exegetical emphasis on the "infratextual" underlying concepts (1992, 1), Jacob Milgrom insightfully considers "values" as the uppermost underlying theme of the book of Leviticus: "Values are what Leviticus is all about. . . . Leviticus *does* discuss rituals. However, underlying the rituals, the careful reader will find an intricate web of values that purports to model how we should relate to God and to one another" (2004, 1). In Leviticus 19, keeping YHWH's Sabbath, along with revering father and mother, is the first item of the stipulations—thus, cases and definitions—of holiness. Likewise, in Isaiah 56, keeping the Sabbath (esp. for the lowly peasants and slaves amid their ceaseless hard labor; cf. Exod 20:10; Lev 25:1-6; Deut 5:12-14), alongside keeping one's hands from doing all evil, is the very definition and essence of doing justice and righteousness. Ethos (justice and righteousness) and cultus (Sabbath ritual), therefore, define and complement each other as two theoretical and practical sides of the same coin.

Two groups exhibit the righteous and happy people—immigrants (lit., "son of the foreigner") and eunuchs (v. 3). Read intertextually, in relation to Psalm 1, the happy ones are the righteous people (Ps 1:1) as well as the foreigners and eunuchs who keep the Sabbath and avoid evil (Isa 65:1-3). In a logical syllogistic equation, then, the righteous ones are the outsiders, such as foreigners and eunuchs, rather than the insiders. Furthermore, the theme of the immigrants echoes the meaning and praxis of holiness in the Holiness Code, which culminates not only in Leviticus 19:18 ("You should love your neighbor as yourself") but equally importantly in Leviticus 19:34 ("You should love [the immigrants (or 'sojourners,' 'strangers')] as yourself").

Moreover, in comparison with Deuteronomy 23:1-6 (MT 23:2-7), Ezra 9:1-2, and Nehemiah 13:1-3, and over against the probable setting in the restoration period of Yehud, these groups would represent the outsiders excluded from the identity of the new Israel, let alone the people of Zion. As if subverting elements of the Deuteronomic law code that declares that these outsiders "shall not enter (*lo'-yabo*'; Deut 23:1-3 [MT 23:2-4]), the Isaianic oracle twice annuls the prohibition with similar negative expressions, "shall not say (*'al-yo'mar*)." YHWH will not "separate" (*badal*) these foreigners from "his people" (cf. Ezra 9:1; Neh 9:2), and the eunuchs should not say that they are a "withered tree." If we take these as laments of the excluded outsiders, we then hear the similar resounding divine rebuttal with compassionate care for them. YHWH's assuring responses to the complaints of Jacob-Israel (40:27; 49:4) and of Zion (49:14), therefore, recur in the caring affirmation of these socio-religious outcasts. Put simply, we learn of the status of the immigrants and eunuchs equivalent to that of Jacob-Israel and Zion. This equation certainly works in God's compassionate principle. This God, who heard and replied to the laments of Jacob-Israel and of Zion, now undoubtedly hears and responds to the laments of foreigners and eunuchs with the same compassion and care.

Concerning the *eunuchs*, in the ancient Near East, trees could signify procreative progeny (cf. 6:13; 11:1). Jacob Wright and Michael Chan cite a treaty between Shattiwaza of Mittanni and Suppiluliuma I of Hatti in fourteenth century BCE: "If I, Prince Shattiwaza . . . do not observe the words of this treaty and of the oath, let me, Shattiwaza . . . as a fir tree when it is felled has no more shoots, like this fir tree let me . . . like the fir tree have no progeny" (Wright and Chan 2012, 101). The divine assurance thus does not merely grant a reversal of status for the uprooted tree but promises a more permanent honor and reward. Likewise, in the ancient Near Eastern tradition, it was the king who was often associated with gardens and plants. Accordingly, a person identified with a tree can signify a royal background (Ps 1:5; cf. Brown 2002, 67–70). Admittedly, the eunuch here laments as a "withered" (*yabesh*) tree (v. 3), not unlike that in 40:7, "grass withers (*yabesh*) and flower fades." On the contrary, YHWH promises to bestow a royal honor not upon a king but upon this eunuch. Likewise, just as divine rebuttal asserts that the word of YHWH shall stand "forever" (*'olam*) in 40:8, YHWH vows to give this righteous eunuch an "everlasting" (*'olam*) name (v. 5).

Another "thus says YHWH" phrase opens detailed delineations of how these outside groups will join themselves to YHWH (vv. 4-8). First, in a chiastic relationship to v. 3, YHWH elects the *eunuchs* who keep YHWH's covenant (v. 4). With emphatic descriptions of inclusion, "in my house and in my walls," YHWH promises to confer an "everlasting name" (cf. 51:11; 54:8; 55:3, 13) that will not be cut off (cf. 55:13). Izaak J. de Hulster, in his exegesis of the iconography of 56:5, judiciously argues that the hendiadys "memorial and name" (*yad washem*) denotes a memorial statue. In light of the upright stones throughout ancient Israel "that were used as representatives of human beings (next to deities) and were in particular used as memorial stele," Hulster considers "memorial" (*yad*) a synonym for an upright pillar, a stele (*matseba*, cf. 6:13), thereby signifying the divine promise of a respected, lasting memorial (2009, 168). It was customary to place such stones outside the cultic areas. Accordingly, it is astonishing that YHWH intends to build a memorial statue not just inside the city but especially "*in* my house and *in* my walls," i.e., inside the sanctuary: "by erecting a monument within the temple, the eunuch's acceptance by God is marked for eternity" (Hulster 2015, 188). Also, recognizing that constructing a memorial was the child's duty to maintain the legacy of the ancestors, YHWH ardently "takes up the task of a child by providing the childless with a memorial stele" (Hulster 2009, 168). Indeed, this "memorial *name*" (*yad washem*) or stele is an iconographic, cultural, and theological delineation of the parallel phrase, an "everlasting *name*" (*shem 'olam*; cf. 66:22) that YHWH vows to give to these eunuchs.

Some of these eunuchs may have been descendants of Hezekiah, Davidic dynastic lineage, evidently exiled into Babylon (cf. 39:7; Esther and Daniel). In addition to their physical stance, many ancient iconographic and literary sources commonly stereotyped eunuchs negatively, due to many instances in which eunuchs took advantage of their privileged access to the king to commit acts of conspiracy and betrayal. To loyal eunuchs, however, kings would endow honorific royal burials. By bestowing YHWH's lasting honors and rewards upon the eunuchs, the prophet promotes three underlying themes: first, this oracle counters the negative stereotypes of these outsiders; second, this oracle subverts and transforms imperial ideology in that it is not the imperial kings but YHWH the true King who guarantees such an honor; third, this oracle depicts the destroyed and exiled community as the felled tree or stump, thereby extending the divine acceptance and blessing to all the Judahites, especially those marginalized and ostracized (Wright and Chan 2012, 112–18). Comparable and even equal to the Suffering Servant (Isa 53) and the barren Zion (Isa 54), these devout eunuchs and the dispirited community will have divine honor better than sons and daughters (v. 5; cf. Ruth 4:15).

Likewise, YHWH elects the *foreigners* who desire to convert to faith in YHWH, who want to become "servants" of YHWH, and "all" who keep the Sabbath (v. 6). Again, this radical inclusion of foreigners comes with some qualifications and stipulations. Regarding qualifications, instead of YHWH's people who are to "love YHWH" (cf. Deut 6:5), these foreigners are to "love *the name of* YHWH," which may further hint at the "hypostatization" of YHWH's name, the stronger reverence for the divine name evidenced in the postexilic period (Schniedewind 2003, 235). Regarding stipulations, including the foreigners, the observance of Sabbath is a fundamental practice. Thus, with those qualifications and stipulations, YHWH affirms the acceptance of these foreigners to Jerusalem, "*in* my house" (v. 7).

Intertextual allusions to Isaiah 1–2 are noteworthy here. Whereas the prophet condemned the new moon and "Sabbath" of the corrupt in-groups of Israel (Isa 1:13; note that "Sabbath" occurs elsewhere only in Isa 58:13; 66:23), YHWH acknowledges the Sabbath that these out-groups observe (v. 6). Whereas YHWH took no delight over the "sacrifices (*zebak*)" and "burnt offerings (*'olah*)" of the rulers (1:11), this marginalized group's "burnt offerings (*'olah*)" and "sacrifices (*zebak*)" will become acceptable (v. 7). It is the same "mountain of the house of YHWH" (2:2) on which YHWH embraces "all peoples" and nations (v. 7; cf. 2:2-4). Finally, whereas vain worshipers' "prayers" would not receive a divine response (1:15), YHWH vows to welcome all devout peoples into the house of "prayer" (v. 7; note that the word "prayer" occurs elsewhere only in Isa 37:4; cf. Jer 7:11; Matt 21:13; Mark 11:17; Luke 19:46).

With regard to the thematic implications of the eunuchs and foreigners in this oracle, the text admittedly does not indicate modern-day naturalization per se, but it "certainly envisions an international community of YHWHists centered upon the YHWH-temple in Jerusalem" (Levenson 1996,

163; cf. Kaminsky 2011, 19–20). This theme resonates with the old exodus event when the "mixed multitude" went up with the Israelites out of Egypt (Exod 12:38; cf. Neh 13:3), while it also lays an interpretive foundation for the saying of Rabbi Elazar in the Talmud: "The Holy One (blessed be he) dispersed Israel into exile among the nations only so that converts may be added to them" (*b.Pes.* 87b; Levenson 1996, 163; cf. Kaminsky 2011, 29). Summing up, YHWH declares the gathering of all those "banished" out of Israel, and even more groups with them, presumably including those socially, economically, politically, religiously, and ethnically outcast and ostracized (v. 8; cf. 11:12; 27:12-13).

Verses 9-12 portray the doomed group as the corrupt beasts and greedy dumb dogs—illustrated by sentinels and shepherds. Just as the banquet to all the poor, humble exiles excludes the unrepentant wicked (Isa 55), so here not all can join the ideal, faithful community (cf. Isa 24–27; Hibbard 2006, 107). In an ironic contrast to the emphatic inclusion of "all" who keep the Sabbath (v. 6) and "all" the peoples (v. 7) delineated in 56:1-8, the word "all" in this subunit occurs repeatedly—five times—in expressions concerning the chastisement and exclusion of the wicked.

Remarkably similar to the earlier invitation to the feast, "*all* thirsty ones, *come* to the waters . . . buy and *eat*" (55:1), the prophet invites the menacing neighboring nations described as "wild beasts" to "*come* and *eat*" (v. 9; cf. Jer 12:9; Ezek 39:17). What are they to devour? They are cordially invited to vanquish the stubborn, self-serving leaders of Israel, described as sentinels—"all of them do not know" (v. 10)—and shepherds—who "have no understanding" (v. 11; cf. 6:9).

If the opening chapter of the entire book of Isaiah uses the harshest names for obstinate Israel—"evil seed, sons of perversion" (1:3), we hear virtually equivalent denunciations in slurs of the powers that be in Yehud—"dumb dogs" (v. 10) and "insatiably greedy dogs . . . all turned to their own way, their own gain" (v. 11; cf. 53:6; 55:7-9; Ps 22:16 [MT Ps 22:17]). Joseph Blenkinsopp thus remarks, "One of the tasks of the interpreter of Isaiah 56–66, and by no means an easy one, is to identify the situations which precipitated this name-calling and the groups or factions to which the names correspond" (2006, 111). Whatever the situations may have been, the hypocrisy and corruption of justice masterfully wrought by these inhumane leaders must have so deeply pained the hearts of the devout people, so excruciatingly devastated the morale of the faithful ones, that these righteous "we"-group had to resort to use the most offensive curse words against them. In the pastoral setting, "guard dogs" had the duty to shout out to protect the flocks for the shepherd. These priestly leaders are so corrupt and callous to discard their main duty of righteous barking (i.e., proclaiming) that their "shepherd" status as leaders have been degraded to that of "mute dogs" (vv. 10-11; Blenkinsopp 2003, 146–47).

In the ancient Mediterranean world, the term "dog" could also suggest a strong insult (similar to today's slur, "SOB"), because "dogs were considered scavengers (like rats to an American), not domestic pets," as can be noted from the NT story of the Gentile woman in Matthew 15:26-27 and Mark 7:27-28 (Malina and Rohrbaugh 2003, 177). In our passage, the wicked "dogs" must have wielded and abused the unjust power toward the righteous to the maximum capacity possible so that the righteous victims who were disempowered and falsely accused had no choice but to explode their fuming emotion. We have so many lament psalms of such torment and agony against the wicked enemies as dogs in the Psalter (Pss 22:16, 20 [MT 22:17, 21]; 59:6, 14 [MT 59:7, 15]).

At the end of this chapter, we observe an inclusio within Isaiah 55–56. The key word "wine" both starts (55:1) and ends (56:12) these two chapters. Also, there is a contrast between the thirsty, impoverished group (55:1-5) and the intoxicated, privileged group (56:9-12). The devout group, depicted as the Servant's disciples, is also called the "people of loyalty" (57:1), "tremblers" (66:2, 5), and "servants" of YHWH (54:17; 56:6; 63:17; 65:9, 13-15; 66:14). On the contrary, the corrupt shepherds who boast of their riches and their ability to afford "wine" do not know their impending misery (v. 12; cf. 55:1). They are the wicked who will encounter the opposite fate of the righteous in the following passages.

The Righteous, Outnumbered by the Wicked, Will Inherit Zion, 57:1-21

The section about the fate of the righteous Servant and daughter Zion (Isa 49–57) culminates in the contrast between the staunch condemnation of the wicked (vv. 1-13) and the impassioned uplifting of the righteous—the crushed and the lowly (vv. 14-21). Paul Niskanen likewise claims this core theme of salvific righteousness (*tsedaqah*) as the single most important word of the entire book of Isaiah (2014, 3). This society is not unlike the unfairly imbalanced world of disparate communities in *The Hunger Games* (2008), the first book of bestselling trilogy by Suzanne Collins. In the book, many poverty-stricken and mistreated people of various Districts can neither change their inhumane plight nor access the Capitol, where excessive luxury and consumption are galore. As the rest of us pondered whether our future is heading toward such dystopia, one student in my Introduction class discussion said, "Our current world is already like that." For that matter, the ancient biblical world too was like that, with the harsh reality of injustice and brutality. Such a society, in reality, is governed and driven by the money game, power game, and ego game. What readers have heard of the radical community with the divine compassion and care for the disciples of the Servant (Isa 53), the offspring of Zion (Isa 54), the destitute (Isa 55), and the marginalized outcasts (Isa 56) all seem like utopian, unrealistic ideals. Now, in Isaiah 57, this future hope guided by the *compassion games* seems remote from the reality where the wicked prosper over the seemingly unfortunate righteous (cf. Ps 109:2-5).

Verses 1-13 disclose the situation in which the righteous and the loyal ones encounter rampant injustice while the wicked prosper. Like Psalm 1, this unit starts with the righteous (vv. 1-2) and concludes with the wicked (vv. 20-21) as brackets—we should note that Psalm 1 is bracketed by the wicked, as inclusio, in v. 1 and v. 6. Whereas the wicked (pl.) will perish in Psalm 1:6, here the righteous one (sg.) is perishing (v. 1; cf. Mic 7:2; Ps 12:1; Eccl 7:15; 8:14; 9:1-2), recalling the righteous Servant who suffered and died (cf. 53:8, 11).

Notably, the dichotomous conflict also links this segment about the righteous (57:1-2) with the preceding segment about the wicked (56:9-12). Joseph Blenkinsopp observes the literary dependence of both segments (which he considers to have been originally one literary corpus) on Jeremiah 12:7-13. The phrase "no one takes it to heart" (*'en 'ish sam 'al-leb*) from Jeremiah 12:11 occurs verbatim in 57:1. These texts' echo of the similar Jeremianic text underscores the social context of unmitigated injustice (Blenkinsopp 2006, 110–11).

Concerning the identity of this righteous one, some consider an individual, most likely the Suffering Servant of Isaiah 53 (Blenkinsopp 2003, 150; 2006: 116), or others consider a collective entity represented in the individual figure (Niskanen 2014, 9). Either way, the oracle asserts that, though unjustly taken away, the righteous will enter into "peace" and the upright will have "rest" (v. 2; cf. Jer 34:5; Ps 1:1, 6).

Now, the oracle accuses the wicked, leaders in moral and religious debauchery, in terms of court trial procedure: subpoena (v. 3); indictment (vv. 4-11); and verdict (vv. 12-13; Paul 2012, 463). As though parodying the society's exclusion of illegitimate children (cf. Deut 23:1-6 [MT 23:2-7]; Isa 56:1-8), the prophet summons the recalcitrant wicked (pl.) directly, calling them the "offspring of an adulterer and a harlot" (v. 3; cf. 1:21; Hos 4:13). As Shalom Paul elucidates, "this trial scene is reminiscent of earlier prophecies, such as 41:1-4; 45:20-21. In these, however, the nations are summoned, whereas here the accused are Israel" (2012, 463).

The interrogative questions (cf. 53:1)—"against whom (*'al-mi*)" in v. 4 forms a chiastic bracket with "whom (*mi*) . . . against (*'al*)" in v. 11—deride this group as the "children of transgression, offspring of deception" (v. 4). The accusation exposes the pagan rituals of child sacrifice practiced in secret, "under the clefts of the rocks" (v. 5; cf. 2:21; 2 Kgs 3:27; Jer 7:31; Ezek 16:21; 23:39).

Personified as a pagan cultic prostitute, this group is addressed in a detailed list in the second-person feminine singular (vv. 6-11). YHWH indicts her rituals and offerings to idols (v. 6). Graphic expressions heighten the sinfulness of her sexual rites both in the public place, on mountaintops (v. 7; cf. 30:25), and behind closed doors, displaying her phallic images and her lovers' genitalia (v. 8; Paul 2012, 467–68). Chris Franke captures the rhetorical force and hermeneutical challenge of these depictions: "The shepherds/sentinels/leaders' adulterous mother, the sorceress, is the focus of the attack in 57:6-13. Her sexual behavior is explicitly described in what can be called the most violent, lurid polemic in the Bible" (2014, 717).

In contrast with God exalted on the high mountain (2:2, 11), the "high and lofty mountain" (57:7) represents "blatant defilement of God's holy name" (Childs 2001, 467). Toward the end of World War II, in 1940s, the colonized Koreans had to participate in the formal religious obeisance to the Shinto shrine (cf. Dan 3:1-7). Although many compromisers interpreted this act as a mere religious or cultural ritual, some vehemently resisted for religious or even political reasons. The colonizing empire reprimanded and imprisoned those who refused; in fact, the empire executed some leadership figures. Read against this comparative backdrop of imperial rituals and the colonized people's capitulation, just as the prophet's denouncement of Israel's religious idolatry actually points to its leaders' political dependence on foreign powers, so the present indictment indeed may attack the leaders' diplomatic submission to the imperial rulers rather than to YHWH.

Thus, their (second-person feminine singular) sending oils, perfumes, and envoys to the king (*melek*—or a pun with "Molech"; cf. 2 Kgs 23:10; Jer 32:35) would mean their eventual descent into Sheol (v. 9). Some scholars claim that the key violation condemned here is not only cultic prostitution or sexual rites but precisely the prohibited ritual of child sacrifice (Moughtin-Mumby 2008, 148–49). Wandering and seeking other lovers, she never grew tired of incessant lust (v. 10). Bracketing the interrogative, rhetorical questions with v. 4, YHWH rebukes the compromisers who, having "dreaded and feared" superpowers that are mere mortals, have deserted and spurned YHWH (v. 11; cf. 50:10; 51:12; 63:17).

The divine condemnation expounds the foundational meaning of "fear of YHWH." What does it mean to fear God? To fear God does not mean to be scared, afraid, or terrified per se. Rather, to fear God connotes to be in reverent awe and utter humility before the miraculous faithfulness and mercy of God. In a theological nutshell, to fear God means *not to fear* anyone or anything else. Irene Nowell delineates this meaning in a simple yet profound way by saying that fear of the Lord is "the recognition that God is God and I am not—and I am glad!" or, put another way, it really means, "Oh my God [OMG]!" (Nowell 2013, 53). Or, to borrow a famous Christian hymn, for Christians to fear God is to confess, "I'd rather have Jesus than silver or gold" (cf. Rom 8:38-39). The recalcitrant leaders had no fear of God but instead fear of other gods, powers, and materials. By fearing all else, they have failed to remember or give a thought and heart to God, ending up not fearing God altogether (cf. Isa 8:12-13).

YHWH casts a solemn verdict upon these crooked leaders. With sarcasm, the judge presents their righteous deeds, or more likely the lack thereof (v. 12). Piles of idols cannot deliver them, since the wind (*ruakh*) will carry them away (v. 13a; cf. Ps 1:4-5). To the contrary, those righteous ones who seek refuge in YHWH will inherit the land, in Zion, upon whom the following subunit turns its focus (v. 13b; cf. 51:1, 7; 65:9). Here, read in connection with Isaiah 56, we find another criterion for inclusion into the community and the temple: ethical behavior rather than ethnic origin: "Open access to the sanctuary is granted, but only to those who follow the precepts of Yahwistic religion" (Middlemas 2007, 175).

Verses 14-21 pronounce the unfailing divine comfort for the righteous, who have been marginalized and victimized by the wicked leaders who have so casually bent justice. Reverberating the call to "prepare the way" of YHWH's glorious return (40:3), there is a new call to "prepare the way" for the new exodus of the exiles, "my people" (v. 14; note that this phrase to "prepare the way" occurs elsewhere in Isaiah only in 62:10).

With the "thus says YHWH" phrase, YHWH, who is "high and lifted up" (cf. 2:2; 6:1), claims to be with the crushed and the lowly of spirit (v. 15; cf. 66:2; Ps 51:17 [MT 51:19]). In an intertextual connection with Psalm 109, where the righteous speaker laments, and curses, against the wicked that bully "the poor, the needy, and the brokenhearted" all the way to death (Ps 109:16, 22), the oracle here counters with the proclamation that God will take the sides of the poor, needy, and brokenhearted—and thereby implies that God will consider the wicked as enemies. This radical theology reasserts that just as this incomparably majestic God grants lofty status to the meek Servant (cf. 52:13), so now the exalted Lord comes down to revive the humiliated and dispirited people (cf. 1 Sam 1:15). This people's iniquity has caused divine wrath (vv. 16-17). Yet now the divine promise to these repentant mourners rings loudly: "I will restore (*shalem*) their comfort"; "peace, peace (*shalom shalom*) to far and near"—presumably those in exilic locales ("far") and those back in Yehud ("near"); and (twice) "I will heal them" (v. 18 and v. 19).

Returning to the corrupted sociopolitical reality abused by the wicked, this unit once more condemns the wicked, likening them to a troubled sea that finds no peace (v. 20). Indeed, there is no peace (*shalom*) for the wicked (v. 21; cf. 48:22). What may have caused this vehement denunciation of the corrupted city? In many societies, both ancient and contemporary, a newly restored city or people that has just survived unimaginable calamity often falls back to its old system. It is as though bad old habits hardly die but tend to come back again and again. Mark Biddle, identifying this condemned city as Lady Zion, astutely notes Lady Zion's tendency to return to the bad habits and symptoms of Old Jerusalem. New Zion must, the prophet cries out, go through a thoroughgoing transformation in her resolute fight against political corruption, moral inertness, and religious hypocrisy, lest the city's ill practices and wickedness all too easily come back up like weeds and daisies, even after cleansing and restoration (Biddle 1996, 139).

This unit begins with the word "righteous" (*tsaddiq*) in v. 1 and ends with the word "wicked" (*resha'im*) in v. 21. Yet, in the big picture, this unit, which contrasts the divine comfort for the poor, lowly, and marginalized righteous—including the righteous Servant and daughter Zion—with the divine accusation against the greedy, corrupt wicked, wraps up the larger section (Isa 49–57). At the same time, this conflict between the righteous and the wicked will be the central theme of the ensuing section that addresses the reconstruction of Zion and beyond (Isa 58–66).

Glorious Future of Zion for the Righteous Remnants contra the Wicked Perpetrators (Seventh Branch of the Lampstand)

Isaiah 58–66

The issues of the Sabbath (Isa 56) and anti-pagan religious practices (Isa 57) linger from the previous section. The righteous Servant's suffering (Isa 53) and the call for the wicked to repent (Isa 55) came to a serious tension between the righteous minority-marginalized group and the wicked majority-dominant group (Isa 57). Yet now, the schism or chasm between the righteous and the wicked come to the fore in full force.

Moreover, quite common in the postexilic literature, debates and dialogues constitute the key forms of the oracles. Earlier, YHWH addressed the Servant's complaint and Zion's lament (Isa 49) with messages of comfort and assurance, just as the prophetic charges to return to Zion functioned to answer the sorrowful sighs of the exiles and inspired them (Isa 40). Now oracles probe the returnees and remainees alike in the restoration era, especially given the resurfacing rivalries among various groups and sects that the prophetic oracles chastise and accuse head on. Will unity become possible amid ongoing imperial control, or will internal sectarian tensions undermine any possibility for a glorious future?

Scholars have debated many issues related to this section, such as the historical setting, the location of the author(s), and the socio-religious backgrounds of the schism. If we consider Babylon the setting for Isaiah 40–48 (Blenkinsopp 2002, 104), then it seems that some geographical transition occurred in Isaiah 49–57 (such as the author's return from Babylon to Jerusalem; Paul 2012, 321). The traditional view has been that the prophetic oracles address those in Babylon (Isa 40–55) and those in the homeland (Isa 56–66; Uhlig 2009a, 140). Also, the present section (Isa 58–66) contains heated debate and severe criticism among contentious groups, parties, or communities. Readers must contemplate the identities of these groups in the colonial province of Yehud under Persian imperial control, and in the city of Jerusalem where struggles linger and tensions arise, especially between the faithful and the unfaithful.

On the one hand, it is possible that we can conjecturally reconstruct some of the parties in tension. Hence, in comparison with Ezra and Nehemiah, this Isaianic perspective may offer contending and more inclusive perspectives. Alternatively, the tension may betray the disagreement between the returnees (from the Babylonian exile) and the remainees (in Yehud). Moreover, the tension may signify the schism between the Zadokite priests and the less dominant Levites (see the pertinent discussion in the introduction). On the other hand, however, we should remember the prominent ambiguity concerning any clues for distinct parties or groups. As is evident from many of these poetic Isaianic oracles, it is often difficult to make a clear-cut separation regarding the groups' identities, backgrounds, and even evaluations. This can be frustrating but nonetheless raises important hermeneutical options. While it is easy to pinpoint who the wicked are in certain cases, such as Egypt over enslaved Hebrews or Babylon over captive Judah, that may not be the case in many other contexts.

In the aftermath of Korea's liberation after World War II, it has been learned that many of those who became puppet leaders of local farms, factories, and even government offices of imperial Japan ended up occupying elite positions, and even owning immense real estate at the expense of fellow Koreans who lost so much. Despite many efforts to pinpoint the culprits and traitors, it has been extremely difficult to track down all of them and set them apart in a clear-cut manner. Similarly, we learn of the recent identification and sentencing of some former Nazi leader figures who have been hiding in various parts of the world. Such may have been the case for the last section of the book of Isaiah, with the daunting task of restoring and rebuilding a new community amid unsettled injustice and unhealed scars from the Babylonian colonial era.

Structure of Isaiah 58–66
Restoration and Reform of Cultus and Ethos, 58:1–59:21
Zion's Glorious Future, 60:1–62:12
The Penitent Community's Lament to God the Parent and the Potter, 63:1–64:11
YHWH the Righteous Parent Answers, 65:1–66:24

Restoration and Reform of Cultus and Ethos, 58:1–59:21

True Meanings and Practices of Fasting on the Day of Atonement, 58:1-14
This unit explicates and reconceptualizes the topics of religious and ethical reform amid the setting of restoration in Yehud. The present oracle touches

upon the ongoing debates concerning old traditions and values amid new contexts. The responses in the heated debates are radical and subversive. The preceding oracles emphasized divine preference toward the hungry and the poor (Isa 55), foreigners and eunuchs (Isa 56), and the crushed, lowly, yet upright in sociopolitical groups (Isa 57)—all as legitimate and qualified recipients of the divine feast, temple membership, and shalom. Now, the prophet conveys another radical, new definition: concerning problems with the purpose and meaning of the ritual of *fasting* (vv. 1-5), YHWH answers by reconstruing this ritual such that "the fast God desires is to provide food to the destitute, who have no choice but to fast" (vv. 6-12; Paul 2012, 480). A similar reminder and redefinition concerning the *Sabbath* concludes this section (vv. 13-14).

Verses 1-5 present another illustration involving the ritual of fasting, not just to provide a new meaning of fasting but especially to expose the resurfaced problems of distrust and disregard of other groups among the restored community in Yehud. Whereas the call to "proclaim" (*qara'*) in the divine council was to encourage the exiles to wait for YHWH's salvific return (40:6), YHWH now urges the prophet to "proclaim" (*qara'*) the sins of "my people," of the house of Jacob, by raising his voice like "a ram's horn (*shopar*)" on the Day of Atonement (v. 1; cf. Lev 25:9; Mic 3:8; Blenkinsopp 2003, 177). This whole community pretends to earnestly seek to know YHWH (cf. Hos 6:3), as though they were the experts on justice and righteousness (v. 2). They complain that despite their fasting and "self-afflicting" or "fake-afflicting" (cf. Lev 16:31), YHWH does not recognize their needs (v. 3a; cf. Pss 50:8-9, 20; 51:16 [MT 51:18]).

Repeated occurrences of the word "look, behold (*hen*)" in vv. 3b, 4 or the interrogative particle (*ha-*) in v. 5 (three times) imply divine pathos as though a parent explains to and then asks questions of grumbling children (vv. 3b-5). On this Yom Kippur, when they should "not do any work" (Lev 16:29), they rather see to their business and even oppress their lowly workers (v. 3b). Against the complaints of the pious-pretending leaders that God neither "sees" nor "knows" their pious (but fake) affliction in the ritual of fasting (v. 3a), God the real "Boss" rebuts that God does see and know vividly their exploitation of their employees (v. 3b; Goldingay 2014, 85)! They fast but bully and fight with wicked fists, like ferocious kids; it is no wonder their pleas cannot reach "high above" (v. 4; cf. 57:15). Like the indebted slave who, though himself forgiven, extended his fellow slaves harsh treatment (Matt 18:21-35), their humility consists of a superficial bending of heads and pretentious lying in sackcloth and ashes (v. 5).

In verses 6-12, YHWH's rebuttal emphasizes not their ritual formality but instead their ethical actuality, practiced in their neighborly care and communal solidarity. The interrogative question ("is not . . . ?" which is syntactically akin to "if . . .") twice instructs concerning the real meanings of fasting: on the one hand, loosening the shackles of wickedness, untying the ropes of oppression, setting free the crushed, and breaking every yoke (v. 6); on the other hand, breaking bread for the hungry, bringing the homeless into the house, clothing the naked, and not avoiding their own kin or neighbor (v. 7). Situated in Jerusalem in Yehud, the prophet makes theological connections with the concrete, tangible happenings, especially in the reestablished urban capital, where people employ slaves and despise the homeless "wandering the streets of Jerusalem" (Houston 2010, 110; cf. 3:13-15; 10:1-4). In a nutshell, fasting connotes releasing fellow sisters and brothers—including those in the same neighboring blocks and corners—from the economic, social, and judicial bondages: "Freedom is the first and indispensable requisite" (Blenkinsopp 2003, 179).

The prophetic slam against the people's disingenuous solidarity is comparable to that of today's privileged people—including us in the First World—who show off outward charity while inwardly hiding their/our deeply instilled elitism and classism. Just as James Sanders illustrated in his Introduction course lectures at Claremont, we the comfortable and the privileged may react, "Amazing grace, how strange the sound that saved a wretch like him (or her)?" Contrarily, it is for the sake of the underprivileged souls, those impoverished sheep, for whom this God is willing to renounce those self-pious religious bullies (cf. Luke 15:4-6). Throughout human history, it has been the "takers" who tend to end up winning with riches, success, and power (cf. Gen 13:9-13; Mark 10:21-25; Luke 16:19-25). Nevertheless, it is often the "givers" who display and experience a life truly fulfilling and satisfying, blessed and happy, indeed worth living (cf. Gen 18:1-8; Matt 5:3-12; Luke 19:8-9). Such may not have been the reality in many places and epochs. Yet the prophet defiantly preaches that God acknowledges and appreciates the life of the "givers," not that of the "takers."

Twice, following the protases (vv. 6-7), the declarative particle ("then") presents the apodoses (vv. 8-9). The community practicing this definition of fasting will have light and healing surrounded by the vindication and glory of YHWH (v. 8). For those who fast in this genuine way, YHWH promises to answer their prayers, saying, "Here I am" (v. 9a; cf. 6:8; 52:6). The protasis ("if," 'im), which wraps up these conditional sentences in vv. 6-9, highlights what is at stake in this rebuilding society: remove the yoke, finger-pointing, and malicious tongues against one another in your own midst, in your own community (v. 9b)—or, put differently, love your neighbor, especially the disenfranchised, as yourself (Lev 19:18, 34).

Not unlike the famous temple sermons of Jeremiah (cf. Jer 7:1-15; 26:1-19), this oracle reiterates the conditional exhortation associated with fasting now in a broader, interpersonal communal sphere (vv. 10-12; cf. Isa 1:19-20). True fasting is not so much humbling one's "self (*nefesh*)" (vv. 3, 5) but more giving one's "self (*nefesh*)" for the hungry and poor (v. 10a). If they practice so, YHWH—who welcomes the thirsty, the hungry, and the poor (cf. 55:1)—promises to confer blessings upon them and their community. This obedient group will become as a light that shines amid darkness (v. 10b; cf. 42:6; 49:6). Indeed, they will become active partners of divine royalty, as their "light" will break out like the dawn (cf. 60:1-3). In other words, in their actions of solidarity with the homeless and needy, "they perform the originally royal duty to *mediate* YHWH's righteousness" (Uhlig 2009a, 284). YHWH will continue to guide and provide for them (v. 11). Surely, such a group will inherit a rebuilt city and mark a lasting legacy as restorers of walls and streets (v. 12; cf. 61:4).

Thomas Staubli observes traditional and theological parallels between the Egyptian Maat-offering (or "throat-offering") and the Isaianic reconstrual of fasting. In the Egyptian tradition, the Pharaoh (e.g., Pharaoh Ptolemy XIII [51–30 BCE]) would offer to Horus the Maat-figurine, which is associated with a throat ("pipe [cavern] that sends food") and symbolizes the provision of the people with the basic sustenance of life. Similarly, the Isaianic oracle reconceives the tradition of fasting not so much as "suppressing one's throat" but rather as suppressing one's entire self for the sake of feeding those in need. Strikingly, the word, "one's self or soul" (*nefesh*), occurs no less than five times in this pericope (vv. 3, 5, 10 [twice], 11; cf. Deut 6:5). Considering vv. 8-12 in a chiastic pattern, Staubli regards v. 10a as its rhetorical and thematic center—i.e., fasting defined as offering one's "self" (*nefesh*) to the hungry so that the afflicted "soul" (*nefesh*) be nourished and satisfied. Yet there is a thematic shift in this prophetic theology. Whereas it is the Pharaoh who should give the royal provision to the population, the prophet's theology stipulates that "each and every one is now responsible for providing for the poor" (Staubli 2009, 46). Whereas Haggai and Zechariah anticipate a temple where God is to receive the offering, the Isaianic oracle, while by no means abandoning the temple and the cult, reconceptualizes this ritual that offering to the "afflicted souls" is indeed offering to God: "The God who dwells in a temple is replaced by the poor and suffering (dwelling among us)" (Staubli 2009, 46).

Verses 13-14 readdress the ritual of Sabbath in a similar conditional covenant exhortation. Thus, the "if"-statements delineate what is meant by "keeping the Sabbath," as pertaining to the righteous as well as the foreigners (56:2, 6): not pursuing or promoting one's own prerogatives but rather seeking and honoring YHWH's delight (v. 13). Here we should note linguistic and thematic correlations with 1:11-14, expressions such as "trampling my courts" (1:12) and "trampling the Sabbath" (v. 13) or "I do not delight" (1:11) and "you will delight" (v. 14)—although the Hebrew words are not the same. In this intertextual connection, the Sabbath, which people misused as an empty ritual (1:14), is redefined in terms of the practices of social justice (58:13; Niskanen 2014, 18). Contingent upon the rightful practices of such ritual with ethos, they will have delight in YHWH and "eat" the inheritance of Jacob their ancestor (v. 14; cf. 1:19; note the inclusio involving "the house of Jacob" in v. 1 and "Jacob your ancestor" in v. 14), for "the mouth of YHWH has spoken" (cf. 1:20; 40:5).

Accusation, Lament, and Divine Promise to Intervene and Renew, 59:1-21

Accusations continue here concerning the rebuilding community's pervasive sins (vv. 1-8). Peculiarly, however, as if echoing the disciples' confession with regard to the Suffering Servant (cf. 53:1-9), the community laments (first-person plural) their inability to break through the impasse of evil (vv. 9-15a). The prophetic announcement that YHWH will intervene for Zion with forgiveness and deliverance and will renew the covenant for the repentant community closes this unit (vv. 15b-21).

There is a somewhat neatly framed chiasm in this unit:

vv. 1-3—"I" (YHWH), "you" (pl.)
    vv. 4-8—"they" [v. 8, "there is no justice"]
        vv. 9-15a—"we"
    vv. 15b-20—"they," "he" (YHWH) [v. 15, "there is no justice"]
v. 21—"I" (YHWH), "you" (sg.) plus "your offspring"

Verses 1-8 expand the accusation of the community's hypocritical fasting (cf. 58:1-5). Various metaphors, especially of human body parts, underscore the fact that their sins are massive and widespread. The opening segment— led by "look, behold (*hen*)" (cf. 58:3-4)—conveys YHWH's direct, sweeping accusation addressed to the community (vv. 1-3). YHWH's hand is not too short to save (v. 1; cf. 50:2). Rather, "your" sins and iniquities have separated God, hidden God's face, and blocked the divine ears (v. 2; cf. 8:17; 54:8;

64:7 [MT 64:6]). This community's actions ("palms stained with blood" [cf. 1:15] and "fingers with iniquity") and words (lips and tongues that utter lies and malice) block YHWH's hand and ears (v. 3).

The following segment, accusing the community in the third-person plural, portrays a society in utter disarray and lawlessness (vv. 4-8). The repeated negations (*'en*) underscore the complete annihilation of justice or righteousness in the legal system that only conceives harm and begets corruption (v. 4). They are like serpents that hatch more eggs and spiders that weave the web to ensnare more prey (v. 5). Their works only produce malice, and violence is in their palms (v. 6). The expression that "their feet run to evil and they hasten to shed innocent blood" (v. 7) repeats Proverbs 1:16 verbatim (cf. Prov 6:16-18). As expected of the wicked, these sinners follow the crooked paths that have no justice and are devoid of "peace" (v. 8).

Verses 9-15a, which return to first-person plural speech ("we"; cf. 53:1-5), contain the community's lament amid social havoc. This lament, framed in a chiasm by four catchwords, offers a moving confession of their wickedness by the penitent group (cf. 55:7):

v. 9—*justice, righteousness, light, brightness*
    vv. 10-11—we grope . . . stumble . . . murmur . . .
        v. 12—our transgressions are numerous *before you* . . . our transgressions are with us . . . (cf. 7:14; 8:8, 10)
    v. 13—[we] transgress . . . backslide . . . rebel . . .
vv. 14-15a—*justice, righteousness, truth, integrity*

The result of sin begetting more sins is a grim situation of moral chaos and societal collapse. Justice and righteousness are far from this community and, despite their hope for light, darkness overwhelms (v. 9; cf. 50:10; 58:8). Their task to be a "light" to the nations (cf. 42:6; 49:6) has to wait for a while (60:1, 3). Even in the bright noonday, they are blinded without light (v. 10). "All of us" (cf. 53:6) moan but salvation is far from them (v. 11).

At the lowest point, the community solemnly confesses that they themselves have sinned and specify against whom they have transgressed (v. 12). In the chiastic center of this subunit, in fact in this entire chapter, this is the only place where God is directly addressed as "you." Against and before God, "we" have committed enormous crime (cf. Ps 51:4 [MT 51:6]). How burdensome are their wrongdoings? Opposite the pious group's confession that "God is *with us* (*'immanu*)" (cf. 7:14; 8:8, 10), this sin-laden community humbly admits that "our transgressions are *with us* (*'ittanu*)." Indeed, the target of their sins is none other than YHWH against whom they transgressed, God from whom they backslid (v. 13).

Accordingly, the absence of goodness within the rebuilding community of Yehud culminates in the reiterated expressions that "justice went back, righteousness remains *far away* [as opposed to "near"; cf. 57:19]. . . . Uprightness cannot enter, truth is missing, and one who turns away from evil is assaulted" (vv. 14-15a; cf. 5:26; 43:6; 49:12). Paul Hanson's hermeneutical connection to today's society is telling: "In our society, as in that of the struggling community of Third Isaiah, the hopes and expectations of many are raised by glorious promises of prosperity, peace, and divine favor, only to be dashed on the rocks of poverty and marginalization" (1988, 100).

Verses 15b-21 reciprocate the divine response to Yehud's depravity and the lament of its repentant "we"-group. There is a word play: "YHWH saw [*wyr*] and it was evil [*wyr*] in his eyes" (Niskanen 2014, 30). Also, the phrase "there is no justice" (*'en mishpat*) in v. 15b forms a symmetrical bookend with the same phrase in v. 8. Having seen that justice is vacant in the community (v. 15b) and that no one speaks out against rampant evil, YHWH stirs up the divine arm for salvation and vindication (v. 16; cf. 51:9; 52:10). A society cannot stay healthy if it is full of negative naysayers. Alternatively, however, a society can also decay if there is no voice of criticism and truth telling. During the Cold War era of the twentieth century, there were many prophetic voices that raised concerns and even anger toward occurrences of rampant injustice. We wonder whether things have significantly progressed in the twenty-first century, when it is becoming rare to hear voices of outcry and justice against cases of economic discrepancy, police brutality, racial discrimination, human trafficking, environmental pollution, and so on. The Isaianic complaint seems ironically relevant in today's world, if and whenever voices of righteous accusation and justice-pursuing indignation are being muted or obstructed.

Adapting the common Mesopotamian motifs, the text says that YHWH puts on battle equipment to vanquish the enemies (v. 17; Paul 2014, 509). A thematic pun with the verb "to make complete, repay" (*shalem*) hints that YHWH's foes and enemies will receive the exact retribution of divine wrath instead of peace, shalom (v. 18). Many from the east and from the west will fear YHWH (v. 19). Who will be delivered then? It will be those in Zion and those in Jacob who repent and turn away from transgressions (v. 20; cf. 1:27; Jonah 3:10).

In the concluding verse, resuming YHWH's direct address ("you") to this penitent, pious group, YHWH pronounces a new covenant in which the divine spirit (cf. 32:15; 42:1; 44:3) and words (cf. 51:16) will abide by this group for eternity (v. 21; Jer 31:33-34).

Zion's Glorious Future, 60:1–62:12

Jerusalem's Light Will Shine forth and Its Walls Will Be Reestablished, 60:1-22

This unit opens a new section that presents certain new themes and perspectives. Scholars commonly consider chapters 60–62 an originally independent portion and the central core of Isaiah 56–66 (Westermann 1969, 296–300). In particular, many think it may have been a part of a commentary on Isaiah 40–55, with similar styles and themes: "The rhetorical devise, the imagery, and the key words are not unlike Second Isaiah [Isa 40–55]" (Muilenburg 1956, 697; cf. Fishbane 1985, 497–99; Blenkinsopp 2003, 242–44). Nonetheless, as will be addressed below, numerous catchwords, patterns, and themes align this section smoothly with the preceding and following texts. Thus, like most sections in the book of Isaiah, this section has an important linguistic and thematic link to 59:20-21. In a way, Isaiah 60 is a prophetic reply to the divine promise of 59:20. Similarly, 59:21 is a gloss but also a thematic "window" for the surrounding chapters (Niskanen 2014, 31).

Despite various ways to subdivide Isaiah 60, we will pay attention to two thesis verses, i.e., v. 3 and v. 10. Read this way, following the opening call for Zion to arise (vv. 1-2), the oracle announces that nations and kings will march to Zion, bringing the Diaspora expatriates from afar (vv. 3-9), and that nations and kings will then help build the walls, gates, and temple of Zion (vv. 10-22). On the whole, vv. 1-3 and vv. 19-22 can be taken to form an inclusio around the entire chapter as a unit (Niskanen 2014, 35; cf. Polan 2001, 70).

Verses 1-9 project an upcoming new era when Zion's light will shine forth (vv. 1-2) so that nations and kings will make a procession to Zion (vv. 3-9). The profound opening proclamation resumes the previous calls for Zion (second feminine singular) to stand up (*qumi*; cf. 51:17; 52:1-2), while ushering in the coming of Zion's light (v. 1). Notably, many expressions in Isaiah 60 counter those in Isaiah 59 (Paul 2012, 516–17). Read sequentially, against the restored community's lament of darkness (59:1-8), as a result of the "we"-group's repentance (59:9-15a) and the announcement of YHWH's victorious battle (59:15b-21), the time of light is finally imminent (60:1-2).

We should also comment on the motif of "light" briefly. On the one hand, light connotes YHWH, who is the very "everlasting light" and glory (cf. vv. 19-20; cf. Gen 1:3-5, 14-19; Deut 33:2). Embedded in the Egyptian and Mesopotamian, including the Persian, royal solar symbolism (especially the sun-gods Re, Shamash, and Ahuramazda), light is intricately associated with the sun. Representing YHWH as the solar deity, this passage declares that "Jerusalem is the sun, the Lord is the sun, the Lord's glory is the sun and: Jerusalem is God's glory" (Hulster 2009, 228).

On the other hand, at the same time, just as the Servant's call includes the role of light in the sense of salvific hope and peace for Jerusalem and the nations (cf. 42:6; 49:6; 58:8, 10), Zion's light similarly connotes its shining blessing with the divine execution of justice and righteousness. In Egypt, the sun-god Re is said to appoint the king to establish Ma'at (justice)—a daughter of Re—and vanquish Isfet (disorder). In Mesopotamia, Hammurabi claims, "By the command of Shamash, the great judge of heaven and earth, may I make justice to shine forth in the land!" Hence, light entails righteousness and salvation, while darkness signifies judgment (Hulster 2009, 213–14, 221–25).

Accordingly, "the dawning light of salvation" presented in 9:1 (MT 8:23) combined with "the glory of YHWH" in 40:5 culminate in our passage, 60:1-2, which underscores the interrelated dual theme of the advent of light and YHWH's radiant presence (Niskanen 2014, 36): "YHWH is my light and my salvation" (Ps 27:1).

To this light, nations and kings, as well as the children of the Diaspora, will march (v. 3; cf. 2:2-5). Zion's children will come from "far away"—beyond a new exodus in an additional return of the Diaspora (v. 4; cf. 40:26; 49:18). Tributes from the nations will accompany the march to Zion (v. 5). The Arabian kingdoms will bring camels, gold, and frankincense. One of these kingdoms, Sheba, recalls the renowned Solomonic monarchy (v. 6; cf. 1 Kgs 10:1-13). The radical inclusivism encompasses the fact that the offerings of these foreigners will be pleasing on YHWH's altar (v. 7; cf. ch. 56). In the preceding unit, the foreigners who desire to "minister" (*sharat*) to YHWH are assured welcome at the holy mountain, and that their offerings and sacrifices will be "acceptable at my altar" (*ratson mizbeah*, 56:6-7). Here, in this oracle, the flocks and rams of the foreigners will "minister" (*sharat*) to Zion, and these offerings, too, will be "acceptable at my altar" (*ratson mizbeah*). In 56:7, YHWH offers a new name for the temple: "my house will be called a house of prayer (*bet-tefillah*) for all peoples." In our text, 60:7, YHWH affirms a new definition of the temple: "I will glorify my glorious house" (*bet tif'arti*). Read together, although these two texts may be read as two conflicting ideologies (cf. Middlemas 2007, 174–75), there is also a continuity of theology in light of the two interrelated purposes of the temple, i.e., both as "a house of prayer"—not exclusively a building per se (cf. 66:1)—for all peoples (cf. 2:2-4) and as a location that rightfully honors YHWH at its center.

The interrogative question "who . . . ?" contains the expression "like doves" that echo the penitent group's mourning (v. 8; cf. 59:11). Coastlands will assuredly bring Zion's scattered Diaspora from "far away" (v. 9; cf. 43:6; 49:22; on the intertextual correlations between 49:18-26 and 60:4-16 see Wells 2009, 199–214). Shawn Zelig Aster compares key aspects of the Neo-Babylonian and Persian inscriptions on temple and palace constructions with those in our text, such as the influx of tribute from afar, light and solar imagery, and the use of foreign workers in building projects. The prophet's intention thus is to compare Jerusalem and Babylon, thereby underscoring YHWH as the true creator and giver of light while denying the hegemony of Mesopotamian deity and power (Aster 2012, 317–33).

Verses 10-22 further expand the preceding theme of the nations' pilgrimage to Zion with the radical notion of nations' joining the construction of new Zion. Pronounced as theses in parallel, these verses contend that just as nations and kings will escort and accompany Zion's Diasporic offspring from far away to Zion (v. 3), so foreigners and kings will also build the walls, gates, and temple of Jerusalem (v. 10).

Isaiah's theology of universalism versus particularism leaves ambiguity in the composite whole. On the one hand, that foreigners (lit., "sons of foreigners") and kings will build Zion's walls may connote their subjugation in service of Zion, a reversal of fortune. Yet, on the other hand, as Shalom Paul elucidates, this seems to continue the radically inclusive perspectives toward outsiders and unfits: "Just as the prophet includes foreigners in the future Temple service (see vv. 6-7), in stark contrast to the prevalent isolationist policies (see Ezra 4:1-5; Neh 2:17-20; 3:33-38 [Eng. 4:1-6]; 4:1-5 [Eng. 4:7-11]), so too does he envisage them participating in the reconstruction of the walls of the city" (Paul 2012, 526).

The announcement of a reversal of fortune follows, seemingly a dissenting commentary insertion about v. 10. Opposite the history of monarchic Israel and Judah that had to pay tribute in obeisance to the kings of Assyria and Babylon, foreign kings will bring tribute to Jerusalem (v. 11), because the kingdoms that do not serve Zion will perish (v. 12). Scholars consider v. 12 to be a direct echo of Isaiah 56:6-7, as the other side of the same coin; the former passage (60:12) implying salvation for the nations that serve Zion and the latter passage (56:6-7) depicting foreigners as YHWH's servants (Niskanen 2014, 39). Choice wood of Lebanon will decorate the temple, YHWH's footstool (v. 13; cf. 66:1; Ezek 43:7; Ps 132:7). This reversal of fortune underscores the eventual liberation of the righteous offspring of

Zion previously oppressed and despised, analogous to the anticipation that the Egyptian taskmasters or the Babylonian tormentors would bow down to the ridiculed, debased children of Zion (v. 14; cf. 49:23; Tiemeyer 2014, 36–37): "Once humbled before the nations, she is now the recipient of the nations' homage and praise" (Polan 2001, 71).

Two statements that start with the word "instead of . . ." extend the theme of a reversal of fortunes (vv. 15-17; cf. 55:13). In the first statement, instead of Zion's being forsaken and hated (cf. 49:14), Zion with her offspring will become an "everlasting splendor" (v. 15). The words "forsaken" and "hated" connote the context of betrothal (cf. Judg 14:16; 15:2). Likewise, the words "pass by" (*'abar*) and "pride" (*ga'on*) echo the marital metaphor of Ezekiel 16 (esp. vv. 8, 15, 25, 56). Whereas Ezekiel 16 portrays Jerusalem as a wayward, repudiated wife, Isaiah 60 reverses her status with the imagery of radiant pride (Niskanen 2014, 40). Echoing the ancient Near Eastern motif of noble ones suckling the milk of deity, Zion will take that royal esteem (v. 16; cf. 49:23). According to the second statement, gold and silver will replenish Jerusalem, while peace and righteousness will replace her malicious taskmasters (v. 17).

Three statements that start with the word "not . . ." (*lo'*) follow (vv. 18-20). No more violence (cf. 59:6), havoc, or crushing here, "salvation" will be the name of Zion's walls and "praise" of her gates (v. 18). No more need for sun or moon for light or brightness (cf. v. 3); YHWH will be Zion's "everlasting light" (vv. 19-20). According to Brent Strawn's analysis of the iconography of the Apadana reliefs from Persian Persepolis in relation to Isaiah 60, these verses entail a *Pax Jerusalem* polemic against the *Pax Persica* ideology. YHWH supplants the Persian deity Ahuramazda, symbolized by the winged sun disk (Strawn 2007, 103, 115). The sun is one of the brightest solar planets or asteroids in the galaxy. But both the sun and Ahuramazda dim in the presence of YHWH the everlasting light. Therefore, in these verses, possibly the climax of Isaiah 60, "YHWH replaces the sun and the moon as illuminator of Jerusalem" (Aster 2012, 317).

In the concluding subunit (vv. 21-22), YHWH discusses Zion's posterity, "your people," who will be righteous and inherit the land forever (v. 21). In this time of glorious future, the smallest will be great and the least will become a mighty nation (v. 22; cf. 2:11; 51:2).

The Announcement of Jubilee for the Servant's Disciples and Community, 61:1-11

As a counterpart to the dramatic uplifting of Zion—a *female* character—in Isaiah 60, in Isaiah 61 the prophet—a *male* character—receives the dynamic vocation of carrying out the jubilee for the people in Diaspora (compare the combination of the laments of the male servant in 49:1-13 and of the female Zion in 49:14-26). Interestingly, this pattern of both female Zion (Isa 60) and male prophet/Servant's disciple (Isa 61) continues on to concerns about Zion (Isa 62) and voice of the prophet/disciple (Isa 63). Framed by the phrase "Adonay YHWH" in v. 1 and v. 11 as bookends, this unit contains symmetrical arrangement:

vv. 1-3—"I" (servant), "he" (YHWH), and "they"
  vv. 4-9—"I" (YHWH), "you" (Diaspora), and "they"
vv. 10-11—"I" (servant), "he" (YHWH)

Verses 1-3 proclaim the jubilee year—the fiftieth year alluding to the period from captivity in 587 BCE to release in 539 BCE (cf. Lev 25:8-10)—for the Diaspora, announcing the cancellation of debt in captivity and the restoration of their dignity. This speaker is anonymous, but the speaker "anointed" here (v. 1) is not Cyrus. Scholars posit that the speaker—upon whom "the spirit of YHWH" rested—is either the servant (cf. 42:1), the prophet (cf. 49:1; 50:4), or a monarch (cf. 11:2). Alternatively, the speaker may represent a collective community (cf. 32:15; 49:3).

Jacob Stromberg identifies "a pastiche of earlier texts" in vv. 1-3 (e.g., 6:8; 11:1; 40:1-6; 42:1-7; 45:1; 49:9), indicating how the speaker in v. 1 takes over the role of the Servant in Isaiah 42 as well as that of Cyrus (Stromberg 2009, 262). These multiple intertextual allusions provide significant clues as to the identity of the speaker: "The speaker takes to himself the task of proclaiming the future fulfillment of all the as yet unrealized tasks entrusted to a variety of figures in Deutero-Isaiah: Cyrus, the servant, the herald of good news, God's ministers in the heavenly court and the prophet himself" (Williamson 1998b, 187). Given these pluriform layers as a pastiche, we will assume this speaker to be the anonymous prophet, the so-called Deutero-Isaiah (as a counterpart to daughter Zion in the previous chapter), whose voice represents that of the Servant's offspring and disciples in the righteous community.

Regardless of the identity of this speaker, this subunit highlights the commissioned tasks and the target of the tasks. Recurring infinitive verbs accentuate the tasks (vv. 1-3a):

• to bring good news to the afflicted (cf. Isa 40:9; 52:7; 60:6);
• to bind up the brokenhearted (cf. Ps 147:3);
• to proclaim release to captives and freedom to prisoners;

- to proclaim the year of Yhwh's favor and the day of divine vindication;
- to comfort all who mourn (cf. Isa 57:18; 59:11);
- to provide for Zion's mourners;
- to give them a crown instead of ashes. . . .

The rhetorical effect of the seven infinitives may constitute an allusion to the seven days of creation (Gen 1) and thus underscore the notion that each commissioned task is equivalent to participating in the new creation as the servants of Yhwh. Moreover, mirroring the style of the preceding chapter (cf. 60:15, 17), three "instead of . . ." phrases subversively portray the target of these tasks not only as the poor, afflicted, and mourning captives but also as the heirs of Zion who will regain the crown (cf. 3:20), joy, and praise. In fact, they are called oaks of righteousness, Yhwh's pleasant planting (v. 3b; cf. 5:7; 27:2; 60:21). Unlike the unidentified speaker, the objects of this good news are clearly hinted amid the context of the socioeconomically disadvantaged: "This prophetic 'preferential option for the poor' is perhaps the most significant contribution of the Hebrew prophets to the moral tradition of Judaism and Christianity" (Blenkinsopp 2003, 223). At the same time, within the imperial colonial context, the whole people of Yehud—especially the righteous (cf. Ps 109:2, 16, 22)—may be called "the poor of Yhwh" (Blenkinsopp 2003, 224).

Verses 4-9 announce the drastic rebuilding of Jerusalem by a re-identified collective community. It is not clear who "they" are—those who will build the ancient ruins and desolate cities (v. 4)—whether the liberated exilic captives (cf. v. 1 and v. 3b; cf. 49:17) or the strangers and foreigners (v. 5; cf. 58:12; 60:10). What remains certain is that in these verses (vv. 5-7), where the plural "you" occurs uniquely, this community of brokenhearted mourners will attain new statuses—"priests of Yhwh" and "ministers of our God" (v. 6). Also, if "they" here refers to "the mourners of Zion" (cf. v. 3), then these verses imply that "the Israelites share in the manual labor of the foreigners [cf. 60:10]. . . . Seen in this way, the nations are not relegated to second-class status but share in the common work of restoring the neglected lands and cities of Judea" (Niskanen 2014, 46). The pluralized servants (cf. 54:17; 56:6)—the disciples of the Servant and the offspring of Zion—as the righteous community, which includes even eunuchs and foreigners, will attain the priesthood previously given only to the elite Zadokite or Aaronite groups. Now, this righteous "we"-group—that comprises both "you" (pl.) and "they"—shall have a "double portion" (cf. 40:2) and an "everlasting joy" (v. 7; cf. 51:11). Whereas ancient Near Eastern materials (especially legal materials, such as the codices of Ur-Nammu and Hammurabi) focus only on an ideal king, here the plural "we" (whether royal or priestly, whether political or cultic) receives such ideal designations and duties.

Then, in the only verse in this chapter in which YHWH speaks directly, God declares God's love of justice and hatred of stealing and injustice (v. 8; cf. 1:14; Amos 5:21; Zech 8:17; Mal 1:2-3; 2:16). Here the "everlasting covenant" evokes the divine faithfulness promised to the Davidic dynasty, which is now extended to the collective people: "If the Davidic covenant is the starting point (beginning with Isa 55:3) for Trito-Isaiah's reflections on this lasting covenant, it does not end with David or his line but is broadened to some extent to include all the 'servants' of YHWH who also participate in the roles of priest (Isa 61:6) and prophet (Isa 59:21)" (Niskanen 2014, 48). This glorious plan for rebuilding culminates in the divine blessing extended to the seed and offspring of this community (v. 9; cf. Gen 12:2-3).

Verses 10-11 resume the speech of the spirit-filled and anointed figure (cf. v. 1). Similar to Zion, this character's thanksgiving praise sounds like a communal hymn. The speaker ("I") expresses exceeding joy in YHWH for providing garments of salvation and a robe of righteousness (v. 10). This character is both a bridegroom with a crown (cf. v. 3) and a bride with jewelry. This individual and collective praise concludes with the declaration that YHWH will reap righteousness and praise from this community before all the nations (v. 11).

The Divine Bridegroom's Love Song Pledging the Bride Zion's Renewal, 62:1-12

Echoing the marriage metaphor of Hosea 1–3, and picking up the unified imagery of a bridegroom and bride in the first-person hymn (61:10-11), now YHWH speaks a song of love, asserting the unfailing promise to restore Zion's beauty and honor. (Some scholars identify the prophet or the sentinel as the speaker of v. 1, the same "I"-figure of 61:1, 10; Blenkinsopp 2003, 233). Through YHWH's righteous vindication, Zion will regain royal status with new names (vv. 1-5). With God's appointed guards, the city will stand fully restored and secure against any harm (vv. 6-9). Once again, in addition to a highway toward this restored city, Zion and her people will receive new names that guarantee divine protection (vv. 10-12).

Verses 1-5 announce the future of a new Zion, the bride for whom YHWH vows to restore her beauty, granting new names—a new identity. Earlier it was for the sake of Jacob-Israel that YHWH summoned Cyrus (cf. 45:4). Now, YHWH, thought to have been silent for a while (cf. 42:14; 57:11), vows to break silence for the sake of Zion, addressed directly, "you" (v. 1). Thus, Zion's righteousness will go forth like "brightness" (cf. 60:3) and her salvation will burn like a torch (cf. 60:1). "Nations" and "kings" will witness Zion's vindication and splendor, along with her new name (v. 2; cf. 60:3). Zion will regain her beautiful crown and royal status (v. 3; cf. 61:3, 10).

New names can dramatically transform one's identity, whether negatively or positively, as can be found in numerous cases throughout the HB, e.g., Abraham (Gen 17:5), Sarah (Gen 17:15), Jacob (Gen 32:28; 35:10), Joseph (Gen 41:45), Naomi (Ruth 1:20), Jehoiakim (2 Kgs 23:34), Daniel (Dan 1:7), and so on. Thus, her new names signify Zion's new identity: no longer "forsaken" (cf. 49:14; 54:6; 60:15) or "desolate" (cf. 6:11; 61:4), her new names are YHWH's "delight" and "married" (v. 4; cf. Hos 2:23 [MT 2:25]; Ezek 48:35). Zion's builder, YHWH the divine bridegroom, will marry her (v. 5).

Here, the term for Zion's "builder" (*banayik*) in v. 5 can be translated "sons" as well. This word, which can be vocalized in two distinct ways, recalls the similar occurrence in 49:17. In fact, Paul Niskanen proposes that 62:1-6 makes verbal allusions to 49:14-19 (cf. 54:1-5), through the unique catchwords "forsaken" (49:14; 62:4), "palm" (49:14; 62:3), "your walls" (49:16; 62:6), "bride" (49:18; 62:5), "desolate" (49:19; 62:4), and "your sons/ builders" (49:17; 62:5). Read together, the relational imagery of mother and child in Isaiah 49 is transposed to that of bridegroom and bride here (Niskanen 2014, 56–57).

Verses 6-9 add with further details. The phrase—"I will not keep silent (*hashah*) . . . until (*'ad*) . . ." (v. 1)—recurs: the sentinels on Jerusalem's walls "will not keep silent (*hashah*) . . . until (*'ad*)" YHWH restores her reputation (vv. 6-7). Additionally, YHWH swears to reverse the old punishment so that Jerusalem will enjoy the normal life of security, being able to eat her produce and crops (vv. 8-9; cf. 1:19; 3:10; Deut 28:30-33; Amos 9:14).

Verses 10-12 climactically wrap up this unit with a resounding hymn, involving one fanfare after another, echoing various key expressions from the previous texts. Twice-repeated imperatives to "pass through, pass through" the gates continue the preceding repeated commands (v. 10; cf. 40:1; 51:9, 17; 52:1, 11, 14). Whereas the earlier exhortation was to "prepare the way" of YHWH (cf. 40:3), here the call to "prepare the way" is for the people—the Diaspora who aspire to repent and return to Zion (cf. 49:11; 57:14). The "highway" will guide the return of the righteous remnants (cf. 11:16; 40:3). A "signal" raised over the peoples will send a message to the whole world to witness (cf. 11:12; 49:22).

Like the herald of good news, the end of the earth is to broadcast to Zion that YHWH's rewards and treasures are on the way (v. 11; note the phrases shared verbatim with 40:10; cf. 49:4). Echoing 40:1-11, the prophet builds on the opening oracle of Isaiah 40 that announces YHWH's triumphant return through the highway, guiding the exiles back home. Subsequently, the people, the returning Diaspora, will have new names, "holy people" and "redeemed of YHWH," just as Zion will yet have more new names as a city "sought after" and "not forsaken" (v. 12; cf. v. 4; 49:14). The literary echoes of 40:9-10 (cf. 60:11), therefore, ascertain the impending fulfillment of the oracles previously pronounced (Blenkinsopp 2003, 243).

The Penitent Community's Lament to God the Parent and the Potter, 63:1–64:11

Divine Pathos: God the Angry Warrior and God the Wounded Savior, 63:1-19

Explicit expressions of the theme of divine pathos stand out in this unit, palpably recorded in dialogue. Recalling the divine plan to arm for a battle against enemies (cf. 59:15b-20), the prophet reports YHWH's victorious return from that bloody battle, seething with *divine anger* (occurring no less than five times), mostly expressed directly by YHWH (vv. 1-6). Then the prophet speaks, recalling Israel's earlier history that discloses *divine mercy*, deeply embedded not only in divine compassion and love but also in divine pain and wounds inflicted by God's children (vv. 7-14). Then, with the numerous uses of "we," the prophet petitions in a lament psalm for divine forgiveness for YHWH's servants, tribes, and children (vv. 15-19).

Verses 1-6, picking up the motifs not only of 59:15b-20 (e.g., the theme of the absence of justice or intercessor) but also of Isaiah 60–62, convey dialogues between the prophet/sentinel and YHWH, revealing divine anger wrought upon the wicked enemies, exemplified by Edom. In fact, some scholars consider 63:1-6 to be an originally integral part of Isaiah 60–62 (Smith 1995, 38–44). Chris Franke elucidates a major thematic shift from Isaiah 59 to Isaiah 63: "in chapter 59 God's anger is directed against injustices within the Jerusalem community [Yehud]; in chapter 63, it is aimed at Israel's enemies" (2014, 720). The prophet as a vigilant sentinel (cf. 62:6, 10) inquires who the warrior returning from Edom is (v. 1). Perhaps, the question "Who is this?" may not be a rhetorical question but a real one, since it problematizes the warrior's identity—"the speaker does not recognize [YHWH] at first" (Sawyer 1993, 74; cf. Ps 24:8; Job 38:2; 42:3). If so, the divine response would then effectively be, "(Do not be put off by appearance.) Believe me, it is I, [YHWH], mighty to save" (Sawyer 1993, 77).

Following YHWH the warrior's answer, the prophet asks again, another genuine inquiry, about YHWH's garments (cf. 59:17; 61:10) soaked red (*'adom*) with blood—a pun on "Edom (*'edom*)" (v. 2; cf. Gen 25:25). Edom seems out of place here. Commentators have proposed several explanations. Some highlight its intertextual similarities with Isaiah 34: both accounts allude to the bloodshed on the "day of vengeance" (cf. 34:8; 63:4; Blenkinsopp 2003, 249). Others call attention to the importance of its southern location, alluding to the original place of YHWH's triumphal march (Niskanen 2014, 71). Still others point out the word play between "Edom" and bloodstained red in the divine judgment, emending Edom into an adjective "red" for the image of treading and trampling the enemies (Paul 2012, 564).

Now YHWH answers in a lengthy reply that it was YHWH's trampling the wicked peoples that stained all the robes (v. 3; cf. 34:5-7; 59:16). According to the pictorial materials from various ancient Near Eastern inscriptions, the depiction of treading the winepress often involves a company of those who tread, suggesting the motif of trampling an enemy, with the red blood comparable to crushed grapes. In our text, YHWH the vineyard owner (cf. 5:1-7; 27:2-5) will singlehandedly trample those oppressors who heretofore trampled God's vineyard Israel and Judah (cf. 10:6; 26:6). This act of divine trampling of the enemies will usher in the redemption of YHWH's people (Hulster 2009, 230–54). In an inverted chiasm with Isaiah 61, these acts of divine wrath define "the year of YHWH's favor" and "the day of vindication" (cf. 61:2) as "the day of vindication" and "the year of [YHWH's] deliverance" (v. 4). Seeing that there was no supporter (cf. 59:16), YHWH's "arm" sans other aids or voluntary warriors will wield upon the earth, bringing victory and salvation (vv. 5-6; cf. 59:16; 62:8).

Alternatively or paradoxically, however, this portrayal of YHWH whose clothes are spattered with blood may point to the anthropomorphic vulnerability of God. John Sawyer perceptively posits this interpretive clue, since the metaphor of the bloodstained warrior is intertwined, or smeared, with that of a laborer in a winepress. From this perspective, we then see YHWH not just "as a triumphant gloating warrior, swaggering back from battle . . . but as tired and bloodstained, barely recognizable, as someone who knows what it is to suffer" (Sawyer 1993, 80). Not unlike the imagery of God as a compassionate mother in the book of Isaiah, and also in tune with the subsequent imagery of the afflicted, pain-stricken God (63:9-10), this bloodstained Soldier, "alone, weary, unrecognized," epitomizes the pain of divine pathos over the pains of God's children (Sawyer 1993, 81–82).

Additionally, the theme of the messengers in 63:1-6 (cf. 59:15b-20) represents an intertextual extension of the same theme in 40:1-11 and 52:7-10. The preceding texts depict God's charging the messengers to herald good news to Jerusalem. Somewhat contrary to such a pronouncement and anticipation, the present text portrays God's anguish over the absence of the agents of comfort, justice, and good news. Yet, as a consequence, God personally—alone yet powerfully—assumes the role of helper and warrior through the glorious return to Jerusalem (62:11) and the victory over the nations (63:1-6; Tiemeyer 2012, 243–44).

Verses 7-14 present a lament psalm (some scholars isolate and identify 63:7–64:11 as "the longest communal prayer"; Uhlig 2009a, 286), starting with the prophet's recollection of Israel's past, which highlights divine mercy as much as divine anger. Rainer Albertz subdivides this subunit into an introductory praise of YHWH (v. 7), a historical retrospect (vv. 8-9), and a reflection on the past (vv. 10-14; Albertz 2003b, 146). Picking up the previous hymn—"I will rejoice greatly in YHWH" (61:10)—the prophet, as a psalmist rather than a sentinel, remembers ("I will recount") the faithfulness (*hesed*) of YHWH, the praise of YHWH, with all divine goodness toward the house of Israel (v. 7). This is the people YHWH elected as "my people" (v. 8). Divine pathos is astoundingly intensified: in all their affliction, "God was afflicted," as God affectionately lifted and carried them in good old days (v. 9; cf. Hos 11:1, 3-4). These children's rebellion "pained" God's holy spirit (v. 10; cf. Hos 11:2, 7).

In times of trouble, they then remembered the divine mighty acts during the time of Moses, when God empowered Moses to deliver the people, dividing the waters and guiding them through the wilderness, all through God's holy spirit and for God's everlasting name (vv. 11-14). The crucial transitional v. 14 shifts the prophet's address to YHWH from third-person speech to direct address ("you").

Verses 15-19 convey the prophet's intensified petition, representing the communal outcry with repetitive "we" pronouncements (cf. 59:9-15a; 61:1-9). The lamenter beseeches YHWH to look down from heaven, frantically searching for profound divine compassion with the question, "where?" (v. 15). Indeed, the penitent community humbly confesses that they are the children of God, "our father," who earlier begot Abraham and Jacob-Israel (v. 16).

Blaženka Scheuer, in his analysis of the chiastic structure of vv. 15-19, highlights the exhortation in the central verse, "which discloses a firm belief in YHWH's sovereignty which in this case seems to deny human freedom of choice" (2014, 161):

Accusatory statement that YHWH's zeal, might, pity and compassion are withheld. (v. 15)
    Reasons for YHWH to intervene: strong family bonds. (v. 16)
        Accusatory question and direct exhortation: YHWH turn back! (v. 17)
    Reasons for YHWH to intervene: property in ruins. (v. 18)
Accusatory statement: YHWH does not care. (v. 19)

This chiastic center (v. 17) confronts the theological question of theodicy: the disheartened community pleads to understand why God "hardened our heart" (v. 17a; cf. 6:9-10; Exod 7:3-5). In light of the intertextual correlation with 6:9-10, Scheuer posits that 63:15-19 (esp. v. 17) concerns the issue of theodicy in the postexilic setting when divine judgment and mercy seem to transcend human guilt or virtue. Its effect redirects the plea back to God, in the imperative verb "return" or "repent" (*shub*): "It is not just that YHWH needs to intervene to stop the sinning, [YHWH] needs to stop causing it. The lack of fear of YHWH exposes a hard heart which in turn is caused not by the iniquity of the people but by YHWH himself. YHWH is guilty and in need of repentance!" (Scheuer 2014, 171).

This defiant complaint or accusation against the harsh reality of theodicy is not denying but rather confronting and crying out to God amid intense pains and disappointments. Concerning the comparable contexts of trauma and adversity of the prophet Jeremiah, Kathleen O'Connor presents the following forceful insight:

> [Jeremiah's] confessions turn divine justice into a question that forces readers to wonder about it, to let into their spiritual world the possibility that they may not deserve such overwhelming destruction, that their behavior may not be the chief cause of the disaster . . . . Here the search-light of blame settles upon God, but in the process, Jeremiah keeps talking and praying and imploring. He keeps God alive. (2011, 91)

Thus, their earnest outcry appeals to divine care, "return," for the sake of YHWH's servants and tribes (v. 17b). The holy sanctuary where Israel proudly worshiped during the monarchical time is now in ruins—hinting that the second temple is not yet rebuilt (v. 18). Eventually, the accusation resumes in their plea that "we" have become like children lost and abandoned (v. 19).

God the Potter and "We" the Clay amid the Lament Regarding Zion's Impasse, 64:1-11

Just as the call in 51:17–52:12 ("arise, O Jerusalem" [51:17] . . . "awake, awake, put on your strength, O Zion" [v. 1]) follows up on Isaiah 51 ("awake, awake, put on strength, O arm of YHWH" [v. 9]), so now this lament psalm of Isaiah 64 amplifies and extends Isaiah 63. Reiterating the preceding supplication (cf. 63:15-19), the prophet petitions to YHWH that heavens and earth would shatter upon YHWH's appearance (vv. 1-3), because this corrupted society is so mute and indifferent toward prevalent injustice, with no one upright during a period of seeming divine absence (vv. 4-7). The final plea from "all of us" concludes with the acknowledgment of YHWH as their potter, their creator, and "us" as the fragile, remorseful clay (vv. 8-11).

Verses 1-3 emotionally expound the petition of 63:15. There the prophet had entreated YHWH to "look down from heaven and see." Now we hear another plea—"if only you would rend the heavens and come down" (v. 1). The prophet pleads for a potent theophany of the living God with earthquake and fire against God's enemies and nations (v. 2). Like the psalmist encircled by the assailing enemies (Ps 27:2-3), the prophet appeals to the divine presence, if not protection, for the vulnerable yet trusting children of God: "We may have a heightened awareness of all the danger that is around us—adrenaline is a wonderful thing—but, no matter what, we're not letting go of God" (Nowell 2013, 63). With the community, the prophet recalls the history of God's mighty appearances (v. 3; cf. 2 Sam 22:8-18; Ps 18:7-17 [MT 18:8-18]).

Verses 4-7 confess Israel's sins, recounting their obstinacy amid the seeming absence of YHWH. Notably, the word "all of us" (*kullanu*) occurs four times in Isaiah 64 (vv. 5 [two times], 7, 8), emphasizing this community's collective repentance—both past and present. Also, words of negation—"not" (*lo'*) or "none" (*'en*)—occur four times within this subunit, underscoring the society's utter lack of righteousness and recognition of God.

Thus, since ancient times, they have neither heard nor seen God who acts for the obedient ones (v. 4; cf. 6:9), who protects the righteous but shows indignation toward the sinful (v. 5). Now, the community—"all of us" (cf. 53:6; 59:11)—acknowledges their unclean, filthy iniquities (v. 6). With no one righteous to be found, God has hidden the divine face (v. 7; cf. 8:17; 54:8; 59:2).

Verses 8-11 reiterate the entreaty of 63:16-19. As children, this community despondently cries out to God "our" father and potter to rescue and restore the clay (v. 8; cf. 29:16; 41:25; 45:9; 63:16; Ps 27:8-9). Their rationale for this appeal to God is that they are "your people" (v. 9; cf. 63:17).

The petition here that "all of us are your people" hearkens back to the divine assurance that "you are my people" (51:16). This penitent yet trusting confession does not deny the fears of life but amid the overpowering challenges of the enemies, "looking those dangers in the eye, [the community of God] expresses trust in the Lord" (deClaissé-Walford, Jacobson, and Tanner 2014, 271).

Therefore, the defenseless community solemnly describes their onerous environment; Jerusalem remains a desolate desert (v. 10). The sacred temple, burned by fire, still lies in ruins (v. 11; cf. 63:18). Their final heart-wrenching outcry appeals to God, asking, "Will you still restrain yourself, remain silent, and afflict ('anah) us heavily?" (v. 12; cf. 58:10; 63:19; 66:2). The word "to afflict" haunts back to the old Exodus memory of the Egyptians' oppression of the Israelites (Exod 1:11-12). Now the lament accusation by the same verb infers that God's "neglect and punishment are surely excessive" (Goldingay 2014, 84).

YHWH the Righteous Parent Answers, 65:1–66:24

New Heaven and New Earth for "My Servants" but not for the Apostates, 65:1-25

The final two chapters function as the grand finale of the entire book of Isaiah, just as Isaiah 1–2 plays a similar function as the foundational overture. Scholars have long recognized numerous catchwords and thematic similarities between Isaiah 1–2 and 65–66. It is evident that, though some think that Isaiah 66 originated from a different recension (especially in the Septuagint; Baer 2010, 31), Isaiah 1–2 and 65–66 construct the literary frame of the scroll of Isaiah.

This unit also corresponds to the preceding texts, especially in terms of YHWH's answers (Isa 65–66) to the communal laments (Isa 63–64; cf. Hanson 1975, 80–81). Likewise, the complex tension between the righteous (63:8, 11, 18; 64:5) and the wicked (63:10; 64:5-7) reaches its climax in Isaiah 65–66 (Whybray 1975, 266; Paul 2012, 589). YHWH is the speaker throughout the whole chapter. Strikingly, instead of addressing the righteous, penitent remnant—also called "my servants," "my chosen," and "my people," YHWH directly indicts the stubborn and the wicked ("you" pl.)—presumably the compromising, self-serving, privileged group. It is as though God the powerful parent counterattacks the bully, while shielding the abused children with arms around them. Erhard Gerstenberger insightfully expounds the implied theme of the fatherhood of God in the preceding passages (63:16; 64:8; cf. 1:2; 63:8): God being their same father inherently anticipates that all the siblings, God's children, should live in mutual love, care, and solidarity (Gerstenberger 2011, 496; cf. Ps 133:1; 1 John 2:9). The postexilic community sadly displays an opposite situation of internal faction and strife. Thus, this God returns as a powerful judge who will separate the devout servants from their oppressors (cf. Matt 18:32-35).

Since the prophet ardently cried out for God's response (cf. 64:1), God now answers, fiercely accusing the callous people of rebellion, exposing their boundless arrogance (vv. 1-7). Two "thus says YHWH" speeches convey dramatic verdicts of weal for "my servants" and woe for the reprobate "you" (vv. 8-16). The divine announcement promises newly created Jerusalem and its people no more crying or sickness but constant joy and gladness (vv. 17-25).

Verses 1-7 present YHWH's reply to the preceding laments. Whereas the people complained about YHWH's absence or abandonment, the divine rebuttal asserts that YHWH has been fervently calling and reaching out to the rebellious children, repeatedly shouting "here I am, here I am" (v. 1; cf. 6:8; 52:6; 58:9). In an anthropomorphic way, YHWH would "spread out" the divine hand as though pleading to human beings (v. 2a; cf. 1:15). This people rebelled with countless abominations, however: following their own ways and thoughts (v. 2b; cf. 55:7-9), sacrificing to pagan cults in gardens (v. 3; cf. 1:29; 1 Macc 1:41-61; 2 Macc 6:1-6), consulting the dead (v. 4a; cf. Deut 18:11), eating swine's flesh (v. 4b; cf. Deut 14:8; 2 Macc 6:18-20), and jeering at one another, "I am holier than you" (v. 5). In consequence, now YHWH responds to break a prolonged silence, presumably answering to intercessory prayer of Jerusalem (v. 6; cf. 42:14; 57:11; 62:1; 64:11; Blenkinsopp 2003, 233) and exacting "your" iniquities (v. 7; cf. 59:18). Significantly, the descriptions of these self-righteous people contrast sharply with those of the genuine servants—those of humble, crushed, and contrite spirit (cf. 57:15; 66:2). Even in our time, we learn of some notable leaders, whether political or religious, who arrogantly brag about their phony integrity, as though declaring "I am holier than you," only to be exposed of their corruption and falsehood. When we wonder how they have become such fraudulent crooks, oftentimes it is because they have become so desensitized and thick-skinned to evil that they have been incapable of distinguishing between good and evil (cf. Isa 5:20). Perhaps a humble answer by a well-known pastor of a Korean-American megachurch in Los Angeles area, when asked about his philosophy of ministry, sounds more pious and inspiring: "My philosophy of ministry is this prayer: Lord, help me not become a stumbling block to Your glory."

In vv. 8-16 YHWH explicitly portrays a context of schism with regard to a social, religious, and political dichotomy between the righteous and the wicked, between the God-fearers and the self-serving apostates, between "my servants" and "you" (pl.). Admittedly, not all who claim to be the people of YHWH can be identified and included in the newly defined membership. There will be ethical and moral qualifications, as will be explicated in the subsequent oracles.

The first "thus says YHWH" oracle (vv. 8-12) introduces two opposite groups—"my servants" (vv. 8-10) versus "you" (vv. 11-12). On the one hand, like the new wine in the cluster of grapes, YHWH finds "blessing" in the surviving faithful servants (v. 8). Whereas the rotten grapes led to Judah's demise (cf. 5:1-7), now there will be no destruction but sure protection (cf. 27:2-7). This righteous remnant is indeed the "seed" of Jacob and "heirs" of Judah—"my servants" and "my chosen" (v. 9; cf. 2:5; 41:8). For "my people" who seek YHWH (cf. v. 1), YHWH will provide Sharon (Israel's western coastal border) and Achor (Israel's eastern boundary) as fertile pasture (v. 10).

On the other hand, as for "you" who worship the gods of fortune (*gad*) and fate (*meni*), the sword will consume them (v. 11), because when God called them, none of them answered or obeyed (v. 12; cf. 50:2). Here readers can detect leadership in temple priesthood saturated with imperial syncretists. Scholars conjecture that these two foreign deities venerated represent the types of "personal tutelary deity," over against the postexilic context where the Judeans could easily resort to various kinds of foreign cults, amid "a plethora of religious options in the Persian Empire" (Gerstenberger 2011, 204). Therefore, at the root of their outright apostasy, there is this deliberate propensity to social and cultural amnesia: "You who forsake YHWH, you who forget my holy mountain" (v. 11).

Throughout human history, we human beings, especially powers that be, have practiced selective memory by recording self-promoting agendas and erasing self-critical actions. Whether through political coercion or through religious persecution, one's own shameful acts have tended to be hushed or fabricated. Ironically, even in the modern era, similar trends have continued. For example, until fairly recently, many Germans confessed that they had not actually learned of the concentration camp or the Nazis' mass murder of millions of Jews during WWII. Many Japanese did not learn of the imperial regime's systemic oppression of many Far East and South East Asians subsequent to the Pearl Harbor invasion. Nor did many Americans know of the internment camp against so many Japanese Americans within the United States. The Korean government has not officially acknowledged the Korean soldiers' indiscriminate massacre of the Vietnamese, including many civilians, during the Vietnam War. The list can go on, from the recent histories in many other parts of the world, sadly.

In today's education field, due to financial advancement or institutional survival, many universities are investing in the so-called STEM (science, technology, engineering, mathematics) majors at the expense of the humanities, including the subject of history. As an inevitable side effect of the capitalistic system, collective memory of human history is shrinking or disappearing. Nevertheless, history must be taught and continue to teach us not only the atrocities of the others but also *our own* wrongdoings. Otherwise, we may tread the same paths of the self-righteous wicked, who had forgotten their past. We may indeed forget who we are—human beings, not mere robots (with artificial intelligence), created in the image of God—and eventually forget who God is (cf. 51:13).

The second "thus says YHWH" oracle (vv. 13-16) demonstrates a vivid case of reversal of fortune between "my servants" and "you." In this contrary accusation, we can picture a society and leadership where the crooked enjoy riches while the upright suffer unjust hardships:

> Look, my servants will *eat*, but you (pl.) will starve;
> look, my servants will *drink*, but you (pl.) will thirst;
> look, my servants will *rejoice*, but you (pl.) will be ashamed (v. 13; cf. 55:1);
> look, my servants will sing joyfully with a good heart,
> but you (pl.) will cry out with a heavy heart. . . . (v. 14; cf. 63:17)

Thus, the arrogant leaders hear divine curse (v. 15), while the obedient servants will receive blessing from the faithful God (v. 16). Even here, readers can witness vivid pictures of strife and noises of discord, "increasingly acrimonious confrontation between spiritual brothers and sisters, in which one side addresses [or, curses] the other" (Hanson 1988, 96). Contrary to the corrupt group, the servants will attain the basic yet ideal good presented in Qoheleth: "All human beings should *eat, drink,* and *enjoy* [lit., 'see good'] in all their toil—it is a gift of God" (Eccl 3:13).

Verses 17-25 culminate with the proclamation of the new heaven and the new earth, a society completely transformed from all doubts and agonies into longevity and peace. In fact, this societal transformation is so radical that the oracle identifies it as a course of God's creative acts, "new" heaven and "new" earth (cf. Gen 1:1; Isa 66:22). Although a new subunit, the key phrase, "the former things will not be remembered" (65:17), connects to the preceding one, "the former troubles will be forgotten" (65:16), forming a link for compositional continuity (Niskanen 2014, 90). Interestingly, God addresses "my people" in Jerusalem in the third-person plural, as though dispatching a decree in a letter from heaven. Here the word "to create (*bore'*)" occurs three times—all in the active participial form—in vv. 17-18, signifying its urgent imminence. Rebuilt Jerusalem and her inhabitants will become joy and gladness, without any more weeping or crying (v. 19). With no more diseases or threats, "my people" will regain long life as those primordial ancestors in Genesis (v. 20).

This newly established community will "build houses and dwell, and plant vineyards and eat their fruit" in grand Jerusalem (v. 21), contrary to the previous exilic community that had to persevere to "build houses and dwell, and plant gardens and eat their fruit" in exilic Babylon (Jer 29:5, 28). Thus, "my (YHWH's) people" and "my chosen" will not suffer the loss of their houses or food (v. 22; cf. 62:8-9; Deut 28:30; Zeph 1:13). Instead, YHWH will bless them and their offspring (v. 23). Blessing here further implies that YHWH will answer them, even before they call (v. 24; cf. 1:15; 58:9).

This ideal world (v. 25) will be a realization of the earlier peaceable kingdom, reconceived with intertextual echoes of 11:6-9: "Wolf and lamb will graze together [cf. 11:6], lion will eat straw like an ox [11:7] . . . they will not do evil or violence on all my holy mountain [11:9]." Thus, the previous vision of the paradisiacal world is about to arrive soon. This world will bring about the traditional covenant blessings of longevity and land. Also, with Jerusalem as the center, the future Israel will play a central role for the restoration of the dispersed people, their souls, and their crops. Now, this new impending kingdom of God will be universal, without boundaries, open to all: this radically redefined identity of new Jacob and new Judah, the kingdom of God, "is not determined by ethnicity, lineage, nationality, or geography, but rather on the basis of [religious, ethical, and social] activity" (Middlemas 2011, 117; cf. Gerstenberger 2011, 492). Elie Wiesel, a Holocaust survivor, puts this visionary hope in an astounding way:

> I belong to a generation that has often felt abandoned by God and betrayed by [humankind]. And yet, I believe that we must not give up on it either . . . . I know—I speak from my experience—that even in darkness it is possible to create light and encourage compassion. That it is possible to feel free inside a prison. That even in exile, friendship exists and can become an anchor . . . . I belong, after all, to a generation that has learned that, whatever the question, indifference and resignation are not the answer. Illness may diminish me, but it will not destroy me. The body is not eternal, but the idea of the soul is. The brain will be buried, but the

memory will survive it. Such is the miracle: A tale about despair becomes a tale against despair. (2012, 72–73)

Yet there is one stipulation for this peaceable kingdom: whereas the earlier idealization portrays infants and toddlers playing harmoniously over the dens of snakes and vipers (cf. 11:8), in this vision of a just world, "dust will be serpent's food" (cf. Gen 3:14). Eating dust of the earth is an "expression of humiliation" (Isa 49:23; Mic 7:16-17; Ps 72:9; cf. Mazor 2004, 80). In other words, in contrast to the downtrodden yet faithful servants who will inherit bountiful blessings, the wicked apostates will be served their dessert in curses.

YHWH Comforts the Humble but Judges the Wicked, 66:1-24

This final chapter continues the impassioned divine speech of Isaiah 65 as answers to the outcries of the afflicted, penitent community in Isaiah 63–64. YHWH as "I" now directly addresses the righteous community, "you." Just as YHWH assumes the role of a father and potter (63:16; 64:8), now YHWH takes up the place of a mother who comforts the dejected children (66:13).

Complex literary features of this chapter make it difficult to identify clear-cut subunits. While the structural analyses in this study have primarily paid closer attention to formal features, here we will follow content shifts. Mirroring the schism between "you" (pl.), those who tremble at idols or superpowers and the righteous "my servants" (cf. 65:8-16), YHWH now turns to take the side of "those humble and contrite, who tremble at the word of YHWH" against the hypocritical temple leaders (vv. 1-6). At a central place of this chapter, the divine motherly compassion radiates toward "all those who love [Jerusalem] . . . all those who mourn over her" (vv. 7-14). Finally, as YHWH resumes the role of the divine warrior (Isa 63), in response to the divine indignation against the reprobate enemies who are utterly doomed, YHWH will add to the list of those faithful servants all others from distant nations and coastlands who acknowledge YHWH's name so that some of them will even take the positions of priests and Levites in a newly created society (vv. 15-24).

Verses 1-6 restate the socio-religious tension between the righteous and the wicked in more detailed descriptions. Just as 52:1 reiterates 51:9, and similarly 64:1 retells 63:17, so the catchwords "heaven" and "earth" of 65:17 recur here as references to YHWH's throne and footstool (v. 1a; cf. 1:2; 66:22). YHWH, whose robe is larger than the temple (cf. 6:1-2), contends that mortal worshipers cannot contain God in a house (v. 1b; cf. 2 Sam 7:5-7; 1 Chr

17:4-6). Scholars have discovered a rough chiasm in this unit (Middlemas 2007, 178–81):

v. 1—concerning the temple
   v. 2—"who tremble (*hared*) at my [YHWH's] word"
      vv. 3-4—condemnation on the practitioners of apostate, idolatrous worship
   v. 5—"who tremble (*hared*) at his [YHWH's] word"
v. 6—concerning the temple

Here divine criticism is not a repudiation of the legitimacy of the Jerusalem temple per se, although there is a tone of criticism against the dogma that human beings can box God into a temple and thereby God cannot leave the Jerusalem temple (cf. Jer 7:4, 14; Ezek 10:2-4, 18-19). Rather, considering the likely setting of the controversy about who should build the second temple, who may become members of this new community, and who should take charge of the cultic office, divine criticism may directly counter temple leaders who corruptly benefit and wield power. Considering the ongoing context of Yehud's colonial subjugation under the Persian imperial domination, we should note that these Jewish temple leaders must have built intimate political and religious ties with their overlords. During the monarchical era, the Israelite and Judean kings frequently kept their vassal alliances with their imperial suzerains, adopting the foreign imperial customs and practices. Now, in the post-monarchic reconstruction era, the temple leaders of Yehud would follow the same policies by paying political and religious homage to their colonial rulers. In both contexts, their own people (of Judah and of Yehud) would suffer socioeconomic, political, and religious hardship and injustice (cf. Adams 2014, 130–45).

Against this backdrop, to their dismay, YHWH declares solidarity with the poor and the brokenhearted, those who tremble at the word of YHWH (v. 2; cf. 57:15; Ps 51:17 [MT 51:19]). The catchphrase "to whom (*'el-zeh*)" of v. 2 links with the phrase "where (*'e-zeh*)" of v. 1, involving assonance and thematic similarity (Middlemas 2007, 180). The locale of YHWH's lofty throne and sacred footstool thus profoundly coincides with the locale of none other than the very people who are humble and contrite! Admittedly, they are those humble and contrite "of spirit," denoting emotional and religious place. Yet the words "humble" and "contrite" also connote being "afflicted" and "crushed," i.e., in their socioeconomic and political locale, oppressed by the wealthy and powerful. The adjectival word "humble" (*'oni*) in v. 2 comes from the verbal root, "to afflict" (*'anah*), which is the same word in the descriptions that Sarah "afflicted/oppressed" (*'anah*) Hagar in Genesis 16:6 and that the Egyptian taskmasters "afflicted/oppressed" (*'anah*) the Hebrew slaves with forced labor in Exodus 1:11-12. They are thus not only those who are penitent of their wrongs but also those who have been cruelly oppressed by the more powerful (Isa 11:4; 58:10; 61:1) or unjustly persecuted for the sake of righteousness (Isa 53:4; cf. Matt 5:10-12).

Isaiah's theology affirms that YHWH as the *exalted* divine King not only takes the place of a human king but also takes the side of the *lowly*, powerless, and afflicted (cf. 2:5-22). If we radicalize this theology, God's *compassion game* goes to the extreme in deserting the heaven and earth (v. 1) so as to give the prominent care for the vulnerable, common people (v. 2). As is the rightful duty of the virtuous king (11:3-5; cf. Deut 17:19-20), YHWH the divine King concerns the common people (Korean *minjung*—especially "the oppressed, poor, and underprivileged mass populace") and their hearts, first and foremost. In other words, in terms of divine care and concern, how shall we please God? To obey God, and to tremble at God's word (v. 2), is to work out our solidarity with the vulnerable and disenfranchised. Or, what should be the fundamental premise of a just ruler? A line from the 2006 movie *V for Vendetta* contains a good insight: "People should not fear their government; governments should fear their people."

To reiterate from another angle, it is not how pious or holy we claim to be or behave (1:15; 65:5; cf. Luke 18:9-14) but rather how we treat the fellow common people that functions as the measuring barometer for a just community God would approve and bless (cf. Matt 25:40, 45; Luke 10:30-35). If the poor and at-risk people among us (*minjung*) are in agony, God will not be pleased. A society is good and healthy when its peace and prosperity are "of the people, by the people, for the people," as opposed to "of the people, by the people, for the less than one-percent rich and powerful." To push this theology further, when one or a few fellow human beings are victimized, like in the tragedy of the Ferguson, Missouri, police shooting of an unarmed black man, the society may express a perfunctory regret about such an "unfortunate" incident or casualty. Such expressions, however, do not reflect the principle of the God of justice and the God of compassion. When one member is hurting, the entire community is hurting. When one part is suffering, the entire body must care (cf. 1 Cor 12:22-26): "In a closely knit solidarity under [YHWH] such as this [Judaic community of the exilic and postexilic period], there really must not be any 'poor,' and the community must support all of its members" (Gerstenberger 2011, 498). Alas, the temple priests and leaders of the restoration community of Yehud did not care for those in the margin, those on the social fringe, at all. To save their skin and satiate their greed, they would rather invest in serving and pleasing their colonial/imperial overlords, at the cost of trampling their own kindred and even God!

YHWH lashes out in divine accusation against the temple priests who are cold-blooded masters in murdering fellow human beings, bringing offerings of swine's blood, and blessing an idol (v. 3). Indeed, despite God's earnest calling and speaking to them, these egotistic leaders became experts of evil (v. 4; cf. 65:12). The imperative to hear "the word of YHWH" addresses those who tremble at "the word of YHWH" (cf. Ezra 9:4; 10:3)—who are in fact hated and excluded by their own brothers, sisters, and neighbors (v. 5; cf. 56:3; Lev 19:17-18). The identification of the wicked as "your *brothers*, who hate you and exclude you because of my name" recognizes the nasty strife and corruption within the restoring community. Such arrogant, judgmental haters who oversee jurisdictions in temple leadership are YHWH's "enemies" who will receive divine retribution (v. 6; cf. 65:6).

Verses 7-14 get to the heart of this unit, accentuating divine consolation for those stripped of identity and status in the rebuilding community, through *maternal* imagery for YHWH—as a counterpart to *paternal* imagery (cf. 63:16; 64:8). In the trying times, Zion was too weak (cf. 37:3) or barren (cf. 54:1) to give birth (cf. 65:23). Now, however, just as God promises to answer before they call (cf. 65:24), so before her pangs come, Zion will give birth (v. 7). Zion will beget her whole nation in a day, attended to by YHWH her midwife (vv. 8-9; cf. 54:1-4). Then another imperative calls the faithful community—"all who love . . . and lament over" Jerusalem—to rejoice for the miraculously rejuvenated city (v. 10; cf. v. 5). Her offspring will enjoy plentiful nursing milk (v. 11).

The "thus says YHWH" oracle further explicates the metaphor of YHWH as a mother. Zion will enjoy peace like a gentle river, as her righteous descendants will savor tender nursing care (v. 12). YHWH pledges to comfort this devout, afflicted community as a mother comforts her child (v. 13): "The book of Isaiah begins and ends with images of children: in Isaiah 1 YHWH laments that the children [YHWH] has reared have rebelled. . . . The end of the book offers a strikingly different portrait of that relationship: God as a mother, tenderly holding and playing with Israel . . . Mother and child are now reconciled" (Lapsley 2008, 101). At the same time, no longer hardened or discouraged, their heart will rejoice when they see and witness YHWH's righteous acts: the divine hand will sustain the devoted servants (cf. 7:14; 8:8, 10), but divine rage will overtake their foes (v. 14). Paul Niskanen elucidates the dichotomous yet reciprocal aspects of YHWH as a loving parent: "YHWH can be described in one moment as a nursing mother and in the very next as a conquering warrior (Isa 66:13-14). The varied and complex imagery that the prophet employs to speak of YHWH and [YHWH's] actions reveals a sophisticated and nuanced theology of the ultimate incomparability of YHWH" (2014, xvii).

Zion's positive role here is equally significant, albeit complex. Comparing Isaiah's overwhelmingly optimistic depictions of Zion with other prophetic texts, Sharon Moughtin-Mumby presents a trenchant summary:

> Having lingered on the difficult aspects of this poetry, however, it seems important to re-stress the message of hope that *Isaiah* brings to women and all those who seek equality. . . . This poetry may have its problems, but it is still an oasis of hope and a breath of fresh air within the prophetic corpus, where Zion rises as a positive role model for both women and men. (2008, 154–55)

Verses 15-24 resume the motif of YHWH as the divine warrior, culminating in the enlarged gap between the faithful, both Israelites and foreigners who will serve as new leaders, and the wicked, those vicious leaders who will have no peace. Ascending with crescendo toward the climactic conclusion, numerous "says YHWH" phrases wrap up each powerful oracle (e.g., vv. 17, 20, 21, 22, 23). With fury, YHWH the divine warrior is about to return to punish the wicked with fire, storm, and sword (vv. 15-16). How wicked are they, and how rotten is this priestly leadership? These would-be sanctified leaders with priestly titles and levitical status outright sneak into the gardens to engage in pagan rituals (cf. 1:29; 65:3) and blatantly eat the swine, reptiles, and mice (v. 17; cf. v. 3; 65:4):

> All in all, what transpires from the fourth Servant Song is the great yet ultimately illusionary hope of the returnees that the entire nation of Israel would acknowledge their various suffering as being a redemption of guilt that was pleasing to God. The opposite is the case: The *Servants*, successors of the returning exilic congregation, are those who are being excluded from the temple congregation in Jerusalem at the end of the Book of Isaiah (Isa 65–66)! (Berges 2012b, 494)

Subsequently, turning away from these hypocritical leaders and apostates, YHWH announces that a new era has come when all nations and tongues gather to see YHWH's glory (v. 18; cf. 2:2-4; 40:5). These pilgrims will come from the farthest corners—as far as Tarshish (or Spain), Pul (Libya in west of Egypt), Lud (Lydia in Asia Minor), and Javan (Greece)—to revere the divine glory (v. 19; cf. Matt 2:1-12). They will march together with all Israel's kindred to Jerusalem, "says YHWH" (v. 20). These returnees, outsiders, and even foreigners will join the devout remainees, some of whom will assume the treasured priestly and levitical offices, "says YHWH" (v. 21).

Regarding the culminating segments, Paul Niskanen suggests linguistic and thematic bookends with Isaiah 1–2: "For surrounding the vision of the gathering of all nations to Mount Zion (Isa 2:2-4; 66:18-23) are the opening and closing judgments against those who rebel (Isa 1:2; 66:24)" (2014, 103). John Goldingay posits that all these nations and coastlands may have shared the common denominator of having "survived" the empire's brutal crushing and thereby becoming witnesses to YHWH's powerful salvific works (2014, 81). Contrary to the apostate inside-leaders who will not escape the divine punishment of fire and sword (vv. 15-17), those humble pilgrims from various outside-nations, regardless of ethnicity and class, shall not only receive the divine acceptance of their worship and offerings but also become priests and Levites.

Moreover, within Isaiah 65–66, we find additional linguistic and thematic bookends. In one respect, according to Andrew Abernethy's astute analysis, the condemnation of the apostates who eat swine's flesh both starts (65:4) and ends (66:17) this section. These wonton, gluttonous leaders will starve, thirst (65:12-13, 25; 66:3-4), and be excluded from a grand future. On the contrary, the penitent and upright servants of YHWH will joyfully eat and drink (65:13, 21-22; 66:11) "in" the new kingdom (Abernethy 2014, 144–62).

As long as the new heaven and the new earth will remain, so this newly constructed community and their generations will prevail forever (v. 22; cf. Gen 8:22). Irrespective of background, status, or ethnicity, "all flesh" (cf. v. 16; 40:5; 49:26) will join the pilgrimage to worship YHWH at valuable festivals like new moon and Sabbath (v. 23; cf. 1:13; Zech 14:16). Such will be the astonishing future blessings for the transformed community led by the penitent, upright "we"-group as well as God-fearing outsiders. Not so the wicked. The cold-blooded sinners, the self-centered transgressors, will meet their doom. As though portraying what the devout worshipers would be witnessing while processing from the temple, the reprobate will perish in the midst of unquenchable worms and flames (Blenkinsopp 2003, 317). "All flesh" will learn that there is no peace for the wicked (v. 24; cf. 39:8; 48:22; 57:21; Mal 4:1-6 [MT 3:19-24]; Ps 1:6).

Thus concludes the great scroll of Isaiah. To modern readers who anticipate a conclusion with a dandy happy ending, the final verse would certainly give a somewhat anticlimactic or disturbing feeling. In fact, the TNK version thus ends the book of Isaiah with the repetition of v. 23 right after v. 24. Yet this is not too dissimilar from the conclusion of the Psalter, according to the aspect of its open-endedness, invitation, or call to the readers. The Psalter with repeated Hallelujah psalms at the end (Pss 146–50) certainly appears to have a grand finale of perfect completion. However, Irene Nowell claims that "Psalm 150 is unfinished—it has only the call to praise but no reasons. . . . We are left to finish the doxology, to give the reasons for praise, with our lives" (2013, 85). So, the concluding oracles of the Isaiah scroll, with the visions of new heavens and new earth as well as the candid reminder of corruption and brutality in this complex world, cast the theological and hermeneutical invitations to the readers. Thus, the Hebrew text's originally controversial ending powerfully and accurately paints the ancient world—not too different from today's world—with the reality of the righteous servants' difficult yet praiseworthy struggles to maintain, build, and work for justice and shalom, overwhelmingly surrounded by the rapacious exertion of power by the wicked. The wicked are still around everywhere, at times within us. However, the prayers and efforts of the righteous will not be in vain, as God the Light of the world has promised to continue to abide, Immanuel (7:14; 8:8)!

Works Cited

Abernethy, Andrew T. 2014. *Eating in Isaiah: Approaching the Role of Food and Drink in Isaiah's Structure and Message.* Leiden: Brill.

Abou-Chaar, Iskandar. 2013. "Rereading Isaiah 40–55 as 'Project Launcher' for the Books of the Law and the Prophets." Pages 101–28 in *Festschrift in Honor of Professor Paul Nadim Tarazi: Vol. 1, Studies in the Old Testament.* Edited by N. Roddy. New York: Lang.

Achtemeier, Elizabeth. 1988. "Isaiah of Jerusalem: Themes and Preaching Possibilities." Pages 23–37 in *Reading and Preaching the Book of Isaiah.* Edited by C. R. Seitz. Philadelphia: Fortress.

Ackroyd, Peter R. 1987. *Studies in the Religious Tradition of the Old Testament.* London: SCM.

Adams, Jim W. 2006. *The Performative Nature and Function of Isaiah 40–55.* London/New York: T&T Clark.

Adams, Samuel L. *Social and Economic Life in Second Temple Judea.* Louisville: Westminster John Knox, 2014.

Ahn, John J. 2008. "Psalm 137: Complex Communal Laments." *JBL* 127 (2008): 267–89.

———. 2011. *Exile as Forced Migrations: A Sociological, Literary, and Theological Approach on the Displacement and Resettlement of the Southern Kingdom of Judah.* BZAW 417. Berlin: de Gruyter.

Albertz, Rainer. 2003a. "Darius in Place of Cyrus: The First Edition of Deutero-Isaiah (Isaiah 40.1–52.12) in 521 BCE." *JSOT* 27:371–83.

———. 2003b. *Israel in Exile: The History and Literature of the Sixth Century B.C.E.* Translated by David Green. Atlanta: SBL.

Asen, Bernhard A. 1996. "The Garlands of Ephraim: Isaiah 28:1-6 and the *Marzeah.*" *JSOT* 71:73–87.

Aster, Shawn Zelig. 2007. "The Image of Assyria in Isaiah 2:5-22: The Campaign Motif Reversed." *JAOS* 127:249–78.

———. 2012. *The Unbeatable Light:* Melammu *and Its Biblical Parallels.* AOAT 384. Münster: Ugarit-Verlag.

Baer, David A. 2010. "What Happens in the End? Evidence for an Early Greek Recension in LXX Isaiah 66." Pages 1–31 in *The Old Greek of Isaiah: Issues and Perspectives: Papers Read at the Conference on the Septuagint of Isaiah, Held in Leiden 10-11 April 2008.* Leuven: Peeters.

Balogh, Csaba. 2008. "'He Filled Zion with Justice and Righteousness': The Composition of Isaiah 33." *Biblica* 89:477–504.

———. 2009. "Blind People, Blind God: The Composition of Isaiah 29,15-24." *ZAW* 121:48–69.

———. 2011. *The Stele of YHWH in Egypt: The Prophecies of Isaiah 18–20 concerning Egypt and Kush.* OtSt 60. Leiden: Brill.

———. 2013. "Isaiah's Prophetic Instruction and the Disciples in Isaiah 8:16." *VT* 63:1–18.

Baltzer, Klaus. 2001. *Deutero-Isaiah: A Commentary on Isaiah 40–55.* Translated by M. Kohl. Hermeneia. Minneapolis: Fortress.

Barré, Michael L. 2000. "Textual and Rhetorical-Critical Observations on the Last Servant Song (Isaiah 52:13–53:12)." *CBQ* 62:1–27.

Barstad, Hans. 1996. *The Myth of the Empty Land: A Study in the History and Archaeology of Judah during the "Exilic" Period.* Oslo: Scandinavian University Press.

Becking, Bob. 2011. "A Fragmented History of the Exile." Pages 151–69 in *Interpreting Exile: Displacement and Deportation in Biblical and Modern Contexts.* Edited by B. E. Kelle, F. R. Ames, and J. L. Wright. SBLAIL 10. Atlanta: SBL.

———. 2013. "Between *Realpolitiker* and Hero of Faith: Memories of Hezekiah in Biblical Traditions and Beyond." Pages 182–98 in *Remembering Biblical Figures in the Late Persian and Early Hellenistic Periods: Social Memory and Imagination.* Edited by D. V. Edelman and E. Ben Zvi. Oxford: Oxford University Press.

Ben Zvi, Ehud. 2010. "A Contribution to the Intellectual History of Yehud: The Story of Micaiah and Its Function within the Discourse of Persian-Period Literari." Pages 89–102 in *The Historian and the Bible: Essays in Honour of Lester L. Grabbe.* Edited by P. R. Davies and D. V. Edelman. New York: T&T Clark.

Berges, Ulrich F. 2011. "Zion and the Kingship of YHWH in Isaiah 40–55." Pages 95–119 in *'Enlarge the Site of Your Tent': The City as Unifying Theme in Isaiah: The Isaiah Workshop – De Jesaja Werkplaats.* Edited by A.L.H.M. van Wieringen and A. van der Woude. *OtSt* 58. Leiden: Brill.

———. 2012a. *The Book of Isaiah: Its Composition and Final Form.* Translated by M. C. Lind. Sheffield: Sheffield Phoenix Press.

———. 2012b. "The Fourth Servant Song (Isaiah 52:13 – 53:12): Reflections on the Current Debate on the Symbolism of the Cross from the Perspective of the Old Testament." *OTE* 25:481–99.

———. 2012c. *Isaiah: The Prophet and His Book.* Sheffield: Sheffield Phoenix Press.

———. 2014. "Where Does Trito-Isaiah Start in the Book of Isaiah?" Pages 63–76 in *Continuity and Discontinuity: Chronological and Thematic Develoment in Isaiah 40–66.* Edited by L.-S. Tiemeyer and H. M. Barstad. Göttingen: Vandenhoeck & Ruprecht.

Bergmann, Claudia D. 2008. "'We Have Seen the Enemy, and He Is Only a "She"': The Portrayal of Warriors as Women." Pages 129–42 in *Writing and Reading War: Rhetoric, Gender, and Ethics in Biblical and Modern Contexts.* Edited by B. E. Kelle and F. R. Ames. SBLSymS 42. Atlanta: SBL.

Beuken, Willem A. M. 1991. "Jesaja 33 als Spiegeltext im Jesajabuch." *ETL* 67:5–35.

———. 1998. "Women and the Spirit, the Ox and the Ass: The First Binders of the Booklet Isaiah 28–32." *ETL* 74:5–26.

———. 2000a. *Isaiah 28–39.* Translated by Brian Doyle. Leuven: Peeters.

———. 2000b. "The Prophet Leads the Readers into Praise: Isaiah 25:1-10 in Connection with Isaiah 24:14-23 Seen against the Background of Isaiah 12." Pages 121–56 in *Studies in Isaiah 24–27: The Isaiah Workshop – De Jesaja Werkplaats.* Edited by H. Jan Bosman et al. Leiden: Brill.

———. 2002. "'Lebanon with Its Majesty Shall Fall. A Shoot Shall Come Forth from the Stump of Jesse' (Isa 10:34–11:1): Interfacing the Story of Assyria and the Image of Israel's Future in Isaiah 10–11." Pages 17–33 in *The New Things: Eschatology in Old Testament Prophecy: Festschrift for Henk Leene.* Edited by F. Postma, K. Spronk, and E. Talstra. Maastricht: Uitgeverij Shaker.

———. 2003. "The Unity of the Book of Isaiah: Another Attempt at Bridging the Gorge between Its Two Main Parts." Pages 50–60 in *Reading from Right to Left: Essays on the Hebrew Bible in Honour of David J. A. Clines.* Edited by J. C. Exum and H. G. M. Williamson. JSOTSup 373. London: Sheffield Academic Press.

———. 2004a. "The Literary Emergence of Zion as a City in the First Opening of the Book of Isaiah (1,1–2,5)." Pages 457–70 in *Gott und Mensch im Dialog: Festschrift für Otto Kaiser zum 80. Geburtstag.* Edited by M. Witte. BZAW 345.1. Berlin: de Gruyter.

———. 2004b. "The Manifestation of Yahweh and the Commission of Isaiah: Isaiah 6 Read against the Background of Isaiah 1." *CTJ* 39:72–87.

———. 2004c. "A Song of Gratitude and a Song of Malicious Delight: Is Their Consonance Unseemly?: The Coherence of Isaiah Chs. 13–14 with Chs. 11–12 and Chs. 1–2." Pages 96–114 in *Das Manna fällt auch heute noch: Beiträge zur Geschichte und Theologie des Alten, Ersten Testaments: Festschrift für Erich Zenger.* Edited by F.-L. Hossfeld and L. Schwienhorst-Schönberger. Freiburg: Herder.

———. 2005. "Obdurate Short-Sightedness in the Valley of Vision: How Atonement of Iniquity is Forfeited (Isa 22:1-14)." Pages 45–63 in *One Text, A Thousand Methods: Studies in Memory of Sjef van Tilborg.* Edited by P. C. Counet and U. Berges. Leiden: Brill.

———. 2007. *Jesaja 13–27.* Freiburg: Herder.

———. 2010. "The King Diseased and Healed (Isaiah 38), the King Embarrassed and Comforted (Isaiah 39): What Do These Figures Add to the King Beleaguered and Rescued (Isaiah 36–37)?" *ETL* 86:379–91.

———. 2011. "From Damascus to Mount Zion: A Journey through the Land of the Harvester (Isaiah 17–18)." Pages 63–80 in *'Enlarge the Site of Your Tent': The City as Unifying Theme in Isaiah: The Isaiah Workshop – De Jesaja Werkplaats*. Edited by A.L.H.M. van Wieringen and A. van der Woude. *OtSt* 58. Leiden: Brill.

———. 2014. "Shifting Settings in (Post-)Exilic Prayer from the Hebrew to the Old Greek Text of Isaiah 26." *HeBAI* 3:249–75.

Bhabha, Homi K. 1984. "Of Mimicry and Man: The Ambivalence of Colonial Discourse." *October* 28:125–33.

———. 1994. *The Location of Culture*. London: Routledge.

Biddle, Mark E. 1996. "Lady Zion's Alter Egos: Isaiah 47.1-15 and 57.6-13 as Structural Counterparts." Pages 124–39 in *New Visions of Isaiah*. Edited by R. F. Melugin and M. A. Sweeney. JSOTSup 214. Sheffield: Sheffield Academic Press.

Blenkinsopp, Joseph. 2000a. *Isaiah 1–39*. AB 19. New York: Doubleday.

———. 2000b. "Judah's Covenant with Death (Isaiah xxviii 14-22)." *VT* 50:472–83.

———. 2001. "Cityscape to Landscape: The 'Back to Nature' Theme in Isaiah 1-35." Pages 35–44 in *'Every City Shall Be Forsaken': Urbanism and Prophecy in Ancient Israel and the Near East*. Edited by L. L. Grabbe and R. D. Haak. JSOTSup 330. Sheffield: Sheffield Academic Press.

———. 2002. *Isaiah 40–55*. AB 19A. New York: Doubleday.

———. 2003. *Isaiah 56–66*. AB 19B. New York: Doubleday.

———. 2006. "Who Is the *Ṣaddiq* of Isaiah 57:1-2?" Pages 109–20 in *Studies in the Hebrew Bible, Qumran, and the Septuagint Present to Eugene Ulrich*. Edited by P. W. Flint, E. Tov, and J. C. VanderKam. Leiden: Brill.

———. 2013. *David Remembered: Kingship and National Identity in Ancient Israel*. Grand Rapids MI: Eerdmans.

———. 2014. "Continuity-Discontinuity in Isaiah 40-66: The Issue of Location." Pages 77–88 in *Continuity and Discontinuity: Chronological and Thematic Development in Isaiah 40–66*. Edited by L.-S. Tiemeyer and H. M. Barstad. Göttingen: Vandenhoeck & Ruprecht.

Boda, Mark J. 2010. *1–2 Chronicles*. Carol Stream IL: Tyndale.

Boling, Robert G. 1999. "Kings and Prophets: Cyrus and Servant: Reading Isaiah 40–55." Pages 171–88 in *Ki Baruch Hu: Ancient Near Eastern, Biblical, and Judaic Studies in Honor of Baruch A. Levine*. Edited by R. Chazan, W. W. Hallo, and L. H. Schiffman. Winona Lake: Eisenbrauns.

Brenner, Athalya. 1997. "Identifying the Speaker-in-the-Text and the Reader's Location in Prophetic Texts: The Case of Isaiah 50." Pages 136–50 in *A Feminist Companion to Reading the Bible: Approaches, Methods and Strategies*. Edited by A. Brenner and C. Fontaine. Sheffield: Sheffield Academic Press.

Brett, Mark G. 2013a. "Negotiating the Tides of Empire." Pages 198–204 in *Isaiah and Imperial Context: The Book of Isaiah in the Times of Empire*. Edited by A. T. Abernethy et al. Eugene OR: Pickwick.

———. 2013b. "Unequal Terms: A Postcolonial Approach to Isaiah 61." Pages 243–55 in *Biblical Interpretation and Method: Essays in Honour of John Barton*. Edited by K. J. Dell and P. M. Joyce. Oxford: Oxford University Press.

Brown, William P. 2002. *Seeing the Psalms: A Theology of Metaphor*. Louisville: Westminster John Knox.

Brueggemann, Walter. 1984. *The Message of the Psalms: A Theological Commentary*. Minneapolis: Augsburg.

———. 1986. "The Costly Loss of Lament." *JSOT* 36: 57-71.

———. 1998a. *Isaiah 1–39*. Westminster Bible Companion. Louisville: Westminster John Knox.

———. 1998b. *Isaiah 40–66*. Westminster Bible Companion. Louisville: Westminster John Knox.

———. 2014. *From Whom No Secrets Are Hid: Introducing the Psalms*. Louisville: Westminster John Knox.

Burke, Aaron A. 2011. "An Anthropological Model for the Investigation of the Archaeology of Refugees in Iron Age Judah and Its Environs." Pages 41–56 in *Interpreting Exile: Displacement and Deportation in Biblical and Modern Contexts*. Edited by B. E. Kelle, F. R. Ames, and J. L. Wright. SBLAIL 10. Atlanta: SBL.

Carr, David M. 2014. *Holy Resilience: The Bible's Traumatic Origins*. New Haven: Yale University Press.

Chan, Michael. 2009. "Rhetorical Reversal and Usurpation: Isaiah 10:5-34 and the Use of NeoAssyrian Royal Idiom in the Construction of an Anti-Assyrian Theology." *JBL* 128: 717–33.

Chaney, Marvin L. 1999. "Whose Sour Grapes?: The Addressees of Isaiah 5:1-7 in the Light of Political Economy." *Semeia* 87:105–22.

—————. 2006. "Micah—Models Matter: Political Economy and Micah 6:9-15." Pages 145–60 in *Ancient Israel: The Old Testament in Its Social Context*. Edited by P. F. Esler. Minneapolis: Fortress.

Childs, Brevard S. 2001. *Isaiah*. OTL. Louisville: Westminster John Knox.

Cho, Paul Kang-Kul and Janling Fu. 2013. "Death and Feasting in the Isaiah Apocalypse (Isaiah 25:6-8)." Pages 117–42 in *Formation and Intertextuality in Isaiah 24–27*. Edited by J. T. Hibbard and H. C. P. Kim. SBLAIL 17. Atlanta: SBL.

Clements, Ronald E. 1989. "Isaiah 14,22-27: A Central Passage Reconsidered." Pages 253–62 in *The Book of Isaiah/Le Livre D'Isaïe*. Edited by J. Vermeylen. Leuven: Leuven University Press.

—————. 1996. "A Light to the Nations: A Central Theme in the Book of Isaiah." Pages 57–69 in *Forming Prophetic Literature: Essays on Isaiah and the Twelve in Honor of John D. W. Watts*. Edited by J. W. Watts and P. R. House. JSOTSup 235. Sheffield: Sheffield Academic Press.

—————. 1997. "'Arise, Shine: For Your Light Has Come': A Basic Theme of the Isaianic Tradition." Pages 441–54 in *Writing and Reading the Scroll of Isaiah: Studies of an Interpretive Tradition*. Vol. 1. Edited by C. C. Broyles and C. A. Evans. Leiden: Brill.

Clifford, Hywel. 2010. "Deutero-Isaiah and Monotheism." Pages 267–89 in *Prophecy and Prophets in Ancient Israel: Proceedings of the Oxford Old Testament Seminar*. Edited by J. Day. New York: T&T Clark.

Cohn, Robert L. 2000. *2 Kings*. Berit Olam. Collegeville MN: Liturgical.

Collins, John J. 2010. "The Sign of Immanuel." Pages 225–44 in *Prophecy and Prophets in Ancient Israel: Proceedings of the Oxford Old Testament Seminar*. Edited by J. Day. New York: T&T Clark.

Conrad, Edgar W. 1985. "The Community as King in Second Isaiah." Pages 99–111 in *Understanding the Word: Essays in Honor of Bernhard W. Anderson.* Edited by J. T. Butler, E. W. Conrad, and B. C. Ollenburger. JSOTSup 37. Sheffield: JSOT Press.

———. 1991. *Reading Isaiah.* OBT. Minneapolis: Fortress.

Cook, Stephen L. 2010. "An Interpretation of the Death of Isaiah's Servant." Pages 108–24 in *The Bible as a Human Witness to Divine Revelation: Hearing the Word of God through Historically Dissimilar Traditions.* Edited by R. Heskett and B. Irwin. LBH/OTS 469. New York: T&T Clark.

———. 2015. "Second Isaiah and the Aaronide Response to Judah's Forced Migrations." Pages 47–61 in *The Prophets Speak on Forced Migration.* Edited by M. J. Boda et al. Atlanta: SBL.

Cuéllar, Gregory Lee. 2008. *Voices of Marginality: Exile and Return in Second Isaiah 40-55 and the Mexican Immigrant Experience.* New York: Lang.

Davidson, Richard M. 2007. "The Messianic Hope in Isaiah 7:14 and the Volume of Immanuel (Isaiah 7–12)." Pages 85–96 in *"For You Have Strengthened Me": Biblical and Theological Studies in Honor of Gerhard Pfandl in Celebration of His Sixty-Fifth Birthday.* Edited by M. Pröbstle. St. Peter am Hart, Austria: Seminar Schloss Bogenhofen.

Davidson, Steed Vernyl. 2011. *Empire and Exile: Postcolonial Readings of the Book of Jeremiah.* LHB/OTS 542. New York: T&T Clark.

Day, John. 1985. *God's Conflict with the Dragon and the Sea: Echoes of a Canaanite Myth in the Old Testament.* Cambridge: Cambridge University Press.

De Jong, Matthijs J. 2010. "A Window on the Isaiah Tradition in the Assyrian Period: Isaiah 10:24-27." Pages 83–107 in *Isaiah in Context: Studies in Honour of Arie van der Kooij on the Occasion of his Sixty-Fifth Birthday.* Edited by M. N. van der Meer et al. Leiden: Brill.

deClaissé-Walford, Nancy, Rolf A. Jacobson, and Beth LaNeel Tanner. 2014. *The Book of Psalms.* NICOT. Grand Rapids: Eerdmans.

Dekker, Jaap. 2007. *Zion's Rock-Solid Foundations: An Exegetical Study of the Zion Text in Isaiah 28:16.* OtSt 54. Leiden: Brill.

Dell, Katharine J. 2010. "The Suffering Servant of Deutero-Isaiah: Jeremiah Revisited." Pages 119–34 in *Genesis, Isaiah and Psalms: A Festschrift to Honour Professor John Emerton for His Eightieth Birthday*. Edited by K. J. Dell, G. Davies, and Y. V. Koh. Leiden: Brill.

Dempsey, Carol J. 2012. *Isaiah: God's Poet of Light*. St Louis MO: Chalice.

Dicou, Bert. 1991. "Literary Function and Literary History of Isaiah 34." *BN* 58:30–45.

Dijkstra, Meindert. 2002. "'He Who Call the Eras from the Beginning' (Isa 41:4): From History to Eschatology in Second Isaiah." Pages 61–76 in *The New Things: Eschatology in Old Testament Prophecy: Festschrift for Henk Leene*. Edited by F. Postma, K. Spronk, and E. Talstra. Maastricht: Uitgeverij Shaker.

Dille, Sarah J. 2004. *Mixing Metaphors: God as Mother and Father in Deutero-Isaiah*. JSOTSup 398. London: T&T Clark.

Dion, Paul-Eugène. 2006. "Ahaz and Other Willing Servants of Assyria." Pages 133–45 in *From Babel to Babylon: Essays on Biblical History and Literature in Honour of Brian Peckham*. Edited by J. R. Wood, J. E. Harvey, and M. Leuchter. LHB/OTS 455. New York: T&T Clark.

Dobbs-Allsopp, F. W. 1993. *Weep, O Daughter of Zion: A Study of the City-Lament Genre in the Hebrew Bible*. Roma: Editrice Pontificio Istituto Biblioco.

Doyle, Brian. 2002. "Fertility and Infertility in Isaiah 24–27." Pages 77–88 in *The New Things: Eschatology in Old Testament Prophecy: Festschrift for Henk Leene*. Edited by F. Postma, K. Spronk, and E. Talstra. Maastricht: Uitgeverij Shaker.

Duhm, Bernhard. 1892. *Das Buch Jesaja: Übersetzt und Erklärt*. Göttingen: Vandenhoeck & Ruprecht.

Eidevall, Göran. 2009. *Prophecy and Propaganda: Images of Enemies in the Book of Isaiah*. Winona Lake, Ind.: Eisenbrauns.

Erickson, Carlton K. 2007. *The Science of Addition: From Neurobiology to Treatment*. New York: W. W. Norton.

Exum, J. Cheryl. 1981. "Of Broken Pots, Fluttering Birds and Visions in the Night: Extended Simile and Poetic Technique in Isaiah." *CBQ* 43:331–52.

Fanon, Frantz. 2008 (1952). *Black Skin, White Masks.* Translated by Richard Philcox. New York: Grove.

Faust, Avraham. 2011. "Deportation and Demography in Sixth-Century B.C.E. Judah." Pages 91–103 in *Interpreting Exile: Displacement and Deportation in Biblical and Modern Contexts.* Edited by B. E. Kelle, F. R. Ames, and J. L. Wright. SBLAIL 10. Atlanta: SBL.

Finkelstein, Israel. 2015. "Migration of Israelites into Judah after 720 BCE: An Answer and an Update." *ZAW* 127:188–206.

Finitsis, Antonios. 2011. "The Other in Haggai and Zechariah 1–8." Pages 116–31 in *The 'Other' in Second Temple Judaism: Essays in Honor of John J. Collins.* Edited by D. C. Hawlow et al. Grand Rapids: Eerdmans.

Fischer, Irmtraud. 2008. "World Peace and 'Holy War.'" Pages 151–65 in *Isaiah's Vision of Peace in Biblical and Modern International Relations: Swords into Plowshares.* Edited by R. Cohen and R. Westbrook. New York: Palgrave Macmillan.

Fishbane, Michael. 1985. *Biblical Interpretation in Ancient Israel.* Oxford: Clarendon.

Fohrer, G. 1966. *Das Buch Jesaja. I. Kapitel 1–23.* ZBK. Zurich: Zwingli Verlag.

Franke, Chris A. 1994. *Isaiah 46, 47, and 48: A New Literary-Critical Reading.* Winona Lake: Eisenbrauns, 1994.

———. 2014. "Isaiah 40–66." Pages 699–724 in *Fortress Commentary on the Bible: The Old Testament and Apocrypha.* Edited by G. A. Yee, H. R. Page, and M. J. M. Croomber. Minneapolis: Fortress.

Frechette, Christopher G. 2012. *Mesopotamian Ritual-prayers of "Hand-lifting" (Akkadian Šuillas): An Investigation of Function in Light of the Idiomatic Meaning of the Rubric.* AOAT 379. Münster: Ugarit-Verlag.

Fretheim, Terence E. 1999. *First and Second Kings.* Westminster Bible Companion. Louisville: Westminster John Knox.

———. 2013. *Reading Hosea–Micah: A Literary and Theological Commentary.* Macon GA: Smyth & Helwys.

———. 2014. "What Kind of God Is Portrayed in Isaiah 5:1-7?" Pages 53–67 in *New Studies in the Book of Isaiah: Essays in Honor of Hallvard Hagelia.* Edited by M. Zehnder. Piscataway NJ: Gorgias.

Ganzel, Tova. 2015. "Isaiah's Critique of Shebna's Trespass: A Reconsideration of Isaiah 22.15-25." *JSOT* 39:469–87.

Glazov, Gregory Yuri. 2001. *The Bridling of the Tongue and the Opening of the Mouth in Biblical Prophecy.* JSOTSup 311. Sheffield: Sheffield Academic Press.

Gerstenberger, Erhard S. 2011. *Israel in the Persian Period: The Fifth and Fourth Centuries B.C.E.* Translated by S. S. Schatzmann. Atlanta: SBL.

Goldingay, John. 2001. *Isaiah.* Carlisle: Paternoster.

———. 2014. *The Theology of the Book of Isaiah.* Downers Grove IL: IVP Academic.

Goldingay, John and David Payne. 2006a. *Isaiah 40–55.* ICC. Vol. 1. London: T&T Clark.

———. 2006b. *Isaiah 40–55.* ICC. Vol. 2. London: T&T Clark.

Goswell, Greg. 2014. "The Literary Logic and Meaning of Isaiah 38." *JSOT* 39:165–86.

Goulder, M. 2002. "Behold My Servant Jehoiachin." *VT* 52:175–90.

Groenewald, Alphonso. 2012. "Isaiah 2:1-5: A Post-Exilic Vision of the Pilgrimage of the Nations to Zion." Pages 53–69 in *Zugänge zum Fremden: Methodisch-hermeneutische Perspektiven zu einem biblischen Thema.* Edited by G. Baumann et al. Frankfurt am Main: Lang.

Hägglund, Fredrik. 2008. *Isaiah 53 in the Light of Homecoming after Exile.* FAT 2.31. Tübingen: Mohr Siebeck.

Hallo, William H., and K. Lawson Younger, eds. 2003. *The Context of Scripture.* Vol. 2. Leiden: Brill.

Hanson, Paul D. 1975. *The Dawn of Apocalyptic.* Philadelphia: Fortress.

———. 1988. "Third Isaiah: The Theological Legacy of a Struggling Community." Pages 91–103 in *Reading and Preaching the Book of Isaiah*. Edited by C. R. Seitz. Philadelphia: Fortress.

———. 1995. *Isaiah 40–66*. Interpretation. Louisville: John Knox.

Haran, Menahem. 2010. "Isaiah as a Prophet to Samaria and His Memoirs." Pages 95–103 in *Genesis, Isaiah and Psalms: A Festschrift to Honour Professor John Emerton for His Eightieth Birthday*. Edited by K. J. Dell, G. Davies, and Y. V. Koh. Leiden: Brill.

Harrelson, Walter. 1994. "Isaiah 35 in Recent Research and Translation." Pages 247–60 in *Language, Theology and the Bible: Essays in Honour of James Barr*. Edited by S. E. Balentine and J. Barton. Oxford: Clarendon.

Hays, Christopher B. 2010. "The Covenant with Mut: A New Interpretation of Isaiah 28:1-22." *VT* 60:212–40.

———. 2013. "Isaiah as Colonized Poet: His Rhetoric of Death in Conversation with African Postcolonial Writers." Pages 51–70 in *Isaiah and Imperial Context: The Book of Isaiah in the Times of Empire*. Edited by A. T. Abernethy et al. Eugene, Ore.: Pickwick.

Hens-Piazza, Gina. 2006. *1–2 Kings*. AOTC. Nashville: Abingdon.

Heschel, Abraham J. 1962. *The Prophets*. New York: Harper & Row.

Hibbard, J. Todd. 2006. *Intertextuality in Isaiah 24–27: The Reuse and Evocation of Earlier Texts and Traditions*. FAT 2.16. Tübingen: Mohr Siebeck.

Hobson, Russell. 2013. "The Memory of Sennacherib in Late Persian Yehud." Pages 199–220 in *Remembering Biblical Figures in the Late Persian and Early Hellenistic Periods: Social Memory and Imagination*. Edited by D. V. Edelman and E. Ben Zvi. Oxford: Oxford University Press.

Holston, M. Jan. 2011. "Imagining Hope and Redemption: A Salvation Narrative among the Displaced in Sudan." Pages 217–33 in *Interpreting Exile: Displacement and Deportation in Biblical and Modern Contexts*. Edited by B. E. Kelle, F. Ritchel Ames, and J. L. Wright. SBLAIL 10. Atlanta: SBL.

Holter, Knut. 2014. "Isaiah and Africa." Pages 69–90 in *New Studies in the Book of Isaiah: Essays in Honor of Hallvard Hagelia.* Edited by M. Zehnder. Piscataway NJ: Gorgias.

Hopkins, Denise Dombkowski. 2002. *Journey through the Psalms.* St. Louis MO: Chalice.

Hossfeld, Frank-Lothar and Erich Zenger. 2005. *Psalms 2.* Hermeneia. Minneapolis: Fortress.

Houston, Walter J. 2010. "Exit the Oppressed Peasant?: Rethinking the Background of Social Criticism in the Prophets." Pages 101–16 in *Prophecy and Prophets in Ancient Israel: Proceedings of the Oxford Old Testament Seminar.* Edited by J. Day. New York: T&T Clark.

Huffmon, Herbert B. 2006. "Jezebel—The 'Corrosive' Queen." Pages 273–83 in *From Babel to Babylon: Essays on Biblical History and Literature in Honour of Brian Peckham.* Edited by J. R. Wood, J. E. Harvey, and M. Leuchter. New York: T&T Clark.

Hulster, Izaak J. de. 2009. *Iconographic Exegesis and Third Isaiah.* FAT 2:36. Tübingen: Mohr Siebeck.

———. 2015. "'A Monument and a Name': Isaiah 56 and the Aniconic Image." Pages 181–96 in *Iconographic Exegesis of the Hebrew Bible/ Old Testament: An Introduction to Its Method and Practice.* Edited by I. J. de Hulster, B. A. Strawn, and R. P. Bonfiglio. Göttingen: Vandenhoeck & Ruprecht.

Hurowitz, Victor. 1989. "Isaiah's Impure Lips and Their Purification in Light of Mouth Purification and Mouth Purity in Akkadian Sources." *HUCA* 60:39–89.

Ibn Ezra, Abraham. 1873. *The Commentary of Ibn Ezra on Isaiah.* New York: P. Feldheim.

Jacobson, Rolf A. 2009. "A Rose by Any Other Name: Iconography and the Interpretation of Isaiah 28:1-6." Pages 125–46 in *Images and Prophecy in the Ancient Eastern Mediterranean.* Edited by M. Nissinen and C. E. Carter. Göttingen: Vandenhoeck & Ruprecht.

Japhet, Sara. 1983. "People and Land in the Restoration Period." Pages 103–25 in *Das Land Israel in biblischer Zeit.* Edited by G. Strecker. Göttingen: Vandenhoeck & Ruprecht.

———. 1989. *The Ideology of the Book of Chronicles and Its Place in Biblical Thought*. Frankfurt: Lang.

Kaiser, Otto. 1974. *Isaiah 13–39*. Translated by R. A. Wilson. OTL. London: SCM.

Kaminsky, Joel S. 2011. "Israel's Election and the Other in Biblical, Second Temple, and Rabbinic Thought." Pages 17–30 in *The "Other" in Second Temple Judaism: Essays in Honor of John J. Collins*. Edited by D. C. Harlow et al. Grand Rapids MI: Eerdmans.

Kaminsky, Joel S. and Joel. N. Lohr. 2015. *The Hebrew Bible for Beginners: A Jewish and Christian Introduction*. Nashville: Abingdon.

Kelle, Brad E. 2011. "An Interdisciplinary Approach to the Exile." Pages 5–38 in *Interpreting Exile: Displacement and Deportation in Biblical and Modern Contexts*. Edited by B. E. Kelle, F. R. Ames, and J. L. Wright. SBLAIL 10. Atlanta: SBL.

Kim, Hyun Chul Paul. 1999. "An Intertextual Reading of a 'Crushed Reed' and a 'Dim Wick' in Isa 42:3." *JSOT* 83:113–24.

———. 2003. *Ambiguity, Tension, and Multiplicity in Deutero-Isaiah*. New York: Peter Lang.

———. 2004. "The Song of Moses (Deut 32:1-43) in Isaiah 40–55." Pages 149–74 in *God's Word for Our World: In Honor of Simon John De Vries*. Edited by J. H. Ellens et al. Vol. 1. JSOTSup 388. London: T&T Clark.

———. 2007. "Jonah Read Intertextually." *JBL* 126:497–528.

———. 2009. "The Spider-Poet: Signs and Symbols in Isaiah 41." Pages 159–79 in *The Desert Will Bloom: Poetic Visions in Isaiah*. Edited by A. J. Everson and H. C. P. Kim. SBLAIL 4. Atlanta: SBL.

———. 2012. "Cyrus." Page 1043 in *Encyclopedia of the Bible and Its Reception*. Vol. 5. Edited by Hermann Spieckermann et al. Berlin: de Gruyter.

———. 2013. "City, Earth, and Empire in Isaiah 24-27." Pages 25–48 in *Formation and Intertextuality in Isaiah 24-27*. Edited by J. T. Hibbard and H. C. P. Kim; SBLAIL 17. Atlanta: SBL.

———. 2014. "Little Highs, Little Lows: Tracing Key Themes in Isaiah." Pages 141–66 in *The Book of Isaiah: Enduring Questions Answered Anew: Essays Honoring Joseph Blenkinsopp and His Contribution to the Study of Isaiah*. Edited by R. J. Bautch and J. T. Hibbard. Grand Rapids: Eerdmans.

———. 2015a. "A Farewell to Trito-Isaiah?: An Inner-Biblical Exegesis of Isaiah 54–57 in Light of Isaiah 1–2 and Psalm 1." *Canon and Culture* 35–70.

———. 2015b. "Isaiah 22: A Crux or a Clue in Isaiah 13–23?" Pages 3–18 in *Concerning the Nations: Essays on the Oracles against the Nations in Isaiah, Jeremiah, and Ezekiel*. Edited by E. Holt, H. C. P. Kim, and A. Mein. LHB/OTS 612. London: T&T Clark.

Klein, Ralph W. 2006. *1 Chronicles*. Hermeneia. Minneapolis: Fortress.

Knierim, Rolf P. 1968. "The Vocation of Isaiah." *VT* 18:47–68.

———. 1992. *Text and Concept in Leviticus 1:1-9: A Case in Exegetical Method*. Tübingen: Mohr Siebeck.

Knight, George A. F. 1984. *Isaiah 40–55*. ITC. Grand Rapids MI: Eerdmans.

Korpel, Marjo C. A. 1999. "Second Isaiah's Coping with the Religious Crisis: Reading Isaiah 40 and 55." Pages 90–113 in *The Crisis of Israelite Religion: Transformation of Religious Tradition in Exilic and Post-Exilic Times*. Edited by B. Becking and M. C. A. Korpel. Leiden: Brill.

Kratz, Reinhard G. 1993. "Der Anfang des Zweiten Jesaja in Jes 40,1 f. und seine literarischen Horizonte." *ZAW* 105:400–19.

———. 1994. "Der Anfang des Zweiten Jesaja in Jes 40,1f. und das Jeremiabuch." *ZAW* 106:243–61.

———. 2003. "From Nabonidus to Cyrus." Pages 143-56 in *Melammu Symposia III (Milano 2002)*. Edited by A. Panaino and G. Pettinato. Helsinki: Università di Bologna.

———. 2006. "Israel in the Book of Isaiah." *JSOT* 31:103–28.

———. 2010. "Rewriting Isaiah: The Case of Isaiah 28–31." Pages 245–66 in *Prophecy and Prophets in Ancient Israel: Proceedings of the Oxford Old Testament Seminar*. Edited by J. Day. New York: T&T Clark.

———. 2012. "The Two Houses of Israel." Pages 167–79 in *Let Us Go Up to Zion: Essays in Honour of H.G.M. Williamson on the Occasion of His Sixty-Fifth Birthday.* Edited by I. Provan and M. J. Boda. Leiden: Brill.

Kruger, Paul A. 2012. "A World Turned on Its Head in ancient Near Eastern Prophetic Literature: A Powerful Strategy to Depict Chaotic Scenarios." *VT* 62:58–76.

Kuhrt, Amélie. 2007. *The Persian Empire.* Vol. 1. London: Routledge.

Launderville, Dale. 2013. "'Mysogyny' in Service of Theocentricity: Legitimate or Not?" Pages 193–214 in *Prophets Male and Female: Gender and Prophecy in the Hebrew Bible, the Eastern Mediterranean, and the Ancient Near East.* Edited by J. Stökl and C. L. Carvalho. SBLAIL 15. Atlanta: SBL.

Lapsley, Jacqueline E. 2008. "'Look! The Children and I Are as Signs and Portents in Israel': Children in Isaiah." Pages 82–201 in *The Child in the Bible.* Edited by M. J. Bunge. Grand Rapids MI: Eerdmans.

LeMon, Joel M. 2015. "On Wings in a Prayer: Multistable Images for God in Psalm 63." Pages 263-79 in *Iconographic Exegesis of the Hebrew Bible/Old Testament: An Introduction to Its Method and Practice.* Edited by I. J. de Hulster, B. A. Strawn, and R. P. Bonfiglio. Göttingen: Vandenhoeck & Ruprecht.

Levenson, Jon D. 1996. "The Universal Horizon of Biblical Particularism." Pages 142–69 in *Ethnicity and the Bible.* Edited by M. G. Brett. Leiden: Brill.

Lim, Bo H. 2010. *The "Way of the Lord" in the Book of Isaiah.* LHB/OTS 522. London: T&T Clark.

Lipschits, Oded. 2011. "Shedding New Light on the Dark Years of the 'Exilic Period': New Studies, Further Elucidation, and Some Questions regarding the Archaeology of Judah as an 'Empty Land.'" Pages 57–90 in *Interpreting Exile: Displacement and Deportation in Biblical and Modern Contexts.* Edited by B. E. Kelle, F. Ritchel Ames, and J. L. Wright. SBLAIL 10. Atlanta: SBL.

Liverani, Mario. 2014. *The Ancient Near East: History, Society and Economy.* Translated by Soraia Tabatabai. London: Routledge.

Logan, James S. 2016. "*Everywhere Ferguson* and the Racial Crucible of the Christian Churches." Lecture on "Faithful Justice: Confronting Mass Incarceration" at Methodist Theological School in Ohio.

Løland, Hanne. 2008. *Silent or Salient Gender? The Interpretation of Gendered God-Language in the Hebrew Bible, Exemplified in Isaiah 42, 46 and 49.* FAT 2.32. Tübingen: Mohr Siebeck.

Long, Thomas G. 2014. "Four Ways to Preach a Psalm." *Journal for Preachers* 37:21–32.

Lund, Øystein. 2007. *Way Metaphors and Way Topics in Isaiah 40–55.* FAT 2.28. Tübingen: Mohr Siebeck.

MacDonald, Nathan. 2011. "Monotheism and Isaiah" Pages 43–61 in *Interpreting Exile: Displacement and Deportation in Biblical and Modern Contexts.* Edited by B. E. Kelle, F. R. Ames, and J. L. Wright. SBLAIL 10. Atlanta: SBL.

Machinist, Peter. 1983. "Assyria and Its Image in the First Isaiah." *JAOS* 103:719–37.

Macintosh, A. A. 1980. *Isaiah XXI: A Palimpsest.* Cambridge: Cambridge University Press.

Maier, Christl M. 2008. *Daughter Zion, Mother Zion: Gender, Space, and the Sacred in Ancient Israel.* Minneapolis: Fortress.

Malina, Bruce J. and Richard L. Rohrbaugh. 2003. *Social-Science Commentary on the Synoptic Gospels.* 2nd ed. Minneapolis: Fortress.

Mathews, Claire R. 1995. *Defending Zion: Edom's Desolation and Jacob's Restoration (Isaiah 34–35) in Context.* BZAW 236. Berlin: de Gruyter.

Mays, James L. 1994. *Psalms.* Interpretation. Louisville: John Knox.

Mazor, Lea. 2004. "Myth, History, and Utopia in the Prophecy of the Shoot (Isaiah 10:33–11:9)." Pages 73–90 in *Sefer Moshe: The Moshe Weinfeld Jubilee Volume: Studies in the Bible and the Ancient Near East, Qumran, and Post-Biblical Judaism.* Edited by C. Cohen, A. Hurvitz, and S. M. Paul. Winona Lake: Eisenbrauns.

McCann, J. Clinton. 1996. "The Book of Psalms." Pages 639–1280 in *The New Interpreter's Bible.* Vol. 4. Edited by L. E. Keck et al. Nashville: Abingdon.

McKenzie, Steven L. 2004. *1–2 Chronicles.* AOTC. Nashville: Abingdon.

Melugin, Roy F. 1976. *The Formation of Isaiah 40–55.* BZAW 141. Berlin: de Gruyter.

———. 2009. "Poetic Imgaintaion, Intertextuality, and Life in a Symbolic World." Pages 7–15 in *The Desert Will Bloom: Poetic Visions in Isaiah.* Edited by A. J. Everson and H. C. P. Kim. Atlanta: SBL.

Middlemas, Jill. 2007. "Divine Reversal and the Role of the Temple in Trito-Isaiah." Pages 164–87 in *Temple and Worship in Biblical Israel: Proceedings of the Oxford Old Testament Seminar.* Edited by J. Day. LHB/OTS 422. London: T&T Clark.

———. 2011. "Trito-Isaiah's Intra- and Internationalization: Identity Markers in the Second Temple Period." Pages 105–25 in *Judah and the Judeans in the Achaemenid Period: Negotiating Identity in an International Context.* Edited by O. Lipschits, G. N. Knoppers, and M. Oeming. Winona Lake: Eisenbrauns.

Milgrom, Jacob. 2004. *Leviticus.* CC. Minneapolis: Fortress.

Miller, J. Hillis. 2007. "Boundaries in *Beloved.*" *Symplok* 15:24–39.

Mitchell, Christine. 2014. "A Note on the Creation Formula in Zechariah 12:1-8; Isaiah 42:5-6; and Old Persian Inscriptions." *JBL* 133:305–308.

Mobley, Gregory. 2009. "1 and 2 Kings." Pages 119–43 in *Theological Bible Commentary.* Edited by G. R. O'Day and D. L. Petersen. Louisville: Westminster John Knox.

Morrow, William. 2011. "Tribute from Judah and the Transmission of Assyrian Propaganda." Pages 183–92 in *"My Spirit at Rest in the North Country" (Zechariah 6.8): Collected Communications to the XXth Congress of the International Organization for the Study of the Old Testament, Helsinki 2010.* Edited by H. M. Niemann and M. Augustin. Frankfurt am Main: Lang.

Moughtin-Mumby, Sharon. 2008. *Sexual and Marital Metaphors in Hosea, Jeremiah, Isaiah, and Ezekiel.* Oxford: Oxford University Press.

Muilenburg, James. 1956. "The Book of Isaiah: Chapters 40–66." Pages 381–773 in *The Interpreter's Bible.* Vol. 5. Edited by G. A. Buttrick et al. Nashville: Abingdon.

Na'aman, Nadav. 2014. "Dismissing the Myth of a Flood of Israelite Refugees in the Late Eighth Century BCE." *ZAW* 126:1–14.

Newsom, Carol A. 2014. *Daniel.* OTL. Louisville: Westminster John Knox.

Niskanen, Paul V. 2014. *Isaiah 56–66.* Berit Olam. Collegeville MN: Liturgical, 2014.

Nissinen, Martti. 2001. "City as Lofty as Heaven: Arbela and Other Cities in Neo-Assyrian Prophecy." Pages 172–209 in *'Every City shall be Forsaken': Urbanism and Prophecy in Ancient Israel and the Near East.* Edited by L. L. Grabbe and R. D. Haak. JSOTSup 330. Sheffield: Sheffield Academic Press.

Noegel, Scott B. 1994. "Dialect and Politics in Isaiah 24–27." *Aula Orientalis* 12:177–92.

Nogalski, James D. 2011. *The Book of the Twelve: Hosea–Jonah.* SHBC 18a. Macon GA: Smyth & Helwys.

Nowell, Irene. 2013. *Pleading, Cursing, Praising: Conversing with God through the Psalms.* Collegeville MN: Liturgical.

O'Connor, Kathleen M. 2011. *Jeremiah: Pain and Promise.* Minneapolis: Fortress.

Odell, Margaret S. 2005. *Ezekiel.* SHBC 16. Macon GA: Smyth & Helwys.

Oosting, Reinoud. 2002. "Returning (to) Zion: Isaiah 52:8 in Light of Verbal Valency Patterns." Pages 159–66 in *The New Things: Eschatology in Old Testament Prophecy: Festschrift for Henk Leene.* Edited by F. Postma, K. Spronk, and E. Talstra. Maastricht: Uitgeverij Shaker Publishing.

Oswalt, John N. 1986. *The Book of Isaiah: Chapters 1–39.* NICOT. Grand Rapids MI: Eerdmans.

———. 2004. "The God of Newness: A Sermon on Isaiah 43:14-21." *CTJ* 39:386–90.

Paul, Shalom M. 1996. "Polysemous Pivotal Punctuation: More Janus Double Entendres." Pages 369–74 in *Texts, Temples, and Traditions: A Tribute to Menahem Haran.* Edited by M. V. Fox et al. Winona Lake: Eisenbrauns.

———. 2012. *Isaiah 40–66: Translation and Commentary.* Grand Rapids MI: Eerdmans.

Perdue, Leo G. and Warren Carter. 2015. *Israel and Empire: A Postcolonial History of Israel and Early Judaism.* London: T&T Clark.

Pixley, Jorge. 1999. "Isaiah 52:13–53:12: A Latin American Perspective." Pages 95–100 in *Return to Babel: Global Perspectives on the Bible.* Edited by P. Pope-Levison and J. R. Levison. Louisville: Westminster John Knox.

Polan, Gregory J. 2001. "Zion, the Glory of the Holy One of Israel: A Literary Analysis of Isaiah 60." Pages 50–71 in *Imagery and Imagination in Biblical Literature: Essays in Honor of Aloysius Fitzgerald.* Edited by L. Boadt and M. S. Smith. CBQMS 32. Washington, D.C.: Catholic Biblical Association of America.

Polaski, Donald C. 2001. *Authorizing an End: The Isaiah Apocalypse and Intertextuality.* Leiden: Brill.

Roberts, J. J. M. 2002. *The Bible and the Ancient Near East: Collected Essays.* Winona Lake: Eisenbrauns.

———. 2007. "The End of War in the Zion Tradition: The Imperialistic Background of an Old Testament Vision of Worldwide Peace." Pages 119–28 in *Character Ethics and the Old Testament: Moral Dimensions of Scripture.* Edited by M. D. Carroll R. and J. E. Lapsley. Louisville: Westminster John Knox.

Rofé, Alexander. 1985. "Isaiah 66:1-4: Judean Sects in the Persian Period as Viewed by Trito-Isaiah." Pages 205–17 in *Biblical and Related Studies Presented to Samuel Iwry.* Edited by A. Kort and S. Morschauser. Winona Lake, Ind.: Eisenbrauns.

Rom-Shiloni, Dalit. 2013. *Exclusive Inclusivity: Identity Conflicts between the Exiles and the People Who Remained (6th-5th Centuries BCE).* New York: T&T Clark.

Routledge, Robin L. 1992. "The Siege and Deliverance of the City of David in Isaiah 29:1-8." *TynBul* 43:181–90.

Ruff-O'Herne, Jan. "Fifty Years of Silence: Cry of the Raped." Pages 3–8 in *Listening to the Silences: Women and War.* Edited by Helen Durham and Tracey Gurd. Leiden: Martinus Nijhoff, 2005.

Rumfelt, Janet L. 2011. "Reversing Fortune: War, Psychic Trauma, and the Promise of Narrative Repair." Pages 323–42 in *Interpreting Exile: Displacement and Deportation in Biblical and Modern Contexts.* Edited by B. E. Kelle, F. R. Ames, and J. L. Wright. SBLAIL 10. Atlanta: SBL.

Samet, Nili. 2010. "Two Sumerian Parallels to Isaiah 55,10." *ZAW* 122:439–40.

Sawyer, John F. A. 1993. "Radical Images of Yahweh in Isaiah 63." Pages 72–82 in *Among the Prophets: Language, Image and Structure in the Prophetic Writings.* Edited by P. R. Davies and D. J. A. Clines. JSOTSup 144. Sheffield: JSOT Press.

Schaudig, Hanspeter. 2008. "'Bēl Bows, Nabû Stoops!': The Prophecy of Isaiah xlvi 1-2 as a Reflection of Babylonian 'Processional Omens.'" *VT* 58:557–72.

Scheuer, Blaženka. 2014. "'Why Do You Let Us Wander, O Lord, from Your Ways?' (Isa 63:17). Clarification of Culpability in the Last Part of the Book of Isaiah." Pages 158-73 in *Continuity and Discontinuity: Chronological and Thematic Development in Isaiah 40–66.* Edited by L.-S. Tiemeyer and H. M. Barstad. Göttingen: Vandenhoeck & Ruprecht.

Schmidt, Uta. 2011. "Servant and Zion: Two Kinds of Future in Isaiah 49." Pages 85–91 in *"My Spirit at Rest in the North Country (Zechariah 6.8)": Collected Communications to the XXth Congress of the International Organization for the Study of the Old Testament, Helsinki 2010.* Edited by H. M. Niemann and M. Augustin. Frankfurt am Main: Lang.

Schniedewind, William M. 2003. "The Evolution of Name Theology." Pages 228–39 in *The Chronicler as Theologian: Essays in Honor of Ralph W. Klein.* Edited by M. P. Graham, S. L. McKenzie, and G. N. Knoppers. JSOTSup 371. London: T&T Clark.

Schökel, Luis Alonso. 1987. "Isaiah." Pages 165–83 in *The Literary Guide to the Bible.* Edited by R. Alter and F. Kermode. Cambridge, Mass.: Harvard University Press.

Schramm, Brooks. 1995. *The Opponents of Third Isaiah: Reconstructing the Cultic History of the Restoration.* JSOTSup 193. Sheffield: Sheffield Academic Press.

Schultz, Richard L. 2009. "Nationalism and Universalism in Isaiah." Pages 122–44 in *Interpreting Isaiah: Issues and Approaches*. Edited by D. G. Firth and H. G. M. Williamson. Downers Grove IL: IVP Academic.

Scott, James C. 1990. *Domination and the Arts of Resistance: Hidden Transcripts*. New Haven: Yale University Press.

Seow, C. L. 1999. "The First and Second Books of Kings." Pages 1–295 in *The New Interpreter's Bible*. Vol. 3. Edited by L. E. Keck et al. Nashville: Abingdon.

Seitz, Christopher R. 1993. *Isaiah 1–39*. Interpretation. Louisville: Westminster John Knox.

———. 2001. "The Book of Isaiah 40–66." Pages 307–552 in *The New Interpreter's Bible*. Vol. 6. Edited by L. E. Keck et al. Nashville: Abingdon.

Seters, John Van. 1999. "In the Babylonian Exile with J: Between Judgment in Ezekiel and Salvation in Second Isaiah." Pages 71–89 in *The Crisis of Israelite Religion: Transformation of Religious Tradition in Exilic and Post-Exilic Times*. Edited by B. Becking and M. C. A. Korpel. Leiden: Brill.

Shaper, Joachim. 2014. "Divine Images, Iconophobia and Monotheism in Isaiah 40–66." Pages 145–58 in *Continuity and Discontinuity: Chronological and Thematic Development in Isaiah 40–66*. Edited by L.-S. Tiemeyer and H. M. Barstad. Göttingen: Vandenhoeck & Ruprecht.

Smith, Mark S. 1981. "*BERIT 'AM/BERIT 'OLAM*: A New Proposal for the Crux of Isa 42:6." *JBL* 100:241–48.

Smith, Paul Allan. 1995. *Rhetoric and Redaction in Trito-Isaiah: The Structure, Growth and Authorship of Isaiah 56–66*. VTSup 62. Leiden: Brill.

Smith-Christopher, Daniel L. 1996. "The Book of Daniel." Pages 17–152 in *The New Interpreter's Bible*. Vol. 7. Edited by L. E. Keck et al. Nashville: Abingdon.

———. 2002. *A Biblical Theology of Exile*. OBT. Minneapolis: Fortress.

Sommer, Benjamin D. 1998. *A Prophet Read Scripture: Allusion in Isaiah 40–66*. Stanford: Stanford University Press.

Stansell, Gary. 1996. "Isaiah 28–33: Blest Be the Tie That Binds (Isaiah Together)." Pages 68–103 in *New Visions of Isaiah*. Edited by R. F. Melugin and M. A. Sweeney. JSOTSup 214. Sheffield: Sheffield Academic Press.

Staubli, Thomas. 2009. "Maat-Imagery in Trito-Isaiah: The Meaning of Offering a Throat in Egypt and in Israel." Pages 41–50 in *Images and Prophecy in the Ancient Eastern Mediterranean*. Edited by M. Nissinen and C. E. Carter. Göttingen: Vandenhoeck & Ruprecht.

Steck, Odil Hannes. 1972. "Bemerkungen zu Jesaja 6." *BZ* 16:188–206.

———. 1985. *Bereitete Heimkehr: Jesaja 35 als redaktionelle Brücke zwischen dem Ersten und dem Zweiten Jesaja*. SBS 121. Stuttgart: Katholisches Bibelwerk.

———. 1989. "Tritojesaja im Jesajabuch." Pages 361–406 in in *The Book of Isaiah/Le Livre D'Isaïe*. Edited by J. Vermeylen. Leuven: Leuven University Press.

Strawn, Brent A. 2007. "'A World under Control': Isaiah 60 and the Apadana Reliefs from Persepolis." Pages 85–116 in *Approaching Yehud: New Approaches to the Study of Persian Period*. Edited by J. L. Berquist. Atlanta: SBL.

Stromberg, Jacob. 2009. "An Inner-Isaianic Reading of Isaiah 61:1-3." Pages 261–72 in *Interpreting Isaiah: Issues and Approaches*. Edited by D. G. Firth and H. G. M. Williamson. Downers Grove IL: IVP Academic.

———. 2011. *An Introduction to the Study of Isaiah*. New York: T&T Clark.

Stulman, Louis and Hyun Chul Paul Kim. 2010. *You Are My People: An Introduction to Prophetic Literature*. Nashville: Abingdon.

Sweeney, Marvin A. 1988a. *Isaiah 1–4 and the Post-Exilic Understanding of the Isaianic Tradition*. BZAW 171. Berlin: de Gruyter.

———. 1988b. "Textual Citations in Isaiah 24–27: Toward an Understanding of the Redactional Function of Chapters 24–27 in the Book of Isaiah." *JBL* 107:39–52.

———. 1996. *Isaiah 1–39*. FOTL 16. Grand Rapids MI: Eerdmans, 1996.

———. 2001. "Micah's Debate with Isaiah." *JSOT* 93:111–24.

—. 2006. "On the Road to Duhm: Isaiah in Nineteenth-Century Critical Scholarship." Pages 243–61 in *"As Those Who Are Taught": The Interpretation of Isaiah from the LXX to the SBL*. Edited by C. M. McGinnis and P. K. Tull. Atlanta: SBL.

—. 2013. *Reading Ezekiel: A Literary and Theological Commentary*. Macon GA: Smyth & Helwys.

—. 2014. "Isaiah 1–39." Pages 673–97 in *Fortress Commentary on the Bible: The Old Testament and Apocrypha*. Edited by G. A. Yee, H. R. Page, and M. J. M. Coomber. Minneapolis: Fortress.

Tiemeyer, Lena-Sofia. 2007. "Geography and Textual Allusions: Interpreting Isaiah xl-lv and Lamentations as Judahite Text." *VT* 57:367–85.

—. 2011. *For the Comfort of Zion: The Geographical and Theological Location of Isaiah 40–55*. VTSup 139. Leiden: Brill.

—. 2012. "The Coming of the Lord—and Inter-textual Reading of Isa 40:1-11; 52:7-10; 59:15b-20; 62:10-11 and 63:1-6." Pages 233–44 in *Let Us Go Up to Zion: Essays in Honour of H. G. M. Williamson on the Occasion of His Sixty-Fifth Birthday*. Edited by I. Provan and M. J. Boda. VTSup 153. Leiden: Brill.

—. 2014. "Continuity and Discontinuity in Isaiah 40–66: History of Research." Pages 13–40 in *Continuity and Discontinuity: Chronological and Thematic Development in Isaiah 40–66*. Edited by L.-S. Tiemeyer and H. M. Barstad. Göttingen: Vandenhoeck & Ruprecht.

Tov, Emanuel. 1997. "The Text of Isaiah at Qumran." Pages 481–522 in *Writing and Reading the Scroll of Isaiah: Studies of an Interpretive Tradition*. Vol. 2. Edited by C. C. Broyles and C. A. Evans. Leiden: Brill.

Tull, Patricia K. 1997. *Remember the Former Things: The Recollection of Previous Texts in Second Isaiah*. SBLDS 161. Atlanta: Scholars Press.

—. 2010. *Isaiah 1–39*. SHBC 14a. Macon GA: Smyth & Helwys.

Tutu, Desmond. 1995. *An African Prayer Book*. New York: Doubleday.

Uffenheimer, Benjamin. 1995. "The 'Desert of the Sea' Pronouncement (Isaiah 21:1-10)." Pages 677–88 in *Pomegranates and Golden Bells: Studies in Biblical, Jewish, and Near Eastern Ritual, Law, and Literature in Honor of Jacob Milgrom*. Edited by D. P. Wright, D. N. Freedman, and A. Hurvitz. Winona Lake: Eisenbrauns.

Uhlig, Torsten. 2009a. *The Theme of Hardening in the Book of Isaiah: An Analysis of Communicative Action*. FAT 2.39. Tübingen: Mohr Siebeck.

———. 2009b. "Too Hard to Understand? The Motif of Hardening in Isaiah." Pages 62–83 in *Interpreting Isaiah: Issues and Approaches*. Edited by D. G. Firth and H. G. M. Williamson. Downers Grove, Ill.: IVP Academic.

Vanderhooft, David. 2006. "Cyrus II, Liberator or Conqueror?: Ancient Historiography concerning Cyrus in Babylon." Pages 351–72 in *Judah and the Judeans in the Persian Period*. Editedy by O. Lipschits and M. Oeming. Winona Lake, Eisenbrauns.

Waters, Matt. 2014. *Ancient Persia: A Concise History of the Achaemenid Empire, 550–330 BCE*. New York: Cambridge University Press.

Watts, John D. W. 2001. "Jerusalem: An Example of War in a Walled City (Isaiah 3–4)." Pages 210–15 in *'Every City Shall Be Forsaken': Urbanism and Prophecy in Ancient Israel and the Near East*. Edited by L. L. Grabbe and R. D. Haak. JSOTSup 330. Sheffield: Sheffield Academic Press.

———. 2005. *Isaiah 34–66*. Rev. ed. WBC. Nashville: Thomas Nelson.

Weinfeld, Moshe. 1986. "The Protest against Imperialism in Ancient Israelite Prophecy." Pages 169–82 in *The Origins and Diversity of Axial Age Civilizations*. Edited by S. N. Eisenstadt. Albany: State University of New York Press.

Wells, Roy D. 2009. "'They All Gather, They Come to You': History, Utopia, and the Reading of Isaiah 49:18-26 and 60:4-16." Pages 197–216 in in *The Desert Will Bloom: Poetic Visions in Isaiah*. Edited by A. J. Everson and H. C. P. Kim. Atlanta: SBL.

Westermann, Claus. 1969. *Isaiah 40–66*. OTL. Philadelphia: SCM.

———. 1980. *The Psalms: Structure, Content and Message*. Minneapolis: Augsburg.

White, Ellen. 2014. *Yahweh's Council: Its Structure and Membership.* FAT 2.65. Tübingen: Mohr Siebeck.

Whybray, R. Norman. 1975. *Isaiah 40–66.* NCB. Grand Rapids MI: Eerdmans.

Widyapranawa, S. H. 1990. *Isaiah 1–39.* ITC. Grand Rapids MI: Eerdmans.

Wieringen, Archibald L.H.M. van. "2015. The 'I'-Figure's Relations in the Poem in Isa 38,10-20." *Biblica* 96:481–97.

Wiesel, Elie. 2012. *Open Heart.* New York: Knopf.

Wildberger, Hans. *Isaiah 1–12.* 1991. Translated by T. H. Trapp. CC. Minneapolis: Fortress.

———. 1997. *Isaiah 13–27.* Translated by T. H. Trapp. CC. Minneapolis: Fortress.

Williamson, Hugh G. M. 1977. *Israel in the Books of Chronicles.* Cambridge: Cambridge University Press.

———. 1998a. "The Messianic Texts in Isaiah 1–39." Pages 238–70 in *King and Messiah in Israel and the Ancient Near East: Proceedings of the Oxford Old Testament Seminar.* Edited by J. Day. JSOTSup 270. Sheffield: Sheffield Academic Press.

———. 1998b. *Variations on a Theme: King, Messiah and Servant in the Book of Isaiah.* Carlisle: Paternoster.

———. 1989. "The Concept of Israel in Transition." Pages 141–61 in *The World of Ancient Israel: Sociological, Anthropological and Political Perspectives.* Edited by R. E. Clements. Cambridge: Cambridge University Press.

———. 1994. *The Book Called Isaiah: Deutero-Isaiah's Role in Composition and Redaction.* Oxford: Clarendon.

———. 1996. "Hezekiah and the Temple." Pages 47–52 in *Texts, Temples, and Traditions: A Tribute to Menahem Haran.* Edited by M. V. Fox et al. Winona Lake: Eisenbrauns.

———. 1997. "Relocating Isaiah 1:2-9." Pages 263–77 in *Writing and Reading the Scroll of Isaiah: Studies of an Interpretive Tradition.* Edited by C. C. Broyles and C. A. Evans. VTSup 70:1. Leiden: Brill.

—————. 2003. "Judgment and Hope." Pages 423–34 in *Reading from Right to Left: Essays on the Hebrew Bible in Honour of David J. A. Clines*. Edited by J. C. Exum and H. G. M. Williamson. JSOTSup 373. London: Sheffield Academic Press.

—————. 2006. *Isaiah 1–5*. ICC. London: T&T Clark.

—————. 2007. "Temple and Worship in Isaiah 6." Pages 123–44 in *Temple and Worship in Biblical Israel: Proceedings of the Oxford Old Testament Seminar*. Edited by J. Day. LHB/OTS 422. London: T&T Clark.

—————. 2010. "Prophetesses in the Hebrew Bible." Pages 65–80 in *Prophecy and Prophets in Ancient Israel: Proceedings of the Oxford Old Testament Seminary*. Edited by J. Day. New York: T&T Clark.

—————. 2014. "Jacob in Isaiah 40–66." Pages 219–29 in *Continuity and Discontinuity: Chronological and Thematic Development in Isaiah 40–66*. Edited by L.-S. Tiemeyer and H. M. Barstad. Göttingen: Vandenhoeck & Ruprecht.

Willis, John T. 2013. "Yahweh Regenerates His Vineyard: Isaiah 27." Pages 201–207 in *Formation and Intertextuality in Isaiah 24–27*. Edited by J. T. Hibbard and H. C. P. Kim. SBLAIL 17. Atlanta: SBL.

Wright, Christopher J. H. 2016. *How to Preach and Teach the Old Testament for All Its Worth*. Grand Rapids MI: Zondervan.

Wright, Jacob L. 2011. "The Deportation of Jerusalem's Wealth and the Demise of Native Sovereignty in the Book of Kings." Pages 105–33 in *Interpreting Exile: Displacement and Deportation in Biblical and Modern Contexts*. Edited by B. E. Kelle, F. R. Ames, and J. L. Wright. SBLAIL 10. Atlanta: SBL.

—————. 2008. "Warfare and Wonton Destruction: A Reexamination of Deuteronomy 20:19-20 in Relation to Ancient Siegecraft." *JBL* 127:423–58.

Wright, Jacob L. and Michael J. Chan. 2012. "King and Eunuch: Isaiah 56:1-8 in Light of Honorific Royal Burial Practices." *JBL* 131:99–119.

Yee, Gale A. 2003. *Poor Banished Children of Eve: Woman as Evil in the Hebrew Bible*. Minneapolis: Fortress.

Younger, Brett. 2013. "Calorie Counting Ministers in a Starving World: Amos 5:14-24." *Review & Expositor* 110:295–300.

Zenger, Erich. 1996. *A God of Vengeance?: Understanding the Psalms of Divine Wrath.* Louisville: Westminster John Knox.

Reading Judges
A Literary and Theological Commentary
Mark E. Biddle

Reading the Old Testament book of Judges presents a number of significant challenges related to social contexts, historical settings, and literary characteristics. Acknowledging and examining these difficulties provides a point of entry into the world of Judges and promises to enrich the reading experience.   *978-1-57312-631-1 240 pages/pb* **$32.00**

Reading Samuel
A Literary and Theological Commentary
Johanna W. H. van Wijk-Bos

Interpreted masterfully by pre-eminent Old Testament scholar Johanna W. H. van Wijk-Bos, the story of Samuel touches on a vast array of subjects that comprise the rich fabric of human life. The reader gains an inside look at royal intrigue, military campaigns, occult practices and the significance of religious objects of veneration.

978-1-57312-607-6 256 pages/pb **$32.00**

Reading Job
A Literary and Theological Commentary
James L. Crenshaw

At issue in the Book of Job is a question with which most all of us struggle at some point in life, "Why do bad things happen to good people?" James Crenshaw has devoted his life to studying the disturbing matter of theodicy—divine justice—that troubles many people of faith.

978-1-57312-574-1 192 pages/pb **$32.00**

Reading Ezekiel
A Literary and Theological Commentary
Marvin A. Sweeney

In this volume, biblical scholar Marvin A. Sweeney considers one of the most interesting and compelling books of the Hebrew Bible. Ezekiel is simultaneously one of the Bible's most difficult and perplexing books as it presents the visions and oracles of Ezekiel, a Judean priest and prophet exiled to Babylonia in the sixth century BCE.   *978-1-57312-658-8 264 pages/pb* **$32.00**

Reading Hosea–Micah
A Literary and Theological Commentary

Terence E. Fretheim

In this volume, Terence E. Fretheim explores themes of indictment, judgment, and salvation in Hosea–Micah. The indictment against the people of God especially involves issues of idolatry, as well as abuse of the poor and needy.

978-1-57312-687-8 224 pages/pb **$32.00**

Reading Nahum–Malachi
A Literary and Theological Commentary

Steven Tuell

Nahum–Malachi, the last six books of the Christian Old Testament, span the period from the end of the Assyrian empire in the 7th century BCE to the fall of the Neo-Babylonian Empire and the emergence of Persia in the 5th century BCE. But these books also have a collective identity as the latter half of the Book of the Twelve—the ancient Jewish and Christian designation for the so-called "minor" prophets. This commentary maintains a balance between reading each of these six books in its own historical and social setting and considering the interrelationships and canonical functions of these books within the Book of the Twelve as a whole.

978-1-57312-848-3 304 pages/pb **$33.00**

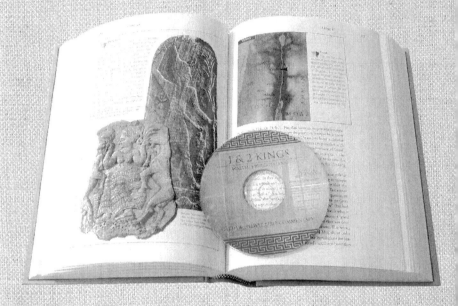

THIS SERIES WILL MAKE AN ENORMOUS IMPACT ON THE LIFE AND FAITH OF THE CHURCH.

Walter Brueggemann, author of *1 & 2 Kings*

The *Smyth & Helwys Bible Commentary* includes "commentary" and "connections" information within each chapter. The "commentary" provides an analysis of the passage, consisting of interpretation of the passage, its language, history, and literary form, and discussion of pertinent theological issues. "Connections" offers application of analytical insight for (1) teaching of the passages, including suggested approaches for instruction and additional resources for further study, and (2) preaching based on the passage, including suggested approaches, themes, and resources. Most Bible commentaries are limited to providing only "commentary," without the helpful "connections" included in this series.

Additional Features

- CD-ROM with powerful search & research tools
- Unique hyperlink format offers additional information
- Includes maps, photographs, and other illustrations relevant for understanding the context or significance of the text
- Quality craftsmanship in printing and binding
- Distinctive sidebars/special interest boxes printed in color
- Footnotes that offer full documentation

OLD TESTAMENT
GENERAL EDITOR

Samuel E. Balentine
Union Presbyterian Seminary
Richmond, Virginia

PROJECT EDITOR

R. Scott Nash
Mercer University
Macon, Georgia

NEW TESTAMENT
GENERAL EDITOR

R. Alan Culpepper
McAfee School of Theology
Mercer University
Atlanta, Georgia

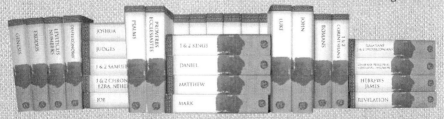

Choose our **Standing Order Plan** and receive a **25% discount** on every volume. To sign up or for more information call **800-747-3016** or visit **www.helwys.com/commentary**